85

Years Of Great Writing in TIME

1923-2008

[EDITED BY CHRISTOPHER PORTERFIELD]
TIME BOOKS

Managing Editor	Richard Stengel
Deputy Managing Editor	Adi Ignatius
Editor	Christopher Porterfield
Designer	Arthur Hochstein
Editorial Production Director	Richard Prue
Editorial Production Manager	Lionel P. Vargas
Copy Editor	Joseph McCombs
Researcher	Harsharn K. Dhah

The editor wishes to thank Bill Hooper, Time Inc. archivist, for his expert, unstinting help; Isaiah Wilner for his illumination of TIME's early years; and countless current and former TIME journalists for their invaluable suggestions. This book would not have been possible without them.

TIME INC. HOME ENTERTAINMENT

Publisher	Richard Fraiman
General Manager	Steven Sandonato
Executive Director, Marketing Services	Carol Pittard
Director, Retail & Special Sales	Tom Mifsud
Director, New Product Development	Peter Harper
Assistant Director, Brand Marketing	Laura Adam
Associate Counsel	Helen Wan
Book Production Manager	Suzanne Janso
Design & Prepress Manager	Anne-Michelle Gallero
Senior Brand Manager	Joy Butts
Associate Brand Manager	Shelley Rescober

SPECIAL THANKS TO:
Bozena Bannett
Alexandra Bliss
Glenn Buonocore
Robert Marasco
Brooke Reger
Mary Sarro-Waite
Ilene Schreider
Adriana Tierno
Alex Voznesenskiy

ISBN 10: 1-60320-018-5
ISBN 13: 978-1-60320-018-9
Library of Congress Number: 2007909111

We welcome your comments and suggestions about TIME Books. Please write to us at:
TIME Books
Attention: Book Editors
P.O. Box 11016
Des Moines, IA 50336-1016

If you would like to order any of our hardcover Collector's Edition books, please call us at 1-800-327-6388 (Monday through Friday, 7:00 a.m.–8:00 p.m., or Saturday, 7:00 a.m.–6:00 p.m., Central Time).

85 Years Of Great Writing in TIME

TABLE OF CONTENTS

Tentative identification

[WAR ZONES]

[ALL BUSINESS]

Tentative identification

[THE ARTS SCENE]

[FRONTIERS OF SCIENCE AND MEDICINE]

[The Social Fabric]

[Persons of the Year]

*The inset at the beginning of each article is
the cover image of the issue in which the article appeared.*

[Introduction]

Agony, Poetry and Baking a Soufflé

BY RICHARD STENGEL

WHEN I STARTED AT TIME as a writer, we placed our finished stories in a scuffed wooden in-box in front of the copy desk on the 23rd floor of the Time & Life Building. This was in the early 1980s, when computers were still exotic and most of the older writers wrote their stories on humming IBM Selectrics. During my second week I was assigned a very modest one-column story, and when I was turning it in on a Friday morning a veteran writer was also dropping off his copy. "Finished your story?" I said rather inanely, trying to make conversation. "Yup," he said breezily, "I'm turning it in for joke removal."

The attitude among writers in those days was that editors were the enemy and that writers needed to do their best to prevent them from cutting, flattening, rewriting or otherwise sucking the life out of a story. TIME writers were a proud if slightly careworn species. We were craftsmen—craftsmen who could take a story and figure out a snappy opening, a smart "billboard" paragraph, a compelling narrative with unexpected twists, some clever turns of phrase and a memorable ending (or "kicker")—all in a limited number of words and in an amount of time that was always too short. We wore blue blazers and khaki pants. We smoked. We drank. And yes, a liquor cart was still wheeled down the corridors on Thursday and Friday evenings.

We younger writers were in awe of the older writers. They seemed like giants—Nation writers Ed Magnuson and George Church, essayists Lance Morrow and Roger Rosenblatt, the art critic Bob Hughes, the drama critic Ted Kalem and the always versatile Otto Friedrich. During my first few years at TIME, I sat next to an easygoing writer who would drink two six-packs of Budweiser on Friday while calmly tapping out a lucid cover story. Another one of my neighbors would bang the walls and yell and scream but turn out beautiful, lyrical copy. I had another colleague who stripped down to his boxer shorts to write. The idea was that you labored and struggled to make the prose seem effortless. We all believed it was agony to write, and that if it wasn't difficult, it wouldn't be good. Eccentricity was treasured. Great ledes (that is, opening paragraphs), wonderful similes and clever puns were admired and read aloud. We debated the virtues of different ledes and kickers.

TIME stories were a genre unto themselves. Newspaper writing, we felt, was straightforward, stolid and dull. Longer pieces in other magazines were lazy, indulgent and unstructured. A TIME story was a poem by comparison. When I was hired, the editor who offered me a job said, "We can't teach journalists to be poets, but we can teach poets to be journalists."

I became a TIME writer because of one man: John McPhee. He was my writing teacher in college and had been a staff writer at TIME for seven years before becoming an icon at the *New Yorker.* He said that if you want to learn to write, there's no better place to learn than at TIME. There, he said, you had to write several stories a week; all of them had to be models of concision, with clear prose and clear thinking; and the editors were tough but fair. I signed up. TIME was a writer's boot camp in those days. The newest recruit usually spent a year writing Milestones—the nimble little notes on deaths, births, marriages and the like—and A Letter from the Publisher, which the publisher never actually wrote. Every sentence was meticulously edited and checked and copy read and polished, and within six months I felt like a pro.

Editors rarely told you what you did right or wrong, but you learned in part through watching what they did. Your lede might be shortened and punched up, the billboard graph might be strengthened and made clearer, the paragraphs moved around to create a more transparent structure, the kicker tweaked to make it sing. Editors often had idiosyncratic ways of explaining what they wanted. I remember one of TIME's earliest woman editors, Martha Duffy, who spoke so softly that you had to lean across her desk to hear her, explaining the story she wanted me to write by saying: "Bake me a soufflé." I knew exactly what she meant.

The two most dreaded words to a TIME writer were "new version." When a new version was ordered up, it meant that you had to go back to square one, that there was nothing salvageable from the story except "and" and "the," that you had to toss it all out, every last sentence, and start over. It was most dispiriting. Once when I was called to my editor's office for a new version, he said, "I want you to gird your loins and go back and write." I'd never heard a human being say the words "gird your loins" before—and I've never heard one since.

People in those days used to ask me, How can you write in that TIME style? The dirty little secret is that there really was no such thing as TIME style. Yes, there had been. In the early days, and up until World War II, there were the terse, choppy sentences; the brash mannerisms; the Homeric epithets; the clever coinages and labored neologisms ("cinemactress," "sexational"); and the famous backward-reeling sentences. And yes, in the 1950s and '60s, TIME, under Henry Luce, was the voice of America's growing and prospering upper-middle class, and the writing often reflected that: a bit stiff, a little institutional, at times lofty and all-knowing. But by the late '60s, the writing loosened up and became more colloquial, more nuanced and open-minded. Today's magazine has more voice and a stronger point of view, but it has all evolved from the same DNA. What people still think of as TIME style comes more from function than from form: the stories are characterized by brevity and concision, with a taut structure, a clear thematic line, precise details and a relentless forward flow with no dead spots.

TIME writing—like most things in life—divides into two categories. Lance Morrow once observed that TIME writers tended to be either Roundheads or Cavaliers. The terms come from the 17th century English Civil War, in which the aristocratic Cavaliers supported Charles I and the puritanical Roundheads advocated a more republican form of government. The Cavaliers, Morrow said, favored the packaging over the product and tended to be more decorative, stylish and elaborate. The Roundheads embraced a plainer, more direct style. Perhaps it was due to subject matter, but TIME's Cavaliers tended to cluster at the "back of the book" where arts and culture lived, while its Roundheads collected at the front, writing about war and politics and the economy.

In the pieces and excerpts that were masterfully put together in this book by Chris Porterfield, one of TIME's greatest editors and a graceful writer himself, you can see the two styles and much else as well. There are the clean, clear and firmly constructed Washington narratives of George Church, Ed Magnuson and Jim Atwater. The more showy and dazzling writing tends to be on culture, not politics. There is T.E. Kalem on the poignant death of Ernest Hemingway; John McPhee on the larger-than-life figure of Jackie Gleason; Paul Gray on the elegance of Joe DiMaggio; Robert Hughes on the genius of Picasso. But many pieces combine both styles: A.T. Baker's courageous indictment of Joseph McCarthy; James Agee's famous essay on the atomic bombs that ended World War II; John Elson's memorable 1966 cover story that asked, "Is God Dead?"; Roger Rosenblatt's sensitive exploration of *Children of War;* Walter Isaacson's intimate portrait of Bill Gates; and Nancy Gibbs' moving and powerful account of the 9/11 attacks.

The pieces are among the finest examples of what we at TIME have been doing for 85 years: explaining the world for our readers. From the beginning, we have not just reported the news but put it in context and perspective. We have offered clarity in a confusing world, explaining not just what happened but why it mattered. We don't just provide information, we convert it into knowledge and meaning. That's what the writing in this book offers— and what we strive for every week. How's that for a kicker? ∎

BUZZ ALDRIN ON THE MOON, 1969, BY NEIL ARMSTRONG

TIME The National Experience

Flight

BY NEWTON HOCKADAY*

[
*Charles Lindbergh's pioneering transatlantic flight
launched not only an iconic American hero but, as the writer
perceived, a new chapter in the commerce of celebrity*
]

May 30, 1927

THE ATLANTIC IN ITS immense indifference was not aware that man-made cables on its slimy bottom contained news, that the silent heavens above pulsed with news—news that would set thousands of printing presses in motion, news that would make sirens scream in every U. S. city, news that would cause housewives to run out into backyards and shout to their children: *"Lindbergh is in Paris!"*

Late one evening last week Capt. Charles A. Lindbergh studied weather reports and decided that the elements were propitious for a flight from New York to Paris. He took a two-hour sleep, then busied himself with final preparations at Roosevelt Field, L. I. Four sandwiches, two canteens of water and emergency army rations, along with 451 gallons of gasoline were put into his monoplane, *Spirit of St. Louis.* "When I enter the cockpit," said he, "it's like going into the death chamber. When I step out at Paris it will be like getting a pardon from the governor."

He entered the cockpit. At 7:52 a. m. he was roaring down the runway, his plane lurching on the soft spots of the wet ground. Out of the safe-

* Tentative identification

ty zone, he hit a bump, bounced into the air, quickly returned to earth. Disaster seemed imminent; a tractor and a gully were ahead. Then his plane took the air, cleared the tractor, the gully; cleared some telephone wires. Five hundred onlookers believed they had witnessed a miracle. It was a miracle of skill.

Captain Lindbergh took the shortest route to Paris—the great circle—cutting across Long Island Sound, Cape Cod, Nova Scotia, skirting the coast of Newfoundland. He later told some of his sky adventures to the aeronautically alert New York *Times* for syndication: "Shortly after leaving Newfoundland, I began to see icebergs. . . . Within an hour it became dark. Then I struck clouds and decided to try to get over them. For a while I succeeded at a height of 10,000 feet. I flew at this height until early morning. The engine was working beautifully and I was not sleepy at all. I felt just as if I was driving a motor car over a smooth road, only it was easier. Then it began to get light and the clouds got higher. . . . Sleet began to cling to the plane. That worried me a great deal and I debated whether I should keep on or go back. I decided I must not think any more about going back. . . .

"Fairly early in the afternoon I saw a fleet of fishing boats. . . . On one of them I saw some men and flew down almost touching the craft and yelled at them, asking if I was on the right road to Ireland. They just stared. Maybe they didn't hear me. Maybe I didn't hear them. Or maybe they thought I was just a crazy fool.

"An hour later I saw land. . . . I flew quite low enough over Ireland to be seen, but apparently no great attention was paid to me. . . ."

Captain Lindbergh then told how he crossed southwestern England and the Channel, followed the Seine to Paris, where he circled the city before recognizing the flying field at Le Bourget. Said he: "I appreciated the reception which had been prepared for me and had intended taxiing up to the front of the hangars, but no sooner had my plane touched the ground than a human sea swept toward it. I saw there was danger of killing people with my propeller and I quickly came to a stop."

He had completed his 3,600-mile conquest of the Atlantic in 33 hours, 29 minutes, at an average speed of 107½ miles per hour.

He did not collapse in his cockpit immediately after landing, as some early despatches stated. His first words were, "Well, here we are. I am very happy"; and *not* "Well, I did it" or "I got my pardon."

Some of the crowd of 25,000 attempted to strip souvenirs from the *Spirit of St. Louis,* while the majority escorted Captain Lindbergh, on somebody's shoulders, to a nearby clubhouse. Then, there were congratulations from U. S. Ambassador Myron Timothy Herrick and French officials, a massage and some coffee (he had refused to take coffee on the flight), a motor trip through dense traffic to Paris and ten hours' sleep in the U. S. Embassy.

Next day, he talked with his mother over radiophone, related his flight to newspapermen, glanced at hundreds of cablegrams.

Some say he had "a boyishly stern squint"; others proclaim him a practical joker and tell how he once answered his roommate's desire for a drink of water with a glass of kerosene. He is 25, more than six feet tall, rangy, handsome, blond. He knows flying as the barnstormer with a $250 plane and as the chief pilot for the St. Louis-Chicago air mail route. He is a prominent member of the Caterpillar Club, having four times become a butterfly and descended to earth in a parachute. In the Missouri National Guard he earned the rank of captain. As his next exploit, he is considering a flight from California to Australia (6,500 miles), with a stop at Hawaii.

His father, the late Congressman Charles A. Lindbergh of Minnesota, was born in Stockholm, the son of a member of the Swedish Parliament. Congressman Lindbergh was progressively a Republican, a "Bull Moose," a Farmer-Laborite. In Washington he was known as "the early bird of Congress."

Mrs. Evangeline Lodge Lindbergh continued her duties as chemistry teacher, at the Cass Technical High School in Detroit, while her son was somewhere in the atmosphere between New York and Paris. Said she: "I am proud to be the mother of such a boy."

A 27-year-old engineer, Donald Hall, designed the Ryan monoplane, *Spirit of St. Louis*. It was built in 60 days at San Diego, Calif. It was christened in St. Louis while Captain Lindbergh was pausing in his flight across the continent. The fact that it is equipped with a 200-horsepower Wright whirlwind motor caused Wright Aeronautical Corp. stock, usually inactive, to jump from 29¾ to 34⅜, with the news of Captain Lindbergh's progress.

Over and over again "Lucky" had repeated that his "luck" had consisted chiefly in a faultless motor, a periscope by which he watched ahead without exposure, and in an earth induction compass by which alone he steered to a point within three miles of his theoretic arrival point in Ireland.

Not only did Captain Lindbergh win the $25,000 prize offered by Raymond Orteig, Manhattan hotelman, for the first New York-Paris nonstop flight, but he established for himself the immemorial right of extract-

ing dollars from the hero-gaping U. S. public by appearing on the vaudeville stage, in the cinema, etc. A money-minded New York *Herald Tribune*
writer figured out that Captain Lindbergh, as a professional hero, could
(if he chose) earn $1,000,000 in one year in the following manner:

Cinema	$200,000
Vaudeville	400,000
Radio	50,000
Book	50,000
C. C. Pyle spectacle	150,000
Articles for the press	50,000
Advertising concessions	75,000
Orteig prize	25,000

Drought, Dust, Disaster

BY MANFRED GOTTFRIED

[*The writer, the first hired by* TIME *at its founding
and eventually its managing editor, strikingly evoked the
devastation that hit U.S. farmers during the Depression*]

May 21, 1934

LAST WEEK THE AGRICULTURAL Adjustment
Administration reported it had spent $67,600,000 to reduce
the U. S. wheat crop for 1934. At the same time the Department
of Agriculture gave out its May estimate for the winter wheat
crop:* 461,000,000 bu., which was 31,000,000 bu. less than
the April estimate and 171,000,000 bu. less than the five-
year average. There was little connection between the expenditure and the
shrinkage, for a crop reduction agent more potent than AAA was at work.
From Saskatchewan to Texas, from Montana to Ohio, hardly any rain had
fallen for a month. As dry day followed dry day, crop estimators lopped
2,000,000 bu. from their wheat prediction every morning. Before the week
was out the winter wheat estimate had fallen to 442,000,000 bu.

In Washington these were dry statistics, but in the Midwest, disastrous
facts. In North Dakota, which had barely an inch of rain in four months,
there was no grass for cattle. Farmers tramped their dusty fields watching
their dwarfed stand of grain shrivel and perish. A baking sun raised temperatures to 90°, to 100°. And still no rain fell. Water was carted for miles

---

* *Winter wheat, planted the autumn before from Texas through Kansas, accounts for about two-thirds of the
U. S. crop. Spring wheat, planted after the first thaw in Montana and the Dakotas, accounts for the other third.*

for livestock. Towns rationed their water supplies. In Nebraska the State University agronomist gloomily predicted that many fields would not yield over 5 bu. of wheat per acre (normal average: 15 to 20 bu.). In Minnesota they mocked Washington's crop predictions as gross overestimates. Farmers planting corn raised clouds of dust like columns of marching troops.

Then came the wind, great gusty blasts out of the Northwest. It lifted the dust from the parched fields and swirled it across the land. It tore the powdery soil from the roots of the wheat and deposited it like snowdrifts miles away. Concrete highways were buried under six inches of dust. The rich fertility of a million farms took to the air: 300,000,000 tons of soil billowing through the sky. Housewives in Des Moines could write their names in grime upon their table tops. Aviators had to climb 15,000 ft. to get above the pall. A dust storm 900 mi. wide, 1,500 mi. long swept out of the drought-stricken West.

In dust-darkened Chicago excited Board of Trade brokers bid up wheat prices 5¢ in one day (the maximum), raised the price to 93¢ a bu.— up 17¢ in two weeks. That day 6,000 tons of finely divided wheat fields fell on Chicago's roofs and sidewalks. And the dust swept on, until its thick haze could be seen from the windows of the Department of Agriculture in Washington. It hung for five hours like a fog over Manhattan—the greatest dust storm in U. S. history, proof to the East of an unbelievably successful crop reduction in the Midwest.

But the Administration was not grateful for this help from the Hand of God. No fear did it have of a real wheat shortage, for the U. S. consumes only 600,000,000 bu. of wheat a year, has 250,000,000 bu. left over from last year. With a winter wheat crop of 442,000,000 bu., in addition to a spring wheat crop of probably half as much, the U. S. will not starve. But how farmers will make out is another matter. They would have so little wheat to sell that, in spite of a high price, they would lose severely. Moreover, the drought had dried up pastures and ruined the hay crop.

God's crop reduction may cost the U. S. far more for relief than man's crop reduction cost in processing taxes. The Cabinet devoted an entire session to the problem. Relief Administrator Harry L. Hopkins promised $450,000 cash to Wisconsin, North Dakota, South Dakota. The Government also promised to buy cattle in drought areas, to ask railroads to reduce freight charges on cattle going out and feed coming into desolated states.

Finally soft drizzles began throughout the Midwest, enough to lay the dust. But soaking rains were needed to save what was left of the crops and soaking rains had not yet come. ∎

"A Soldier Died Today"

BY JAMES AGEE

[*President Franklin Roosevelt's death in the waning days of World War II shook the world, but the writer found its deepest impact in the quiet grief of ordinary Americans*]

April 23, 1945

IN CHUNGKING THE SPRING dawn was milky when an MP on the graveyard shift picked up the ringing phone in U.S. Army Headquarters. At first he heard no voice on the other end; then a San Francisco broadcast coming over the phone line made clear to him why his informant could find no words. A colonel came in. The MP just stared at him. The colonel stared back. After a moment the MP blurted two words. The colonel's jaw dropped; he hesitated; then without a word he walked away.

It was fresh daylight on Okinawa. Officers and men of the amphibious fleet were at breakfast when the broadcast told them. By noon the news was known to the men at the front, at the far sharp edge of the world's struggle. With no time for grief, they went on with their work; but there, while they worked, many a soldier wept.

At home, the news came to people in the hot soft light of the afternoon, in taxicabs, along the streets, in offices and bars and factories. In a Cleveland barbershop, 60-year-old Sam Katz was giving a customer a shave when the radio stabbed out the news. Sam Katz walked over to the water cooler, took a long, slow drink, sat down and stared into space for nearly ten minutes. Finally he got up and painted a sign on his window:

"Roosevelt Is Dead." Then he finished the shave. In an Omaha poolhall, men racked up their cues without finishing their games, walked out. In a Manhattan taxicab, a fare told the driver, who pulled over to the curb, sat with his head bowed, and after two minutes resumed his driving.

Everywhere, to almost everyone, the news came with the force of a personal shock. The realization was expressed in the messages of the eminent; it was expressed in the stammering and wordlessness of the humble. A woman in Detroit said: "It doesn't seem possible. It seems to me that he will be back on the radio tomorrow, reassuring us all that it was just a mistake."

It was the same through that evening, and the next day, and the next; the darkened restaurants, the shuttered nightclubs, the hand-lettered signs in the windows of stores: "Closed out of Reverence for F.D.R."; the unbroken, 85-hour dirge of the nation's radio; the typical tributes of typical Americans in the death-notice columns of their newspapers (said one, signed by Samuel and Al Gordon: "A Soldier Died Today").

It was the same on the cotton fields and in the stunned cities between Warm Springs and Washington, while the train, at funeral pace, bore the coffin up April's glowing South in re-enactment of Whitman's great threnody.

It was the same in Washington, in the thousands on thousands of grief-wrung faces which walled the caisson's grim progression with prayers and with tears. It was the same on Sunday morning in the gentle landscape at Hyde Park, when the burial service of the Episcopal Church spoke its old, strong, quiet words of farewell; and it was the same at that later moment when all save the gravemen were withdrawn and reporters, in awe-felt hiding, saw how a brave woman, a widow, returned, and watched over the grave alone, until the grave was filled. ∎

Weighed in the Balance

BY A.T. BAKER

[*With a verve and flair that matched the Senator's,
the writer posed an early, forceful challenge to the
fear-mongering demagoguery of Joe McCarthy*]

October 22, 1951

"MAN IS BORN TO do something," says restless Joe McCarthy. Joe is doing something. His name is in headlines. "McCarthyism" is now part of the language. His burly figure casts its shadow over the coming presidential campaign. Thousands turn out to hear his speeches. Millions regard him as "a splendid American" (a fellow Senator recently called him that). Other millions think McCarthy a worse menace than the Communist conspiracy against which he professes to fight.

McCarthy does not face some questions which the nation cannot evade:

1) Precisely what has McCarthy done?
2) Is his effect on the U.S. good or bad?
*3) Does he deserve well of the republic, or should
   he be treated with aversion and contempt?*

McCarthy's jump from obscurity to the national limelight began nearly two years ago, when he made a speech in Wheeling, W. Va. He said: "I have here in my hand a list of 205, a list of names made known to the Secretary of State as being members of the Communist Party and who nevertheless are still working and shaping policy in the State Department." Next day in Salt Lake City, he declared: "I hold in my hand the names of 57 card-carrying Communists" working in the State Department. Ten days later, on the Senate floor, he cited 81 "cases," particularly "three big Communists." Said McCarthy: "While there are vast numbers of other Communists with whom we must be concerned, if we can get rid of these big three, we will have done something to break the back of the espionage ring within the State Department."

In a nation that had finally learned (without any help from McCarthy) that it was locked in a life-or-death struggle with world Communism, these charges were as grave as any that could be made. The underlying accusation was that its State Department was harboring Communists, knew they were Communists, and was doing so deliberately. To investigate these charges, the Senate set up a committee headed by conservative Democrat Senator Millard Tydings of Maryland.

McCarthy, who had said that he "held in his hand" the names of 205 Communists then in the State Department, did not give the Tydings committee the names of 205. He did not give it the names of 57. He did not produce the name of even one Communist in the State Department.

Logically, that failure might have been expected to end the rocketing flight of Joe McCarthy. That it was a beginning, not an end, is partly explained by McCarthy's personality. Another man, humiliated by failure to produce evidence he said he held, would have retreated and wiped a bloody nose. McCarthy, who was a boxer in college, says: "I learned in the ring that the moment you draw back and start defending yourself, you're licked. You've got to keep boring in." This is not necessarily true of either boxing or politics—but Joe McCarthy thinks it is true.

He bored in, hitting low blow after low blow. He set up a barrage of new accusations which caught the headlines, drawing attention away from the fact that he had not made good on his original charge. He even began to produce some names. But most of the men he has named never were in the State Department. His most sensational charge was that he knew the name of "the top Soviet espionage agent" in the U.S. The man so accused turned out to be Owen Lattimore, a Johns Hopkins professor and writer on Far Eastern affairs. Lattimore, in fact, had great influence in U.S. academic and journalistic circles dealing with the Far East. He was an important factor in leading the U.S. toward policies which many Americans regard as tragically wrong.

But that was not what McCarthy said about Lattimore. He said that Lattimore was "the top Soviet espionage agent"—and to this day McCarthy has not produced a scrap of evidence indicating that Lattimore was a spy or in any way disloyal. The question of whether Lattimore's analysis of the Far East was correct or incorrect—which is still a highly relevant and important question—does not interest Joe. Such questions have no appeal to demagogues.

Before the Tydings committee, Joe demonstrated the technique that he still uses: kicking up a storm of denunciation and then shifting his ground. When he first made his charges, he explained: "Everything I have here is from the State Department's own files." When the Tydings committee asked for proof, Joe set up a chant: "Get the files. If you do, you will find that every word I have said is the truth." Harry Truman refused to let the committee have the files, on the sound ground that it was necessary to protect the reputations of those who might be subsequently cleared.

Joe's chant became deafening. How could he supply the proof without the files? Then Truman changed his mind. Before McCarthy even saw what the State Department turned over to the committee, he pronounced it "a phony offer of phony files." The files had been "raped," he cried. Tydings had the FBI send over a copy of all investigative reports it had; two security officers checked, and found everything there. But Tydings carelessly announced that the FBI had checked the files. McCarthy promptly got a letter from FBI Director J. Edgar Hoover saying that the FBI itself had not made the check. Tydings then had the FBI check in person. But Joe insisted that, by the time the FBI got there, the damning papers had been sneaked back.

Finally, when the Democratic majority brought out a report denouncing his charges as "a fraud and a hoax on the American people," Joe was ready. "Whitewash," he cried.

Tydings made the mistake of underestimating Joe McCarthy. He bickered impatiently with Joe, defended the Administration at every turn, including some points where it was not readily defensible.

Tydings was up for re-election to a seat he had held since 1926. Franklin Roosevelt in 1938 vainly tried to beat Tydings on the ground that he was too conservative. McCarthy, by accusing Tydings of sympathy for Communism, succeeded where Roosevelt had failed. The campaign against Tydings included a faked photograph showing Tydings and Communist Earl Browder cheek by jowl. On other occasions, Joe has said: "You have to play rough if you are going to root out this motley crew."

The Tydings defeat made Joe a power. If he could successfully smear one of the most conservative and best entrenched Senators, was any man safe from his furious onslaught?

The Reds in Government, if any, were safe. After nearly two years of tramping the nation, shouting that he was "rooting out the skunks," just how many Communists has Joe rooted out? The answer: none. At best, he might claim an assist on three minor and borderline cases which Government investigators had already spotted. Joe tries to include himself in by saying: "We got Alger Hiss out, we got Marzani out, Wadleigh, George Shaw Wheeler and a few others." McCarthy had nothing to do with any of them. Hiss was flushed by the House Un-American Activities Committee. Wadleigh, like Hiss, was named by Whittaker Chambers. Judith Coplon (who was employed in the Justice Department) was arrested by the FBI. Marzani was uncovered by the State Department's own loyalty investigation in 1946. George Shaw Wheeler was never in the State Department, but with the U.S. Military Government in Germany; he was denounced by Michigan's Representative George A. Dondero in 1947 and eased out while facing an Army checkup.

On such a miserable showing as an exposer of Reds, how has Joe McCarthy created such an uproar and kept it roaring? A large part of the answer is that Joe McCarthy in 1950 had hit a highly sensitive public nerve. When McCarthy first spoke up, Hiss, whose case Truman had called "a red herring," had just been convicted, and Acheson had declared: "I do not intend to turn my back on Alger Hiss." The U.S. people had just begun to realize fully the malevolence of the enemy they faced. Abroad, the West had suffered a grievous setback in the loss of China to Communism.

The public, quite correctly, thought that someone must be to blame. Joe McCarthy went into the business of providing scapegoats. It was easier to string along with Joe's wild charges than to settle down to a sober examination of the chuckle-headed "liberalism," the false assumptions and the fatuous complacency that had endangered the security of the U.S. That he got a lot of help from the Administration spokesmen who still insist that nothing was wrong with U.S. policy helps to explain McCarthy's success—although it in no way excuses McCarthy.

Joe, like all effective demagogues, found an area of emotion and exploited it. No regard for fair play, no scruple for exact truth hampers Joe's political course. If his accusations destroy reputations, if they subvert the principle that a man is innocent until proved guilty, he is oblivious. Joe, immersed in the joy of battle, does not even seem to realize the gravity of his own charges. On countless rostrums, he has in effect accused Ambassador at Large Philip Jessup and Secretary of State Acheson of treason. This is a crime punishable by death in the U.S. Asked what he would do with Jessup if he were in charge, McCarthy has a simple answer: "Fire him." When he met Acheson in a Senate elevator, Joe grinned, introduced himself, and shook hands as if the meeting were a cordial encounter between rival baseball managers.

OUTSIDE THE POLITICAL ARENA, McCarthy is an ingratiating and friendly fellow. "He comes up to you with tail wagging and all the appeal of a tramp dog," said one colleague. "And he's just about as trustworthy." Joe was liked and respected in college, liked and respected in the Marines, liked and respected in his home town. Within five minutes or so, everyone he meets is calling him "Joe." At 41, he has a candid eye for a pretty girl, but he has never married. "I can't work at politics if I can't stay away from supper when I want to," says Joe. He dotes on children, to whom he talks gravely as equals.

Burly, ham-handed, McCarthy has a furious physical energy. He is always in a hurry. He rushes through a newspaper in five minutes, looking just for items of special interest or use to him; he has little general curiosity. His pockets are always stuffed with notes which he can't find, and he can never keep a comb or a pencil or a handkerchief.

A two-fisted drinker who holds his liquor very well, McCarthy does not smoke. He detests cigars. Joe always begins a lunch or dinner speech by coughing raucously into his fist, saying: "Before I begin [cough-cough], I want to ask So & So [cough-cough] just what he has been smoking. It reminds me of my days back on the farm." This serves a double purpose: it gets a laugh, and all head-table smokers stub out their cigars.

McCarthy's idea of a meal is steak, very well done. "Cremate it," he tells the waiter. He almost always has steak for dinner, often for breakfast. He rarely eats lunch, but when he does, he is likely to order steak. He keeps irregular hours, gets up late, goes to bed usually long after midnight. A favorite McCarthy recreation is poker, but many find playing with him too nerve-racking, and somewhat like opposing him in politics. In seven-card stud, McCarthy will raise, raise again and then again without even bothering to look at his hole cards. Said one opponent: "You get to the point where you don't care what McCarthy's got in the hole—all you know is that it's too costly to stay in the game."

In Washington, Joe lives with his office manager Ray Kiermas and his wife. He gets back to Wisconsin about every two weeks, usually to give speeches. There he lives with the Urban P. Van Susterens in Appleton. Van, a lawyer and proprietor of a fleet of taxis, managed Joe's last campaign. Last time he got back to Appleton, Joe arrived, as usual, in the middle of the night. He went into the kitchen, dumped some baking soda into his hand, threw it into his mouth, and washed it down with cold water. Margery Van Susteren winced. Next, he took off his coat and tie and shoes, dropping them where he happened to be. Joe has no interest in clothes. After every road trip, hotels send on clothing he has forgotten.

Joe seldom misses Sunday Mass, although he sometimes cannot pass up a steak on Friday. A dogged churchgoer, Joe calls himself "a good Catholic, but not the kiss-the-book, light-the-candle Catholic."

Joseph Raymond McCarthy, who always signs himself plain Joe McCarthy these days, was born on a farm in Grand Chute, a few miles north of Appleton. One of seven children, he quit school early, parlayed 50 chickens into a flock of 10,000, but lost nearly all of them one winter when he came down with pneumonia and turned over his flock to some friends. At 18 he wangled a job as manager of a grocery store in nearby Manawa (pop. 990).

Joe's merchandising methods showed the instincts of a born political campaigner. He walked up & down the country roads, calling on farmers. Soon his store became a town meeting place. On Saturday nights, other Manawa grocers were so lonely that they would come over to help Joe wait on the crowds.

Joe's landlady, Mrs. Osterloth, nagged at him to go back to school. "You're smart, McCarthy, you're smart," she insisted. Joe went back. With typically furious energy he signed up for 16 subjects, and finished the four-year high-school course in one year.

At Marquette, Joe started in engineering, switched to law. A slugging, savage attacker, he became the college boxing champion. He worked as short-order cook, sold gravestones and calking compound, worked in a filling station until 1 a.m. On the campus he was president of his class one year, a perennial chairman of events, and he knew everybody's name.

After only four years as a lawyer, Joe decided to run for circuit judge, at the age of 29. He made few speeches, but he met every farmer in the district. His specialty was sick cows. He would get the cow's symptoms, drive on to the next farm and ask the farmer what he would do for a cow with those symptoms. He kept a Dictaphone in his car, and as he drove away he would dictate a letter to the first farmer, giving the second farmer's advice as Joe's own. Both farmers would be flattered by his attention. He would get a little careless and refer to "my 89-year-old opponent"—though the rival candidate, who had served for 24 years, was only 73. Joe won handily.

Justice in Judge McCarthy's court was breezy, informal and swift. As an appellate judge observed: "There was some bad law practiced in Joe's court, and there were some good decisions—which is what happens in all lower courts." When he went on the bench, Joe practically memorized the three volumes of Jones's rules of evidence. He always made a great show of citing his reasons for a ruling, was rarely reversed. Curiously, Senator McCarthy seems never to have understood the spirit of fair play behind the rules that Judge McCarthy memorized.

After Pearl Harbor, Judge McCarthy took leave of absence and signed up with the Marines. McCarthy's war record was good but not spectacular, and he has made the most of it. He shipped overseas as an intelligence officer with a scout-bombing squadron. Nearly ten years older than most of his squadron, "Father Mac" was very popular, always scrounging beer and extra food for his unit, organizing sports, starting bull sessions. Joe volunteered to defend enlisted men, and boasts of how many courts-martial he beat for his clients.

As an intelligence officer, Joe often went along on missions in the rear gunner's seat. He had his picture taken there, and saw that it made Wisconsin papers. Joe used to shoot up everything in sight, on the theory that any coconut tree might hide a Jap. He hated to see a crew come home with any ammunition left. On his tent, marines hung a sign: "Protect the coconut trees—Send McCarthy back to Wisconsin."

In 1944 Joe, having finished his overseas tour of duty, campaigned in Wisconsin as "Tail-Gunner Joe" against Senator Alexander Wiley, and lost. Early in 1945 Joe applied for discharge and got it.

McCarthy had entered the Marines a poor man. He had sold everything he owned for $3,000, turned most of it over to a broker to buy International-Great Northern Railroad bonds on margin. This investment prospered. When he returned he sold out, switched to other securities, pledged them at an Appleton bank, and played the market with the borrowed money. From 1946 to 1949, McCarthy paid no state income tax. In each year, his listed losses or interest payments exceeded his taxable income. Asked how he lived, McCarthy snaps: "Who I borrow from is none of your damned business."

Re-elected circuit judge without contest, Joe in 1946 brashly decided to take on Senator Robert ("Young Bob") La Follette in the Republican primary. He beat Young Bob by a slim 5,000 votes.

Nobody in Washington paid much attention to the new Senator from Wisconsin, not even after McCarthy invited eight women reporters to dinner and cooked them fried chicken himself. He showed little practical interest in the fight against Communism. He voted for 7 out of 16 of the amendments to limit the scope or cut the amount of ECA and other foreign aid bills. This year, he voted for a $500 million cut in the Mutual Security Act extending military and economic aid to Europe. Commented a fellow Republican Senator: "McCarthy simply has never been in the picture. He's off on that stuff of his own."

McCarthy never answers criticisms, just savagely attacks the critic. Anyone who voices reservations about his methods is blasted as a "defender of Communists." The Senate resolution of Connecticut's William Benton asking his ejection charges McCarthy with misrepresentation, deception and outright perjury. Last week a subcommittee of Senators decided that the charges warranted a full investigation. McCarthy's response: the committee is trying to throw him out of the Senate "because of my fight against Communism."

He regularly tries to intimidate reporters by going over their heads to their bosses. When he denounced Drew Pearson (who is not always careful in his own accusations) as a "Kremlin mouthpiece," he demanded that Pearson's radio sponsor, Adam Hat Stores, Inc., drop him immediately, and urged the public to boycott Adam hats. The company dropped Pearson as promptly as the voters of Maryland had dropped Tydings—apparently fearing that their customers would do what McCarthy suggested.

To get action that fast gives a man a sense of power. McCarthy's infatuation with his own crusade has showed signs recently of being stronger than his sense of what his audience will stand. Last summer, when he spent three hours accusing General George Marshall of conspiracy to "make common cause with Stalin," all but three Senators walked out on him.

West of the Alleghenies, Joe McCarthy is still bamboozling audiences. On the speaker's platform he has a sweat-stained, shirtsleeved earnestness. He stumbles, mixes his grammar, bangs the lectern hard with his fist. He dives into a huge briefcase for "documentation." He flourishes affidavits, reads from congressional hearings, waves photostats. "Listen to this, if you will—unbelievable!", he cries.

SOME HAVE ARGUED that McCarthy's end justifies his methods. This argument seems to assume that lies are required to fight Communist lies. Experience proves, however, that what the anti-Communist fight needs is truth, carefully arrived at and presented with all the scrupulous regard for decency and the rights of man of which the democratic world is capable. This is the Western world's greatest asset in the struggle against Communism, and those who condone McCarthy are throwing that asset away. As the New York *Times* put the case: "He has been of no use whatever in enabling us to distinguish among sinners, fools and patriots, except in the purely negative sense that many of us have begun to suspect that there must be some good, however small, in anybody who has aroused Senator McCarthy's ire."

A very practical danger lies in this inevitable, negative reaction to McCarthy. The Administration supporters have gradually come to see that they could make capital out of "McCarthyism." If anybody criticizes the judgment of any State Department official in his past or present analysis of Communism, the cry of "McCarthyism" is raised. This McCarthyism in reverse was apparent last week in the Senate hearings over the confirmation of Ambassador Jessup. Harold Stassen had been careful to say that he was raising no question of Jessup's loyalty or his affiliations; he was simply questioning Jessup's past record of judgment. One observer quickly concluded that Stassen was "the rich man's McCarthy," presumably because McCarthy had also attacked Jessup—on different and far shakier grounds.

On the other hand, a larger share of responsibility for the confusion of McCarthyism belongs to those Republican leaders who have either openly encouraged McCarthy or failed to disavow him, in the belief that he was making votes. Republican Senate Leader Kenneth Wherry recently declared that McCarthy had done the U.S. a "great service." Even Ohio's Robert A. Taft came to McCarthy's defense when Truman described Joe as "a Kremlin asset."

In less McCarthyesque language, McCarthy can be summed up this way:

1) His antics foul up the necessary examination of the past mistakes of the Truman-Acheson foreign policy.

2) His constant imputation of treason distracts attention from the fact

that patriotic men can make calamitous mistakes for which they should be held politically accountable.

3) There are never any circumstances which justify the reckless imputation of treason or other moral guilt to individuals in or out of office.

4) McCarthy's success in smearing Tydings and others generates fear of the consequences of dissent. This fear is exaggerated by the "liberals" who welcome McCarthyism as an issue; but the fear exists—and it is poison in a democracy.

More than Joe McCarthy went into the making of McCarthyism. It would never have become a force if mistakes of policy had not led the U.S. into a position that alarmed the public. Long before McCarthy, the U.S. had been slipping into the lazy fallacy that all ideas, policies and political systems are approximately equal—a state of mind very different from the valid principle that all men have a right to express their ideas, however bad. Part of the U.S. public, over-tolerant of bad ideas, was a sucker for McCarthy's bigoted effort to prove that bad policy must be the work of evil, traitorous men.

In the vital debates of the day, this charge is totally irrelevant. But it is an irrelevance that compels attention. Like a man busily shooting off firecrackers in a legislative hall, McCarthy may not be persuasive, but he must be dealt with before any debate at all can progress.

Some of the sentries of the republic were asleep after the war—and some are still drowsy. The finding that they were not traitors does not answer the charge that they were bad sentries.

And the drowsy sentry is no worse sentry than the one who maliciously cries wolf, shoots up the coconut trees, and keeps the camp in a state of alarm and confusion. ■

Laughing Matter

BY PAUL O'NEIL

[*A mob hit as slapstick comedy? In the hands of a gifted writer, this improbable notion produced a wry but compelling account of the death of Murder Inc.'s boss*]

November 4, 1957

THE HUMOROUS ASPECTS OF premeditated murder are almost identical with those of custard-pie comedy: connoisseurs of both can enjoy the victim's splendid initial innocence, his growing disbelief and alarm, and, finally, his absurd response to the inexorable offices of fate. It takes a trained mind to really appreciate the drolleries of the rubout, however; when the gaudiest murder of the year was staged one morning last week in the barber shop of Manhattan's Park Sheraton Hotel, nobody in the U.S. was as well qualified to enjoy its subtleties as bulky, greying Albert Anastasia—onetime Lord High Executioner of Brooklyn's Murder Inc. But this time Al was straight man rather than critic.

Al managed to be pretty funny in his new role, although doubtless not as comical as the fellow his practical jokers once threw into a lake, alive, weighted down with slot machines. At 55, Al was ripe for the part; he had grown rich, fleshy, imperious and sentimental on the rewards of death. He wore the big tipper's air of assurance as he walked into the bright, mirrored, roomy barber shop and ordered a haircut; he closed his eyes contentedly as he felt the clippers on his thick neck. He was completely oblivious of two dark, sallow men who entered with their hats on, after him. Each

36

of the pair wore the sort of dark, metal-rimmed glasses affected by high-way cops. Each wore a scarf over his mouth. Each wore a black glove on his right hand, and each black hand gripped a pistol. They pushed the barber aside and stood on either side of the chair.

Al's eyes were still closed when the first bullet made a hole in his pudgy left hand. Both gunmen fired at him. Another slug went through Al's clothes, made him jump as though he had been hit with a baseball bat, and bloodied the soft, warm, white, middle-aged flesh of his right side. Al just had time to realize he was being killed. He kicked out in such convulsive fright that he broke the chair's metal footrest. Then he lurched up in adenoidal agony and knocked over a bottle of bay rum. The two men who were killing him went placidly on with their work, and when Al crashed to the floor he was a pleasantly scented cadaver—a five holer, as it were, and badly in need of a new head.

The killers inspected the remains with professional care. Then they joined the horrified barbers, customers and shoeshine boys who went bursting into a hall off the hotel lobby. They left Al as evidence that history repeats itself—he had gotten it in the same hotel in which Gambler Arnold Rothstein was shot back in 1928.

Al had earned the honor. A murderous, grasping and illiterate slob, he had thwarted the law for 40 years, twisted the politics, and opened the economic veins, of the greatest city in the world. He had done it, at bottom, simply by killing people, personally and by proxy, with ice picks, knives, pistols, the garrote and the bludgeon.

Al, who was born in Tropea, Italy (real name: Umberto Anastasio), started his career almost as soon as he jumped ship in New York in 1917 to become a dock-walloper on the Brooklyn piers. In 1921 and 1922 he spent 18 months in the death house at Sing Sing for the murder of another long-shoreman named George Turrello. The experience taught him the efficacy of wholesale death; when his lawyer got him a new trial, his pals killed off so many witnesses that Al was released. After that he prospered; the waterfront offered, as it still does, wonderful opportunities in pilferage, shake-downs, strikebreaking and extortion. He met a lot of other rising young men: Al Capone, Louis ("Lepke") Buchalter, Lucky Luciano. He was often arrested (murder, 1928; murder, 1932; murder, 1933), but never convicted. A stool pigeon named John Bazzano, who took an interest in him in 1932, was found cut into stew meat in a burlap bag.

When the mobs syndicated, after Prohibition, Al became "The Law"—

his Brooklyn mob handled executions for the chieftains of the underworld. Some victims went into the Hudson in concrete kimonos. Some were buried in quicklime in a Lyndhurst, N.J. chicken yard that the boys used as a private cemetery. In all, Al was credited with 63 corpses during this phase of his career. He never paid a day in jail for them. Abe ("Kid Twist") Reles sang about Murder Inc. in 1940, but Reles, though locked in a Coney Island hotel room and guarded by cops, somehow managed to fall out the window and kill himself before Brooklyn Prosecutor Bill O'Dwyer saw fit to bring Al to trial. Al disappeared and joined the Army (he trained soldiers as longshoremen during the war), and for "clerical reasons," the "wanted" card with Al's name was removed from the files of the New York Police Department.

After the war Al built a tile-roofed, Spanish-style mansion at the edge of the Hudson River palisades in New Jersey, built a 10-ft. metal fence topped by barbed wire, installed lights and Doberman pinscher watchdogs, and settled down to the good life. He went to race tracks and took the sun in Florida and Hot Springs, Ark. This existence was interrupted in 1954 when the Government charged him with evading a paltry $12,000 in federal income taxes. Before the matter was settled two Government witnesses, an elderly couple, disappeared from their bloodstained Miami house. Al got off with a year in Milan, Mich.

Still, Al grew to resent reference to the vulgar necessities of his sort of life. So did his brother, Tough Tony, who ran the Brooklyn piers for him. "Murderer?" Tony once rasped to a reporter. "He kill anybody in your family yet?" Al was proud of his children and became a heavy spender in New York toy stores. He was mourned last week, however, in a very narrow circle. Only Tough Tony gave any public display of grief. When a New York *Daily News* reporter called him and announced that Al had been shot to death, Tony said: "What the hell kind of a joke do you call that?" "It's no joke," said his informant. "Oh, my God," moaned Tony. "Oh, my God. No . . . no . . . no." He hurried to the hotel and threw himself, weeping hysterically, upon his brother's corpse.

But servants at Anastasia's home seemed unmoved at the news (although a maid did set the dogs on reporters), and Al's family decided not to ask the Roman Catholic Church to bury him (another brother, the Rev. Salvatore Anastasio, is a Bronx priest). He was put away quietly in a plain old $900 coffin—although another brother, Joe, got a $6,000 box when he passed on (of natural causes) last year, and $15,000 worth of flowers to boot.

Only the New York cops seemed genuinely stirred. Al had hardly been lugged out of the hotel before they were questioning the first of hundreds of underworld characters. The two killers had dropped their pistols on the way out; one was a .32 Smith & Wesson, the other a .38 Colt which originally had been sold in the Middle West in the 1930s. That was all anybody knew. The police were intensely curious as to why Al's bodyguard, one Anthony Coppola, was in a drugstore across the street when Al was ventilated. Anthony was just doing what his kind always does; he was having a cup of coffee.

There were dozens of theories: that it was Al who had ordered Frank Costello shot last spring and that he had paid the price; that a new, young mob was responsible for both the Costello and Anastasia shootings; that Al had declared himself the new "boss" of Manhattan garment-district rackets and doomed himself in the process.

At week's end it was only possible to wonder who in what city tenement or guarded country home was laughing hardest at the joke on Al—who had gotten the chair at last.   ■

"A Giant Leap for Mankind"

BY LEON JAROFF

[*More than a U.S. victory in the cold war, more than a scientific breakthrough, the first moon landing was a milestone in man's perpetual quest for the unknown*]

July 25, 1969

THE GHOSTLY, WHITE-CLAD FIGURE slowly descended the ladder. Having reached the bottom rung, he lowered himself into the bowl-shaped footpad of *Eagle,* the spindly lunar module of Apollo 11. Then he extended his left foot, cautiously, tentatively, as if testing water in a pool—and, in fact, testing a wholly new environment for man. That groping foot, encased in a heavy multi-layered boot (size 9½B), would remain indelible in the minds of millions who watched it on TV, and a symbol of man's determination to step—and forever keep stepping—toward the unknown.

After a few short but interminable seconds, U.S. Astronaut Neil Armstrong placed his foot firmly on the fine-grained surface of the moon. The time was 10:56 p.m. (E.D.T.), July 20, 1969. Pausing briefly, the first man on the moon spoke the first words on lunar soil:

"That's one small step for man, one giant leap for mankind."

With a cautious, almost shuffling gait, the astronaut began moving about in the harsh light of the lunar morning. "The surface is fine and powdery, it adheres in fine layers, like powdered charcoal, to the soles and sides of my foot," he said. "I can see the footprints of my boots and the treads in the fine, sandy particles." Minutes later, Armstrong was joined by Edwin Aldrin. Then, gaining confidence with every step, the two jumped and loped across the barren landscape for 2 hrs. 14 min., while the TV camera they had set up some 50 ft. from *Eagle* transmitted their movements with remarkable clarity to enthralled audiences on earth, a quarter of a million miles away. Sometimes moving in surrealistic slow motion, sometimes bounding around in the weak lunar gravity like exuberant kangaroos, they set up experiments and scooped up rocks, snapped pictures and probed the soil, apparently enjoying every moment of their stay in the moon's alien environment.

After centuries of dreams and prophecies, the moment had come. Man had broken his terrestrial shackles for the first time and set foot on another world. Standing on the lifeless, rock-studded surface he could see the earth, a lovely blue and white hemisphere suspended in the velvety black sky. The spectacular view might well help him place his problems, as well as his world, in a new perspective.

Although the Apollo 11 astronauts planted an American flag on the moon, their feat was far more than a national triumph.* It was a stunning scientific and intellectual accomplishment for a creature who, in the space of a few million years—an instant in evolutionary chronology—emerged from primeval forests to hurl himself at the stars. Its eventual effect on human civilization is a matter of conjecture. But it was in any event a shining reaffirmation of the optimistic premise that whatever man imagines he can bring to pass.

It was appropriate that the event was watched by ordinary citizens in Prague as well as Paris, Bucharest as well as Boston, Warsaw as well as Wapakoneta, Ohio. In practically every other corner of the earth, newspapers broke out what pressmen refer to as their "Second Coming" type to hail the lunar landing. Poets hymned the occasion. Wrote Archibald MacLeish:

> O
> silver evasion in our farthest thought—
> "the visiting moon" . . . "the glimpses of the moon" . . .
> and we have touched you! . . .
>
> Three days and three nights we journeyed,
> steered by farthest stars, climbed outward,
> crossed the invisible tide-rip where the floating dust

* In any case, the U.S. could not have claimed sovereignty over the moon, even if it had been so inclined. A treaty drafted in 1966, and since signed by both Washington and Moscow, asserts that the moon is terra nullius, or no-man's-land, open to exploration and use by all nations.

falls one way or the other in the void between,
followed that other down, encountered
cold, faced death—unfathomable emptiness.

U.S. space officials, normally as detached and professionally cool as the astronauts they sent into space, in their own way also grew poetic. "We have clearly entered a new era," said Thomas O. Paine, Administrator of NASA. "The voices coming from the moon are still hard to believe."

For those who watched, in fact, the whole period that began with *Eagle's* un-docking from *Columbia,* the command module, and its descent to the moon seemed difficult to believe. No work of the imagination, however contrived, could have rivaled it for excitement, suspense and, finally, triumph.

As the orbiting command module and the lunar module emerged from behind the moon, having undocked while they were out of radio communication, an anxious capsule commentator in Houston inquired: "How does it look?" Replied Armstrong: "The *Eagle* has wings." The lunar module was on its own, ready for its landing on the moon.

Behind the moon again, on their 14th revolution, *Eagle's* descent engine was fired, slowing the module down and dropping it into the orbit that would take it to within 50,000 ft. of the lunar surface. The crucial word from Houston was relayed by Michael Collins, *Columbia* pilot, when a burst of static momentarily cut *Eagle* off from the ground: "You are go for PDI [powered descent insertion]." Again *Eagle's* descent engine fired, beginning a twelve-minute burn that was scheduled to end only when the craft was within two yards of the lunar surface. One of the most dangerous parts of Apollo 11's long journey had begun.

Now the tension was obvious in the voices of both the crew and the controller. Just 160 ft. from the surface Aldrin reported: "Quantity light." The light signaled that only 114 seconds of fuel remained. Armstrong and Aldren had 40 seconds to decide if they could land within the next 20 seconds. If they could not, they would have to abort, jettisoning their descent stage and firing their ascent engine to return to *Columbia.*

At that critical point, Armstrong, a 39-year-old civilian with 23 years of experience at flying everything from Ford tri-motors to experimental X-15 rocket planes, took decisive action. The automatic landing system was taking *Eagle* down into a football-field-size crater littered with rocks and boulders. Armstrong explained: "It required a manual takeover on the P-66 [a semiautomatic computer program] and flying manually over the rock field to find a reasonably good area." The crisis emphasized the value of manned flight. Had *Eagle* continued on its computer-guided course, it might well have crashed into a boulder, toppled over or landed at an angle of more than 30° from the vertical, making a later takeoff impossible. Said a shaken Paine in Houston's Mission Operations Control Room: "It crossed my mind that, boy, this isn't a simulation. Perhaps we should come back for just one more simulation."

Now the craft was close to the surface. "Forty feet," called Aldrin, rattling off altitudes and rates of descent with crackling precision. "Things look good. Picking up some dust [stirred up on the surface by the blasting descent engine]. Faint shadow. Drifting to the right a little. Contact light—O.K. Engine stop." Armstrong quickly recited a ten-second check list of switches to turn off. Then came the word that the world had been waiting for.

"Houston," Armstrong called. "Tranquillity Base here. The *Eagle* has landed." The time: 4:17:41 p.m., E.D.T., just about 1½ minutes earlier than the landing time scheduled months before. It was a wild, incredible moment. There were cheers, tears and frantic applause at Mission Control in Houston. "You got a lot of guys around here about to turn blue," the NASA communicator radioed to *Eagle*. "We're breathing again." A little later, Houston added: "There's lots of smiling faces in this room, and all over the world." "There are two of them up here," responded *Eagle*. "And don't forget the one up here," Collins piped in from the orbiting *Columbia*.

FOR THE NEXT 3 HRS. 12 MIN., Armstrong and Aldrin busily read through check lists and punched out computer instructions, making all *Eagle* systems ready for a quick takeoff if it should become necessary. Aldrin took time to describe the landing site: "It looks like a collection of just about every variety of shapes. Angularities, granularities, every variety of rock you could find."

After it became evident that the sturdy, 16-ton craft had survived the landing unscathed, the astronauts, eager to explore their new world, requested permission to skip their scheduled sleep period and leave *Eagle* around four hours earlier than planned. "Tranquillity Base," radioed Houston, "we've thought about it. We will support it."

Armstrong and Aldrin struggled to put on their boots, gloves, helmets and backpacks (known as PLSS, or Portable Life Support System), then depressurized *Eagle's* cabin and opened the hatch. Wriggling backward out of the hatch on his stomach, Armstrong worked his way across the LM "porch" to the ladder and began to climb down. On his way he pulled a lanyard that opened the MESA (Modularized Equipment Storage Assembly) and exposed the camera that televised the remainder of his historic descent. Thus the miracle of the moon flight was heightened by the miracle of TV from outer space, made possible by a special miniature camera. Because the camera had to be stowed upside down, for a few seconds Armstrong was turned topsy-turvy in the picture; a NASA television converter quickly righted it. On the moon, even the taciturn Armstrong could not contain his excitement. He could not, of course, have known about the gentle admonition made by his wife Janet as she watched the mission on TV: "Be descriptive now, Neil." Yet suddenly he began to bubble over with detailed descriptions and snap pictures with all the enthusiasm of the archetypal tourist. Houston had to remind him four times to quit clicking and get on with a task of higher priority: gathering a small "contingency" sample of lunar soil that would guarantee the return of at least some moon material if the mission had to be suddenly aborted.

"Just as soon as we finish these pictures," said Armstrong. Scooping up the soil, he reported: "It's a very soft surface. But here and there, where I probe with the contingency sample collector, I run into very hard surface." Even his geologic descriptions bordered on the rhapsodic. "It has a stark beauty all its own. It's like much of the high desert of the United States. It's different, but it's very pretty out here."

Aldrin, obviously itching to join Armstrong, asked: "Is it O.K. for me to come out?" As soon as he touched the surface, he jumped back up to the first rung of the ladder three times to show how easy it was. Then, delighted with his new-found agility despite the 183 lbs. of clothing and gear that he carried, he became the first man to run on the lunar surface.

Armstrong moved the still-operating camera to its panorama position on a tripod aimed at the lunar module. During the next two hours, the astronauts went busily about their appointed tasks, moving in and out of the camera's view. They planted a 3-ft. by 5-ft. American flag, stiffened with thin wire so that it would appear to be flying in the vacuum of the moon. Effortlessly they set up three scientific devices: 1) a solar wind experiment, consisting of a 4-ft.-long aluminum-foil strip designed to capture particles streaming in from the sun; 2) a seismometer to register moonquakes and meteor impacts and report them back to earth; and 3) a reflector for measuring precise earth-moon distances by bouncing laser beams from earth directly back to the source.

The seismometer went to work immediately. It recorded and transmitted to earth evidence of the tremors caused when Aldrin hammered tubes into the lunar surface to collect core samples. It also registered the thud when the astronauts dropped their backpacks from *Eagle's* hatch. But the first test of the laser reflector failed when a beam shot from California's Lick Observatory missed the reflector by about 50 miles.

Fifty-three minutes after Armstrong first set foot on the moon, Houston urged him and Aldrin to move within camera range. "The President of the United States would like to say a few words to you," Mission Control advised. The President has been eager all along to associate himself with the mission. Now, as both astronauts stood stiffly at attention near the flag, Nixon told them: "This certainly has to be the most historic phone call ever made. . . . All the people on this earth are truly one in their pride of what you have done, and one in their prayers that you will return safely."

In the remaining time, Armstrong and Aldrin scooped up about 60 lbs. (earth weight) of rocks for one of the lunar sample boxes. They managed to collect 20 lbs. of rocks for the sample box that was supposed to hold sorted and identified rocks. Unfortunately, with time running out, none of the rocks were actually catalogued. At the urging of controllers ("Head on up the ladder"), the astronauts rolled up the solar wind experiment, placed it in a sample box, sealed both boxes, and hauled them via a clothesline-like pulley into the lunar module. Two hours and 31 minutes after Armstrong first emerged, both men had climbed back inside *Eagle,* and the hatch was closed.

In addition to the flag, the astronauts left behind a number of mementos from the earth. There was a 1½-in. silicon disk bearing statements (reduced in size 200 times) by Presidents Eisenhower, Kennedy, Johnson and Nixon, and words of good will from leaders of 72 different countries. The disk also bore a message from Pope Paul VI quoting from the Eighth Psalm, a hymn to the Creator:

> *When I behold your heavens, the work of your fingers, the moon and the stars which you set in place—*
> *What is man that you should be mindful of him, or the son of man that you should care for him?*
> *You have made him little less than the angels, and crowned him with glory and honor.*

You have given him rule over the works of your hands, putting all things under his feet . . .

Attached to a leg of the lunar module's lower stage, which would remain on the moon when the upper portion blasted off, was the already famous "We came in peace" plaque signed by President Nixon and Apollo 11 Astronauts Armstrong, Aldrin and Collins. Also to be left behind: medals and shoulder patches in memory of Yuri Gagarin, Vladimir Komarov, Virgil Grissom, Roger Chaffee and Edward White, five men who have died while in Soviet or U.S. space programs.

Their lunar excursion successfully completed, they settled down to a relaxed meal and a rest. It was strange to think that while much of the U.S. slept, two Americans were also sleeping in their cramped quarters on the distant and silent moon. Some 21 hours after landing on the moon, Armstrong and Aldrin were ready to blast off in the five-ton upper stage of the lunar module. Later, they were to rendezvous and dock with the orbiting *Columbia.*

Other stages of the flight had been—and would be—dangerous enough. At any point during the eight-day journey, a massive failure of the electrical or oxygen systems, or a collision with a large meteor would almost surely result in tragedy. But lift-off was the most nerve-racking part of the mission. If the ascent engine had failed to start, *Eagle* would have been stranded on the lunar surface. Too short a burn would have tossed the module into a trajectory that would send it smashing back onto the lunar surface. Had the LM achieved an orbit with an apocynthion (high point) much less than 50,000 ft., *Columbia* would have been unable to reach it. As it turned out, departure from the moon was triumphantly smooth. Of course, even after lift-off and redocking, there were still the dangers of the homeward trip. Control failures could cause the spacecraft to re-enter the earth's atmosphere at too steep an angle and burn to a cinder, or at so flat an angle that it would bounce off the outer fringes of the atmosphere far into space. There its oxygen would be exhausted before it could loop back to the earth.

The early part of Apollo 11's epic journey had been as uneventful as the later part was suspenseful. Lift-off was nearly perfect. Rising Phoenix-like above its own exhaust flames, a scant 724 milliseconds behind schedule, the giant rocket shook loose some 1,300 lbs. of ice that had frozen on its white sides. Although it was the heaviest space vehicle ever fired aloft—

6,484,289 lbs. at ignition—it cleared the launch tower in twelve seconds.

Less than twelve minutes after lift-off, a brief boost from the S-4B third stage placed Apollo into a circular 119-mile orbit at a velocity of 17,427 m.p.h. Over the Pacific for the second time, just 2½ hrs. after launch, the spacecraft was cleared by Houston for "translunar insertion" (TLI). Firing for five minutes, the reliable S-4B engine accelerated the ship to 24,245 m.p.h., fast enough to tear it loose from the earth's gravitational embrace and send it toward the moon. At a point 43,495 miles from the moon, lunar gravity exerted a force equal to the gravity of the earth, then some 200,000 miles distant. Beyond that crest, lunar gravity predominated, and Apollo was on the "downhill" leg of its journey.

The astronauts zoomed past the western rim of the moon at 5,645 m.p.h. They were whipped behind the far side and into lunar orbit by the moon's gravity and a 5-min. 57-sec. burn of the reliable SPS engine that reduced their speed to 3,736 m.p.h. When they emerged from behind the eastern edge, after 34 minutes during which radio communication was blocked, they had dropped into a 70- by 196-mile-high orbit.

THAT WAS ABOUT AS CLOSE as Collins, the affable, relaxed Air Force lieutenant colonel, would get. Before the trip, he complained good-humoredly that because he would be piloting *Columbia* during the moon walk, he would be "about the only person in the world who won't get to see the thing on television." He asked Houston to save a videotape for him. At least, said Collins, "I'm going 99.99% of the way."

Coming around the eastern limb of the moon on their first revolution, the astronauts focused the camera on the desolate landscape below. After a long period of silence, a Houston capsule communicator pleaded: "Would you care to comment on some of those craters as we go by?" At last the astronauts came to life.

"Just going over Mount Marilyn," said Armstrong, referring to a triangular-shaped peak named for the wife of Apollo 8 Astronaut James Lovell. "Now we're looking at what we call Boot Hill. On the right is the crater Censorinus P." The spacecraft passed over Sidewinder and Diamondback, two of the sinuous rills that had caused Apollo 10 Astronaut John Young to wonder "if some time long ago fish hadn't been jumping in those creeks." Commented Collins: "It looks like a couple of snakes down there in the lake bed."

None of the astronauts slept very long before awakening to the most momentous day of their lives. Collins got six hours, Aldrin and Armstrong five apiece. During Apollo's eleventh revolution of the moon, Aldrin and Armstrong donned their space suits and crawled through a tunnel for a final checkout of the lunar module before its long separation from the command module. They paid particular attention to *Eagle's* propulsion systems—the tanks containing the hypergolic fuels that fire the descent and ascent engines, and the pressure gauges on the helium that forces the fuels into the combustion chambers, where they burn upon contact with one another. Efficient and businesslike, they completed the check 30 minutes ahead of schedule. Two minutes before the spacecraft disappeared behind the moon on its 13th revolution, Houston advised: "We're go for undocking." Tense minutes followed until the spacecraft emerged from the far side and Armstrong reported that *Eagle* had wings.

Thus did Armstrong and Aldrin set out on that last, epochal one-hundredth of 1% of the outbound journey. Some nine hours later, while *Columbia* was out of contact on the far side of the moon, Armstrong and Aldrin stepped down from the ungainly looking *Eagle*—and into history. It was a moment that would surely survive long after the criticism that has accompanied every step of the space program is forgotten—understandable as that criticism may be in view of the pressing problems back on earth. It was, too, a moment that symbolized man's wondrous capacity for questing, then conquering, then questing yet again for something just beyond his reach. But the black vastness that served as a backdrop for the two astronauts' walk on the moon also was a reminder of something else. Stargazer, now star-reacher, man inhabits a smallish planet of an ordinary sun in a garden-variety galaxy that occupies the tiniest corner of a universe whose scope is beyond comprehension.   ■

The Unmaking of the President

BY ED MAGNUSON

[*In this gripping narrative of the climax of the Watergate
scandal, the U.S. government was in crisis and Richard Nixon
had to face the decisive moment in his long, turbulent career*]

August 19, 1974

WHEN THE NATION'S WORST political scandal finally rendered the presidency of Richard Nixon inoperative,
it did so with savage swiftness. Hopelessly entrapped in the
two-year tangle of his own deceit, forced into a confession of
past lies, he watched the support of his most loyal defenders
collapse in a political maelstrom, driven by their bitterness
over the realization that he had betrayed their trust. Yet, as throughout his
self-inflicted Watergate ordeal, Nixon remained unwilling to admit, perhaps even to himself, the weight of his transgressions against truth and the
Constitution. He was among the last to appreciate the futility of his lonely
struggle to escape removal from office.

Fittingly, the prelude to collapse began on July 24, when three "strict
constructionist" Supreme Court Justices appointed by Nixon searchingly
scoured the Constitution and joined in a unanimous finding that it contained no legal basis for his withholding 64 White House tape recordings
from Special Prosecutor Leon Jaworski. The President on May 6 and 7
had listened to some of those tapes and abandoned a proposed compromise under which he would turn twelve of them over to Jaworski. He did

not tell his chief Watergate lawyer James St. Clair that those tapes would destroy his professions of innocence in the cover-up conspiracy. Instead, Nixon allowed St. Clair to carry a claim of absolute Executive privilege to the Supreme Court and to argue before the House Judiciary Committee that the President was unaware of that cover-up until informed of it on March 21, 1973, by John Dean.

Incredibly, St. Clair had taken on the job of defending the President without any assurance that he would have access to all of the evidence.* But just two days after the Supreme Court decision, St. Clair was jolted into a full awareness of his responsibilities by Federal Judge John J. Sirica, whose judicial inquisitiveness has played a pivotal role in unraveling the Watergate deceptions. "Have you personally listened to the tapes?" Sirica asked St. Clair in court, well aware from news reports that St. Clair had not. "You mean to say the President wouldn't approve of your listening to the tapes? You mean to say you could argue this case without knowing all the background of these matters?" Visibly flustered for the first time in his presidential-defense role, St. Clair promised to analyze each tape submitted to the court.

That promise set the trap. Nixon insisted upon listening to each tape once more before transmitting it to the court. Even if he had wanted to, there was no way he could now alter the evidence. The erase mechanism on the President's Sony recorder had been disconnected by the Secret Service. Even more important, Nixon Aide Stephen Bull delivered duplicate tapes rather than the originals to the President. After Nixon listened to the tapes, trusted secretaries prepared verbatim transcripts, and, in accordance with Sirica's wishes, copies went to St. Clair.

For the President's lawyer, the awful moment of truth came on Wednesday, July 31. On that day, he received and read the transcripts of three conversations held on June 23, 1972, between Nixon and his top aide, Chief of Staff H.R. Haldeman. Instantly, the stunned St. Clair knew that the contents were devastating to Nixon's defense. The transcripts showed that just six days after the Watergate wiretap-burglary, Nixon was fully aware that Re-Election Campaign Director John Mitchell and two former White House consultants, E. Howard Hunt and G. Gordon Liddy, had been in-volved—even though Hunt and Liddy had not then been arrested. He was told by Haldeman that "the FBI is not under control," and that agents were

---

* Robert Bork, U.S. Solicitor General, had turned down an offer to become Nixon's chief defense lawyer precisely because he was not assured such access.

tracing money found on the burglars to Nixon's re-election committee.

Nixon immediately proposed cover-up actions. His first suggestion to Haldeman, according to the transcripts, was that each campaign contributor whose check was traced to the burglary by the FBI should claim that the burglars had approached him independently for the money. Haldeman objected that this would involve "relying on more and more people all the time." Haldeman relayed a suggestion from Mitchell and Dean that the CIA should be asked to tell the FBI to "stay to hell out of this" because the FBI probe would expose unnamed—and actually nonexistent—secret CIA operations. Asked Haldeman about the FBI, "You seem to think the thing to do is get them to stop?" Replied Nixon: "Right, fine." Added Nixon later: "All right, fine, I understand it all. We won't second-guess Mitchell and the rest."

With those words, Nixon authorized the cover-up, a criminal obstruction of justice that was eventually to destroy his presidency. The transcripts show that Nixon ordered Haldeman to call in CIA Director Richard Helms and Deputy CIA Director Vernon Walters and get them to tell Acting FBI Director L. Patrick Gray "to lay off" his investigation of the Watergate burglary money. Nixon suggested that Haldeman could claim that "the President believes" that such an investigation would "open the whole Bay of Pigs thing up again" (as a CIA agent, Hunt had helped organize the disastrous 1961 invasion of Cuba), and that the CIA officials "should call the FBI in" and tell Gray, "Don't go any further into this case, period!"

The June 23 conversations hinted, moreover, that Nixon had been concerned even earlier about the FBI investigation touching the White House. "We're back in the problem area," Haldeman said early in the first meeting with Nixon that day, indicating a prior discussion. One such occasion almost certainly was on June 20, the day on which the two held an 18½-minute Watergate discussion—the tape of which was later manually erased by someone with access to the White House–held recordings.

Reading the transcripts, St. Clair had no doubt about what should be done: they must be released promptly and publicly. He knew that once Jaworski got them under the Supreme Court order, they would eventually become public, if only at the cover-up conspiracy trial of six Nixon aides. He knew that the Senate could acquire them for its probable trial of the President, and he feared that their contents might leak out earlier. Release in any of those forms would look involuntary. That would not only destroy Nixon but it could ruin St. Clair professionally, since he could be accused of having withheld evidence and argued falsely in Nixon's behalf.

The President's lawyer showed the transcripts to White House Chief of Staff Alexander Haig, who also realized at once their awesome potential. At that point, both men knew that Nixon was finished. Their delicate problem was gently to persuade the President that he must resign. Haig, in turn, went immediately to Secretary of State Henry Kissinger. He too saw no way out for Nixon and joined in the careful diplomatic exercise of convincing a proud Chief of State that he must step down.

With Haig's backing, St. Clair braced Nixon. Stressing the dire dangers, legal and political, in withholding the damaging information any longer, the lawyer urged its release. Implicit in St. Clair's appeal was the threat that he would have to resign from the Nixon defense if his advice was not taken. Fatalistically, Nixon finally concurred. "What's done is done," he said. "Let it go."

Just how to explain the transcripts publicly was a dilemma. Before the details were worked out, Nixon could conceivably change his mind. In a move that seemed designed to block any such possibility and to assess Congressional reaction, Haig and St. Clair on Friday, Aug. 2, asked the President's ablest defender on the House Judiciary Committee, California's Charles Wiggins, to come to the White House. He had never been in Haig's office before.

HAIG, ST. CLAIR AND WIGGINS gathered round the coffee table in Haig's office. Haig thanked Wiggins for his efforts on Nixon's behalf during the televised impeachment deliberations of the Judiciary Committee. Wiggins was preparing to carry that fight to the floor of the House and had already scheduled briefings on the evidence for Republican Congressmen whom he hoped to persuade to join the battle to save Nixon. Then St. Clair handed Wiggins the June 23 transcripts. Wiggins read them. "The significance was immediately apparent," he explained later. Wiggins reread the documents, looked up, and asked St. Clair what he intended to do with the adverse information. Before St. Clair could answer, the alarmed Wiggins gave his own advice: "The President really has only two options: 1) claim the Fifth Amendment and not disclose, or 2) disclose."

St. Clair assured Wiggins that Nixon had agreed to give the transcripts to the Judiciary Committee. Wiggins asked how long St. Clair had known of this evidence. Only since the tapes had been transcribed for delivery to

Judge Sirica two days before, St. Clair replied. "Haig said that was true for him too, and I believed them," Wiggins recalled. "St. Clair was very apologetic that the case had proceeded on an incomplete-fact basis."

Heartsick, Wiggins studied the document for a third time. He told the Nixon aides that "the case in the House will be hopelessly lost because of this," and that "you have to face the prospect of conviction in the Senate as well." Moreover, he advised, "somebody has to raise with the President the question of his resigning. The country's interest, the Republican Party's interest and Richard Nixon's interest would be served by resignation." St. Clair and Haig acknowledged as much, but observed that it was very difficult for them to broach the subject to Nixon. Returning to Capitol Hill, Wiggins instructed an assistant to cancel his briefings for the Republican defenders of the President. The aide looked puzzled.

Next day President Nixon helicoptered to Camp David, joined by his family and his friend Bebe Rebozo. Richard Nixon was there as the last week of his presidency began, and the events he had set in motion swept him through four fateful days of irresistible outside pressure, internal anguish and ultimate decision.

Nixon secluded himself in Aspen Cabin, his favorite, rustic four-bedroom retreat, and summoned five aides: St. Clair, Haig, Press Secretary Ronald Ziegler and Speechwriters Raymond Price and Patrick Buchanan. Arriving in the afternoon, they worked on the release of the confessional transcripts. Assembled in Laurel, the camp's main dining lodge, the distraught aides were diverted by larger worries. St. Clair and Buchanan saw the President's position as doomed and suggested that he must consider resigning. Haig and Ziegler shuttled between the two buildings, expressing these concerns. "I wish you hadn't said that," Nixon told the pair when resignation was proposed.

Although giving it some consideration, Nixon stiffly resisted that choice. "He kept mentioning the importance of not short-circuiting the constitutional process and of avoiding the setting of a dangerous precedent," said one Nixon aide. Nixon proposed that he take his case once more to the people in a last-ditch television appeal, thought about it, then rejected his own idea. As so often in the Watergate saga, his perception was poor, almost disconnected from reality: he was not at all certain that the effect of the newest tape disclosure would be that fatal. He ordered his aides to draft a statement to accompany the release of the transcripts. He would take his chances with the result. Price moved into an unoccupied cabin and began drafting the President's explanation. St. Clair insisted on a paragraph making it clear that he had been unaware of this damaging evidence. With the statement still unfinished, the aides returned to the capital.

Word of the unusual activity at Camp David had rapidly spread through Washington. Speculation grew that some major new Nixon move was imminent. The Senate's second-ranking Republican, Michigan's Robert Griffin, announced that he had sent a letter to the President warning that he would vote for conviction if Nixon defied any subpoenas for tapes and documents issued by the Senate. Already, Nixon's congressional support appeared to be shaky and shrinking.

FLYING BACK TO THE capital from a weekend in Michigan, Senator Griffin worked on a statement that went beyond his previous warning. He too had learned that adverse evidence was about to be revealed. Stepping before television cameras outside the House Rules Committee room, he urged Nixon to resign "in both the national interest and his own interest." Added Griffin in a quavering voice: "It's not just his enemies who feel that way. Many of his best friends—and I regard myself as one of those—believe now that this would be the most appropriate course." Griffin said later that he considered the suggestion to resign as the earnest advice of one friend to another.

At the White House, General Haig began telephoning Cabinet members to prepare them for the shock of the coming revelations. After informing the Cabinet, Haig asked some 150 members of the White House staff to assemble in a large conference room in the Executive Office Building. "I hate to be the harbinger of bad news," he said, before reading the President's incriminating statement. "You may feel depressed or outraged by this," he concluded, "but we must all keep going for the good of the nation. And I also hope you would do it for the President too." Haig was warmly applauded. Explained one staff member: "The applause was not for what he said. It was for Haig himself. Everybody knows he's been under the gun for a year."

A similar but more difficult notification chore was undertaken by Lawyer St. Clair. He headed for the Capitol in a black limousine to brief the men who had stuck their political necks out for the President in the House Judiciary Committee meetings: the ten Republicans who had opposed every article of impeachment. All but Mississippi's Trent Lott and Iowa's Wiley Mayne were able to attend the meeting in the office of Republican House Whip Leslie Arends.

"Gentlemen, I'm sorry to say it, but I'm not the bearer of good tidings," St. Clair began. Then he explained the nature of the new evidence, which was soon to be described as more than the long-sought "smoking pistol" and actually, in the apt phrase of Columnist George F. Will, akin to a "smoking howitzer." St. Clair said flatly that he had been ready to resign if Nixon had opposed release of the material. "I have my professional reputation to think about," he explained, adding that any other action would have been to withhold evidence of a possible criminal conspiracy.

The Republicans' reaction was a mixture of anger and dismay. "We were just dumbfounded," said Ohio's Delbert Latta. "We'd put our trust in the President. We felt he was telling us the truth. I think every American has that right—to put his trust in the President. It was a terrible, let-down feeling." Indiana's David Dennis said that he was "shocked and disappointed." He had planned to fight for Nixon on the House floor. But now Dennis was convinced that Nixon's "lack of frankness" had undercut his case and that he was impeachable under Article I as a member of the cover-up conspiracy.

Within hours of the publication of the transcripts, all ten Republicans on the Judiciary Committee announced that they would vote for the impeachment of the President. On Article I, at least, that would make the committee unanimously in favor of sending Nixon to trial in the Senate. Barely controlling his emotions, Wiggins read a statement saying that the new facts were "legally sufficient in my opinion to sustain at least one count against the President of conspiracy to obstruct justice." It was time, he added, for "the President, the Vice President, the Chief Justice and the leaders of the House and Senate to gather in the White House to discuss the orderly transition of power from Richard Nixon to Gerald Ford."

"Devastating—impeachable," rumbled New Jersey's Charles Sandman, who had been the President's most vocal champion on the committee; now he finally found the "specificity" he had declared lacking in the evidence. When he learned of the news, Iowa's mild-mannered Mayne declared that "the President has today admitted deceiving the American people, the Judiciary Committee and his own lawyer. This is direct evidence."

The burdened St. Clair pushed on to give the same shocking message to Senate leaders, assembled in Republican Leader Hugh Scott's office. "I have some very bad news," he repeated. After relating it, he added: "I was tempted to resign. I framed the issue that the President would either have to make this disclosure or he'd lose a lawyer." Perhaps wishfully, St. Clair insisted: "I think I can honorably continue to defend him. There are elements here on which I can continue to make a case." He could no longer argue that there was no evidence against the President, he seemed to say, but he could still claim that the President should not be convicted since the investigation had been only briefly delayed.

Then St. Clair revealed some of the same lack of political awareness that has marked the President's own flawed self-defense. "Before this," he told the Senate leaders, "we had the case won." "Where?" asked the incredulous Scott. "I mean as a lawyer," St. Clair replied. To a man, the Senate leaders—Scott, Griffin, Texas' John Tower, Utah's Wallace Bennett and New Hampshire's Norris Cotton—were stunned by the evidence of Nixon's deception. "We were shaken," said one of them. "It's the worst thing we've had."

When the Nixon statement and the transcripts were finally released late in the afternoon in a mobbed White House pressroom, the words of the conversations were indeed damning. But the Nixon explanation glossed over the import with patronizingly mild language. Nixon implied that he had forgotten all about those June 23 conversations with Haldeman until he had reviewed his tapes in May. Only then, he suggested, had he "recognized that these presented potential problems." But he did not tell his counsel or the Judiciary Committee because "I did not realize the extent of the implications which these conversations might now appear to have."

Both his forgetfulness and lack of appreciation of the implications were incredible. Nixon did admit, however, that "those arguing my case, as well as those passing judgment on the case, did so with information that was incomplete and in some respects erroneous. This was a serious act of omission for which I take full responsibility and which I deeply regret." The tapes, he also conceded, "are at variance with certain of my previous statements"—a euphemism for the fact that he had lied repeatedly.

Somewhat reluctantly, Nixon observed that "this additional material I am now furnishing may further damage my case"—clearly one of the grossest understatements of his many Watergate pronouncements. Noting more realistically that "a House vote of impeachment is, as a practical matter, virtually a foregone conclusion," he said that he would voluntarily give the Senate every tape transferred to Special Prosecutor Jaworski by Judge Sirica. If he did *not,* of course, the Senate would readily have acquired them during its trial.

Still pursuing the cover-up to the end, Nixon blandly and unpersuasively asserted that "when all the facts were brought to my attention, I insisted on a full investigation and prosecution of those guilty. I am firmly convinced that the record, in its entirety, does not justify the extreme step of impeachment and removal of a President." At a Washington press conference last March 6, Nixon had agreed that "the crime of obstruction of justice is a serious crime and would be an impeachable offense."

As his precarious support on Capitol Hill now crumbled under the revelations, Nixon remained unconvinced that his survival prospects had vanished. He set sail on the Potomac with his family and Rose Mary Woods. At dinner on a refreshingly breezy night, Pat and his daughters Tricia and Julie argued that there still was no reason for the President to consider resignation. After the cruise, Nixon sent word for the Cabinet to assemble next morning. He wanted to rally their continued support.

THE CABINET MEETING WAS bizarre. For 40 minutes, the remarkably composed President engaged in a monologue about the new tapes disclosures. Recounting the Viet Nam War, his diplomatic breakthroughs with China and the Soviet Union, Nixon sought to show how preoccupied he had been as his re-election campaign of 1972 approached. "One thing I have learned," he said, rerunning an old refrain, "is never to allow anybody else to run your campaign." That was meant to explain how he could have forgotten those telltale cover-up talks with Haldeman in June of that distant year. "In my opinion and in the opinion of my counsel, I have not committed any impeachable offense," he said. Therefore, he insisted, "the constitutional process should be followed out to the end—wherever the end may be."

The Cabinet members said nothing. Nixon neither sought their advice nor paused for comment. Neither did any agree with his apparent decision to cling to office. Only Vice President Ford finally offered an observation, explaining that he felt that "the public interest is no longer served" by his making statements in defense of the President. "I understand," said Nixon. Then he abruptly shifted into a discussion of the economy. Vaguely, he suggested setting up a domestic "summit meeting" to grapple with inflation. He wanted it to be held immediately.

Finally, Attorney General William Saxbe broke the air of unreality. "Mr. President, wouldn't it be wise to wait on this until next week anyway—until we see what's going to happen?" Republican National Chairman George Bush joined in. "Shouldn't we wait until the dust settles? Such a meeting ought to wait." Glaring at Saxbe, Nixon replied stonily: "No. This is too important to wait." Without explaining the nature of the proposed anti-inflation conference, he then rose and left the room.

The Cabinet members came away with two strong convictions: Nixon wanted them to carry on with their jobs, and he was not about to quit. But if he seemed politically naive about his desperate situation, Nixon showed no signs of emotional instability. There were no "Captain Queeg" mannerisms, Saxbe recalled later. "We were all looking for something like that. He was calm, in control of himself, and not the least bit tense."

After the meeting, the President called Kissinger into his office. Despite Nixon's resolution against resignation only moments before, the President's doubts began to surface. Kissinger did not reinforce Nixon's determination to stay on; it is not certain but he may have actually suggested that the President should resign. After the conversation, Kissinger told newsmen that despite the crisis, U.S. foreign policy remained stable.

The political realities were very much on the minds of the participants of another Washington meeting. The 15 members of the Senate Republican policy committee, joined by other Republican Senators, held their regular weekly luncheon on Capitol Hill. As they met on a day in which rumors of possible resignation were running wild, initially sending the Dow Jones industrial average up a startling 25 points by midday, the Senators were grim. Explained Tower later: "There was considerable concern that the President did not really understand the mood of the Senate, that he did not fully comprehend the peril he faced if he came to trial here."

Vice President Ford, arriving for the luncheon, did not dispel that atmosphere. Ford reported on the Cabinet meeting and left the impression that Nixon was far more concerned about the economy than about his Watergate weakness and would not resign. As the angry Senators plunged into a freewheeling discussion of Nixon's plight, Ford felt it was inappropriate to stay. Once Ford was gone, the talk turned tough. "There are only so many lies you can take, and now there has been one too many," complained Arizona's Conservative Barry Goldwater. "Nixon should get his ass out of the White House—today!"

During the G.O.P. meeting, Goldwater was called away to accept a telephone call from Haig. How many Senators would stand by the President? Haig wondered. No more than twelve or 15, Goldwater estimated. Returning to the meeting, the former presidential candidate was even more pessimistic. He said he doubted that Nixon could get more than nine votes, and if pressed, he could only name offhand two certainties: Curtis and South Carolina's Strom Thurmond. It became obvious at the meeting that Nixon had hopelessly lost the Republican leaders he needed for survival, including Goldwater and Tower. General agreement was reached that Nixon should be informed of his grave predicament in the Senate and that a majority of the Senators at the luncheon thought that the President must resign. But no decision was made on who should do it or just how it should be done.

That came in a smaller meeting later in the day of the official Republican Senate leadership—Scott, Tower and Griffin—and two invited Senators representing opposite wings of the party: Goldwater and New York's Liberal Jacob Javits. The group selected Goldwater as the man who ought to seek a meeting with the President to warn him of the tremendous odds against his acquittal. It was a role long ago foreseen for Goldwater in any ultimate resignation scenario.

A flurry of phone calls between Scott, Goldwater and three White House aides, Haig, Dean Burch and William Timmons, quickly followed. Goldwater's intention was unmistakably clear to Nixon's men: he wanted to let the President know that his Senate support had collapsed and that many Republican Senators favored his immediate resignation. The aides carried the grim news to Nixon. Finally aware of the depth of his troubles, Nixon deferred such a meeting, but his last option, resignation, loomed larger.

Repeatedly throughout the afternoon, Timmons was asked by the President for soundings on the sentiment in the Senate. Each time, Timmons' telephoned report was distressing. At most, Timmons could count only 20 of the vital 34 votes Nixon would need to survive, and even that insufficient band kept dwindling.

Nixon was now under a continuous barrage of public declarations by other influential members of Congress. Rhodes, long a Nixon loyalist, described the new tapes as "a cataclysmic affair" and declared that "cover-up of criminal activity and misuse of federal agencies can neither be condoned nor tolerated."

Even the Judiciary Committee's Edward Hutchinson made his turnabout official. "I feel that I have been deceived," he said, declaring that he would vote for impeachment "with a heavy heart." Arriving in Washington from Mississippi, Lott also confirmed his reversal on impeachment. He had reacted to the new evidence, he said, with "disbelief at first, then extreme disappointment and a letdown feeling." He was "dumbfounded, and then it turned to anger." House leaders, including the Judiciary Committee's Democratic Chairman Peter Rodino, laid plans to cut the House debate on impeachment from two weeks to one week. The third-ranking Republican in the House,

Illinois' John Anderson, asked: "Why should we need more than a day?"

Richard Nixon had received the message. When he held a private talk with one of his last-ditch supporters, Rabbi Baruch Korff, in the President's Executive Office Building hideaway at 3:30 p.m., he told Korff that he was seriously considering resignation.

In the evening, the troubled President telephoned Kissinger five times for wide-ranging talks about his predicament and how it might affect foreign policy. As the conversation turned to what kind of legacy in that field Nixon would leave, his decision to resign seemed certain. Already, Speechwriter Price was working on a draft of the President's resignation address.

BY WEDNESDAY MORNING, the decision was irrevocable. On instructions from Nixon, Gerald Ford was called to the White House to meet with General Haig. Ford got the summons in his limousine as he was heading for a meeting of the Chowder and Marching Society, a House Republican social club. Deputy Press Secretary Gerald Warren announced only that Ford had been invited to discuss "the current situation." In fact, Haig told Ford to prepare to assume the presidency.

Tricia's husband Edward Cox arrived at the White House from New York to join his wife, Mrs. Nixon, Julie and David Eisenhower in the family quarters. That gathering, too, signaled the fast-approaching end of the Nixon presidency. Rumors of resignation caused banner headlines and dominated news broadcasts. The stock market rallied again, with the Dow Jones industrials rising almost 24 points. Crowds gathered along the fences surrounding the White House; mostly somber and curious, they had the quiet air of a death watch.

In the Senate, the Republican Conference, chaired by Cotton, held its regular meeting. Massachusetts Republican Ed Brooke proposed that a delegation be sent to the White House. He was told that a meeting had already been arranged. In fact, Nixon had told Timmons that he would now see Goldwater, but wanted the regular Republican leaders, Rhodes and Scott, to attend as well. The time was set for late morning, then 12:30, then 2 p.m., 4 p.m. and finally 5 p.m. Rhodes was chauffeured to the White House in his limousine; Scott picked up Goldwater in his.

The President greeted the delegation cordially in the Oval Office, then sat at his large desk, with his visitors ranged in front of it. "He was anxious to put us at ease," said Scott later, "because I'm sure he knew we weren't."

Nixon reminisced about the Eisenhower years, and all chatted as the trio waited for him to broach the momentous topic. "What I need to do," Nixon finally began, "is to get your appraisal of the floor. I have a decision to make. I've got maybe 15 in the Senate and ten in the House."

"There's not more than 15 Senators for you," Goldwater agreed. Nixon turned to Scott. "I think twelve to 15," declared Scott, who once had proclaimed Nixon's Watergate innocence on the basis of an edited White House transcript privately shown him. Nixon next asked Rhodes about the House count. The reply: "I think the substance is about as you have portrayed it."

His feet propped on the desk, Nixon was surprisingly amiable. Could the severe assessment change? he wondered. "It's pretty gloomy," said Scott. "It's damn gloomy," agreed the President. "In the decision I've got to make," he added, "I have very few options." But he did not want to talk, he said, "about emoluments or benefits or anything that people think that I'd be concerned about. I'm only thinking about the national interest. Whatever decision I make, I'll make in the national interest. The decision has to be made in the best interest of the people."

The expression of public concern slipped only fleetingly. Near the end of the half-hour talk, Nixon said: "I campaigned for a lot of people. Some were turkeys, but I campaigned for all of them." Where were they now? he mused. Most of them were voting to impeach him. But he abruptly broke that bitter mood. "Thank you, gentlemen," he said in dismissal.

Nixon had not asked for advice on whether he should resign. His visitors did not offer it. But they knew that his mind was made up. The meeting was merely a formality, a final confirmation of Richard Nixon's worst fears. The three emerged to tell the waiting press and nation only that the President would put the national interest first.

Next morning the President summoned Gerald Ford to notify him, officially and privately, that he was about to succeed to the national summit. For the country, the worst of Watergate was finally over. There would be more trials, perhaps even startling revelations, but they would no longer taint the Oval Office. The renewal had begun. ∎

The Man in the Water

BY ROGER ROSENBLATT

[*In the aftermath of a plane crash in Washington's Potomac River, the writer zeroed in not on the disaster and loss, but on an anonymous, triumphant act of heroism*]

January 25, 1982

AS DISASTERS GO, THIS one was terrible, but not unique, certainly not among the worst on the roster of U.S. air crashes. There was the unusual element of the bridge, of course, and the fact that the plane clipped it at a moment of high traffic, one routine thus intersecting another and disrupting both. Then, too, there was the location of the event. Washington, the city of form and regulations, turned chaotic, deregulated, by a blast of real winter and a single slap of metal on metal. The jets from Washington National Airport that normally swoop around the presidential monuments like famished gulls are, for the moment, emblemized by the one that fell; so there is that detail. And there was the aesthetic clash as well—blue-and-green Air Florida, the name a flying garden, sunk down among gray chunks in a black river. All that was worth noticing, to be sure. Still, there was nothing very special in any of it, except death, which, while always special, does not necessarily bring millions to tears or to attention. Why, then, the shock here?

Perhaps because the nation saw in this disaster something more than a mechanical failure. Perhaps because people saw in it no failure at all, but rather something successful about their makeup. Here, after all, were two forms of nature in collision: the elements and human character. Last Wednesday, the elements, indifferent as ever, brought down Flight 90. And on that same afternoon, human nature—groping and flailing in mysteries of its own—rose to the occasion.

Of the four acknowledged heroes of the event, three are able to account for their behavior. Donald Usher and Eugene Windsor, a park police helicopter team, risked their lives every time they dipped the skids into the water to pick up survivors. On television, side by side in bright blue jumpsuits, they described their courage as all in the line of duty. Lenny Skutnik, a 28-year-old employee of the Congressional Budget Office, said: "It's something I never thought I would do"—referring to his jumping into the water to drag an injured woman to shore. Skutnik added that "somebody had to go in the water," delivering every hero's line that is no less admirable for its repetitions. In fact, nobody had to go into the water. That somebody actually did so is part of the reason this particular tragedy sticks in the mind.

But the person most responsible for the emotional impact of the disaster is the one known at first simply as "the man in the water." (Balding, probably in his 50s, an extravagant mustache.) He was seen clinging with five other survivors to the tail section of the airplane. This man was described by Usher and Windsor as appearing alert and in control. Every time they lowered a lifeline and flotation ring to him, he passed it on to another of the passengers. "In a mass casualty, you'll find people like him," said Windsor. "But I've never seen one with that commitment." When the helicopter came back for him, the man had gone under. His selflessness was one reason the story held national attention; his anonymity another. The fact that he went unidentified invested him with a universal character. For a while he was Everyman, and thus proof (as if one needed it) that no man is ordinary.

Still, he could never have imagined such a capacity in himself. Only minutes before his character was tested, he was sitting in the ordinary plane among the ordinary passengers, dutifully listening to the stewardess telling him to fasten his seat belt and saying something about the "no smoking" sign. So our man relaxed with the others, some of whom would owe their lives to him. Perhaps he started to read, or to doze, or to regret some harsh remark made in the office that morning. Then suddenly he knew that the trip would not be ordinary. Like every other person on that flight, he was desperate to live, which makes his final act so stunning.

For at some moment in the water he must have realized that he would not live if he continued to hand over the rope and ring to others. He *had* to know it, no matter how gradual the effect of the cold. In his judgment he had no choice. When the helicopter took off with what was to be the last survivor, he watched everything in the world move away from him, and he deliberately let it happen.

Yet there was something else about the man that kept our thoughts on him, and which keeps our thoughts on him still. He was *there,* in the essential, classic circumstance. Man in nature. The man in the water. For its part, nature cared nothing about the five passengers. Our man, on the other hand, cared totally. So the timeless battle commenced in the Potomac. For as long as that man could last, they went at each other, nature and man; the one making no distinctions of good and evil, acting on no principles, offering no lifelines; the other acting wholly on distinctions, principles and, one supposes, on faith.

Since it was he who lost the fight, we ought to come again to the conclusion that people are powerless in the world. In reality, we believe the reverse, and it takes the act of the man in the water to remind us of our true feelings in this matter. It is not to say that everyone would have acted as he did, or as Usher, Windsor and Skutnik. Yet whatever moved these men to challenge death on behalf of their fellows is not peculiar to them. Everyone feels the possibility in himself. That is the abiding wonder of the story. That is why we would not let go of it. If the man in the water gave a lifeline to the people gasping for survival, he was likewise giving a lifeline to those who observed him.

The odd thing is that we do not even really believe that the man in the water lost his fight. "Everything in Nature contains all the powers of Nature," said Emerson. Exactly. So the man in the water had his own natural powers. He could not make ice storms, or freeze the water until it froze the blood. But he could hand life over to a stranger, and that is a power of nature too. The man in the water pitted himself against an implacable, impersonal enemy; he fought it with charity; and he held it to a standoff. He was the best we can do. ■

"Home Is Where You Are Happy"

BY HENRY GRUNWALD

[*For the author, editor-in-chief of Time Inc., immigration was a personal matter: the son of a Viennese librettist, he came to America as a teenager in 1940. In 1987 he went back as U.S. ambassador to Austria*]

July 8, 1985

EVERY IMMIGRANT LEADS A double life. Every immigrant has a double identity and a double vision, being suspended between an old and a new home, an old and a new self.

The very notion of a new home, of course, is in a sense as impossible as the notion of new parents. Parents *are* who they are; home *is* what it is. Home is the wallpaper above the bed, the family dinner table, the church bells in the morning, the bruised shins of the playground, the small fears that come with dusk, the streets and squares and monuments and shops that constitute one's first universe. Home is one's birthplace, ratified by memory.

Yet home, like parentage, must be legitimized through love; otherwise, it is only a fact of geography or biology. Most immigrants to America found their love of their old homes betrayed. Whether Ireland starved them, or Nazi Germany persecuted them, or Viet Nam drove them into the sea, they did not really abandon their countries; their countries abandoned them. In America, they found the possibility of a new love, the chance to nurture new selves.

Not uniformly, not without exceptions. Every generation has its

65

Know-Nothing movement, its fear—often understandable—and hatred of alien invasion. That is as true today as it always was. In spite of all this, the American attitude remains unique. Throughout history, exile has been a calamity; America turned it into a triumph and placed its immigrants in the center of a national epic. It is still symbolized by that old copper-plated cliché, the Statue of Liberty, notwithstanding the condescension and the awful poetry of the famous Emma Lazarus lines ("the wretched refuse of your teeming shore").

The epic is possible because America is an idea as much as it is a country. America has nothing to do with allegiance to a dynasty and very little to do with allegiance to a particular place, but everything to do with allegiance to a set of principles. To immigrants, those principles are especially real because so often they were absent or violated in their native lands. It was no accident in the '60s and '70s, when alienation was in flower, that it often seemed to be "native" Americans who felt alienated, while aliens or the children of aliens upheld the native values. The immigrant's double vision results in a special, somewhat skewed perspective on America that can mislead but that can also find revelation in the things that to native Americans are obvious. Psychiatrist Robert Coles speaks of those "who straddle worlds and make of that very experience a new world."

It is not easy. Successive waves of immigration differ, of course, and a refugee from wartime Europe does not have the same experiences as a refugee from postwar Viet Nam 40 years later. But all immigrants have certain things in common, and all know the classic, opposite impulses: to draw together in protective enclaves where through churches, clubs, cafés, newspapers, the old culture is fiercely maintained; and on the other hand to rush headlong into the American mainstream, seeking to adopt indiscriminately new manners, clothes, technology and sometimes names.

Inevitably, the immigrant is a student, and his more or less permanent occupation is learning. That is a nervous business ("Have I got it right?"); depending on one's temperament, it is also a series of joyful discoveries. For younger immigrants, those discoveries begin in school, and the initial, most amazing one is the openness, the absence of the compulsion and petty tyranny that characterize the classroom almost everywhere else in the world. But if that openness is indeed joyful and liberating to young minds, the accompanying lack of discipline is also frightening and destructive: the heart of the perennial American conflict between freedom and order.

The immigrant's education continues everywhere. He must master not only a new history but a whole new imagination. The process goes on at various speeds, and odd gaps can appear. The immigrant carries different nursery rhymes in his head, different fairy tales. He may have just graduated from college Phi Beta Kappa but not know who Mary Poppins is. He may be taking the bar examination and be rather dim about Popeye. Prince Eugene of Savoy lodges stubbornly in the mind (song learned at the age of seven: "Prince Eugene, the noble knight . . ."), while Patrick Henry appears as a stranger, an image full of gaps, like an unfinished sketch.

A continuing part of the immigrant's education is the comparison between the anticipated or imagined America and the real country. The anticipation depends on time and place, but the reality is always startling. If the vision of America was formed by Ginger Rogers and Fred Astaire dancing atop glittering skyscrapers, how to accept the slums? If the vision was noise and materialist chaos, how to account for a Quaker meeting house or the daily, relentless idealism of legions of American do-gooders? If the vision was a childhood fantasy of the Wild West, how can one grasp the fact that Sitting Bull was a real man fighting a real Government and dying a real death?

A new language: nagging impediment to some, liberation to others. There is the constant struggle to achieve the proper accent, like trying to sing one's way into some strange and maddeningly elusive music. There is the pain and bother of trying as an adult or near adult to learn new words and meanings. But these words and meanings have a certain innocence, a certain freshness, free of the constraint, the boredom, the touches of shame that are imposed on one's native language in the classroom or the nursery.

English is illogical and headily free compared, for example, with the grammatical rigidities of French or German. Some newcomers are lost in this malleable structure; others fall upon English with an instinctive sense of recognition, as one might discover a hitherto unknown brother. Shakespeare and Melville gradually replace Goethe and Racine, though drilled-in passages never quite fade; the experience can begin as vague disloyalty and end in passion. Immigrants who know English as one of the great unifiers of America will never be reconciled to those others—many Hispanics, for instance—who refuse to accept English fully, thus creating an ominous dual culture in many parts of the U.S. Language is life. For many immigrants, the true act of naturalization occurs when they start having dreams in English.

More puzzling and complicated than language is the American social syntax. The first impression is one of dazzling and rather unsettling
informality, an indiscriminate camaraderie. But one learns that going to
the opera in shirt-sleeves (an outrage, surely!) does not mean contempt
for culture or even necessarily a lack of rules. Calling the boss by his first
name, which takes some effort, does not mean that he and the office boy
are equals. Indeed, equality is both the great illusion and the great reality
of America. The immigrant is slow to understand that below the egalitar-
ian surface there are hierarchies and tribes, proper and improper addresses, great names and lowly names, old money looking down on new money,
older immigrants looking down on newer—a topography to which there
are very few maps.

But after this discovery there gradually comes yet another insight that
whipsaws the immigrant back toward the original perception: there really is no fixed social structure after all. There is above everything else that
much vaunted mobility—from place to place, career to career, status to
status—which turns so many native-born Americans into immigrants in
their own country.

In philosophical terms, Europe (or Asia or Africa) is the world of being; America is the world of becoming. In Europe, one is what one is; in
America, one is what one does. To the immigrant this is a discovery of high
excitement and also of some anxiety. Opportunity is not just opportunity
but an imperative and a reproach. If anyone can make it in America, why
haven't you? If anyone can be what he wants to be, why aren't you more?

There follows the suspicion that making it is the only American morality. But no—it can't be that simple. The first tangible hint of American
moral attitudes comes on the immigration form: the solemn requirement
to swear that you are not a Communist, or not a prostitute, or whatever. To
those coming from older and more cynical societies, this is the utmost sort
of naiveté. For the immigrant, it foreshadows the American conviction that
one can mandate, even legislate morality. That conviction represents an
amalgam of Puritanism, with its belief in a permanently flawed human nature, and the Enlightenment tradition, with its belief in the perfectibility
of man. Cotton Mather, meet Thomas Jefferson. This contradictory combination bespeaks the sheer and sometimes hopelessly unrealistic determination to overcome any evil that cannot be ignored, the refusal to accept
the status quo in the universe.

The moral landscape the immigrant left behind was usually dominated by the spires of one church or perhaps of two churches living in uneasy peace after centuries of bloody contest. He is therefore overwhelmed by the dizzying variety of religion in America, by the churches, sects, subsects and cults that proliferate in a sort of spiritual shopping mall. But he learns to appreciate the fact that a country that can create God in so many images, no matter how eccentric, has never used fire and sword to impose a faith on its citizens.

The most awesome thing to learn about America is the land itself. No newcomer is ever prepared for its size: the vastness of a country that is a continent. The quintessential American landscape is not found in the mountains or on the shore but in the Great Plains. Space (terrestrial space, not space out there) is the true metaphor for the American condition. Speed can conquer it, but nothing built by man can dominate it. That is perhaps one reason why even the most imposing American skylines can look strangely impermanent and fragile. America does not build for the ages. There are no American palaces and no (convincing) American cathedrals.

BUT THE BEAUTY OF AMERICA is not in its buildings, not in its artifacts or its arts. Its greatest beauty is in its ideas. Freedom is the ultimate value, whether aesthetic or political. Sooner or later most immigrants learn that freedom is not about what one wants but about what one can do and, ultimately, must do. Freedom won't let one be. It pursues one relentlessly, like a secular hound of heaven, challenging, provoking, driving.

The absence of orthodoxy, the lack of any fixed intellectual system is sometimes hard to bear, especially for many older immigrants; it is easier for the young. And it is often the children who truly lead the elders into America, the sons who take their fathers to their first baseball game or shepherd them to their first rock concert or give them a real sense that they have a stake in America's future.

The hardest situation for the immigrant comes when the future seems in doubt and when America seems about to default on its promise. It happened during the Great Depression, and it happened again during Viet Nam. It happens today whenever one contemplates the dark and yet quite visible underside of American life: the New York City subway or the filth of a roadside service station, the American infernos of drugs and crime and sexual decadence, the dregs of the cities—"wretched refuse" indeed. At such moments it sometimes seems that many of the lands the immigrants left behind are actually doing better than America, that they have in a sense "won." Of course, it is not so. It would be dishonest and thus disloyal to ignore the dreadful scars and blemishes of America, but they are themselves to a large extent the result of freedom—sometimes an excess of freedom. For freedom can be dangerous. Yet freedom also holds within it the means to correct its defects, for it allows, indeed encourages, people to criticize their society, to tinker with it, to improve it.

Ultimately, the education of every immigrant is personal, individual. No immigrant can speak for all others. But a Viennese librettist, Alfred Grunwald, who came to America in 1940 and sought to continue practicing his art, wrote some lyrics that sum up much of the immigrant experience in America: *"Deine Heimat ist wo das Glück dich grüsst . . ."* Roughly translated, "Home is where you are happy." Sentimental, perhaps, and certainly not conventionally patriotic, but appropriate for a country that wrote the pursuit of happiness into its founding document.

That pursuit continues for the immigrant in America, and it never stops. But it comes to rest at a certain moment. The moment is hard to pin down, but it occurs perhaps when the immigrant's double life and double vision converge toward a single state of mind. When the old life, the old home fade into a certain unreality: places one merely visits, in fact or in the mind, practicing the tourism of memory. It occurs when the immigrant learns his ultimate lesson: above all countries, America, if loved, returns love. ∎

In the Blazing Eye of the Inferno

BY PICO IYER

[*Caught in a raging California brushfire, the writer was able to turn a keen journalistic eye on the scene even though one of the houses destroyed was his own*]

July 9, 1990

THE IRONIES, OF COURSE, begin to multiply as soon as a life comes unraveled: in retrospect, everything seems an augury. One night before, the local TV station had announced that the conditions—106° heat, gale-force winds and drought-stricken hills—were the best for a fire in 100 years. That day, at lunch, I had been talking with a friend whose mother had just died, about the pathos of going through old belongings. And when, at the optician's office that evening, my doctor stepped out to go and sniff at what he thought might be a fire, I sat back and fumed with impatience.

By 6 o'clock I was in my home, a remote hillside house alone on a ridge, surrounded by acres of wild brush. The fire started along our road, just half a mile away, at 6:02. Two friends, arriving at that moment, pointed to the jagged line of orange tearing down the hillside like a waterfall and splitting the brush open like a knife through fruit. Then the electricity went off. Then the phones went dead. By 6:10, huge curls of flame were hurtling over the ridge a few feet from the house.

I had time only to grab my ancient cat, Minnie, and the manuscript of a book just two weeks from completion. By the time I tried to jump into my

71

car to drive away, walls of flame were jumping over the driveway, scorching my face and shrouding the house in an angry orange haze. The three of us leaped, pursued by flames, into a van, and started to race down the mountain road. Within 50 yards, we knew we could go no farther. Flames 70 feet high were cresting over the curve of the hill on one side, and on the other, currents of orange were slicing up the slope toward us. Everywhere I turned, rivulets of orange were pouring across the hills like molten lava, sweeping up trees and feasting on houses. At times we were unable to breathe as the 70 m.p.h. wind whipped ashes all around, so strong we could not open the door. Our van was alone in the heart of the inferno, and there was nothing we could do but pray.

Only one other person was in view, a man in shorts with a water truck, standing alone in the road trying, through smarting eyes, to contain the flames with a hose. Alone, he aimed his hose at waves of flame that crashed like waves around us, now coming to a crest, and now, for a while, subsiding, until suddenly they were there again, leaping over a ridge and bearing down upon us.

Soon we were gagging at the fumes. The cat was panting feverishly, we were hosing down our van and our bodies with water from the truck. I had never before known how swift fire could be, and how efficient. Occasionally, the air would clear, and we would see the blue above the mountains; then the smoke was around us again, and a column of orange looming above. Someone pointed out that the one book we'd inadvertently managed to bring with us was called *All the Right Places*.

We waited, stranded, for about two hours, two of us with Minnie in the van, while the other two heroically battled the flames. The fire surged up the hill like dogs jumping at a fence. A helicopter appeared, but then was lost again in the smoke and the spitting ashes. A fire truck came up the road at last, but its consolation was brief: we could not go down the hill, they said, nor up. We squeezed together in the van, Verdi playing on the radio, and watched my room turn into a gutted skeleton.

As darkness fell, the scene grew ever more surreal. A car came racing up the hill, snatched and chased by licking flames. In front of us, the hulks of other cars were blazing. A man caked in soot appeared, looking for his horse. As night began to deepen, the dark hills acquired necklaces of orange, and the sky around us was a locust-cloud of ashes. And, when we were told that it was the time to make a break for it, we finally raced down the mountain through a scene more beautiful and unreal than any

Vietnam-movie fire fight: beside us, houses were turning into outlines of themselves, the blackness was electric with orange, and cars were burning as calmly as a family hearth. Burning logs and the corpses of small animals blocked the middle of the road as we sped through clouds of ashes, the sky above us turning an infernal dusty yellow.

By dawn next morning, everything was gone. Smoke hissed out of melting cracks, and an occasional small fire burned. All the signs of life were there, but everything was hushed. Later, officials announced that the fire was probably caused by arson. On Saturday, Santa Barbara was declared a federal disaster area. Fifteen years of daily notes and books half written, of statues and photos and memories, were gone. My only solace came from the final irony. In the manuscript I had saved, I had quoted the poem of the 17th century Japanese wanderer Basho, describing how destruction can sometimes bring a kind of clarity:

> *My house burned down.*
> *Now I can better see*
> *The rising moon.*   ■

The Nightmare After Katrina

BY NANCY GIBBS

[*Even after a stunned nation had seen Hurricane Katrina's devastation on television for a week, this vivid, powerful account brought the tragedy home with renewed force*]

September 12, 2005

NEW ORLEANS LIVES BY the water and fights it, a sand castle set on a sponge nine feet below sea level, where people made music from heartache, named their drinks for hurricanes and joked that one day you'd be able to tour the city by gondola.

A city built by rumrunners and slave traders and pirates was never going to play by anyone's rules or plan for the future. So as Katrina, wicked and flirtatious, lingered in the Gulf with her eye on the town, many citizens decided they would stay, stubborn or stoic or too poor to have much choice. As for the ones packing up to go, disaster officials told them to take a look around before they left, because it might never look the same again.

But by the time President Bush touched down in the tormented region on Friday, more than just the topography had changed. Shattered too was a hope that four years after the greatest man-made disaster in our history, we had got smarter about catastrophe, more nimble and visionary in our ability to respond. Is it really possible, after so many commissions and commitments, bureaucracies scrambled and rewired, emergency supplies stockpiled and prepositioned, that when a disaster strikes, the whole newfangled system just seizes up and can't move?

it may be weeks before the lights come back on and months before New Orleans is mopped out, a year before the refugees resettle in whatever will come to function as home, even without anything precious from the days before the flood. But it may take even longer than that before the nature of this American tragedy is clear: whether the storm of '05 is remembered mainly as the worst natural disaster in our history or the worst response to a disaster in our history. Or both.

Watching helpless New Orleans suffering day by day left people everywhere stunned and angry and in ever greater pain. These things happened in Haiti, they said, but not here. "Baghdad under water" is how former Louisiana Senator John Breaux described his beloved city, as state officials told him they feared the death toll could reach as high as 10,000, spread across Louisiana, Mississippi and Alabama. No matter what the final tally, the treatment of the living, black and poor and old and sick, was a disgrace. The problem with putting it all into numbers is that they stop speaking clearly once they get too big: an estimated half a million refugees, a million people without power, 30,000 soldiers, up to $100 billion in damage. "This is our tsunami," said Biloxi, Miss., Mayor A.J. Holloway. The overstatement is forgivable, for at some point suffering becomes immeasurable, reduced to a hopeless search for a place to sleep, or a bottle of water or a body to bury.

Mother Nature behaved as everyone warned one day she would, but human nature never fails to surprise. Stripped of safety and comfort, survivors made their choices: greed, mercy, mischief, gallantry, depravity or a surrender to despair. So nurses hand-pumped the ventilators of dying patients after the generators and then the batteries failed, while outside the hospitals, snipers fired at ambulances, and invading looters with guns demanded that doctors turn over whatever drugs they had. Hijackers shot the tires of fleeing vehicles, slapped the spares on after the owners escaped and drove the cars away themselves. Some police officers battled the looters; others joined them. As the floodwaters rose, EMS technicians told TIME they were left stranded at the downtown Hampton Inn by panicking cops who jumped into their private cars to flee the city. In the wretched Superdome, where several people died before they could get out, a young violinist took out his instrument and played a Bach adagio. "These people have nothing," he told a Los Angeles *Times* reporter. "I have a violin. And I should play for them."

Around the country, people watched the scene in growing horror, as babies and old people and diabetics and those worn out surviving the storm died on live television for all to see. Churches started assembling comfort kits; 500,000 hot meals a day are being prepared by Red Cross disaster volunteers. "I just had a gentleman walk in off the street and write a $10,000 check," said a Red Cross director in Massachusetts. She'd never seen him before; he had no family down there. He just said it seemed the right thing to do.

The private response was all the more urgent because the public one seemed so inept. Somehow Harry Connick Jr. could get to the New Orleans Convention Center and offer help, but not the National Guard. Bush praised the "good work" on Thursday, then called the results "not acceptable" on Friday. By then, 55 nations had offered to pitch in—including Sri Lanka, whose disaster scars are still fresh. "Get off your asses, and let's do something," New Orleans Mayor C. Ray Nagin raged in a radio interview that he ended in tears. But he of all people was in a position to understand the odds. A city known both for its charm and its rot, not just from the termites consuming whole neighborhoods but from a corrupt police force, dissolving tax base, neglected infrastructure, rising poverty and a murder rate that inspired old-timers to pack a gun beneath their tuxes on their way to the Mardi Gras parade, could hardly have been less equipped to cope with a catastrophe that everyone knew was coming. "Half of Louisiana is under water," former lawmaker Billy Tauzin used to say, "and the other half is under indictment." Three of the top state emergency officials were recently indicted for mishandling disaster funds.

Louisiana staggered under the blow, but others all along the Gulf Coast were ravaged as Katrina, still spitting tornadoes and spraying wood and shingles and glass, made her way slowly up to Canada to die at last. A sudden twirl coming ashore meant that the Mississippi coast got smacked the hardest. In many towns, what the winds spared the floods claimed, as the gusts flung water into the streets in storm surges as high as 25 ft. "It was like the houses were playing bumper cars around here," said Biloxi fisherman Alan Layne. There were cemetery coffins tossed around the beach, and disemboweled slot machines, and boats perched up in trees like ridiculous overweight birds. In Gulfport, Miss., the sea-salty air smelled of corpses. At one Catholic church, only the foundation remained—and a sign that read MASS AT 9 A.M. BRING A CHAIR.

John Padgett, a boat captain in Pass Christian, Miss., who runs supplies to the off-coast oil rigs, saw his cottage disappear. But he was able to throw his dogs, a tent, a sleeping bag and a Coleman stove and lantern into his pickup before the storm arrived. He's living in the woods just north of Gulfport off Highway 49. "Everything I own now is in that truck," he told TIME, "but the shelters are too overcrowded and uncomfortable. I was born and raised on this coast, so I'm a good little redneck. I got a bow and arrow to kill food, and that's what I'm going to be eating." Where will he go from here? "I don't know," he said. "But at least in the woods I don't have to smell the dead bodies."

BUT IT WAS IN NEW ORLEANS where the cameras converged, a city that had braced for the worst, then briefly exhaled when it looked as if the threat had passed. Several hours after the storm moved through on Monday, some streets were essentially dry. Then shortly after midnight, a section almost as long as a football field in a main levee near the 17th Street Canal ruptured, letting Lake Pontchartrain pour in. The city itself turned into a superbowl; roadways crumbled like soup crackers as the levees designed to protect them were now holding the water in. Engineers tried dropping 3,000-lb. sandbags, but the water just swallowed them. As the days passed, the Army Corps of Engineers, which oversees the levees, admitted they weren't able to assess what might work. Part of the problem was a lack of heavy helicopters; the choppers were all busy doing search and rescue.

The levee breach left 80% of the city immediately submerged and 100,000 people stranded. Canal Street lived up to its name. As the temperature rose, the whole city was poached in a vile stew of melted landfill, chemicals, corpses, gasoline, snakes, canal rats; many could not escape their flooded homes without help. Among those who could, only a final act of desperation would drive them into the streets, where the caramel waters stank of sewage and glittered with the gaudy swirls of oil spills. A New Orleans TV station reported that a woman waded down to Charity Hospital, floating her husband's body along on a door.

For the first time ever, a major U.S. city was simply taken offline, closed down. Food and water and power and phones were gone; authority was all but absent. Most of the people left to cope were least equipped: the ones whose Social Security checks were just about due, or those who made for the Greyhound station only to find it already closed, or those confined to bed or who used a wheelchair. "We're seeing people that we didn't know exist," declared Federal Emergency Management Agency (FEMA) director Michael Brown in a moment of hideous accidental honesty. Rescue workers could hear people pounding on roofs from the inside, trapped in attics as the waters rose. The lucky ones were able to cut holes with knives and axes to reach the open air. Emergency workers hovered from house to house, plucking out the living, leaving bodies behind. The potential for a disaster in the air was such that pilots told TIME reporter Adam Pitluk, who was embedded with them, to help scan the skies for stray news helicopters and sightseers in Cessnas among the flocks of military craft. "It was like a pickup game," said Lieut. Commander Bill Howey, a Navy helicopter pilot. "You got three or four different types of Army helicopters, same for the Navy. Then there's Customs, Coast Guard, Marines, and then there are the news helicopters." While rescuing a group of blind people trapped for five days, a Marine helicopter pilot told TIME's Tim Padgett, "It's like flying into a hornets' nest."

When Dr. Greg Henderson, a pathologist turned field medic, arrived at the Convention Center on Friday, he was the only doctor for 10,000 people. "They're stacking the dead on the second floor," he told TIME by phone. "People are having seizures in the hallway. People with open running sores, every imaginable disease and disorder, all kinds of psychiatric problems. We have people who haven't had dialysis in several days. They'll be going into kidney failure. I just closed the door on a man who ran out of medicine for his kidney transplant. Very soon his body is going to go into rejection." Henderson went in with New Orleans police, and when people saw him in scrubs, they surged at him from every side. He tried to tend the sickest and the babies first. "The crowds here have gotten a bad rap. There are not many human beings you could cram into a building with 10,000 others, in 105° heat, that wouldn't get just a little pissed off." He tried to get them settled and asked them to show him the sickest. "And they lead me. It's not a subtle thing. It's generally the ones who are seizing on the floor."

Helicopters airlifted the sick from around the city to the airport, converted into a field hospital where patients were being pushed around on luggage carts and triaged for evacuation. At Lakefront Airport on the edge of the city, fights broke out for seats on the departing choppers. "The gang bangers," said Jimmy Dennis, 34, a Lakefront Airport fire fighter who had been up for two nights trying to keep order, "couldn't understand that we had to get the sick people out first." Frightened, the small band of fire fighters called in 10 New Orleans police with semiautomatic weapons to settle the crowd.

In the few hospitals left operating, the staff fought to keep people alive until rescue came, only to have days pass with no relief. At Charity Hospital, in the dark but for a lone generator and dying flashlights, nurses who hadn't bathed in days tried to sterilize themselves with hand sanitizer. Two patients on the parking deck died waiting to be evacuated. Caregivers wept as they begged for help that did not come. "They'd been keeping these patients alive for a week with very little in terms of resources," says TIME contributor and CNN correspondent Dr. Sanjay Gupta, "and to see them die on the deck—it really was very difficult."

After Gupta arrived by helicopter on Wednesday, hours passed before it was safe to ferry him past the snipers and across a putrid moat into the hospital building. With a full evacuation still several days away, "people came to me and said, 'Why haven't they taken care of us? Why did they forget us?' " The food supply was down to beans and a few raw vegetables; candy vending machines had long since been emptied. "One of the guys here has been trying to call FEMA, and all he gets is a busy signal or voice mail," Gupta said. The stress was so overwhelming that perhaps half a dozen hospital staff members had to be treated in the psychiatric ward. The basement morgue was flooded, so the growing numbers of bodies were stacked in body bags in the stairwells.

The seething center of the angry Crescent City was the Superdome, refuge of utterly last resort for 25,000 people who had waited out the worst of the storm while the sheet-metal roof peeled like fruit, letting the rains pour in. Soon there was no light, no air, no working toilets. Reports came that four of the weakest died that first night. An elderly man, playing cards and seemingly fine, threw himself over a railing inside the stadium and committed suicide, witnesses told TV reporters. Members of the city's EMS team made their way there only to find anarchy. "We tried to start triaging and getting the special needs in one section," a technician recalls, but his team was overwhelmed by the hungry crowd and retreated with armed guards to Army trucks outside. When a 4th Infantry Division helicopter arrived, all but three of the evacuees had to be wheeled onto the Chinook, the elderly panting like animals suffering heatstroke, their mouths sagging and their tongues heavy and swollen. One paraplegic woman looked as if she had been broiled, her motionless legs beet red on the front and ghostly white on her calves. The evacuees were frightened, of both their plight and the booming helicopter that was there to save them. As the chopper pulled away, mothers down below screamed after it for rescue, holding their children high and sobbing.

Opportunity and desperation make a flammable mix. All along the coast, people broke into parked cars to siphon gas. Police reported that a man in Hattiesburg, Miss., shot his sister in the head in a fight over a bag of ice. A rescue team from Texas that had ferried hundreds of people to safety in their flat-bottom boats were told by a New Orleans sheriff that unless they were armed, they should get out of the city. At one point, rescuer Randy White says, "Someone yelled out to me, 'If you don't get us out by 12 o'clock, we're going to start shooting all the rescuers.' " One man was standing on Canal Boulevard with water up to his chest wearing a mink coat that he had liberated from a store. "This natural disaster is beginning to look like a Watts riot," said a worried congressional aide in Washington as he watched the chaos. "There's something really ugly going on here, something wrong at a deeper level."

One thing that was wrong may have been that right and wrong had jumped their tracks. For all the scorching images of armed thugs making off with sneakers and wide-screen TVs, the larger reality wasn't as simple as the President's call for "zero tolerance" of looting. Was it wrong to take a bottle of milk from a store when your baby was sobbing and there was no way to pay for it if you tried? When cans of food are scattered in the debris, does taking them amount to theft, or salvage? At one point, police with guns drawn escorted Dr. Henderson through a Walgreens as he emptied the pharmacy of drugs to use in a French Quarter bar turned makeshift clinic. Dudley Fuqua, tall and lean in baggy blue shorts, broke into neighborhood shops and took canned goods, frozen chicken and ribs and cigarettes to his neighbors, who called him a hero. "I was in a building with no food, no water for five nights," Fuqua's neighbor Mohammed Ally, 70, told TIME's Brian Bennett. "They were taking care of the elderly people." Fuqua saw a neighbor using his empty refrigerator as a rowboat to paddle through the water to get help for his pregnant wife. When the buoyant refrigerator tipped, Fuqua dove off a second-story balcony to help and sliced his feet on a rain gutter. "I was going to make sure everyone was O.K."

Only by Friday did some palpable help arrive, in the form of thousands of National Guard troops and lumbering convoys of supplies. Virtually alone, Lieut. General Russel Honore, commanding Joint Task Force Katrina, whom Mayor Nagin referred to as the John Wayne dude, seemed to be moving pieces into place. He was out in the streets with his troops, directing convoys and telling anxious Guardsmen to keep their weapons pointed down. He "came off the doggone chopper," Nagin said, "and he started cussing, and people started moving. And he's getting some stuff done. They ought to give that guy full authority to get the job done, and we can save some people."

Americans sometimes ask what the government does and where their tax money goes. Among other things, it pays for all kinds of invisible but essential safety nets and life belts and guardrails that are useless right up until the day they are priceless. Furious critics charged last week that the government had not heard the warnings. Instead it cut the funds for flood control and storm preparations, mangled the chain of command, missed every opportunity. And an angry debate opened about how much the demands of the Iraq war, on both the budget and the National Guard, were eating into the country's ability to protect itself at home. Louisiana Republican Congressman Jim McCrery—working the phones with FEMA, the Army, the White House, state officials—argues that Katrina revealed how much doesn't work. "Clearly, with all the money we've spent, all the focus we have put on homeland security, we are not prepared for a disaster of this proportion whether it's induced by nature or man."

And this time a crucial consolation was missing. After 9/11, whatever the evidence of intelligence failures, many people still saw that attack as almost unimaginable, so brutal and brazen an assault. But Katrina was in the cards, forewarned, foreseen and yet still dismissed until it was too late. That so many officials were caught so unprepared was a failure less of imagination than will, a realization all the more frightening in light of what lies ahead. For if we couldn't help our citizens in an hour of desperate need, how well will we do in six months or a year, when many are still jobless and homeless, but no longer center stage? ■

—WITH REPORTING BY MIKE BILLIPS/BILOXI, MASSIMO
CALABRESI, SALLY B. DONNELLY, MARK THOMPSON AND
DOUGLAS WALLER/WASHINGTON, ELLIN MARTENS, COCO MASTERS AND
CAROLINA A. MIRANDA/NEW YORK AND GREG FULTON/ATLANTA

PROTESTER AT CHINA'S TIANANMEN SQUARE, 1989

TIME The Global Arena

Prince Edward

BY LAIRD S. GOLDSBOROUGH *

[*The writer brought a lofty irony to the scandal that had transfixed the world—the love affair between the King of England and a divorced American commoner*]

December 21, 1936

DIGNITY, LIKE THE IMPERIAL mantle which is placed upon England's King at his Coronation, clothed Edward VIII and his every act last week after the decision of His Majesty to abdicate and become not "Mr. Windsor" but Prince Edward, newly created Duke of Windsor, and still Knight of the Most Ancient & Most Noble Order of the Thistle, Knight of the Most Illustrious Order of St. Patrick, Knight Grand Commander of the Most Exalted Star of India, Knight Grand Cross of the Royal Victorian Order, Grand Master of the Most Distinguished Order of St. Michael & St. George, Grand Master of the Most Excellent Order of the British Empire, Knight of the Golden Fleece of Spain, Knight of the Order of the Annunziata of Italy.

Scarcely anyone failed to tune in on Edward VIII as he took leave of his country or to read within a few hours the simple words with which His Royal Highness said good-by to very nearly all except "the woman I love."

Prince Edward was scrupulous not to betray his class, and to do and say all he could to uphold the Kingdom and the Empire, giving no opportuni-

* *Tentative identification*

84

ty to irresponsible groups of the masses to harm Britain. Long after His Majesty's instrument of abdication was signed, sealed, published and in course of certain enactment by Parliament, one of the greatest mass gatherings in British history was still roaring outside of Buckingham Palace, "WE WANT EDWARD!" He was not there.

Neither as King Edward, nor later last week as Prince Edward, did the eldest son of the Royal House enter London. This idol of the British masses (for such His Majesty unquestionably was) vanished, and after a little space other idols (for such King George VI, Queen Elizabeth and crown princess Elizabeth will soon be) were substituted. The basic English truth which emerged is that the Kingdom long ago became and is today neither a democracy nor a monarchy but an efficient oligarchy, more or less benevolent. Its symbol is the Crown, but the really effective British crowns are the top hats worn by Prime Minister Stanley Baldwin and a few hundred others. They rule over millions of British soft hats, tens of millions of caps and hundreds of millions of Indian noddles. Members of the British Royal Family have long had this basic reality embedded in their natures, and last week in King Edward VIII's hour of sorest indecision it tipped the scales. He left England as the eldest son who has locked a rattling skeleton in the Empire's closet and thrown away the key. Not ungrateful to opportune Winston Churchill, who had offered and sought to form a party of "King's men" to fight the issue out in Parliament, His Majesty rewarded this active British son of a U. S. mother last week with a discreetly private lunch.

With Prince Edward supplying all necessary dignity, the British Broadcasting Corp. found it possible to send out a "children's hour" message to the moppets of the Empire, a description in words of one and two syllables of the relations between Edward VIII and Mrs. Simpson. Only a few days prior these had been so "scandalous" (because undignified) that they were supposed to be something which only a few nasty-minded British adults would stoop to read in the "American press."*

---

* *Edward VIII came to the Throne in January, and* TIME *then omitted all mention of Mrs. Simpson until June. Reason: His Majesty had every right to benefit from an assumption that, once on the Throne, he would rapidly begin to conduct his private life in private, as did his grandfather King Edward VII. Had he done so, it would in all probability still be private, and he still on the Throne. In May, His Majesty with his own hand broke open the story of the King's Mrs. Simpson by inserting her name in his public Court Circular. He introduced her to the present King George VI and Queen Elizabeth, as well as to Mr. & Mrs. Stanley Baldwin, other Cabinet members and their wives, next took her on a Balkan yachting tour. Repeatedly the King intervened with Balkan police to let photographers snap him in informal scenes with Mrs. Simpson. Although these pictures were not printed in the United Kingdom, U. S. editors felt specifically free to print them. They were, in September, sure evidence that the crisis, which did not come until December, must come.*

In his historic broadcast, Prince Edward did not defend either himself or Mrs. Simpson. That would have been undignified. The skeleton must not be jangled. Unmentioned therefore by Prince Edward was the clash of wills between himself and the Church of England over whether the Archbishop of Canterbury would refuse or consent to officiate at the Coronation and *consecration* of a King who intended to marry a woman such as Mrs. Simpson. In the House of Lords, the Archbishop spoke volumes when he said in a broken voice, "Of the motive which compelled the renunciation we dare not speak."

The Archbishop's motive had to do with a feature of the Coronation service scarcely noticed by laymen who suppose that the whole point of a coronation must be that somebody is crowned. There have been British coronations for 1,000 years and until comparatively recent generations the whole emphasis was on the "anointing" of the King, as a newly created bishop is anointed—thus making him a *persona mixta* or "person of mixed nature," part layman, part priest. Queen Victoria was of the opinion that she was the head of the Church of England, virtually a female Pope. Although Prime Minister Gladstone gently dispelled this impetuous pretension (pointing out certain ambiguities in the Coronation ceremony), Her Majesty was far more right than she was wrong in the eyes of English churchgoers. The unspeakable dilemma in the case of Edward VIII in recent weeks has been: "Can there be consecrated, as a part-priest or part-Pope, one who we all know has done everything to face us with the fact that he is resolved to marry a lady with a past, even if we did our best to keep him from making this known to us?"

Such was the obstacle which proved insuperable last week, and there were several others, nearly insuperable and nearly unutterable. A minor and utterable obstacle was that Mrs. Simpson is not the daughter of either a king or a peer.

Dignified Prince Edward, after dining for a last time with his Queen Mother, new King George VI, the Duke of Gloucester and the Duke of Kent, drove last week at great speed through night and fog to Portsmouth, intending to embark on the Admiralty Yacht. At the last moment this plan was changed; the name of the yacht is the *Enchantress*. It was dignified to sail instead on the British destroyer *Fury,* and "His Grace, the Duke of Windsor"—as Prince Edward was created this week by King George VI—debarked at Boulogne into a private car and a new life of wealth, ease and perhaps happiness.

Rolling down to Austria, he established himself high on a crag 25 mi. from Vienna at the castle of Baron Eugene Rothschild, who was host to the King & Mrs. Simpson last summer. Said the Duke of Windsor: "I am remaining here at Castle Enzesfeld until after Christmas."

Baron Rothschild closely accompanied his Baroness and the Duke when they played a round of golf on the castle's private links, and the Austrian caddy said that his Royal Highness continually sang snatches of popular tunes.

On the ex-King's first Sunday away from England, the Archbishop of Canterbury broadcast: "A new morning has dawned.... Yet let there be no boasting in our pride!" The proud Primate went on to describe the Duke of Windsor as "alien," called him as though already dead "our late King," denounced his "craving for private happiness" and referred to the present War Secretary of Great Britain, Captain Alfred Duff-Cooper and other close intimates of Edward VIII, thus: "Let those who belong in this circle know that today they stand rebuked!"

A steward on the Britannic: "In the pubs at Southampton they say 'he's a bloody fool. If he'd kept quiet, he could have had her on the side. But trying to put this over—it's too thick!' "

U. S. Senator Gore of Oklahoma: "If I had been King, I would have had the Coronation in due course, then married this woman, then said to the world, 'it's your move next.' "

Arthur Brisbane: "Magnificent, perhaps, but perhaps unnecessary ... The Throne and the life around it breeds weakness.... It is not necessary to tell ambitious young American women ... how Mrs. Simpson will feel when she marries what is left of the 'king.' "

Masses, crowding Manhattan's No. 1 newsreel theatre, the Embassy in Times Square, behaved as follows at sight on the screen of: Prince Edward (*cheers*); Mrs. Simpson (*cheers*); her first husband Commander Spencer, U.S.N. (*boos*); her second and present husband Mr. Simpson (*cheers & boos*); the Archbishop of Canterbury (BOOS); new Crown Princess Elizabeth (*boos*); new King George & Queen Elizabeth (*boos!*); Prime Minister Baldwin (PROLONGED CATCALLS AND BOOS!); King Edward & Mrs. Simpson bathing in the Mediterranean (CHEERS!).　■

The Ghosts on the Roof

BY WHITTAKER CHAMBERS

[
*When Roosevelt, Churchill and Stalin met to plan the peacetime
era after World War II, the writer—a former Party member turned
vehement anti-Communist—took a puckish, unfashionably dire
view of the Soviet Union's geopolitical ambitions*
]

March 5, 1945

*The Big Three conferees dispersed under cover of an all but news-
less fog of military security. But here & there was vouchsafed a
glimpse—such as Franklin Roosevelt's afterdeck chats with Near
Eastern potentates; here & there a sound, like the short snort from
Socialism's old warhorse, George Bernard Shaw. Snorted Shaw:
"[The Yalta Conference is] an impudently incredible fairy tale....
Will Stalin declare war on Japan as the price of surrender of the other two over
Lublin? Not a word about it. Fairy tales, fairy tales, fairy tales. I for one should
like to know what really passed at Yalta. This will all come out 20 years hence ...
But I shall not then be alive—I shall never know."*

Taking Mr. Shaw's lead, one of TIME's *editors has written the following
political fairy tale. Since fairy tales, like more solemn reports, have their implications and their moral,* TIME *wishes to make it clear that it admires and respects
our heroic ally, recognizes great mutuality of interests between the U.S. and
the U.S.S.R.—but that in any argument between Communism and Democracy,*
TIME *is on the side of Democracy.*

WITH THE SOFTNESS OF BATS, seven ghosts settled down on
the flat roof of the Livadia Palace at Yalta. They found someone else already

there: a statuesque female figure, crouching, with her eye glued to one of the holes in the roof (it had been through the Russian revolution, three years of civil war, 21 years of Socialist reconstruction, the German invasion and the Russian reoccupation).

"Madam," said the foremost ghost, an imperious woman with a bullet hole in her head, "what are you doing on our roof?"

Clio, the Muse of History (for it was she), looked up, her finger on her lips. "Shh!" she said, "the Big Three Conference is just ending down there. What with security regulations, censorship and personal secretiveness, the only way I can find out anything these days is by peeping. And who are you?" she asked, squinting slightly (history is sometimes a little short-sighted). "I've seen you somewhere before."

"Madam," said a male ghost, rising on tiptoe to speak over his wife's shoulder (he also had a bullet hole in his forehead), "I am Nicholas II, Emperor and Autocrat of All the Russias, Tsar of Moscow, Kiev, Novgorod, Kazan, Astrakhan, of Poland, Siberia and Georgia, Grand Duke of Smolensk, Lithuania, Podolia and Finland, Prince of Estonia, Livonia and Bialystok, Lord of Pskov, Riazan, Yaroslavl, Vitebsk and All the Region of the North, Lord. . . ."

"Nicholas—how nice to see you again!" cried History. "Wherever have you been? And the Tsarina Alix! Your four charming daughters, I presume—gracious, but those bullet holes are disfiguring. And the little hemophiliac—Tsarevich Alexei! Ah, yes, I understand—doomed for a certain term to walk the night. . . . Why, I've scarcely given you a thought since that time when the Communists threw your bodies down the mine shaft in Ekaterinburg [now Sverdlovsk]. Whatever brings you here?"

"This, Madam," said the imperial ghost, "is no strange place to me. It is our former estate of Livadia. Allow me to cite the *Intourist's Pocket Guide to the Soviet Union:* 'This estate occupies 350 hectares of land, and includes a large park, two palaces and many vineyards. The newer palace [you are standing on its roof], built in 1911 by Krasnov in the style of the Italian Renaissance, is of white Inkerman stone, and contains nearly a hundred rooms. It has now been changed into a sanatorium for sick peasants, although certain of the rooms have been reserved as a museum. . . .

" 'From the alleyways of the Livadian Park. . . .' " Here the Tsarina cut her husband short with a stamp of her ghostly foot.

"Don't hedge, Nicky," she cried. "He never could come to the point. He's trying to cover up the fact that he wanted to eavesdrop on the Big

Three Conference. He doesn't like to admit it in front of the Tsarevich," she added in a stage whisper, "but His Imperial Majesty is simply fascinated by Stalin—*mais tout à fait épris!*"

"Stalin! You?" gasped the Muse of History.

"Yes, yes, oh yes," said the Tsar eagerly, elbowing his wife's ghost out of the way. "What statesmanship! What vision! What power! We have known nothing like it since my ancestor, Peter the Great, broke a window into Europe by overrunning the Baltic states in the 18th Century. Stalin has made Russia great again!"

"It all began," said the Tsarina wearily, "with the German-Russian partition of Poland. . . ."

"I always wanted to take those Poles down a peg," the Tsar broke in, "but something was always tying my hands."

"Until then," the Tsarina went on, "we enjoyed a pleasant, if rather insubstantial, life. We used to haunt the Casino at Monte Carlo. But after the partition of Poland, Nicky insisted on returning to Russia. He began to attend the meetings of the Politburo. The Politburo! Oh, those interminable speeches. . . . *Ah, Katorga!*"*

"Couldn't you stay home?" asked the Muse of History.

"And leave Nicky alone with those sharpers! He never could do anything without me. Besides, I doubt if you know what it's like to be a ghost: *le silence éternel de ces espaces infinis m'effraie*—The eternal silence of these infinite spaces terrifies me. Pascal said that, you know. Not bad for a man who had never been liquidated. And then," the Tsarina added, "Stalin overran Estonia, Latvia, Lithuania."

"Bessarabia," cried the Tsar, "was recovered from Rumania."

"And Northern Bukovina," cried the Tsarina, "which had never been Russian before."

"Foreign Minister Saracoglu of Turkey was summoned to Moscow," said the Tsar, "and taken over the jumps. For a moment I thought we had the Straits."

"Constantinople," breathed the Tsarina, "the goal of 200 years of Russian diplomacy."

"After that," said the Tsar, "it could not be put off any longer."

"What?" asked the Muse of History.

"Why, my conversion," said the Tsar. "I—I became a Marxist."

---

* *Meaning: Hard Labor—An expletive used by Old Bolsheviks instead of Oh, Hell!*

"He means a Leninist-Stalinist," said the Tsarina. "By official definition Leninism-Stalinism is the Marxism of this historical period."

"Stalinists!" cried the Muse of History.

"I don't see any reason why *you* should be so surprised, Madam," said the Tsarina. "After the way you have favored Communism for the last 27 years, you are little better than a fellow traveler yourself!"

"Of course, we could not formally enter the Party," the Tsar explained. "There was the question of our former status as exploiters in Russia. Even worse was our present status as ghosts. It violates a basic tenet of Marxism which, of course, does not recognize the supernatural."

"One might suppose, though," said the Tsarina, "that since the Party was, so to speak, responsible for making us what we are, the Central Control Commission would stretch a point in our case."

"And now," said the Tsar, peering through the chink in the roof, "the greatest statesmen in the world have come to Stalin. Who but he would have had the sense of historical fitness to entertain them in my expropriated palace! There he sits, so small, so sure. He is magnificent. Greater than Rurik, greater than Peter! For Peter conquered only in the name of a limited class. But Stalin embodies the international social revolution. That is the mighty, new device of power politics which he has developed for blowing up other countries from within."

"With it he is conquering Rumania and Bulgaria!" cried the Tsarina.

"Yugoslavia and Hungary!" cried the Tsar.

"Poland and Finland," cried the Tsarina.

"His party comrades are high in the Governments of Italy and France."

"A fortnight ago they re-entered the Government of Belgium."

"Soon they will control most of Germany."

"They already control a vast region of China."

"When Russia enters the war against Japan, we shall take Manchuria, Inner Mongolia, Korea, and settle the old score with Chiang Kai-shek."

"Through the meddling of the imperialist, Churchill, we have suffered a temporary setback in Greece. But when the proper time comes, we shall sweep through Iran and reach the soft underbelly of Turkey from the south. Turkey and Greece are Britain's bastions to defend the Middle East. . . ."

" 'You have a world to win,' " cried the Tsarina, " 'You have nothing to lose but your chains.' "

"I must ask you, Madam," said the Muse of History, "to stop dancing up & down on this roof. These old palaces are scarcely more substantial than you ghosts. I am glad to see that Marxism has had the same psycho-therapeutic effect on you as on so many neurotics who join the Communist Party. But your notions about Russia and Stalin are highly abnormal. All right-thinking people now agree that Russia is a mighty friend of democracy. Stalin has become a conservative. In a few hours the whole civilized world will hail the historic decisions just reached beneath your feet as proof that the Soviet Union is prepared to collaborate with her allies in making the world safe for democracy and capitalism. The revolution is over."

"*Grazhdanka!* (citizeness)," cried the Tsarina, "you have been reading banned books. Those are the views of the renegade Leon Trotsky."

"The Muse cannot help being an intellectual," said the Tsar generously, "but I do not think that we should charge her with Trotskyism. I must say, though, that for a Muse of History, you seem to have a very slight grasp of the historical dialectic. It is difficult for me to understand how a contemporary of the dialectician, Heraclitus of Ephesus, can still think in the static concepts of 19th-Century liberalism. History, Madam, is not a suburban trolley line which stops to accommodate every housewife with bundles in her arms."

"I think I liked you better, Nicholas," said the Muse of History, "when you were only a weakling Tsar. You are becoming a realist."

"Death," said the Tsarina, "is a somewhat maturing experience. What Nicky means is that between two systems of society, which embody diametrically opposed moral and political principles, even peace may be only a tactic of struggle."

"But have not the gentlemen downstairs," asked History, "just agreed to solve the Polish and Yugoslav questions in a friendly fashion?"

"What makes Stalin great," said the Tsar, "is that he understands how to adapt revolutionary tactics to the whirling spirals of history as it emerges onto new planes. He has discarded the classical type of proletarian revolution. Nevertheless, he is carrying through basic social revolutions in Rumania, Bulgaria, Yugoslavia, Hungary and Poland. Furthermore, we Marxists believe that in the years of peace Britain and the U.S. will fall apart, due, as we Marxists say, to the inability of capitalism to solve its basic contradiction—that is, its inability to provide continuous work for the masses so that they can buy the goods whose production would provide continuous work for the masses. Britain and America can solve this problem only by becoming Communist states."

"If that were true, Stalin would be wrong," said History, "because

America and Britain, though they may undergo great changes, will not become Communist states. More is at stake than economic and political systems. Two faiths are at issue. It is just that problem which these gentlemen below are trying to work out in practical terms. But if they fail, I foresee more wars, more revolutions, greater proscriptions, bloodshed and human misery."

"Well," said the Tsarina, "if you can foresee all that, why don't you do something to prevent it?"

The Muse of History drew the Tsarevich to her, for he had become restless. "Poor little bleeder," she said, stroking his hair, "different only in the organic nature of your disease from so many others who have bled and died. In answer to your question, Madam," she said, glancing at the Tsarina, "I never permit my fore-knowledge to interfere with human folly, if only because I never expect human folly to learn much from history. Besides, I must leave something for my sister, Melpomene, to work on."* ∎

* In the Greek Pantheon, Melpomene was the Muse of Tragedy.

End of Forever

BY HERBERT LAING MERILLAT

[
*Despite the nonviolence urged and exemplified by
Gandhi, British India's bloody transition into two
new nations presaged postcolonial tensions
that plague the world to this day*
]

June 30, 1947

ON A TURF-COVERED PLAIN near Delhi, a splendid assemblage gathered Jan. 1, 1877. The High Officers and Ruling Chiefs of India took their seats behind a gilt railing in an amphitheater of blue, white, gold and red, to hear Queen Victoria proclaimed first Empress of India. They rose to their feet as a flourish of trumpets announced the arrival, across 800 feet of red carpet, of His Excellency the Viceroy, Edward Robert Bulwer-Lytton, Second Baron Lytton. The proclamation was read, the Royal Standard was hoisted, and artillery fired a grand salute of 101 salvos. Mixed bands played *God Save the Queen,* then trumpeted the blaring march from *Tannhäuser.* Richly caparisoned elephants trumpeted too, and rushed wildly about with trunks erect when they heard the roll of musketry.

His Highness the Maharaja Sindia was first to congratulate (*in absentia*) the new Empress: "*Shah-en-Shah Padishah* [Queen of Queens]. May God bless you. The Princes of India bless you and pray that your sovereignty and power may remain steadfast forever."

"Forever" might have been a longer time if it had not been for a scrawny, timid schoolboy then in the northwest India town of Porbandar on the Arabian Sea, 700 miles away. Mohandas Kamarchand Gandhi was eight years old at the time of the Great Durbar at Delhi. He was already sensitive about his British rulers. His schoolmates used to recite a bit of doggerel:

> *Behold the mighty Englishman!*
> *He rules the Indian small,*
> *Because being a meat eater*
> *He is five cubits* tall.*

Although his parents were pious Vaishnavas (a Hindu sect which strictly abstains from meat eating), Gandhi was goaded a few years later into sampling goat meat to emulate the British. "Afterwards," he reported, "I passed a very bad night. . . . Every time I dropped off to sleep, it would seem as though a live goat were bleating inside me; and I would jump up full of remorse."

Gandhi's frail body never grew beyond 110 pounds, but the youthful conscience matured into a towering spirit that laid the meat eaters low, five cubits or not. Winston Churchill had once called Gandhi "a half-naked, seditious fakir. . . . These Indian politicians," he said in 1930, "will never get dominion status in their lifetimes." But 70 years after the Great Durbar both Gandhi and Churchill were still alive, and freedom was only 50 days away.

Last week in New Delhi, Queen-Empress Victoria's great-grandson, Rear Admiral Viscount Mountbatten of Burma, Viceroy of India, was working hard to get out of India as fast as he could. To Hindu and Moslem politicos responsible for setting up two new dominions in India before mid-August he sent memos reminding them "only 62 more days," "only 55 more days." The British did not rely on Hindu and Moslem leaders' continuing to work together. The British wanted to clear out before India blew up in their faces.

On the outskirts of New Delhi, in the dingy, dungy Bhangi (untouchable) Colony, Gandhi was not jubilant, although the British were leaving at last. To him, the violence and disunity of India were a personal affront. To Gandhi, *ahimsa* (nonviolence) is the first principle of life, and *satyagraha* (soul force, or conquering through love), the only proper way of life. In the whitewashed, DDT-ed compound which serves him as headquarters, Gandhi licked his soul wounds: "I feel [India's violence] is just an indication," he told his followers, "that as we are throwing off the foreign yoke,

---

* *Length of biblical (and British) cubit: 18 inches. David's Goliath towered six cubits and a span (9 ft. 9 in.).*

all the dirt and froth is coming to the surface. When the Ganges is in flood the water is turbid."

Ironically, Gandhi himself, who has spent a lifetime trying to direct the waters into disciplined channels, had helped to roil his people into turbulence. What he had called the "dumb, toiling, semi-starving millions," who revered (and sometimes worshiped) Gandhi, could understand him when he cried for their freedom; they could not always understand him when he told them they must not use violence to win that freedom. "To inculcate perfect discipline and nonviolence among 400,000,000," he once said, "is no joke."

Gandhi seriously began his own self-discipline when he went to South Africa as a London-educated *vakil* (barrister) at the age of 23. There he first felt the full weight of the white man's color bar. More & more he neglected a lucrative law practice to lead his fellow Indians in a fight against local anti-Indian laws.

A British friend lent him Count Leo Tolstoy's *The Kingdom of God Is Within You.* The Russian Christian's doctrine of nonviolent resistance to unjust rule gripped the Hindu lawyer's mind. "Young birds," wrote Tolstoy, ". . . know very well when there is no longer room for them in the eggs. . . . A man who has outgrown the State can no more be coerced into submission to its laws than can the fledgling be made to re-enter its shell."

Gandhi broke his shell. He decided manual labor was essential to the good life; he still thinks Indians will find peace only through making their own clothes on the *charka* (spinning wheel). So he gave up a legal practice bringing in about £5,000 a year, moved to a farm settlement where his helpers worked the ground, and began to get out a newspaper, *Indian Opinion.*

Gandhi mobilized local Indians for his first civil disobedience campaign. They won repeal of some anti-Indian laws from an obstinate South African Government. In 1915, aged 45, he returned to Bombay, the hero of India.

The first year after his return Gandhi toured much of India. The gentle ascetic in loincloth, walking among the villages, won the hearts of millions of Indians. "Gandhi says" became synonymous with "The truth is," for many a peasant and villager. When simple peasants crowded round to see him (many tried to kiss his feet), Gandhi tried to stop "the craze for *darshan*" (beholding a god).

The Mahatma (Great Soul), as he came to be called, insisted he was a religious leader, not a politician. "If I seem to take part in politics," he said, "it is only because politics today encircle us like the coils of a snake from which one cannot get out no matter how one tries. I wish to wrestle with the snake.... I am trying to introduce religion into politics."

Applied to India, that meant to Gandhi that people could not be pure in thought, word and deed unless they were their own masters. So he began to work for Indian independence. He found India's "struggle" for independence in the hands of a few well-educated Indians. The Indian National Congress* was a polite debating society, pledged to win dominion status for India by "legitimate" means. Gandhi converted it into a mass movement. Indian peasants did not worry about independence until Gandhi told them to.

British repressive measures after World War I convinced Gandhi that the British would never willingly give India dominion status. So he organized *satyagraha*. This first campaign came near to unseating the British Raj. "Gandhi's was the most colossal experiment in world history, and it came within an inch of succeeding," admitted the British governor of Bombay.

But passive resistance always erupted into violence. When he saw the bloodshed that followed his call for resistance, Gandhi was overwhelmed with remorse. He called off his campaign in 1922, admitted himself guilty of a "Himalayan miscalculation." His followers were not yet self-disciplined enough to be trusted with *satyagraha*. To become a "fitter instrument" to lead, Gandhi imposed on himself a five-day fast.

The pattern repeated itself in later years. The ways of passive action—the sari-clad women lying on railway tracks, the distilling of illicit salt from the sea, the boycotting of British shops, the strikes, the banner-waving processions—would lead to shots in the streets, to burning and looting. Gandhi always punished himself for his followers' transgressions by imposing a fast on himself.

With each fast, each boycott, and each imprisonment (by a British Raj which feared to leave him free, feared even more that he would die on their hands and enrage all India), Gandhi came closer to his goal of a free India. With the same weapons he got in some blows at his favorite social evils—untouchability, liquor, landlord extortions, child marriages, the low status of women.

But as he wrestled, India and Indian politics changed along the road.

---

* *Allan Octavian Hume, a British theosophist and retired civil servant, founded the Congress in 1885. He persuaded the Viceroy, Lord Dufferin, that the best way to combat growing unrest in the villages was to let Indian leaders discuss political development.*

The Indian National Congress, which claimed to represent Indians of every religious community, finally had to admit that Mohamed Ali Jinnah spoke for the Moslems. Left-wing groups left the Congress. Communists led by Puran Chandra Joshi threatened the placid order of the agricultural, home-industrial India which Gandhi strove for. The Congress leadership (since 1941 Gandhi has ruled only from the sidelines) passed more & more to a group of well-to-do conservatives bossed by Sardar Vallabhbhai Patel.

The only outstanding exception was socialistic Jawaharlal Nehru. Indian independence was certain to be followed by a struggle for economic power. For all these bewildering problems Gandhi had an answer: hurt no living thing; live simply, peacefully, purely. But fewer & fewer listened to that part of his advice. Just as Gandhi had outgrown the shell of the British Raj, so Indian nationalism, Hindu and Moslem, showed signs of outgrowing Gandhi's teachings.

THE INDIA OF NEW Delhi politicians was little concerned with soul force. Old (70), rabble-rousing Mohamed Ali Jinnah, head of the Moslem League, was greeted by followers with shouts of *"Shah-en-Shah Zindabad"* (Long live the King of Kings). His birthplace, Karachi, would probably be capital of the new Pakistan, possibly be renamed Jinnahabad.

Jinnah was already using his new power to disrupt India further. In the face of Jawaharlal Nehru's blunt warning to the Indian princes ("We will not recognize the independence of any state in India"), Jinnah began courting them. Most princes had already decided to join Hindu India, but the Nizam of Hyderabad (a Moslem) and Maharaja of Travancore (a Hindu) had each said he would go it alone. Jinnah dangled alliance-bait before them: "If states wish to remain independent . . . we shall be glad to discuss with them and come to a settlement." Big Kashmir, still on the fence, was ruled by a Hindu, but its 76% Moslem population would probably bring it into Pakistan sooner or later.

Last week Harry St. John B. Philby, Briton-turned-Moslem, familiar intriguer in the Arab world and intimate of Saudi Arabia's King Ibn Saud, arrived in India "to buy tents." He went into a huddle with Moslem Leaguers and Hyderabad officials. Delhi was sure Jinnah was angling for the support of Moslem states in the Middle East.

His Pakistan would be strong agriculturally (with a wheat surplus in the rich Punjab, 85% of the world's jute in eastern Bengal), but weak industrially. Pakistan would begin its career with no cotton mills, jute mills, iron or steel works,* copper or iron mines. Jinnah hoped to compensate for this weakness with foreign support, might keep Pakistan a British dominion even if Hindu India declared complete independence.

But these maneuverings were remote from the India of mud and dung and endless toil, which wondered in bewilderment what was happening to it. The little man in India had never asked for Pakistan or Hindustan or even for independence, except when his leaders told him. He was scarcely aware who ruled him. Recently a tattered Hindu peasant helped to repair a blowout on a car in the Punjab. Asked what he thought of the Government in New Delhi (now a temporary, joint Hindu-Moslem Cabinet, operating under viceregal veto), he replied, "I never heard of it."

If the symbol of unity at New Delhi was remote, the communal hatred that had forced the partition now faced was real enough. On both sides of the new dividing line, between Pakistan and Hindu India, minority groups wondered what to do. A Moslem tonga (two-wheeled carriage) driver, who had lived 20 years in Delhi, thought of moving to the Punjab. "I will wait and see what happens," he said. "If there is any trouble, I will send for my mother, my sister and my two buffalo, on my farm in the United Provinces." But it would cost him $50 to move to the Punjab—and the meager amount he collects in fares barely pays for food on the black market. Besides, he was still paying off a $200 debt incurred when he had tried vainly to save the life of a typhoid-stricken son.

A Hindu milkman in Bombay thought of moving his 68-year-old father from the Lahore district (which will go to Pakistan). "We own half a dozen cows and bullocks and three-quarters of an acre of land. My father would hate to leave our village and breathe the foul air of Bombay. I, my wife and five children are sharing a one-room apartment with another couple with three children. How can I accommodate my father? But I must bring him down. I cannot abandon him to Pakistan."

A Pathan watchman from the North-West Frontier Province thought he might have to go back to the barren soil of his native district. "The Hindu who owns the firm where I work has given me notice, saying he cannot trust foreigners to guard his shop. Who will give me jobs now? What will happen to my family?"

A Hindu *chaprasi* (office boy) in a Delhi Government office, who owned three acres of land in a Pakistan district, thought he had better bring his

---

* *The great 1,2500,000-ton plant at Jamshedpur is owned by the Parsi Tata clan and manned mostly by Hindus.*

wife and family to Delhi. But then he would have to sell his land. "Who will pay a good price for my property?" he asked. "I tried to sell it recently, but some Moslems who were originally prepared to purchase it now say they will get it anyway, once Pakistan comes into being, for little or no money."

All along the prospective border between Pakistan and Hindu India, minorities were on the move. From little villages in the Moslem Punjab, Hindu and Sikh traders and money-lenders trekked to Delhi or the United Provinces. Among them were men who had been in charge of rationing food and clothing during the war, and men who profited by high wartime prices.

Returning Punjabi soldiers last year had turned in hate against the money-lenders, merchants and all their co-religionists. In Bengal it had been the same. While 1½ million died of famine, landowners and food dealers, Moslem and Hindu alike, had reaped profits of 1½ billion rupees. "Every death in the famine," estimated the Woodhead Famine Enquiry Commission two years ago, "was balanced by roughly a thousand rupees of excess profit." The economic grievance of peasants against landlords and profiteers became a religious fight.

In the cities, as always, the warnings of conflict and disorder were sharpest. Throngs of wartime jobholders were idle. In sweltering Calcutta, it took but the flick of a Moslem cigaret butt against the flanks of a sacred Hindu cow, or a Hindu tonga driver's bumping a Moslem child, to start a fight that would engulf the city. Last week Calcutta was still divided into "Pakistan" and "Hindustan" quarters, with strong points bristling with barbed wire and machine guns. A Hindu driver dared not cross into a Moslem quarter, nor a Moslem into "Hindustan." In Bombay, where Hindus and Moslems had formerly lived mixed in together, streetcar signs now said "Pakistan Bombay," meaning the Moslem quarter.

With the political leaders' agreement to partition India had come a lull in communal fighting. But last week it flared again at Lahore in the Punjab. In the Gurgaon district near Delhi, Moslem and Hindu-Sikh tribes still burned and looted each other's villages. There, for the first time in communal riots, firearms were used on a big scale by each side. The embattled tribes had been turning out homemade wooden rifles, six feet long. In a divided India, where 38 million Moslems are still within the borders of Hindu India, 18 million Hindus and two million Sikhs within Pakistan, few supposed that political deals in Delhi could really repair the breach between religious communities.

One Moslem, who had lost his leather works in riots at Amritsar, no longer cared whether he was in Pakistan or Hindustan. Unshaven and ragged, Chaudhri Ahmen Hasan wandered aimlessly among the ruins of his property, carrying a big framed photograph of Jinnah. From time to time Hasan paused and addressed the picture: "Are you happy now, *Qaid-e-Azam* [Great Leader]? You have at last achieved Pakistan."

One Hindu, Mohandas Gandhi, still hoped to bring Hindus and Moslems together in a united India. If, in spite of divisive forces, India's 400 million really form themselves into a nation in the modern sense, Gandhi will have brought off (almost as a by-product of his larger purpose) a revolution greater than Danton's, bigger than Lenin's. The subcontinent had never been a nation; its separate peoples had, however, tolerated each other's very different ways of life. As both a politician and a Great Soul, Gandhi knew that if tolerance was replaced by permanent hatred, there would be not just two Indias, but no India. For India's future, nonviolence was not a philosopher's dream, but a political necessity.

Far closer than Queen Victoria's little isle was the Soviet Union which might, like Britain before it, exploit the weakness of a divided India to win hegemony. Already Puran Chandra Joshi, India's grinning Communist leader, and other Russian agents had a small (50,000), growing, tightly organized machine within India. If dissension grew in India, Joshi's grin (and Russia's chance) would grow with it.

Across the northern frontier, in the Tajik Socialist Soviet Republic, loomed Mt. Stalin (24,590 ft.) and Mt. Lenin (23,386 ft.), mightiest peaks of the U.S.S.R. Gandhi's thoughts last week turned to the lowest part of India, the mushy flats of Noakhali at the mouth of the Ganges. That part of Bengal, where Moslems and Hindus are mixed, will become part of Pakistan.

Noakhali was the first place Gandhi visited last spring in his tour of India's riot areas. Barefoot, staff in hand, leaning on his grandniece Manu, he had padded through the water-soaked fields and the mixed Moslem-Hindu villages, preaching peace. Last week Gandhi planned a symbolic return. "My work is in Noakhali," he said. "Nobody will prevent me from going there." For Gandhi considered himself a citizen of both new Indian states. "I will go freely to all parts of India . . . without a passport." The question was, would other Indians be able to do the same? ∎

The Showdown

BY JAMES ATWATER

[*This swift-paced narrative of the Cuban missile crisis recounted a two-week period in which the U.S. and the Soviet Union brought the world to the brink of nuclear war*]

November 2, 1962

FOR DAYS AND WEEKS, refugees and intelligence sources within Cuba had insisted that the Soviet Union was equipping its Caribbean satellite with missiles, manned by Russians, that could carry nuclear destruction to the U.S. But the reports were fragmentary and sometimes contradictory. And U.S. reconnaissance planes, photographing Cuba from the Yucatan Channel to the Windward Passage, could detect no such buildup. President Kennedy was not yet persuaded to take decisive action.

On Oct. 10 came aerial films with truly worrisome signs. They showed roads being slashed through tall timber, Russian-made tents mushrooming in remote places. The order went out to photograph Cuba mountain by mountain, field by field and, if possible, yard by yard.

For four long days, Hurricane Ella kept the planes on the ground. Finally, on Sunday, Oct. 14, Navy fighter pilots collected the clinching evidence. Flying as low as 200 ft., they made a series of passes over Cuba with their cameras whirring furiously. They returned with thousands of pictures—and the photographs showed that Cuba, almost overnight, had been transformed into a bristling missile base.

As if by magic, thick woods had been torn down, empty fields were clustered with concrete mixing plants, fuel tanks and mess halls. Chillingly clear to the expert eye were some 40 slim, 52-ft., medium-range missiles, many of them already angled up on their mobile launchers and pointed at the U.S. mainland. With an estimated range of 1,200 miles, these missiles, armed with one-megaton warheads, could reach Houston, St. Louis— or Washington. Under construction were a half-dozen bases for 2,500-mile missiles, which could smash U.S. cities from coast to coast. In addition, the films showed that the Russians had moved in at least 25 twin-jet Ilyushin-28 bombers that could carry nuclear bombs.

Throughout Monday, Oct. 15, the experts pored over the pictures. There could be no doubt. Early on Oct. 16 a telephone call went to CIA Director John McCone, who was in Seattle mourning the death there of his stepson. It was 4 a.m. on the Coast, but McCone came awake in shocked realization of the grave impact of the news. When he had heard the last detail, he ordered the pictures taken to the President at once.

While the pictures were being prepared for the President, CIA officials outlined the information by phone to McGeorge Bundy, Kennedy's adviser on national security. Bundy hurried out of his office in the west wing of the White House, rode the tiny elevator up to the President's living quarters on the second floor, and walked into Kennedy's bedroom. The President, who was dressed and had just finished breakfast, put down the morning papers and listened. His expression did not change as Bundy spun out the startling story.

At 10:30 a.m., Kennedy first saw the pictures of the missiles. At 11:45 he sat down in his rocking chair for a conference with the top members of his Administration that began the most crucial week of his term in office. It was a week of intensive analysis and planning, a week of round-robin meetings at State and the Pentagon—and above all, a week of decisions of surpassing importance to the U.S. and the world today.

Throughout that week, U.S. planes kept Cuba under their photographic magnifying glass. Air Force RB-47s and U2s prowled high over the island. Navy jets swooped low along the coastlines. With the passing of each day, each hour, the missile buildup burgeoned. In speed and scope it went far beyond anything the U.S. had believed possible. By conservative estimate, the Soviet Union must have been planning it in detail for at least a year, poured at least $1 billion into its determined effort.

But why? That was the question that kept pounding at President Kennedy. He knew all too well that the Soviet Union had long had the U.S.

under the Damoclean sword of intercontinental ballistic missiles in the Russian homeland. There thus seemed little real need for such a massive effort in Cuba. Yet, as Kennedy pondered and as he talked long and earnestly with his top Kremlinologists—among them former U.S. Ambassadors to Moscow Llewellyn Thompson and Charles Bohlen—some of the answers began to emerge. More and more in Kennedy's mind, the Cuban crisis became linked with impending crisis in Berlin—and with an all-out Khrushchev effort to upset the entire power balance of the cold war.

"Chip" Bohlen, about to leave for Paris as U.S. ambassador there, supplied a significant clue. Talking to Kennedy, he recalled a Lenin adage that Khrushchev is fond of quoting: If a man sticks out a bayonet and strikes mush, he keeps on pushing. But when he hits cold steel, he pulls back.

Khrushchev's Cuban adventure seemed just such a probe. He hoped to present the U.S. with a *fait accompli,* carried out while the U.S. was totally preoccupied—or so, at least, Khrushchev supposed—with its upcoming elections. If he got away with it, he could presume that the Kennedy Administration was so weak and fearful that he could take over Berlin with impunity.

The theory gained credence when, on the very day that Kennedy learned about the missiles in Cuba, Khrushchev did his best to cover up the operation by assuring U.S. Ambassador Foy D. Kohler during a relaxed, three-hour talk that the arms going to Cuba were purely defensive. Two days later, Foreign Minister Andrei Gromyko showed up in the White House with the same soothing message. But all was not bland during Gromyko's 2¼-hour visit. Noting that he knew Kennedy appreciated frank talk, Gromyko declared that U.S. stubbornness had "compelled" Russia to plan to settle the Berlin crisis unilaterally after the Nov. 6 elections.

Khrushchev already had requested a November meeting with Kennedy. As Kennedy came to see it, Khrushchev planned to say something like this: We are going to go right ahead and take Berlin, and just in case you are rash enough to resist, I can now inform you that we have several scores of megatons zeroed in on you from Cuba.

If such a scene would hardly be dared by novelists, it was well within Khrushchev's flair for macabre melodrama. In this baleful light, it became completely clear to Kennedy that the U.S. had no course but to squash the Soviet missile buildup. But how? In his long, soul-trying talks with Defense Secretary Robert McNamara, State Secretary Dean Rusk, the CIA's McCone and other top civilian and military officials, the plan was arduously worked out. Direct invasion of Cuba was discarded—for the time being. So was a surprise bombing attack on the missile sites. Both methods might cause Khrushchev to strike back instinctively and plunge the world into thermonuclear war. More than anything else, Kennedy wanted to give Khrushchev time to understand that he was at last being faced up to—and time to think about it.

The best answer seemed to be "quarantine"—a Navy blockade against ships carrying offensive weapons to Cuba. That would give the Premier time and food for thought. It would offer the U.S. flexibility for future, harsher action. It seemed the solution most likely to win support from the U.S.'s NATO allies and the Organization of American States. And it confronted the Soviet Union with a showdown where it is weakest and the U.S. is mighty: on the high seas. For the U.S. Navy, under Chief of Naval Operations George Anderson, 55, has no rival.

To Anderson went the job of setting up the blockade with ships and planes and making it work. While the Bay of Pigs fiasco had involved heltery-skeltery White House amateurs, now the pros were taking over. Anderson worked closely with Joint Chiefs of Staff Chairman Maxwell Taylor and with McNamara, who had been eating and sleeping in the Pentagon.

Speed was vital. Already plowing through the Atlantic were at least 25 Soviet or satellite cargo ships, many of them bringing more missiles and bombers for Cuba. They were shadowed by Navy planes from bases along the East Coast. Now, under Anderson's direction, U.S. warships prepared to intercept them.

All this took place in an eerie atmosphere of total secrecy in a notably voluble Administration. As part of the security cover, Kennedy took off on a scheduled campaign tour. But by Saturday, Oct. 20, he knew he could stay away from Washington no longer. Press Secretary Pierre Salinger announced that the President had a cold. Kennedy, a dutiful deceiver muffled in hat and coat, climbed aboard his jet and sped back to Washington.

ON THE MORNING OF Monday, Oct. 22, Kennedy worked over the TV speech that would break the news to the nation that night. The order went out to round up congressional leaders—wherever they were—and fly them back to Washington. The Air Force brought House Speaker John McCormack from his home in Boston, House Republican Leader Charles Halleck from a pheasant-hunting trip in South Dakota, Senate Minority Whip Thomas Kuchel from a handshaking visit to a San Diego factory.

House Democratic Whip Hale Boggs was fishing in the Gulf of Mexico when an Air Force plane flew over his boat and dropped into the water a plastic bottle attached to a red flag. The message in the bottle told Boggs to phone the White House. His boat pulled over to a nearby offshore oil rig. The Congressman donned a life jacket, swung by rope to a spindly ladder, and climbed 150 feet to the rig's platform, where a helicopter was awaiting him. At an airbase on the mainland, they crammed Boggs into a flight suit, strapped him into a two-seat jet trainer, clapped an oxygen mask on his face, took away the sandwich he had been clutching, and rocketed him back to Washington.

While the Senators and Congressmen were converging on Washington, Kennedy called in his Cabinet members. Some of the members still did not know what was going on. Silently they filed in. Silently they listened to the briefing, and silently they departed. Next came the congressional leaders. They studied the enlargements of the missile pictures and, in the words of one, their blood ran cold. The President then said simply: "We have decided to take action."

When he was done outlining the quarantine plan, Kennedy asked for comments—and found himself opposed by two of his fellow Democrats. Sitting directly across from the President, Georgia's Richard Russell, chairman of the Senate Armed Services Committee, told the President that the blockade was not enough and came too late. Russell was for immediate invasion. He argued that the U.S. was still paying for the Bay of Pigs debacle, so why fiddle around any longer? Russell was supported, surprisingly, by Arkansas' William Fulbright, chairman of the Senate's Foreign Relations Committee, who had led the fight in April 1961 against the Bay of Pigs invasion.

Kennedy turned away the criticism without anger, stuck by his decisions, and even managed to send the legislators away laughing. Said the President to Minnesota's Hubert Humphrey as the meeting broke up: "If I'd known the job was this tough, I wouldn't have trounced you in West Virginia." Said the Senator to the President: "If I hadn't known it was this tough, I never would have let you beat me."

That night, all America seemed to be watching as Kennedy went on television. It was a grim speech, delivered by a grim President. The U.S., he said, had two goals: "To prevent the use of these missiles against this or any other country, and to secure their withdrawal or elimination from the Western Hemisphere."

Kennedy explained that the quarantine would cut off offensive weapons from Cuba without stopping "the necessities of life." He warned that "any nuclear missile launched from Cuba against any nation in the Western Hemisphere" would be regarded by the U.S. as an attack by the Soviet Union and would bring full-scale nuclear reprisal against Russia.

Around the world, U.S. forces braced for combat. Under Admiral Anderson's orders, the Navy's Polaris submarines prowled the seas on courses known only to a handful of ranking officials. The Air Force went on a full-scale alert, put a fleet of B-52 bombers into the air, dispersed hundreds of B-47 bombers from their normal bases to dozens of scattered airfields. In West Berlin, the Army's contingent of 5,000 went on maneuvers.

As for the blockade itself, it was precisely directed by Anderson, working in his blue-carpeted Pentagon office bedecked with pictures of historic Navy battles. Several times a day he briefed McNamara, red-eyed from lack of sleep, in front of huge wall maps. He signed countless cables—pink paper for secret, green for top secret. At all times, Anderson delegated heavy responsibility to his subordinates—most of all to an old friend he called Denny. This was Admiral Robert Lee Dennison, 61, who is both Commander in Chief of the U.S. Atlantic Fleet and NATO's Supreme Allied Commander, Atlantic.

As the Russian ships headed toward Cuba on their collision course with the blockading force, Dennison walked to a wall map in his Norfolk headquarters and outlined the Navy's problem. "The approaches to Cuba are pretty well funneled down. Most ships headed for Cuba come out of the North Atlantic and have to come through the Bahamas or the Lesser Antilles, and both the Bahamas and the Lesser Antilles have relatively few channels. We don't really have any headaches. We have plenty of force. There are a lot of ships out there."

So there were. They belonged to Task Force 136, commanded by Vice Admiral Alfred G. Ward, 53, a gunnery specialist who has developed into one of the Navy's most respected strategists. Under Ward were approximately 80 ships. In reserve was the nuclear-powered carrier *Enterprise*. Navy P2V, P5M and P3V patrol planes, flying out of bases all along the East Coast and Florida, and from carriers encircling Cuba, put the Soviet ships under constant surveillance within 800 miles of Cuba.

Anderson's orders were clear. All Cuba-bound ships entering the blockade area would be commanded to heave to. If one failed to halt, a shot would be fired across its bow. If it kept on, the Navy would shoot to sink. If it stopped, a boarding party would search it for offensive war materials. If it had none, it would be allowed to go on to Cuba. But if it carried proscribed cargo, the ship would be required to turn away to a non-Cuban port of its captain's own choosing. Similarly, Cuba-bound cargo aircraft would be intercepted and forced to land at a U.S. airport for inspection, or be shot down.

Although there was a strong national sense of relief when Kennedy finally announced that he was "doing something" about Cuba, tension mounted almost unbearably in the hours that followed. What would happen? Would Khrushchev press the thermonuclear button? On Tuesday night, Kennedy signed a proclamation outlining the quarantine. The first indication of Russia's reaction came when a few Soviet freighters changed course away from Cuba. But others steamed on, and the moment of showdown came closer.

Two days after proclamation of the blockade, about 180 miles northeast of the Bahamas, the destroyers *John R. Pierce* and *Joseph P. Kennedy Jr.** took up stations behind a Russian-chartered Lebanese freighter named the *Marucla* (built in Baltimore during World War II). At daybreak on Friday, in a scene reminiscent of the 19th century, the *Kennedy* lowered away its whaleboat and sent a boarding party aboard the *Marucla,* which cooperatively provided a ladder. Wearing dress whites, Lieut. Commander Dwight G. Osborne, executive officer of the *Pierce,* and Lieut. Commander Kenneth C. Reynolds, the exec of the *Kennedy,* led the party aboard the ship. After politely serving his visitors coffee, the Greek captain allowed them the run of his ship. The cargo turned out to be sulphur, paper rolls, twelve trucks, and truck parts.

"No incidents," radioed the boarding party. "No prohibited material in evidence. All papers in order. *Marucla* cleared to proceed course 260, speed 9 knots to Havana via Providence Channel. Maintaining surveillance."

While the *Marucla* was being searched, a far more important event of the blockade was happening elsewhere in the Atlantic. After days of steaming toward Cuba and closer and closer to the Navy's line of ships, the remaining Soviet arms-carrying merchantmen were heading for home. Khrushchev had decided not to collide with the U.S. Navy on the high seas.

---

* *Asked how the destroyer named for the President's older brother, who was killed in World War II, happened to be at the right place at the right time, a Defense official said: "Pure coincidence." The* Pierce *is named for a lieutenant commander who won the Navy Cross and lost his life in 1944 while commanding the U.S.S.* Argonaut *against the Japanese. In the battle, the* Argonaut *went down with all guns firing.*

The blockade was a success.

Still, there could be no sense of relaxation. A way had to be found to get those already installed missiles out of Cuba. The U.S. effort was two-pronged: one was diplomatic, the other military.

On the diplomatic front, Adlai Stevenson urged Acting U.N. Secretary-General U Thant to impress upon the Russians the fact that the missiles must go. Making prompt action even more necessary was the fact that the Navy's twice-daily, low-level reconnaissance flights showed that the Russians were speeding up the erection of missile sites.

While the talks with U Thant were going on, Khrushchev suddenly proposed a cynical swap: he would pull his missiles out of Cuba if Kennedy pulled his out of Turkey. His long, rambling memorandum was remarkable for its wheedling tone—that of a cornered bully. Wrote Khrushchev: "The development of culture, art and the raising of living standards, this is the most noble and necessary field of competition . . . Our aim was and is to help Cuba, and nobody can argue about the humanity of our impulse."

Kennedy bluntly rejected the missile swap and increased the speed of the U.S. military buildup. The President considered choking Cuba's economy with a complete blockade. To knock the missiles out in a hurry, the White House discussed sabotage, commando raids, naval bombardment or a pinpoint bombing attack. And there was the strong possibility that invasion might finally be required.

Squadrons of supersonic F-100s and F-106s zoomed into Florida's Patrick and MacDill Air Force Bases. In the Caribbean were 10,000 Marines who had been about to go on maneuvers. McNamara ordered to active duty 24 troop carrier squadrons of the Air Force Reserve—more than 14,000 men.

Kennedy's course carried with it the obvious risk of casualties and finally, after a week of talk and maneuver, an Air Force reconnaissance plane was lost. But the flights went on as the U.S. prepared to move against Cuba if Khrushchev did not destroy his missiles.

To underline the need for urgent action, Kennedy sent Khrushchev a letter at week's end stating that no settlement could be reached on Cuba until the missiles came down under U.N. supervision.

Next day—just two weeks after the clinching recon photos were taken—Khrushchev said he was giving in. In his message, Khrushchev mildly told Kennedy: "I express my satisfaction and gratitude for the sense of proportion and understanding of the responsibility borne by you for the preservation of peace throughout the world, which you have shown. I understand very well your anxiety and the anxiety of the people of the U.S. in connection with the fact that the weapons which you describe as offensive are in fact grim weapons. Both you and I understand what kind of weapons they are."

To try and save some face, Khrushchev took full credit for preserving the peace of the world by dismantling the missiles. He also asked for a continued "exchange of opinions on the prohibition of atomic and thermonuclear weapons and on general disarmament and other questions connected with the lessening of international tension." And he said that Russia would continue to give aid to Cuba, which might mean that he had a lingering hope of still using the island as a base for Communist penetration of Latin America.

Within three hours, President Kennedy made his reply: "I welcome Chairman Khrushchev's statesmanlike decision to stop building bases in Cuba, dismantling offensive weapons and returning them to the Soviet Union under United Nations verification. This is an important and constructive contribution to peace . . . It is my earnest hope that the governments of the world can, with a solution to the Cuban crisis, turn their earnest attention to the compelling necessities for ending the arms race and reducing world tensions."

Thus, President John Kennedy appeared to have won in his courageous confrontation with Soviet Russia. There would, of course, be other crises to come. Looking ahead, Kennedy said several times last week: "I am sure we face even bigger, more difficult decisions." Such decisions—if met as boldly and carried out as shrewdly as those so far—present him with an opportunity for a major breakthrough in the cold war.   ■

Fangs a Lot

BY JOHN BLASHILL, ROBERT F. JONES
AND JASON McMANUS

[*What began as an office April Fools' gag, based on events in Ghana after President Nkrumah's ouster, ended up setting a new high—or low—for punning in* TIME]

April 8, 1966

"The soldiers now left in Flagstaff House, residence of the former President, are, I am told, eating their way through his private zoo," reported a columnist in West Africa *magazine last month. Full details were hard to come by, but the report set correspondents and writers to speculation about what might be going on in the cages of Kwame Nkrumah's private zoo.*

SOMEHOW THE OLD ELAND was missing. Neither hide nor hair of him had been seen since the day that Kwame Nkrumah had been ostrichized, accused of being the biggest cheetah in Ghana, but safaris anyone knew, no fowl play was involved.

First sign that anything was cooking at Flagstaff House came when Lieut. General Joseph Ankrah got on the horn and was told by the operator: "I'm sorry, the lion is busy." "Rhino what you're up to," he roared, with the phone still Ringling in his ears, "but I don't know vulture doing it for." In a frightful stew, Ankrah headed for the waterfront zoo (known as Hyenasport) for an on-the-spots investigation.

The bear facts, as Ankrah herd them, suggested that the garrison had been reluctant at first about eating up the zoo. But hesitation quickly

111

gave way to hunger, and it soon became a matter of gibbon take. For the first time they could remember, the ill-paid troops at Flagstaff House were all in plover.

To some, of course, it was spoor sportsmanship, killing defenseless animals and all, but Nkrumah had made chimps of his soldiers too long, and they had lots of bones to pick. The animals, they decided, were fair game. So while Nkrumah sat in Conakry, turning himself into a Guinea pig and pondering whether he should pack his trunk and join his friend Nasser at his Nile perch, the boared soldiers decided what they needed was some good gnus. One night when they were all croc-ed, they turned the zoo into Nkrumah's Bar & Gorilla.

It was aardvark. One apprentice cook was kept beesy making hamster sandwiches, but he won no kudus for his efforts: the troops were looking for fancier fare, such as peppered leopard or antelope with cantaloupe. The troops washed down their meals with giraffes of wine, and afternoon visitors to Flagstaff House were offered tea and simba-thigh, followed by lemon meringue python.

By the time Ankrah arrived on the scene, the zoo was nearly empty. Why hadn't someone phoned to inform him? he growled. "We orang-utang but ewe did not answer," the zookeeper replied tsetsely. After a halfhearted tour of the cages, he returned to headquarters, sank wearily into a chair and, realizing it was too late to save the animals, told the garrison commander to allow his troops to continue the feast. "As a matter of fact," said Ankrah, "as long as you're up, get me a Grant's gazelle." ■

The Temptations of Revenge

BY LANCE MORROW

[*With Iranian militants holding 66 Americans hostage in the U.S. embassy in Tehran, the writer traced a fine line in diplomacy between weakness and restraint*]

May 12, 1980

"LIFE BEING WHAT IT IS," said Baudelaire, "one thinks of revenge." Americans found themselves thinking about it a little more than usual last week as they watched Iranians displaying charred American bodies in front of the Tehran embassy that the dead had been sent to liberate. They thought of it again when Moussavi Garmoudi, the Iranian President's "cultural affairs adviser," appeared before cameramen, reached into a box and brought out a burned human foot (American), which he laid on a table before them.

Such scenes open a little trap door at the base of the brain. From that ancient root cellar they summon up dark, flapping fantasies of revenge. During the six-month imprisonment of their hostages, Americans have on the whole reacted with a surprising forbearance toward the Iranians. But beneath the surface they have marinated in an odd, atavistic cross-cultural rage. Their anger has been ripened by the long spectacle of their nation's ineffectuality and the humiliation of the failed rescue raid, by the nightly TV pageant of Iranian mobs pumping their fists in the air and screaming death threats in Farsi, and by the image of Sadegh Ghotbzadeh's cretinous smirk. Dark impulses that

113

normally stay below, like Ahab's harpooners, begin to straggle up on deck.

If aggression is the most basic and dangerous of human impulses, revenge gains a step on it by being premeditated. The urge for lurid, annihilating retaliation—vindication, satisfaction, the no-good bastard's head upon a plate—fetches far back to a shrouded moment when the spontaneous animal reflex of self-protection turned to a savage brooding. The human mind, newly intelligent, began to dream of the barbarously fitting ways in which it would get even. Emanating from hurt and the pain of failure and unfairness, the fantasy of revenge became, it may be, even stronger than the imperative of sex.

The gods of man's myths were elaborately, even bizarrely, vengeful. In the *Inferno,* Dante's Deity was satanically inventive in making the vengeance fit the crime. The best tragic theater (*Hamlet,* for example) and some of the worst has been built around the deep urge to settle someone's hash. In an orgy of horrific finality and emotional overstatement, Medea murders her two sons and hurls their corpses at Jason. That, God knows, ought to teach him.

History has been just as imaginative as theater and myth. The South American Tupinamba tribe would take a prisoner of war, make him consort with a woman of their tribe, then allow the woman to bear a child so that they could increase the tragedy by slaughtering both the prisoner and his baby. Sometimes in New Zealand, when a chieftain was killed during a war between two tribes, hostilities were broken off while the body of the leader was chopped up by his opponents, roasted and devoured. Among the southern Slavs a mother has been known to lay her infant son down in the cradle to sleep upon the bloodstained shirt of his murdered father. The child was raised to avenge; it became his vocation.

Under the protocols of the blood feud, one act of revenge begot another, so that violence originating in some forgotten crime or slight could reverberate for generations. Eventually the old brutal arrangement was superseded by the laws of the state, which undertook to end the freelance savageries of personal revenge by meting out justice uncomplicated by private passion.

Revenge detonates a little explosion of doom for the sake of personal—and usually rather temporary—satisfaction. But some say the practice of vengeance has its salutary, cleansing effect. Better for the circulation, they say, to liberate that maniacal little Nietzsche doll that jumps up and down inside all of us than to let him tear apart his cage.

Furthermore, revenge has its practical uses. The Mafia, first tutored in the exquisitely touchy finishing schools of Sicily, practices revenge as a matter of dispassionate business; the man who ordered the hit sends a horseshoe of flowers. Athletes have some instinct for keeping retaliatory accounts as a practical matter. Reggie Jackson of the New York Yankees was brushed back by two pitches last year by Mike Caldwell of the Milwaukee Brewers. Jackson went out and throttled him. Strictly business, Jackson explained later. If he had let the pitcher get away with it twice, he would have subtly lost respect and a competitive edge on the field.

Is there a practical counterpart in relations among nations? At the end of World War II the U.S. wisely declined to exact vengeance upon Japan and Germany, but instead helped to rebuild them, turning them at last, ironically, into the real economic victors of war. In the nuclear era, revenge may be too hairy a form of redress and self-gratification to be endured. Yet a cautionary super-revenge, in the latent form of a cataclysmic threat, is the governing principle of the nuclear age. The global balance of power is maintained by a threat of revenge that is designed by its sheer unthinkable horror to forestall the first blow.

Revenge is especially dangerous when it lumbers around shaggily between two cultures—like those of Iran and the U.S.—that profoundly misunderstand each other, that in some ways inhabit different centuries. The Iranians consider that they are exacting revenge for the years of America's association with the Shah. Thus grievances and countergrievances accumulate in some evolutionary rhythm, the way that grazing animals over the millenniums developed better teeth and, simultaneously, nutritional plants evolved harder thorns.

The cycle of revenge and counterrevenge should be broken, but not by the abject submission of Americans in an Iranian psychodrama. In the first place, American meekness invites contempt not only in Iran but elsewhere in the world. Without acting with the pathological ferocity of revenge, Americans might want to administer a little of what psychologists call negative reinforcement, when the time is right, something like the message that a hot stove delivers to someone who tries to sit on it. Both sides should remember, if they can, the Persian proverb: "Blood cannot be washed away with blood." Revenge has its undeniable satisfactions. It is a primal scream that shatters glass. But revenge is not an intelligent basis for a foreign policy. This century has already fulfilled its quota of smoke and rage and survivors, gray with bomb dust, staggering around in the rubble, seeking what is left of the dead they loved. ■

City of Protest and Prayer

BY OTTO FRIEDRICH

[*Published during Holy Week, this story offered a rich, evocative portrait of historic Jerusalem, the site of centuries of religious and political strife between Arabs and Jews*]

April 12, 1982

What can I say that others have not said already... told many times over and drawn again and again?... What can these places say to you, if in your mind's eye you do not see... the fearful day of the death on the Cross within the walls of Jerusalem?

—NIKOLAI GOGOL, LETTER ON JERUSALEM, 1850

THE FIRST THING TO BE SAID about Jerusalem, even if it has been said before, is that the ancient city is eternally new. In this magical place, sacred to three religions, the slopes outside the Jaffa Gate are ablaze with orange tulips, and rows of golden hyacinths sprout beneath the outstretching arms of the Moses Montefiore windmill. An unusual sight among the orange trees of the Mediterranean? "Ah, yes," a handsome Israeli woman sighs, "the Dutch sent us 100,000 bulbs when they moved away their embassy. So we planted them."

In Gogol's time, three centuries of Ottoman rule had reduced the City of God to a crumbling Levantine village of no more than 15,000 inhabitants (slightly fewer than half of them Jews). "Jerusalem is mournful and dreary and lifeless," Mark Twain wrote in *Innocents Abroad.* "Everything in it is rotting," said Gustave Flaubert, "the dead dogs in the streets, the religions in the churches." Today, after a turbulent sequence of British, Jordanian and Israeli conquests, after years of sporadic bombings and gunfire, this beautiful and richly diverse city is vibrant with growth and prosperity.

Since the Israelis forcibly reunified Jerusalem in 1967, the population has climbed from 275,000 to 407,000, and more than 1.1 million visitors pour in every year. The fortress-like apartment towers clustered on the once bare hills surrounding the city now extend to the very edge of the desert wilderness where Satan tempted Jesus; and though the walled Old City surrounding the holy shrines is still redolent of cinnamon and roasting lamb and hashish and donkey turds, the twisting alleys leading onto the Via Dolorosa (Sorrowful Way) are covered with paving stones rather than mud. Even the cats—Jerusalem has a remarkable quantity of cats—look content.

Yet all this exuberant rebirth is, in a strict sense, illegal. Not a single nation in the world recognizes the Israeli annexation of East Jerusalem. And when the Knesset voted in 1980 that a reunited Jerusalem was, in the words of Prime Minister Menachem Begin, "the eternal capital of our country, our people, our faith, our civilization," the United Nations promptly voted that it was no such thing. Hence the departure, under strong Arab pressure, of the Dutch diplomats.*

Of all the conflicts between Jews and Arabs, that over Jerusalem is the most complex and intractable. It is so deeply rooted in centuries of political and religious strife that each side is passionately determined to have its way. As long as there is no settlement, every terrorist bomb on the West Bank contains the danger of escalation: rioting, warfare, spreading oil cutoffs, a new confrontation of the superpowers. Arab claims on Jerusalem range from demands for Islamic sovereignty over the Muslim holy places to more contentious proposals for a Palestinian Arab capital in the east of the city, and even to wild-eyed cries that all Israelis should be expelled. The Israelis are willing to bargain on many things, but not on Jerusalem.

International controversy tends to imbue not just flowers but everything about Jerusalem with a nervous symbolism. Particularly state visitors. When Egypt's President Hosni Mubarak balked at extending his state visit to Jerusalem out of fear of appearing to condone Israeli control, there was talk for a time of his dashing through the Israeli capital without spend-

---

* *All twelve other embassies in Jerusalem, all from Latin America, also went to Tel Aviv.*

ing the night, a bizarre compromise that failed to satisfy anyone. Begin finally put off Mubarak's entire tour.

The paradoxical symbolism of Jerusalem flickers all through its commercial life. Just across the street from the Damascus Gate, near the East Jerusalem bus station, which still displays signs announcing the nonexistent express bus to the Jordanian capital of Amman, the British Bank of the Middle East stands apparently abandoned. Its front windows are covered by rusty metal shutters, the shutters covered with Arab handbills. "The Israelis wanted the bank to stay open," says an Arab wise in local charades, "but then it might be closed down in all Arab countries. So the manager remains here to do business, but you must call him at home, and then he comes down here, and there is a back way. Look here." The Arab points to an unmarked entrance on a side street, where an old woman is selling baskets of white and yellow daisies. Behind her is a little door that opens into the bank whenever someone comes to unlock it.

But this Friday is Good Friday—what Gogol called "the fearful day of the death on the Cross within the walls of Jerusalem"—and in Holy Week the city seems to become for a time the center of the world, as it was on the maps of the Middle Ages. As Holy Week starts on Palm Sunday, brown-robed Franciscan monks and white-robed Dominicans march in a long procession of the faithful, each with his own palm frond, along the route that Christ rode on his donkey from the village of Bethany up over the Mount of Olives, past the ancient olive trees in the Garden of Gethsemane and through St. Stephen's Gate into the Old City.

Good Friday is more somber. The zigzagging Via Dolorosa, so named only in the 16th century, is packed with pilgrims following in Christ's footsteps to Calvary. "We adore thee, O Christ . . . Thou hast redeemed the world," the Franciscan monks chant in Latin as they lead their flocks through the Arab market, through the 14 stations of the Cross.

Calvary is believed by many to be within the Church of the Holy Sepulcher. Near the entrance stands the rock of Golgotha, thought to have held the Cross. It is only dimly visible behind a small sheet of plate glass set in the surrounding wall. A few scattered coins lie at its base. The sepulcher where Christ lay is more elaborately bedecked with the trappings of worship. Dozens of thin white candles cast their flickering light over the sacred stone slab and the icons that survey it from the marble walls of the encompassing chapel.

After centuries of conflict and even bloodshed among rival groups of clerics, the ruling Turks in 1757 divided up all rights in this church among six Christian groups—the Franciscans, the Greek Orthodox, the Armenians, Syrians, Copts and Ethiopians—and these six still conduct the Easter ceremonies at Christ's tomb, each in its own time and according to its own ritual. Only on the Saturday following Holy Week do the Eastern faiths unite in the climactic ceremony of Holy Fire. The men dance, the women ululate, the church is darkened. The Greek Orthodox patriarch enters the tomb, prays and then thrusts from a porthole to the expectant crowd a lighted torch that symbolizes the Resurrection of the Light of the World.

These traditional Easter ceremonies can prove dismaying to Protestant pilgrims. Since Jerusalem offers all things to all believers, some now worship at a completely different burial site known as the Garden Tomb. It was Charles ("Chinese") Gordon, British conqueror of the Taiping rebels, who in the 1880s popularized the idea that the whole tradition of the Holy Sepulcher might be mistaken, and that Golgotha, which means "the place of the skull," might actually be a skull-shaped cliff about 500 yards to the north, behind what is now the main East Jerusalem bus station.

Modern scholars generally agree, however, that such shrines as the Via Dolorosa and the stone of Golgotha are no more than approximations of what is historically unprovable. They argue that exact geographical details simply do not matter a great deal, that a unique religious event took place in Jerusalem nearly two millenniums ago, and that the whole city commemorates it.

To the large majority of people who actually live in Jerusalem, however, Easter is an essentially alien rite. It is the Jewish Sabbath, or *Shabbat,* that closes down West Jerusalem's stores and even stops the buses at sundown every Friday, and this week is *Pesach* (Passover) of the year 5742. For the past week, schools have been closed so that everyone can prepare for Wednesday night's Seder. The flower shops are bursting with anemones, chrysanthemums, carnations. The housewives have been cooking and cleaning and cooking and cleaning.

While the male head of the house retells the story of the Exodus from Egypt, everyone shares in the ritual foods: bitter herbs for the Israelites' slavery, salt water for their tears, unleavened bread (matzo) to represent their haste in flight, a roasted egg for the triumph of life over death. When the ceremony ends, the eating becomes festive: *kneidlach* (dumplings) in chicken soup, cakes boiled in honey and spiced with ginger, coconut macaroons.

Every Seder for centuries has ended with the words "Next year in Jerusalem" (in Israel, the pledge is: "Next year in Jerusalem rebuilt"). And to honor the ancient injunction, an estimated 200,000 Jews are pouring into Jerusalem for this week's holidays. "Jerusalem," says Israel's Chief Rabbi, Shlomo Goren, "is our brain, our head, our soul."

The physical attachment of the Jews to Jerusalem helped them to survive the centuries of Diaspora. "I was born in one of the cities of the exile," said S.Y. Agnon, a native of Galicia, when he won the Nobel Prize for Literature in 1966, "but I always regarded myself as one who was born in Jerusalem."

This Jewish combination of religious and national feeling reaches its epitome in the mystical veneration for Jerusalem's Western Wall, or "Wailing Wall." To an alien eye, the limestone retaining wall looks impressive but hardly sacred. It rises nearly 60 ft. high, 1,580 ft. long, on the western edge of where the Temple stood 2,000 years ago. Some of its boulders are huge, 40 ft. long and weighing 100 tons. There is nothing here but these stones, yet Jews from all over the world flock to the wall to pray, to meditate, to dance, to take photographs, to hold bar mitzvahs or simply to be awed. According to tradition, a prayer said here will pass through the stones into the buried Holy of Holies, and a prayer left in writing between the stones will reach God. "This is where the Presence resides," says one white-bearded worshiper in a prayer shawl. "This is where he will always be. Forever."

TO THE MUSLIMS, WHO MAKE UP more than a quarter of Jerusalem's people, every Friday is holy, this week in the Muslim year 1402 no more or less so than any others, and even as the great bronze bells toll in the Church of the Holy Sepulcher, the chant of the muezzin in the minaret of the neighboring Mosque of Omar summons all Muslims to prayer. It is customary for both Christians and Jews to acknowledge Islam as Jerusalem's third religion, but also to patronize it as a latecomer. It angers many Jews and puzzles Christians that the Muslim conquerors of the 7th century built their magnificent Dome of the Rock squarely atop the ruins of Solomon's Temple. That Muhammad ascended to heaven there, from the same sacred rock on which Abraham prepared to sacrifice Isaac, is recounted in guidebooks as a picturesque legend.

But for the Arabs, who shut the gates of the Temple Mount against all infidel intruders before every prayer service at the mosques, five times a day, that Temple Mount is Haram as-Sharif (Noble Sanctuary). Jerusalem—known as Al-Quds, or the Holy City—is more sacred to them than any other city except Mecca and Medina, and according to the Hadith, "one act of worship there is like a thousand acts of worship anywhere else." Although Jews are forbidden to worship on the Temple Mount—partly because Moshe Dayan so decreed as a conciliatory gesture after the 1967 takeover, partly because rabbinical law warns that such an intrusion might unwittingly profane the uncertain site of the Temple's Holy of Holies—the Muslims sometimes feel they are under siege. Just last month, a group of Jewish extremists pushed their way onto the Temple Mount, began chanting prayers and stabbed an Arab guard who tried to prevent them.

For all the antiquity of its three religions, Jerusalem was there before any of them. When David first conquered the city from the Jebusites about 1000 B.C., the founders of "eternal Rome" had not yet been suckled by the legendary she-wolf. But Jerusalem was already 1,000 years old. And bloodshed has remained the city's motif through its four millenniums. It has been conquered 37 times, according to one reckoning. The Babylonians destroyed King Solomon's Temple of cedar wood and gold in 587 B.C. and carried the Jews off into exile ("By the rivers of Babylon, there we sat down, yea, we wept, when we remembered Zion . . . If I forget thee, O Jerusalem, let my right hand forget her cunning . . ."). The Romans not only destroyed the Second Temple, built by Herod, but tore the city to the ground in A.D. 135. They renamed it Aelia Capitolina and banished all Jews forever. (Not until two centuries later were exiles permitted to return just once a year to pray and mourn at the Western Wall outside what had once been their temple.) Where are the imperial Romans now? Where is Babylon?

The very stones of Jerusalem still echo the names of its many conquerors. The Church of the Holy Sepulcher was built by the Crusaders, who stormed Jerusalem in 1099 and killed all the Muslims and Jews they could find in the city. Salah el-Din (Saladin) Street, the main commercial thoroughfare of East Jerusalem, commemorates the Muslim warrior who expelled the Crusaders in 1187. The mighty walls that still gird the Old City are the creation of Suleiman the Magnificent, the 16th century Turkish Sultan. Even the brief reign of the British under a League of Nations mandate still has its monuments in King George V Street and Allenby Square, named for the general who entered the Old City on foot in 1917 because he would not ride where Jesus had walked.

Today's Jerusalem was born in the violence of Israel's creation. The

British had promised Palestine to both Jews and Arabs, then clung to power through World War II. Hitler's Holocaust made the need for a Jewish homeland inescapable. But after the U.N. voted in 1947 to partition the mandated territory into Jewish and Arab states, with an autonomous Jerusalem under international supervision, the violence worsened. British patrols proved unable or unwilling to prevent Arab guerrillas from ambushing trucks supplying Jerusalem. Food and even water had to be rationed as the city underwent a two-month siege.

May 14, 1948. The British depart. Israel is proclaimed. Five Arab nations attack. The Israelis beat them back. Jordan's British-trained Arab Legion seizes Jerusalem's Old City, and Jordanian mortars wreck much of the Jewish Quarter . . .

The armistice left Jerusalem divided as brutally as Berlin. Concrete barriers and barbed wire and land mines extended from the Cathedral of St. George to the hospice of Notre Dame and south to the tomb of David. The Israeli city hall was hit periodically by sniper fire from the New Gate, across the street (bullet holes still ornament the façade). Jordanian troops not only barred Jews from the Old City but opened fire on virtually anyone trying to reach the Hebrew University and Hadassah Hospital in the encircled Israeli enclave on Mount Scopus. And so passed nearly two decades.

June 5, 1967. At the demand of Egypt's Gamal Abdel Nasser, the U.N. withdraws its peace-keeping forces from the Sinai frontier. Nasser mobilizes his troops, declares he will blockade Israeli access to the Gulf of Aqaba. Israel strikes first by bombing Nasser's air force . . .

The Israelis claimed that they had no designs on Jerusalem and even told Jordan's King Hussein that they wanted no two-front war. The Jordanians responded by shelling West Jerusalem, hitting the Knesset, Prime Minister Levi Eshkol's house and several hospitals. The very afternoon of the first Monday's fighting, a mechanized brigade of Israeli reservists launched a counterattack. They were joined by paratroopers who encircled the strongly defended Old City. Then, on Wednesday morning, from a halftrack in front of the Inter-Continental Hotel atop the Mount of Olives, the paratroop commander, Mordechai Gur, ordered the final assault: "For two thousand years our people have prayed for this moment. Let us go forward."

Colonel Gur could not wait. He raced his halftrack down the mountain at top speed, hurtling past the burned-out hulks of tanks and the sprawling bodies of slain paratroopers, then dodged by a flaming truck partly blocking St. Stephen's Gate and burst right into the Old City. White flags were beginning to appear on all sides. While his paratroopers roared in behind him, the colonel turned left, crashed through another gate and then sent back his message to GHQ: "The Temple Mount is ours. Repeat: The Temple Mount is ours." And despite the crackle of continuing sniper fire, the first paratroopers rushed to the Western Wall, touched and kissed the sacred stones, then burst into tears at their triumph.

The battle for Jerusalem lasted just three days, the whole war just six, but after 2,000 years of saying "Next year in Jerusalem," the victors had no real plan of what to do with their recaptured capital. It took almost three weeks for the Knesset to declare the city united, and only then, at dawn on June 29, did the army start blowing up the walls that had divided the city for nearly 20 years. The army had already evacuated and bulldozed the slum hovels of the Moroccan quarter, which obstructed most of the Western Wall, thus making possible the vast plaza that faces it today.

Jerusalem's mayor, Teddy Kollek, a rotund Viennese, now 70, is an assertive politician but also a shrewd and humane one. To help keep the developers within bounds, he organized an international Jerusalem Committee of prestigious figures such as Buckminster Fuller, Isamu Noguchi and Pablo Casals. With their backing, he blocked all superhighways within the city and put a limit of eight stories on buildings. He re-enforced the British regulation that all new buildings be faced with Jerusalem stone, the soft dolomite limestone that gives the city its unique rosy, peachy, golden color. And all along the scarred no man's land that once divided the city, Kollek has erected theaters, concert halls and other stone symbols of reunification. Says Moshe Safdie, 43, the celebrated architect who is building a complex of modern apartment houses in the revived Jewish Quarter of the Old City: "Jerusalem before 1967 was a village . . . a dead end for both Jews and Arabs. It had lost its original purpose for existence. Since 1967, it has become a city again."

Jerusalem remains, of course, a city of wildly diverse communities. There are not just Jewish Jerusalem and Arab Jerusalem but official Jerusalem of the Knesset and the monolithic government ministries, commercial Jerusalem of the Bank Leumi le-Israel, and intellectual Jerusalem of the 15,000-student Hebrew University and the renowned Israel Philharmonic Orchestra. The city's Jews come from some 70 nations (70% of them from Muslim lands), and every nationality has its own neighborhood. The wealthy Rehavia section, where all Prime Ministers live, was settled largely by early refugees from Nazism, and German can still be heard there. In the Nahlaot district, one little synagogue is for Kurdish Jews from Iran, and another little synagogue standing right next to it is for Kurdish Jews from Iraq.

Christian communities are no less diverse. The White Russians congregate in the bulb-domed convent church of St. Mary Magdalene, near the Garden of Gethsemane, but there is also a Soviet-run order of Russian Orthodox monks, which is reputed to include the KGB agent for Jerusalem. The entire southwest corner of the Old City belongs to the black-frocked Armenian clerics, who live behind high stone walls and lock all their doors to the world at 10 p.m.

TO PRESIDE OVER SUCH a conglomeration requires lots of money, and like most mayors, Kollek does not have enough. Indeed, Jerusalem's finances would make a less visionary mayor start cutting back. Local taxes, the highest in the country, raise only one-third of the municipal budget of $150 million; the rest has to be wheedled out of the national government. But Kollek is a master fund raiser in Europe and America (his Jerusalem Foundation has dispensed $50 million), and he has been known to scoff at a half-million-dollar check as "not enough."

Kollek's efforts also require constant negotiation. Before 1967, many houses in the Old City had no sewers or running water, for example, but to install new plumbing means rooting around amid buried archaeological treasures. Every official innovation tends to be regarded with dire suspicion not only by Arabs but by ultra-Orthodox Jews.

The most controversial aspect of the rebuilding of Jerusalem derives from the Israeli government's decision to establish Jewish housing projects in the Arab East. In 1968, the year after their victory, the Israelis began confiscating land, and in 1969 the first 200 Jewish families moved into the new suburb of Ramat Eshkol. The Arabs protested, the U.N. voted censure, all to no avail. When the U.S. State Department joined in the protests, the Jerusalem city council responded by adding two more stories to the buildings being planned. Today there are 15,000 Jewish families in ten suburban projects from Neve Yaakov in the north to Gilo in the south, and the number is still growing. In 1967 the population in the 28 sq. mi. of East Jerusalem was 65,000 Arabs and no Jews; today the figures are 115,000 Arabs and 70,000 Jews.

The new projects are almost defiantly ugly—great Bronx-like block-houses on what had been bare hills. "The idea always used to be that there would be no suburban sprawl," grumbles Architect Art Kutcher. "That has been destroyed." Adds one Israeli: "The purpose of this whole program is to make Israeli possession of the united city irreversible."

A few idealists see hope in the social integration of Jews and Arabs, but most people are skeptical. "I have Arab friends," says Architect Kutcher, "but we don't invite each other to our homes. We just live side by side." Kollek's aides admit as much, and one spokesman talks of Jerusalem as being "a mosaic rather than a melting pot." Though Arab and Israeli children now learn each other's languages in Jerusalem classrooms, they still go to separate schools.

No Israeli reforms, however, will ever satisfy the Arabs. To accept any benefits of Israeli rule implies an acceptance of Israeli rule itself—an implication the Arabs emotionally resist. They see Israel, in Kollek's words, as "an occupier, maybe the best possible occupier, but an occupier." Like any benign occupier, Kollek leans over backward to be sympathetic to his Arab constituents. Before every election, he courteously asks some prominent Arabs to join his ticket; they respectfully but unfailingly decline. When the Israelis annexed East Jerusalem in 1967, they offered Arab residents the choice of becoming Israeli citizens or remaining Jordanian. About 99% remained Jordanian. Though Arabs are allowed to vote in Israeli elections, only about 10% do so.

Like all peoples in occupied lands, the Arabs claim to see slights and denigrations everywhere. Sometimes this feeling is justified, sometimes paranoiac, sometimes both. The Hadassah Hospital, for example, now provides Arab patients with better service than any Arab hospital, but many Arab patients are dismayed that the doctors address them in Hebrew and that the food is Jewish. Such resentments are aggravated by class differences: the Arabs of East Jerusalem increasingly serve as the maids, waiters and construction workers of the Jewish West. "The Israelis are more capable at running a city," concedes a garage owner in East Jerusalem, "so the roads are better, the traffic, the sewage system, but there is no joy any more. We don't enjoy our lives." Adds his son: "It is impossible to deal with an Israeli, because his point of view is impossible. They believe it is their land, and that is that."

This half-suppressed Arab anger over Israeli rule periodically erupts in violence. "The P.L.O. doesn't like me being here, so we have a lot of problems," says Shraga Rozenzweig, 38, who has been bombed six times since he opened the prosperous Dolphin Restaurant in East Jerusalem in 1967. Two troopers with automatic rifles are stationed outside the restaurant's door.

Actual terrorism in Jerusalem is not very widespread. But bomb scares remain part of the city's everyday life. Signs warn of "suspicious objects," and handbags are searched at the Western Wall and at the great mosques. Phone calls to the police frequently bring a blue-and-white bomb-squad truck to investigate a dropped briefcase or a child's broken doll lying on the sidewalk. The rifle-carrying Israeli soldiers are all over downtown Jerusalem, usually in groups of two or three, lounging on street corners, sauntering watchfully through the Arab markets. The Jerusalem police force, which is about 10% Arab, boasts a number of Jewish-Arab teams, like Sasson Ovadia, a Kurdistan Jew, and Khalil Doube, a Jerusalem Arab. Says Khalil: "Policemen are a different breed. We let others deal with the politics. We don't make laws, we enforce them."

Such an attitude helps keep alive the idea that there must be some "solution" to the question of Jerusalem, some peaceable kingdom in which the wolf shall dwell with the lamb. But in the strenuous negotiations at Camp David that brought a compromise on other Arab-Israeli disputes in 1978, the only agreement that could be reached on Jerusalem was an agreement to omit all mention of the subject. Says a Western diplomat in Israel: "There are no solutions for Jerusalem. There are just next steps, new frameworks."

Most Arabs and Israelis agree on a few basic points: that the city should never again be partitioned, that there should be free access to the holy places, and that these shrines should be administered by the religious groups. U.S. officials support all these points, always adding that the overall question of sovereignty remains to be negotiated. But those who have tried to negotiate have never come closer than Moses wandering in the wilderness in search of the Promised Land just beyond the horizon.

Mayor Kollek, as usual, has some plans of his own, which would concentrate on making the city function better. Specifically, he wants to provide the diverse neighborhoods with greater autonomy. In five neighborhoods (four Jewish and one Arab), authorities appointed activists to local councils in 1981 and asked them what they needed most. At A-Tur, a Muslim village, the council wanted new sewage lines so badly that it solicited contributions and even organized citizens to volunteer for digging. At Gilo, which had more children than the Education Ministry had expected, the council wanted temporary classrooms. "These may sound like picayune things," says a ranking city official, "but they are the start of something important."

They may also be the beginning of the only solution that has any realistic prospect of being fulfilled. It is not a solution that will satisfy the rival demands of international power politics or of sectarian ideology, but it may hold out the best prospects for the citizens involved.

Listen for a moment to an Arab who was supervising a construction gang at work in Ben Yehuda Street last month. "Right after the war, I didn't want the walls taken down," he said, "but then I went out with my children to walk around Jewish Jerusalem, and I saw that even though the people weren't like us, they had worked hard to make the city beautiful. These men here, they would rather be working for an Arab city. But they aren't, so I tell them, 'We have to do what we can.' This isn't the Jews' city or the Arabs' city. It's our city."

To which, in Holy Week, Amen.　■

—REPORTED BY DAVID AIKMAN AND ROBERT ROSENBERG/JERUSALEM

Was He Normal? Human? Poor Humanity

BY ELIE WIESEL

[*As France prepared to try a notorious Nazi war criminal,* TIME *asked a distinguished Holocaust survivor to frame the case's larger issues of memory, truth and honor*]

May 11, 1987

The author, winner of the 1986 Nobel Peace Prize, was 15 years old when the Nazis entered his hometown of Sighet, Hungary, in 1944. Miraculously he managed to survive the death camps of Auschwitz and Buchenwald, and at war's end he became a journalist in Paris. He would not speak out about the unspeakable for ten years. When that self-imposed vow of silence ended, he devoted his life to writing and talking, with rare eloquence and power, about the despair of the past and the concerns of the present. Now a U.S. citizen, Wiesel, 56, has written some 30 books and is widely acknowledged, in the words of the Nobel committee chairman, as a "messenger to mankind." Later this month he will testify in the case of The State of France v. Klaus Barbie.

I REMEMBER THE NEARSIGHTED, balding man in his glass cage in Jerusalem. During the April-to-December trial in 1961, I listened to witnesses whose words and silences contained the tormented memory of an entire people. Yet I was not watching them. Most of the time I was watching the defendant. It was to see him that I had come to Israel, anxious to find out for myself if he was human, if there was any humanity in him. I had hoped to find myself in the presence of a disfigured creature, a monster whose unspeakable crimes would be clearly legible in his three-eyed face. I was disappointed: Adolf Eichmann seemed quite normal, a man like other men—he slept well, ate with good appetite, deliberated coolly, expressed himself clearly and was able to smile when he had to. The architect of the Final Solution was banal, just as Hannah Arendt had said.

Will the same now be said of Klaus Barbie, who was less important but whose work was no less cruel? Barbie's trial is bound to attract worldwide attention. People are already saying this will be the last great courtroom drama to result from the Holocaust. They may be right.

For even behind bars, Barbie throws a long shadow. From the day of his capture, there were whispers that retribution could bring political catastrophe: the prisoner knows too much about too many. His lawyer is Jacques Vergès, most recently the defender of the Arab terrorist Georges Ibrahim Abdallah, sentenced last February to life imprisonment by a French tribunal for complicity in the killings of two diplomats, one of them an American, and in the attempted murder of a third. With Vergès' help, Barbie is quite capable of turning the tables, of forcing a trial of France under the Occupation.

But despite these fears, there will be a Judgment Day. The official examination of Klaus Barbie begins on May 11 in Lyons, France. No one knows how the story will end. But we know now how it all began.

Barbie, who grew up in Trier, a small town in Germany, and dreamed of becoming a minister, first arrived in Lyons at the age of 28. He was assigned the task of fighting the Resistance and getting rid of the Jews. The young, dedicated Nazi excelled at his job. He is accused of having executed 4,000 people and deported 7,500 Jews. His career grew so bloodstained that he was dubbed the "Butcher of Lyons." Yet only a fragment of that past will be weighed in the deliberations: the accusation is primarily concerned with the 44 Jewish children who, along with their guardians, were arrested on his orders in the village of Izieu and then sent to the gas chambers of Auschwitz.

How can Barbie justify what was done to the children of Izieu? Here, the proofs of his crimes are beyond dispute: the Nazi hunters Beate and Serge Klarsfeld, the best known of his pursuers, have turned up a striking document: "This morning, the Jewish children's home, 'Children's Colony,' at Izieu has been removed. 41 children in all, aged 3 to 13, have been captured. Beyond that, the arrest of all the Jewish personnel has taken place, namely 10 individuals, among them 5 women. It was not possible to secure any money or other valuables. Transportation to Drancy will take place on 4/7/44." The arrest order is signed in the name of Klaus Barbie.

This trial represents an extraordinary victory for Beate Klarsfeld, who, as it happens, was born and raised in Germany. A victory over the forgetfulness, the willingness to compromise, the indifference that an overly politicized world has shown for too long toward escaped SS killers. A victory too over the governments that helped Barbie. It was the Klarsfelds who picked up his trail—he had disappeared for almost 40 years into the identity of a prosperous and peaceful businessman named Klaus Altmann living in Bolivia. They were the ones who managed to persuade François Mitterrand's Socialist government to act, to induce the Bolivian government to expel "Altmann" so that he could be returned to the country of his crimes.

The former head of the Gestapo at Lyons re-entered France on Feb. 5, 1983. On orders from Minister of Justice Robert Badinter, he was locked in the same Montluc prison where his own victims had been subjected to maltreatment and torture. It is said he spent his first night in the very cell Badinter's father occupied before he was deported to Auschwitz, never to return.

How had Barbie eluded prosecution, not to say detection, for so long? For one thing, he had collaborated with the American Counter Intelligence Corps in postwar Europe, supplying information about Communist activities in Germany and Austria. The services of the CIC made it possible for him to flee to South America. (Most ironically, it was a young Jewish officer, 23-year-old Leo Hecht, who was ordered to provide him with his false travel documents.) For another, he had powerful friends throughout Europe. It is known that an international network existed after World War II to aid war criminals. No such escape system was ever created for their victims.

Will Barbie tell us how the network operated? Will he reveal the identity of his highly placed friends? If he does, other questions are certain to arise. The upper echelons of the CIC knew what Barbie had done; how could they reward him for it? Even in the first frosts of the cold war, was it really necessary to call upon individuals like the Butcher of Lyons? Where was honor in all this? And memory?

The French have even more to fear from the revelations or digressions of their special prisoner. Ever since Marcel Ophuls's documentary *The Sorrow and the Pity* unreeled in Europe and America, people have stopped believing in the myth that France united to resist the occupying forces. On the contrary, France under Pétain fully collaborated with Hitler's Germany. It handed its Jews over to the Nazi executioners—76,000 were deported, few came back. French militia competed with the Gestapo for efficiency. French police organized the roundups. Will the nation be forced to remember its sins? Or will its citizens allow themselves to be manipulated by Barbie and Vergès, who will certainly try to show that even the Resistance was not blameless? That Jean Moulin, a leader of the Resistance who died under the hands of Barbie, was betrayed by his own comrades? In a different domain and on another level, there is some concern that the trial will conveniently and simplistically group the various victims together—dump them all into the same file: Jews and Resistance fighters, Jews and anti-Nazis, Jews and political prisoners. In other words, that the specific, the unique, even ontological aspect of the Jewish tragedy will be lost.

Vergès and Barbie will probably try to blur the distinctions. They may go further and remind France that the nation was itself guilty of torture and murder during the Algerian conflict. War is war, they may say. In war everything is allowed. As Barbie remarked to one journalist, "The point is to win. It doesn't matter how."

In fact, *The State of France v. Klaus Barbie* is not a matter of war. It is a matter of truth. In Lyons, Barbie will have to answer not for his war crimes but for his crimes against humanity. For these there is no statute of limitations.

He will have to explain, for example, why he condemned the Jewish children of Izieu. Listen to the words of one of those children, eleven-year-old Liliane Gerenstcin, in a letter scrawled to God before she was taken on the road that led to the gas chambers: "It is thanks to You that I enjoyed a wonderful life before, that I was spoiled, that I had lovely things, things that others do not have. God? Bring back my parents, my poor parents, protect them (even more than myself) so that I may see them again as soon as possible. Have them come back one more time. Oh! I can say that I have had such a good mother, and such a good father! I have such faith in You that I thank You in advance." Of what was this child guilty?

No, Lyons will not provide a restaging of the Eichmann trial. Barbie did not make policy. He was only a regional executioner, a local hangman—he merely participated, did what he was told. His operations only extended to Lyons and its surroundings. Yet if Klaus Barbie was not "important," his trial is. It can serve a vital purpose, for future generations and for our own. Certain witnesses have to be heard; certain truths have to be uttered, repeated. Will they clarify the mystery of what happened? It does not seem possible. The determination of the killer to kill, the passivity of the bystander are likely to remain incomprehensible. There is something about this Event that eludes rational thought. Only those who were there know what it meant to be there. The others can, at best, come close to the gate. There they must stop. They will never see the fire. They will never witness the sight of children thrown into flames alive. They will never experience the fear of selections for the execution chambers. Knowledge can be shared; experience cannot. Surely not in matters related to Auschwitz.

Still, we must hear the testimonies, from the victims, and from Klaus Barbie himself. For in the end they may help us to understand the deeper motivations of a Nazi killer who chose to make himself the enemy of those children and who even now thinks of himself as innocent. Was he normal, like Eichmann? Human, perhaps?

Poor humanity. ∎

Defiance

BY STROBE TALBOTT

[*A dramatic confrontation in China's Tiananmen Square was viewed as part of a worldwide pattern by* TIME'*s foreign-affairs columnist, later a Deputy Secretary of State in the Clinton Administration*]

June 19, 1989

ONE MAN AGAINST AN army. The power of the people versus the power of the gun. There he stood, implausibly resolute in his thin white shirt, an unknown Chinese man facing down a lumbering column of tanks. For a moment that will be long remembered, the lone man defined the struggle of China's citizens. "Why are you here?" he shouted at the silent steel hulk. "You have done nothing but create misery. My city is in chaos because of you."

The brief encounter between the man and the tank captured an epochal event in the lives of 1.1 billion Chinese: the state clanking with menace, swiveling right and left with uncertainty, is halted in its tracks because the people got in its way, and because it got in theirs.

Knowing something is not the same as watching it happen. There is nothing new in the proposition that Marxism is riven with contradictions as fatal to the system as they are brutal to its subjects. For decades critics of Communism have been saying that the party has no legitimacy; that its claims of representation are a tattered veil for its true function of repression; that for all their apparent obedience, passivity and discipline, many or even most of the populace are not just unhappy but deeply angry and increasingly overt in their defiance.

Still, the seven-week-long student protest in Tiananmen Square hit with the impact of a revelation, especially since it coincided with a very different sort of democratization taking place in the Soviet Union and Eastern Europe. While the leaders of China dithered over what to do about the students' occupation of the political heart of the country, President Mikhail Gorbachev presided over the opening of a Congress whose members included purged former comrades, dissident intellectuals and outspoken non-Russian nationalists. In Poland the first halfway-open election in four decades produced a humiliating defeat for the Communist Party.

Whether the men in power were resisting the forces of democracy in China or trying to harness those forces in the Soviet Union and Poland, they could not escape potent reminders of the most ominous and fundamental of all of Marxism's contradictions: the one between people power and the power that Mao Zedong said comes from the barrel of a gun.

The unevenness of the match has always been obvious, and the outcome has been taken for granted. In a showdown between the rulers and the ruled, the rulers would have their way. After all, it was a well-established truism of the 20th century that a Communist regime is a military regime in disguise. The disguise came off in Hungary in 1956, in Czechoslovakia in 1968, in Poland in 1981—and in China last week.

Still, history seemed to be deviating from its script. The trade union founded by a spunky electrician won the election in Poland, but the military seemed to stay in the barracks. The Soviet press blazoned news of violent ethnic unrest in Uzbekistan to a public it formerly kept in the dark about domestic strife. And even in China, where old men reverted to the only kind of power they knew, there was at least the phantom suggestion of tanks against tanks. But in the end, the name of the People's Liberation Army still turned out to be a cruel mockery.

It was as though everyone, whatever his assigned role, understood the larger meaning of the drama. Something is happening in the Communist world, a revolt against the system. From the Baltic to the China Sea, people are straining against the confines of Communism, demanding a greater share in the world's riches and a fair share in their own governance.

And so the unnatural act was the massacre on the square, not the peaceful democracy protests that preceded it. It was the party's attempt to reimpose order that brought chaos to the world's most populous nation.

As the turmoil spread from Beijing to Shanghai to Guangzhou to Xian to Chengdu, the shock waves reverberated throughout the Communist world. Publicly the Poles congratulated themselves on the contrast between their political accomplishments and the calamity unfolding in China. But privately many said they feared what they might yet have in common with the Chinese—a system that has still to prove it can tolerate genuine democracy.

In the Soviet Union, the latest outbreak of ethnic unrest in Uzbekistan was a reminder of what may be the operative difference between Deng Xiaoping's realm and Mikhail Gorbachev's: in the Middle Kingdom, things fall apart from the center outward, while in the U.S.S.R. it is the other way around. Both face a common challenge in devising ways to meet the demands of their citizens.

It was a week that should concentrate the mind as never before on the real Communist threat: not conquest but collapse. Again the proposition is familiar, but the confirmation by events that it may be true has the shock of an epiphany.

Throughout history, empires in their death throes have often caused as much trouble as when they were in the ascendant. What spasms of military desperation might accompany the crumbling of the Soviet bloc? What if some new Chinese warlord in a breakaway province ended up with a few of his country's nuclear-armed missiles?

It has been almost a given among experts for some time that part of the challenge to the U.S. and its allies is to bring global Communism in its decline to a soft landing rather than let it crash and burn. American politicians and statesmen have understood as much, at least in theory. Ronald Reagan spoke of Marxism as "inherently unstable" and doomed. But in the policies that went with this confident rhetoric, he, like his predecessors, concentrated on the task of matching Communism's strength and deterring its expansion, not on the more subtle and relevant dilemma of coping with the consequences of its weakness, decay and retrenchment.

George Bush seems to see the problem clearly. He has said that the industrialized democracies, led by the U.S., should move "beyond containment" and "integrate the Soviet Union into the world order." But he has spoken of that opportunity—which is really an obligation—in the future tense, as something we should think about now but do something about later, if current trends continue.

The work of reinventing Communism belongs to a new generation of party leaders who must first grasp what much of the world already knows:

that economic reform and political reform are impossible without each other. That generation, personified and led by Gorbachev, may have arrived at the pinnacle of power in the Soviet Union. In China it is still waiting for Deng Xiaoping and his fellow aged revolutionaries to accept the judgment of that lone, anonymous man in front of the tanks.

Last week's message was that the trends have continued long and conclusively enough to put new and primary emphasis on the management of Communism's decline, perhaps its disintegration, certainly its transformation. We saw it coming. But that is different from seeing it happening, before our eyes. ■

Freedom!

BY GEORGE J. CHURCH

[*The opening of the Berlin Wall not only freed millions of East Germans but, as the writer made clear, symbolically breached a barrier between tyranny and democracy*]

November 20, 1989

FOR 28 YEARS IT had stood as the symbol of the division of Europe and the world, of Communist suppression, of the xenophobia of a regime that had to lock its people in lest they be tempted by another, freer life—the Berlin Wall, that hideous, 28-mile-long scar through the heart of a once proud European capital, not to mention the soul of a people. And then—poof!—it was gone. Not physically, at least yet, but gone as an effective barrier between East and West, opened in one unthinkable, stunning stroke to people it had kept apart for more than a generation. It was one of those rare times when the tectonic plates of history shift beneath men's feet, and nothing after is quite the same.

What happened in Berlin last week was a combination of the fall of the Bastille and a New Year's Eve blowout, of revolution and celebration. At the stroke of midnight on Nov. 9, a date that not only Germans would remember, thousands who had gathered on both sides of the Wall let out a roar and started going through it, as well as up and over. West Berliners pulled East Berliners to the top of the barrier along which in years past many an East German had been shot while trying to escape; at times the Wall almost disappeared beneath waves of humanity. They tooted trumpets and danced on the top. They brought out hammers and chisels and whacked away at the hated symbol of imprisonment, knocking loose chunks of concrete and waving them triumphantly before television cameras. They spilled out into the streets of West Berlin for a champagne-spraying, horn-honking bash that continued well past dawn, into the following day and then another dawn. As the daily *BZ* would headline: BERLIN IS BERLIN AGAIN.

Nor was the Wall the only thing to come tumbling down. Many who served the regime that had built the barrier dropped from power last week. Both East Germany's Cabinet and the Communist Party Politburo resigned en masse, to be replaced by bodies in which reformers mingled with hard-liners. And that, supposedly, was only the start. On the same day that East Germany threw open its borders, Egon Krenz, 52, President and party leader, promised "free, general, democratic and secret elections," though there was no official word as to when. Could the Socialist Unity Party, as the Communists call themselves in East Germany, lose in such balloting? "Theoretically," replied Günter Schabowski, the East Berlin party boss and a Politburo member.

Thus East Germany probably can be added, along with Poland and Hungary, to the list of East European states that are trying to abandon orthodox Communism for some as-yet-nebulous form of social democracy. The next to be engulfed by the tides of change appears to be Bulgaria; Todor Zhivkov, 78, its longtime, hard-line boss, unexpectedly resigned at week's end. Outlining the urgent need for "restructuring," his successor, Petar Mladenov, said, "This implies complex and far from foreseeable processes. But there is no alternative." In all of what used to be called the Soviet bloc, Zhivkov's departure leaves in power only Nicolae Ceausescu in Rumania and Milos Jakes in Czechoslovakia, both old-style Communist dictators. Their fate? Who knows? Only a few weeks ago, East Germany seemed one of the most stolidly Stalinist of all Moscow's allies and the one least likely to undergo swift, dramatic change.

The collapse of the old regimes and the astonishing changes under way in the Soviet Union open prospects for a Europe of cooperation in which the Iron Curtain disappears, people and goods move freely across frontiers, NATO and the Warsaw Pact evolve from military powerhouses into merely formal alliances, and the threat of war steadily fades. They also raise the question of German reunification, an issue for which politicians in the West or, for that matter, Moscow have yet to formulate strategies.

Finally, should protest get out of hand, there is the risk of dissolution into chaos, sooner or later necessitating a crackdown and, possibly, a painful turn back to authoritarianism.

In East Germany the situation came close to spinning out of control. Considered a hard-liner, Krenz succeeded the dour Erich Honecker as party chief only three weeks ago, and eleven days after a state visit by Mikhail Gorbachev. Ever since, Krenz has had to scramble to find concessions that might quiet public turmoil and enable him to hang on to at least a remnant of power. He has been spurred by a series of mass protests—one demonstration in Leipzig drew some 500,000 East Germans—demanding democracy and freedoms small and large, and by a fresh wave of flight to the West by many of East Germany's most productive citizens. So far this year, some 225,000 East Germans out of a population of 16 million have voted with their feet, pouring into West Germany through Hungary and Czechoslovakia at rates that last week reached 300 an hour. Most are between the ages of 20 and 40, and their departure has left behind a worsening labor shortage. Last week East German soldiers had to be pressed into civilian duty to keep trams, trains and buses running.

THE WALL, OF COURSE, was built in August 1961 for the very purpose of stanching an earlier exodus of historic dimensions, and for more than a generation it performed the task with brutal efficiency. Opening it up would have seemed the least likely way to stem the current outflow. But Krenz and his aides were apparently gambling that if East Germans lost the feeling of being walled in, and could get out once in a while to visit friends and relatives in the West or simply look around, they would feel less pressure to flee the first chance they got. Beyond that, opening the Wall provided the strongest possible indication that Krenz meant to introduce freedoms that would make East Germany worth staying in. In both Germanys and around the world, after all, the Wall had become the perfect symbol of oppression. Ronald Reagan in 1987, standing at the Brandenburg Gate with his back to the barrier, was the most recent in a long line of visiting Western leaders who challenged the Communists to level the Wall if they wanted to prove that they were serious about liberalizing their societies. "Mr. Gorbachev, open this gate!" cried the President. "Mr. Gorbachev, tear down this wall!" There was no answer from Moscow at the time; only nine months ago, Honecker vowed that the Wall would remain for 100 years.

When the great breach finally came, it started undramatically. At a press conference last Thursday, Schabowski announced almost offhand-edly that starting at midnight, East Germans would be free to leave at any point along the country's borders, including the crossing points through the Wall in Berlin, without special permission, for a few hours, a day or forever. Word spread rapidly through both parts of the divided city, to the 2 million people in the West and the 1.3 million in the East. At Checkpoint Charlie, in West Berlin's American sector, a crowd gathered well before midnight. Many had piled out of nearby bars, carrying bottles of cham-pagne and beer to celebrate. As the hour drew near, they taunted East German border guards with cries of *"Tor Auf!"* (Open the gate!).

On the stroke of midnight, East Berliners began coming through, some waving their blue ID cards in the air. West Berliners embraced them, offered them champagne and even handed them deutsche mark notes to finance a celebration (the East German mark, a nonconvertible currency, is almost worthless outside the country). "I just can't believe it!" exclaimed Angelika Wache, 34, the first visitor to cross at Checkpoint Charlie. "I don't feel like I'm in prison anymore!" shouted one young man. Torsten Ryl, 24, was one of many who came over just to see what the West was like. "Finally, we can really visit other states instead of just seeing them on television or hearing about them," he said. "I don't intend to stay, but we must have the possi-bility to come over here and go back again." The crowd erupted in whistles and cheers as a West Berliner handed Ryl a 20-mark bill and told him, "Go have a beer first."

Many of the visitors pushed on to the Kurfürstendamm, West Berlin's boulevard of fancy stores, smart cafés and elegant hotels, to see prosperity at first hand. At 3 a.m., the street was a cacophony of honking horns and happily shouting people; at 5 some were still sitting in hotel lobbies, wait-ing for dawn. One group was finishing off a bottle of champagne in the lobby of the Hotel Am Zoo, chatting noisily. "We're going back, of course," said a woman at the table. "But we must wait to see the stores open. We must see that."

Gorbachev may have done more than merely support the East German opening. It was no coincidence that Honecker resigned shortly after the Soviet President visited East Berlin, and that the pace of reform picked up sharply after Krenz returned from conferring with Gorbachev in Moscow two weeks ago. In pursuing *perestroika*—in his eyes not to be limited to the U.S.S.R.—and preaching reform, Gorbachev has made it clear that Moscow will tolerate almost any political or economic system among its allies, so long as they remain in the Warsaw Pact and do nothing detrimental to Soviet security interests. The Kremlin greeted the opening of the Wall as "wise" and "positive," in the words of Foreign Ministry spokesman Gennadi Gerasimov, who said it should help dispel "stereotypes about the Iron Curtain."

West Germany, the country most immediately and strongly affected, was both overjoyed and stunned. In Bonn members of the Bundestag, some with tears in their eyes, spontaneously rose and sang the national anthem. It was a rare demonstration in a country in which open displays of nationalistic sentiment have been frowned on since the Third Reich died in 1945.

"Developments are now unforeseeable," said West German Chancellor Helmut Kohl, who interrupted a six-day official visit to Poland to fly to West Berlin for a celebration. "I have no doubt that unity will eventually be achieved. The wheel of history is turning faster now." At the square in front of the Schöneberg town hall, where John F. Kennedy had proclaimed in 1963 that *"Ich bin ein Berliner,"* West Berlin Mayor Walter Momper declared, "The Germans are the happiest people in the world today." Willy Brandt, who had been mayor when the Wall went up and later, as federal Chancellor, launched a Bonn *Ostpolitik* that focused on building contacts with the other Germany, proclaimed that "nothing will be the same again. The winds of change blowing through Europe have not avoided East Germany." Kohl, who drew some boos and whistles as well as cheers, repeated his offer to extend major financial and economic aid to East Germany if it carried through on its pledges to permit a free press and free elections. "We are ready to help you rebuild your country," said Kohl. "You are not alone."

Running through the joy in West Germany, however, was a not-so-subtle undertone of anxiety. Suppose the crumbling of the Wall increases rather than reduces the flood of permanent refugees? West Germany's resources are being strained in absorbing, so far this year, the 225,000 immigrants from East Germany, as well as 300,000 other ethnic Germans who have flocked in from the Soviet Union and Poland. According to earlier estimates, up to 1.8 million East Germans, or around 10% of the population, might flee to the West if the borders were opened—as they were last week all along East Germany's periphery. (Within 48 hours of the opening of the Wall, nearly 2 million East Germans had crossed over to visit the West; at one frontier post, a 30-mile-long line of cars was backed up.) West Germans fear they simply could not handle so enormous a population shift.

Thus West German leaders' advice to their compatriots from the East was an odd amalgam: We love you, and if you come, we will welcome you with open arms—but really, we wish you would stay home. In Bonn, Interior Minister Wolfgang Schäuble warned would-be refugees that with a cold winter coming on, the country is short of housing. Hannover Mayor Herbert Schmalstieg, who is also vice president of the German Urban Council, called for legal limits on the influx—an act that federal authorities say would be unconstitutional since West Germany's Basic Law stipulates that citizenship is available to all refugees of German ethnic stock and their descendants.

Much will depend, of course, on whether, and how soon, Krenz delivers on his rhetoric of freedom. The conviction that they will be able to decide their future could indeed keep at home most East Germans who are now tempted to flee; it is difficult to see anything else that might. Until the opening of the Wall, however, Krenz's reformist inclinations had seemed ambiguous. For many years he had been a faithful follower of Honecker's, and as recently as September defended the Chinese government's bloody suppression of pro-democracy demonstrators in Beijing's Tiananmen Square. His conversion seemed sparked less by ideological conviction than by a desperate desire to cling to power in the face of street protest and refugee hemorrhage.

The initial reforms, in any case, did not satisfy the opposition. "Dialogue is not the main course, it is just the appetizer," proclaimed Jens Reich, a molecular biologist and leader of New Forum, the major dissident organization. Founded only in September, it claims 200,000 adherents and has just been recognized by the government, which originally declared it illegal. The opposition pledged to keep up the pressure for a free press, free elections and a new constitution stripped of the clause granting the Communist Party a monopoly on power.

The Central Committee responded in co-opting language. "The German Democratic Republic is in the midst of an awakening," it declared. "A revolutionary people's movement has brought into motion a process of great change." Besides underlining its commitment to free elections, the committee promised separation of the Communist Party from the state, a "socialist planned economy oriented to market conditions," legislative oversight of internal security, and freedom of press and assembly.

Thus, rhetorically at least, the opposition no longer gets an argument from the government. Gerhard Herder, East German Ambassador to the

U.S., pledged reforms that "will radically change the structure and the way the G.D.R. will be governed. This development is irreversible. If there are still people alleging that all these changes are simply cosmetic, to grant the survival of the party, then let me say they are wrong."

Yesterday, with the Wall still locking people in, such talk might have been hard to believe. Today, with the barrier chipped, battered and permeable, it is a good deal easier to accept. In the end it does not matter whether Eastern Europe's Communists are reforming out of conviction or if, as one East German protest banner put it, THE PEOPLE LEAD—THE PARTY LIMPS BEHIND. What does matter is that the grim, fearsome Wall, for almost three decades a marker for relentless oppression, has overnight become something far different, a symbol of the failure of regimentation to suppress the human yearning for freedom. Ambassador Herder declared that the Wall will soon "disappear" physically, but it might almost better be left up as a reminder that the flame of freedom is inextinguishable—and that this time it burned brightly. ■

—REPORTED BY MICHAEL DUFFY WITH BUSH,
JAMES O. JACKSON/BONN AND KEN OLSEN/BERLIN

History in a Handshake

BY HUGH SIDEY

[*Time's longtime White House correspondent captured the symbolic drama in a small—but momentous—gesture between two leaders, Palestinian and Israeli*]

September 27, 1993

A JUBILANT BUT STRANGE pledge of peace. No large armies lying smashed and smoking in the far deserts. No victors, no vanquished. This was a search for peace in quieted minds and hearts, though no less perilous for that. Yet it was a profound statement of hope, this singular coming together of Yitzhak Rabin and Yasser Arafat on the broad green South Lawn of the White House, with chrysanthemums in bloom and robins calling.

History was sealed less with paper and pens than with a brief handshake that was caught in the click of hundreds of cameras, a scene beamed to millions of people in a world nurtured for 45 years on a diet of hate and death in the arid lands of Israelis and Arabs. This, more than the Declaration of Principles, was the affirmation of a new era that watchers could believe. The parchment signed out on the lawn was a framework for interim Palestinian self-government, and it was for the archives, a document meant to bind Israel and the Palestine Liberation Organization to further constructive deliberation. It was the handshake between the Israeli Prime Minister and the chairman of the P.L.O. that mattered. Men, not papers, make peace.

Bill Clinton felt the weight of the moment. He went to bed at 10 the night before, but woke at 3 a.m. to roam the White House corridors as so many of his predecessors had done—Johnson, Nixon, Bush. They had paced away the dark hours contemplating war, the enduring curse of Middle East policymaking. Clinton read the Book of Joshua, hearing in his mind the trumpet blasts that rent the walls of Jericho, wanting to be sure to make the point in the ceremony that this time the trumpets "herald not the destruction of that city but its new beginning." He wandered into the kitchen "to see the morning light," and was worried it might rain. At 6:30 someone made him fresh coffee. "I just couldn't sleep," recalled Clinton. "My mind was so full of the day."

Nobody was sure the touch of hands would happen. No formal request had been sent through diplomatic channels. Arafat wanted desperately to come; Rabin didn't. Arafat wanted to show up on the lawn with his holster holding his faithful Smith & Wesson and, with a great flourish, to unstrap the gun and hand it to Clinton. That was vetoed: too much theater even on that day. One hour before the ceremony, the Israelis and the Palestinians both threatened to boycott over trifles: then Rabin swallowed his objections to Arafat's uniform and agreed the P.L.O. could be named in the accord. Arafat and Rabin avoided each other at the reception before the ceremony, but Clinton recalled that as the three of them left the Blue Room, "they looked at each other, really clearly in the eye, for the first time, and the Prime Minister said, 'You know we are going to have to work very hard to make this work.' And Arafat said, 'I know, and I am prepared to do my part.'"

From the moment he appeared silhouetted against the White House, in sharp-pressed khakis and trademark kaffiyeh, Arafat couldn't stop smiling. This was the arrival on the world stage he had always dreamed of. Rabin was plainly of a different mind, uncomfortable and stiff. His body language throughout the ceremony—the tics, the cocking of his head, the eyes cast toward the sky, the ground, anywhere but Arafat—gave away just how uneasy he was.

Time for a handshake was worked into the 26-page script meticulously crafted by the White House and the State Department. The President rehearsed with aides in the Oval Office minutes before he was to step onto the sunny lawn, where 3,000 of the old warriors and the new trustees of peace had been summoned. For four days the diagram of the proceedings had been drawn and redrawn, the seven chief figures moved like chessmen on their tiny stage, chairs put in the blueprint, then withdrawn, until finally it was agreed they all would stand to talk, sit to sign, stand again. Clinton was to act as stage manager. He would reach for the hand of Rabin at the crucial moment, turn next to shake the hand of Arafat, then step back half a pace and enfold the two in a wide and gentle extension of his arms with the expectation that the weight of history would bring their two hands together. It did. First Arafat reached out, then after what seemed like endless minutes, Rabin responded. Simple, shattering.

Oded Ben-Ami, a spokesman for Rabin, watched it in wonder. "It was a handshake with someone who just a moment ago was the devil in person," he said, "and from now on is your partner in negotiation." The Lebanese daily *L'Orient–Le Jour* made a cooler but no less momentous assessment: "A prodigious moment this handshake, soberly, none too warmly exchanged between Rabin and Arafat, as if they were crushed by the terrible responsibility that their historic gesture condemned them to share." This is the stuff of modern diplomatic power. It is impulsive and ephemeral and can vanish with the morning mist, but it plants in the minds of millions of people a solemn promise, making it harder for leaders to go on defying logic and decency.

The young people invited were suitably impressed, but for the old it was something truly special. Clark Clifford, 86, still recovering from heart surgery, glanced at the Oval Office and thought of the day in 1948 when at the last minute word came that "the Jewish State" would be called "Israel" and the documents for recognition had to be altered by pen before Harry Truman could sit down and firmly stroke his name. Present at the creation—and now at what Clifford thought could be a renewal for the entire Middle East.

Henry Kissinger, Secretary of State for both Richard Nixon and Gerald Ford and so often a player in the Middle East game, seemed subdued, even misty-eyed. He walked slowly, graying head bent. "A stunning moment," he murmured. James Baker, Secretary of State for George Bush, thought time had done its work as he watched the tableau of peace. He had convened meetings, pushing the old adversaries together at Madrid 23 months ago. Clinton knew how much that legwork had counted. He reached through three rows of people to make sure Arafat and Rabin shook hands with Baker.

It was a triumphant but curious time for Bill Clinton. He deserved credit not for what he had done but for what he had not done. This agreement was the work of others over decades. Clinton stayed out of the way in the last act and let it happen naturally. He did not posture or seek personal acclaim, but paid tribute to those who had long carried the heavy burden. Such acts are far too rare in the presidency, but they are just as much a measure of honor. Bill Clinton enhanced himself as well as those who had braved the road to the South Lawn by the courage of his restraint.　■

NORMANDY INVASION, JUNE 6, 1944, BY ROBERT F. SARGENT

War
Zones

Death of an American Illusion

BY ROY ALEXANDER

[*Early in World War II, the Japanese, still riding the momentum of their strike at Pearl Harbor, cornered the last U.S. resistance in the Philippines and crushed it*]

April 20, 1942

BATAAN FINALLY FELL. In a military sense the big news meant that 150,000-200,000 Jap fighters were now released, to be used on other fronts. But that was not the fact that struck home to the U.S. Not until the last burned-out man put down his rifle on the soil of a Bataan that was now Japanese did Americans learn their lesson.

Bataan taught the U.S. a thing it had forgotten: pride of arms, pride in what the young men could do when tested.

Bataan taught America a humiliating thing, too: that U.S. soldiers could be beaten, could be taught the fullest ignominy of unconditional surrender. And they could be given this lesson by the funny, myopic, bucktoothed, bandylegged, pint-sized Jap—who, it suddenly appeared, was taut-muscled, courageous, vastly menacing.

The Jap had not changed. He was the same fellow who ran the curio shop in Rockefeller Center, or fished off California's coast. What had changed was a U.S. state of mind almost as old as the Republic. Before Pearl Harbor there was only one world to U.S. citizens. The world, the only world that Americans believed in or cared about, was the U.S. The rest of mankind was, in an American sense, unreal. The American might—and did—throng the tourist spots like London and Paris, "discover" Bali or the Dalmatian Coast, but he could never quite believe that these outlandish foreign parts could have a real connection with his world.

The Jap lived in the U.S. and worked against it, but his image was even mistier than the forms of the white men of Europe. Even after he had smashed at Pearl Harbor, his true form did not emerge. Americans did not yet believe what Pearl Harbor and Wake and Guam told them. They did not believe it because these first reverses of the war had a newsreel quality of unreality.

Bataan's end was different. Here was no blow that could be repaired in a navy yard. With Bataan went 36,000 or more courageous U.S. soldiers—heroes, three out of four of whom were sons of the Philippines. They had been worn to hollow shadows of men by 15 days of smashing by the finest troops of the Son of Heaven. Because the U.S. had been well satisfied with the world it lived in, had pinched its boundless flood of pennies and sat alone, those U.S. soldiers had stumbled ragged, sleepless and half-starved through the last days of the most humiliating defeat in U.S. history. In no previous battle had so many U.S. fighting men gone down before a foreign enemy, and seldom had any beaten U.S. soldiers been in such pitiable condition—believing until the last hour of destruction that their country could and surely would send them aid.

The end was slow and agonizing and struck home the harder because Lieut. General Jonathan M. Wainwright's communiqués were terse and professional. For 15 days the Jap struck at Bataan with everything he had. Dive-bombers blew great craters in forward positions. Artillery roared endlessly day & night; the nervous chatter of Jap machine guns rattled until it rasped men's nerves like a file. The Jap even struck again at the hospital, scattered the wounded like straws.

Jonathan Wainwright's soldier's eye saw that the end was near. From the shores of the Bay he withdrew his naval forces to the island of Corregidor. He tried to strike one last blow. Against a Jap breakthrough on the Manila Bay side of the peninsula he threw a corps in desperate counter-attack. It was too much. The glassy-eyed soldiers went forward like men in a dream, so exhausted that many of them could hardly lift their feet, and the Jap mowed them down. The flank folded up.

The men on Corregidor saw only a little of the ghastly end. The last, pitifully small ammunition dump on Bataan went up in smoke and flame; the three ships at the water's edge were dynamited. Finally, from one of the heights on Bataan, a white flag went up. How many of the 36,000 died fighting, only the Japs knew.

Men still swam the shark-infested stretch from Bataan to Corregidor, and in the last few hours boats got across with nurses and a few survivors. But the biggest part of the battle-trained Philippine Army was gone. From the heights the Jap, with artillery already emplaced, began slamming away at Corregidor. The soldiers there and the few civilians who had fled from Bataan knew it could not be long before they were finished too. No gunners had ever been in finer positions than the Jap. From Bataan's heights he could pour fire night & day across two miles of water into Corregidor and see where every shell fell.

In the Islands, as in the U.S., hundreds of cities and villages mourned their men. The survivors of the 9,000 American troops and 27,000 Filipinos fell into the hands of the Jap—all of them U.S. soldiers and U.S. losses. Alongside troops from the mainland, Tagalog and Moro and Igorot had fought just as bravely, died just as tight-lipped and with just as little fuss as their white comrades. It took that fighting and those deaths to make the U.S. know that the men from the Islands were their brothers and their equals.

They were all Americans on Bataan.   ■

The Hills of Nicosia

BY JOHN HERSEY

The writer, who became a noted novelist and chronicler of the Hiroshima bombing, accompanied U.S. troops as they battled their way into a town in central Sicily

August 9, 1943

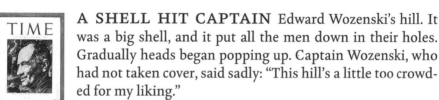

A SHELL HIT CAPTAIN Edward Wozenski's hill. It was a big shell, and it put all the men down in their holes. Gradually heads began popping up. Captain Wozenski, who had not taken cover, said sadly: "This hill's a little too crowded for my liking."

A telephone bell rang. It was such an absurd sound out there some men jumped. An enlisted man answered: "Hello ... wait a minute," and he shouted: "Hey, where's that wireman, anyone seen that wireman?"

Wozenski said: "Every time a shell lands on this hill, everybody calls up from the other hills to see if their buddies are okay."

A shell hit the top of the hill. A dark lump flew up with the smoke and blasted dust and went higher and fell in a gentle arc. A man screamed: "Help! help! help! help!"

Wozenski said: "Damn," and walked wearily up the hill.

A mumbled message was passed down the hill: "Send up some litter bearers ... they say they need some litter bearers...."

Captain Wozenski came down the slope. Here & there the men gathered to talk over who had been killed and who had been wounded up there.

Captain Wozenski shouted in a clear, deep voice: "All right. Let's not have these great goddam gatherings. Spread out."

The wounded men and their helpers began trickling down from the crest. A man with most of his shoulder shot away was guiding a blinded man. One limped along. The litter team carried a sergeant whose leg was bad and whose face was cut. Captain Wozenski had to detail some whole men to help. I took the arm of the blinded man.

The man with the shot-out shoulder said: "Let's go back there and get those bastards." The blind man was apologetic. He hoped he was causing me no trouble. He was sorry to have to be guided when he could walk and all.

The litter bearers stopped to rest. When they put the sergeant down he said: "Say, Doc, would you mind straightening my leg out?" What was left of his leg could be no straighter, for it was splinted between two rifles.

The going was very rough. The blind man lifted his feet high and put them down wherever they fell. He had none of the cautious grace of men long blind, but struck out with his legs as if angry at the path. A mule skinner came up the path riding a mule and singing a song about Georgia. One of the litter bearers said: "Here you, what you doing on that mule? Get off and let one of these fellows ride who need it." So the skinner got off and we lifted the blind soldier on to the mule's bare back. After that my job was to balance the blind man up there.

As we started down Wozenski's hill, our artillery had gone to work on the German hills. Shelling these hills was like shaking lice out of old clothes. Each pounding seemed to bring one or two Germans out to surrender. Now another prisoner walked across the lines. One of our men spoke to the prisoner in German and the prisoner answered. He said he had been two days without food or water.

The blind man said: "Is that a kraut? The next German I see walking, by God, he won't be walking any more after that." It was not then certain that he would ever see a German walking, or any man.

The wounded sergeant said to the man who could speak German: "Say, will you ask the German for a souvenir? Tell him I promised an old lady." The German did not understand, but finally he gave the sergeant a five-mark piece.

The climb grew very steep and we were all quiet. Wounds began to hurt and shock began to set in seriously. The sergeant moaned: "Doc, can't you keep my leg straight?"

No one had spoken for a long time when the blinded soldier said to me, very softly: "Eyes are very delicate things."

We turned the wounded men over to a doctor, and I rejoined the battalion commander, Lieut. Colonel John H. Mathews. He said he was going to Wozenski's hill to launch an attack.

The attack on all the hills went well. The enemy was human. On the second evening, just before dark, our men launched the final attack. All units moved—even the tanks, which punched along the road in the face of well-placed anti-tank guns. The attacks by the tanks and by three infantry combat teams were beautifully timed. The enemy was bewildered, shattered by deadly accurate artillery and demoralized by dwindling supplies, which our air attacks far behind his lines had diminished. The enemy pulled out, and our men walked into Nicosia. ∎

Those Who Fought

BY DUNCAN NORTON-TAYLOR

[*This sweeping account of the vast Normandy invasion portrayed a turning point from which the Allies would begin their drive across Europe to Berlin and victory*]

June 19, 1944

THE NORMANDY POPPIES WERE pale with dust. The Normandy sky was heavy with smoke. Land and sky rumbled and trembled with battle.

In the fair fields where the tide had rolled, the ground was littered with the debris of battle—tanks, jeeps, rifles, ration tins, bulldozers, first-aid kits, canteens. Everywhere lay the dead—weltering in the waves along the shore, lying heaped in ditches, sprawling on the beaches. Here & there in trees hung the shattered body of a paratrooper. In field hospitals, the wounded lay. The smell of ether mingled with the smell of earth. Probably no one yet knew the price that had been paid for the first week in Normandy.

That first day the paratroopers had landed near midnight—six hours before H-hour—to prepare the way for the glider-borne divisions which had swooped like hell's witches into the area behind the German lines. A paratroop lieutenant survived to return and tell how the Germans "were machine-gunning us all the way down." One officer told of seeing German tracers ripping through other men's parachutes as they descended. In one plane nine soldiers had dived through the plane's door; the tenth, laden with his 90 pounds of equipment, got momentarily stuck. A 20-mm. shell hit him in the belly. Fuse caps in his pockets began to go off. Part of the wounded man's load was TNT. Before this human bomb could explode, his mates behind him pushed him out. The last they saw of him, his parachute had opened and he was drifting to earth in a shroud of bursting flame.

The airborne divisions captured gun positions, pillboxes, road junctions, destroyed bridges. Some of them made contact later with ground troops. Some of them, the Germans claimed, were annihilated.

It was at 5:35 a.m. that morning that the Allied armada had begun to pour its fire onto the French coast, where brightly colored German ack-ack was streaking the morning sky. In the fleet were old ladies like the *Arkansas,* belching with twelve 12-in. guns, the *Texas* and the *Nevada,* each with ten 14-inchers; the British *Warspite,* veteran of Jutland, the new British *Black Prince,* the British monitor *Erebus.* Closer inshore stood the cruisers and, even closer, the destroyers—the whole great armada, spread out from horizon to horizon, trying to batter down the Atlantic Wall. Overhead were 8,000 planes of the R.A.F. and the U.S. Eighth and Ninth Air Forces, adding their big and little bombs to the destruction. Grey-black clouds puffed up from the land to shroud the sun rising over Normandy.

Under the fiery canopy the engineers and Army & Navy demolition units had crawled ashore. Hidden by the sea at high tide were concrete piers, pointed steel and wooden stakes. At low tide, they were visible. On the beach itself were great tripods of steel rails, braced steel fences, all of them ingeniously mined. The demolition units went to work clearing paths while German shells fell among them and German machine gunners hidden in tunnels and six-foot-thick concrete pillboxes raked them. An assault engineer said: "We had to work with water up to our necks, sometimes higher. Then there were snipers. They were nipping us off. As I was working with two blokes on a tough bit of element, I suddenly found myself working alone. My two pals just gurgled and disappeared under the water."

In those early hours Rangers had gone ashore in LCTs under cover of darkness. At one point, atop a 200-ft. cliff, were six 155-mm. guns which could sweep the sea approaches. The Rangers shot a grappling hook to the top of the cliff. One of them climbed a rope hand over hand, carrying rope ladders which he made secure. Up swarmed the Rangers; took the gun positions, knocked them out with TNT.

On the heels of the demolition units went the infantry. It was not announced which divisions were in the first wave, but two U.S. divisions were identified as taking part in the invasion: the storied 1st, once predominant-ly a Brooklyn outfit, now a rainbow division of men from many states, vet-erans of the North African campaign; the 29th, a National Guard outfit whose ranks were originally filled with men from Maryland and Virginia. Beside them fought the Canadian 3rd Division and the tough little men of England's 50th Northumbrians, who had fought in France and Flanders four years before, had covered the evacuation of Dunkirk, had chased the Nazis across North Africa, across Sicily and up Italy.

The British and Canadians were on the eastern water flank, which was churned by a brisk wind across the Bay of the Seine. Some small landing craft were swamped or impaled on the water barriers, or bobbed help-lessly offshore, targets for German 88s and 155s which had survived the bombardment. Bert Brandt, an Acme photographer, later reported: "Boats were burning and a pall of smoke hung over the beach. I saw some bodies of soldiers who had been killed in the first landings floating in the water. . . . There were tremendous rafts floating offshore, jammed with trucks, tanks, ambulances."

As the ramps went down and khaki-clad men plunged shorewards, German fire mowed them down. Others ran over them. The living lay be-side the dead and fought with flame-throwers, grenades, bazookas and ban-galore torpedoes, which blasted holes in barbed-wire entanglements. From the sea the naval guns did their best to pin down Nazi emplacements. The ancient *Texas* laid her guns on a 155-mm. battery, blew it up. New waves of men poured ashore like waves of the Channel.

Mortar fire from the cliffs fell like rain on one beach. Over the radio came a pleading voice to R.A.F. Spitfire pilots wheeling overhead: "For God's sake get those mortars quick. Dig them out, boys, they are right down our necks." The Spitfires dipped down and dug the Nazis out.

Not until late afternoon of D-day were some of the beaches secured. All night, while the naval guns boomed in the roadstead and explosions flashed along the embattled coast, the drenched wounded lay in the sand, some whimpering in delirium. Then the invasion rolled on—beyond the dreadful jetsam on the beaches.

On the third day, the wind moderated, and the great fleet of ships from England worked mightily to make up for the delays caused by weather and rough water. Standing on the flanks, the warships guarded the great ma-rine bridge which the Allies had thrown across the Channel.

At week's end LSTs were crawling steadily back to English ports.

Negro stretcher bearers lifted out the men whose up-ended feet were dusty with the sands of France. Medical Corpsmen moved among them, looking at their wound tags. Some of the wounded were smoking. A homesick U.S. soldier said wryly: "Is that really England? I never thought I wanted to see the goddam country again but now it looks like heaven." Some of the men had their eyes closed. Over the faces of some, blankets had been drawn.

As the wounded and the dead came back, other soldiers, with flowers stuck in the camouflage netting of their tin hats, marched past them through the streets of the English town. They avoided looking at the returning troops. Now it was their turn. ■

Art For History's Sake

TIME co-founder Henry Luce called the Twentieth Century the *American* Century. And almost from the magazine's inception in 1923, the cover of TIME has been a cultural touchstone in American life. The famous and the infamous, the heroes and the scoundrels, the significant trends and the momentous events of the day have appeared on it, portrayed by artists and photographers who gave the magazine its signature visual style. Herewith, a gallery of favorites.

The first cover:
Speaker of the House
Joseph G. Cannon
March 3, 1923
Artist: William Oberhardt

TIME

THE WEEKLY NEWSMAGAZINE

MAN OF THE YEAR

Blood, toil, tears, sweat—and untold courage.

(Foreign News)

Winston Churchill
January 6, 1941
Artist: Ernest Hamlin Baker

Rita Hayworth
November 10, 1941
Artist: George Petty

Fleet Admiral Osami Nagano
February 15, 1943
Artist: Boris Artzybasheff

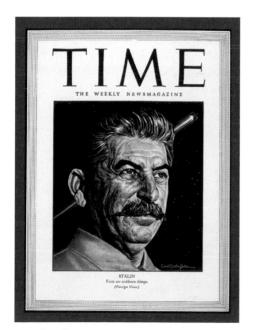

Joseph Stalin
February 5, 1945
Artist: Ernest Hamlin Baker

General Dwight D. Eisenhower
January 1, 1945
Artist: Ernest Hamlin Baker

Adolf Hitler
May 7, 1945
Artist: Boris Artzybasheff

Laurence Olivier
April 8, 1946
Artist: Boris Chaliapin

Mohandas Gandhi
June 30, 1947
Artist: Boris Chaliapin

Eva Perón
July 14, 1947
Artist: Boris Chaliapin

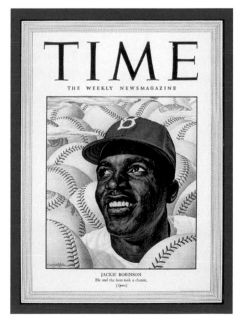

Jackie Robinson
September 22, 1947
Artist: Ernest Hamlin Baker

TIME

THE WEEKLY NEWSMAGAZINE

Artzybasheff

LOUIS ARMSTRONG
When you got to ask what it is, you never get to know.
(Music)

Louis Armstrong
February 21, 1949
Artist: Boris Artzybasheff

Diego Rivera
April 4, 1949
Artist: Self-Portrait

Coca-Cola
May 15, 1950
Artist: Boris Artzybasheff

The Amateur Photographer
November 2, 1953
Artist: Boris Artzybasheff

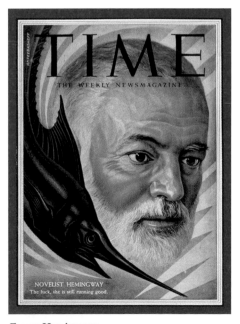

Ernest Hemingway
December 13, 1954
Artist: Boris Artzybasheff

The U.S. Taxpayer
March 10, 1952
Artist: Boris Artzybasheff

Dave Brubeck
November 8, 1954
Artist: Boris Artzybasheff

Charles de Gaulle
January 5, 1959
Artist: Bernard Buffet

Alec Guinness
April 21, 1958
Artist: Ben Shahn

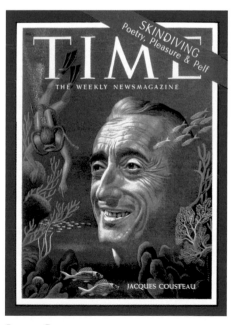

Jacques Cousteau
March 28, 1960
Artist: Boris Artzybasheff

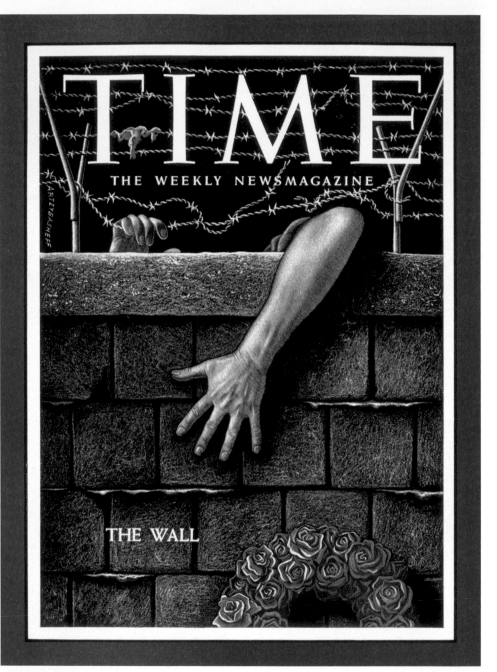

The Berlin Wall
August 31, 1962
Artist: Boris Artzybasheff

John Fitzgerald Kennedy
January 5, 1962
Artist: Pietro Annigoni

R. Buckminster Fuller
January 10, 1964
Artist: Boris Artzybasheff

Thelonious Monk
February 28, 1964
Artist: Boris Chaliapin

Sophia Loren
April 6, 1962
Artist: J. Bouché

Bob Hope
December 22, 1967
Artist: Marisol

Robert F. Kennedy
May 24, 1968
Artist: Roy Lichtenstein

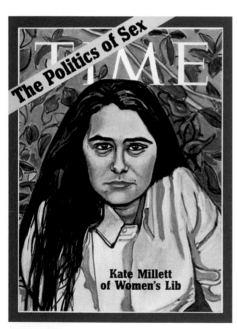

Kate Millett
August 31, 1970
Artist: Alice Neel

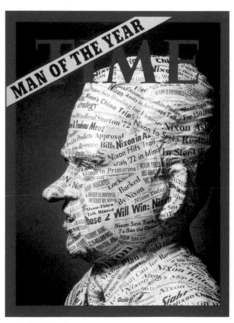

Richard M. Nixon
January 3, 1972
Artist: Stanley Glaubach

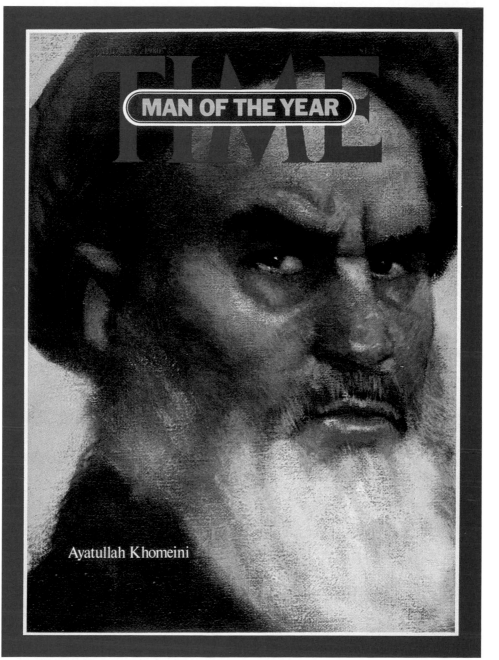

MAN OF THE YEAR

Ayatullah Khomeini

Ayatullah Khomeini
January 7, 1980
Artist: Brad Holland

Vladimir Horowitz
May 5, 1986
Artist: R.B. Kitaj

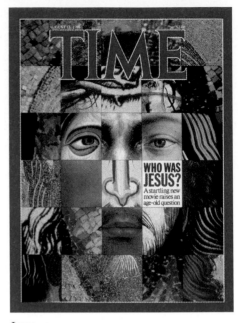

Jesus
August 15, 1988
Artist: Tom Bentkowski

Endangered Earth
January 2, 1989
Artist: Christo

Homo Erectus
March 14, 1994
Artist: Matt Mahurin

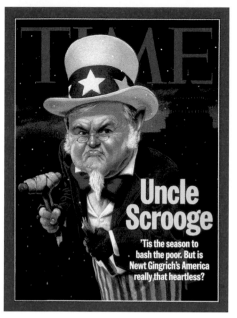

Newt Gingrich
December 19, 1994
Artist: C.F. Payne

World Trade Center
September 14, 2001
Photographer: Lyle Owerko

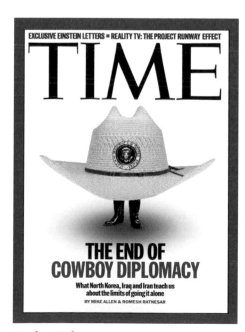

Cowboy Diplomacy
June 7, 2007
Artist: Arthur Hochstein

Modern-Day Rosie the Riveter
September 10, 2007
Artist: Eric Bowman

Leaders & Revolutionaries of the 20th Century
April 13, 1998
Artist: Robert Rauschenberg

Flight Through Kweichow

BY THEODORE H. WHITE

[*As Japanese forces pushed into central China, half a million Chinese fled their homes and set out for the hinterland.* TIME's *China correspondent was with them*]

January 8, 1945

ALL DAY AND THROUGH the evening we drove down the road toward Kwangsi. Refugees flanked us in unbroken columns. This was the tail end of one of the longest treks in the history of the China war. I had seen these refugees start their march five months before on the dusty roads of Hunan, where the sun leeched sweat from every pore, where human bodies and the fields about them were parched moistureless. Now, 600 miles away, these refugees were still trudging—the friendless, the halt and the sick—overtaken by the merciless blast of the Kweichow winter.

There are certain clinical phenomena that characterize mass flight in China. First is exhaustion. Second is a beastlike silence broken only by children's chattering. You get technical after you have seen millions of people suffering for years. You examine the children's hair to see whether it is dry and brittle; when a child starts to go, his hair loses oil and it cracks easily. You look down at people's feet to see how many are pus-laden and split by wind or frost. Most of all you listen to the quality of their silence. The longer the trek, the more intense the silence, the more deadly the apathy.

The silence on this road was prodigious. Faces were expressionless, beyond the point of suffering. They were carved blocks of puffy human flesh with holes for eyes, a red spot for a nose, two cracking flaps for a mouth. Some had rags on their feet. Those who had no rags trudged in straw sandals, the flesh of their feet peeling away in frostbitten rawness.

Only the children laughed or talked loudly, still resilient in suffering. One man carried a child pickaback (he stopped us and asked in good, crisp English what the news was from the German battlefront). Others carried children in baskets slung from shoulder staves. One enormous Bactrian camel bore a little child between its two humps. Family groups in fours and fives pushed and pulled at carts loaded with all their possessions. There were trucks of all kinds, American trucks almost new and G.M.C.s ready for the junk yard. There were old German trucks burning stinking diesel oil, commercial trucks burning sweet-smelling alcohol. Every truck was piled five to ten feet high with baggage or goods. Humanity clustered over the baggage on the trucks, over the mudguards, over the driver's cab.

Every mile of road had its quota of trucks stopped for repairs, with mechanics under the chassis or the hood, and frigid passengers thawing themselves by the roadside with a fire of rice stubble. Some vehicles were parked for the evening with passengers and crew sleeping underneath for shelter against the wind. Others had broken down completely. They had been stripped bare of every useful article—tires, lamps, seats, even motors. Abandoned beside them lay cargoes of bombs and ammunition, shining and useless in the biting cold.

Along the route of flight lay little towns, deserted by their inhabitants and now only stopping places for the refugees. They stank of humanity. In huts and booths people gathered, warmed themselves at feeble fires of rice stubble. We passed a large lumber dump. Refugees clustered about it, hacking off wood slivers for fires with knives and sharp stones. Occasionally we saw what was left of a horse, donkey or cow. Always the carcass had been stripped to its skeleton, for the refugees fell on any dead thing and picked its bones clean. Only once we saw a freshly dead animal; refugees were thick about it, tearing voraciously at the still warm corpse. A food vender passed one column as we stopped to talk, and the famished marchers were on him in an instant, wolfing his hot buns while he wailed to the heavens.

And there were the human dead as they had fallen, on roadsides, in ditches, and nearby paddies. They were shriveled and brown. Even the body of a teen-age boy looked older than time in its silent rest. Some bodies were twisted and torn, but most were quiet and calm. The freshly dead were still encased in woolen paddings or blue uniforms. But the older bodies lay bare. Of what use is warm padding to dead men when the living must shiver?

One more evil thing we saw, in the evening of this long trip. Across the beam of our headlights ran a wolf, a grey, lithe creature. He looked well-fed. ■

The Bomb

BY JAMES AGEE

[*As World War II ended with the dropping of the atomic bomb, the Nuclear Age began, and the writer pondered the fearful, awesome prospect it conjured up*]

August 20, 1945

THE GREATEST AND MOST terrible of wars ended, this week, in the echoes of an enormous event—an event so much more enormous that, relative to it, the war itself shrank to minor significance. The knowledge of victory was as charged with sorrow and doubt as with joy and gratitude. More fearful responsibilities, more crucial liabilities rested on the victors even than on the vanquished.

In what they said and did, men were still, as in the aftershock of a great wound, bemused and only semi-articulate, whether they were soldiers or scientists, or great statesmen, or the simplest of men. But in the dark depths of their minds and hearts, huge forms moved and silently arrayed themselves: Titans, arranging out of the chaos an age in which victory was already only the shout of a child in the street.

With the controlled splitting of the atom, humanity, already profoundly perplexed and disunified, was brought inescapably into a new age in which all thoughts and things were split—and far from controlled. As most men realized, the first atomic bomb was a merely pregnant threat, a merely infinitesimal promise.

All thoughts and things were split. The sudden achievement of victory

179

was a mercy, to the Japanese no less than to the United Nations, but mercy born of a ruthless force beyond anything in human chronicle. The race had been won, the weapon had been used by those on whom civilization could best hope to depend; but the demonstration of power against living creatures instead of dead matter created a bottomless wound in the living conscience of the race. The rational mind had won the most Promethean of its conquests over nature, and had put into the hands of common man the fire and force of the sun itself.

Was man equal to the challenge? In an instant, without warning, the present had become the unthinkable future. Was there hope in that future, and if so, where did hope lie?

Even as men saluted the greatest and most grimly Pyrrhic of victories in all the gratitude and good spirit they could muster, they recognized that the discovery which had done most to end the worst of wars might also, quite conceivably, end all wars—if only man could learn its control and use.

The promise of good and of evil bordered alike on the infinite—with this further, terrible split in the fact: that upon a people already so nearly drowned in materialism even in peacetime, the good uses of this power might easily bring disaster as prodigious as the evil. The bomb rendered all decisions made so far, at Yalta and at Potsdam, mere trivial dams across tributary rivulets. When the bomb split open the universe and revealed the prospect of the infinitely extraordinary, it also revealed the oldest, simplest, commonest, most neglected and most important of facts: that each man is eternally and above all else responsible for his own soul, and, in the terrible words of the Psalmist, that no man may deliver his brother, nor make agreement unto God for him.

Man's fate has forever been shaped between the hands of reason and spirit, now in collaboration, again in conflict. Now reason and spirit meet on final ground. If either or anything is to survive, they must find a way to create an indissoluble partnership. ■

The Ugly War

BY JOHN OSBORNE

[
*Years before Viet Nam, the writer presciently recognized
that the Korean conflict was confronting America with a
new kind of warfare and new cultural challenges*
]

August 21, 1950

THIS IS A STORY that no American should ever have
to write. It is the ugly story of an ugly war. Because there is
so much to tell that is sorrowful and sickening, let the story
begin with a few good and heartening things that also can be
said about our war in Korea.

The American effort and the American soldier in Korea
are magnificent. Doubtless we could and should have been better prepared.
But the more important fact is that never before in all our history have we
been so nearly prepared at the start of any war as we were at the start of
this one. Today we have in Korea more men and more arms than we sent
to the invasion of North Africa in November of 1942, eleven months after
Pearl Harbor.

Already, though still outnumbered, we have the greater weight of arms,
on the ground and in the air and at sea. We know how to use and coordinate the arms, as we did not know for many months after the start of World
War II. It is a wonderful and thrilling thing to see, as I have just seen, infantry in action with the support of fighters from the Air Force, bombers
from a naval carrier, and, if the field commander had wanted it, bombardment from warships standing offshore.

It is wonderful and thrilling, too, to ride the pipeline into Korea. The C-54s, the C-46s and 47s stream into the airports of Japan, laden with everything from battlewise noncoms to dismantled artillery.

We might yet be pushed out of Korea. But the buildup of American power has been achieved at a pace and on a scale that would never before have been possible so early in a war so far from home.

Then there are the soldiers. They are boys, most of them, in their teens and early 20s, many of them lately trained only in the softening and vitiating duty of the occupation in Japan. They were scared at first. In some places, they abandoned positions that seasoned troops might have held. But in a land and among a people that most of them dislike, in a war that all too few of them understand and none of them want, they became strong men and good soldiers—fast. Quite literally overnight they learned all there is to know about sticking, fighting, killing and dying. The business of soldiers is not to die but to live, and they are learning to do that, too. I have seen boys who by rights should have been freshmen in college transformed by a week of battle into men wise in the terrible ways of this especially terrible war.

I say that this is an especially terrible war. It is so for reasons which every American must understand if we are to grasp the extent, the nature and the immense complexities of our problem in Asia. Much of this war is alien to the American tradition and shocking to the American mind. For our men in Korea are waging this war as they are forced to wage it and as they will be forced to wage any war against the Communists anywhere in Asia.

Our soldiers will continue to be forced to war in this fashion—until our political and military leaders acquire and apply an understanding of war in Asia that they have not as yet displayed in Korea. Above all, our leaders must grasp one quite simple fact: war against the Communists of Asia cannot be won—not really won—by military means alone.

To attempt to win it so, as we are now doing in Korea, is not only to court final failure but also to force upon our men in the field acts and attitudes of the utmost savagery. This means not the usual, inevitable savagery of combat in the field, but savagery in detail—the blotting out of villages where the enemy *may* be hiding; the shooting and shelling of refugees who *may* include North Koreans in the anonymous white clothing of the Korean countryside, or who *may* be screening an enemy march upon our positions.

And there is savagery by proxy, the savagery of the South Korean police and (in some sectors) South Korean marines upon whom we rely for contact with the population and for ferreting out hidden enemies. I am not presuming to issue righteous indictments—or to ignore the even greater savagery of the North Korean army. I am simply stating the elementary facts of war in Korea. The South Korean police and the South Korean marines whom I observed in front line areas are brutal. They murder to save themselves the trouble of escorting prisoners to the rear; they murder civilians simply to get them out of the way or to avoid the trouble of searching and cross-examining them. And they extort information—information our forces need and require of the South Korean interrogators—by means so brutal that they cannot be described.*

Let it be understood that I do not refer to the South Korean army, which has fought with great bravery and effectiveness, but only to the South Korean police and marine units which I have seen in action behind our lines.

IN SOME PARTS OF Asia we would be hard put to it to find enough Americans who can speak the language and who know the ways of the country concerned. But this is not so in South Korea. We occupied it for nearly three years and in this time we should have accumulated a considerable staff of military and civilian officials who came to know the country, the people, the language.

It is true that many of the American civilian officials who were stationed in Korea before the war are there now. But I saw none of them at work in the field. We could have assembled and can still assemble a staff adequate to put our field forces in effective communication with the people of South Korea. Why haven't we done it? I know of only one reason. It is that our leaders still have not recognized the union of politics and arms in war.

We laugh at the "commissars" whom the Communists take good care to have with their military forces, and we refuse to see that with our enemies the "politics" comes first, the fighting second. We, in short, persist in thinking of political warfare as something to be practiced by rear-area pamphleteers and tolerated by the fellows doing the real fighting. However we may fare again in Europe with our chronic neglect of the political aspects of war, we cannot get by with it in Asia. That is the lesson of Korea.

In Korea today our military and political positions are intimately inter-

---

* *A reporter for Britain's* Manchester Guardian *tells the story of an overcoat which was stolen from a U.S. vice consul in Pusan and which the local authorities were anxious to recover. A few days after the theft, Pusan's chief of police personally reported to the coat's owner. "All is well," said the chief, "as I am currently torturing two suspects."*

woven. For this is a guerrilla war, waged amongst and to some extent by the population of the country. For proof of this, come with me to South Korea and see with me some of the scenes that I have lately witnessed or heard of at firsthand.

A hilltop in southwest Korea. The hillside falls steeply to a river and a valley of paddies. Just across the valley is a schoolhouse, now the forward command post of an American infantry unit. Twice on this day, just before our arrival, this post had been attacked by hundreds of North Koreans who emerged without warning from the hills and very nearly overran our position. From the hilltop where we now stand, soldiers of an American machine gun squad had seen the repulsed enemy retire beyond the range and then, in plain sight of our men, calmly change from the green uniforms of the North Korean army to the white trousers and blouses of Korean peasants. The soldiers watching from the hill do not forget; every time they see a column of peasants coming toward them they reach for their guns, and sometimes they use their guns.

It is 6 o'clock on another morning at another place. Our command post is in a village at the foot of a valley, our men disposed across the rusty hills 2,000 and 3,000 yards beyond the post, and now, in the half-light of early morning, distant figures in white are walking down a road from the hills.

A few G.I.s, tired after a harassing night of intermittent alarms and firing, go taut, take up their rifles and walk stiff-legged toward the end of the village street nearest the oncoming people in white. One of the G.I.s says, "Christamighty, look there," and points across the paddies to our right. An old man with a stick in his hand leads the column on the road. Other men, not young, seem to be leading their families across the paddies.

They are evidently in their Sunday best—small white blouses, black cotton trousers on the boys and skirts on the little girls standing out like little dots from the all-white clothing of the men & women. Some of the boys have small packs on their backs, and already—they are three, four, five years old—their legs move in the piston motion of the Asian coolie. Now they stand, halted for a moment, looking with the bright interest of any children anywhere at the G.I.s who also stand, stiff, with rifles at the ready. Here there is none of the camaraderie of G.I. and child everywhere else that the U.S. Army has gone.

A G.I. mutters, "Where in hell are the goddam gooks?" meaning the South Korean policemen who should be here to handle the refugees. ("Gook" is the universal G.I. word for any & all Koreans.) The thin file of soldiers and the still, dumb hundreds of refugees stand in the road facing each other. Then the moment is broken, the danger passes. A sergeant walks up to the old man with the stick, puts a hand on his shoulder and wheels him around, not roughly. The women break into a quick protesting chatter, and some of them move, as though blindly, down the road of their choice, toward us. The old man lifts his stick and waves imperatively, and slowly the column turns and the people take the road that, quite evidently, leads to nowhere for them.

It is midnight and all around the hills are astir. Here a sharp burst of small-arms fire, there the flashing life & death of an American shell, searching out the enemy who we know are gathering within 5,000 yards of this command post. One of the field telephones rings, an officer of the staff picks it up, listens a moment and says, "Oh, Christ, there's a column of refugees, three or four hundred of them, coming right down on B company." A major in the command tent says to the regimental commander, "Don't let them through."

And of course the major is right. Time & again, at position after position, this silent approach of whitened figures has covered enemy attack. Finally the colonel says, in a voice racked with wretchedness, "All right, don't let them through. But try to talk to them, try to tell them to go back."

"Yeah," says one of the little staff group, "but what if they don't go back?"

"Well, then," the colonel says, as though dragging himself toward some pit, "then fire over their heads."

"O.K.," an officer says, "we fire over their heads. Then what?"

The colonel seems to brace himself in the semi-darkness of the blacked-out tent.

"Well, then, fire into them if you have to. *If you have to,* I said."

An officer speaks into the telephone, and the order goes across the wire into the dark hills.

Another afternoon, another place. The way lies through an area into which the U.S. Marines have just moved. It's good to see them, beautifully equipped and so obviously well trained. Once again I see refugees on this road. But there's a difference. Our own men, marines, surround them. As the jeep comes toward them I witness something of an advance in American communication with the people of the country. A marine is passing a mine detector over the clothing and packs of the refugees. Any metal—a rifle barrel, a pistol, a clip of ammunition, maybe the parts of a radio—will presumably be spotted by the detector. Anyhow, it is better than guns and the policemen whom I have seen at work.

A way down the road I enter the busy port of Pusan. Over its outskirts two helicopters are flying. Most of the Koreans on the highway look briefly up, then down again, as the helicopters hover and pass. But one, a boy of perhaps seven or eight, stares upward at the monstrous things with a gaze of fixed and bright fascination. His eyes shine, his lips are parted, and I think of an American boy gazing at his first bicycle on a Christmas morning.

The mine detector, the helicopters, the boy on the roadside—here, after a fashion, was communication between the American West and the people of South Korea. And, so thinking, I reflected as the jeep bumped into Pusan that the machine age and the machine man of the West can be pretty wonderful. But machines still can't talk to people, not as we must learn—and learn very soon—to talk to the people of Asia. ∎

The General's Gamble

BY JASON McMANUS

[
*Belying sanguine predictions by American politicians
and generals, North Viet Nam's audacious Tet offensive
jolted the U.S. into a sobering realization: the war
in Viet Nam might not be winnable*
]

February 9, 1968

THOUGH OMINOUS HARBINGERS OF trouble
had been in the air for days, most of South Viet Nam lazed
in uneasy truce, savoring the happiest and holiest holiday of
the Vietnamese year. All but a few Americans retired to their
compounds to leave the feast of *Tet* to the Vietnamese celebrators filling the streets. Vietnamese soldiers made a special
effort to rejoin their families. Relative visited relative, threading through
thousands of firecrackers popping and fizzing in the moonless night. The
Year of the Monkey had begun, and every Vietnamese knew that it was
wise to make merry while there was yet time; in the twelve-year Buddhist
lunar cycle, 1968 is a grimly inauspicious year.

Through the streets of Saigon, and in the dark approaches to dozens
of towns and military installations throughout South Viet Nam, other
Vietnamese made their furtive way, intent on celebrating only death—and
on launching the Year of the Monkey on its malign way before it was many
hours old. After the merrymakers had retired and the last firecrackers had
sputtered out on the ground, they struck with a fierceness and bloody de-
structiveness that Viet Nam has not seen even in three decades of nearly
continuous warfare. Up and down the narrow length of South Viet Nam,

more than 36,000 North Vietnamese and Viet Cong soldiers joined in a widespread, general offensive against airfields and military bases, government buildings, population centers and just plain civilians.

The Communists hit in a hundred places, from Quang Tri near the DMZ [Demilitarized Zone] in the north all the way to Duong Dong on the tiny island of Phu Quoc off the Delta coast some 500 miles to the south. No target was too big or too impossible, including Saigon itself and General William Westmoreland's MACV [Military Assistance Command, Vietnam] headquarters. In peasant pajamas or openly insigniaed NVA [North Vietnamese army] uniforms, by stealth or attacks marshaled by bullhorn, the raiders struck at nearly 40 major cities and towns.

They attacked 28 of South Viet Nam's 44 provincial capitals and occupied some, destroyed or damaged beyond repair more than 100 allied planes and helicopters. South Viet Nam's capital, which even in the worst days of the Indo-China war had never been hit so hard, was turned into a city besieged and sundered by house-to-house fighting. In Hué, the ancient imperial city of Viet Nam and the architectural and spiritual repository of Vietnamese history, the Communists seized large parts of the city—and only grudgingly yielded them block by block under heavy allied counterattacks at week's end.

Allied intelligence had predicted that there would be some attempted city attacks during *Tet,* but the size, the scale and, above all, the careful planning and coordination of the actual assaults took the U.S. and South Vietnamese military by surprise. In that sense, and because they continued after five days of fighting to hang on to some of their targets, the Communists undeniably won a victory of sorts. "This is real fighting on a battlefield," admitted Brigadier General John Chaisson, Westmoreland's combat operations coordinator for South Viet Nam. The Communist attack was, he said, "a very successful offensive. It was surprisingly well coordinated, surprisingly intensive and launched with a surprising amount of audacity."

In the raid on the poorly defended U.S. embassy in Saigon, the attackers embarrassed and discomfited the U.S. They succeeded in demonstrating that Communist commandos can still strike at will virtually anywhere in the country.

The allied command reported nearly 15,000 of the attackers killed. Even if the total is only half that—and some observers think that that may be the case when all the combat reports filed in the swirl of battle are cross-checked—it would still represent a huge bloodletting of the enemy's forces in South Viet Nam. Even the lower estimates leave no doubt about who won the actual battles: U.S. dead numbered 367 and South Vietnamese military dead about 700.

In its timing and total effect, the Communist offensive changed the rules of the war in a way that will make it more difficult for the enemy in the future. In making a mockery of the *Tet* truce, proposed in the first instance by the Viet Cong and reluctantly agreed to by the allies, the Communists, as U.S. Ambassador Ellsworth Bunker indicated, made it highly unlikely that there would ever be a holiday truce again. By demonstrating their resources of manpower, the resiliency of their communications and command networks and the quality and quantity of their weaponry in the widespread attacks, the Communists also made it highly unlikely, as President Johnson all but said, that there would be any bombing pause over North Viet Nam.

There was no doubt about who was the strategist behind the Communists' desperate thrust: North Viet Nam's Defense Minister General Vo Nguyen Giap, the charismatic victor over the French at Dienbienphu in 1954 and creator of the North Vietnamese army. In its surprise, its boldness, the sweep of its planning and its split-second orchestration, the general offensive bore all the unmistakable marks of Giap's genius. All the evidence indicated, in fact, that probably for the first time since the war against the French, Giap was personally directing the entire campaign in South Viet Nam.

As always in Communist military doctrine, Giap doubtless considered the political effect at least as important as the outcome on the battlefield. Some of Giap's political aims were evident: to embarrass the U.S. and undercut the authority of the South Vietnamese government, to frighten urban South Vietnamese and undermine pacification in the countryside, to give the impression to the U.S. public that the war is in a stalemate. Some U.S. officials also see the offensive as a prelude to North Viet Nam's coming to the conference table, aimed at enhancing Hanoi's hand in negotiations.

Whatever Giap's immediate aims, it has been clear to Hanoi for some time that something drastic had to be done in South Viet Nam. Captured cadre notes spoke of a "counteroffensive." Depressed by constant defeats on the battlefield and consigned to stay in South Viet Nam until the war was over, the infiltrated North Vietnamese regulars were growing weary and restive. They badly needed a victory to bolster their morale, or at least a major initiative that they could call their own. A dramatic demonstration of Communist power and prowess was required. To Giap, the countryside general offensive seemed tailormade for the task.

It was undoubtedly an extraordinary tour de force, unprecedented in modern military annals: the spectacle of an enemy force dispersed and unseen, everywhere hunted unremittingly, suddenly materializing to strike simultaneously in a hundred places throughout a country. Nowhere was the feat more impressive, or its art more instructively displayed, than in the assault on Saigon, the capital city of 2,000,000 people and the core of the allied commands.

INTO SAIGON IN THE days just before *Tet* slipped more than 3,000 Communist soldiers armed with weapons ranging up to machine-gun and bazooka size. Some came openly into the open city, weapons concealed in luggage or under baskets of food, riding buses, taxis and motor scooters, or walking. Others came furtively: some of the Viet Cong who attacked the U.S. embassy had ridden into town concealed in a truckload of flowers. Once in town, they hid their weapons. Only after the attack did Vietnamese intelligence realize that the unusual number of funerals the previous week was no accident: the Viet Cong had buried their weapons in the funeral coffins, dug them up on the night of the assault. They even test-fired their guns during the peak of the *Tet* celebrations, the sound of the shots mingling with that of the firecrackers going off.

In the An Quang Buddhist pagoda, the Communists set up a fully equipped command post for the attack. Shortly after midnight, the raiders assembled in units ranging from small suicide squads to well-armed company-size teams, and were led to their targets by local Communist guides. Some were dressed in neat, white button-down shirts and khakis, others in parts of ARVN [South Vietnamese army] uniforms or ragtag sports clothes. Dark clouds hung over the city, and only an occasional Jeep moved quickly through the eerie silence. Warned to expect something through captured enemy documents, military police had donned flak jackets and guard duty had been doubled. Saigon was a city waiting for trouble.

It began when a guard in his cement-lined outpost at the side entrance of the Independence Palace saw a distant blur of moving men. There was a shout: "Open the palace gates! We are the Liberation Army!" Then, rockets blazing, the Viet Cong commandos charged. From that moment on, fighting broke out all over the city, to the crack and boom of rockets, mortars and bazookas, the chop of machine-gun fire and the whine of ricocheting bullets. For the would-be liberators of the Independence Palace, the reply was a hail of fire. Retreating across the streets, the Communists took up positions in a half-completed hotel, killed the first two Jeep loads of U.S. MPs who raced to the scene and commandeered their M-60 machine gun. In a pattern of stubborn pocket resistance to be repeated throughout Viet Nam, it took two days to shoot the Viet Cong out of the hotel.

An enemy force of at least 700 men tackled the city's most vital military target: Tan Son Nhut airstrip and its adjoining MACV compound housing Westmoreland's headquarters and the 7th Air Force Command Center, the nerve centers of U.S. command in the war. The Communists breached the immediate base perimeter, slipping past some 150 outposts without a shot being fired, and got within 1,000 feet of the runways before they were halted in eight hours of bloody hand-to-hand combat. All told, the Communists attacked from 18 different points around Tan Son Nhut, getting close enough to MACV to put bullets through Westy's windows.

Communist units raced through the city shooting at U.S. officers' and enlisted men's billets (BOQs and BEQs), Ambassador Ellsworth Bunker's home, Westmoreland's home, the radio and TV stations. Wearing ARVN clothes, raiders seized part of the Vietnamese Joint General Staff Headquarters, turned the defenders' machine guns against helicopters diving in to dislodge them.

Other Viet Cong had less militant assignments. Near the Free World Force Headquarters, a score of Viet Cong paraded through the streets singing songs and waving flags and shouting: "This is the Liberation Force come to liberate the city! Please be compatriots! Help us liberate the city!" Two- and three-man teams with the same message went from door to door, like census takers, asking for the names of local police and government officials, the addresses of ARVN and government families. Those they got—or found—they killed on the spot.

In nearby Bien Hoa, Viet Cong took over the town and set up their own roadblocks. When two American G.I.'s were stopped, the Viet Cong hauled them from their car, delivered a "verdict" on them and summarily shot them for the benefit of the gathered townspeople. Some of Saigon's worst fighting took place in Cholon, the Chinese sector and a traditional stronghold of anti-government feeling. As elsewhere in the city, where resistance was heavy in house-to-house fighting, the ARVN warned the civilians out of the area, then called in helicopters to strafe and Skyraiders to dive-bomb.

At week's end, Saigon was still a city shuddering with the roar of bombs and the splat of bullets. After five days of fighting, the stubborn attackers of Tan Son Nhut airstrip were still entrenched near the field as F-100 jets, Skyraiders and helicopters blasted at their positions. Fighting flared in one part of the city and, when troops moved in with air support to damp it down, broke out in another area.

The violence in Saigon was only a small portion of the fighting that raged through the rest of the country. The first attack fell on Danang, site of the giant Marine base, where 300 Viet Cong infiltrated to the boundary of the Danang airfield and the walls of the South Vietnamese I Corps Headquarters before being driven back. Then, in a domino pattern, the attacks moved southward through the coastal cities of Qui Nhon, Tuy Hoa and Nha Trang, leapfrogged over into the highland cities of Kontum and Pleiku and continued southward into the Delta—where some of the first attacks came only at week's end. The timing was as sequential as a mammoth string of *Tet* firecrackers going off one after the other, obviously aimed at tying down allied forces the progressive length of the country.

In Dalat, pleasure spot for South Vietnamese generals and site of the nation's fledgling military academy, the cadets got an early introduction to combat. The Viet Cong seized the highland town, still held it at week's end. On the Bong Son plain, where the 1st Cavalry (Airmobile) has so often punished the enemy, the Communists hit an Air Cav base, destroyed two helicopters and penetrated the perimeter before being repulsed. At the Dong Ba Thien airfield just north of Cam Ranh Bay, attackers using satchel charges destroyed nine helicopters. In the Mekong Delta, long a Viet Cong haven, the situation seemed even more serious. The Communists held half the important city of My Tho and parts of several provincial capitals.

In the fighting throughout the country, the Communists, as Westmoreland pointed out, showed "a callous disregard for human life," attacking hospitals as well as military compounds, using churches and schools as defense posts and captured civilians as shields. In the highland town of Ban Me Thuot, the Viet Cong killed six American missionaries in a sweep through a leprosarium operated by the Christian and Missionary Alliance, leaving their bodies wired with booby traps.

Such tactics no doubt contributed to the failure of the Vietnamese to heed the call to a "general uprising." No sooner had the general offensive got under way than both the Viet Cong radio and Radio Hanoi began calling for the South Vietnamese to greet the attackers as liberators, for ARVN soldiers to throw in their arms with the Communists and help overthrow the government of President Nguyen Van Thieu. But throughout South Viet Nam there were few takers. In Danang, when a Viet Cong rose at a Buddhist *Tet* service with a pistol in one hand and a bullhorn in the other, bidding the crowd to support the "uprising," the Buddhists seized him and his two comrades and turned them over to the South Vietnamese police.

It was in Hué, sitting on the lush banks of the Perfume River, that the Communists, recognizing both its symbolic importance and the greater likelihood of some support from the population, made a maximum effort. There, for the time being, they enjoyed their most signal success. The seat of South Viet Nam's militant Buddhists and the home of many disaffected university students, Hué has long been South Viet Nam's capital of discontent. Into Hué last week Giap sent elements of five of his North Vietnamese regulars, supported by Viet Cong local soldiers—an estimated 2,000 men in all. They seized the Citadel of the ancient royal palace, dug in and raised the Viet Cong flag atop its crumbling battlements. Then they released from jail some 2,500 prisoners, including 400 Viet Cong.

South Vietnamese infantry units closed in on the city from all sides, and three companies of U.S. Marines, spearheaded by a platoon of army tanks, moved in to rescue a besieged U.S. military advisory unit trapped in its command. That mission accomplished, they turned to aid the South Vietnamese in rooting out the NVA, who reportedly were being guided and fed by Hué students. In the twisting alleyways of the old city, digging out the Communists turned out to be a tough task. After two days of combat, President Thieu phoned ARVN 1 Corps Commander Lieut. General Hoang Xuan Lam and demanded that he get Hué back in allied hands—and "get it back fast."

Lam and U.S. Marine Lieut. General Robert E. Cushman Jr. knew how to get it back fast, but only at the cost of reducing it to ruins, and turning much of Viet Nam's heritage to crumbled stone. So the Skyraiders, wheeling and diving over Hué in support of the allied counterattack, at first used only guns and rockets no larger than 2.5 in. in order to protect the city's buildings and royal tombs and monuments. When after four days the Communists still held more than half the city, heritage was reluctantly sacrificed to necessity and the bombs loosed on the Citadel. The U.S., however, insisted that the South Vietnamese do the bombing themselves.

Hué, with Route 1 running through it, lies directly astride the main allied supply line from the Marine bases at Danang and Phu Bai to the encircled outpost of Khe Sanh. One of Giap's aims in his general offensive is to stretch U.S. lines—and U.S. troop deployments—as thin and as wide as he can, forcing General Westmoreland to make difficult choices of priority.

Westmoreland sees the assault on Khe Sanh as the capstone of a three-phase campaign devised by Giap last September to win the war. The first phase, which produced the battles of Loc Ninh and Dak To along the Cambodian border, was designed to draw American forces away from population centers and rural pacification areas and "force us," as Westmoreland said, "to dissipate our military strength." The second phase erupted in the past week's widespread attacks on population centers and military installations, aimed at rendering impotent for a time the U.S. ability to react quickly to the third-phase "main attack" against the Marines in northern Viet Nam.

There is much in Giap's new strategy that flies in the face of his own guerrilla doctrine of warfare. One of his maxims is to fight only when the odds are overwhelmingly in his favor and success is certain, a precept that his troops violated nearly everywhere they struck in the course of his general offensive last week. What lies behind Giap's turnabout, which in its sanction of attacks on cities and towns constitutes the most important change of tactics by either side in the war?

In the argument within the Hanoi hierarchy on how to meet the allies' growing momentum, Giap, true to his own maxims and proven experience against the French, argued for an abandonment of large-scale or big-unit fighting and a return to guerrilla warfare in the south that might last for 10 or 20 years. His chief opponent and longtime rival, General Nguyen Chi Thanh, wanted to stick with big-unit warfare. Thanh had the advantage of being closest to the action as head of all Communist operations in South Viet Nam from his headquarters northwest of Saigon along the Cambodian border, and he prevailed in the Politburo.

Then Thanh died last summer, and no successor appeared in South Viet Nam. Instead, Giap disappeared from Hanoi, even missing the 23rd anniversary party on Dec. 22 of the founding of his own army. The best evidence is that he has set up a headquarters just north of the DMZ, determined, even if it is against his own instincts, to make big-unit war work against the U.S. He has said, in effect, to the Politburo: If this is what you want to do, I'll show you how to do it. ∎

Report from a Captured Correspondent

BY   ROBERT   SAM   ANSON

[*While covering the war in Cambodia, the writer was taken prisoner by North Vietnamese soldiers. His three weeks of captivity were not what he expected*]

September 7, 1970

I WAS LOOKING FOR the buses, the gaudy red, yellow and blue buses in which the Cambodian army rides off to fight and sometimes die. When you see the empty buses parked by the side of the road, their drivers sleeping in their shade, you know that you should stop. Ahead is the battle.

I drove confidently, foolishly, toward Skoun, not looking for the other signs that were all around me. Six kilometers from Skoun, my eye caught a South Vietnamese gunship making lazy circles over what had to be the city. I watched carefully now, but saw only the plane. Then I saw them, out the left window, standing in the heavy underbrush by the side of the road.

There were two of them, both with Chinese-made AK-47s. They looked Cambodian. I waved and drove past. They waved back. Seconds later, their costumes registered: they were dressed in black, and their helmets were camouflaged with leaves and small branches. They seemed as surprised to see me as I was to see them. They might run. I turned the car and started slowly back down the road. Then, 300 yards away, the soldiers appeared again, this time out on the road itself, signaling that I stop. I pulled off the road. They came, guns at the ready. Two Vietnamese. My hands went up, and I whispered the word for journalist: *"Bao-chi."* Then *"Hoa-binh,"* the Vietnamese words for peace. Then louder: *"Bao-chi, bao-chi, bao-chi."* One of the soldiers looked at me confusedly. With his rifle, he motioned me out of the car. I got out, hands raised, and spoke again: *"Hoa-binh, hoa-binh, hoa-binh."* One soldier nodded and repeated the word.

Within moments, my captors and I were trotting into the jungle. We came to a small command post, and once again I blurted out: *"Bao-chi, hoa-binh."* They were Viets, all 15 of them, and they understood. Now they began talking, asking me the question I feared most: *"My? My? My?"* (American? American? American?) I feigned ignorance, and we moved off again, deeper into the trees. The soldiers guided me into a bunker. So this is how it ends, I thought. In some rotten little hole, where no one will find me.

The soldiers approached and pointed their guns in. I tensed and closed my eyes. But they were speaking to me, telling me in Vietnamese to get out. We were leaving. There were too many mortars, too many planes. They tied my arms loosely behind my back, and two of them took up guard in front of and behind me. As we began to march off, I looked back at the others and said again, *"Hoa-binh."*

We walked for two hours. Then, almost suddenly, the brush country gave way to paddies, and we entered a small village. My guards motioned me to sit down, and someone brought a cup of water. In a few moments, I was directed inside a Khmer-style house sitting high off the ground on stilts. A young Vietnamese appeared and squatted down beside me. In broken French, he asked who I was. I told him that and much more: "I am a journalist. I come in peace. Once, after a massacre at Takeo, I helped some of your people." He listened stolid-faced, then broke into a grin and slapped my leg. "I know," he said. "Thank you."

The next night I left the village and, on foot and by car in the rain, was led to a small factory. Inside, the soldiers found several boards and laid them on the earthen floor as my bed. Drenched by the rain, I lay down and tried to sleep. The boards rattled beneath me as I quivered from the cold. One of the soldiers fetched a blanket from his pack and wrapped it around me. As I drifted into sleep, the ground again shook beneath me, and then again. It was the rumble of bombs from a B-52.

I awoke to find two visitors sitting quietly a few feet away from me. It was some moments before they spoke, then one of them said in broken French and English: "We understand you are a journalist. We would like to talk to you."

Talk we did about politics, my family, my views on the war. As they were preparing to go, I impulsively snatched up a journal that I had been keeping and showed it to them. Their reaction was surprise: "The soldiers permit you pen and paper?" But when I explained what it was and they had paged through it, they nodded their approval. They were especially interested in a few small poems I had written, including a verse about one of my guards, a young North Vietnamese soldier.

> *Ti*
> *A boy*
> *A boy like any other boy*
> *A boy*
> *Like me.*

A poem? the older man asked. An attempt at a poem, I answered. Then I added: "Ho Chi Minh was a poet, was he not?" "Yes," said the man. "Yes, Ho Chi Minh was a poet."

That evening we moved once again, not far this time, to a small village schoolhouse that would serve as my home for the next ten days. Slowly my life was settling into the semblance of a routine. Morning would be announced by the crowing of the village cocks. Rising from the tabletop that served as my bed, I would strip off my clothes and don a red-and-white checkered sarong for the first of three daily baths, accomplished by the simple expedient of pouring three pails of ice-cold water over my head.

I had four windows, but they were seldom opened. I was told that the danger from planes and spies was too great. In the afternoon, when the air was still and oppressive, I retreated to my tabletop and tried to sleep till the cool of the evening. Invariably, I lay wide awake, watching the rats scurry across the ceiling rafters or marveling at the industry of the hornets building their nests.

My guard was now permanently established: six North Vietnamese and nine Khmers. None of us spoke the other's language, but we talked just the same and in a short time became remarkably close. When I asked for water, I said *"nuoc,"* or *"bat lua"* when I wanted a light for my cigarette, or *"cam on"* when the light was provided. For every Vietnamese or Khmer word I learned, they demanded to know the equivalent in "Washington." I found out that the small oil lamp every soldier carries with him is called a *cai-den*. After I used the word the first time, one of the soldiers held up the lamp and asked, "Washington? Washington?" "Torch," I replied.

"Tors, tors," they all repeated, unable to form the difficult English *ch* sound with their mouths. I laughed and shook my head. "Not tors. Call it lamp. L-a-m-p."

The meals originally came at a rate of five a day: two in the morning, then lunch, a hefty afternoon snack, and finally dinner. *"Tumtum,"* one of the Khmers said, slapping my fat stomach. Then, slapping his own rock-hard middle, he boasted, *"Kampuchea, tut-tut." Kampuchea* means Cambodia in Khmer.

A bond was forming between us. Earlier, when they clicked their weapons in the darkness, I would instinctively catch my breath, never quite sure what would happen next. After a week, the windows came open a tiny crack, and finally they were flung open altogether. Increasingly, I was left alone for long periods. After ten days, the soldiers gave me a pair of sandals—or *gap,* as I learned to call them—cut from an old automobile tire. The North Vietnamese soldier who presented them to me told me they were "sandals of the Resistance." Then, with a grin, he whispered, *"Gap Ho Chi Minh."* They even began leaving their weapons around my room while they went on their errands—knives, carbines, AK-47s, Chinese-made grenades. I was astonished.

ON THE SEVENTH DAY after my capture, three North Vietnamese officers, including the older man who had questioned me before, appeared at the door. This time the interrogation was far more detailed. For the next several hours, we talked politics and personalities. They were especially interested in what I thought of the war. The questioning climaxed with a single query. "Do you believe," said one of the officers, leaning forward until his face was only a few inches from mine, "in the inevitable victory of the Indochinese peoples?" I pulled back and thought for a moment. "I believe," I said at last, "in self-determination of all peoples."

Two days later the older man walked into my room and told me in French that on Aug. 12 I would be released.

Aug. 12 came and went. I was still their prisoner. Mentally, I had prepared myself for the disappointment. Days went by. I was slipping into depression. But my spirits rose on the night of Aug. 16, when we moved from the schoolhouse to a large Khmer-style house across the village. I learned that the peasants, after being told that I was an American journalist and had not come to hurt them, had insisted that I be moved to better quarters.

Evenings were my favorite time of day. One night after the village was asleep, the soldiers took me outside for exercise and let me bask in the cool evening air. Sitting on a chair they had provided, I watched as some of the Vietnamese taught the Khmers how to crawl quietly through the grass, dragging their rifles behind them. Then the soldiers invited me to show them how Americans crawl. I got down on all fours and promptly split the seat of my pants, and the evening solitude dissolved in laughter.

I seldom moved from my bed the next day. I lay on my back, smoking cigarette after cigarette, thinking about what I had seen. Weeks before in Phnom-Penh, around the swimming pool at the Hotel Royal, we correspondents had told each other that Premier Lon Nol's regime was in trouble. But we had never guessed how deeply the trouble ran. Now I had seen the beginnings of a Khmer liberation army, and it seemed to be growing stronger, fed both by volunteers and prisoners. In less than three weeks, I had seen scores of Khmer soldiers with Sihanouk badges pinned to their chests. Wherever I had gone, there had been Khmers guiding the Vietnamese and in turn being trained by them. This was no phantom army. A civil war was building.

Aug. 21 was the most memorable day I spent in the village. Early that afternoon, the English-speaking North Vietnamese officer appeared with a small group of other officers, both Vietnamese and Khmer. He said what he had to say quickly: "You are going home. There will be a ceremony tomorrow, and you will be released as soon after that as possible. We will talk later."

Later, when we did talk, he outlined the release procedures, told me my possessions would be returned to me, including my car, and concluded with a surprise. "There will be a gathering of the peasants, and we would like you to make a statement. We want you to tell us your impressions of your stay here." I nodded, and he gave me a pencil and paper. I thought for a few long moments and then began to write. In minutes, I had finished what I wanted to say. He took my copy and walked over to read it by the light of the window. His face creased into a frown. "Some of this is good," he said, in the tone of a schoolmaster, "but there is some you left out, don't you think? You should begin by confessing your mistake. Write again. This time think more carefully. I will help you."

He certainly did. In an hour, the statement was finished. He nodded with satisfaction, then added, "But you must sign it." Then another surprise: "We would like to tape-record your voice so all the people of Kampuchea can hear you."

For the rest of the day, I received visitors, the people of the village. Almost all of them brought some gift—a few bananas, a rice cake, a package of cigarettes. In Buddhist fashion, I would fold my hands and bow my head, whispering in Khmer "Thank you" and "Long life." Then we would sit cross-legged on the floor facing one another, not saying a word, drinking tea, smiling and, with the children, laughing. In a few minutes they would go, and I would bow again. They would bow in return.

Next morning, I went through the promised ceremony and received my release order from the Khmer representatives of the Skoun front. Two photographers recorded the event after carefully removing a North Vietnamese helmet from the picture. A Vietnamese officer asked me, "How does it feel to be a free man?" I answered with a smile: "I've always felt I was a free man."

Toward 6 in the evening, I gathered my things and made my final goodbyes to the soldiers. They had brought my Hertz car to the schoolhouse. As I walked to the auto, people came out of their houses. First dozens of them, then several hundred. They came to applaud and say goodbye. Children tagged along after me, yelling and laughing, sometimes darting up to touch my arm. I got into the back seat of the car, and the driver started off. After a few moments I looked back. The people were still waving.

Gingerly, we picked our way through the darkness, heading for a point close to the main road, where we would spend the night. At 4:30 the next morning, we rose and slowly drove to the release point. Suddenly, the car was braking to a halt. Three miles ahead, my escorts told me, government forces waited. "You must be careful that they don't harm you," an officer warned. I half laughed at his remark, and he looked at me questioningly. I didn't bother to explain.

Thirty minutes dragged by. Finally, the English-speaking Vietnamese officer said, "It is time for the separation." We shook hands. "You are a man of the people," he said. "Remember them." "The people have been good to me," I replied. "I won't forget them." I slid into the front seat, started the engine and then sat there a long moment. At last, I began moving forward, away from the past three weeks. In a few minutes, I looked into the rear-view mirror. The soldiers had gone. Ahead, the sun was beginning to come up.   ∎

"This Is It! Everybody Out!"

BY ROY ROWAN

[*As Saigon fell to Communist troops, bringing the war in Viet Nam to its dismal end, the writer was one of the last Americans to be evacuated before escape routes were cut off*]

May 12, 1975

THE EMERGENCY PLAN HAD called for the evacuation of the remaining Americans in three stages—on Tuesday morning, afternoon and evening. But by 10:30 a.m. Tuesday, with Tan Son Nhut airbase under pounding by rockets, mortars and 130-mm. artillery, word came from the American embassy: "This is it! Everybody out!"

Correspondents and cameramen in the Continental Palace Hotel swarmed down the stairs, through the lobby and out across Lam Son Square in single file, a ragtag army lugging typewriters, shoulder bags, TV cameras and sound gear. Our designated assembly point was down near the Saigon River four blocks away. Armed policemen in the square eyed us menacingly. There was no question: this formation clearly signaled the final departure of Americans from the Indochina war.

The day before, Lam Son Square had echoed with the sound of carbines, M-16s and rooftop machine guns. Now the square was quiet, the pavement under our feet baked to cooking temperature by the morning sun. I glanced at my watch: it was 10:42. People peered through iron gates that had been pulled shut because of the 24-hour curfew. Their eyes were easy to read. "You're leaving us," they said.

Our assembly point faced the statue of Viet Nam's 6th century naval hero, Trang Hung Dao. A landing zone had been prepared atop the building. But the South Vietnamese navy had placed 50-cal. machine guns on top of the building next door, posing a threat to the departing Americans. Picking up our gear, we trooped on to another assembly point.

Nobody knew what the plan was. Would the "helos" pick us up from a pad on the roof? Or would buses take us to Tan Son Nhut, which had been under Communist attack for twelve hours? At 35 Gia Long we discovered that the building door had been padlocked. There were no instructions, only a faded sign: UNIVERSITY OF MARYLAND, SAIGON EDUCATION CENTER. A few French civilians joined our group. Mme. Madeleine Morton, owner of the best restaurant in Saigon, the Guillaume Tell, greeted her customers. "I am trying to go to Bridgeport, Con-nec-ticut," she announced. At 12:20 two black buses finally arrived and were quickly filled.

Rumbling along in low gear, the buses began a circuitous tour of Saigon. Were they searching out more Americans? We didn't know. "[U.S. Ambassador] Graham Martin sightseeing excursions," cracked one correspondent. Every few blocks the buses stopped, perhaps unsure if the road ahead was clear. An ARVN soldier rushed up to our bus and banged against the door. "Take me out!" he yelled. The Marine guard on our bus slapped him hard across the back. "Goddam, we took out 25,000 Vietnamese."

Over a VHF radio we tuned in to the mission wardens' control center (code-named "Dodge City") and learned that the U.S. embassy was in trouble. "Marines to the gate as soon as possible," the operator called. Minutes later: "There are 2,000 people in front of the gate. It's getting hostile." Still later: "The gates are open. We've lost control of the crowd."

The buses began to move again and headed toward Tan Son Nhut—right into the rocket belt. Guards at the gate were firing at the buses. Pillars of black smoke rose from the airbase ahead. Over the radio we heard our own Marine escort ("Wagon Master") ask Dodge City, "What's the situation at the gate?" "Bust it if necessary," came the reply.

We did not have to. Inside the airbase, a damaged American helicopter, one skid broken off, lay on the ground, its rotor still spinning. A tremendous explosion rocked our bus as a North Vietnamese 130-mm. shell hit the Air America terminal just across the road. "Don't panic!" shouted our Marine escort.

Crouching and running, the passengers raced into the Defense Attaché's Office, a reassuring structure with thick cement walls. From time to time we could feel the building shudder from incoming rockets. About 500 evacuees were already waiting in line. One Marine passed out green tags ("For you, not your baggage," he explained). Another, stripped to the waist, walked down the line with a bucket of ice water, reviving the dehydrated evacuees.

One woman, caught between a bus and the building when a shell burst, was carried inside unconscious, but only from fright. A European walked down the line asking everybody to sign a 500-piaster note he wanted to keep as a souvenir. Sister Fidema of the Good Shepherd Convent in Saigon knelt over her suitcase and prayed. "I've been here four years," she said later. "These have been good years until this week. But this has been the saddest ever."

For the first time all day we began to get information. "The helos," we were told, "are on the way." Word was passed down the line: one suitcase and one handbag per evacuee. Just as our group of 50 prepared to leave, that rule was changed to make way for more passengers: the Marine at the door shouted, "No baggage!" Suitcases and bags were ripped open as evacuees fished for their passports, papers and other valuables. I said goodbye to my faithful Olivetti, grabbed my tape recorder and camera and got ready to run like hell. The door opened. Outside I could see helmeted, flak-jacketed Marines—lots of them—crouched against the building, their M-16s, M-79 grenade launchers and mortars all at the ready.

We could view the whole perimeter. There was a road leading to a parking lot, and on the left was a tennis court that had been turned into a landing zone. Two Sikorsky CH-53 Sea Stallions were sitting in the parking lot. I raced for it. Marines, lying prone, lined the area, but they were hard to see because their camouflaged uniforms blended with the tropical greenery. I almost stepped on a rifle barrel poking out from under a bush as I entered the lot.

The Sea Stallion was still 200 ft. away, its loading ramp down and its rotors slashing impatiently. Fifty people, some lugging heavy equipment despite the order to abandon all baggage, piled in, one atop another: correspondents, photographers and Vietnamese men, women and children. The loadmaster raised the ramp, the two waist gunners gripped the handles of their M-16s, and, with about a dozen passengers still standing like subway straphangers, the helicopter lifted off. As the tail dipped, I could see towers of smoke rising from all over Tan Son Nhut.

Beside us was a second Sea Stallion. Tilting and swaying in unison, the two machines gained altitude. Saigon lay below, brown and smoky in the afternoon light, its serpentine river cutting a wide and winding swath through the city. I glanced at my watch: 3:52, five hours and ten minutes since our evacuation had commenced at the Continental Palace Hotel. I tried to pick out the hotel from the air, but we were already too high, slipping southeast over veined paddyfields toward the sea. ∎

Nothin's Worth Killing Someone

BY ROGER ROSENBLATT

[
Part of the author's sequence Children of War, *set in
five trouble spots from Lebanon to Cambodia, this story
focused on children tragically caught up in the ancient
enmity between Protestants and Catholics in Belfast*
]

January 11, 1982

*Our fathers and ourselves sowed dragon's teeth. Our children
know and suffer the armed men. —Stephen Vincent Benét*

IF YOU WANT THE full account of Frank Rowe's murder, it will not be provided by Paul. Paul is 13 now, was seven
at the time, yet he can still only get so far into the story—to
the point where "Daddy, he ran to the back, to the next house"—before he
starts crying. He has a woman's face, still dimpled, along with the absolutely blue eyes of most Belfast children, and brown hair parted carelessly
down the middle: the sort of face the old masters sought. His school tie
hangs cockeyed; it was knotted in a hurry.

"What do you feel about your father's death now?"

His friend Joseph answers for him. Joseph, also 13, has a small, tight
head, a high, clear voice, and his ambition is to grow up and join the Provos.
"Revenge. That's what you want. Isn't it, Paul?" Paul says nothing.

"*I'd* want revenge," says Joseph, looking again to Paul.

Paul eventually nods; then says faintly: "Aye. Revenge."

As if to make his case forever, Joseph thrusts his face toward the
American stranger. "You. You'd take revenge too, wouldn't you, Mister?"

The two boys sit in low plastic chairs beside each other in a classroom of the Stella Maris Secondary School, a brick-and-stucco series of after-thoughts that could pass for a warehouse. Stella Maris is in an unusual po-sition because it is a Roman Catholic school located in a Protestant area, and it holds a special place in modern Belfast history because Bobby Sands is an alumnus. Yet the Stella Maris students make no big thing of their con-nection to the hunger striker. A couple of boys were once caught playing a game called Bobby Sands, but that's about the extent of it. Ask Stephen and Malachy, both 15, what they think of Sands' decision, and they answer simultaneously, "Brave." "Foolish."

Joseph would undoubtedly say "Brave," and he would probably urge the same answer on Paul. But alone, away from Joseph, Paul is more himself.

"That business about revenge. Is that really what you want?"

The boy looks helpless. "No. It doesn't matter who done it. Nothin's worth killing someone."

According to most accounts, Paul is a very odd, timid exception in a city that has become famous for its violent children. In fact, the reverse is true. There are plenty of violent children in Belfast, to be sure: kids who kill time stealing cars for joyrides or lobbing petrol bombs at the army. But they are a small knot of a minority. Most Belfast children are like Paul. They have not all suffered so directly from the Troubles, but their response to the Troubles is similar. They carry no hatred in their hearts, they show a will to survive, and they are exceptionally gentle with grownups and with one another. This seems especially remarkable when one considers the dark, moaning city of their home—the once clanging port that made great ships and sailed them down the Belfast Lough for the world to see. It is now shut tight like a corpse's mouth, its brown terrace houses strung out like teeth full of cavities, gaps and wires.

The wires hold. Belfast is rich in wire, coiled and barbed, and in corru-gated iron. (You could make your fortune in corrugated iron here.) Great sheets of it are slabbed up in front of government buildings and on the "peace line" that separates the Catholic Falls Road from the Protestant Shankill. In the centers of the streets are "dragon's teeth"—huge squares of stone arranged in uneven rows to prevent fast getaways. Downtown in the "control zone," no car may be parked unattended. Solitary figures sit like dolls behind the wheels to prove there is no bomb. Armored personnel car-riers, called "pigs" by the children, poke their snouts around corners and lurch out to create sudden roadblocks. The Andersonstown police station, like a fly draped in a web, is barely visible behind what looks like a baseball backstop. The fence is slanted inward at the top, to fend off any rockets.

To the children of the city the message is clear: Keep behind your lines; stay with your own people. In effect, the war has caged them. They have limited freedom of movement, little freedom of speech and, in some cases, no freedom of childhood itself.

Bernadette Livingstone, for example, cannot leave the house much these days because her mother has commanded most of her attention since Julie's death. Julie was 14, a year younger than Bernadette when she was killed last May by a plastic bullet fired from a British army Saracen. It happened during a protest demonstration involving mostly women.

"One of the hunger strikers had just died—you know? Francis Hughes, I think it was. Yeah, it was. And Julie and her friend had just come out of a shop. And there was the bangin' of the lids [garbage can lids—a signal of mourning and anger]. Suddenly people started running. And the army Saracens came down the road—you know? Six-wheeler Saracens? And Julie dove. But when her friend tried to pick her up, she couldn't move. She was still conscious on the way to the hospital. But she wasn't all there, like, when we left her. Mommy kept ringing the doctors all night to see how she was. The thing they were afraid of was the blood leakin' into her brain."

Bernadette is a fifth-former in the Cross and Passion Secondary School— all girls—in Andersonstown, a hard-line Catholic area. The school is located next to a brewery, and the sidewalk out front bears burn marks where a car was set afire in a riot. Inside, all is composed and pleasant. Nuns shush the light chatter. The girls swish by in their green-and-yellow uniforms; their heels click on the linoleum. On the wall of the room where Bernadette sits is a Pope John Paul II calendar and a poster with the words GOD IS NEARER TO US THAN WE ARE TO OURSELVES. Bernadette holds her hands clasped below her green-and-yellow tie, except when she brushes a wisp of blond hair away from her eyes. The eyes are at once soft and stubborn.

"My mother will never get over it. She had Julie late in life—you know? My father doesn't express his feelings. I think that's worse. He used to do a bit of singin', but he doesn't sing so much any more—you know?"

You don't know, of course, but this is the way most Belfast kids tell stories. Each statement of fact is turned up at the end like a question. It isn't as if they are asking you anything that requires an answer. The statement carries the assumption that you probably already know what they have been telling you. That she and Julie didn't get along—you know? That

Julie was the nervous one. That Julie was the youngest—you know? "Now I'm the youngest."

Like Paul, Bernadette seeks no revenge against the other side, not even the army men who ride the Saracens. She points out that they are not much older than herself. She does have Protestant friends, but it's difficult because of the neighborhood she lives in. The Livingstones are residents of Lenadoon, where Julie's death is memorialized by a white cross on a small green. The neighborhood is loud with graffiti: DON'T LET THEM DIE; TOUTS WILL BE SHOT; and in bold white letters across the jerry-built walls, WELCOME TO PROVOLAND. In a sense the Livingstones are a Provo family, since Bernadette's two older brothers, Patrick, 30, and Martin, 24, are serving time in the H block; one of them is up for murder. But Bernadette has her own politics: "I don't support the I.R.A. because I know what death is."

That is true two ways. Bernadette may be the youngest in her family, but Julie's death has imposed a different sort of death on her. Now her mother clings to her like death, and Bernadette must stay home with her mother and talk with her about Julie, for that is all her mother wishes to talk about. In a single shot she has been propelled into adulthood, while her mother, in Bernadette's view, has retreated to the past, and, for the time being at least, has locked her daughter in with her.

"Do you think of Julie yourself?"

"All the time," says Bernadette. "She's *everywhere*."

WHAT HAS HAPPENED OVER the long years is that chaos has become normal, and in its normality lies a basic feature of a child's life in Belfast. Alexander Lyons, a Belfast psychiatrist, points out that in a chaotic world, antisocial behavior is acceptable. That is why he finds so little of what might be termed "emotional disturbance," in the clinical sense, among the Belfast children, since, in a way, the whole place is emotionally disturbed. The kids play war games, but there is nothing unique in that. Indeed, their war games are made more normal by the fact that the grown-ups play them too.

In such an atmosphere, Lyons is far more impressed by the resilience of the children than by their fears or rampages. A girl who had three limbs blown off by a bomb managed to hold on to her mind and eventually marry. But Lyons stresses that resilience is a short-term effect. "In the long run [his voice is calm and certain] we are raising a generation of bigots."

If that is so, it is hard to see now. Bigotry is not something that people generally boast about; still, you catch almost none of it in the conversations of these children. A Catholic girl in Stella Maris expressed the deepest sorrow for the pregnant widow of a murdered Protestant policeman. "His baby will never know him." Protestant children display the same feelings. Keith Fletcher is still stunned by the story of his Catholic friend whose father, like Paul's, was murdered in his own hallway. "They walked in, very polite. The mother didn't know what they wanted. She gave them tea. They drank it. When the father came home, they shot him."

It is the closeness of the lives that makes the war intense for the children, like a terrible, endless family fight, but it also confuses their feelings. Each side is carefully taught to be suspicious of the other, yet there is an unspoken affinity between the two sides as well, an affinity that does not exist between the Protestant Northern Irish and the English, or even between the Catholics in the north and south. The connections show up in indirect ways. Teen-age girls in Belfast adore the romantic novels of Joan Lingard, especially *Across the Barricades* ("when Catholic Kevin and Protestant Sadie are old enough for their hitherto unacknowledged attraction to flower into love"). It is not wishful thinking, exactly; Bernadette admits she would never date a Prod, because "nothing could come of it." But the possibility exists, nonetheless—a fact that infuriates the gunmen at the doors.

What the terrorists do to keep the children in line is to use them in their battles, and the children recognize this. Here, as in Lebanon and elsewhere, children are often deliberately placed at the head of demonstrations, marches and funeral processions. Their mere presence gives moral authority to the cause. A booklet under the prosaic title *Rubber & Plastic Bullets Kill & Maim* contains pictures and stories of child victims; the more brutal the better. Such devices work especially well in Belfast, where everyone gives the impression of knowing everyone else, where people like Paul and Bernadette achieve a dubious celebrity for having had their lives shot out from under them.

But the stories of those two are not nearly as famous as Elizabeth Crawford's. Elizabeth, 16, like Bernadette, goes to Cross and Passion, but even across town in Stella Maris they know all about the Crawfords. A girl in Stella Maris recalled how beautiful Patrick Crawford was—then blushes to think that she is flirting with the dead. Patrick was 15. He was very tall, wore his hair cut short and resembled a policeman. They say that is how he was shot by mistake. Dead too is Elizabeth's grandfather, who was run down by a car in what appeared to be a sectarian killing. And then there was Elizabeth's mother, killed mistakenly in a crossfire between the I.R.A. and the army.

"There were ten of us at the time—seven brothers, two sisters and myself. I can't really remember much about the happenin'. I was seven. My mother was out doin' the shoppin'. I was sittin' in a neighbor's house, and I seen my older sister being brought inside, and seen that she'd been cryin' and all. That was when we found out that Mother had been shot. And everybody kept tellin' us that she was going to be O.K. Then later the doctor came in and he was tryin' to calm us down, and sayin' that she was dead and gone to heaven and all this here. Just before she died, me daddy had been talkin' to her. He was very upset, he was, though he's fairly settled now. When Mother died, we all found it hard to be close to him. He was always thinkin' of her—that's the way we seen it. I don't mean to criticize him. It's just that we were left aside, like, for a while. That was only a matter of weeks. After that we began to get close again."

Elizabeth sits in the Cross and Passion office where Bernadette was sitting. Her voice is quiet, her smile hesitant. Every feature is gentle—the way the long hair waves; the way the lidded eyes give solace. She may have the face of her mother.

"Did they ever find out who did the shooting?"

"The bullets in her body were from the I.R.A. They've got two fellas in jail for it now. My father works with their fathers in the brewery. He's quite friendly with them, actually. He just has pity for the ones who done it."

The man jailed for the killing of her grandfather was a member of the militant Ulster Volunteer Force.

"And Patrick? How was he killed?"

"It was a Catholic fella. They have him locked up too." All three, then, died in different parts of the violence. "When we were younger we couldn't understand it. We didn't know where to turn or who to blame. We asked the adults, and the adults, they all had different views on it.

"I kept askin': Why is all this happenin' to *us*?"

"Did it shake your belief in God?"

"Not in God. In man."

She goes on about her life; about cooking and cleaning for her father, about the occasional movie she gets to (*Friday the 13th*—"a good scare") and the occasional book (*Across the Barricades*). She suddenly seems invested with an ancient image. She is Ireland, this girl; not Northern Ireland, but the whole strange place, that western chip of Europe stuck out in the Atlantic with no natural resources but its poetic mind and a devouring loneliness. In peacetime that loneliness is desolate but beautiful. In time of war it is merely desolate. Here is Elizabeth at the window watching rain. Or Elizabeth shopping for groceries. Or Elizabeth walking home under that tumultuous blue-black sky. Children love to be alone because alone is where they know themselves, and where they dream. But thanks to the war, Elizabeth is alone in a different way. She is not dreaming of what she will be. She looks about her and knows quite well what she will be—what her life and that of her children will be in that dread city. And like many Belfast children, she wants out.

"Do you think that you could marry a Protestant boy?"

"If I find one nice enough. [A graceful laugh.] But if I ever did get married, I'd end up emigratin'. I would not want to live here, bringin' my own children up in the Troubles. 'Cause I was hurt. And I wouldn't want that to happen to them."

It is easy to picture Elizabeth as a parent because she seems a parent already. Like Bernadette, she has been rushed into adulthood. Now she must take care of her father as if she were his parent—he who does not like to talk about the Troubles, or about the past, and who seems to have settled, quite justifiably, for a life of determined peace and quiet. He may never change. A grownup parent sees life in stages, knows fairly well when a child will outgrow or overcome this and that. But how does a child-parent know the same about grownups? In a sense, more patience and understanding are asked of these children than of any real parent.

"Do you think that one side in the Troubles is more right than the other?"

"No," says Elizabeth, "neither is wrong. But they need somethin' to bring them together. I really don't know where fightin' gets anybody. It's only goin' to bring more dead, more sadness to the families."

She is told the story of Paul and Joseph.

"Don't *you* want revenge?"

"Against whom?" she says.   ∎

If You Want to Humble an Empire

BY NANCY GIBBS

[*War came home to America on 9/11. The writer, using reporting by the entire* TIME *staff and working on an intensely short deadline, pieced together an indelible panorama of a nation coping with catastrophe*]

September 14, 2001

IF YOU WANT TO humble an empire, it makes sense to maim its cathedrals. They are symbols of its faith, and when they crumple and burn, it tells us we are not so powerful and we can't be safe. The Twin Towers of the World Trade Center, planted at the base of Manhattan island with the Statue of Liberty as their sentry, and the Pentagon, a squat, concrete fort on the banks of the Potomac, are the sanctuaries of money and power that our enemies may imagine define us. But that assumes our faith rests on what we can buy and build, and that has never been America's true God.

On a normal day, we value heroism because it is uncommon. On Sept. 11, we valued heroism because it was everywhere. The fire fighters kept climbing the stairs of the tallest buildings in town, even as the steel moaned and the cracks spread in zippers through the walls, to get to the people trapped in the sky. We don't know yet how many of them died, but once we know, as Mayor Rudy Giuliani said, "it will be more than we can bear." That sentiment was played out in miniature in the streets, where fleeing victims pulled the wounded to safety, and at every hospital, where the lines to give blood looped round and round the block. At the medical-supply companies, which sent supplies without being asked. At Verizon, where a worker threw on a New York fire department jacket to go save people. And then again and again all across the country, as people checked on those they loved to find out if they were safe and then looked for some way to help.

This was the bloodiest day on American soil since our Civil War, a modern Antietam played out in real time, on fast-forward, and not with soldiers but with secretaries, security guards, lawyers, bankers, janitors. It was strange that a day of war was a day we stood still. We couldn't move—that must have been the whole idea—so we had no choice but to watch. Every city cataloged its targets; residents looked at their skylines, wondering if they would be different in the morning. The Sears Tower in Chicago was evacuated, as were colleges and museums. Disney World shut down, and Major League Baseball canceled its games, and nuclear power plants went to top security status; the Hoover Dam and the Mall of America shut down, and Independence Hall in Philadelphia, and Mount Rushmore. It was as though someone had taken a huge brush and painted a bull's-eye around every place Americans gather, every icon we revere, every service we depend on, and vowed to take them out or shut them down, or force us to do it ourselves.

Terror works like a musical composition, so many instruments, all in tune, playing perfectly together to create their desired effect. Sorrow and horror, and fear. The first plane is just to get our attention. Then, once we are transfixed, the second plane comes and repeats the theme until the blinding coda of smoke and debris crumbles on top of the rescue workers who have gone in to try to save anyone who survived the opening movements. And we watch, speechless, as the sirens, like some awful choir, hour after hour let you know that it is not over yet, wait, there's more.

It was, of course, a perfect day, 70° and flawless skies, perfect for a nervous pilot who has stolen a huge jet and intends to turn it into a missile. It was a Boeing 767 from Boston, American Airlines Flight 11 bound for Los Angeles with 81 passengers, that first got the attention of air-traffic controllers. The plane took off at 7:59 a.m. and headed west, over the Adirondacks, before taking a sudden turn south and diving down toward the heart of New York City. Meanwhile American Flight 757 had left Dulles; United Flight 175 left Boston at 7:58, and United Flight 93 left Newark three minutes later, bound for San Francisco. All four planes on transcontinental flights, plump with fuel, ripe to explode. "They couldn't carry anything—other than an atom bomb—that could be as bad as what they were flying," observed a veteran investigator.

The first plane hit the World Trade Center's north tower at 8:45, ripping through the building's skin and setting its upper floors ablaze. People thought it was a sonic boom, or a construction accident, or freak lightning on a lovely fall day; at worst, a horrible airline accident, a plane losing altitude, out of control, a pilot trying to ditch in the river and missing. But as the gruesome rains came—bits of plane, a tire, office furniture, glass, a hand, a leg, whole bodies began falling all around—people in the streets all stopped and looked, and fell silent. As the smoke rose, the ash rained gently down, along with a whole lost flock of paper shuffling down from the sky to the street below, edges charred, plane tickets and account statements and bills and reports and volumes and volumes of unfinished business floating down to earth.

Almost instantly, a distant wail of sirens came from all directions, even as people poured from the building, even as a second plane bore down on lower Manhattan. Louis Garcia was among the first medics on the scene. "There were people running over to us burnt from head to toe. Their hair was burned off. There were compound fractures, arms and legs sticking out of the skin." Of the six patients in his first ambulance run, two died on the way to St. Vincent's Hospital.

The survivors of the first plot to bring down the Twin Towers, the botched attempt in 1993 that left six dead, had a great advantage over their colleagues. When the first explosion came, they knew to get out. Others were paralyzed by the noise, confused by the instructions. Consultant Andy Perry still has the reflexes. He grabbed his pal Nathan Shields from his office, and they began to run down 46 flights. With each passing floor more and more people joined the flow down the steps. The lights stayed on, but the lower stairs were filled with water from burst pipes and sprinklers. "Everyone watch your step," people called out. "Be careful!" The smell of jet fuel suffused the building. Hallways collapsed, flames shot out of a men's room. By the time they reached the lobby, they just wanted to get out—but the streets didn't look any safer. "It was chaos out there," Shields says. "Finally we ran for it."

They raced into the street in time to see the second plane bearing down. Even as they ran away, there were still people standing around in the lobby waiting to be told what to do. "There were no emergency announcements—it just happened so quickly nobody knew what was going on," says Perry. "This guy we were talking to saw at least 12 people jumping out of [the tower] because of the fires. He was standing next to a guy who got hit by shrapnel and was immediately killed." Workers tore off their shirts to make bandages and tourniquets for the wounded; others used bits of clothing as masks to help them breathe. Whole stretches of street were slick with blood, and up and down the avenues you could hear the screams of people plunging from the burning tower. People watched in horror as a man tried to shimmy down the outside of the tower. He made it about three floors before flipping backward to the ground.

Gilbert Richard Ramirez works for BlueCross BlueShield on the 20th floor of the north tower. After the explosion he ran to the windows and saw the debris falling, and sheets of white building material, and then something else. "There was a body. It looked like a man's body, a full-size man." Someone pulled an emergency alarm switch, but nothing happened. Someone else broke into the emergency phone, but it was dead. People began to say their prayers.

"Relax, we're going to get out of here," Ramirez said. "I was telling them, 'Breathe, breathe, Christ is on our side, we're gonna get out of here.' " He prodded everyone out the door, herding stragglers. It was an eerie walk down the smoky stairs, a path to safety that ran through the suffering. They saw people who had been badly burned. Their skin, he says, "was like a grayish color, and it was like dripping, or peeling, like the skin was peeling off their body." One woman was screaming. "She said she lost her friend, her friend went out the window, a gust sucked her out." As they descended, they were passed by fire fighters and rescue workers, panting, pushing their way up the stairs in their heavy boots and gear. "At least 50 of them must have passed us," says Ramirez. "I told them, 'Do a good job.' " He pauses. "I saw those guys one time, but they're not gonna be there again." When he got outside to the street there were bodies scattered on the ground, and then another came plummeting, and another. "Every time I looked up at the building, somebody was jumping from it. Like from 107, Windows on the World. There was one, and then another one. I couldn't understand their jumping. I guess they couldn't see any hope."

Desks and chairs and people were sucked out the windows and rained down on the streets below. Men and women, cops and fire fighters watched and wept. As fire and debris fell, cars blew up; the air smelled of smoke and concrete, that smell that spits out of jackhammers chewing up pavement. You could taste the air more easily than you could breathe it.

The first crash had changed everything; the second changed it again. Anyone who thought the first was an accident now knew better. This was not some awful, isolated episode, not Oklahoma City, not even the first World Trade Center bombing. Now this felt like a war, and the system responded accordingly; the emergency plans came out of the drawers and clicked one by one into place. The city buckled, the traffic stopped, the bridges and tunnels were shut down at 9:35 as warnings tumbled one after another; the Empire State Building was evacuated, and the Metropolitan Museum of Art, the United Nations. First the New York airports were closed, then Washington's, and then the whole country was grounded for the first time in history.

AT THE MOMENT THE second plane was slamming into the south tower, President Bush was being introduced to the second-graders of Emma E. Booker Elementary in Sarasota, Fla. As he was getting ready to pose for pictures with the teachers and kids, chief of staff Andy Card entered the room, walked over to the President and whispered in his right ear. The President's face became visibly tense and serious. He nodded. Card left and for several minutes the President seemed distracted and somber, but then he resumed his interaction with the class. "Really good readers, whew!" he told them. "These must be sixth-graders!"

Meanwhile, in the room where Bush was scheduled to give his remarks, about 200 people, including local officials, school personnel and students, waited under the hot lights. Word of the crash began to circulate; reporters called their editors, but details were sparse—until someone remembered there was a TV in a nearby office. The President finally entered, about 35 minutes late, and made his brief comments. "This is a difficult time for America," he began. He ordered a massive investigation to "hunt down the folks who committed this act."

Even as the President spoke, the second front opened. Having hit the country's financial and cultural heart, the killers went for its political and military muscles. David Marra, 23, an information-technology specialist, had turned his BMW off an I-395 exit to the highway just west of the Pentagon when he saw an American Airlines jet swooping in, its wings wobbly, looking like it was going to slam right into the Pentagon: "It was 50 ft. off the deck when he came in. It sounded like the pilot had the throttle completely floored. The plane rolled left and then rolled right. Then he caught an edge of his wing on the ground." There is a helicopter pad right in front of the side of the Pentagon. The wing touched there, then the plane cartwheeled into the building.

Two minutes later, a "credible threat" forced the evacuation of the White House, and eventually State and Justice and all the federal office buildings. Secret Service officers had automatic weapons drawn as they patrolled Lafayette Park, across from the White House. Police-car radios crackled with reports that rogue airplanes had been spotted over the White House. The planes turned out to be harmless civilian aircraft that air-traffic controllers at National Airport were scrambling to help land so they could clear the air space over the nation's capital.

But that was not all; there was a third front as well. At 9:58 the Westmoreland County emergency-operations center, 35 miles southeast of Pittsburgh, received a frantic cell-phone call from a man who said he was locked in the restroom aboard United Flight 93. Glenn Cramer, the dispatch supervisor, said the man was distraught and kept repeating, "We are being hijacked! We are being hijacked!"

The flight had taken off at 8:01 from Newark, N.J., bound for San Francisco. But as it passed south of Cleveland, Ohio, it took a sudden, violent left turn and headed inexplicably back into Pennsylvania. As the 757 and its 38 passengers and seven crew members blew past Pittsburgh, air-traffic controllers tried frantically to raise the crew via radio. There was no response.

The rogue plane soared over woodland, cattle pastures and cornfields until it passed over Kelly Leverknight's home. Her husband, on his regular tour of duty with the Air National Guard's 167th Airlift Wing in Martinsburg, W.Va., had just called to reassure his wife that his base was still operating normally when she heard the plane rush by. "It was headed toward the school," she said, the school where her three children were.

Had Flight 93 stayed aloft a few seconds longer, it would have plowed into Shanksville-Stonycreek School and its 501 students, grades K through 12. Instead, at 10:06 a.m., the plane smashed into a reclaimed section of an old coal strip mine. The largest pieces of the plane still extant are barely bigger than a telephone book. "I just keep thinking—two miles," said elementary principal Rosemarie Tipton. "There but for the grace of God—two miles."

Vice President Dick Cheney was in his West Wing office when the Secret Service burst in, physically hurrying him out of the room. "We have to move; we're moving now, Sir; we're moving," the agents said as they took him to a bunker on the White House grounds. Once there, with members of the National Security staff and Administration officials, they told Cheney that a plane was headed for the White House. Mrs. Cheney and Laura Bush were brought in as well.

Washington was supposed to have contingency plans for disasters like this, but the chaos on the streets was clear evidence that plans still needed work. By 10:45 a.m. the downtown streets around the Capitol, government buildings and White House were laced with cars pointing in every direction, unable to move. A security officer for one of the buildings sat on a park bench. He had been locked out of his building, so he didn't have a clue if the senior officials inside were out and in a safe place. "I'm not surprised at this," he said. "We aren't prepared. We were supposed to have a plan to evacuate our Cabinet officer to a place 50 miles out, but none of that has been done."

Senator Robert Byrd, the Senate's president pro tempore and fourth in line to the presidency, was put in a chauffeured car and driven to a safe house, as were Speaker Dennis Hastert and other congressional leaders. There were rumors flying that the fourth plane, the one that went down in Pennsylvania, had been headed for the Capitol or Camp David. The Secret Service has similar safe houses where they can take the Vice President and other top Administration officials as well. They are homes, offices, in some cases even fire stations, that have secure phones so that the leaders can still communicate.

Meanwhile, the mood on board Air Force One could not have been more tense. Bush was in his office in the front of the plane, on the phone with Cheney, National Security Adviser Rice, FBI director Robert Mueller and the First Lady. Cheney told him that law-enforcement and security agencies believed the White House and Air Force One were both targets. Bush, the Vice President insisted, should head to a safe military base as soon as possible. The plane's TV monitors were tuned in to local news broadcasts; Bush was watching as the second tower collapsed. About 45 minutes after takeoff, a decision was made to fly to Offut Air Force Base in Nebraska, site of the nation's nuclear command and one of the most secure military installations in the country.

IN NEW YORK, THE chaos was only beginning. Convoys of police vehicles raced downtown toward the cloud of smoke at the end of the avenues. The streets and parks filled with people, heads turned like sunflowers, all gazing south, at the clouds that were on the ground instead of in the sky, at the fighter jets streaking down the Hudson River.

Jim Gartenberg, 35, a commercial real estate broker with an office on the 86th floor of 1 World Trade Center, kept calling his wife Jill to let her know he was O.K. but trapped. "He let us know he was stuck," says Jill, who is pregnant with their second child. "He called several times until 10. Then nothing. He sounded calm, except for when he told me how much he loved me. He said, 'I don't know if I'll make it.' He sounded like he knew it would be one of the last times he would say he loved me." That was right before the building turned to powder.

The tower's structural strength came largely from the 244 steel girders that formed the perimeter of each floor and bore most of the weight of all the floors above. Steel starts to bend at 1000°. The floors above where the plane hit—each floor weighing millions of pounds—were resting on steel that was softening from the heat of the burning jet fuel, softening until the girders could no longer bear the load above. "All that steel turns into spaghetti," explains retired ATF investigator Ronald Baughn. "And then all of a sudden that structure is untenable, and the weight starts bearing down on floors that were not designed to hold that weight, and you start having collapse." Each floor drops onto the one below, the weight becoming greater and greater, and eventually it all comes down.

The south tower collapsed at 10, fulfilling the prophecy of eight years ago, when last the terrorists tried to bring it down. The north tower came down 29 minutes later, crushing itself like a piston. All that was left of the New York skyline was a chalk cloud. The towers themselves were reduced to jagged stumps; the atrium lobby arches looked like a bombed-out cathedral.

The streets filled with masked men and women, cloth and clothing torn to tie across their noses and mouths against the dense debris rain. Some streets were eerily quiet. All trading had stopped on Wall Street, so those canyons were empty, the ash several inches thick and gray, the way snow looks in New York almost before it hits the ground. Sounds were both muffled and magnified, echoing off buildings, softened by the smoke. You could hear the chirping of the locator devices the fire fighters wear, hear the whistle of the respirators, see only the lights flashing red and yellow through the haze.

Mayor Giuliani took to the streets, walking through the raining dust and ordering people to evacuate the entire lower end of the island. Medical teams performed triage on the streetcorners of Tribeca, doling out medical supplies and tending the walking wounded. Police and fire fighters realized even as they worked that hundreds of their colleagues, the first to respond, were dead.

The refugee march began at the base of the island and wound up the highways as far as you could see, tens of thousands of people with clothes dusted, faces grimy, marching northward, away from the battlefield. There was not a single smile on a single face. But there was remarkably little panic as well—more steel and ingenuity: Where am I going to sleep tonight? How will I get home? "They can't keep New Jersey closed forever," a man said. Restaurant-supply companies on the Bowery handed out wet towels. A cement mixer drove toward the Queensboro Bridge with dozens of laborers holding onto it, hitching a ride out of town. Overcrowded buses, one after another, shipped New York's workers north. Ambulances, some covered with debris, sped past them, ferrying the injured to the waiting hospitals.

There were no strangers in town anymore, only sudden friends, sharing names, news and phones. Lines formed, at least 20 people long, at all pay phones, because cell phones were not working. Should we go to work? Is the subway safe? "Let's all have a good look at each other," a passenger said to the others in her car. "We may be our last memory."

At St. Vincent's Hospital in Greenwich Village they were running out of Silvadene to treat burn victims, and began raiding the local drug stores. A hospital staff member wheeled around a grocery cart with a sign on the side reading WE NEED CLOTHING DONATIONS. Within the hour, local residents had brought dozens of shopping bags full of blazers, shoes and pants for patients whose clothes had been burned off.

Outside the N.Y. Blood Center, the line of prospective donors stretched halfway down the block, around the corner, all the way to 66th Street and around that corner—more than a thousand, all told. Type O donors, the universal donors, were handed little yellow movie tickets and asked to form a separate line. Eventually some blood centers turned everyone else away, told them to come back another day. "It's just amazing," said nurse Anne Taylor, standing in the donors' line. "There'll be a three- or four-hour wait, and just look at all of these people standing here."

Meanwhile, the U.S. government reassembled and mobilized. Secretary of State Colin Powell cut short his trip to Latin America to return to the U.S. By mid-afternoon, members of Congress were calling on their leaders to summon a special session, to show the world the government was up and running. Eavesdroppers at the supersecret National Security Agency had picked up at least two electronic intercepts indicating the terrorists had ties to Osama bin Laden. By nightfall, less than 12 hours after the attacks, U.S. officials told TIME that their sense that he was involved had got closer to what one senior official said was 90%. U.S. intelligence believes a bin Laden cell in Florida was a support group helping with the aviation aspects of the attack.

It was clear that some things had changed forever. The attacks will become a defining reference point for our culture and imagination, a question of before and after, safe and scarred. When one world ended at 8:45 on Tuesday morning, another was born, one we always trust in but never see, in which normal people become fierce heroes and everyone takes a test for which they haven't studied. As President Bush said in his speech to the nation, we are left with both a terrible sadness and a quiet unyielding anger. He was wrong, though, to talk of the steel of our resolve. Steel, we now know, bends and melts; we need to be made of something stronger than that now—not excluding an unseasoned President new to his job.

Do we now panic, or will we be brave? Once the dump trucks and bulldozers have cleared away the rubble and a thousand funeral Masses have been said, once the streets are swept clean of ash and glass and the stores and monuments and airports reopen, once we have begun to explain this to our children and to ourselves, what will we do? What else but build new cathedrals, and if they are bombed, build some more. Because the faith is in the act of building, not the building itself, and no amount of terror can keep us from scraping the sky. ■

—REPORTED BY THE STAFF OF TIME MAGAZINE

Portrait of a Platoon

BY ROMESH RATNESAR
AND MICHAEL WEISSKOPF

[*Only after coalition forces took Iraq did the war
there enter its most difficult phase. The writers spent
three weeks with U.S. troops in Baghdad, sharing their
daily lives, their dangers, their losses*]

December 29, 2003

THE PATROL HAS LASTED an hour, the three humvees slashing and darting through hairpin turns and blind
alleyways, looking for attackers. It's 9 o'clock on a clear,
mild December night in Adhamiya, one of Baghdad's oldest
neighborhoods and these days among the most restive. The
soldiers are out to draw fire. They cruise the streets and make
themselves targets in order to flush insurgents into the open.

But they encounter nothing. So now the convoy is heading back to base,
a mile away. The platoon rolls into Adhamiya's main marketplace. The atmosphere is festive. Patrons of the teahouses and restaurants overflow
onto the one-lane street. Traffic is running in both directions, and the convoy slows to a crawl. Just across Imam Street, the district's main thoroughfare, sits the Abu Hanifa mosque, where Saddam Hussein was last seen in
public before his arrest by U.S. forces. A large crowd of Iraqis mills outside
it. Private First Class Jim Beverly, 19, and Private Orion Jenks, 22, stand in
the bed of the convoy's second vehicle, a roofless high-back humvee, which
resembles a large pickup truck and is generally used to transport troops.
Also riding in the back are two TIME journalists. As the convoy begins
moving again, Jenks and Beverly chat casually and laugh. Sergeant Ronald

Buxton, who is riding shotgun in the cab of the high-back, whips around. "I don't care if you joke or if you smoke," he tells the privates, "but make sure you watch our back."

The vehicles cross Imam Street and move toward the mosque. TIME senior correspondent Michael Weisskopf glances up at the mosque's clock tower, damaged by U.S. tank shells during a fierce battle in April. As he does, he hears a clunk and sees that an oval-shaped object has landed on the seat beside him. For a split second he thinks it's a rock, then he realizes it isn't. He reaches to throw it out. Suddenly there is a flash. The object explodes in Weisskopf's hand.

Shrapnel ricochets off the walls of the humvee, hitting Beverly, Jenks and TIME photographer James Nachtwey. Smoke rises from the high-back. Blood pours from Weisskopf's right arm; when he holds it up, he realizes the grenade has blown off his hand. Specialist Billie Grimes, a medic attached to the platoon, sprints out of the third humvee and hoists herself onto the high-back. She uses a Velcro strap tied to her pant leg as a tourniquet to stop Weisskopf's bleeding and applies a field dressing to the wound while loudly asking the three other passengers if they are injured. Nachtwey, who has taken shrapnel in his left arm, abdomen and both legs, briefly snaps pictures of Grimes treating Weisskopf before losing consciousness. For several seconds Jenks slumps motionless, stunned, but then instinctively slides his gun's safety to semiautomatic, preparing to return fire. Only later does he learn that shrapnel has fractured his leg.

The convoy halts in front of the mosque. Buxton turns around. "Are there any casualties?" he asks. "Yes! Yes!" replies Beverly. Shrapnel has hit him in the right hand and right knee. Two of his front teeth have been knocked out, and his tongue is lacerated. "Let's go!" he says. "Let's go!" The humvees peel out and roar for home.

This is not the war this Army unit—officially known as the Survey Platoon, Headquarters Battery, 2nd Battalion, 3rd Field Artillery Regiment of the 1st Armored Division—was trained to fight. On a traditional battlefield, field-artillery survey units stay behind the front lines and use gyroscopic devices to measure the distance to enemy positions so the Army's big guns can hit their targets. That was the job this platoon, based in Giessen, Germany, pictured for itself when it received deployment orders in March, before the start of the war with Iraq. The group, now nicknamed the "Tomb Raiders," was told to prepare for combat in the event of a prolonged siege of Baghdad. That battle never came. The platoon reached the capital in late May, nearly a month after President Bush declared the end of major combat operations. But the demands of the occupation of Iraq forced the Tomb Raiders to assume the duties of infantrymen—patrolling streets, conducting raids, hunting insurgents and imposing order in one of the most volatile neighborhoods of Baghdad. In that respect, the platoon embodies the ways in which the 120,000 American men and women in arms serving in Iraq have had to adapt to the evolving challenges of making the country secure.

Drawn from disparate backgrounds, the platoon's members provide a portrait of the military's diversity as well as insight into the motivations—and fears—of America's fighting forces. Its soldiers include Sergeant Marquette Whiteside, 24, an African-American gunner who pines for his 6-year-old daughter; Specialist Sky Schermerhorn, 29, an idealist now gnawed by doubt about what he is fighting for; and Buxton, 32, a brainy Gulf War I veteran who since being deployed has taught himself Arabic and missed the birth of a son. Specialist Bernard Talimeliyor, 24, a native of the U.S. protectorate of Yap, Micronesia, was so moved by the events of 9/11 that he decided to enlist, even though he had never seen mainland U.S. Two noncommissioned officers, Staff Sergeant Abe Winston, 42, and Sergeant David Kamont, 34, serve as mentors to the platoon's three youngest G.I.s, Private Lequine Arnold, 20, an African American from Goldsboro, N.C.; Beverly, an amateur artist from Akron, Ohio; and Jenks, who joined the platoon in late November. Grimes, 26, the only female soldier attached to the unit, maintains a steely grit around the guys but cries on the phone to her father when she talks about what she has witnessed in Iraq. Sergeant José Cesar Aparicio, 31, a reservist, heads a psychological-operations team attached to the platoon. The leader of the Tomb Raiders, First Lieutenant Brady Van Engelen, 24, took over command two months ago and is still fighting for his soldiers' respect.

In three weeks with the Tomb Raiders, over the course of 30 patrols with the unit and sister platoons, TIME journalists witnessed the tedium and the terror, the sacrifice and resolve that epitomize the lives of G.I.s across Iraq. Like thousands of Americans in this war, the Tomb Raiders have absorbed losses that have changed their lives forever. Theirs is the story of what the Army looks like today and what this war has become.

Nov. 25: Marquette Whiteside is standing up in the gunner's hatch, swinging his machine gun in the direction of the Iraqis who stop to watch as the Americans drive by. The two-vehicle convoy curls past the Adhamiya police station and heads north along the Tigris River, which bounds the neighborhood on two sides. Of the 88 sectors in Baghdad, Adhamiya is rated by the U.S. command among the six most dangerous for coalition forces. The 1.2-sq.-mi. area is home to 400,000 people, most of them Sunni Muslims. The anti-American graffiti that blankets the walls of neighborhood buildings attests to the strong resistance to the U.S. presence here. Spray-painted in Arabic and English, it reads DOWN USA. LONG LIVE SADDAM. YES TO MARTYRDOM FOR THE SAKE OF IRAQ.

The platoon stops on a largely deserted road along the river and sets up a checkpoint. After fruitlessly searching a dozen cars for weapons, the Tomb Raiders head home. Whiteside unloads his gear and lays his machine gun next to his cot, which sits below a gallery of pictures of half-clad women clipped from magazines. "It's like *Groundhog Day*," he says. "It's the same thing every day. You just don't know whether you're going to live or die."

Nov. 26: Sky Schermerhorn writes his name on a tile wall in the common area that serves as a reservation sheet for the platoon's single Internet terminal. Most members of the platoon communicate daily with family members through e-mail. The Tomb Raiders' two-story house—the hooch, as the G.I.s call it—lies within the perimeter of the Azimiya palace compound, built by Saddam in the mid-1990s for his oldest son Uday. It can be eerily antisocial, largely because today's G.I. can spend so much time in front of TV and computer screens. Schermerhorn spends the next hour instant messaging his girlfriend of three months, Nicole, a German he met while based in Giessen. The two speak three times a week on a satellite phone, and Schermerhorn tape-records 90-minute soliloquies for her when he is on guard duty. But he doesn't tell her everything. "I have to be cautious to preserve her sanity," he says. "If she knew what we did every day, she couldn't sleep at night."

Nov. 27: The platoon lives in two worlds—one beyond the steel coils that drape the compound, where the soldiers rely on one another to survive, and one "inside the wire," where they struggle to find space of their own. "Out here, I'd take a bullet for any one of these guys," says Schermerhorn. "But there are probably three people here I'd give a s___ about keeping in touch with when I get home." Says Whiteside: "We get on each other's nerves because we see each other every day. But being stuck with someone 24/7, all there is to do is talk. Basically, it's like one big dysfunctional family."

Outside the wire, the dysfunction ends. Everyone attributes the unit's cohesion to the man who became their platoon leader shortly after they arrived in Baghdad, Second Lieutenant Benjamin Colgan, 30. He was originally attached to the Tomb Raiders' battalion as a chemical and biological officer, responsible for managing preparations for unconventional attacks. But that position is a desk job, and Colgan, a 12-year veteran of the special forces, longed to be on the streets. "Use my skills," he told Lieut. Colonel William Rabena, the battalion's commanding officer. At the time, the Tomb Raiders were leaderless, their original commander having remained in Germany for the birth of his first child, so Colgan got the job.

Colgan was determined to transform the platoon into a combat unit that could handle street patrols and raids on enemy safe houses, neither of which the Tomb Raiders had ever conducted. And so the hooch became a training center. Every afternoon the platoon practiced close-quarters combat and house-clearing techniques in the basement. Colgan rearranged the furniture to simulate different settings and ordered three $300 battering rams for kicking in doors. "Get in loud, fast and violent," he told them, while insisting that they treat those they found inside with respect. "They're young, they're new," Colgan wrote of the platoon in an e-mail to his sister Liz. "But they're doing good."

Over the next three months, the platoon conducted more than 40 raids on houses of suspected insurgents and former members of Saddam's regime in Adhamiya. In July, Colgan led the platoon on midnight searches of a Muslim cemetery next to the Abu Hanifa mosque, where insurgents were believed to be storing weapons. Colgan instructed the soldiers to bang the lid of each crypt; if it sounded hollow, the troops hoisted the 250-lb. granite slab and looked inside. On its second graveyard hunt, on July 4, the platoon netted a rocket-propelled-grenade launcher and 31 RPGs. A later search turned up a stash of the explosive C4. Afterward, the platoon nicknamed itself the Tomb Raiders.

Colgan's most valuable asset was his skill at gathering intelligence. He cultivated informants on the streets and dined in the houses of new Iraqi friends. He memorized the names, residences and descriptions of top Baathists. On patrols, Colgan tirelessly chatted up locals, recording their complaints in a green notebook he kept in a Ziploc bag. "When that notebook comes out," Schermerhorn says, "we know we're going to be there another hour."

With Colgan at the helm, the platoon's morale soared. Even in 130° heat, the Tomb Raiders sometimes ran patrols five times a day on four hours' sleep. No one minded. "There are very few people who can break into your house, arrest your husband and then by the time he leaves, have everyone waving and smiling. It takes a special person," says Whiteside. "We all thought, This cat is invincible."

Dec. 1: Ronald Buxton walks into the hooch and slumps onto the sofa, exhausted. "I just made the call," he tells Sergeant Kamont. In August Buxton's wife Audrey gave birth to the couple's second child, Jared. Buxton was scheduled to leave Iraq this month to see the baby for the first time, but he received word in November that his redeployment had been delayed two months. Tonight he delivered the news to Audrey over a satellite phone. She and the couple's 7-year-old son broke down crying.

When they are inside the wire, Buxton and the rest of the soldiers in the platoon wrestle with how much to tell their families about the risks of life outside it. Grimes keeps the worst details out of her letters to avoid worrying her mother. The really "bad stuff" she saves for phone conversations with her dad. Buxton says his wife "knows I'm here, but she doesn't know specifics. She knows what she doesn't know." Which means she does not know any of the details of the night of Nov. 1.

IN THE RUN-UP TO that date, insurgents were increasingly attacking military convoys with homemade bombs known as improvised explosive devices (IEDs)—typically, munitions disguised as roadside trash and detonated by remote control. By the beginning of Ramadan in late October, the 2nd Battalion was finding five IEDs a week in Adhamiya. At the same time, the palace compound was taking fire from mortars and rocket-propelled grenades nearly every night. On Oct. 31, after a mortar attack on the palace injured two soldiers, the Tomb Raiders combed the streets of Adhamiya looking for the perpetrators. They came up empty, but Colgan believed he had obtained a fix on the coordinates of a suspected insurgent cell leader.

On the night of Nov. 1, an RPG landed inside the walls of the palace. Members of a sister platoon to the Tomb Raiders were on patrol at the time and opened fire on a vehicle they believed had launched the grenade, but the car got away. The Tomb Raiders loaded into three humvees and joined the chase, Colgan riding shotgun in the lead vehicle and Schermerhorn driving. When the convoy reached a bridge leading out of Adhamiya, Colgan told Schermerhorn to swing around to cut off traffic going toward it. His window was down.

As the vehicle turned, an explosion went off under the humvee's right tire. "It felt like we hit a boulder," Schermerhorn recalls. "A shock wave went through the vehicle." Whiteside, who was in the gunner's turret, was knocked unconscious by the blast and fell onto Buxton's lap. Buxton patted him in the dark, feeling for blood, but found none. As Whiteside righted himself, Schermerhorn waited for Colgan's instructions. But Colgan was unconscious. Blood poured out of the left side of his forehead. His eye was bulging and purplish. "Get him home!" Buxton yelled.

Schermerhorn sped away, the humvee's flat tire flapping crazily. Whiteside climbed out of the turret and began trying to resuscitate the lieutenant. Colgan made a gurgling sound. He has a wife and kids, Whiteside thought. We've got to keep him alive. Colgan's eyes were open when the three soldiers carried him into the aid station inside the palace compound. Two special-forces medics began to stabilize him. They asked Colgan his name. "Ben," he said. "What happened?" The medics performed a tracheotomy to help him breathe. Colgan's face was covered in blood, and his eye was protruding out of its socket, but his pulse was stable. A medevac helicopter took Colgan to the 28th Combat Support Hospital in central Baghdad. Grimes reported that Colgan was responsive and that his eye had been damaged but it might be salvageable.

What Grimes did not know was that shrapnel had penetrated all the way to the back of Colgan's head. By the time the chopper reached the hospital, Colgan was brain-dead. He was kept alive by a respirator while Rabena, who had driven to the hospital, completed paperwork that promoted him to first lieutenant and gave him a "medical retirement"—a step that allows his family to receive more generous benefits.

At 8:30 a.m., the platoon was told to fall into the horseshoe formation that commanders use to disclose personal information to troops. Captain Mike Kielpinski, the Tomb Raiders' battery commander, sobbed as he broke the news of Colgan's death. Talimeliyor ran back to his cot, disconsolate. "I didn't read my Bible," he remembers. "I didn't wash my clothes. I just wanted to lay in my bed." Whiteside recalls, "I cried for the first day and a half." The rest of the platoon went numb. Says Beverly: "Everything just died. All sounds stopped."

The soldiers still have to remind themselves that he is gone. His name remains on the satellite-phone bill the platoon updates on a wall of the hooch. "Sometimes I think that I'll wake up," Whiteside says, "and that he's going to walk through the door and get his coffee and watch SportsCenter.

And he'll say good morning, and I'll ask him how he's doing. And then I realize, that's never going to happen again."

Dec. 2: A desert chill cuts through the air as the Tomb Raiders prepare for a pre-dawn raid. The target house belongs to a man called Abu Taha, a former officer in the Fedayeen Saddam militia who is suspected of organizing attacks against the Americans. In the month since Colgan's death, the soldiers have been slow to warm to his replacement, Van Engelen, a stolid, tobacco-spitting 24-year-old who lacks his predecessor's charisma. "I still ain't used to him," mutters Whiteside. "There's a difference of experience." As the Tomb Raiders grease their guns and pack flashlights and zip-ties (for cuffing hands) into their flak vests, Winston, the platoon's weathered senior sergeant, briefs them on Abu Taha, a middle-aged, overweight man who may be a "major supplier" of weapons to the insurgents. The room falls silent as Winston outlines evacuation procedures in the event that the troops encounter resistance at the house. Since Colgan's death, Winston says, the platoon's anxiety has grown. Every piece of trash now looks like a hidden bomb. "Everyone is afraid," he says. "If they're not, they're lying. People are cringing." Some soldiers have turned to God. Whiteside reads Scripture and recites the Lord's Prayer before leaving the gates.

The loss of Colgan has tested another kind of faith—the belief that their mission in Iraq is worth the ultimate sacrifice. "It's hard to see headway," Schermerhorn says. "The same guys who are waving at you and saying 'Good Bush' are firing at us. I'd like to see these people enjoy what I have on a daily basis. But I don't know that anything we've accomplished since we've been here was worth the L.T.'s life or—thinking about it—my own."

The raid on the house of Abu Taha kicks off just before 2 a.m. Driving without lights, the platoon moves past the Abu Hanifa mosque and pulls up in front of a darkened one-story structure. A three-man "breach team" hurdles the front wall and attempts to force its way into the house. It takes Schermerhorn 10 tries before he finally smashes open the metal door with a battering ram. In the front room, the breach team finds a woman sitting calmly on the floor with her three children. She identifies herself as Abu Taha's wife and says she has not seen him in a year. The soldiers search the house but find no sign of an adult male. Finally, Van Engelen apologizes and tells the woman the Army will replace her front door, and will give her one three times as nice if she brings her husband by the compound. She thanks him. "My daughters gave your soldiers flowers," she says. "We love the Americans very much."

Dec. 5: Sergeant Aparicio is a popular guy. As his vehicle rolls through a graceful old neighborhood on the northern edge of Adhamiya, hordes of children chase after him, grabbing for the U.S.-produced Arabic news-papers and leaflets he is passing out to locals through his window. As head of the reservist psychological-operations team attached to the Tomb Raiders' battalion, Aparicio is responsible for canvassing the area, hand-ing out pro-U.S. literature and listening to the complaints of residents. When he stops at a teahouse in a peaceful, predominantly Shi'ite area of Adhamiya, locals surround him and deluge him with complaints about the lack of electricity, shortage of medical supplies, chronic unemployment and high price of gas. Aparicio listens patiently, jotting down each petition in his notebook and promising to report them to his superiors. The crowds thank him and wish him well. As Aparicio climbs back into his humvee, he shakes his head. "We're going to hear the same thing all day," he says. "It's just a circle. You can never give enough."

The mood on the street darkens as Aparicio's convoy heads down Imam Street, the Sunni heart of Adhamiya. "You are animals!" a shop owner shouts at the soldiers. At one point Aparicio hands a newspaper to a well-dressed elderly man, who looks at it, tears it up and tosses it back at the humvee. Aparicio shrugs. "The people who are going to be won over have been won over," he says. "We've been here so long that we're not go-ing to get anyone new on our side."

Dec. 10: In response to a mortar attack the previous night, the battal-ion commanders decide to flood Adhamiya with troops from four batteries to deny the insurgents territory to fire from. The Tomb Raiders are told to move out at 8 p.m., around the time when mortar attacks typically occur. It is on the return trip from this mission that Jenks, Beverly and the two TIME journalists are wounded.

Dec. 12: Beverly and Jenks are recovering from surgery in the inten-sive-care ward of the 28th Combat Support Hospital in Baghdad. Both show visitors plastic cups that contain shrapnel fragments removed from their bodies. There is no bitterness or self-pity. Says Beverly: "You've al-ways got to expect the worst, and I'm glad that's not what happened." Jenks is more frustrated about leaving Iraq so soon after arriving. "I didn't have a chance to do anything positive or productive," he says. The Tomb Raiders are now stretched thin. With Beverly likely to remain out-side of Iraq for the rest of the deployment and Whiteside preparing for reassignment to another unit, only six soldiers who were part of the platoon when it was constituted in Kuwait will still be in the country in 2004. Tonight is a test of their fortitude. "We're trying something different," Van Engelen tells the Tomb Raiders as they gather around a gray satellite map of Adhamiya, preparing for their first patrol since the grenade attack. Van Engelen believes that the platoon will draw less attention without the humvees. The soldiers can hardly remember when they last did a foot patrol of any kind, and this will be the first one they have ever done at night. Van Engelen wants the soldiers to walk in a cigar-shaped formation, rather than the typical V, so they can stay in the shadows on one side of the street. He tells them that if they spot anything suspicious, they have approval to shoot. "I'm telling you right now," he says, "if you can ID the target, you don't have to wait for your buddy to do the same thing."

The soldiers line up, cinching down their vests and adjusting their packs, checking the action on their rifles. Then they open the door and head out onto the street.

Dec. 14: Like all the other American soldiers in Iraq, the members of the platoon have been tempered by the fires of the occupation, the raw emotions of war now forged into something harder and more durable. The news of Saddam's capture on this day is a jolt of euphoria for the Tomb Raiders, but it does little to alter their cool assessment of the perils ahead. "This country is still up for grabs, as far as these people are concerned," says Schermerhorn. "It's still going to be crazy around here for us."

Ultimately, that's where you discover the heroism of the soldiers serving in Iraq today—not so much in their battlefield bravery or the firmness of their resolve as in their acceptance of uncertainty and the courage of their restraint. "There is nobody to shoot back at. That's every soldier's biggest complaint," Buxton says. "But we are not cold-blooded killers. We are not going to kill innocent civilians. That's just a part of who we are." He thinks back to the grenade attack. "A couple of us saw some guys running away and thought about pulling the trigger. But when you see a guy running through a crowd, do you spray the crowd to get the guy? If in a situation like that you can control your impulse for revenge, then that means you are fighting for something larger." ∎

—WITH REPORTING BY BRIAN BENNETT/BAGHDAD,
MARGOT ROOSEVELT/LOS ANGELES,
ELI SANDERS/KENT AND MAGGIE SIEGER/CHICAGO

RAYON YARN ON SPOOLS, 1939, BY MARGARET BOURKE-WHITE

TIME

All
Business

Race of Three

BY RALPH D. PAINE JR. *

[
*Henry Ford had seen other companies surpass his own
in the industry he founded. But at 72, in the midst of the
Depression, he could still assert his pioneering spirit*
]

January 14, 1935

FORD MOTOR CO. IS a Delaware corporation. Its main plant—the most magnificent aggregation of industrial equipment in the modern world—is at River Rouge, Mich. At the start of last year it had assets of $639,000,000, over one-half of which was in cash or liquid paper. During the past 30 years it has sold more than 22,000,000 automobiles, approximately the total number on the road today. Its principal stockholder once turned down an offer of a billion dollars for the company as a going concern. Since it was founded in 1903 with $28,000 of paid-in capital, it has grossed a few hundred millions in excess of $11,000,000,000, retained as net gain nearly $800,000,000. No man in all history has made so much money so quickly or so cleanly as Henry Ford.

Mr. Ford is not an officer of Ford Motor Co. His only connection with the corporation is his ownership of 58½% of the stock and a seat on the board of directors. With him on the board sits his son, President Edsel Bryant Ford, who owns the rest of the stock, and Vice President Peter E. Martin, one of the few survivors of the countless upheavals in Ford

* Tentative identification

management. There is a secretary and assistant treasurer, and an assistant secretary of the corporation, but no other title within the whole Ford organization. Henry Ford does not believe in titles.

It takes an efficient executive staff to run a business whose payroll at one plant alone has been as high as 104,000 persons, whose purchases have run as high as $40,000,000 per month and whose operations include coal mines, glass factories, steel mills and a fleet of 37 ships. Yet the Ford staff is small. All the key men in the company can sit down together at a lunch table in a maple-paneled corner room at the Engineering Laboratory where the elder Ford makes his headquarters. There for counsel and advice go untitled Fordlings like William Cowling (sales), Albert M. Wibel (purchasing) and Charles Sorensen, hard-boiled superintendent of the mighty Rouge works.* Also high in Ford councils are William J. Cameron, Mr. Ford's official spokesman, and Harry H. Bennett, who handles personnel and directs Ford Motor's notoriously efficient police. But the one & only boss of Ford Motor Co. is Henry Ford.

Last week the spare, stooped grey-haired dean of the premier U. S. industry launched a 1935 edition of the Ford V-8, Model 48. And for the first time in his life he launched a model at the New York Automobile Show, No. 1 of the great fairs where the men from the motormaking provinces of the Midwest each year exhibit their newest and finest transportation wares.

Mr. Ford used to exhibit only Lincolns at the Automobile Shows because Lincoln was a member of the National Automobile Chamber of Commerce (now the Automobile Manufacturers Association) which sponsored the exhibits. But Ford, characteristically, never joined the industry's trade association. This year the show was staged not by the manufacturers but by their local dealers. Hence Mr. Ford exhibited. He sent cross-section displays, a team of two mechanics who could pull down a V-8 motor in six minutes, assemble it in ten, a cut-away car on a traveling belt which, when big blocks were tossed under its wheels, demonstrated what Ford calls "Center-Poise," balanced riding quality.

But what made the 1935 Fords more interesting than other Fords was the fact that their maker announced last autumn with considerable fanfare that he planned to sell 1,000,000 of them—"or better"—in the third year

---

* Once at the Rouge works, where sitting down is not encouraged, Superintendent Sorensen spied a workman squatting on a box fiddling with a length of wire. Up strode Mr. Sorensen, kicked the box from beneath the workman. When he got to his feet, the workman knocked Mr. Sorensen to the floor. "You're fired!" said Mr. Sorensen as he in turn uprose. "The hell I am," yelled the workman. "I work for the Bell Telephone Co."

of Roosevelt II. A dozen years ago when Chevrolet sales were 76,000 and Plymouth was not even an idea in Mr. Chrysler's head, Mr. Ford was turning out Model T's at the rate of 2,000,000 per year. But Chevrolet has outsold Ford in six of the past eight years, and the last million-car year at River Rouge was 1930. Last year Mr. Ford had a head start over Chevrolet, which was delayed by the tool & die strike. Yet in combined truck and passenger car sales Chevrolet again nosed out Ford.

Said Mr. Ford in 1933: "I don't know how many cars Chevrolet sold last year. I don't know how many they're selling this year. I don't know how many they may sell next year. And—I don't care."

Mr. Ford's indifference to his competitors is no pose. His sole interest is in building the best car he can for the money. To him merchandising is merely a necessary nuisance. If a person chooses to buy a Chevrolet or a Plymouth, the loss, Mr. Ford feels, is the buyer's, not his. Even the staggering deficits rolled up in the Depression—$132,000,000—do not bother him. It is, to Henry Ford, merely money "spent."

Mr. Ford's competitors, however, have stockholders to think of, and last year the Man of Dearborn increased his share of the national business from 20% in 1933 to 28% of all cars sold. Relatively, both Chevrolet and Plymouth lost ground. What they will do in 1935 no man knows.

Chevrolet is General Motors' biggest unit and the finest merchandising organization in the industry. The fact that President Marvin E. Coyle surmounted his early production difficulties and again pushed Chevrolet to the front of the field is generally regarded as the outstanding selling job of 1934. Now 48, dynamic, little-publicized President Coyle has been with G. M. for 23 years, 17 of them in Chevrolet. William S. Knudsen picked him as his successor when that all-round motorman stepped up to executive vice president of General Motors Corp.

Until 1928 when Plymouth was first marketed, Ford and Chevrolet had the low-priced field pretty much to themselves. Under B. Edwin Hutchinson, Plymouth board chairman and Chrysler vice president & treasurer, Plymouth has on at least one occasion pressed Ford hard for second place in the Big Three's race. And even last year Plymouth lost less ground to Ford than did Chevrolet. More notable, the man who has multiplied Plymouth's sales by five is one of the few crack motormen who did not rise from the bench. Mr. Hutchinson is primarily a financial man, having raised the money to keep old Maxwell Motor alive when Walter P. Chrysler was fashioning that company into a personal springboard.

Messrs. Coyle and Hutchinson certainly do not reciprocate Mr. Ford's indifference to competition but they are by no means in mortal terror of the Man of Dearborn. What they fear, if anything, is a new force evident in Ford merchandising. And that force is powered by Edsel Bryant Ford, 41, heir-apparent to the last and greatest personal empire of U. S. industry.

Ford advertising and promotion have always been spasmodic, and Ford dealers have usually been treated as a necessary evil. But in the past few years dealers' commissions have been boosted. Ford's advertising appropriation of about $8,000,000 in 1934 is supposed to have been boosted for 1935. Last year Ford sent a big exhibit to the second edition of the Chicago World's Fair and last week Ford sent Edsel to the Show in Manhattan, where he nervously munched cough drops through various salesmeetings. But the most impressive sign of Edsel's growing power is the 1935 Ford, a modern car in comfort and appearance as well as engineering.

Henry Ford will be 72 next July. A lean, lonely figure roaming through his museum or fiddling with his old music boxes, he has lived five years of Depression without apparent change. He is trying to decentralize the vastest concentration of industry the world has ever seen by establishing small accessory plants in rural districts where workers can live on the land. He and his lady are seen more frequently at Detroit social functions. His spat with the Administration over his stubborn refusal to sign the Automobile Code is forgiven & forgotten.

But when Henry Ford steps to a drawing board or tinkers with a Ford part the years drop away from his thin shoulders, and he seems a different person from the aging man who has an earthy platitude for every interviewer. Ruralist and antiquarian though he has become, the Henry Ford who in 1934 laid out $20,000,000 for plant expansion when Big Business was shivering for reassurances or who boldly announced that he would spend nearly $500,000,000 for wages and materials in 1935, is the Henry Ford who motorized the U. S.

Last month in Manhattan in answer to the uneasy rumbling voiced by businessmen at a Congress of American Industry, Donald Richberg taunted: "Unless the businessmen of America have been shell-shocked into nervous impotence, there must come a time when they will respond to the fighting spirit of that old admiral who signaled, 'Damn the torpedoes. Go ahead!'"

Henry Ford damned the torpedoes two months ago and has been going ahead ever since. ■

Women & Machines

BY ANNA NORTH

[*During World War II, as men joined the Armed Forces, women flooded into factory jobs. The workplace—and relations between the sexes—would never be the same*]

May 11, 1942

THE U.S. MANPOWER PROBLEM is rapidly coming round to the inevitable solution: womanpower. Slacks and hairnets dot the nation's warplants now—and thousands on thousands of women stand ready to rear munitions as well as children. The U.S. had no trouble in converting women to war—the problem was to get enough war work for the women to do.

Last week the President announced that registration of women for war work had to be abandoned because 1,500,000 women who want jobs are already registered at U.S. Employment Service offices. And of the 750,000 women who have applied for work in factories, only 79,000 can be absorbed by July 1, according to a survey of 12,500 plants which plan to take on 675,000 new workers by then.

Industry is taking on women workers slowly now. The rate must increase if the U.S. is to have a fighting force of 10,000,000 men. Employers find it impossible to save a man from his draft board, no matter what his industrial skill is. "Train another," has been the answer. Lately the answer often is: "Train a woman."

In Caldwell, N.J., a miss just out of high school carefully, quickly smoothes the edges of brass propeller-fittings. Three minutes are allotted to each fitting. In Detroit an ex-schoolmarm holds valve tappets for Wright engines to the light, and feels each one with her fingers. There must be no tiny scratch or rough spot—to wreck a plane, cost a life. In Ford's great bomber hatchery at Willow Run a woman flyer (Mary Elizabeth Von Mach) inspects motors for the big B-24s. In San Diego a young war widow strings numbered wires of an electrical sub-assembly, attaching the end of each to its proper terminal. In Dallas a bridge champion's wife assembles hydraulic devices which raise & lower landing gear. All her salary goes to war bonds. In Flint, Mich., a Polish girl carefully fastens the bolt of a .50-caliber machine gun in a grinder, adjusts a machine which smoothes its face. In a noisy Detroit cellar-school a mother of three works with a hand riveter—inserting rivets, inspecting them, and drilling them out if imperfect. And thousands of girls all over the U.S. are making small parts on machines, inspecting, filling shells, putting fabric on non-stress areas of bomber wings, bending tubing to fit into fuselages, making rubber boats, assembling machine guns and small arms. They work as long as ten hours a day on day, "swing," and "graveyard" shifts.

Patriotism is one feminine motive for war work. But the strongest is the pay. Even college-trained girls seldom hope for more than $25 a week on their first jobs. But war-factory jobs start at $25 to $40 a week and applicants need not have graduated from anything. After a training period—from two to six weeks—they are in.

Work in a war plant also has more charm for the female worker than work in an old-fashioned factory. Aircraft plants, for instance, are likely to be brand-new, one-floor, fluorescent-lighted places, with plenty of space. The atmosphere is air-conditioned and stimulating—signs, flags, mottoes, charts exhort speed and more speed. Machinery is compact, beltless, quiet. And management constantly concerns itself with worker morale.

War fever has removed the social stigma from factory work: many women enlisting for industry are nurses, teachers, saleswomen, even Junior Leaguers, who would not have dreamed of factory work a year ago. White-collar girls in plant offices ask for transfers to the shop, where life is "more exciting."

Women are no problem in such places as the AC Spark Plug in Flint, which has employed women for years, easily converted men & women alike to machine-gun making. Briggs Mfg. Co. in Detroit simply took women from the upholstering department, taught them to put fabric on bomber wings and rivet framework.

But in most war plants, women are a novelty. The attitude of plant managers ranges all the way from that of Bell Aircraft in Buffalo, which wonders why it did not employ women before, to that of Cadillac in Detroit which keeps its first 25 women workers behind a *padlocked* door. Says an executive: "You know how men are."

Ford never had a woman in plant production before, was chary of letting them even do clerical work. Vultee, which now employs women in all but the drop-hammer department, figured the distraction caused by a woman walking through the plant in the old days at $250. Once upon a time Consolidated barred women entirely.

The attitude of men fellow workers toward their new competitors is a mixture of nose-out-of-joint and gallantry. They either let Minnie strictly alone or are much too helpful. Said one workman last week as news photographers posed a redhead at her lathe: "I ran that machine two years and nobody ever took *my* picture."

But the influx of women, all agree, has spruced up male workers. When a pert miss came into Curtiss Wright's St. Louis plant as a tool designer, the men, after one dumbfounded day, began wearing ties and shaving with great frequency. In some still womanless departments of North American Aviation in Kansas City men workers complain in the plant's paper that the promised blondes haven't arrived.*

Recovering from the novelty of women workers in slacks (usually too tight), plant managers are beginning to estimate the contribution women can make: 1) they have greater finger dexterity than men (Westinghouse has known this all along, has used women in electrical assembly since the days of fancy aprons and high lace collars); 2) they are more immune to monotony than men, will keep at a tiresome job long after a man starts hanging around the canteen or water cooler; 3) they excel at inspection work where keen eyes and sensitive fingers often find flaws a man misses (Newton A. Woodworth, maker of engine parts, says it is easier to make a woman "quality conscious" than a man); 4) women workers are more docile than men workers; 5) last but not least, they stick at their jobs, respond readily to speed-up campaigns.

The National Association of Manufacturers has summed up the diffi-

---

* *At Douglas in Santa Monica girls cured male coworkers of "whewing" and whistling after lunch by doing the same in reverse. Said one trim girl: "Look at Tarzan." Said another: "What a build that guy's got." The men couldn't take it.*

culties in employing women as 1) they generally need assistance in setting up machinery and in lifting heavy objects; 2) they are absent from work more often than men; 3) they are more susceptible to fatigue; 4) it is difficult to make foremen out of them because they are likely to abuse authority ("They're cats," said one plant manager); 5) a woman worker has a shorter industrial life than a man. Plant managers who have been changing women over from peacetime factory work to wartime work would also add that a woman takes longer to adjust to a new job.

Some objections to women workers can be explained by the fact that women usually have had no experience with machines before coming into a factory—only months ago few U.S. women ever even had to change a tire. As for fatigue—the housewives show it worst, at the end of an afternoon shift. (Some plants, notably Bell Aircraft, find women have surprising endurance.) One big difficulty is getting women to work for women. And there is a prejudice, partly fostered by the girls themselves, against letting a woman assume the final responsibility on a motor that means life or death.

As time goes on women will learn how to set up heavy machinery. Women will take on harder jobs as men are drawn off and they gain seniority. Where heavy lifting now prevents their working, new lifting devices or unskilled labor will do the lifting. Women are likely to take over whole departments, like inspection and electrical sub-assembly, fine acetylene welding—jobs they do better than men.

The first big wave of women into war plants came last November. Each successive clampdown by the Selective Service System has given the trend a great shove. By the end of 1943—if the war is still chewing up U.S. manpower—war industry will have absorbed 4,000,000 women. ■

The Coffee Hour

BY A.T. BAKER

[*A half-century before the advent of Starbucks, the writer highlighted the moment when a casual trend, the coffee break, solidified into a business and social institution*]

March 5, 1951

SOME EMPLOYERS FLUNG themselves hopelessly against the moving horde. Others, already defeated, just watched the tide, making mental notes. But there was nothing to be done about it. Every morning, in every city in the U.S., the bosses watched glumly as the last stenographer disappeared down the hall with a departing flirt of her skirt, purse clutched firmly in one hand, cigarettes and matches in the other.

The morning coffee break had become as deeply entrenched in U.S. custom as the seventh-inning stretch and the banana split. Clerks, secretaries, junior executives and salesgirls had come to consider it an inalienable right of the American office worker. In the face of that terrible, soft insistence, the fuming employer could only take his finger off the unanswered buzzer, jam on his hat, and follow along after the crowd to the coffee shop. As a matter of fact, he kind of liked a cup himself.

"The war, the war, it is all because of the war," growled one employer. In the drum-tight labor market of World War II, when trained workers were hard to find and hard to keep, the wise boss had indulged such little liberties. Later, the men came back from the wardrooms and mess halls of the armed forces, where the percolators chuckle day & night, and gave the custom new impetus.

These days, no time clock daunts the coffee-breakers, and no office manager's frown. The office worker who arrives at 9 o'clock runs the risk of being trampled by the 8:30 arrivals who have had time to hang up their coats, fix their faces and conscientiously flutter a few papers. Young stenographers have found that they can squeeze in a few minutes of extra sleep by dashing for the office, dashing right out again for breakfast coffee and a cruller. Said a Boston stenographer: "If I couldn't look forward to some coffee and a cigarette after the first hour's dictation, I'd scream."

From Seattle to Miami, every coffee spot has its mid-morning knots of wind-jamming men, its gaggle of gossiping women. In Chicago, policemen complain that Loop traffic is all but halted between 9:45 and 10 by swarming office workers out for the morning cup. In Washington, Ohio's Representative George Bender grumbled: "The Government buildings at coffee hour turn into skeletons. They look like recess time at school. The boys & girls dash off for coffee as if rehearsing for fire drill."

Since the war, the coffee break has been written into union contracts and authorized by state labor laws. No truly modern office building is designed without its grid of coffee dispensaries. Small-town and suburban housewives have adopted "morning coffee" as an excuse to go neighboring after the beds are made, the baby is changed and the breakfast dishes washed. In the Pacific Northwest, youths make their first date with a new girl an invitation for coffee. "Gives the guy a chance to case the babe, cheap," explained a young blade from Walla Walla.

Employers have tried wanly to check their work losses by various stratagems—by serving coffee at desks and from pushcarts at factory benches, by setting aside definite coffee periods in the hope that, at least part of the morning, everybody will be at his desk. They find what solace they can in surveys showing that workers are more alert and make fewer mistakes after they get back to work. But for the habit itself, no cure seems to be in sight. In fact, thousands of office workers are taking more & more to the custom of popping out for a cup of coffee in the afternoon as well. ∎

The Little King

BY MICHAEL DEMAREST

[*This scintillating profile depicted an entrepreneur and "walking ad agency" who was as lively and entertaining as the toys he made and promoted so masterfully*]

December 12, 1955

 **THROUGH THE SWINGING GLASS** doors of Manhattan's "21" Club one night last week popped a roly-poly, melon-bald little man with the berry-bright eyes and beneficent smile of St. Nick touching down on a familiar rooftop. Louis Marx, America's toy king and café-society Santa, was arriving at his favorite workshop. With his beautiful blonde wife Idella—who looks the way sleigh bells sound—59-year-old Lou Marx toddled regally toward a table in the center of the downstairs room. The table is always reserved for Millionaire Marx by the divine right of toy kings—and the fact that he has never been known to let anyone else pay the check.

While most celebrities go to "21" to play, Lou Marx also goes to ply. From the enlarged pockets of his $200 suits flows a tantalizing trickle of toys for his friends, who seem to include the entire world, and number such cronies as Baseballer Hank Greenberg (best man at his wedding), Comedian Edgar Bergen, Lieut. General Emmett ("Rosie") O'Donnell, Boxer Gene Tunney, and Netherlands Prince Bernhard. For them, there are walking penguins and tail-twirling Donald Ducks, statuettes of the Presidents and lightly clad miniature nymphs, tiny cars and pistol-shaped flashlights, lapel buttons urging "Sit Tight with Ike" or "I Like Lou."

While other toymakers spend millions of dollars each year to promote their wares, Toycoon Marx is his own walking ad agency; he spent only $312 for advertising in 1955. He collects the famed and the publicized as though he were following the slogan on all his toy boxes: "One of the many Marx toys—have you all of them?" Marx, who still has a few notables to go, scrupulously includes those he knows in his endless fund of anecdotes and puts their children's names on his Christmas list. Among the thousands of gifts going out this week from Marx's toy shop are a 20-in. convertible coupe and a remote-control walking puppy for President Eisenhower's grandchildren. Altogether, Marx is a real-life Santa to more than 100,000 children. To the children of cops and waiters and charwomen, boys and girls in orphanages and other institutions, he gives a million toys a year.

Marx considers toys one of the higher forms of human ingenuity, and thinks a lot of the world's problems can be solved through them. "Apart from being good business," he intones, "it's important to buy children a lot of toys. When you keep a child supplied with toys, it gives him security, like an Indian woman gives her child by carrying him on her back. Toys give children love and attention synthetically."

Lou Marx, whose toys spread synthetic love as well as old-fashioned fun from Hamburg to Hiroshima, can well afford his lavish standard of giving. This year he will gross more than $50 million (and net $5,000,000), produce some 10% of all toys sold in the U.S. Marx's output includes every type of plaything (except bicycles and dolls), from plastic baby beakers to $2.98 toy sports cars that can be assembled by a seven-year-old. More than 10% of the 5,000 items made by Marx are mechanical, *e.g.,* a clockwork Bonny Braids, who ambles realistically across the floor, an electric bingo game, a xylophone-playing Mickey Mouse. His 1955 best-sellers include:

• A battery-powered robot ($5.98) that clanks forward and backward, hurls a baby robot to the ground, grunts in Morse code, flashes defiance from light-bulb eyes.

• A plastic-covered shooting arcade ($4.98) with moving ducks for targets.

• A 7,500-piece kit ($9.98) from which skilled children and patient parents can make a 2½-ft. clipper ship with bellying plastic sails. Assembly time: 100 hours.

This year, for the first time in history, more than $1 billion worth of toys will be sold in the U.S. Few industries have soared so high so fast.

Until 1914, inexpensive German toys reigned unchallenged in the U.S. When World War I pinched off European imports, U.S. makers, who had specialized in expensive dolls and ingenious metal playthings, whirred ahead with a legion of low-priced toys. American production methods proved more than a match for postwar foreign competition. Since 1919, when 644 domestic toymakers produced goods with a retail value of $150 million, U.S. toydom has grown to include some 2,000 manufacturers.

Under U.S. Christmas trees this year there will be such high-priced items as a 5-ft., battery powered Thunderbird ($395) that whisks two children along at 5 m.p.h.; a monkey ($250) that puffs cigarettes; a lion-sized lion ($300) with a man-eating roar; a 9-ft. giraffe ($250); an 8-ft. marionette ($300) that hangs from the ceiling and shimmies like sister Kate. Lionel Corp., No. 2 toymaker (1955 sales: $23 million), has a $100 model of the crack *Congressional*. A. C. Gilbert ($12.5 million sales) has a fork-lift truck and driver ($12.95) that swings oil drums from loading platform to flatcar. There are Teddy bears in storm coats ($24.95); a robot-driven bulldozer ($9.98) that backs up when it hits an obstacle; a mamma whale ($2.49) that swallows a baby whale; a remote-control Continental ($6.98); a Playskool lockup garage ($6); and aluminum armor for $125.

Ideal Toy Corp. ($20 million sales) has a "Magic Lips" doll ($15) that purses its mouth for kissing, and a 13-in.-long rocket car that blasts off at 20 m.p.h.; Lynn Pressman has a "Fever" doll ($5) that turns a sickly scarlet.

Toymaker Marx discovered early that children like to play with the things they see around them, and most of his toys are as realistic as he can make them, whether they are trains or cars, carpet sweepers, miniature stoves or boats. But he has little patience with psychologist-blessed "educational" toys that are sold not as playthings but as "combinations of coordination influences." Snorts Marx: "The ones who buy them are the spinster aunts and spinster uncles and hermetically sealed parents who wash their children 1,000 times a day."

There is an increasing demand, however, for build-it-yourself toys that develop a child's imagination and dexterity. Marx, for example, has a station wagon whose transparent-plastic V-8 engine comes in 64 colored parts for the child to assemble himself. To teach his own children about the human body, Marx this year imported from Japan life-size life-like male and female papier-mâché figures that can be taken apart, organ by organ. Next year Marx plans to make smaller versions (probable price: $14.98).

Even his competitors admit that Louis Marx is the Henry Ford of the toy industry. Like Ford, Marx has used mass production and mass distribution to turn out cheap toys, *e.g.,* electric trains had seldom been sold for less than $10 before Marx brought out a sturdy $3.98 train in the early '30s. Today, some 75% of Marx's toys sell for less than $5.

In the highly competitive toy industry, where piracy is almost second nature, the race is to the swift, the daring and the shamelessly self-imitating. Marx is all three. "There is no such thing as a new toy," he says. "There are only old toys with new twists." With a new mechanical twist, last year's submarine becomes next year's rocket ship; a flop may be face-lifted to stardom. After a 25¢ truck had saturated the market in the mid-'30s, Marx loaded it with plastic ice cubes (then a new product), called it an ice truck and had a new hit. With a new twist on an old friction motor, Marx three years ago was able to redesign an old firehouse so that it catapulted a hook and ladder through closed doors. He used the same motor last year for a heliport that shoots a helicopter to the ceiling.

IN 1928 MARX GOT the greatest idea in toydom's history. Rounding a corner in Los Angeles one day, he stopped to watch a Filipino whittle away at a circular block of wood, attach it to a string and then bounce the block up and down the string—as his fellow-countrymen had been doing for as long as anyone could remember. The Yo-Yo, transformed by Marx from a primitive, island plaything into a universal preoccupation, sold more than 100 million and is still going strong.

Since most toymakers "knock off" (*i.e.,* copy) their competitors' products, new toys are as elaborately guarded—and as inevitably filched—as Detroit's new car designs. Doll manufacturers solemnly lead buyers to a vault and there show them a Betsy Wetsy or a Tiny Tears. At Manhattan's Toy Fair last March, one manufacturer chained his gun to a radiator so no one could make off with it. The Ideal Toy Corp. sequesters its 18 designers in a closely guarded room that can only be reached by a secret passageway.

The gentle art of toy piracy consists of changing a competitor's successful design just enough to evade paying royalties to its originator. "When they copy you, it's piracy," cracks Lou Marx, who pays no royalties in the U.S. "When you copy them, it's competition." When Marx "competes," he often cuts the price, but he always makes small improvements, *e.g.,* when he "knocked-off" Ideal's bestselling mechanical robot, he put in a battery motor.

With the best idea in the world, a toymaker still takes a tremendous gamble. To put a new narrow-gauge train under Christmas trees two years from now, Marx will invest $500,000 in dies and materials. Unlike most toymakers, Marx finances his operation out of capital, thus can push a toy into production faster than anyone in the industry.

Marx is out ahead in other ways. His production lines are among the smoothest and most fully automatic in the business. Marx constantly analyzes machine layouts to cut wasteful operations. "When we find a machine that will do a 30-second job in 25," he says, "we'll scrap the old one, even if it's new." Marx was one of the first U.S. toymakers to switch to plastic. Though the first plastic toys broke too easily, he now makes most small toys of polyethylene, a durable material that can be turned out up to 64 times faster than metal. Unlike most toy manufacturers, who virtually close down for six months when the Christmas lights go off, Marx sells 90% of his output to the big chains, *e.g.,* Woolworth and Walgreen's, which do a brisk year-round toy business, and Sears, Roebuck and J. C. Penney, which order in huge quantities early in the year. Thus he cuts costs, keeps his plants humming and most of his work force busy three shifts a day all year.

When Marx goes off the day shift at 5:30 p.m., he switches from manual output to intellectual intake. In 1942, after his first wife died, Marx enrolled in a night course on Western civilization at the New School for Social Research. "I'd get to feeling morose," he explains, "and hit the bottle." He and Idella now attend five or six classes a week at the New School and New York University in such courses as "American Political Parties" and "Psychology of Religion." He finds that being a night-school student at N.Y.U. gives him a formidable fund of information with which to confound his friends, many of whom are experts in their own lines.

He is also quick to convert night-school theory into practical business use. Two department-store buyers who were moaning about discount-house competition in Marx's office one day were flabbergasted when the toymaker interrupted them: "It's like this guy *Toy*-nbee says. It's a question of challenge and response. These discount houses are the challenge that is going to make department stores into merchants again."

In addition to collecting culture, Marx is frequently accused by competitors of "collecting" generals. Actually, he has known most of his brass-hat friends since they were young officers. His love affair with the military started in the early '30s, when he was able to give a hard-to-get toy-train switch to the late Air Force General H. H. ("Hap") Arnold, who was then a major at Bolling Field. Arnold introduced Marx to General Walter Bedell

Smith, now vice chairman of the American Machine & Foundry board, who was then a captain. Said "Beedle" Smith recently: "If anyone had asked me then if I would trade my chance at making brigadier general for a quarter, I would have grabbed the money."

When Marx sent Beedle Smith some caviar, Smith, who had no taste for caviar, passed it on to his next-door neighbor at Fort Myer, Brigadier General Eisenhower. Later, Ike dropped in to thank Marx. The toymaker's other military friends include NATO's General Alfred Gruenther, Strategic Air Command's General Curtis LeMay, General Omar Bradley, now a Bulova top executive, and General George Catlett Marshall. Even after they leaped into the headlines in wartime, Marx says, he was sure that the generals would be "forgotten like Bliss and Pershing," worried about the generals' financial future. In 1946, when he formed a cosmetic company called Charmore, Marx decided to help out some of his military friends by selling them shares in the profitable company at a nominal price.

About the same time that the generals were returning from the war, Idella Ruth Blackadder, then 21 and an RKO starlet, came back from an overseas stint with a U.S.O. troupe and met Marx at a party the next day. Idella, who is Ecdysiast Lili St. Cyr's half sister, married Marx. When Marx took Idella, who is two inches taller and 28 years younger, to meet General Gruenther on a European trip, Gruenther greeted Idella with: "What on earth did you marry him for?" Declared Marx: "I'm the one with the brains." Although some acquaintances had predicted that the marriage would not last two minutes, Lou and Idella are now the happy parents of four sons. Each son has two generals as godfathers. The "second shift," as Marx calls them (to distinguish Idella's offspring from the four children by his first wife), boasts a total of 35 sponsoring stars. The eldest boy, six-year-old Spencer Bedell (the only second-shift Marx with a nonmilitary first name) is a godchild of President Eisenhower and Bedell Smith. Ike volunteered again when Emmett Dwight, now five, came along; his other godfather is Rosie O'Donnell. The other sons: Bradley Marshall, 3, and Curtis (for Curtis LeMay) Gruenther, 1.

Marx says he has never received one good idea for a toy from the generals. But Marx was one of the many who kept telling Ike about his political future. "You're on pages one, two and three of every newspaper," Lou told Ike in 1946. "You're the political Coca-Cola." His proudest possessions: an oil painting of the West Point chapel—Ike's first picture—and a portrait of Marx in a frame inscribed "Dwight D. Eisenhower—American-Born."

The first- and second-shift Marxes occupy a rambling, white-pillared Georgian mansion on a 20-acre estate in suburban Scarsdale, just off the Hutchinson River Parkway. Marx bought the red brick house for his first wife during World War II, but before they could move in, Renee Freda Marx died of cancer. After that, says Rosie O'Donnell, "Lou was both father and mother" to his children: Barbara, now 26, wife of Artist-Writer Earl Hubbard; Louis Jr., 24, a Princeton graduate, now a Marine lieutenant; Jacqueline ("Jackie"), a pretty, dark-haired Vassar graduate who joins New Jersey Republican Senator Case's Washington staff next month; and Patricia ("Patty"), 17, a freshman at Stanford.

Says O'Donnell: "Lou did a wonderful job with the kids. I'd go to his place, and we'd be having breakfast and the six dogs would be running all over the place. And he'd be telling his daughter, right in the middle of it: 'White is the color of purity, so if you want to get married in white, be sure that you live morally. Otherwise, get married in Reno or something. Or don't wear white.' "

Roughhousing with the second shift, Lou Marx likes to pummel and chase them frantically up and down the three-story house, allows the boys to squirt water guns and smash toys to their hearts' content. (Idella feels the boys are working off their aggressive instincts.) Once a week the Marx brothers pile into their parents' 13-ft.-wide bed for the night. There they are treated to a bedtime-story session in which Marx spins chiller-dillers about such bad guys as a deformed villain who sautés children's eyeballs for supper. The "mean-man stories," as the children call them, are intended, says Marx, to "immunize them against fear." Like the first shift before them, the boys are also being treated to Idella's digests of the classics, bedtime concerts of Brahms, Beethoven, etc. piped into their rooms, French lessons and word-building.

Led by Lou and Idella, the family swoops down periodically on a new branch of learning, *e.g.,* for months they smothered visitors with I.Q., vocabulary and personality tests. Although Marx is an agnostic, both shifts belong to the Episcopal Church. Marx stays at home when the family attends services, but ships argosies of toys to the annual bazaar of Scarsdale's Church of St. James the Less.

Marx, a fresh-air fiend as well as culture fan, likes to bask in the sun on winter days at the bottom of his swimming pool, which is drained in September. There he sits puffing six-inch cigars (Jack & Charlie's "21" Selection), dictating letters to his Audiograph or reading a dictionary and marking the words and phrases he wants to transfer to his vocabulary. These are later typed by a secretary in a series of black books that Marx carries everywhere, studies in idle moments. For an hour, three or four times a week, he dons sneakers, a grey sweat suit and a Mother Hubbard bonnet that ties under his chin. With a black book in hand, he trots briskly around his driveway or the roof of his office building on lower Fifth Avenue as he memorizes new words. "After a stiff workout," says a friend, "Lou's breath comes in polysyllables."

Marx has puffed his way through Webster in twelve years. Now, on the second time around, his favorite expression is *Dum Vivimus, Vivamus,* which can be freely translated as "Live It Up." He found the exhortation so appealing that he had it embroidered on a batch of silk neckties that he gives away.

PERHAPS ONE REASON MARX is so anxious to expand his English vocabulary is that he spoke only German until the age of six. He was born (Aug. 11, 1896) in Brooklyn, where his Berlin-born parents, Jacob and Clara Lou, owned a small drygoods store and left most of the job of raising young Louis to a German maid. By the time Louis reached P.S. 11, he was known derisively as "The Dutchman." Marx still speaks with a guttural rasp and nurses a distrust for German. On annual toy trips to Germany, Marx hires an interpreter, although, as he admits, "I understand like mad."

As a boy Marx excelled at baseball, basketball, ice skating and shop lifting. "Everyone stole," he recalls complacently. "You weren't anyone if you couldn't steal." When he was nine, Lou proved he was someone by recruiting an accomplice and going to Brooklyn's Abraham & Straus department store. There they picked out a canoe, hefted it over their heads and walked out through the delivery exit unchallenged. The rest of that summer Louis and friends spent boating on Prospect Park Lake nearby.

The Marx parents shifted their little store from neighborhood to neighborhood with scant success, and there were few luxuries for Louis, his elder sister Rose and younger brother Dave. "But I don't remember feeling my life was tough," says Louis. "People in Brooklyn were warm and understanding, and I learned a lot about democracy. The class struggle? Someone sold that idea. We never felt it."

Lou studied hard to get ahead. He graduated from elementary school at twelve and finished Fort Hamilton High in three years. At nights he pored over books "on how to become a $5,000-a-year man." After a short-lived job with a druggists' syndicate, Marx stumbled "by sheer happenstance" into an office-boy's job with Ferdinand Strauss, whose Zippo the Climbing Monkey was one of the first mechanical toys mass-manufactured in the U.S. Within four years, Marx had been promoted to manage the company's East Rutherford, N.J. plant, and soon afterward he had his first idea for a toy. One of Strauss's products was a toy horn that bleated "Mamma, Papa." Marx amplified the sound effects, redesigned the horn to resemble a carnation and brought it out as a paper lapel flower that doubled as a noisemaker at parties.

The horn sold well, and Marx was made a Strauss director. One day the directors discussed whether the company should continue to manufacture and sell in its four retail stores in New York or give up selling. Marx alone urged Strauss to get out of the retail field. Instead of getting rid of the stores, Strauss got rid of Marx.

In his next job, as salesman for a Vermont wood-products company, Marx redesigned a line of wooden toys, and sales soared from 15,000 to 1,500,000 in two years. At the same time, Louis and brother Dave set themselves up as middlemen. Their specialty was to figure out how to cut costs on a 10¢ toy. Then they would land an order, farm out the manufacturing and pocket the profit. Before he was 21, Lou Marx had served a hitch in the Army, risen from private to sergeant, and, back in civilian clothes, realized his ambition of making $5,000 a year.

In 1921 brothers Louis and Dave started in to make toys themselves. They bought the dies for Zippo after Strauss had gone bankrupt. The monkey had been on the market for more than 20 years, but Marx gave it bright new colors, brought out bigger models, and sold 8,000,000 of them. By the time he was 26, Marx was a millionaire and convinced that, in the toy industry, there is nothing new under the sun. To prove his point, he brought Zippo back this year, redesigned, rechristened (Jocko) and repriced.

Hard-driving Louis and easygoing brother Dave (known to friends as "Mako" and "Spendo") now have six U.S. factories, wholly owned British and Canadian subsidiaries, and toy-manufacturing interests in Germany, France, Mexico, South Africa, Japan, Australia, and Brazil. Peak U.S. employment: 8,000.

This year, while U.S. toymakers clamored for higher tariffs to keep out Japanese imports (current share of U.S. toy sales: about 6%), Marx provided Tokyo toymakers with the cash and know-how to turn out toys that he contracted to sell in the U.S. as well as in foreign markets such as South Africa. This Christmas Japanese toys make up 5% of the Marx line and include many items, *e.g.,* a $2.98 remote-control model auto that Japanese toymakers can turn out with 10¢-an-hour labor for less than half as much as it would cost to produce in the U.S. Marx bargained so closely with the crafty Japanese toymakers that Tokyo newspapers accused him of trying to ruin the industry. Marx was unabashed. "When in Rome," he shrugged, "shoot Roman candles."

As Christmas anticipation began to spread across the U.S. last week, Toy King Marx was busy wrapping up ideas for the presents that Santa Claus will be bringing two and three years from now. For Lou Marx, Christmas doesn't come just once a year, or even on Dec. 25. "When you come out with a real great hit," he says, "that's Christmas." ■

What Is the Point of Working?

BY LANCE MORROW

[
Although the work ethic had weakened, the essayist argued, workers still found in their jobs dignity, rewards and social ties—in short, a sense of their own identity
]

May 11, 1981

WHEN GOD FORECLOSED ON Eden, he condemned Adam and Eve to go to work. Work has never recovered from that humiliation. From the beginning, the Lord's word said that work was something bad: a punishment, the great stone of mortality and toil laid upon a human spirit that might otherwise soar in the infinite, weightless playfulness of grace.

A perfectly understandable prejudice against work has prevailed ever since. Most work in the life of the world has been hard, but since it was grindingly inevitable, it hardly seemed worth complaining about very much. Work was simply the business of life, as matter-of-fact as sex and breathing. In recent years, however, the ancient discontent has grown elaborately articulate. The worker's usual old bitching has gone to college. Grim tribes of sociologists have reported back from office and factory that most workers find their labor mechanical, boring, imprisoning, stultifying, repetitive, dreary, heartbreaking. In his 1972 book *Working*, Studs Terkel began: "This book, being about work, is, by its very nature, about violence—to the spirit as well as to the body." The historical horrors of industrialization (child labor, Dickensian squalor, the dark satanic mills) translate into the

20th century's robotic busywork on the line, tightening the same damned screw on the Camaro's firewall assembly, going nuts to the banging, jangling Chaplinesque whirr of modern materialism in labor, bringing forth issue, disgorging itself upon the market.

The lamentations about how awful work is prompt an answering wail from the management side of the chasm: nobody wants to work any more. As American productivity, once the exuberant engine of national wealth, has dipped to an embarrassingly uncompetitive low, Americans have shaken their heads: the country's old work ethic is dead. About the only good words for it now emanate from Ronald Reagan and certain beer commercials. Those ads are splendidly mythic playlets, romantic idealizations of men in groups who blast through mountains or pour plumingly molten steel in factories, the work all grit and grin. Then they retire to flip around iced cans of sacramental beer and debrief one another in a warm sundown glow of accomplishment. As for Reagan, in his presidential campaign he enshrined work in his rhetorical "community of values," along with family, neighborhood, peace and freedom. He won by a landslide.

Has the American work ethic really expired? Is some old native eagerness to level wilderness and dig and build and invent now collapsing toward a decadence of dope, narcissism, income transfers and aerobic self-actualization?

The idea of work—work as an ethic, an abstraction—arrived rather late in the history of toil. Whatever edifying and pietistic things may have been said about work over the centuries (Kahlil Gibran called work "love made visible," and the Benedictines say, "To work is to pray"), humankind has always tried to avoid it whenever possible. The philosophical swells of ancient Greece thought work was degrading; they kept an underclass to see to the laundry and other details of basic social maintenance. That prejudice against work persisted down the centuries in other aristocracies. It is supposed, however, to be inherently un-American. Edward Kennedy likes to tell the story of how, during his first campaign for the Senate, his opponent said scornfully in a debate: "This man has never worked a day in his life!" Kennedy says that the next morning as he was shaking hands at a factory gate, one worker leaned toward him and confided, "You ain't missed a god-damned thing."

The Protestant work ethic, which sanctified work and turned it into vocation, arrived only a few centuries ago in the formulations of Martin Luther and John Calvin. In that scheme, the worker collaborates with God to do the work of the universe, the great design. One scholar, Leland Ryken of Illinois' Wheaton College, has pointed out that American politicians and corporate leaders who preach about the work ethic do not understand the Puritans' original, crucial linkage between human labor and God's will.

During the 19th century industrialization of America, the idea of work's inherent virtue may have seemed temporarily implausible to generations who labored in the mines and mills and sweatshops. The century's huge machinery of production punished and stunned those who ran it.

And yet for generations of immigrants, work *was* ultimately availing; the numb toil of an illiterate grandfather got the father a foothold and a high school education, and the son wound up in college or even law school. A woman who died in the Triangle Shirtwaist Co. fire in lower Manhattan had a niece who made it to the halcyon Bronx, and another generation on, the family went to Westchester County. So for millions of Americans, as they labored through the complexities of generations, work worked, and the immigrant work ethic came at last to merge with the Protestant work ethic.

The motive of work was all. To work for mere survival is desperate. To work for a better life for one's children and grandchildren lends the labor a fierce dignity. That dignity, an unconquerably hopeful energy and aspiration—driving, persisting like a life force—is the American quality that many find missing now.

THE WORK ETHIC IS not dead, but it is weaker now. The psychology of work is much changed in America. The acute, painful memory of the Great Depression used to enforce a disciplined and occasionally docile approach to work—in much the way that older citizens in the Soviet Union do not complain about scarce food and overpopulated apartments, because they remember how much more horrible everything was during the war. But the generation of the Depression is retiring and dying off, and today's younger workers, though sometimes laid off and kicked around by recessions and inflation, still do not keep in dark storage that residual apocalyptic memory of Hoovervilles and the Dust Bowl and banks capsizing.

Today elaborate financial cushions—unemployment insurance, union benefits, welfare payments, food stamps and so on—have made it less catastrophic to be out of a job for a while. Work is still a profoundly respectable thing in America. Most Americans suffer a sense of loss, of diminution, even of worthlessness, if they are thrown out on the street. But the blow seldom carries the life-and-death implications it once had, the sense of personal ruin. Besides, the wild and notorious behavior of the economy takes a certain amount of personal shame out of joblessness; if Ford closes down a plant in New Jersey and throws 3,700 workers into the unemployment lines, the guilt falls less on individuals than on Japanese imports or American car design or an extortionate OPEC.

Because today's workers are better educated than those in the past, their expectations are higher. Many younger Americans have rearranged their ideas about what they want to get out of life. While their fathers and grandfathers and great-grandfathers concentrated hard upon plow and drill press and pressure gauge and tort, some younger workers now ask previously unimaginable questions about the point of knocking themselves out. For the first time in the history of the world, masses of people in industrially advanced countries no longer have to focus their minds upon work as the central concern of their existence.

In the formulation of Psychologist Abraham Maslow, work functions in a hierarchy of needs: first, work provides food and shelter, basic human maintenance. After that, it can address the need for security and then for friendship and "belongingness." Next, the demands of the ego arise, the need for respect. Finally, men and women assert a larger desire for "self-actualization." That seems a harmless and even worthy enterprise but sometimes degenerates into self-infatuation, a vaporously selfish discontent that dead-ends in isolation, the empty face that gazes back from the mirror.

Of course in patchwork, pluralistic America, different classes and ethnic groups are perched at different stages in the work hierarchy. The immigrants—legal and illegal—who still flock densely to America are fighting for the foothold that the jogging tribes of self-actualizers achieved three generations ago. The zealously ambitious Koreans who run New York City's best vegetable markets, or boat people trying to open a restaurant, or chicanos who struggle to start a small business in the *barrio* are still years away from est and the Sierra Club. Working women, to the extent that they are new at it, now form a powerful source of ambition and energy. Feminism—and financial need—have made them, in effect, a sophisticated-immigrant wave upon the economy.

Having to work to stay alive, to build a future, gives one's exertions a tough moral simplicity. The point of work in that case is so obvious that it need not be discussed. But apart from the sheer necessity of sustaining life, is there some inherent worth in work? Carlyle believed that "all work, even cotton spinning, is noble; work is alone noble." Was he right?

It is seigneurial cant to romanticize work that is truly detestable and destructive to workers. But misery and drudgery are always comparative. Despite the sometimes nostalgic haze around their images, the preindustrial peasant and the 19th century American farmer did brutish work far harder than the assembly line. The untouchable who sweeps excrement in the streets of Bombay would react with blank incomprehension to the malaise of some $17-an-hour workers on a Chrysler assembly line. The Indian, after all, has passed from "alienation" into a degradation that is almost mystical. In Nicaragua, the average 19-year-old peasant has worked longer and harder than most Americans of middle age. Americans prone to restlessness about the spiritual disappointments of work should consult unemployed young men and women in their own ghettos: they know with painful clarity the importance of the personal dignity that a job brings.

Americans often fall into fallacies of misplaced sympathy. Psychologist Maslow, for example, once wrote that he found it difficult "to conceive of feeling proud of myself, self-loving and self-respecting, if I were working, for example, in some chewing-gum factory . . ." Well, two weeks ago, Warner-Lambert announced that it would close down its gum-manufacturing American Chicle factory in Long Island City, N.Y.; the workers who had spent years there making Dentyne and Chiclets were distraught. "It's a beautiful place to work," one feeder-catcher-packer of chewing gum said sadly. "It's just like home." There is a peculiar elitist arrogance in those who discourse on the brutalizations of work simply because they cannot imagine themselves performing the job. Certainly workers often feel abstracted out, reduced sometimes to dreary robotic functions. But almost everyone commands endlessly subtle systems of adaptation; people can make the work their own and even cherish it against all academic expectations. Such adaptations are often more important than the famous but theoretical alienation from the process and product of labor.

Work is still the complicated and crucial core of most lives, the occupation melded inseparably to the identity; Freud said that the successful psyche is one capable of love and of work. Work is the most thorough and profound organizing principle in American life. If mobility has weakened old blood ties, our co-workers often form our new family, our tribe, our social world; we become almost citizens of our companies, living under the protection of salaries, pensions and health insurance. Sociologist Robert Schrank believes that people like jobs mainly because they need other people; they need to gossip with them, hang out with them, to schmooze. Says Schrank: "The workplace performs the function of community."

Unless it is dishonest or destructive—the labor of a pimp or a hit man, say—all work is intrinsically honorable in ways that are rarely understood as they once were. Only the fortunate toil in ways that express them directly. There is a Renaissance splendor in Leonardo's effusion: "The works that the eye orders the hands to make are infinite." But most of us labor closer to the ground. Even there, all work expresses the laborer in a deeper sense: all life must be worked at, protected, planted, replanted, fashioned, cooked for, coaxed, diapered, formed, sustained. Work is the way that we tend the world, the way that people connect. It is the most vigorous, vivid sign of life—in individuals and in civilizations. ■

Panic Grips the Globe

BY GEORGE J. CHURCH

[*Certainly there was drama in Wall Street's worst collapse—yes, worse than 1929's—but the writer also found it in the underlying issues of debt, inflation and confidence*]

November 2, 1987

FIRST CAME A VAGUE foreboding, a kind of free-floating anxiety. The U.S., said worriers, could not go on forever spending more than it would tax itself to pay for, buying more overseas than it could earn from foreign sales, and borrowing more abroad than it could easily repay. There had to be a day of reckoning, and it could unhinge the whole world economy. But when might it come? What form would it take? How bad might it be? No one could say, and so the forebodings could be pushed to the back of the mind.

But then, slowly at first, the anxiety began to take on a shape that could be sensed if not exactly foreseen. On all the world's stock exchanges, prices had leaped up too far, too fast, to be sustained. The mood in the markets shifted from fantasy about instant wealth to nervousness about an inevitable "correction" (a wonderful euphemism). By Monday morning the concern was no longer vague but had taken on physical form—piles of papers littering brokers' desks, each representing a hastily scribbled order to sell stock; rows of numbers flashing on computer screens, bringing news of alarming price breaks in all the early-opening markets: Tokyo, Hong Kong, London, Paris, Zurich . . .

Then trading began in New York, and the unimaginable happened: a collapse on a scale never seen before—no, not even in 1929. Prices went down, down, down, swiftly wiping out an entire year's spectacular gains. "I just can't believe that this is happening," moaned one trader, as he took nonstop sell orders at Donaldson, Lufkin & Jenrette. At lunchtime, brokers across the U.S. went hungry or ate sandwiches at their desks while trying to keep phone receivers pressed to both ears. "This is going to make '29 look like a kiddie party," shouted a trader on the Los Angeles floor of the Pacific Stock Exchange.

Almost an entire nation became paralyzed with curiosity and concern. Crowds gathered to watch the electronic tickers in brokers' offices or stare at television monitors through plate-glass windows. In downtown Boston, police ordered a Fidelity Investments branch to turn off its ticker because a throng of nervous investors had spilled out onto Congress Street and was blocking traffic. George Finch, 66, a retired businessman in San Francisco, summed up the bewilderment: "I don't know what the hell is going on."

By the time the 4 p.m. closing bell rang at the New York Stock Exchange on what instantly became known as Black Monday, the Dow Jones industrial average had plunged 508 points, or an incredible 22.6%, to close for the day at 1738.74. Some $500 billion in paper value, a sum equal to the entire gross national product of France, vanished into thin air. Volume on the New York exchange topped 600 million shares, nearly doubling the all-time record. Brokers could find only one word to describe the rout, an old word long gone out of fashion but resurrected because no other would do: panic. The frenzy rose as it spread once again around the globe. On Tuesday stock prices fell by 12.2% in London, 15% in Tokyo, 6% in Paris and 6.7% in Toronto, on top of huge losses Monday.

Then, since blind panic is no more sustainable than unthinking euphoria, came a crazy whipsawing that continued virtually all week and in markets all around the world. Up, down, up, down, with trends reversing in hours, and then reversing again. And always the questions: Would the stock crisis cause a recession? Or even a global depression like the one ushered in by the 1929 Crash? What would happen to the dollar, to interest rates, to world trade? What might Ronald Reagan do to calm the markets? Could a President who was so weakened by the Iran-*contra* affair and the impending defeat on the Bork nomination, and who was distracted by war in the Persian Gulf and his wife's cancer operation, possibly quell the financial turmoil?

By Thursday night, Reagan showed that he recognized the serious-ness of the situation—and the need for action. "We shouldn't assume that the stock market's excess volatility is over," he asserted at a White House press conference, and he acknowledged that public fear spread by those gyrations "could possibly bring about a recession." More important, he an-nounced that he was summoning the leaders of Congress to a bipartisan deficit-cutting conference at which, through his top aides, he was "putting everything on the table with the exception of Social Security, with no other preconditions." Including a tax increase? Though he could not quite bring himself to pronounce those words, Reagan clearly indicated that, well, yes, he would at least discuss the subject. Reminded again and again by re-porters of his many previous pledges to veto anything resembling a tax in-crease, he refused to repeat any such pledge; he merely said both spending and taxes should be kept "as low as possible."

The impact of the President's words was hard to gauge. Exchanges in Asia and Europe suffered additional heavy losses Friday, but that might have been more a response to a bad Thursday on Wall Street. Despite a lukewarm reaction in the New York financial community to the President's statements, prices on the Big Board steadied, perhaps from exhaustion. The Dow average eked out a .33 gain to close the week at 1950.76. Two bits of news helped: the Consumer Price Index rose at an annual rate of only 2.1% in September, less than half the 5.8% pace in August; the GNP grew at an annual rate of 3.8%, after adjustment for inflation, in the third quarter, up from 2.5% in the second quarter. Those figures seemed to indicate that the American economy, if not exactly sound in its fundamentals, was at least not deteriorating as drastically as the Black Monday stock-price col-lapse might have led an unsophisticated observer to believe.

Nonetheless, the week as a whole will go down as the worst in finan-cial history. The Dow's Black Monday plunge of 22.6% was almost double the record 12.8% fall on Oct. 28, 1929. Despite a spirited rally on Tuesday and Wednesday, the Dow was still down an unprecedented 295.98 points, or 13.2%, for the week. That immediately eclipsed the record 235.48-point decline the market had suffered the previous week. From its peak of 2722 in August to its Friday close, the average has fallen 28.3%, burning up an es-timated $870 billion in equity values. Volume for the week was inconceiv-ably greater than ever before, totaling 2.3 billion shares on the Big Board; the four heaviest trading days in New York exchange history all occurred last week. The turnover strained the exchange's computer network to the limit, and the Big Board decided to knock off trading two hours early on Friday and this Monday and Tuesday to allow exhausted brokers time to catch up on their paperwork.

At best, the President may have bought some time for the White House and Congress to come up with a program to convince investors that something worthwhile will be done to bring budget and trade deficits under control. Probably not much time, either. Wildly gyrating markets are better than those that plunge straight down, but they are hard on the nerves of stockholders who have already proved they are ready to jump at the first sign of trouble. The continued drop on the foreign exchanges Friday cannot be brushed off. If the wild week proved anything, it was that in an era when the U.S. is dependent on foreign goods and capital, no exchange is an island. Price breaks overseas can touch off panic in the U.S., which can then hammer prices down further abroad; that, in fact, is roughly what happened Monday and Tuesday.

Moreover, even if prices stabilize—a gargantuan if, given the extreme jumpiness of the markets—the bust that has already occurred darkens prospects for business. Even in an economy the size of the U.S.'s, the nearly $385 billion in asset values that vanished last week alone is a sum large enough to have a strong impact. Not all those losses are theoretical; for many people who sold on Monday, the damage is painfully real. And investors who sat tight and saw the value of their stocks recover a bit at midweek have had an unforgettable demonstration that they cannot count on eventually being as rich in reality as they once looked on paper.

TO BE SURE, HARDLY anyone expects a rerun of the Great Depression that followed the 1929 Crash. Main reasons: the economy has developed many safeguards, and the Government, if it cannot yet be trusted to resolve the nation's fundamental financial problems, at least knows enough to avoid making the situation drastically worse. The banking system collapsed in the wake of the 1929 debacle, but it is much sounder today, shored up by federal deposit insurance, among other things. Says James Wilcox, an economist at the University of California, Berkeley: "In the 1930s when things looked bad, people ran from the banks out of fear. In 1987 people run to the banks to put their money in, because this time the banks are among the safest things around."

The Federal Reserve Board, in hindsight, is widely considered to have played a role in converting the 1929 Crash into the 1930s Depression by allowing the U.S. supply of money and credit to shrink substantially at the worst possible time. Last week the Fed took exactly the opposite tack. Chairman Alan Greenspan on Monday was denounced by some critics for having inadvertently helped trigger the stock-market break by pushing up interest rates in early September. But on Tuesday morning he became something of an instant hero by reversing policy: just before the markets opened, he announced that the Federal Reserve, "consistent with its responsibilities as a central bank," would make as much money available as might be needed—for example, to banks that might be hurt by suddenly uncollectible loans to stockbrokers. Greenspan seemed to be as good as his word; by week's end the Fed was apparently pumping enough money into banks to bring interest rates down again slightly. Led by Citicorp, the major U.S. banks dropped the benchmark prime rate that they charge corporate customers from 9.25% to 9%. The move came only two weeks after the banks had boosted the prime from 8.75% to 9.25%.

But if no depression is in the cards, the market crack could cause a recession all by itself. Frank Korth, senior vice president of Shearson Lehman, explains the mechanism by which market cracks get translated into slowdowns or recessions: "If you lose $4,000 in the stock market, you don't go out and spend $1,200 on a new color TV or $4,000 on a new motorboat. As a result, the man on the street whose job is in the boat plant is out of a job because there is no market for his company's product. Boatbuilders don't want to build inventory, so they close down their plants. Everybody loses: the plant workers, the suppliers, the corner grocer, the shoe store."

This is, of course, a highly simplified scheme, and there is nothing inevitable about it; it could be averted by Government action that would restore confidence. But what kind of action? An answer must begin with an analysis of what triggered the market crash.

Superficially, the bust might seem, to put it bluntly, insane. By no rational calculation could the asset value and earning power of American corporations be 22.6% less on Monday night than they had been the previous Friday. But that statement assumes that their values on Friday were realistic, and in hindsight there is widespread agreement that they were not. In other words, the crash to some extent really was—oh, all right—a correction, though one on a scale to make that word seem ludicrously inadequate.

Says Korth of Shearson Lehman: "The market should not have reached 2700 [on the Dow Jones average] in the first place. We probably should have been trading around 1900 or 2100; maybe 2000 would have been the right number based on interest rates, corporate earnings and other fundamentals. We were 700 points ahead on sheer greed." As early as August, when the American bull market celebrated its fifth birthday, some investing pros were noting apprehensively that stock prices were getting out of line with expected corporate earnings, and dividend yields had fallen well below the interest return on bonds, making the fixed-income securities potentially a better investment. But the general feeling then was that the Dow might go as high as 3000, on pure momentum if nothing else, so why not stick around for the end of the ride? A similar psychology ruled overseas, according to Nils Lundgren, chief economist of Sweden's PKbanken. Says he: "The market was really overspeculated, with people saying to themselves, 'I won't get out now, but as soon as stocks start to fall, I will sell.' When you have that mentality operating, you are ready for a big fall."

ONE FACTOR BEHIND THE speed of the market's descent was the almost complete computerization of the New York exchange and other markets. There is immense dispute, even days after the fact, as to what part computers that make trades semiautomatically played in touching off the gigantic volume of sell orders. Taking no chances, however, the Big Board after the Monday debacle instituted restrictions on so-called program trades of large portfolios of stock carried out by computer, in order to damp down price swings.

In a broader sense, computers unquestionably had an all-important role. They enable the exchanges to execute trades swiftly, in volume that would have been inconceivable a few years ago. So at times of market excitement, the volume that would once have been stretched over a week or so gets squeezed into a day. When the orders are predominantly on one side, prices run up or down violently.

But never so violently as on Black Monday. Tickers and news reports flashed the story of huge price declines on heavy volume. With each sale, more investors became convinced that a collapse had begun and they had better get out while they still could. Mutual-fund managers tried to hold on but could not; they had to dump stock to get cash to pay off investors who clamored to redeem their fund shares. Margin calls to investors who had bought stock on credit aggravated the frenzy. Some could not put up additional collateral and were sold out.

Why, then, did the rout give way to a rally? Traditionally, that happens after every so-called selling climax (even in 1929), because most investors who were thinking of selling have been cleaned out in one grand sweep and buyers start looking for newly cheap shares. The rally in the middle of last week was given particularly powerful support by some 200 major corporations that started buying up their own stock at bargain prices, in part to keep it out of the hands of would-be raiders. The crash put at least a temporary damper on mergers and acquisitions anyway. Several deals fell through because the bids made for the target companies suddenly looked unrealistically high after the general decline in stock prices.

But it is anyone's guess whether the small degree of stability so painfully achieved on Friday—volume dwindled as the Dow average stood almost still—will hold even for days or hours. Alan Meltzer, professor of political economy at Pittsburgh's Carnegie Mellon University, thinks the "markets will remain volatile because there are still too many unanswered questions."

The most fundamental questions, economists agree with the closest approach to unanimity they ever achieve, are: How long will the U.S. try to live it up on borrowed money? And can it summon the will to start the painful readjustment necessary to kick the habit—a readjustment that grows more painful the longer it is put off?

The problem is hideously complicated in detail but simple enough in outline. Ever since the giant tax cuts of 1981, the U.S. has been running deficits on a scale never seen before. True, Reagan announced at his press conference that the deficit in fiscal 1987, which ended on Sept. 30, dropped to $148 billion, from $221 billion the prior fiscal year. But the new figure is still far too high, and it is likely to rise again soon; much of the 1987 reduction was due to one-shot effects of the tax-reform law. Concurrently, the U.S. has swung from a surplus of exports over imports of $3 billion as recently as 1975 to a trade deficit of $156 billion last year.

One result is that America has run up a foreign debt of about $250 billion. Economists across a broad spectrum of ideological positions warn almost with one voice that this situation is precarious in the extreme. Foreigners will not continue forever to finance American profligacy, and the stock-market crash was a relatively mild foretaste of what could happen if they pull their money out. The nation would then face a grim choice of financing the deficit by ruinous printing-press inflation or a sudden, brutal cutback in spending that might trigger a real economic bust.

No wonder, then, that stock investors have been nervous. Whatever the precise mix of emotions and events that triggered last week's collapse—and to establish that mix would require probing into millions of minds around the world—its root cause was a dim but accurate perception that U.S. prosperity was not sustainable with present policy. And with Congress and the President perpetually wrangling over the most modest proposals to reduce the budget deficit, they could see no sign that policy was about to change.

In truth, even with the most brilliant policy, the passage to a sounder prosperity is likely to be tricky, dangerous and painful. Lowering the trade deficit will take years, and will probably require a cut in American consumption—meaning, in other words, at least a temporary reduction in the standard of living. Many economists think the dollar will have to fall further too, reluctant as both U.S. and foreign moneymen are to see that happen. The reluctance is understandable. Unless a decline is carefully managed, it will raise two dangers: a renewal of inflation and a panic flight of foreign capital from the U.S. (since foreigners would not be eager to hold dollar-denominated investments that shrank in value against their own currencies).

But there is an impressive consensus, in the U.S. and abroad, on how to begin to correct the imbalances in the American economy. The President and the Democratic-controlled Congress must agree, right away, on a package of measures that hold some real promise of reducing the budget deficit steadily and substantially. Certainly these must include painful spending cuts. But they must also include tax increases, much as Reagan hates the thought. Not because they are any panacea; indeed they carry a serious risk. Higher taxes might reduce consumer spending just when a recession is beginning, and deepen the slump. But no significant budget cut is possible without at least some sort of modest tax increase, and no progress toward solving the nation's fundamental economic problems is possible without a real deficit reduction.

The decisive meeting occurred Tuesday after the market close. Treasury Secretary James Baker, by then back in his office after having cut short a trip to Europe, first called in White House Chief of Staff Howard Baker, Greenspan and Council of Economic Advisors Chairman Beryl Sprinkel to coordinate what they would tell the President. Then, joined by White House Aide Kenneth Duberstein, they went upstairs in the White House to the brightly colored West Sitting Room, which the Reagans use as a living room. James Baker opened by telling Reagan that the world seemed to be looking for some movement on the President's part, and the quickest way he could display leadership was by reaching a compromise with Congress on reducing the budget deficit. Everyone knew that would have to include a tax increase.

Greenspan, who had been an informal economic adviser to Reagan before the President chose him to head the Federal Reserve, voiced a somewhat perverse but effective argument: in effect, the only way to keep taxes low was to agree to raise them a bit. If there was no budget compromise with Congress, he said, the financial markets might continue to weaken and the economy might take a real turn for the worse. That, he continued, might give the Democrats enough political clout to shove through a big increase severely trimming back Reagan's cherished tax cuts, either by ramming one through over the President's veto or by winning the 1988 election and enacting a stiff boost after Reagan left office. The President showed great reluctance to accept the advice that he should compromise on a modest boost now. But, says one participant, eventually the "President bought the [Greenspan] argument that if the economy goes down the tubes you lose the whole thing, the whole legacy."

The budget negotiations were set to begin early this week. If a budget compromise is not worked out and enacted by Nov. 20, some $23 billion of automatic spending cuts go into effect under a modified version of the Gramm-Rudman Act. They would slash away with idiot impartiality at defense and social spending, at good programs and bad. And that would just about end any chance that Washington would give the stock markets the signal they yearn for.

What if the negotiations break down and the market gets the opposite signal: that the U.S. is unable or unwilling even to start working out some long-range solution to its gargantuan budget and trade deficits? As last week's wild price whipsawing demonstrated, no one can predict stock prices and volume for even a few hours. But if the U.S. continues to float on a sea of red ink and foreign debt—well then, many financial experts suggest, sooner or later the markets can expect the *real* crash. How it could be much worse than Black Monday is as difficult to imagine as was Black Monday itself just days before. But the world had better hope it never finds out what that ultimate bust would be like. ∎

—REPORTED BY ROSEMARY BYRNES AND BARRETT SEAMAN/WASHINGTON
AND FREDERICK UNGEHEUER/NEW YORK, WITH OTHER BUREAUS

In Search of the Real Bill Gates

BY WALTER ISAACSON

[*Written by TIME's managing editor, this long, detailed profile set a new model for the magazine of intimate reporting and personal involvement by the author*]

January 13, 1997

WHEN BILL GATES WAS in the sixth grade, his parents decided he needed counseling. He was at war with his mother Mary, an outgoing woman who harbored the belief that he should do what she told him. She would call him to dinner from his basement bedroom, which she had given up trying to make him clean, and he wouldn't respond. "What are you doing?" she once demanded over the intercom.

"I'm thinking," he shouted back.

"You're thinking?"

"Yes, Mom, I'm thinking," he said fiercely. "Have you ever tried thinking?"

The psychologist they sent him to "was a really cool guy," Gates recalls. "He gave me books to read after each session, Freud stuff, and I really got into psychology theory." After a year of sessions and a battery of tests, the counselor reached his conclusion. "You're going to lose," he told Mary. "You had better just adjust to it because there's no use trying to beat him." Mary was strong-willed and intelligent herself, her husband recalls, "but she came around to accepting that it was futile trying to compete with him."

A lot of computer companies have concluded the same. In the 21 years since he dropped out of Harvard to start Microsoft, William Henry Gates III, 41, has thrashed competitors in the world of desktop operating systems and application software. Now he is attempting the audacious feat of expanding Microsoft from a software company into a media and content company.

In the process he has amassed a fortune worth $23.9 billion. The 88% rise in Microsoft stock in 1996 meant he made on paper more than $10.9 billion, or about $30 million a day. That makes him the world's richest person, by far. But he's more than that. He has become the Edison and Ford of our age. A technologist turned entrepreneur, he embodies the digital era.

His success stems from his personality: an awesome and at times frightening blend of brilliance, drive, competitiveness and personal intensity. So too does Microsoft's. "The personality of Bill Gates determines the culture of Microsoft," says his intellectual sidekick Nathan Myhrvold. But though he has become the most famous business celebrity in the world, Gates remains personally elusive to all but a close circle of friends.

Part of what makes him so enigmatic is the nature of his intellect. Wander the Microsoft grounds, press the Bill button in conversation and hear it described in computer terms: he has "incredible processing power" and "unlimited bandwidth," an agility at "parallel processing" and "multitasking." Watch him at his desk, and you see what they mean. He works on two computers, one with four frames that sequence data streaming in from the Internet, the other handling the hundreds of E-mail messages and memos that extend his mind into a network. He can be so rigorous as he processes data that one can imagine his mind may indeed be digital: no sloppy emotions or analog fuzziness, just trillions of binary impulses coolly converting input into correct answers.

"I don't think there's anything unique about human intelligence," Gates says over dinner one night at a nearly deserted Indian restaurant in a strip mall near his office. Even while eating, he seems to be multitasking; ambidextrous, he switches his fork back and forth throughout the meal and uses whichever hand is free to gesture or scribble notes. "All the neurons in the brain that make up perceptions and emotions operate in a binary fashion," he explains. "We can someday replicate that on a machine." Earthly life is carbon based, he notes, and computers are silicon based, but that is not a major distinction. "Eventually we'll be able to sequence the human genome and replicate how nature did intelligence in a carbon-based system." The notion, he admits, is a bit frightening, but he jokes that it would also be cheating. "It's like reverse-engineering someone else's product in order to solve a challenge."

Might there be some greater meaning to the universe? When engaged or amused, he is voluble, waving his hands and speaking loudly enough to fill the restaurant. "It's possible, you can never know, that the universe exists only for me." It's a mix of Descartes' metaphysics and Tom Stoppard's humor. "If so," he jokes, "it's sure going well for me, I must admit." He laughs; his eyes sparkle. Here's something machines can't do (I don't think): giggle about their plight in the cosmos, crack themselves up, have fun.

Right? Isn't there something special, perhaps even divine, about the human soul? His face suddenly becomes expressionless, his squeaky voice turns toneless, and he folds his arms across his belly and vigorously rocks back and forth in a mannerism that has become so mimicked at Microsoft that a meeting there can resemble a round table of ecstatic rabbis. Finally, as if from an automaton, comes the answer: "I don't have any evidence on that." Rock, rock, rock. "I don't have any evidence on that."

The search for evidence about the soul that underlies Bill Gates' intellectual operating system is a task that even this boyish man might find a challenge.

"As a baby, he used to rock back and forth in his cradle himself," recalls Gates' father, a man as big and huggable as his son is small and tightly coiled. A retired lawyer, he still lives in the airy suburban Seattle house overlooking Lake Washington where Bill III—the boy he calls "Trey"—grew up. (The name comes from the card term for three, though the father is now resigned to being called Bill Sr.)

His mother Mary was "a remarkable woman," Bill Sr. says. A banker's daughter, she was adroit in both social and business settings, and served on numerous boards, including those of the University of Washington, the United Way, USWest and First Interstate Bancorp. After her death in 1994, the city council named the avenue leading into their neighborhood after her.

"Trey didn't have a lot of confidence in social settings," says his father. "I remember him fretting for two weeks before asking a girl to the prom, then getting turned down. But Mary did. She was a star at social intercourse. She could walk into a room . . ." He has the same toothy smile as his son, the same smudgy glasses covering twinkling eyes. But now, for just a moment, he is starting to tear up. His mind does not seem like a computer. He folds his arms across his stomach and starts to rock, gently.

He gets up to show some more pictures of Mary and of her mother. Both loved cards, and they would organize bridge games, as well as Password and trivia contests, after the big family dinners they held every Sunday. "The play was quite serious," Bill Sr. recalls. "Winning mattered."

As he wanders through the house, he points out more framed pictures of his son: Trey, the towheaded Cub Scout; Trey with sister Kristi, a year older, who now has the joy of being his tax accountant; and with Libby, nine years younger, who lives a few blocks away raising her two kids; with Bill Sr. and his new wife Mimi, the director of the Seattle Art Museum; and hugging his wife Melinda while listening to Willie Nelson play at their New Year's Day 1994 wedding in Hawaii.

"He's a busy guy," says Bill Sr., "so we don't see him a lot, but we spend holidays together." Thanksgiving was in Spokane, Washington, at Kristi's house, Christmas playing golf in Palm Springs, California, where Bill Sr. and Mimi have a place. They communicate mainly by E-mail. Just this morning he got one describing a photocopier Trey bought him for his birthday.

He lumbers over to a table where he has gathered some pictures of summer vacations they used to take with friends at a cluster of rental cabins known as Cheerio on the Hood Canal, about two hours away. There were nightly campfires, family skits and the type of organized competitive games the Gates family loved. "On Saturdays there was a tennis tournament, and on Sundays our Olympics, which were a mixture of games and other activities," Bill Sr. recalls. "Trey was more into the individual sports, such as water skiing, than the team ones."

In 1986, after Microsoft became successful, Gates built a four-house vacation compound dubbed Gateaway for his family. There his parents would help him replicate his summer activities on a grander scale for dozens of friends and co-workers in what became known as the Microgames. "There were always a couple of mental games as well as performances and regular games," says Bill Sr. as he flips through a scrapbook. These were no ordinary picnics: one digital version of charades, for example, had teams competing to send numerical messages using smoke-signal machines, in which the winners devised their own 4-bit binary code.

"We became concerned about him when he was ready for junior high," says his father. "He was so small and shy, in need of protection, and his interests were so very different from the typical sixth grader's." His intellectual drive and curiosity would not be satisfied in a big public school. So they decided to send him to an élite private school across town.

Walking across the rolling quad of the Lakeside School, Bill Sr. points out the chapel where his son played the lead in Peter Shaffer's *Black Comedy.* "He was very enthusiastic about acting. But what really entranced him was in there," he says, pointing to a New England–style steepled classroom building. With the proceeds from a rummage sale, the Mothers' Club had funded a clunky teletype computer terminal.

Learning BASIC language from a manual with his pal Paul Allen, Trey produced two programs in the eighth grade: one that converted a number in one mathematical base to a different base, and another (easier to explain) that played tic-tac-toe. Later, having read about Napoleon's military strategies, he devised a computer version of Risk, a board game he liked in which the goal is world domination.

Trey and Paul were soon spending their evenings at a local company that had bought a big computer and didn't have to pay for it until it was debugged. In exchange for computer time, the boys' job was to try (quite successfully) to find bugs that would crash it. "Trey got so into it," his father recalls, "that he would sneak out the basement door after we went to bed and spend most of the night there."

The combination of counseling and the computer helped transform him into a self-assured young businessman. By high school he and his friends had started a profitable company to analyze and graph traffic data for the city. "His confidence increased, and his sense of humor increased," his father says. "He became a great storyteller, who could mimic the voices of each person. And he made peace with his mother."

"In ninth grade," Gates recalls over dinner one night, "I came up with a new form of rebellion. I hadn't been getting good grades, but I decided to get all A's without taking a book home. I didn't go to math class, because I knew enough and had read ahead, and I placed within the top 10 people in the nation on an aptitude exam. That established my independence and taught me I didn't need to rebel anymore." By 10th grade he was teaching computers and writing a program that handled class scheduling, which had a secret function that placed him in classes with the right girls.

His best friend was Kent Evans, son of a Unitarian minister. "We read FORTUNE together; we were going to conquer the world," says Gates. "I still remember his phone number." Together with Paul Allen, they formed the official-sounding Lakeside Programmers Group and got a job writing a payroll system for a local firm. A furious argument, the first of many, ensued when Allen tried to take over the work himself. But he soon realized he needed the tireless Gates back to do the coding. "O.K., but I'm in charge," Gates told him, "and I'll get used to being in charge, and it'll be hard to deal with me from now on unless I'm in charge." He was right.

To relieve the pressures of programming, Evans took up mountain climbing. One day Gates got a call from the headmaster: Evans had been killed in a fall. "I had never thought of people dying," Gates says. There is a flicker of emotion. "At the service, I was supposed to speak, but I couldn't get up. For two weeks I couldn't do anything at all."

After that he became even closer to Paul Allen. They learned an artificial-intelligence language together and found odd jobs as programmers. "We were true partners," Gates says. "We'd talk for hours every day." After Gates went off to Harvard, Allen drove his rattletrap Chrysler cross-country to continue their collaboration. He eventually persuaded Gates to become that university's most famous modern dropout in order to start a software company, which they initially dubbed Micro-Soft (after considering the name Allen & Gates Inc.), to write versions of BASIC for the first personal computers. It was an intense relationship: Gates the workaholic code writer and competitor, Allen the dreamy visionary.

Over the years they would have ferocious fights, and Allen would, after a Hodgkin's disease scare, quit the company and become estranged. But Gates worked hard to repair the relationship and eventually lured Allen, who is now one of the country's biggest high-tech venture-capital investors (and owner of the Portland Trail Blazers), back onto the Microsoft board. "We like to talk about how the fantasies we had as kids actually came true," Gates says. Now, facing their old classroom building at Lakeside is the modern brick Allen/Gates Science Center. (Gates lost the coin toss.)

STEVE BALLMER, BIG AND balding, is bouncing around a Microsoft conference room with the spirit of the Harvard football-team manager he once was. "Bill lived down the hall from me at Harvard sophomore year," he says. "He'd play poker until 6 in the morning, then I'd run into him at breakfast and discuss applied mathematics." They took graduate-level math and economics courses together, but Gates had an odd approach toward his classes: he would skip the lectures of those he was taking and audit the lectures of those he wasn't, then spend the period before each exam cramming. "He's the smartest guy I've ever met," says Ballmer, 40, continuing the unbroken sequence of people who make that point early in an interview.

Ballmer nurtured the social side of Gates, getting him to join one of the college's eating clubs (at his initiation Gates gave a drunken disquisition on an artificial-intelligence machine), playing the video game Pong at hamburger joints and later wandering with him to places like the old Studio 54 during visits to New York City. "He was eccentric but charismatic," says Ballmer.

When Microsoft began to grow in 1980, Gates needed a smart non-techie to help run things, and he lured Ballmer, who had worked for Procter & Gamble, to Seattle as an equity partner. Though he can be coldly impersonal in making business decisions, Gates has an emotional loyalty to a few old friends. "I always knew I would have close business associates like Ballmer and several of the other top people at Microsoft, and that we would stick together and grow together no matter what happened," he says. "I didn't know that because of some analysis. I just decided early on that was part of who I was."

As with Allen, the relationship was sometimes stormy. "Our first major row came when I insisted it was time to hire 17 more people," Ballmer recalls. "He claimed I was trying to bankrupt him." Gates has a rule that Microsoft, rather than incurring debt, must always have enough money in the bank to run for a year even with no revenues. (It currently has $8 billion in cash and no long-term debt.) "I was living with him at the time, and I got so pissed off I moved out." The elder Gates smoothed things over, and soon the new employees were hired.

"Bill brings to the company the idea that conflict can be a good thing," says Ballmer. "The difference from P&G is striking. Politeness was at a premium there. Bill knows it's important to avoid that gentle civility that keeps you from getting to the heart of an issue quickly. He likes it when anyone, even a junior employee, challenges him, and you know he respects you when he starts shouting back." Around Microsoft, it's known as the "math camp" mentality: a lot of cocky geeks willing to wave their fingers and yell with the cute conviction that all problems have a right answer. Among Gates' favorite phrases is "That's the stupidest thing I've ever heard," and victims wear it as a badge of honor, bragging about it the way they do about getting a late-night E-mail from him.

The contentious atmosphere can promote flexibility. The Microsoft Network began as a proprietary online system like CompuServe or America Online. When the open standards of the Internet changed the game, Microsoft was initially caught flat-footed. Arguments ensued. Soon it became clear it was time to try a new strategy and raise the stakes. Gates turned his company around in just one year to disprove the maxim that a leader of one revolution will be left behind by the next.

During the bachelor years in the early '80s, the math-camp mentality was accompanied by a frat-boy recreational style. Gates, Ballmer and friends would eat out at Denny's, go to movies and gather for intellectual games like advanced forms of trivia and Boggle. As friends started getting married, there were bachelor parties involving local strippers and skinny-dipping in Gates' pool. But eventually, after Gates wed, he took up more mature pursuits such as golf. "Bill got into golf in the same addictive way he gets into anything else," says Ballmer. "It gets his competitive juice flowing."

It's a rainy night, and Gates is bombing around in his dark blue Lexus. He is not wearing a seat belt. (A dilemma: Is it too uncool to use mine?) He rarely looks at you when he talks, which is disconcerting, but he does so when he's driving, which is doubly disconcerting. (I buckle up. As his mother and others have learned, it's not always prudent to compete.) He turns into a dark drive with a chain-link fence that slides open as the Lexus approaches. It's nearing midnight, and the security guard looks a bit startled.

Gates' home of the future has been under construction for more than four years, and is not expected to be completed until this summer. Built into a bluff fronting Lake Washington, it has 40,000 sq. ft. of space and will cost about $40 million. Looming against the night sky are three connected pavilions of glass and recycled Douglas fir beams, looking a bit like a corporate conference center masquerading as a resort.

Gates swings into a vaulted 30-car garage carved into the hillside. In the corner, like a museum piece, sits his parents' red Mustang convertible that he drove as a kid. "The first pavilion is mainly for public entertaining," he says as he picks his way past construction debris down four levels of stairs. Despite the hour, three technicians are working in the ground-floor reception hall, with its view of the Olympic Mountains across Lake Washington, adjusting two dozen 40-in. monitors that will form a flat-screen display covering an entire wall. "When you visit, you'll get an electronic pin encoded with your preferences," he explains. "As you wander toward any room, your favorite pictures will appear along with the music you like or a TV show or movie you're watching. The system will learn from your choices, and it will remember the music or pictures from your previous visits so you can choose to have them again or have similar but new ones. We'll have to have hierarchy guidelines, for when more than one person goes to a room." Like Gates himself, it's all very fascinating, fun and a little intimidating.

Gates chose the austere and natural architectural style before he got married, but Melinda is now putting her own imprint on it. "The exposed concrete is going to have to go," he says, expressing some concern about how the architect might take this.

Gates met Melinda French 10 years ago at a Microsoft press event in Manhattan. She was working for the company and later became one of the executives in charge of interactive content. Their daughter Jennifer was born last April. Melinda, 32, is no longer at Microsoft, and she is active in charity work and on the board of Duke, where she studied computer science as an undergraduate and then got a graduate degree in business. Like Gates, she is smart and independent. Like his mother, she is also friendly and social, with an easy manner of organizing trips and activities. But she zealously guards her privacy and doesn't give interviews.

If Ballmer is Gates' social goad, his intellectual one is Nathan Myhrvold (pronounced Meer-voll), 37, who likes to joke that he's got more degrees than a thermometer, including a doctorate in physics from Princeton. With a fast and exuberant laugh, he has a passion for subjects ranging from technology (he heads Microsoft's advanced-research group) to dinosaurs (he's about to publish a paper on the aerodynamics of the apatosaurus tail) to cooking. He sometimes moonlights as a chef at Rover's, a French restaurant in Seattle.

"There are two types of tech companies," Myhrvold says over dinner at Rover's, in between pauses to inhale the aroma of the food. "Those where the guy in charge knows how to surf, and those where he depends on experts on the beach to guide him." The key point about Gates is that he knows—indeed loves—the intricacies of creating software. "Every decision he makes is based on his knowledge of the merits. He doesn't need to rely on personal politics. It sets the tone."

Myhrvold describes a typical private session with Gates. Pacing around a room, they will talk for hours about future technologies such as voice recognition (they call their team working on it the "wreck a nice beach" group, because that's what invariably appears on the screen when someone speaks the phrase "recognize speech" into the system), then wander onto topics ranging from quantum physics to genetic engineering. "Bill is not threatened by smart people," he says, "only stupid ones."

Microsoft has long hired based on I.Q. and "intellectual bandwidth." Gates is the undisputed ideal: talking to most people is like sipping from a fountain, goes the saying at the company, but with Gates it's like drinking from a fire hose. Gates, Ballmer and Myhrvold believe it's better to get a brilliant but untrained young brain—they're called "Bill clones"—than someone with too much experience. The interview process tests not what the applicants know but how well they can process tricky questions: If you wanted to figure out how many times on average you would have to flip the pages of the Manhattan phone book to find a specific name, how would you approach the problem?

Warren Buffett, the Omaha, Nebraska, investor whom Gates demoted to being merely the second richest American, seems an unlikely person to be among his closest pals. A jovial, outgoing 66-year-old grandfather, Buffett only recently learned to use a computer. But as multibillionaires go, both are unpretentious, and they enjoy taking vacations together. Buffett's secretary apologetically explains that Buffett isn't giving interviews these days and at the moment is traveling, but she promises to pass along the request. Less than three hours later, Buffett calls to say he happens to be in the Time & Life Building with some free time between meetings in Manhattan, and he would be happy to come by to be interviewed. He likes to talk about Gates.

When Gates decided to propose to Melinda in 1993, he secretly diverted the chartered plane they were taking home from Palm Springs one Sunday night to land in Omaha. There Buffett met them, arranged to open a jewelry store that he owned and helped them pick a ring.

Last October Gates brought Melinda and their new daughter to visit Buffett and his wife in San Francisco. They ended up playing bridge for nine hours straight. Another marathon session in Seattle started in the morning and lasted—with a break for Melinda to pick up lunch at Burger King—until guests started arriving for dinner. "He loves games that involve problem solving," Buffett says. "I showed him a set of four dice with numbers arranged in a complex way so that any one of them would on average beat one of the others. He was one of three people I ever showed them to who figured this out and saw the way to win was to make me choose first which one I'd roll." (For math buffs: the dice were nontransitive. One of the others who figured it out was the logician Saul Kripke.)

Their relationship is not financial. Buffett, who does not invest in technology stocks, bought 100 shares of Microsoft just as a curiosity back when he met Gates ("I wish I'd bought more," he laughs), and Gates describes his investment with Buffett as "only" about $10 million ("I wish I'd invested more," he likewise jokes). But Gates shares Buffett's interest in the media world and even likes to joke that he has created a digital encyclopedia called Encarta that now outsells *World Book,* which is controlled by Buffett. So far Microsoft has mainly treated content as something that its software managers can create from scratch. But given the relative cheapness of some media stocks compared with that of Microsoft, Gates may someday look for some big acquisitions (he was in serious talks about taking a $2 billion stake in CNN before Time Warner merged with Turner Communications), and Buffett would be a useful partner.

Another of Gates' vacation companions is Ann Winblad, the software entrepreneur and venture capitalist he dated during the 1980s. They met in 1984 at a Ben Rosen–Esther Dyson computer conference and started going on "virtual dates" by driving to the same movie at the same time in different cities and discussing it on their cell phones. For a few years she even persuaded him to stop eating meat, an experiment he has since resolutely abandoned.

They were kindred minds as well as spirits. On a vacation to Brazil, he took James Watson's 1,100-page textbook, *Molecular Biology of the Gene,* and they studied bioengineering together. On another vacation, to a Santa Barbara, California, ranch, she took tapes of Richard Feynman's lectures at Cornell, and they studied physics. And on a larger excursion with friends to central Africa, which ended at some beach cottages on an island off Zanzibar, among their companions was anthropologist Donald Johanson, known for his work on the human ancestor Lucy, who helped teach them about human evolution. In the evenings on each trip they would go to the beach with four or five other couples for bonfires, Hood Canal–style games and a tradition they called the sing-down, where each team is given a word and has to come up with songs that feature it. Winblad remembers Gates disappearing on a dark beach after his group had been given the word sea, and then slowly emerging from the mist singing a high-pitched solo of *Puff, the Magic Dragon.*

They broke up in 1987, partly because Winblad, five years older, was more ready for marriage. But they remain close friends. "When I was off on my own thinking about marrying Melinda," Gates says, "I called Ann and asked for her approval." She gave it: "I said she'd be a good match for him because she had intellectual stamina." Even now, Gates has an arrangement with his wife that he and Winblad can keep one vacation tradition alive. Every spring, as they have for more than a decade, Gates spends a long weekend with Winblad at her beach cottage on the Outer Banks of

North Carolina, where they ride dune buggies, hang-glide and walk on the beach. "We can play putt-putt while discussing biotechnology," Gates says. Winblad puts it more grandly. "We share our thoughts about the world and ourselves," she says. "And we marvel about how, as two young over-achievers, we began a great adventure on the fringes of a little-known industry and it landed us at the center of an amazing universe."

AFTER A RECENT WHIRL of travel that included a speech in Las Vegas and a meeting in Switzerland, Gates detoured to a secluded resort in New York's Adirondacks to spend a weekend with Melinda and Jennifer. There they played with 1,000-piece jigsaw puzzles from a craftsman in Vermont who makes them for customers like Gates. Melinda has helped broaden her husband. Instead of studying biotechnology together, they find time to take singing lessons.

Gates is ambivalent about his celebrity. Although he believes that fame tends to be "very corrupting," he is comfortable as a public figure and as the personification of the company he built. Like Buffett, he remains unaffected, wandering Manhattan and Seattle without an entourage or driver.

The phone in Gates' office almost never rings. Nor do phones seem to ring much anywhere on the suburban Microsoft "campus," a cluster of 35 low-rise buildings, lawns, white pines and courtyards that resemble those of a state polytechnic college. Gates runs his company mainly through three methods: he bats out a hundred or more E-mail messages a day (and night), often chuckling as he dispatches them; he meets every month or so with a top management group that is still informally known as the BOOP (Bill and the Office of the President); and most important, taking up 70% of his schedule by his own calculation, he holds two or three small review meetings a day with a procession of teams working on the company's various products.

There is a relaxed, nonhierarchical atmosphere as the seven young managers of the "WebDVD" group, all in the standard winter uniform of khakis and flannel shirts, gather in a windowless conference room near Gates' office. They have been working for almost a year on a digital video-disc intended to provide content along with Web browsing for television sets, and he wants to review their progress before leaving for Japan, where he will meet with such potential partners as Toshiba.

Craig Mundy, the veteran Microsoft exec who oversees all noncomputer consumer products, lets the younger team members lead the discussion. Gates quickly flips ahead through the deck of papers and within minutes has the gist of their report. He starts rocking, peppering them with questions that segue from the politics of their potential partners, the details of the technology, the potential competition and the broad strategy. The answers are crisp, even as Gates drills down into arcane details. No one seems to be showing off or competing for attention, but neither do any hesitate to speak up or challenge Gates. To a man (and they all are), they rock when they think.

Gates doesn't address anyone by name, hand out praise or stroke any egos. But he listens intently, democratically. His famous temper is in check, even when he disagrees with someone's analysis of the DVD's capability to handle something called layering. "Educate me on that," he says in challenging the analysis, and after a minute or so cuts off the discussion by saying, "Send me the specs."

Gates does not hide his cutthroat instincts. "The competitive landscape here is strange, ranging from Navio to even WebTV," he says. He is particularly focused on Navio, a consumer-software consortium recently launched by Netscape and others designed to make sure that Windows and Windows CE (its consumer-electronics cousin) do not become the standard for interactive television and game machines. "I want to put something in our product that's hard for Navio to do. What are their plans?" The group admits that their intelligence on Navio is poor. Gates rocks harder. "You have to pick someone in your group," he tells Mundy, "whose task it is to track Navio full time. They're the ones I worry about. Sega is an investor. They may be willing to feed us info." Then he moves on to other competitors. "What about the Planet TV guys?" Mundy explains that they are focusing on video games, "a platform we haven't prioritized." Gates counters: "We can work with them now, but they have other ambitions. So we'll be competitive with them down the line."

Though the videodisc is not at the core of Microsoft's business, this is a competition Gates plans to win. The group argues that the $10-per-unit royalty is too low. "Why charge more?" he asks. They explain that it will be hard to make a profit at $10, given what they are putting in. Gates turns stern. They are missing the big picture. "Our whole relationship with the consumer-electronic guys hangs in the balance," he declares. "We can get wiped." Only the paranoid survive. "The strategic goal here is getting Windows CE standards into every device we can. We don't have to make money over the next few years. We didn't make money on MS-DOS in its first release. If you can get into this market at $10, take it." They nod.

His mother may have come to terms with this competitive intensity, but much of the computer world has not. There are Websites dedicated to reviling him, law firms focused on foiling him and former friends who sputter at the mention of his name. Companies such as Netscape, Oracle and Sun Microsystems publicly make thwarting his "plan for world domination" into a holy crusade.

The criticism is not just that he is successful but that he has tried to leverage, unfairly and perhaps illegally, Microsoft's near monopoly in desktop operating systems in ways that would let him dominate everything from word processing and spreadsheets to Web browsers and content. The company is integrating its Internet Explorer browser and Microsoft Network content into its Windows operating system, a process that will culminate with the "Active Desktop" planned for Windows 97, due out in a few months.

Critics see a pattern of Microsoft's playing hardball to make life difficult for competing operating systems and applications. "They are trying to use an existing monopoly to retard introduction of new technology," says Gary Reback, the Silicon Valley antitrust lawyer representing Netscape and other Microsoft competitors. The stakes are much higher than whose Web browser wins. Netscape is enhancing its browser to serve as a platform to run applications. "In other words," says Reback, "if Netscape is successful, you won't need Windows or a Microsoft operating system anymore." On the other hand, if Microsoft is allowed to embed its Web browser into its operating system in a manner that maintains its monopoly, Reback warns, "where will it stop? They'll go on to bundle in content, their Microsoft Network, financial transactions, travel services, everything. They have a game plan to monopolize every market they touch."

Gates makes no apologies. "Any operating system without a browser is going to be f____ out of business," he says. "Should we improve our product, or go out of business?" Though the stakes are clear, the law (which was developed in the era of railway barons) is not. After deadlocking, the Federal Trade Commission in 1993 surrendered jurisdiction over Microsoft to the Justice Department. FTC Commissioner Christine Varney, an expert in the field, says it's hard to apply antitrust law in a fluid situation. "My concern is with the law's ability to keep pace with market conditions in fields that change so rapidly," she says. "Once it's clear a practice is anticompetitive, the issue may already be moot."

Longtime competitors raise a more philosophical issue about Gates: his intensely competitive approach has poisoned the collaborative hacker ethos of the early days of personal computing. In his book *Startup,* Jerry Kaplan describes creating a handwriting-based system. Gates was initially friendly, he writes, and Kaplan trusted him with his plans, but he eventually felt betrayed when Gates announced a similar, competing product. Rob Glaser, a former Microsoft executive who now runs the company that makes RealAudio, an Internet sound system, is an admirer who compliments Gates on his vision. But, he adds, Gates is "pretty relentless. He's Darwinian. He doesn't look for win-win situations with others, but for ways to make others lose. Success is defined as flattening the competition, not creating excellence." When he was at Microsoft, for example, Glaser says the "atmosphere was like a Machiavellian poker game where you'd hide things even if it would blindside people you were supposed to be working with."

It comes down to the same traits that his psychologist noted when Gates was in sixth grade. "In Bill's eyes," says Glaser, "he's still a kid with a startup who's afraid he'll go out of business if he lets anyone compete." Esther Dyson, whose newsletter and conferences make her one of the industry's fabled gurus, is another longtime friend and admirer who shares such qualms. "He never really grew up in terms of social responsibility and relationships with other people," she says. "He's brilliant but still childlike. He can be a fun companion, but he can lack human empathy."

"If we weren't so ruthless, we'd be making more creative software? We'd rather kill a competitor than grow the market?!?" Gates is pacing around his office, sarcastically repeating the charges against him. "Those are clear lies," he says coldly. "Who grew this market? We did. Who survived companies like IBM, 10 times our size, taking us on?" He ticks off the names of his rivals at Oracle, Sun, Lotus, Netscape in an impersonal way. "They're every bit as competitive as I am."

"We win because we hire the smartest people. We improve our products based on feedback, until they're the best. We have retreats each year where we think about where the world is heading." He won't even cop a plea to the charge that Microsoft tends to react to competitors' ideas—the graphical interface of Apple, the Web browser of Netscape—more than it blazes new trails of its own. "Graphical interfaces were done first at Xerox, not Apple. We bet on them early on, which is why Microsoft Office applications became the best."

Gates is enjoying this. Intellectual challenges are fun. Games are fun.

Puzzles are fun. Working with smart people is superfun. Others may see him as ruthless, cold or brutal; but for him the competition is like a sport, a blood sport perhaps, but one played with the same relish as the summer games at Hood Canal. He sprawls on a couch, uncoils and pops open a Fresca. Though rarely attempting the social warmth of his mother (he doesn't actually offer me a Fresca but acquiesces when I ask), Gates has an intensity and enthusiasm that can be engaging, even charming. He takes a piece of paper and draws the matrix of strategies he faced when creating applications to compete with WordPerfect and Lotus. See what an exciting puzzle it was? His language is boyish rather than belligerent. The right stuff is "really neat" and "supercool" and "hardcore," while bad strategies are "crummy" and "really dumb" and "random to the max."

His office is rather modest, sparsely decorated and filled with standard-issue furniture. The biggest piece of art is a huge photo of a Pentium processor chip. There are smaller pictures of Einstein, Leonardo da Vinci and Henry Ford, though he admits that he has little admiration for the latter.

He hopes to be running Microsoft for another 10 years, he says, then promises to focus as intensely on giving his money away. He says he plans to leave his children about $10 million each. "He will spend time, at some point, thinking about the impact his philanthropy can have," Buffett says. "He is too imaginative to just do conventional gifts." Already he's given $34 million to the University of Washington, partly to fund a chair for human genome–project researcher Leroy Hood; $15 million (along with $10 million from Ballmer) for a new computer center at Harvard; and $6 million to Stanford. An additional $200 million is in a foundation run by his father, and he has talked about taking over personally the funding of Microsoft's program to provide computers to inner-city libraries, to which he's donated $3 million in book royalties. "I've been pushing him gently to think more about philanthropy," his father says. "I think his charitable interests will run, as they do now, to schools and libraries."

Especially since Jennifer's birth, friends say, he has begun to reflect more on his life and what he might end up contributing. He speaks of the promise of computing, not just in business terms but in social ones. "Everyone starts out really capable," he says. "But as you grow and turn curious, either you get positive feedback by finding answers or you don't, and then this incredible potential you have is discouraged. I was lucky. I always had a family and resources to get more and more answers. Digital tools will allow a lot more people to keep going the next step rather than hitting a wall where people stop giving them information or tell them to stop asking questions."

He has also become less enamored with pure intelligence. "I don't think that I.Q. is as fungible as I used to," he says. "To succeed, you also have to know how to make choices and how to think more broadly."

So has family life dulled Gates' intensity? "Well, predictably, he's pumped and focused on Jennifer," says Ballmer. "He showed a picture of her at our last sales conference and joked that there was something other than Netscape keeping him awake at nights. He may be a bit less exhausting and a bit more civil. But he still pushes as hard, still keeps score." Gates likes repeating Michael Jordan's mantra—"They think I'm through, they think I'm through"—and the one Intel's CEO Andrew Grove used as a book title, "Only the paranoid survive." As Ballmer says, "He still feels he must run scared." Gates puts another spin on it: "I still feel this is superfun."

And what about his feeling that there is nothing unique about the human mind, that intelligence can someday be replicated in binary code? Has watching a daughter learn to smile at a father's face changed that at all? At our last meeting, these questions don't seem to engage him. As I wander out of his office, he offers none of life's standard see-you-again-someday pleasantries, but he agrees that I should feel free to E-mail him. So I pose the questions, along with some more mundane technical ones, in a message a few days later. Answers to the tech issues come promptly. But he ignores the philosophical ones. Finally, weeks later, a note pops up in my mailbox, dispatched from storm-swept Seattle:

"Analytically, I would say nature has done a good job making child raising more pleasure than pain, since that is necessary for a species to survive. But the experience goes beyond analytic description... Evolution is many orders of magnitude ahead of mankind today in creating a complex system. I don't think it's irreconcilable to say we will understand the human mind someday and explain it in software-like terms, and also to say it is a creation that shouldn't be compared to software. Religion has come around to the view that even things that can be explained scientifically can have an underlying purpose that goes beyond the science. Even though I am not religious, the amazement and wonder I have about the human mind is closer to religious awe than dispassionate analysis." ■

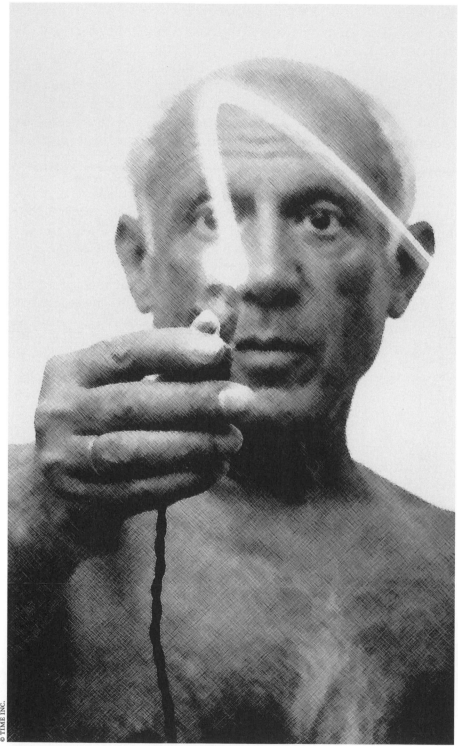

PABLO PICASSO, 1949, BY GJON MILI

The Arts Scene

He Is Kindly

BY JOHN FARRAR

[*A glimpse of a figure destined to be an American classic, couched in a style reflecting the clubby, Ivy League atmosphere of* TIME *in its earliest days*]

January 28, 1924

THE OTHER EVENING AT a dancing club a young man in a gray suit, soft shirt, loosely tied scarf, shook his tousled yellow hair engagingly, introduced me to the beautiful lady with whom he was dancing and sat down. They were Mr. and Mrs. F. Scott Fitzgerald, and Scott seems to have changed not one whit from the first time I met him at Princeton, when he was an eager undergraduate bent upon becoming a great author. He is still eager. He is still bent upon becoming a great author. He is at work now on a novel which his wife assures me is far far better than either *This Side of Paradise* or *The Beautiful and Damned,* but like most of our younger novelists he finds it imperative to produce a certain number of short stories to make the wheels go around. That *The Vegetable,* his play, did not receive a Manhattan presentation seems to have disappointed rather than discouraged him. He is still eminently light-hearted, charmingly outrageous—the complete play-boy.

I have always considered him the most brilliant of our younger novelists. No one of them can touch his glowing bitterness, his style, nor the superb quality of his satire. He has yet to fuse them in a novel with carefulness of conception and profound development of character. He can become almost any kind of writer that his peculiarly restless temperament will allow.

Born in St. Paul, he attended Princeton, served in the Army, wrote his first novel in a training camp, achieved fame and fortune, married a Southern girl, has a child and lives in Great Neck, L. I. At heart, he is one of the kindliest of the younger writers. Artistry means a great deal to F. Scott Fitzgerald—and into his own best work he pours a real torrent of artistic endeavor. This he demands in the work of others, and when he does not find it he criticizes with passionate earnestness. I have known him, after reading a young fellow-novelist's book, to take what must have been hours of time to write him a lengthy, careful and penetrating analysis.

Just what he will write in the future remains cloudy. With a firmer reputation than that of the other young people, he yet seems to me to have achieved rather less than Robert Nathan and rather more than Stephen Vincent Benet, Cyril Hume or Dorothy Speare. His coming novel should mean a definite prophecy for future work. It is to be hoped that from it will be absent the seemingly inevitable flapper. ∎

Ulysses Lands

BY T. S. MATTHEWS

[*When one of the most famous novels of the 20th century finally became legal and respectable—if not completely comprehensible—in the U.S., it was major news*]

January 29, 1934

WATCHERS OF THE U.S. skies last week reported no comet or other celestial portent. In Manhattan no showers of ticker-tape blossomed from Broadway office windows, no welcoming committee packed the steps of City Hall. No call to nation-wide thanksgiving was sounded by Nicholas Murray ("Nicholas Miraculous") Butler. No overt celebration marked the day with red. Yet many a wide-awake modern-minded citizen knew he had seen literary history pass another milestone. For last week a much-enduring traveler, world-famed but long an outcast, landed safe and sound on U. S. shores. His name was *Ulysses.**

Strictly speaking, *Ulysses* did not so much disembark as come out of hiding, garbed in new and respectable garments. Ever since 1922, when the first edition of *Ulysses* was published in Paris, hundreds of U. S. citizens have smuggled copies through the customs or bought them from bookleggers. But this week, on the strength of Federal Judge John Munro Woolsey's decision that *Ulysses* is not obscene, *Random House* was able to publish the first edition of the book ever legally printed in any English-speaking country.

*Ulysses—*James Joyce*—Random House ($3.50)*

For every first-hand reader of *Ulysses* there have been scores of second-hand gossipers. Censorship rather than sound criticism has spread its reputation throughout the Western world. What the man in the street has heard of *Ulysses* has made him prick up his ears. Usually his first question is:

Is it dirty? To answer the man in the street in his own language, Yes. With the exception of medical books and out & out pornography, the only book of modern times that can compare with it for outspokenness in barnyard and backhouse terms is the late D. H. Lawrence's *Lady Chatterley's Lover*. But *Ulysses* is far from being "just another dirty book." Judge Woolsey decided that its purpler passages are "emetic," rather than "aphrodisiac"; that the net effect of its 768 big pages is "a somewhat tragic and very powerful commentary on the inner lives of men and women." But even granting *Ulysses* a bill of moral health an intelligent adult may well smite his brow and cry:

What is it all about? Trusting readers who plunge in hopefully to a smooth beginning soon find themselves floundering in troubled waters. Arrogant Author Joyce gives them no help, lets them sink or swim. But thanks to the exploratory works of critics, and notably such an exegetical commentary as Stuart Gilbert's *James Joyce's Ulysses,* the plain reader can now literally find out what *Ulysses* is all about. Lacking the sleuth-nose, the slot-trained paws of scholarship, even an intelligent reader will miss much the first time over the ground. At that, however, the main outlines of the story are plain.

Ulysses opens early on a summer morning (June 16, 1904) on an old tower outside Dublin. Here three young men are living together: Stephen Dedalus, embittered, ambitious intellectual; Malachi ("Buck") Mulligan, medical student and japer extraordinary; a minor character named Haines. After breakfast Haines and Mulligan walk to the sea and Mulligan bathes while Stephen sets off to his teaching at a boys' school. At about the same hour one Leopold Bloom, middle-aged Jew who makes his living as an advertisement-canvasser, rises from his bed to cook his wife's breakfast and bring her a letter from her latest paramour. Bloom knows all about Molly's constant infidelities, but is too crafty and too resigned to do anything about them. Leaving her in bed, he goes about his day's business. He visits the public baths, attends a funeral, calls at a newspaper office, has lunch at a pub, drops in at the National Library, goes to Sandymount beach to take the air. In the evening he calls at the Lying-in Hospital to inquire after a friend's wife who is having a hard delivery. There he meets

Stephen, carousing in the common room with some medical students, and joins the party. Bloom takes a liking to Stephen, and when the party breaks up follows him to "nighttown" to take care of him. After a wildly drunken scene in a brothel and a brawl between Stephen and two soldiers, Bloom persuades Stephen to come home with him. When they have had a cup of cocoa in the kitchen, Stephen, now fairly sober, takes his leave. Bloom goes up to bed, where he makes a drowsy but cautious report of his day's doings and goes to sleep. Molly lies awake, thinking over what he has told her and what they have not told each other. The book ends with her famed soliloquy.

The plainest reader will also see that there is a great deal more to *Ulysses* than this record of two men's day in Dublin. Without a key to its plan this stream-of-consciousness Bible, with its elliptical shorthand, its apparently confused and formless method, may well seem an esoteric work of art. Confusing *Ulysses* sometimes is, but rather from too much plan than too little. The key to the plan is the title.

Why "Ulysses"? Every schoolboy knows the story of the *Odyssey,* epic-sequel to the *Iliad,* which recites the ten-year wanderings of the wily Odysseus (Latin—Ulysses) in his long-thwarted attempts to get home to his island kingdom after the siege of Troy. The Ulysses of the *Odyssey* is a cunning, common-sensible, nervy, not-too-scrupulous man, an opportunist who triumphs at last not so much by virtue as endurance.

Joyce first conceived the tale of Leopold Bloom as a short story, only to discover too many possibilities in it. In his strolls down the beaches of literature he stumbled on the *Odyssey,* an archaic old bottle but still stout, decided it was just the thing for his 20th Century wine. Thus Ulysses became Bloom, the wanderer in search of home, wife and son. Penelope was his wife Molly; Telemachus, Stephen. Other obvious parallels: Hades, the graveyard; the Cave of Aeolus, the newspaper office; the Isle of Circe, the brothel. A less obvious parallel: the passage between Scylla and Charybdis, Bloom's walk through the National Library while Stephen and some literary men are discussing Aristotelianism (the rock of Dogma), Platonism (the whirlpool of Mysticism). Ulysses' slaying of Penelope's suitors has its counterpart in Bloom's casting from his mind scruples and false sentiment about himself and Molly. Almost every detail of the *Odyssey's* action can be found, in disguised form, in *Ulysses.*

On a third stratum of Joyce's book even deeper meanings appear. Stephen represents the intellect, the creative imagination; Mrs. Bloom the earth, the flesh; Bloom the average half-intelligent, half-sensual man. Like ancient Troy, *Ulysses* is many cities on one foundation. If the plain reader keeps on digging he may discover that each of *Ulysses'* 18 episodes is written in its own style, in which Joyce has tried to blend the minds of the characters, the place, atmosphere, feeling of the time of day. Each episode turns on an organ of the body, an art and a particular symbol. Thus in the 11th episode (the Sirens), the scene of which is the Concert Room at 4 p. m., the bodily organ represented is the ear; the art, music; the symbol, barmaids; the technique, *fuga per canonem* (repetition and elaboration of a theme, as in music). Without such foreknowledge, no one could make much of this:

> "*Bronze by gold heard the hoofirons, steelyringing.*
> *Imperthnthn thnthnthn.*
> *Chips, picking chips off rocky thumbnail, chips.*
> *Horrid! And gold flushed more.*
> *A husky fifenote blew.*"

A great book? If greatness is measured by universality of appeal, *Ulysses* cannot be called great. It will never be a best-seller. Old-line critics have mostly found it too hot to handle. But a growing body of modern critical opinion on both sides of the Atlantic has already acclaimed *Ulysses* as a work of genius and a modern classic. For readers to whom books are an important means of learning about life, it stands preeminent above modern rivals as one of the most monumental works of the human intelligence.

Ulysses is an epic constructed on the principles of solid geometry, a synthetic dissection. Showing a thick segment (in time: 20 hours) of one day's life in Dublin, it cuts through many a solid slice of human tissue. It slices through "literary" brain cells:

"Ineluctable modality of the visible: at least that if no more, thought through my eyes. Signatures of all things I am here to read, seaspawn and seawrack, the nearing tide, that rusty boot. Snotgreen, blue-silver, rust: coloured signs. . . . Airs romped around him, nipping and eager airs. They are coming, waves. The white-maned seahorses, champing, brightwind-bridled, the steeds of Mananaan. . . . Broken hoops on the shore; at the land a maze of dark cunning nets; farther away chalkscrawled backdoors and on the higher beach a dryingline with two crucified shirts. Ringsend: wigwams of brown steersmen and master mariners. Human shells. . . . He turned his face over a shoulder, rere regardant. Moving through the air high spars of a threemaster, her sails brailed up on the crosstrees, homing, upstream, silently moving, a silent ship."

And through lusty arteries: "and the night we missed the boat at Algeciras the watchman going about serene with his lamp and O that awful deepdown torrent O and the sea the sea crimson sometimes like fire and the glorious sunsets and the figtrees in the Alameda gardens yes and all the queer little streets and pink and blue and yellow houses and the rosegardens and the jessamine and geraniums and cactuses and Gibraltar as a girl where I was a Flower of the mountain yes when I put the rose in my hair like the Andalusian girls used or shall I wear a red yes and how he kissed me under the Moorish wall and I thought well as well him as another and then I asked him with my eyes to ask again yes and then he asked me would I yes to say yes my mountain flower and first I put my arms around him yes and drew him down to me so he could feel my breasts all perfume yes and his heart was going like mad and yes I said yes I will Yes."

The wanderings of *Ulysses* have been longer if less arduous than those of its namesake. Joyce finished his seven-year job of writing it at Paris in 1921, but could find no publisher. Editors Margaret Anderson and Jane Heap printed several installments of it in their *Little Review,* mailed copies of which were promptly suppressed by the U. S. postal authorities. Then Poet Ezra Pound, good friend to Joyce, introduced him to Sylvia Beach, liberal daughter of a Princeton, N. J. Presbyterian parson, who ran a bookshop in Paris, Shakespeare & Co. Bookseller Beach had *Ulysses* printed at a French press in Dijon, presented the first copy to Author Joyce on his 40th birthday (1922). In the twelve years since then there have been ten editions in Paris and London. Of the second printing (2,000 copies), 500 were burned by the New York postal authorities. Of the third (500), only one copy escaped the holocaust of the British customs at Folkestone.

Since the U. S. is not a member of the International Copyright Union, there was nothing to prevent any U. S. scalawag from pirating *Ulysses* and 'legging copies. Some scalawags did. After the fate that met Joyce's book of short stories, *Dubliners,* in his own country ("Some very kind person," says Joyce, "bought out the entire edition and had it burnt in Dublin") there was no chance of publishing *Ulysses* there. And Joyce had not increased the honor in which Ireland held him by referring in *Ulysses* to his native land as "the old sow that eats her farrow."* In Manhattan in 1924 the sale of the

* *Some two years ago Ireland tried to bury the hatchet by selecting Joyce as a member of the newly-founded Irish Academy of Letters. Joyce refused the honor with typical arrogance, because "living in France, he finds it difficult to realize how important the academy seems to men of Irish letters."*

manuscript of *Ulysses* at auction brought $1,975—about half a cent a word. For years it looked as though the censors of the English-speaking world had determined that Joyce's book, like himself, should remain in exile.

The Author is variously regarded by those who have never read his books as either a dirty-minded old man or a young crackpot. He is neither. Though critics may bark up different trees in assaying his work, most of them agree that Joyce, as an experimentalist with language, is farther out on a limb than any other writer of English.

Born 52 years ago in Dublin, James Joyce was educated by Jesuits at Clongowes Wood College, Belvedere College, Royal University. In his early 20's he left Ireland and the Church for good, took himself and his sleek blonde Galway wife, Nora Barnacle, to Italy. In Trieste, where they spent ten years, and where Joyce supported his family by teaching languages, his son George and daughter Lucia were born. When the War came Joyce found himself an enemy alien (Trieste was then Austrian), managed to move his family to Switzerland. Friends who have seen the series of letters he later wrote the Swiss Customs, in a finally successful attempt to get some trunks out of their official clutches, say it is a model of practical epistolary art. After the War Joyce moved to Paris, where he still lives, a shy, proud private citizen with a worldwide reputation. His few intimate friends include Padraic Colum, James Stephens, Lord and Lady Astor, John McCormack, Sylvia Beach. He rarely misses a chance to hear opera. Himself no mean tenor, he often sings at his mildly convivial parties, at which he urges red wine on his guests, drinks only white himself. Joyce-addicts may now purchase a phonograph record of his voice. Like his predecessor "Homer" who was reputed to be blind, Joyce has long had trouble with his eyes, with periods of virtual blindness. After more than ten operations he can see just well enough to read newspaper headlines, to scrawl his own writing hugely on vast strips of paper. Behind his thick glasses he often wears a black patch over his left eye.

He has proved his hatred of publicity by never granting an interview. Some three years ago he made newshawks wild by remarrying his wife at the London Registry office without offering explanations. His attorney's guarded comment: "For testamentary reasons it was thought well that the parties should be married according to English law." Some months later Joyce became a grandfather when his son's first son (Stephen James) was born.

Enthusiasts have hailed James Joyce as an invigorator and inventor of language. But perhaps he will be longest remembered as the man who made "unprintable" archaic. ∎

Masterpiece

BY JAMES AGEE

[*A noted film critic—and future Pulitzer Prize–winning novelist—hailed a work that made Shakespeare fresh and timely and made the movies, well, Shakespearean*]

April 8, 1946

THE MOVIES HAVE PRODUCED one of their rare great works of art.

When Laurence Olivier's magnificent screen production of Shakespeare's *Henry V* was first disclosed to a group of Oxford's impassive Shakespeare pundits, there was only one murmur of dissent. A woman specialist insisted that all the war horses which take part in the Battle of Agincourt should have been stallions.

The film was given its U.S. première* this week (in Boston's Esquire Theater). This time, the horses engendered no complaint. At last there had been brought to the screen, with such sweetness, vigor, insight and beauty that it seemed to have been written yesterday, a play by the greatest dramatic poet who ever lived. It had never been done before.** For Laurence Olivier, 38 (who plays Henry and directed and produced the picture), the

---

* *Producer Filippo Del Giudice says the film will pay for itself in Great Britain (cost: almost $2,000,000). Paralleling Hollywood's bookkeeping on exports, he looks to the U.S. and elsewhere for profits. But United Artists, uneasy about the mass audience, is handling the film timidly. The plan: after opening in the most English and academic of U.S. cities, Henry V will play twice-a-day in all major cities at legit prices. Heavy play will be made for Mr. Gallup's estimated 15,000,000 who think most movies worthless. There will be special rates for colleges, etc. No date has been set for general release.*
** *A Midsummer Night's Dream and Romeo and Juliet, the two bravest attempts, were neither good cinema nor good Shakespeare.*

event meant new stature. For Shakespeare, it meant a new splendor in a new, vital medium. Exciting as was the artistic development of Laurence Olivier, last seen by U.S. cinemaddicts in films like *Rebecca* and *Wuthering Heights,* his production of *Henry V* was even more exciting.

As Shakespeare wrote it, *The Cronicle History of Henry the fift* is an intensely masculine, simple, sanguine drama of kinghood and war. Its more eloquent theme is a young king's coming of age. Once an endearingly wild Prince of Wales, Henry V (at 28) had to prove his worthiness for the scepter by leading his army in war. He invaded France, England's longtime enemy. He captured Harfleur, then tried to withdraw his exhausted and vastly outnumbered army to Calais. The French confronted him at Agincourt. In one of Shakespeare's most stirring verbal sonnets, Henry urged his soldiers on to incredible victory. English mobility (unarmored archers) and English firepower (the quick-shooting longbow) proved too much for the heavily armored French. Casualties (killed): English, 29; French, 10,000.* With victory came the courtly peacemaking at Rouen, and Henry's triumphant courtship of the French Princess Katherine.

There were important minor touches. In one of the most moving scenes in Shakespeare, Falstaff was killed off. To replace him, his pal, Pistol, the quintessential burlesque of the Elizabethan soul, was played far down to the groundlings. Because in writing *Henry V* Shakespeare was much hampered by the limitations of his stage, there was heavy work for the one-man Chorus, who, in persuasive and beautiful verbal movies, stirred his audience to imagine scenes and movement which the bare and static Elizabethan stage could not provide.

Olivier's *Henry V* frees Shakespeare from such Elizabethan limitations. The film runs two hours and 14 minutes. Seldom during that time does it fudge or fall short of the best that its author gave it. Almost continually, it invests the art of Shakespeare—and the art of cinema as well—with a new spaciousness, a new mobility, a new radiance. Sometimes, by courageous (but never revolutionary) cuts, rearrangements and interpolations, it improves on the original. Yet its brilliance is graceful, never self-assertive. It simply subserves, extends, illuminates and liberates Shakespeare's poem.

It begins with shots of 17th-Century London and Shakespeare's Globe Theater, where *Henry V* is being played. The florid acting of Olivier and

---

* According to Shakespeare and medieval chroniclers, the English lost just 29. (Says Shakespeare's Duke of Exeter in magnificent understatement: " 'Tis wonderful!") English historical estimates: English losses 500, French losses 7,000. French estimates: French losses 10,000, English 1,600.

his prelates and the Elizabethan audience's vociferous reactions are worth volumes of Shakespearean footnotes. For the invasion, the camera, beautifully assisted by the Chorus (Leslie Banks), dissolves in space through a marine backdrop to discover a massive set such as Shakespeare never dreamed of—and dissolves backward in time to the year 1415. Delicately as a photographic print in a chemical bath, there emerges the basic style of Shakespearean cinema.

Voice and gesture exchange Shakespeare's munificence for subtlety, but remain subtly stylized. Faces, by casting, by close-up and reaction, give Shakespeare's lines a limpid, intimate richness of interpretation which has never been available to the stage. One of the prime joys of the picture is the springwater freshness and immediacy of the lines, the lack of antiquarian culture-clogging. Especially as spoken by Olivier, the lines constantly combine the power of prose and the glory of poetry. Photographic perspectives are shallow, as in medieval painting. Most depths end in two-dimensional backdrops. Often as not, the brilliant Technicolor is deliberately anti-naturalistic. Voice, word, gesture, human beings, their bearing and costumes retain their dramatic salience and sovereignty. The result is a new cinema style.

Falstaff's death scene, for which the speeches were lifted bodily from *Henry IV*, Part 2, is boldly invented. The shrunken, heartbroken old companion of Henry's escapades (George Robey, famed British low comedian) hears again, obsessively, the terrible speech ("A man . . . so old and so profane. . . .") in which the King casts him off. In this new context, for the first time perhaps, the piercing line, "The king has kill'd his heart," is given its full power. In the transition scene which takes the audience from Falstaff's death to the invasion of France, the Chorus makes a final appearance alone against the night sky, then recedes and fades as the movie takes over from him. In a flash of imagination, Britain's armada is disclosed through mist as the Chorus, already invisible, says: *Follow, follow. . . .*

The French court, in fragility, elegance, spaciousness and color, is probably the most enchanting single set ever to appear on the screen. Almost every shot of the French court is like a pre-Renaissance painting. The French King (Harcourt Williams) is weak-minded and piteous as he was in history, if not in Shakespeare. There is one beautiful emblematic shot of his balding, pinkish pate, circled with the ironic gold of royalty.

The French Princess (Renee Asherson) has the backward-bending grace of a medieval statuette of the Virgin. Her reedy, birdlike exchange of

French-English with her equally delightful duenna, Alice (Ivy St. Helier), is a vaudeville act exquisitely paced and played beyond anything that Shakespeare can have imagined. Her closing scene with Henry—balanced about equally between Olivier's extraordinarily deft delivery of his lines and her extraordinary deft pantomimic pointing of them—is a charming love scene.

The Battle of Agincourt is not realistic. Olivier took great care not to make it so. To find the "kind of poetic country" he wanted, and to avoid such chance anachronisms as air raids (the picture was made in Britain during the war), Olivier shot the battle sequence in Ireland.*

Making no attempt to over-research the actual fight, he reduced it to its salients—the proud cumbrousness of the armored French chevaliers, and Henry's outnumbered archers, cloth-clad in the humble colors of rural England. A wonderful epitomizing shot—three French noblemen drinking a battle-health in their saddles—is like the crest of the medieval wave. The mastering action of the battle, however, begins with a prodigious truck-shot of the bannered, advancing French chivalry shifting from a walk to a full gallop, intercut with King Henry's sword, poised for signal, and his archers, bows drawn, waiting for it. The release—an arc of hundreds of arrows speeding with the twang of a gigantic guitar on their victorious way—is one of the most gratifying payoffs of suspense yet contrived.

But the most inspired part of Shakespeare's play deals with the night before the Battle of Agincourt. It is also the most inspired sequence in the film. Olivier opens it with a crepuscular shot of the doomed and exhausted English as they withdraw along a sunset stream to encamp for the night. This shot was made at dawn, at Denham (a miniature British Hollywood) against the shuddering objection of the Technicolor expert. It is one of many things that Olivier and Cameraman Robert Krasker did with color which Technicolor tradition says must not or cannot be done.

The invisible Chorus begins the grandly evocative description of the night camps:

> *Now entertain conjecture of a time*
> *When creeping murmur and the poring dark*
> *Fills the wide vessel of the universe.*

---

* *On the estate of land-poor gentry who, perhaps in gratitude for the sudden prosperity the film brought them, named one of their donkeys for Olivier's wife, Cinemactress Vivien Leigh.*

The screen sustains this mood with a generalized shot of the opposed camps, their fires like humiliated starlight. There are no creeping murmurs, neighing steeds, crowing cocks, clanking armorers. Instead, William Walton's score, one of the few outstanding scores in movie history, furnishes subdued, musical metaphors. Midway through the Chorus, the film boldly breaks off to interpolate, to better effect, a scene in the French camp which in Shakespeare's version precedes it.

This scene itself also improves on Shakespeare. His Frenchmen, the night before their expected triumph, were shallow, frivolous and arrogant. By editing out a good deal of their foolishness, by flawless casting, directing and playing, and by a wonderfully paced appreciation of the dead hours of rural night, Olivier transforms the French into sleepy, overconfident, highly intelligent, highly sophisticated noblemen, subtly disunified, casually contemptuous of their Dauphin—an all but definitive embodiment of a civilization a little too ripe to survive.

The hypnotic Chorus resumes; the camera pans to the English camp and strolls, as if it were the wandering King himself, among the firelit tents.

And here poem and film link the great past to the great present. It is unlikely that anything on the subject has been written to excel Shakespeare's short study, in *Henry V,* of men stranded on the verge of death and disaster. The man who made this movie made it midway in England's most terrible war, within the shadows of Dunkirk. In appearance and in most of what they say, the three soldiers with whom Henry talks on the eve of Agincourt might just as well be soldiers of World War II. No film of that war has yet said what they say so honestly or so well.

Here again Olivier helped out Shakespeare. Shakespeare gave to a cynical soldier the great speech: *But if the cause be not good,* etc. Olivier puts it in the mouth of a slow-minded country boy (Brian Nissen). The boy's complete lack of cynicism, his youth, his eyes bright with sleepless danger, the peasant patience of his delivery, and his Devon repetition of the tolled word *die* as *doy,* lift this wonderful expression of common humanity caught in human war level with the greatness of the King.

HENRY V IS ONE OF the great experiences in the history of motion pictures. It is not, to be sure, the greatest: the creation of new dramatic poetry is more important than the recreation of old. For such new poetry, movies offer the richest opportunity since Shakespeare's time, and some of them have made inspired use of the chance. But *Henry V* is a major achievement—this perfect marriage of great dramatic poetry with the greatest contemporary medium for expressing it.

It was chiefly Olivier who did the brilliant casting; he who gave the French court its more-than-Shakespearean character. Many of the most poetic ideas in cutting and transition were also his. Above all, his was the whole anti-naturalistic conception of the film—a true Shakespearean's recognition that man is greater, and nature less, than life.

The career of Laurence Olivier (pronounced O'lívvy yay) was decided at 15, when he played Katherina in a boys-school production of *The Taming of the Shrew*. When he announced that he wanted to go on the stage, his father, a rural Anglo-Catholic clergyman, did not groan: "Better that I should see you dead." Instead, he gave his endorsement and financial support. At 17, young Olivier enrolled at the Central School of Dramatic Art, which is second only to London's Royal Academy of Dramatic Art. At 18, he was able to tell the Oliviers' old housekeeper, who asked what Laurence did in his first professional engagement: "When you're sitting having your tea during the interval [intermission], and you hear the bell summoning you back to your seat, you'll know that my finger is on the bell."

Later, more substantial parts in plays like *Journey's End, The Green Bay Tree, No Time for Comedy* proved Olivier to be one of the thoroughly good English actors. His performances as Hamlet, Sir Toby Belch, Macbeth, Henry V, Romeo, Iago, Coriolanus, Mercutio earned him a solid, if by no means pre-eminent, reputation as a Shakespearean actor—and gave him invaluable experience. He also picked up a good deal of experience, which he scarcely valued at all, acting intermittently in movies.

For years Olivier "just thought of movies as a quick way to earn money." In the '30s, his work with sincere, painstaking Director William Wyler made him realize that they can amount to a lot more. His fine performance as Heathcliff in *Wuthering Heights* first suggested that Olivier might be a great actor in the making. But Olivier was never really happy in Hollywood. He disliked the climate; he was homesick for the stage.

When England went to war, he planned, like his good friend Cinemactor David Niven, to join the air force. But he could not get out of his contract. While sweating it out, he took flying lessons and, in an unusually short time, piled up 200 hours.

In two years' service Olivier became a lieutenant in the Fleet Air Arm. He stepped unhurt out of a number of forced or crash landings, gave ground and gunnery instruction, never saw combat. But when he got back to work once more as an actor, theatrical London realized that a remarkable new artist had appeared. Olivier has no explanation for the change in himself except to say: "Maybe it's just that I've got older."

Now, as co-manager (with his friend, fellow flyer and fellow actor Ralph Richardson and with John Burrell) of London's Old Vic Theater, Olivier works at least ten hours a day. For recreation he spends quiet evenings after work at the home of friends, listening to phonograph music (Mozart is a favorite). When possible, he runs up to his country home, the 15th-Century Notley Abbey in Buckinghamshire, where his second wife Vivien Leigh is convalescing from tuberculosis.

Next month Olivier and Richardson will bring the Old Vic troupe to Manhattan for six weeks of Sophocles, Shakespeare, Sheridan and Chekhov. Later Olivier would like to film *Macbeth, Hamlet* and *Othello.* But he is in no hurry. He has not had enough plain rest to satisfy him since Britain went to war. ∎

The Kid from Hoboken

BY BRAD DARRACH

[
Delightful, violent, sad, sometimes downright terrifying,
Frank Sinatra showed early in his career that his personality
was as extravagant as his talent and ambition
]

August 29, 1955

IN HOBOKEN, A JERSEY waterfront town that does not shrink from comparison with Port Said, the old folks on the front steps tell the tale of a pretty little boy with rosy cheeks and light brown ringlets who went skipping along the sidewalk in one of the nation's hairiest neighborhoods— all dressed up in a Little Lord Fauntleroy suit. "Hey!" said one little denizen of the neighborhood. "Lookit momma's dolling!" It was the work of a moment for the roughneck and his pal to redecorate the object of their interest with a barrage of rotten fruit. Then they opened their mouths to laugh, but no sound came. When last seen, the two boys were disappearing rapidly in the direction of the Erie Railroad tracks, followed hard by Little Lord Fauntleroy himself, who was spouting profanity in a highly experienced manner and carving the breeze with a jagged chunk of broken bottle.

Thirty-odd years have passed over Hoboken since that day, but what was true then still holds true. Francis Albert Sinatra, long grown out of his Little Lord Fauntleroy suit, is one of the most charming children in everyman's neighborhood; yet it is well to remember the jagged weapon. The one he carries nowadays is of the mind, and called ambition, but it takes an ever more exciting edge. With charm and sharp edges and a snake-slick gift of song, he has dazzled and slashed and coiled his way through a career unparalleled in extravagance by any other entertainer of his generation. And last week, still four months shy of 40, he was well away on a second career that promises to be if anything more brilliant than the first.

"Frank Sinatra," says an agent who wishes he had Frank's account, "is just about the hottest item in show business today." Sinatra, who in *Who's Who* lists himself as "baritone" by occupation, has offers of more work than he could do in 20 years, and seems pleasantly certain to pay income tax for 1955 on something close to $1,000,000. Moreover, his new success spreads like a Hoboken cargo net across almost every area of show business.

• In the movies, Frank Sinatra is currently in more demand than any other performer. His portrayal of Private Maggio in *From Here to Eternity*, which won him an Academy Award last year, burst on the public a new and fiercely burning star. To the amazement of millions, the boudoir johnny with the lotion tones stood revealed as a naturalistic actor of narrow but deep-cutting talents. He played what he is, The Kid from Hoboken, but he played him with rage and tenderness and grace, and he glinted in the barrel of human trash as poetically as an empty tin can in the light of a hobo's match.

• In records, according to his worst enemy in show business, Frankie is "the biggest thing . . . so far this year." Whereas three years ago his best record (*Good Night Irene*) sold only 150,000 pressings, he has one on the market now (*Learnin' the Blues*) that is pushing 800,000 and another (*Young at Heart*) that is over the million mark. Furthermore, he is "the only pop singer who is a smash success in the album market." His three recent albums (*Songs for Young Lovers, Swing Easy,* and *In the Wee Small Hours of the Morning*) have reportedly sold 250,000 copies at $4.98 apiece.

• In television, Sinatra is about to star in a Spectacular-type musical version of *Our Town,* and last week NBC was chasing him hard with a five-year contract to do seven shows a year. The proposed nut: about $3,000,000.

• On the nightclub and variety circuit, Frank has a rating that stands second to none in pull or payoff (he can make up to $50,000 a week at Las Vegas).

Said Frank Sinatra last week, as he sat cockily in his ebony-furnished, "agency modern" offices in Los Angeles' William Morris Agency and tilted a white-banded black panama off his forehead: "Man, I'm buoyant. I feel about eight feet tall." Said a friend: "He's got it made. He's come all the way back and he's gone still further. He's made the transition from the bobby-sox to the Serutan set, and if he keeps on going like he's going, he'll step right in when Bing steps out as the greatest all-around entertainer in the business."

Can Frank Sinatra keep on going? If it were only a question of public appeal, there would be no question. But it is also a matter of character, and Frank Sinatra is one of the most delightful, violent, dramatic, sad and sometimes downright terrifying personalities now on public view. The key to comprehension, if comprehension is possible, lies perhaps in one of the rare remarks that Baritone Sinatra has made about himself. "If it hadn't been for my interest in music," he once wrote, "I'd probably have ended in a life of crime."

The man looks, in fact, like the popular conception of a gangster, model 1929. He has bright, wild eyes, and his movements suggest spring steel; he talks out of the corner of his mouth. He dresses with a glaring, George Raft kind of snazziness—rich, dark shirts and white figured ties, with ring and cuff links that almost always match. He had, at last count, roughly $30,000 worth of cuff links. "He has the Polo Grounds for a closet," says a friend. In one compartment hang more than 100 suits. In another there are 50 pairs of shoes, each shoe set on a separate tree that sprouts out of the wall. In another, 20 hats. Frank is almost obsessively clean. He washes his hands with great frequency, takes two or three showers a day, and often gets apparently uncontrollable impulses to empty ashtrays. He hates to be photographed or seen in public without a hat or hairpiece to cover his retreating hairline.

Frankie has his gang. He is rarely to be seen without a few, and sometimes as many as ten, of "the boys" around him, and some look indeed like unfortunate passport photographs. A few of the Sinatra staff—Manager Hank Sanicola, Writer Don McGuire, Makeup-man "Beans" Ponedel—have established and important functions, but most of the others are classified as "beards and hunkers,"* and as they march in bristling phalanx along Sunset Strip, Frank walks lordly at the head of them.

"I hate cops and reporters," Frank was once heard to say. He is an admitted friend of Joe Fischetti, who is prominent in what is left of the

---

*A "beard," in Hollywood parlance, is a man employed by a male star to accompany him when he appears in public with a woman not his wife. Sometimes female stars use them too. The custom is usually successful in averting trouble with the wife or husband, the gossip columnists and the public. "If Hollywood ever took off its beard," a comedian once remarked, "the public would not recognize it." A "hunker" is somebody kept on the payroll to know baseball scores, send out for coffee, and strike matches on.

Capone mob, and he once made himself a lot of trouble by buddying up to Lucky Luciano in Havana—all of which is not to say that he mixes his pleasure with their business; Frankie is too smart for that. On occasion Sinatra, who was trained as a flyweight by his fighter father, has also gone in for slapping people around. He throws pretty frequent crying fits and temper tantrums too, and has even been seen to weep in his secretary's lap. His prodigality with the big green is legend from Hoboken to Hollywood. "Perhaps," says one friend, "Frank is the wildest spender of modern times. He throws it around like a drunken admiral." A member of his family reports that he usually carries nothing smaller than $100 bills and "peels them off like toilet paper." He once financed a $5,000 wedding for a friend. Another got a Cadillac, just because Sinatra liked him. To a third, Frank flung a grand piano one Christmas. In 1948 alone he spent more than $30,000 on last-minute Christmas presents.

The penny has its obverse, and the other side of Frankie can be a shining thing. He has a Janizary's loyalty for his few close friends. Says one: "It's sort of wonderful but frightening, like having a pet cheetah." Says Don McGuire: "You can call him any hour of the night and tell him you've got the flu, and he will bring you minestrone." When Judy Garland was in a Boston sanitarium, Sinatra sent her flowers every day for a year, and once sent a chartered plane full of her friends from Hollywood to Boston for a visit.

Says Actor Robert Mitchum, cinema's No. 1 problem child: "Frank is a tiger—afraid of nothing, ready for anything. He'll fight anything. Here's a frail, undersized little fellow with a scarred-up face who isn't afraid of the whole world."

Sinatra's courage, even his enemies agree, is the courage of burning convictions, however crudely they may be expressed. Many of his worst passages of public hooliganism have proceeded from instances of racial discrimination. He once slugged a waiter who refused to serve a Negro, another time went haywire at an anti-Semitic remark. Baritone Sinatra, riding the wave of success, is no underdog. "But he bleeds for the underdog," says one of his friends, "because he feels like one. Don't ask me why."

By a similar token, Sinatra is doggedly independent. "Don't tell me!" he often tells friends, eyes blazing, as he jabs them with a forefinger. "Suggest. But don't tell me." "Why, he might even vote Republican," one friend surmised, "if I told him to vote Democrat." A friend tells how Frankie walked out on the christening of his son because the priest would not let him have the godfather Frankie wanted, who happened to be a Jew.

Is there an essential Sinatra hidden somewhere in this bony bundle of contradictions? One of his best friends thinks not. "There isn't any 'real' Sinatra. There's only what you see. You might as well try to analyze electricity. It is what it does. There's nothing inside him. He puts out so terrifically that nothing can accumulate inside. Frank is the absolutely genuine article, the diamond in the rough. If you want to understand a diamond, you ask about the pressures that made it. And if you want to understand Frank, you ask about Hoboken."

IN HOBOKEN, IN A coldwater flat ("one can to four families"), Frank was born on Dec. 12, 1915. He weighed 13½ lbs. at birth, and in the delivery his head was badly ripped by the forceps, and one of his ear lobes was torn away; he carries the scars to this day. The doctor laid the unbreathing baby on the bed, thinking him stillborn, and turned to save the mother. Frank survived because his grandmother snatched him up and put him under the cold-water faucet.

Frankie's father, Martin Sinatra, was a run-of-the-gym boxer who fought under the name of "Marty O'Brien," a quiet little man who could stand up to a beer and mind his own business. Frankie's mother, "Dolly" Sinatra, was another slice of pizza altogether. That sturdy little woman could stand up to anything, come Hague or firewater, and minded everybody else's business along with plenty of her own. In 1909 Mayor Griffin made her district leader.

When Frankie came along, mother Dolly had little time to be a mother. She was off, day and night, in the political swim, and if sometimes the water was polluted, Dolly always insisted that she kept her chin above it. Frank was sent to live with his grandmother, Dolly's mother. He also spent a lot of his time with his Aunt Josie, and with a motherly Jewish lady named Mrs. Golden.

Being a well-fixed boy in a poor neighborhood had its disadvantages, but Frankie made the least of them. When the green-eyed little monsters mobbed him, Frankie fought foot and fang, and won their respect. Moreover, those he could not beat he could buy. In short, Frankie soon found himself with a gang at his back, and a gang in Hoboken had to be kept busy.

"We started hooking candy from the corner store," Frankie recalls. "Then little things from the five-and-dime, then change from cash registers, and finally, we were up to stealing bicycles." Pretty soon Frank was involved in some rough gang wars. He got so good at planning jobs that his awe-struck henchmen called him "Angles," and he had plenty of bad examples to follow, pretty close to home. The streets he played in were full of bootleggers and triggermen; there were even a couple of neighborhood gang killings. "School was very uninteresting," he remembers. "Homework ... we never bothered with ..." In his last year in high school he was expelled, he says, on grounds of general rowdiness.

Frankie could not have cared less. He had already decided what he wanted to do with his life, and it didn't require a high-school diploma. At the age of 16, he had seen Bing Crosby on the stage. Cried Sinatra, in a voice that broke in his mouth like raw spaghetti: "I can do that!" Dolly and Marty had a good laugh. But Frankie talked her out of $65 for a public-address system with a rhinestone-studded case, and started hiring out as a single at lodge dances for $3 a night. He worked over his technique meticulously, tirelessly. "My theory was to learn by trial and error," says Sinatra. "Not sing in the shower, but really operate. Execute!"

Pretty soon he won a Major Bowes contest and landed a 39-week contract as lead singer in a quartet called "The Hoboken Four." He also sang in the Rustic Cabin, a roadhouse not far from Hoboken, where he waited table too, and "practically swept the floor," for $15 a week. And there it was, in 1939, that Frank Sinatra got his break.

Bandleader Harry James heard Frank sing, and took him on as a featured vocalist. Six months later the great Tommy Dorsey himself bought Frank away from Harry at the princely price of $110 a week. Two years with the Dorsey band smoothed a lot of rough edges off the kid from Hoboken, and raised at the same time some alarmingly sensual yet sensationally effective bumps on his singing style.

Sinatra would appear onstage, looking, as one contemporary described him, "like a terrified boy of 15 in the presence of his first major opportunity." He would hang for a moment on the microphone, holding it itchily, as if it were a snake. "His face was like a wet rag." His chest caved in, as if from the weight of the enormous zoot shoulders it bore, and a huge, floppy bow tie hung down like the ears of a spaniel. For a moment he would look among his audience, pleadingly, as if searching for his mother, and then he would begin, timidly and with trembling lips, to sing.

The Voice was worth all the buildup. From Bing, of course, Frank borrowed the intense care for the lyrics, and a few of those bathtub sonorities the microphone takes so well. From Tommy Dorsey's trombone he learned to bend and smear his notes a little, and to slush-pump his rhythms in the long dull level places. From Billie Holiday he caught the trick of scooping his attacks, braking the orchestra, and of working the "hot *acciaccatura*"— the "N'awlins" grace note that most white singers flub.

Yet through all these carefully acquired characteristics ran a vital streak of Sinatra. He was the first popular singer to use breathing for dramatic effect. He actually learned to breathe in the middle of a note without breaking it (an old trick of the American Indian singers), and so was able "to tie one phrase to another and sound like I never took a breath." He carried diction to a point of passionate perfection. But what made Sinatra Sinatra, when all came to all, was his naive urgency and belief in what he was saying. As one bandleader put it: "Why, that dear little jerk. He really believes those silly words!"

He believed them, and suddenly large numbers of young girls began to believe Sinatra. They began to make little ecstatic moans when Frankie sang. The boys in the band laughed, and moaned right back, but Frankie took it all in ferocious earnest. He knew his hour had struck, and he asked Dorsey for a release of contract. Tommy refused, but in the end, in return for a fat piece of Frankie's future, let him go, and Frank was booked into the Paramount.

S-day, Dec. 31, 1942, dawned bright. After Frank's first performance, the stage door was congested by some squealing young things who wanted his autograph. The crowds grew until, after some weeks, traffic in Times Square was stopped cold by the massed oblation of thousands of wriggling female children. Out came the riot squad, up went the headlines: FIVE THOUSAND GIRLS FIGHT TO GET VIEW OF FRANK SINATRA. A scrawny, wistful little piper had come to town, and the younger generation was following him in far greater numbers and enthusiasm than ever it had shown for the Hamelin original—or for Rudolph Valentino himself.

Frank's income whooshed up from $750 to $3,500 a week, and kept on going. In 1943 he made more than $1,500,000. In 1944, while Governor Dewey, the Republican candidate for the presidency, was greeting a crowd gathered in front of the Waldorf-Astoria Hotel, Democrat Sinatra made a point of passing by. Two minutes later the governor was facing a handful of hard-core Republicans, while almost everybody else was following Frankie Boy down Park Avenue.

And what did Frankie do while the wine of fame was flowing free? He bought a $250,000 home in Holmsby Hills, then a place in Palm Springs for $162,000. He gave away gold Dunhill lighters ($250 apiece) by the gross. He threw champagne parties day after day. And night after night, there were the women. When Frankie came back to his hotel he almost always found some mixed-up youngster hiding under his bed or in the closet; sometimes it was not a girl but a grown-up woman. One night a well-known society belle walked up and asked him for his autograph— on her brassière. On another occasion a woman walked into his room wearing a mink coat—and nothing underneath. Frank Sinatra coped with each situation as best he could.

Frankie's name was linked with a succession of famous women: Lana Turner, Judy Garland, Marilyn Maxwell, Gloria Vanderbilt, Anita Ekberg. All these goings-on were naturally not calculated to please Mrs. Nancy Sinatra, the pretty girl from Hoboken whom Frank had married back in the Rustic Cabin days, and with whom he has three children— Nancy, 15, Frankie, 11, and Christina, 7. But somehow the Sinatras managed to keep the home fires sputtering along—until Frank one day met up with Ava Gardner.

THE BAREFOOT VENUS of Smithfield, N.C. was in some respects an excellent match for the Little Lord Fauntleroy of Hoboken. They had come from well below the salt, and they loved the high life at the head of the table. Ava, who had been chastened in two marriages and on the analytic couch as well, saw through her martini glass more darkly than did Frank. "If I were a man," she told him, "I wouldn't like me." But Frank liked her very much indeed, left home to keep her stormy, full-time company, finally persuaded Nancy, a steadfast Roman Catholic, to give him a divorce, and married Ava on Nov. 7, 1951.

Even before the wedding, Frank was worn down pretty fine. One night, in Reno, he had taken an overdose of sleeping pills. And after two years of Ava he was admitted to a New York hospital one night with several scratches on his lower arm. The decisive moment, however, came one night in 1952 when Frank threw her out of his house in Palm Springs. Since then, Ava has flirted with both Frankie and a divorce, but gotten together with neither of them.

After the avalanche, there wasn't much left of Frank Sinatra. He was down from 132 to 118 lbs., his voice was shot, his record sales had practically stopped. His relations with the press were in shreds. Church groups were fighting him because of all the scandal. The Government was after him for $110,000 in back taxes. "Anyone know of a bigger bore just now," the *Daily News* inquired, "than Frank Sinatra?" Frankie, said the boys in Toots Shor's and in Chasen's, was done.

They underestimated Angles. Frankie loosened his ties to M-G-M. "Then," says he, "I started all over again with a clean slate." He changed his agent, from M.C.A. to William Morris; he changed his record company, from Columbia to Capitol. His voice came back, better than ever; record sales began to climb. He started to freelance in TV on a larger scale, and to look around for roles he really liked in the movies. Along came *Eternity*. "That's me!" said Frank Sinatra when he read about the roistering, ill-starred little Italian named Maggio. He wanted the part so badly that he offered to play it for only $1,000 a week, made only $8,000 on the picture.

Almost magically, humpty-dumpty was together again. What was he like after his great fall, and his miraculous bounce back to the high wall of fame? In recent months, Frank Sinatra has managed to irritate a crowd of 10,000 in Australia, sue a well-known producer for breach of contract and make it widely known that he "would rather punch him in the face," display scorn in public for Marlon Brando, alienate the affections of Sam Goldwyn, mount a wide-open attack on another entertainer in a prominent newspaper ad ("Ed Sullivan, You're sick . . . P.S. Sick! Sick! Sick!").

But many of Frank's friends insist that he has matured of late. He shows intense devotion to his children, visiting them almost every day and taking them with him wherever he can. He has buttressed the flimsy walls of present success with long-range business enterprises—five music companies, an independent film outfit, a 2% chunk of the enormous Sands gambling hotel in Las Vegas, and eleven shares of the Atlantic City Racetrack. In movies, he picks his parts as carefully as he has always picked songs that suit both his talent and his taste. He works as fiercely as he plays.

The Sinatra day usually begins about 10 a.m. with a mug of hot coffee and a grandiose scattering of transcontinental telephone calls. A dozen people crowd around him as the makeup-man goes to work, all trying to outshout each other and a blaring radio. Off to the set in a bevy of Cadillacs, where the mob grows to 50 or 100 until Frank suddenly stands alone against a sky-blue set and moves his mouth expressively, while his voice drifts out of a distant amplifier. At the first break he piles into a box lunch, then takes a catnap. There are some dialogue loops to make, and then across town in his colossal Cad ("I like lots of armor around me"), with brooding on the way about "them Giants," happy cackling about "Rocky" Marciano or the fun he will have with the boys at Toots Shor's on a scheduled trip to New York.

At the recording studio everything is ready: bare walls, hard chairs and rattling music racks, all neuter in a thin fluorescent light. But as Sinatra stands up to the mike, tie loose and blue palmetto hat stuck on awry, his cigarette hung slackly from his lips, a mood curls out into the room like smoke. He begins to sing, hips down and shoulders hunched, hands shaping the big rhythms and eyes rolling with each low-down line. The musicians come to life, the wallbirds start to smile and weave with the very special sound that is Sinatra. Instead of the old adolescent moo, the Sinatra voice now has a jazzy undertone of roostering confidence, and a kind of jewel hardness that can take on blue and give off fire with subtlety and fascination.

"That does it," a technician says, and Frank hand-shakes his way to the door, purrs off into the California night with his waiting date. They may drop in on some of Sinatra's current set of friends—the Bogarts, Judy (Garland) and Sid Luft—or munch a steak with Montgomery Clift & Co. Frankie loves the clink of ice in well-filled glasses, and the click of Hollywood's oddballs in a well-filled room. But everybody has to go home, sooner or later, and the moment comes sometimes when Frankie is left alone—the thing he seems to hate the most in life. If that should happen, he may ring up a girl he has known for many years. When she arrives, they sit and talk and talk until the sun comes up or she falls asleep, and then Frank may wander next door to have breakfast with Jimmy van Heusen, the songwriter and Sinatra friend. So begins another day in the Arabian Nights of Frank Sinatra.

Sometimes somebody tries to tell him that his way is no way to live, but when they do, Frank has an answer as simple and as emphatic as a punch in the mouth: "I'm going to do as I please. I don't need anybody in the world. I did it all myself." ∎

The Hero of the Code

BY T.E. KALEM

[
*This moving tribute to Ernest Hemingway looked
beyond his decline and suicide to his tenacious, masterly
scrutiny of the crisis in Western belief and values*
]

July 14, 1961

*All stories, if continued far enough, end in death, and he is no
true storyteller who would keep that from you.*

ERNEST HEMINGWAY, THE storyteller who wrote
those lines, was brushing his teeth. It had been, his wife later
recalled, a "calm, good-natured" dinner, and she was sitting
in her bedroom in their house in Ketchum, Idaho, when an Italian song
she had not thought of for years came into her mind—*Tutti Mi Chiamano
Bionda* (Everybody Tells Me I'm Blonde). Mary Hemingway walked across
the hall to her husband's room to sing it for him. "I said, 'I have a present
for you.' He listened to me, and he finished cleaning his teeth to join me in
the last line."

Next morning, shortly after 7 a.m., a pajama-clad Hemingway went
downstairs and from the gun rack took his favorite gun, which, like almost
everything he owned, was not merely a thing but a ceremonial object. A
twelve-gauge, double-barreled shotgun inlaid with silver, it had been spe-
cially made for Hemingway. He put the gun barrel in his mouth and pulled
both triggers. The blast blew his whole head away except for his mouth, his
chin, and part of his cheeks.

313

The small, quiet funeral took place four days later in the placid village cemetery of Ketchum. To the north, the peaks of the rugged Sawtooth Mountains were still capped with snow. To the east lay the lavish summer greenery of the Wood River Valley. Around the rose-covered coffin gathered only about 50 people, mostly Idaho neighbors and some of Hemingway's always-varied circle of friends—a doctor, a rancher, a hotel man, a onetime operator of a gymnasium. "O Lord," prayed Father Robert Waldmann, pastor of Our Lady of the Snows Catholic Church, "grant to thy servant Ernest the remission of his sins. Eternal rest grant unto him, O Lord."

Mary Hemingway kept insisting that, somehow, her husband's death had been an accident. Plainly it could not have been. Moreover, Hemingway had been ill and depressed for a long time. His blood pressure was high, and his doctor suspected incipient diabetes. His eating and drinking were restricted—to shrink more than 40 lbs. from the bearlike physique in which he had always taken a small boy's pride. Literary visitors last winter found Hemingway inarticulate and insecure, pathetically doubting not only his current creative powers but the value of all he had ever done. In two lengthy stays at the Mayo Clinic he got shock treatments for depression. Recently, the death of his friend Gary Cooper depressed him further.

Suicide as a way of ending the story of a life had been much on his mind. Hemingway's physician father, also ill with hypertension and diabetes, had died by his own hand in 1928. Indeed, Hemingway had brooded and passed judgment upon it in print. In *For Whom the Bell Tolls,* Robert Jordan thinks about his suicide-father, "that other one that misused the gun," and calls him a coward. Elsewhere, Hemingway suggested that there was nothing cowardly in suicide—if used to hasten what otherwise might be a slow and messy death. Some years ago, his mother, as a present, sent him the Civil War pistol with which his father had shot himself.

There was a worldwide seismic shock at Hemingway's death, even though for some years younger writers had stopped imitating the master stylist, and despite the fact that in the last two decades, Hemingway had produced only a near parody of himself, *Across the River and Into the Trees,* and a small but immutable achievement, *The Old Man and the Sea.* For the rest, the legend engulfed the man, and he seemed bent on playing the part of a Hemingway character.

From his earliest expatriate days, when he knew James Joyce and Gertrude Stein at Sylvia Beach's Paris bookshop, Hemingway plainly enjoyed being a celebrity among celebrities. He went fishing with Charles

Ritz, the Paris hotel man, and considered fighting a duel over Ava Gardner, whose honor somebody had insulted. In Paris he invariably cultivated Georges Carpentier, the prizefighter turned saloon owner; in New York he befriended Restaurateur Toots Shor, and despite an often-expressed desire for privacy, went on the town with Gossip Columnist Leonard Lyons. He not only allowed but encouraged the world to turn him into a character. He had well-publicized talks about child care with Grandmother Marlene Dietrich ("The Kraut"), jovially referred to himself as Doctor Hemingstein or Old Ernie Hemorrhoid ("The Poor Man's Pyle"), and talked of his literary prowess in prizefighting terms: "I trained hard and I beat Mr. De Maupassant. I've fought two draws with Mr. Stendhal, but nobody is going to get me in any ring with Mr. Tolstoy unless I'm crazy or keep getting better."

But all this could not damage the work he had already done or lessen his world impact, which was, and is, incalculable.

For years, critics skimmed the dazzling prose surface of Hemingway and harped on his tough-guy realism. In one of those flat-out statements that sometimes herald a major critical about-face, at least one U.S. critic, North Carolina State's E. M. Halliday, recently called Hemingway essentially a philosophical writer. His was, of course, never a formal but a sort of visceral philosophy. But though he was leary of metaphysical systems, Hemingway was really on a metaphysical quest. Without the customary marks of the intellectual, in fact often called anti-intellectual, he was nevertheless a tenacious observer of the crisis in belief and values which is the central crisis of Western civilization.

His philosophy—essentially a profound pessimism about the human situation and a stoic sense of tragedy—grew out of war. Like many a child of the times, he was born twice, once in Oak Park, Ill., on July 21, 1899, and a second time during World War I at Fossalta on the Italian Piave on July 8, 1918. At Fossalta, Hemingway, who had switched from ambulance driving to join the Italian infantry, was so badly wounded in a burst of shellfire that he felt life slip from his body, "like you'd pull a silk handkerchief out of a pocket by one corner," and then return. He emerged with 237 bits of shrapnel (by his own count), an aluminum kneecap, and two Italian decorations. It was at Fossalta that he picked up a fear of his own fear and the lifelong need to test his courage.

This experience might not have shaped the philosophic attitudes of his works if the entire climate of intellectual history had not prepared an audience for him. The 20th century was primed for a philosophy of concrete things rather than abstract ideas, was ready for a psychology of sensations—for the brute fact, the tactile thrill, the stream of sensuousness that inundate the pages of Hemingway.

As a fledgling writer in Paris, Hemingway intuitively felt a double betrayal of language and ideals. The first thing the Lost Generation lost was its faith in words, big words. Says Lieut. Henry, the hero of *A Farewell to Arms:* "I was always embarrassed by the words sacred, glorious and sacrifice and the expression in vain . . . I had seen nothing sacred, and the things that were glorious had no glory and the sacrifices were like the stockyards at Chicago if nothing was done with the meat except to bury it." The big words were false, and life itself was "just a dirty trick," as the dying Catherine tells her lover in the same book. Hemingway's image for man's plight in the universe was that of an ant colony on a burning log. There was no hope of heaven or sustaining faith in God. In the short story *A Clean, Well-Lighted Place,* there is a parody of the Lord's Prayer built on the Spanish word *nada,* meaning nothingness ("Our nada who art in nada, nada be thy name"). In *The Gambler, the Nun, and the Radio,* the hero narrator decides that "bread is the opium of the people."

The pattern of what Alberto Moravia aptly calls Hemingway's "ingenuous nihilism" was early set, but even Hemingway could not sustain himself on *nada,* or on bread alone. If life was a short day's journey from nothingness to nothingness, there still had to be some meaning to the "performance en route." In Hemingway's view, the universal moral standard was nonexistent, but there were the clique moralities of the sportsman or the soldier, or, in his own case, the writer. So he invented the Code Hero, the code being "what we have instead of God," as Lady Brett Ashley puts it in *The Sun Also Rises.*

THE CODE HERO IS both a little snobbish and a little vague, but the test of the code is courage, and the essence of the code is conduct. Conduct, in Hemingway, is sometimes a question of how one behaves honorably toward another man or woman. More often, it is a question of how the good professional behaves within the rules of a game or the limits of a craft. All the how-to passages—how to land a fish, how to handle guns, how to work with a bull—have behind them the professional's pride of skill. But the code is never anchored to anything except itself; life becomes a game of doing things in a certain style for the sake of style, a narcissistic ritual—which led Hemingway himself not only to some mechanical, self-consciously "Hemingway" writing but to a self-conscious "Hemingway" style of life.

To raise the Code Hero to something like tragic dignity, there had to be the risk of death. From Fossalta on, Hemingway had death as an obsession; the bullfight gave it to him esthetically, as a ritual, with order and discipline. In *Death in the Afternoon,* he states his tragic creed flatly: "There is no remedy for anything in life." His *Winner Takes Nothing;* his lovers lose all. His fictional stages are strewn with corpses. In *To Have and Have Not,* there are twelve, which compares favorably with the Elizabethans. Nemesis, in the Hemingway tragedy, is bad luck. "I was going good," says Manuel, the gored bullfighter in *The Undefeated,* "I didn't have any luck. That was all." "Never fight under me," says Colonel Cantwell in *Across the River and Into the Trees.* "I'm cagey. But I'm not lucky." Even Santiago, the old fisherman in *The Old Man and the Sea,* says, "I have no luck any more." Under the brilliant physical surface in Hemingway there was always the metaphysical brooding, the glancing reflections on a destiny his characters keep telling themselves not to think about.

What does not bear thinking about is what is going to happen. A Hemingway character does not make things happen; things happen to him. Hemingway's people often seem like masochistic spectators of their own doom. In *The Killers,* Nick Adams rushes to the boardinghouse room of the ex-prizefighter Ole Andreson to warn him that two gangsters are in town to kill him. "There isn't anything I can do about it," says Ole Andreson, lying on his bed and turning his face fatalistically to the wall. There isn't anything any Hemingway character can do about his fate except to take it.

The trouble with the metaphysics of chance is that it is too shallow for a true tragic destiny. Unlike the Greek and Elizabethan heroes, the Hemingway hero does not understand his fate. It's simply a dirty trick. The reader, in turn, is saddened without being purged, resigned without being reconciled to man's destiny.

Whatever Hemingway's merits or demerits as a thinker, he had the greatest technical command of English of any modern writer except Joyce. He performed a major operation on the English sentence. He cut out the adjectives and prompting words that tell a reader how to feel and replaced them with spare, brisk monosyllables that he called the "ugly short infantry of the mind." Hemingway spliced his images together like a film editor, so that the action was always advancing on the reader rather than the reader following the action.

In *For Whom the Bell Tolls,* El Sordo on the hilltop is waiting to squeeze the trigger on an enemy, but it is the reader who sights along the rifle: "Look. With a red face and blond hair and blue eyes. With no cap and his moustache is yellow. With blue eyes. With pale blue eyes. With pale blue eyes with something wrong with them. With pale blue eyes that don't focus. Close enough. Too close. Yes, Comrade Voyager. Take it, Comrade Voyager."

Though he relied on the common speech of the commonest men— race-track touts, prizefighters, soldiers—Hemingway wrote brilliant dialogue that was highly stylized, just as an X ray is a highly stylized picture of the body. It revealed more than it ever laconically said. Though he never went to college, he picked his prose teachers well, starting with the King James Bible. His love of nature and the vernacular, together with a kind of barefoot male camaraderie, linked him fraternally with Mark Twain and Huckleberry Finn. Hemingway was the first of the '20s expatriates to knock on Gertrude Stein's door, and he learned the most. She taught him the impact of simple repetition and the rhythm of words.

From Flaubert, whose bust he used to salute while crossing the Luxembourg Gardens to his Montparnasse flat, Hemingway learned precision, the right word in the right place. But there is an emotional intensity in a random Hemingway sentence that the teachers do not account for and the imitators and parodists never capture. The effect of "In the bed of the river there were pebbles and boulders, dry and white in the sun, and the water was clear and swiftly moving and blue in the channels" depends on a special quality of vision. Everything in Hemingway is seen as it might be looked at by a man on the day he knew he would die.

He never toyed with minor themes. He wrote of life and death, of time and towns (which he called cities), and of the courage he liked to call "grace under pressure." He never had much stomach, or much head, for politics, and his literary reputation may wear the better for it, since nothing dates like a paper barricade.

He once said: "Let those who want to save the world if you get to see it clear and as a whole." Seeing it clear and whole did not involve for him, as it did for Tolstoy, the high politics of a philosophy of history. In *War and Peace,* Tolstoy speculates at length on whether heroes and leaders influence events or whether everything is impersonally determined like the rise and fall of tides. Hemingway had an underdeveloped social sense, and he put his characters in situations where society had already broken down. He pictured the social order as disorder, a kind of natural catastrophe like a river in flood. The individual could save himself only by relying on himself.

Of love, Hemingway wrote with peculiar implausibility. The love affair in *A Farewell to Arms* is a kind of modern *Romeo and Juliet*. Most of the other love stories read like adolescent male fantasies. In Hemingway there are only two kinds of women—the bitches like Margaret Macomber who shoots her husband the moment he displays courage, and the somnambules like Maria, who sleepwalks into Robert Jordan's sleeping bag. Lady Brett Ashley is a special breed, a likable bitch. Ibsen's Nora wanted to be her own woman. Promiscuous, aggressive Brett, with her habit of calling everybody "chap," is both her own woman and her own man, with the fatal sterility of being able to give herself to no one.

Among major modern U.S. writers, Hemingway showed more internal discipline than Faulkner, who has ruined half his books with careless rhetorical obscurity, and more personal integrity than Fitzgerald, who potboiled and drank away the greatest natural gifts of the three as a novelist. Unlike Faulkner and Fitzgerald, Hemingway rarely dealt with the American scene after his early Nick Adams stories of hunting and fishing in the West. Internationally, Hemingway belonged with Eliot, Yeats and Joyce as one of the prime shapers of modern literature, but temperamentally he was more akin to that roving intellectual foreign legion of Malraux, Camus and Koestler, who sent back communiqués from all the battlefronts of the 20th century consciousness and conscience.

Will Hemingway pass the test of timelessness? There are several good reasons for thinking so. Most of his short stories, *The Sun Also Rises, A Farewell to Arms* and *The Old Man and The Sea* have the internal inevitability of masterworks; no one can imagine them happening in some other way. The underlying theme is universal: natural man pitted against the mystery of the universe.

T. S. Eliot once proposed a test for the lasting significance of a writer: "Someone said: 'The dead writers are remote from us because we *know* so much more than they did.' Precisely, and they are that which we know." Through his books, Hemingway is "that which we know" of World War I, the Lost Generation, the mystique of the bullfight, the Spanish Civil War. One can learn all of this without knowing Hemingway, but once having read him, one can never see these subjects again without some angle or tint of his vision. His best books exist at that rare level at which literature becomes experience.

In Hemingway, experience is always a form of fate. It tells of defeat and "the evil-smelling emptiness" of death. It stirs memories of pleasure and desire, "of sunshine and salt water, of food, wine, and making love." Wherever he went, whatever he did, the fate Hemingway yearned for was deceptively simple and impossibly serene—it was "the good place" Nick Adams found on *The Big Two-Hearted River:* "He felt he had left everything behind, the need for thinking, the need to write, other needs. It was all back of him. Now it was done. He was very tired. He had made his camp. He was settled. Nothing could touch him. It was a good place to camp. He was there, in the good place." ∎

The Big Hustler

BY JOHN McPHEE

[*This vivid profile showed how, at the peak of his rowdy, flamboyant career, Jackie Gleason just about lived up to his self-description as "the greatest"*]

December 29, 1961

CLICK. THE NINE BALL plops into the side pocket, the cue ball hits one cushion and stops near the center spot. Big as a water tower but light on his feet, with a diamond ring on a pudgy finger, the fat man moves around the table. For 31 consecutive hours, with an almost incredible repertoire of massé shots, bank shots, gather shots, and combinations, with just enough English and the right amount of draw, he has been defending his reputation as the best there is. He chalks up and shoots again. Click. The 15 ball slams into the corner and disappears. Minnesota Fats is still the greatest pool shark in the world.

It is a relatively small part—in Robert Rossen's movie *The Hustler*—but no one who has seen that fat man will forget him. A man of understated power, Minnesota Fats is played, curiously enough, by Jackie Gleason, and where audiences might have arrived expecting a million laughs from the most celebrated buffoon ever to rise through U.S. television, they leave with a single, if surprised, reaction: inside the master jester, there is a masterful actor. Gleason, the storied comedian, egotist, golfer, and gourmand, mystic, hypnotist, boozer and bull slinger, is now emerging as a first-rank star of motion pictures.

His talent, in fact, is so elastic that he could probably make a living in any form of show business except midget-auto racing. From his start in vaudeville as a boy in Brooklyn, he developed his galloping wit in a string of tough nightclubs before becoming the Jack of all television. Now, as a serious actor and no longer merely a situation comedian, he is surrounded by competing actors schooled in the Method, but he holds his own with unquiet confidence, bellowing, as he always has: "I'm the world's greatest." Entering his new career with appetite akimbo, he has already completed another film, *Gigot,* for which he wrote the story himself, and in Manhattan last week he was at work on still another, *Requiem for a Heavyweight.*

Gleason does his new job with remarkable ease. He memorizes at first sight. While Method actors search their souls and "live" their roles, Gleason riffles through a script and is ready to go. His fellow performers both amuse and irritate him with their warmup exercises: while shooting *The Hustler,* Paul Newman was forever shaking his wrists like a swimmer before a race; and on the *Requiem* set, Anthony Quinn shadowboxes and dances up and down—"marinating," as Gleason puts it—for half an hour before a take. Gleason stands around cracking jokes and shouting: "Let's go! Let's go!" But his directors uniformly report that when they call for action, Gleason snaps instantly into the character he is playing.

In one sense, Gleason's sudden achievements should not be as surprising as they seem. For unlike such masters of the one-line gag as Bob Hope and Mort Sahl, he bases his humor on the creation of comic characters—most of them acted by himself. And as the late James Thurber liked to remark, such comedy may be amusing, but it is also serious commentary on human life. "Gleason has gorgeous creative juices," says *Requiem's* Producer David Susskind with purple accuracy. "He is a thundering talent—the kind of raw, brilliant talent that has gone out of style, with as much instinct in drama as in comedy."

On the *Requiem* set last week—in the locker-room area under the grandstands at Randalls Island stadium—Gleason was finding out that moviemaking on location can be spartan. Against freezing temperatures, heat came from charcoal briquettes in braziers. Cast and crew were breathing contrails. Gleason sat, like a huge frostbitten gourd, in a camp chair labeled THE GREAT ONE.

It was enough to make a penguin take to the bottle; but Gleason, dieting, munched his Ry-Krisp without benefit of sauce. Although he can, as Susskind says, "put away more Scotch per square hour than any man alive," he rarely drinks on the job. The Gleason legend has much to float on, but he proudly insists that he has never missed a show because of drinking. "I'm a heavy drinker when I drink," Gleason generalizes, "because I can put away a bundle of booze before the lights go out. I like it. Some people like to climb mountains. I'm glad I'm not one of them. I'm happy knowing the only thing in danger when I'm getting my kicks is my elbow. There is nothing to fear about drinking if you're honest with yourself as to why you drink. I have never taken a drink to improve my appetite, ward off a cold, or get a good night's sleep. I drink with the honorable intention of getting bagged."

Bagged he gets. He is the national open champion at something called The Challenge, a game of classic simplicity wherein the contestants see who can swallow the greatest quantity of booze before falling over, heels in the air. Dressed in red ties and baseball hats, Gleason and Actor Paul Douglas once got ready for a major league battle, but Gleason said. "Let's fungo a few first." The preliminary rounds were so numerous that the contest never started; both Gleason and Douglas were beaned by the fungoes.

As for his eating, most horses would be embarrassed. Gleason orders pizzas by the stack, has put down five stuffed lobsters at a sitting. He says he has pica, which Webster's *New Collegiate Dictionary* describes as "craving for unnatural food, as chalk, ashes, etc."; but what Gleason really has is merely an unnatural craving. Often—and with great will power—he diets, cutting down his intake to 1,200 calories a day. He once took off 100 lbs.

He is 6 ft. tall, and his mature weight has generally varied from 220, which he calls "slim," to an alltime high of 284. His neck size is 19, and the nose cone has yet to leave Canaveral that could not parachute back to earth dangling from one of Jackie Gleason's shirts. His Manhattan tailor flatteringly but fairly describes him as "the best-dressed stout man I know—above conservative, not afraid to look well-dressed." Gleason orders about a dozen suits a year, paying as little as $285 for a little grey nothing, sometimes going exotic with such items as a cashmere trench coat or pink slacks. He once gave his tailor a single $7,500 order. He is 47 in. at the bulge, but it sometimes swells to 51 in., and he has to keep a triple wardrobe. Each "medium weight" Gleason suit (designed to cover approximately 250 lbs., his present weight) has a larger and smaller counterpart.

The man inside all these textiles has a stupendous ego, and the only characters who come near him in all of fiction are Spenser's Braggadochio and Plautus' Braggart Warrior. "If I didn't have an enormous ego and a monumental pride, how in hell could I be a performer?" he explains. With something for everybody, he is kind, generous, rude and stubborn, explosive, impulsive, bright and mischievous. He is an outgoing, flamboyant man to whom privacy is sacred. Now he is snapping out wisecracks. Now he is sitting alone, quietly unapproachable. He is too often bored. He is a bad listener in general conversation and a good one when acting. He has a great big kettledrum laugh. He is afraid of airplanes and strangers. "He is all fun and jazz until a stranger comes in," says a onetime member of his staff. "Then he goes into that fat shell."

Largely self-educated, he is forever apologizing for his lack of education, but he has no need to: he is informed and knowledgeable. He drops little aphorisms like petals: "A genius is a man who can convince himself he isn't"; "Television critics report accidents to eyewitnesses"; "To make the world go around, men must have two feelings—unhappiness, to make them seek a better life, and egotism, to supply the fuel that keeps them going when they don't find it." He has a huge vocabulary, which sometimes slices into the rough. "Don't misconcept this," he will say, or "That guy is a man of great introspect." But his favorite adjective is "beautiful," his favorite noun is "pal," and his favorite phrase is "beautiful, pal, beautiful."

GLEASON'S HISTORIC HANGOUT IS Toots Shor's restaurant, which reopens on a new site this week on Manhattan's West 52nd Street with Gleason figuring centrally in the ceremonies. "After all," says Jackie, "I'm the elder statesman of the joint." A close friend of Shor for more than 20 years, Gleason calls him Clamhead. He has long since earned Shor's highest accolade: "Jackie drinks good."

With the showbiz-sporting crowd that collects there, Gleason stands around at the bar, communicating in the limited vocabulary of the milieu: "Pal," "Bum," "Tomato," and "Har-de-har-har." Jackie compares Shor's to "the corner candy store when you were a kid, except instead of Jujubes you've got the booze." The famous story is true that Gleason and the 240-lb. Shor once raced each other around the block, running in opposite directions. Gleason was standing coolly at the bar when Shor puffed in. Gleason had used a cab, but Shor, whose giant brain sometimes takes five, paid off the bet before he came to his senses and realized that Gleason had never passed him.

Shor got his revenge one night when he introduced Gleason to "Mr. Joe Shuman," explaining that Shuman was a dress manufacturer from Philadelphia and an old Shor pal. Shuman confided that in his spare time he sometimes liked to shoot a little pool. Gleason prides himself on shooting an excellent stick in his own right, and always has (at the age of 13, he became the pool champion of his neighborhood in the Bushwick section of Brooklyn, upholding the honor and petty bets of the Irish kids against the Italian champion "from up the hill"). He invited Shuman to try his skill at a nearby billiard room. Shuman nicked Gleason for $100 in a close game of straight. "I'll bet you another hundred," said Gleason. Shuman then ran through 70 balls right-handed, 30 more left-handed, and shut Gleason out cold in a 100-point game. "I don't know who the hell I'm playin', but he sure does all right under the name he's usin'," said Jackie Gleason—who had been hustled by Willie Mosconi, the world's pocket-billiard champion (and, later on, technical adviser to *The Hustler*).

Jackie Gleason was born in Brooklyn in the winter of 1916. His father was an auditor for the Mutual Life Insurance Co. who sold candy bars to his fellow employees to supplement the family income. His only brother died before Jackie was three, and Jackie was in effect an only child. When Jackie was eight, his father went to work one day and never came home. His disappearance has never been explained. "He was," says Jackie with a quiet smile, "as good a father as I've ever known."

Thomas Patrick Robinson, Ph.D., a sometime college professor who grew up with Jackie (and was later—as Bookshelf Robinson—given frequent mention on Gleason's TV shows, along with such other neighborhood immortals as Duddy Duddelson, Crazy Guggenham, and Fatso Fogarty), remembers Jackie as "a big hero in the neighborhood—because of the pool, and also because he was so funny. He had a slouchy mannerism, a duck-waddling walk." Gleason's mother worked in a subway change booth and had small regard for her son's comic talents, and when Jackie brought down the house with his clowning in the P.S. 73 eighth-grade graduation play, he shouted at her from the stage: "I told you, Mom! I told you!" His formal education ceased at that level and, to his mother's dismay, he spent the next few years standing around on street corners, usually dressed in a grey suit, a pearl grey double-breasted vest, a yellow polka-dot tie, a polka-dot handkerchief, a polka-dot scarf, a chesterfield, a derby and spats—doing absolutely nothing.

For $3 a night, he started to emcee amateur shows all over the city, keeping a joke book with the dirty ones circled and the clean ones starred.

When his mother died of erysipelas, Jackie, not yet 20, moved to Manhattan and began to seek bookings in nightclubs. During a three-year job at something called Club Miami in Newark, N.J., he kept the crowds amused by insulting them, occasionally stepping into the alley to fight it out with a customer. One night a patron smashed him into unconsciousness. It turned out that the patron was boxing's Two-Ton Tony Galento.

He served as house comic in a burlesque hall, gave a snake-oil spiel for a stunt-driving show, and worked the circuit as a comic diver—but when he was ordered to plunge 90 ft. into a 7-ft. tub of water, he quit, saying "Look, I'm getting $16 a week, and that won't even pay for the iodine." His first big-time comedian's job came at Manhattan's Club 18, a downstairs bin where everybody on the staff took part in the act, even the waiters and chef. One day Hollywood's Jack L. Warner caught his act and signed him to a motion picture contract.

"I'll take Hollywood by storm," Gleason told his friends, but Warner Bros. today does not even remember that he was there. He was miscast (gangster, blue-eyed Arab) in a few pictures and spent most of his time performing at Slapsie Maxie's nightclub. Gleason would drink iced-tea tumblers full of whisky ("No booze, no laughs" was his motto) before going onstage to sing and dance and do improvisations, low comedy, and devastating imitations of more celebrated performers. Retreating to New York, and turned down for service in World War II on physical grounds, Gleason spent several professionally lean years doing club work and bit parts in Broadway shows.

Then in 1949 he began the TV parlay that soon made him television's No. 1 star. He started with *Cavalcade of Stars* on the old Dumont network, a variety show during the course of which he developed the Gleason characters that were to become as nationally familiar as the face on the $1 bill: Reggie Van Gleason, the patrician sot; Charlie Bratton, the loudmouth; the Poor Soul, who always got into trouble trying to do things for other people; Joe the Bartender, the 3¢ philosopher—all played by Gleason and all representing some aspect of Gleason himself.

But no skit on the show caught on like *The Honeymooners*, the ironically titled description of a Brooklyn couple who had been married for ten years and fighting for nine years and twelve months. It was broad, low-median but honest humor, perhaps the best situation comedy that has ever been on television. As Ralph Kramden, husband and bus driver, Gleason stared with massive malevolence at his mother-in-law and pounded the kitchen table, a big man with big gestures under a half-acre of black curls. He looked like a big basset hound who had just eaten W. C. Fields, his expression a mélange of smugness, mischievousness, humility, humor, guilt, pride, warmth, confidence, perplexity, and orotund, bug-eyed naiveté.

"Jackie Gleason is an artist of the first rank," wrote Novelist John O'Hara. "An artist puts his own personal stamp on all of his mature work, making his handling of his material uniquely his own. Millions of people who don't give a damn about art have been quick to recognize a creation. Ralph Kramden is a character that we might be getting from Mr. Dickens if he were writing for TV."

With Art Carney as Ed Norton, the sewer worker, Joyce Randolph as Norton's wife and Audrey Meadows as Alice Kramden, Gleason carried *The Honeymooners* out of *Cavalcade* and into the major leagues on CBS's *The Jackie Gleason Show*, always running nearly every aspect of the production himself, from set designing to bit-part bookings. He worked so hard that he sometimes had to be given oxygen on the set. In 1954 he broke his leg and ankle during a performance.

In 1955 he set *The Honeymooners* up on their own as a half-hour show. Buick signed him up with one of the largest contracts in the history of TV—$11 million for three seasons. At that moment, Gleason was the biggest thing in show business. But, as an accomplished catnapper, he fell asleep at the signing table and had to be awakened to scratch his signature on the contract.

For his headstrong rule of his own roost, Gleason had a mixed reputation around CBS: "There is only one way to do things," said the voices in the washroom, "the Gleason way." He refused to rehearse, treated scriptwriters with such scorn that one producer claims "we had to hire a liaison man between Gleason and his scriptwriters." Nonetheless, the company thought enough of his talents to agree to pay him $100,000 a year every year from 1957 through 1972. Gleason does not have to work for the money. It is paid to him simply to keep him from working for any other network. He called the $100,000 "peanuts," but he took it anyway. It represented another concession from what he calls "the hierarchy"—a general term he often uses to indicate all the "frat-pin boys," the college men with diplomas who make the ultimate rules by which he has to live. "All the buildings on Madison Avenue are conning towers," he says, and "any television executive must have one very important attribute: cologne."

After 39 weeks of *The Honeymooners,* Gleason reports, he called Buick and told them to keep the rest of their $11 million, explaining that it was impossible to maintain good material at the accelerated pace. "You'll have to give us time to think it over," said Buick, nonplused. They thought it over and finally agreed. Like all TV phenomena, Gleason had reached a peak and was apparently in decline. In 1957-58, he took a year off.

BUT THE BOY FROM Brooklyn had it made financially, and he knew it. He became the biggest of the big-time spenders, and has kept it up. Jackie saves little and gambles as if he were using Monopoly scrip. He is willing to bet $100 a hole in a golf game, and he lost $3,000 on a wager that Grace Kelly would never marry the Prince of Monaco. With him, betting is as direct a challenge as Indian wrestling. Says Arthur Godfrey: "I understand that he finds out what his opponent's top wager is and then bets him twice that."

His gifts to friends, usually expensive and conventional, often run wild and combine with a boisterous taste for practical jokes. To various people he has given a pig, a goat, a horse, 600 lbs. of manure, a dozen rabbits, a truckload of used furniture, a tiny monkey, and a basketful of shrunken heads. One recipient retaliated by sneaking into Gleason's bathroom and filling the tub with Jello.

His gifts to charity are also endless—$100 here, $1,000 there, a check to the family of a fireman whose death he read about in the papers, continual subsidies to a Catholic institute in New England of which he is the chief financial supporter. But he never talks about his charitable giving.

Gleason's newest pride is a $30,000, two-toned (opal and burgundy) Rolls-Royce, and he boasts that the front bumper arrives at any selected destination about "three weeks ahead of me." But his most spectacular acquisition is the $650,000 office-home which he has built for himself near Peekskill, N.Y. Comedian George Jessel describes the place as "a sort of bar with a built-in house." It is basically an immense rotunda, with circular rooms, circular terraces, circular shower baths, and a circular sky-dome. It has a 270-ton fireplace-barbecue pit of white Carrara marble, a piano that revolves majestically, and a stereo machine that plays 400 selections. Called "Round Rock," the house would certainly make Samuel Taylor Coleridge think he was back in Xanadu, for past it flows one of the minor rivers of Westchester County, complete with trout, perch, smallmouth bass and fat, fat catfish.

Gleason stoutly asserts that the place is a "studio," designed for business and even for broadcasting TV shows. He points out that he himself lives in another, quite ordinary house elsewhere on the twelve-acre property. So the pool table is covered with light blue felt instead of the standard green—"blue happens to photograph better on television." So the one bed in the house is 8 ft. in diameter and absolutely round—all sorts of people in Brooklyn, says Gleason, are buying round beds these days.

During his year off, Gleason took up golf. As in everything else, he was determined to be "the best." "He was out on the course practicing before the caddies got up," says a friend. Soon he was shooting in the low 80s, occasionally dipping into the 70s. He goes around on an electric cart, playing as many as 72 holes a day. He has played with Toots Shor and says of the great-bellied Clamhead: "If he puts the ball where he can hit it, he can't see it, and if he puts it where he can see it, he can't hit it." Perhaps because of his pool-trained eye, Gleason is best with a putter. Last season, while losing a handicap match on TV to Open Champion Arnold Palmer, he sank putts of well over 40 ft. on two consecutive greens.

He also cut a few records during his "idle" year. For Gleason, a man of innumerable parts, is a writer of music, too. He picks out tunes with one finger and has an arranger dress them up. He has written themes for his TV shows, and he did all of the score for *Gigot*. Since the early '50s, he has turned out some 30 albums with titles like *Music to Change Her Mind* and subtitles like *Music for Sippin', Listenin', Dancin' and Lovin'*. It is mainly quiet, seductive music that suggests Log Cabin syrup poured over a slowly turning pizza. The records have sold close to 5,000,000 copies and have grossed about $17 million.

But the year off seems to have been a time of decision for Gleason. Late in 1958, he took on a role as a serious actor—in a television production of Saroyan's *The Time of Your Life*. To nearly everybody's astonishment, he was enormously impressive. Then Producer David Merrick asked him to play the blissfully besotted Uncle Sid in *Take Me Along*, the musical version of Eugene O'Neill's *Ah! Wilderness*. His collision with Merrick, whose ego matches his, was Homeric. "What's the highest straight salary ever paid to a Broadway actor?" asked Gleason. Merrick said he thought it was $5,000 a week. Gleason demanded and got $5,050. He also insisted on an extra dressing room and a chauffeur-driven car. Once rehearsals began, Merrick grumbles, "he'd say if he couldn't have his way on this or that, 'I'll get sick.' "

Temperamentally unsuited to the night-in-night-out routine of Broadway, Gleason was bored with the show when it was still in Boston, but—bursting onstage saying "Get a load of all the bottle babies," and dancing as lightly as a weather balloon in the stratosphere—he won unreserved praise from such alto-brows as *New Yorker* Critic Kenneth Tynan and Sir Laurence Olivier. He also won the Antoinette Perry award as the season's outstanding actor in a musical.

In Paris last spring for the filming of *Gigot* (in which he plays a deaf-mute), Gleason was asked by an A.P. reporter what he thought of French girls. He refused to comment, saying: "I just happen to be a one-girl guy." The one girl at the moment is Honey Merrill, a bright, pretty, former showgirl who helps in Gleason's office and has loved him devotedly for five years. Before that, Gleason's steady companion was Marilyn Taylor, dancer and younger sister of his choreographer on *The Jackie Gleason Show.* She eventually left him because it was clear that Jackie would never be free to marry her.

In 1936 Gleason had married Genevieve Halford, a dancer. Over the years, Gleason was home-again-gone-again. They got a legal separation in 1954. He takes all the blame. His two daughters are now adults (one is married and the other is finishing college at Washington's Catholic University), and there is no chance that their parents will reunite. Nor is there any chance of a divorce. Although Jackie does not practice Roman Catholicism, as his friend Jack Haley says, "he believes in it."

He not only believes in it, he thinks about it to a degree that would amaze all the people whose impression of Gleason goes no deeper than what they read in the work of Broadway columnists. "Whenever I hear someone say that religion is their own personal affair, I'm irritated," he says. "Religion can't be called personal. The health of your religion determines the compassion, sympathy, forgiveness, and tolerance you give to your fellow man. I have studied different religions to see if there was one more attractive for me. I only discovered I was seeking a religion that was more compatible to my way of living. I remained a Catholic. It wasn't comfortable, but what religion is to a sinner? While I might not carry out my obligations in any manner to be commended, at least I know where I stand."

His study of religions has led to extensive research in the field of psychic phenomena. He has hundreds of volumes on the subject. He is an accomplished hypnotist. He has even held sessions with spiritualists. He has started to write a novel called *Brother Miracle,* tying psychic phenomena to religion in the story of a monk who experiences an extraordinary manifestation of psychic power. The novel's conclusion, says Jackie, is that "faith is to be placed in God and not in bizarre activities."

Last week Jackie Gleason's own activities were not so bizarre as they often are when his time is his own. Working hard at his new film, he was up at dawn every morning, plowing through take after take all day until 7 p.m. But he found time to irradiate at least one afternoon, sitting on a favorite banquette at Manhattan's 21 Club (a temporary off-Shor island), buying drinks for friends, marshaling waiters like a field general.

If he had an air of self-confidence, he was entitled to it. His new career as a movie actor is seemingly unlimited: he has already signed for *Soldier in the Rain,* under the direction of Blake Edwards (*Breakfast at Tiffany's*), and he is completing negotiations for another film, as yet untitled, that will be directed by Robert Rossen (*The Hustler*). But if, by some improbable fiscal catastrophe, all the things he has going for him should come crashing down, if CBS should go bankrupt and his $100,000 a year be cut off, if Hollywood should evaporate, and the $650,000 house in Peekskill were to float away on the little stream it straddles, Jackie Gleason would still have a way to stay solvent. Since the age of 13, he has had something to fall back on. As Paul Newman says at the fadeout of *The Hustler:* "Fat man, you shoot a great game of pool." ∎

The Backstreet Phantom of Rock

BY JAY COCKS

[
When this first of TIME *'s two cover stories on Bruce Springsteen appeared, "the Boss" was new to readers but not to the writer, who captured him with appropriately street-smart eloquence*
]

October 27, 1975

THE ROCK-'N'-ROLL GENERATION: everybody grows up by staying young. Bruce Springsteen is onto this. In fact, he has written a song about it:

> *I pushed B-52 and bombed 'em with the blues*
> *With my gear set stubborn on standing*
> *I broke all the rules, strafed my old high school*
> *Never once gave thought to landing,*
> *I hid in the clouded warmth of the crowd,*
> *But when they said, "Come down," I threw up,*
> *Ooh . . . growin' up.*

He has been called the "last innocent in rock," which is at best partly true, but that is how he appears to audiences who are exhausted and on fire at the end of a concert. Springsteen is not a golden California boy or a glitter queen from Britain. Dressed usually in leather jacket and shredded undershirt, he is a glorified gutter rat from a dying New Jersey resort town who walks with an easy swagger that is part residual stage presence, part boardwalk braggadocio. He nurtures the look of a lowlife romantic even though he does not smoke, scarcely drinks and disdains every kind of drug.

In all other ways, however, he is the dead-on image of a rock musician: street smart but sentimental, a little enigmatic, articulate mostly through his music. For 26 years Springsteen has known nothing but poverty and debt until, just in the past few weeks, the rock dream came true for him. ("Man, when I was nine I couldn't imagine anyone *not* wanting to be Elvis Presley.") But he is neither sentimental nor superficial. His music is primal, directly in touch with all the impulses of wild humor and glancing melancholy, street tragedy and punk anarchy that have made rock the distinctive voice of a generation.

Springsteen's songs are full of echoes—of Sam Cooke and Elvis Presley, of Chuck Berry, Roy Orbison and Buddy Holly. You can also hear Bob Dylan, Van Morrison and the Band weaving among Springsteen's elaborate fantasias. The music is a synthesis, some Latin and soul, and some good jazz riffs too. The tunes are full of precipitate breaks and shifting harmonies, the lyrics often abstract, bizarre, wholly personal.

Springsteen makes demands. He figures that when he sings

> *Baby this town rips the bones from your back*
> *It's a death trap, it's a suicide rap*
> *We gotta get out while we're young*
> *'Cause tramps like us, baby we were born to run,*

everybody is going to know where he's coming from and just where he's heading.

Springsteen first appeared in the mid-'60s for a handful of loyal fans from the scuzzy Jersey shore. Then, two record albums of wired brilliance (*Greetings from Asbury Park, N.J.* and *The Wild, the Innocent & the E Street Shuffle*) enlarged his audience to a cult. The albums had ecstatic reviews—there was continuing and growing talk of "a new Dylan"—but slim sales. Springsteen spent nearly two years working on his third album, *Born to Run,* and Columbia Records has already invested $150,000 in ensuring that this time around, everyone gets the message.

The album has made it to No. 1, the title track is a hit single, and even the first two albums are snugly on the charts. Concerts have sold out hours after they were announced. Last Thursday Springsteen brought his distinctively big-city, rubbed-raw sensibility to a skeptical Los Angeles, not only a major market but the bastion of a wholly different rock style. It remained to be seen how Springsteen would go down in a scene whose characteristic pop music is softer, easier, pitched to life on the beaches and in the canyons, hardly in tune with his sort of dead-end carnival. Springsteen's four-day stand at a Sunset Strip theater called the Roxy was a massive dose of culture shock that booted everyone back to the roots, shook 'em up good and got 'em all on their feet dancing.

Even the most laid-back easy rocker would find it tough to resist his live performance. Small, tightly muscled, the voice a chopped-and-channeled rasp, Springsteen has the wild onstage energy of a pinball rebounding off invisible flippers, caroming down the alley past traps and penalties, dead center for extra points and the top score.

Expecting a monochromatic street punk, the L.A. crowd got a dervish leaping on the tables, all arms and flailing dance steps, and a rock poet as well. In over ten years of playing tank-town dates and rundown discos, Springsteen has mastered the true stage secret of the rock pro: he seems to be letting go totally and fearlessly; yet the performance remains perfectly orchestrated. With his E Street Band, especially Clarence Clemons' smartly lowdown saxophone, Springsteen can caper and promenade, boogie out into the audience, recite a rambling, funny monologue about girl watching back in Asbury Park, or switch moods in the middle of songs.

He expects his musicians to follow him along. Many of the changes are totally spur of the moment, and the band is tight enough to take them in stride. "You hook on to Bruce on that stage and you go wherever he takes you," says Clarence Clemons. "It's like total surrender to him." A Springsteen set is raucous, poignant, brazen. It is clear that he gets off on the show as much as the audience, which is one reason why a typical gig lasts over two hours. The joy is infectious and self-fulfilling. "This music is forever for me," Springsteen says. "It's the stage thing, that rush moment that you live for. It never lasts, but that's what you live for."

He once cautioned in a song that you can "waste your summer prayin' in vain for a savior to rise from these streets," but right now Springsteen represents a regeneration, a renewal of rock. He has gone back to the sources, rediscovered the wild excitement that rock has lost over the past few years. Things had settled down in the '70s: with a few exceptions, like Paul Simon, Jackson Browne and Linda Ronstadt, there was an excess of showmanship, too much din substituting for true power, repetition—as in this past summer's Rolling Stones tour—for lack of any new directions. Springsteen has taken rock forward by taking it back, keeping it young. He uses and embellishes the myths of the '50s pop culture: his songs are populated by bad-ass loners, wiped-out heroes, bikers, hot-rodders, women of soulful mystery. Springsteen conjures up a whole half-world of shattered sunlight and fractured neon, where his characters re-enact little pageants of challenge and desperation.

The *Born to Run* album is so powerful, and Springsteen's presence so prevalent at the moment, that before the phenomenon has had a chance to settle, a reaction is already setting in. He is being typed as a '50s hood in the James Dean mold, defused for being a hype, put down as a product of the Columbia promo "fog machine," condemned for slicking up and recycling a few old rock-'n'-roll riffs. Even Springsteen remains healthily skeptical. "I don't understand what all the commotion is about," he told TIME Correspondent James Willwerth. "I feel like I'm on the outside of all this, even though I know I'm on the inside. It's like you want attention, but sometimes you can't relate to it."

SPRINGSTEEN DEFIES CLASSIFICATION. This is one reason recognition was so long in coming. There is nothing simple to hold on to. He was discovered by Columbia Records Vice President of Talent Acquisition John Hammond, who also found Billie Holiday, Benny Goodman and Bob Dylan, among others. Hammond knew "at once that Bruce would last a generation" but thought of him first as a folk musician.

Casting Springsteen as a rebel in a motorcycle jacket is easy enough—it makes a neat fit for the character he adopted in *Born to Run*—but it ignores a whole other side of his importance and of his music.

Born to Run is a bridge between Springsteen the raffish rocker and the more ragged, introverted street poet of the first two albums. Although he maintains that he "hit the right spot" on *Born to Run,* it is the second album, *The Wild, the Innocent & the E Street Shuffle,* that seems to go deepest. A sort of free-association autobiography, it comes closest to the wild fun-house refractions of Springsteen's imagination. In *Wild Billy's Circus Song,* when he sings, "He's gonna miss his fall, oh God save the human cannonball," Springsteen could be anticipating and describing his own current, perhaps perilous trajectory. In case of danger, however, Springsteen will be rescued by the music itself, just as he has always been. "Music saved me," he says. "From the beginning, my guitar was something I could go to. If I hadn't found music, I don't know what I would have done."

He was born poor in Freehold, N.J., a working-class town near the shore. His mother Adele ("Just like Superwoman, she did everything, everywhere, all the time") worked through his childhood as a secretary. His father, Douglas Springsteen (the name is Dutch), was "a sure-money man" at the pool tables who drifted from job to job stalked by undetermined demons.

"My Daddy was a driver," Springsteen remembers. "He liked to get in the car and just drive. He got everybody else in the car too, and he made *us* drive. He made us all drive." These two-lane odysseys without destination only reinforced Springsteen's already flourishing sense of displacement. "I lived half of my first 13 years in a trance or something," he says now. "People thought I was weird because I always went around with this *look* on my face. I was thinking of things, but I was always on the outside, looking in."

The parents pulled up stakes and moved to California when Bruce was still in his teens. Bruce stayed behind, with some bad memories of hassles with nuns in parochial school, an $18 guitar and random dreams of a phantom father for company. By the time he was 18, he had some perspective on his father. "I figured out we were pretty much alike," Springsteen says, by which he means more than a shared cool skill at the pool table and a taste for long car rides. "My father never has much to say to me, but I know he thinks about a lot of things. I know he's driving himself almost crazy thinking about these things . . . and yet he sure ain't got much to say when we sit down to talk." The elder Springsteen currently drives a bus in San Mateo, a suburb south of San Francisco. Neither he nor his wife made it to Los Angeles for their son's big show.

Bruce bunked in with friends back in Jersey and tried to make it through public high school. He took off on weekend forays into Manhattan for his first strong taste of big-city street life and began making music. He started writing his own because he could not figure out how to tune his guitar to play anyone else's material accurately. "Music was my way of keeping people from looking through and around me. I wanted the heavies to know I was around."

In 1965, while he was still finishing high school, Springsteen began forming bands like the Castiles, which did gigs for short money in a Greenwich Village spot called the Café Wha?. He met up with Miami Steve Van Zandt, current lead guitarist of the E Street Band, around that time. "We were all playing anything we could to be part of the scene," Van Zandt recalls. "West Coast stuff, the English thing, R & B and blues. Bruce was writing five or ten songs a week. He would say, 'I'm gonna go home tonight and write a great song,' and he did. He was the Boss then, and he's the Boss now."

He took his music anywhere they would listen. His bands changed names (the Rogues, the Steel Mill, Dr. Zoom and the Sonic Boom) as frequently as personnel. "I've gone through a million crazy bands with crazy people who did crazy things," Springsteen remembers. They played not only clubs and private parties but firemen's balls, a state mental hospital and Sing Sing prison, a couple of trailer parks, a rollerdrome, the parking lot of a Shop-Rite and under the screen during intermission at a drive-in. A favorite spot for making music, and for hanging out, was Asbury Park. Springsteen lived in a surfboard factory run by a displaced Californian named Carl Vergil ("Tinker") West III, who became, for a time, his manager.

Everybody had a band: not only Springsteen and his buddy Southside Johnny Lyon, but also Miami Steve, Vini ("Mad Dog") Lopez (who played drums on Bruce's first two albums) and Garry Tallent (now bass guitarist for the E Street Band). They all would appear at a dive called the Upstage Club for $15 a night, work from 8 p.m. to 5 a.m., then party together, play records and adjourn till the next afternoon, when they would meet on the boardwalk to check the action and talk music. For sport everyone played Monopoly, adding a few refinements that made the game more like the Jersey boardwalk they knew. There were two special cards: a Chief McCarthy card (named in honor of a local cop who rousted musicians indiscriminately) and a Riot card. The McCarthy card allowed the bearer to send any opponent to jail without reason; whoever drew the Riot card could fire-bomb any opponent's real estate.

Nobody was getting rich outside of Monopoly. In 1970 Asbury Park was the scene of a bad race riot, and the tourists stayed away. "The place went down to the ground, and we rode right down with it," says Miami Steve. There were jobs to be had in a few of the bars, playing easy-listening rock, but Springsteen and his pals disdained them because, as he says simply, "we hated the music. We had no idea how to hustle either. We weren't big door knockers, so we didn't go to New York or Philly." Adds Van Zandt, who lived on a dollar a day: "We were all reading in the papers how much fun rock 'n' roll was—it seemed like another world. We didn't take drugs. We couldn't *afford* any bad habits."

A lot of the life Springsteen saw then and lived through found its way into his songs, but indirectly, filtered through an imagination that discovered a crazy romanticism in the ragtag boardwalk life.

*She worked that joint under the
boardwalk, she was always the girl you
saw boppin' down the beach with the radio,
Kids say last night she was dressed
like a star in one of the cheap little sea-
side bars and I saw her parked with her
loverboy out on the Kokomo.*

Tinker, the surfboard manufacturer and manager, called Mike Appel on Springsteen's behalf. Appel, whose major claim to fame until then was the co-authorship of a Partridge Family hit called *Doesn't Somebody Want to Be Wanted,* was smart enough to see Springsteen's talent and brash enough to spirit him away from Tinker. Appel got Springsteen to work up a clutch of new songs by simply calling him frequently and asking him to come into New York. Springsteen would jump on the bus and have a new tune ready by the time he crossed the Hudson.

Appel also called John Hammond at Columbia. The call was Springsteen's idea, but the come-on was all Appel. He told Hammond he wanted him to listen to his new boy because Hammond had discovered Bob Dylan, and "we wanna see if that was just a fluke, or if you really have ears." Hammond reacted to Springsteen "with a force I'd felt maybe three times in my life." Less than 24 hours after the first meeting, contracts were signed.

Even before Springsteen's first album was released in 1973, Appel was already on the move. He offered the NBC producer of the Super Bowl the services of his client to sing *The Star-Spangled Banner.* Informed that Andy Williams had already been recruited, with Blood, Sweat & Tears to perform during half time, he cried, "They're losers and you're a loser too. Some day I'm going to give you a call and remind you of this, then I'm going to make another call and you'll be out of a job." Says Hammond: "Appel is as offensive as any man I've ever met, but he's utterly selfless in his devotion to Bruce."

Appel and Springsteen understood each other. They agreed that Bruce and the band should play second fiddle to nobody. For two years Springsteen crisscrossed the country, enlarging his following with galvanic concerts. Early last year, playing a small bar called Charley's in Cambridge, Mass., he picked up an important new fan. Jon Landau, a *Rolling Stone* editor, had reviewed Bruce's second album favorably for a local paper, and Charley's put the notice in the window. Landau remembers arriving at the club and seeing Springsteen hugging himself in the cold and reading the review. A few weeks later, Landau wrote, "I saw the rock and roll future and its name is Springsteen."

Some loyalists at Columbia persuaded the company to cough up $50,000 to publicize the quote. Columbia's sudden recommitment caught Springsteen in a creative crisis. He and Appel had spent nine months in the studio and produced only one cut, *Born to Run*. The disparity between the wild reaction to his live performances and the more subdued, respectful reception of his records had to be cleared up. Landau soon signed on as co-producer of the new album and began to find out about some of the problems firsthand.

"Bruce works instinctively," Landau observes. "He is incredibly intense, and he concentrates deeply. Underneath his shyness is the strongest will I've ever encountered. If there's something he doesn't want to do, he won't." Springsteen would work most days from 3 p.m. to 6 a.m., and sometimes as long as 24 hours, without stopping. Only occasionally did things go quickly. For a smoky midnight song called *Meeting Across the River*, Springsteen just announced, "O.K., I hear a string bass, and I hear a trumpet," and, according to Landau, "that was it." Finally the album came together as real roadhouse rock, made proudly in that tradition. The sound is layered over with the kind of driving instrumental cushioning that characterized the sides Phil Spector produced in the late '50s and '60s. The lyrics burst with nighthawk poetry.

> *The screen door slams*
> *Mary's dress waves*
> *Like a vision she dances across the porch*
> *As the radio plays*
> *Roy Orbison singing for the lonely*
> *Hey that's me and I want you only*
> *Don't turn me home again*
> *I just can't face myself alone again.*

If all this effort has suddenly paid off grandly, and madly, Springsteen remains obdurately unchanged. He continues to hassle with Appel over playing large halls, and just last month refused to show up for a Maryland concert Appel had booked into a 10,000-seat auditorium. The money is starting to flow in now: Springsteen takes home $350 a week, the same as Appel and the band members. There are years of debt and back road fees to repay. Besides, Springsteen is not greatly concerned about matters of finance. Says John Hammond: "In all my years in this business, he is the only person I've met who cares absolutely nothing about money."

Springsteen lives sometimes with his girl friend Karen Darvin, 20, a freckled, leggy model from Texas, in a small apartment on Manhattan's East Side. More frequently he is down on the Jersey shore, where he has just moved into more comfortable—but not lavish—quarters, and bought his first decent hi-fi rig. He remains adamantly indifferent to clothing and personal adornment, although he wears a small gold cross around his neck—a vestigial remnant of Catholicism—and, probably to challenge it, a small gold ring in his left ear, which gives him a little gypsy flash.

When he is not working, Springsteen takes life easy and does not worry about it. "I'm not a planning-type guy," he says. "You can't count on nothing in this life. I never have expectations when I get involved in things. That way, I never have disappointments." His songs, which he characterizes as being mostly about "survival, how to make it through the next day," are written in bursts. "I ain't one of those guys who feels guilty if he didn't write something today," he boasts. "That's all jive. If I didn't do nothing all day, I feel great." Under all circumstances, he spins fiction in his lyrics and is careful to avoid writing directly about daily experience. "You do that," he cautions, "and this is what happens. First you write about struggling along. Then you write about making it professionally. Then somebody's nice to you. You write about that. It's a beautiful day, you write about that. That's about 20 songs in all. Then you're out. You got nothing to write."

Some things, however, must change. Southside Johnny recalls that after *Born to Run* was released, "we had a party at one of the band members' houses. It was like old times. We drank and listened to old Sam and Dave albums. Then someone said my car had a flat tire. I went outside to check, and sitting in the street were all these people waiting to get a glimpse of Brucie, just sitting under the streetlights, not saying anything. I got nervous and went back inside."

These lamppost vigilants, silent and deferential, were not teenyboppers eager to squeal or fans looking for a fast autograph. As much as anything, they were all unofficial delegates of a generation acting on the truth of Springsteen's line from *Thunder Road:* "Show a little faith, there's magic in the night." Just at that doorstep, they found it. Growin' up. ∎

The Show of Shows

BY ROBERT HUGHES

[
Through the lens of a spectacular Picasso exhibition,
a critic took the measure not only of the titanic artist but
also of his role in the birth of modernism
]

May 26, 1980

IN IMAGINATIVE FORCE AND outright *terri-bilità,* it is quite possibly the most crushing and exhilarating exhibition of work by a 20th century artist ever held in the U.S. Beginning this week, over the next four months nearly a million people will queue outside New York City's Museum of Modern Art to get a glimpse of it. Pablo Picasso, who died in 1973, is being honored in a show of nearly 1,000 of his works, some never exhibited before, drawn from his estate as well as from collections the world over.

What gives the exhibit its overwhelming character is the range and fecundity of Picasso's talent—the flashes of demonic restlessness, the heights of confidence and depths of insecurity, the relationships (alternately loving and cannibalistic) to the art of the past, but above all the sustained intensity of feeling. "Pablo Picasso: A Retrospective" contains good paintings and bad, some so weak that they look like forgeries (but are not), as well as a great many works of art for which the word masterpiece—exiled for the crime of elitism over the past decade—must now be reinstated. It is the largest exhibition of one artist's work that MOMA has ever held, or probably ever will. It contains pieces ranging in size from *Guernica,* Picasso's 26-ft.-

wide mural of protest against the fascist bombing of a Basque town during the Spanish Civil War, to a cluster of peg dolls he painted for his daughter Paloma. Paintings, drawings, collages, prints of every kind, sculpture in bronze, wood, wire, tin, string, paper and clay; there was virtually no medium the Spaniard did not use, and all are profusely represented.

Not all great painters are precocious, but Picasso was. In a technical way, he was as much a prodigy as Mozart, and his precocity seems to have fixed his peculiar sense of vocation. He was born in Málaga in 1881, the son of a painter named José Ruiz Blasco (a fine-boned *inglés* face, nothing like Pablo's simian mask; that came from his mother), and by 13 he was so good at drawing that his father is said to have handed over his own brushes and paints to the boy and given up painting. If the story is true, it goes some way to explain the mediumistic confidence with which Picasso worked. "Painting is stronger than I am," he once remarked. "It makes me do what it wants." Painting had won him the Oedipal battle before his career had begun. If one were told that *Science and Charity,* Picasso's sickbed scene from 1897, with its rather conventional drawing but adroit paint handling (especially in the details, like the frame of the mirror above the bed), had been done by a 30-year-old Spanish academician, one would have predicted a competent future for the man. Once one realizes that it was painted by a boy not yet 16, the skill seems portentous, like a visitation—and that is the general impression conveyed by Picasso's earliest work.

The point is not that Picasso, as an art student in Barcelona and, after the autumn of 1900, a young artist in Paris, was markedly better at imitating Steinlen or Toulouse-Lautrec than other Spanish artists were, but that he could run through the influences so quickly, with such nimble digestion. What he needed, he kept. He had no use for the tendril-like, decorative line of Spanish art nouveau, for instance, but he retained its liking for large, silhouetted masses, and they, grafted onto the pervasive influence of Toulouse-Lautrec, keep appearing in his Parisian cabaret scenes of 1901. Some of these are of remarkable intensity. Picasso painted Gustave Coquiot, a fashionable Paris art and theater columnist, as a sinister god of urban pleasure, green shadows straining against red lips in a pale mask of a face. Some of the women, their faces blurred by laughter or squinched up into pug masks of greed, seem to predict by ten years the jittery misogyny of German expressionism. *Woman in Blue,* 1901, with her fierce little Aubrey Beardsley whore's head surmounting the dress of a Velázquez court portrait, is an especially compelling example.

For a young artist in Paris at the turn of the century, such material could not last forever, and not all Picasso's experiences were gaslight and garters. Living in poverty in the little Spanish artists' colony in Montparnasse, he identified himself in a sentimental way with the wretched and down-and-out of Paris, the waifs and strays. This wistful *misérabilisme,* verging on allegory, was the keynote of his so-called Blue Period. Late in 1901 he had painted some Gauguin-like figures, using the characteristic flat silhouettes and solid blue boundary lines that Gauguin, in his turn, had extracted from Japanese decorative art. By 1902 the blueness of this line had spread to dominate the whole painting. It had a symbolic value, of course: it spoke of melancholy, of the "blues." But it also enabled Picasso, as the pervasive brown-gray monochrome of analytical cubism later would in a different way, to take color out of his work, so that he could make a compromise between decorative flatness and sculptural volume in terms of pure tone.

Today one is not apt to think of allegory as a "modern" form, since it contradicts the abstraction of modernist painting. But it mattered a great deal to Picasso, and he resorted to it at some of his intense moments—in the construction of *Les Demoiselles d'Avignon* (which began as an allegory of venereal disease, a subject of great interest to the energetic Pablo), of *Guernica,* and on into his "Mediterranean" subjects of the 1930s, with their bulls and horses, virgins and Minotaurs, caves, ruins and nymphs. Allegory was the conscious, intelligible form of Picasso's vast instinctive talent for metamorphosis, whereby a single form could harbor two or more literal meanings: a glass of absinthe including a drunkard's head, a guitar turning into a torso or a vagina, a bicycle seat becoming a bull's head. Moreover, the ability to handle allegory was the proof of high ambition: Gauguin had gone to Tahiti to paint huge emblems of human fate, not just to see papayas.

By the age of 25 Picasso was an able and gifted artist, but not yet a modern one. He had managed to tame the mannerism of the Blue Period, with its wistful elongations and neurotic passivity of form, by studying Degas. The results can be seen in the *Woman with a Fan,* 1905, with its "Egyptian" gesture of the raised hand and gravely extended fan, or in the robust columnar body of the *Boy Leading a Horse,* 1906. At that point he could have kept painting such pictures for the rest of his life and died in honors.

What happened was very different. The detachment of expression in his Rose Period hardened: through 1906 the faces took on an increasingly masklike air, blank, inexpressive, with empty eye sockets. Picasso had been looking at archaic Spanish carvings from Osuna. Now he stressed the sculptural, instead of the linear and atmospheric: solid impacted form, not fleeting mood. His 1906 portrait of Gertrude Stein, almost leaden in its pictorial ineloquence, marked the start of this change, and the pink stony torsos of *Two Nudes,* 1906, delineate the period's end. In between lay some magnificent paintings, such as the *Seated Female Nude with Crossed Legs,* 1906, whose solidities of thigh, trunk and breasts anticipate the swollen torsos of Picasso's "classical" women 15 years later. It was one more element in the predictions, recapitulations and variations of theme that composed the tissue of Picasso's imagination.

HAVING BROUGHT SOLID FORM to such density, having set so absolute a division between figure and field, what choice did Picasso have but to break it all down again? *Les Demoiselles d'Avignon,* 1907, was the painting that provoked cubism, and one of the most astounding feats of ideation in the history of art. These days the word radical is patched on to any newish artistic gesture, no matter how small: a puddle of lead on the floor, or a face pulled on video tape, or an array of bricks. This use of the word cannot begin to convey the newness of *Les Demoiselles.* No painting has ever looked more convulsive and contradictory, and, though one can follow its development through Picasso's early studies, which are part of the MOMA exhibit, the sheer intensity of its making is beyond analysis.

Les Demoiselles is a brothel scene; there had been a whorehouse on the Carrer d'Avinyo, or Avignon Street, in Barcelona, and Picasso and his friends frequented it. But the picture has none of the social irony or even the sensuality with which Toulouse-Lautrec and Degas invested their brothel paintings. More vividly than ever, against the backdrop of earlier Picassos, it becomes clear why his friends thought he had gone crazy, why the painter André Derain actually predicted that Picasso would hang himself behind the big picture. The painting is freighted with aggression, carefully wrought. The nudes are cut into segments, as though the brush were a butcher knife. Their look, eyes glaring from African-mask faces, is accusatory, not inviting. Even the melon in the still life looks like a weapon. The space between the figures is flattened, like a crumpled box: it was in this play of code between solid and void (one apparently as "tactile" as the other) that the formal prophecies of *Les Demoiselles* lay. Though he plundered African motifs such as masks and Bakota funerary figures for *Les Demoiselles* and its sequels, Picasso neither knew nor cared about their tribal meanings or uses. To him, they were merely shapes, conceptually opaque, with perhaps a secondary use as emblems of "savagery" to disrupt the field of "culture." The idea that Picasso had some sympathetic interest in African art as such is a complete illusion. All that counted for him was its ability to furnish alienated examples of form that clearly owed nothing to Raphael.

No *Demoiselles,* no cubism. But there was a long stretch between them while Picasso, grappling with late Cézanne, crossed from an art of paroxysm to one of exquisitely nuanced analysis. In a work like *Bread and Fruit Dish on a Table,* 1909, Picasso picked up on Cézanne's monumentality. Originally Picasso meant to paint a cabaret scene with figures at a table, in homage to Cézanne's *Cardplayers,* but the image mutated into still life, leaving the drinkers' legs fossilized, as it were, in the sloping table legs. The great brown half-moon of the tabletop, the bread loaves and fruit and napkin have a plastic intensity that makes one feel ready to pluck them away.

Gradually this jutting, sculptural quality dissolved in ever more complicated faceting, "cubifying"—though there are no real cubes in cubism—through the landscapes he painted at Horta de Ebro in 1909. By 1910 the cubist surface was reached, with a sort of gray-brown plasma, the color of fiddle backs, zinc bars and smokers' fingers. Objects were sunk in a twinkling field of vectors and shadows, solid lapping into transparency, things penetrating and turning away, leaving behind the merest signs for themselves—a letter or two, the bowl of a pipe, the sound hole of a guitar. This sense of multiple relationships was the core of cubism's modernity. It declared that all visual experience could be set forth as a shifting field that included the onlooker. It was painting's unconscious answer to the theory of relativity or to the principles of narrative that would emerge in Proust or Joyce. The supremacy of the fixed viewpoint, embodied for 500 years in Renaissance perspective, was challenged by the new mode of describing space that Picasso and Braque had developed in a supreme effort of teamwork.

As with painting, so with sculpture. Picasso's *Guitar* of 1912, an array of cut and folded metal sheets that opened to let space in, was the first constructed sculpture in the history of art. It abolished the solidity, the continuous surface that had been, until then, the essential narrative of sculpture. From that unpromising-looking piece of rusty tin, a 60-year tradition of open-form sculpture was born that spread from Russian constructivism to the work of Anthony Caro in England and David Smith in the U.S.

Picasso never painted an abstract picture in his life. His instinct for the real world was so strong that he probably would have produced something woman-shaped every time he took brush in hand. Nevertheless, some of his cubist still lifes of 1911 run close to total abstraction, depending on such slender clues as a glass or a pipestem to pull them back to reality. As he moved forward, he found in collage a way of linking cubism back to the world. Collage, which simply means gluing, brought fragments of modern life—newspaper headlines, printed labels—directly into the painting. Cut them out, put them in. The tonal values of some of his finest collages have been ruined by age. The newsprint, once gray on white, is now cigar-brown. But in better preserved ones, like *Violin and Sheet Music,* 1912, the original effect remains: a magnificently Apollonian interplay of blue, gray, white and black on its ocher ground, stable and forceful at the same time.

The sense of the cubist moment can never come again. It is almost as distant, in its dulcet and inexhaustible optimism, as the faith that built Beauvais. Cubism was the climax of an urban culture that had been assembling itself in Paris since the mid-19th century, a culture renewed by rapid transitions and shifting modes. It was art's first response to the torrent of signs unleashed by a new technology. Not for nothing did Picasso inscribe "Our future is in the air" on several of his cubist still lifes; tellingly, Picasso's nickname for Braque was "Wilbur," after Wilbur Wright. "The world has changed less since the time of Jesus Christ," remarked the French writer Charles Péguy in 1913, "than it has in the last 30 years." Picasso and Braque took it for granted that reality had changed more than art, but their relation to the art of the past was not one of simple conflict. It was more tentative, precise and subtly felt. The sense of being always at the frontiers of history itself is volatile, and it began to evaporate from Picasso's work before the end of World War I. It left behind a residue, however: his virtuosity. Around 1918 he found his first public, a small enough group compared with the worldwide fame he would be juggling by 1939, but much larger and more influential than the poets and painters around the studios of the Bateau-Lavoir. It was a public of admiring consumers, the cultivated *gratin* of Europe, people who needed a modern Rubens. Moreover, there had been a general recoil from extreme avant-garde art, on principle, after 1918. What seemed necessary was reconstruction, not more iconoclasm, or, in the words of Jean Cocteau, a *rappel à l'ordre* (call to order), which would place art under the normalizing sway of classical nostalgia. "Revolutionary" art simply did not look good around the 16th Arrondissement after October 1917.

The Picasso of 1918-24 was made for this situation. With ebullience, he threw himself into the role of the maestro, designing sets and costumes for Diaghilev's Ballets Russes, marrying one of its dancers, and allowing a conventional style of portraiture, often insipid, to alternate with a highly decorative form of cubism. "Decorative," of course, is no longer a cuss word, and his best flat-pattern cubist paintings of the early '20s, with their gravely shuttling collage-like overlaps of bright and dark color, are marvels of pictorial intelligence. The two versions of his *Three Musicians,* 1921, show what Picasso could do when his sense of form was fully engaged. The classicizing drift of the early '20s took its most explicit shape in the *Three Women at the Spring,* 1921. Their dropsical limbs resemble a Pompeian fresco inflated with an air hose, even though the full-size sanguine drawing for the painting, which Picasso kept for himself, has the genuinely classicist air of unforced, continuous modeling.

As solitary virtuoso, Picasso would from now on depend wholly on himself and his feelings. There would be no more collaborations, as with Braque. The corollary was that Picasso gave feeling itself an extraordinary, self-regarding intensity, so that the most vivid images of braggadocio and rage, castration fear and sexual appetite in modern art still belong to the Spaniard. This frankness—allied with Picasso's power of metamorphosis, which linked every image together in a ravenous, animistic vitality—is without parallel among other artists and explains his importance to a movement he never joined, surrealism.

BASICALLY, PICASSO CARED NOTHING about civilization or its discontents. He admired, and tried to embody, the child and the savage, both prodigies of appetite. To feel, to seize, to penetrate, to abandon: these were the verbs of his art, as they were of his cruelly narcissistic relationships with the "goddesses or doormats," as he categorized the women in his life. Hence, the energy of *The Embrace,* 1925, its lovers grappling on a sofa in their orifice-laden knot of apoplectic randiness. Hence, too, the fear (amounting sometimes to holy terror, but more often to a witch-killing misogyny) that emanates from creatures like the bony mantis woman of *Seated Bather,* 1930. Such images are cathartic: they project fears that no French artist (and outside France, only Edvard Munch) would even admit to. One needs colossal self-confidence to expose such insecurities.

On the other side of these chthonic appetites lay some of the most haunting images of metamorphosis and erotic fulfillment in the history of Western art. They were provided by his affair with Marie-Thérèse Walter, a young woman whom Picasso picked up outside a Paris department store in 1927. He was 45, feeling trapped in a sour marriage to the Russian dancer Olga Koklova; Marie-Thérèse was 17.

"Pictures are made the way the prince gets children," Picasso remarked a little later, "with the shepherdess." In Marie-Thérèse, he found a shepherdess—a placid, ill-educated and wholly compliant blond, who had never heard of him or his work, and offered nothing that even Picasso's egotism could interpret as competition. She became an oasis of sexual comfort. His images of Marie-Thérèse reading, sleeping, contemplating her face in a mirror or posing (in the Vollard suite of etchings) for the Mediterranean artist-god, Picasso himself, have an extraordinarily inward quality, vegetative and abandoned. In one sense, the body of Marie-Thérèse, curled up in *Nude Asleep in a Landscape,* 1934, is seen as a graffitist might see it—a lilac-toned pink blob, twisted and curled to show its openings, nipples and navel, the body recomposed in terms of its sexual signs. It is a hieroglyph for arousal, tumescence in paint. Yet it is something more. For in these images of Marie-Thérèse, Picasso demonstrated his power to materialize his sensations. The body is not merely a sign, but a direct translation of desire into plastic terms, and that is what graffitists cannot do.

His metamorphic sculptures of Marie-Thérèse from the early '30s, involutes of swollen dreaming bronze in which cheek is conflated with buttock, mouth with vagina, have a wonderful tenderness and power as plastic surfaces. Even the plumpness of the bronze cast provides the suggestion of skin, while the slightly fuzzy texture of the metal further equivocates, not with the look, but with the feel of flesh. In some ways, the shapes of Marie-Thérèse, smooth and closed, are like the totemic bone forms of Picasso's grotesque anatomies of the '30s, the projects for immense figure-based sculptures that he fantasized building along the Côte d'Azur. But their whole import is different. There is no dislocation or fear in them: they are, as William Blake put it, "the lineaments of gratified desire."

The climate of sexual politics has changed so irreversibly in the past 50 years that one cannot imagine a painter trying such images today. In that sense, Picasso closed another tradition in the act of reinventing it. The same applies to his visions of the classical Mediterranean from the 1930s. Picasso felt the Greeks in the ground and was the last modern artist to raise them. The river gods, nymphs, Minotaurs and classical heads that fill the Vollard suite and spill over into innumerable drawings and gouaches of the 1930s are not the conventional décor of antiquity. They are more like emblems of autobiography, acts of passionate self-identification. Picasso's Minotaur, now young and self-regarding, fresh as a Narcissus with horns, now bowed under the bison-like weight of his own grizzled head, is Picasso himself. His Mediterranean images are the last appearance, in serious art, of the symbols of that once Arcadian coast.

Picasso's climactic work of the '30s was *Guernica,* 1937. In its way it is a classicizing painting, not only in its friezelike effect, but also in its details. The only modern image in it is a light bulb; but for its presence, the mural would scarcely seem to belong in the world of Heinkel bombers and incendiary bombs. Yet its black, white and gray palette also suggests the documentary photo, while the texture of strokes on the horse's body is more like collaged newsprint than hair.

Guernica was the last masterpiece of painting to be provoked by political catastrophe. World War II and the Holocaust evoked nothing to match it, and the monuments to the Gulag are books, not paintings. *Guernica's* power flows from the contrast between its almost marmoreal formal system and the terrible vocabulary of pain that Picasso locked into it. It is shown at MOMA with all its preliminary studies, and to see Picasso developing these hieroglyphs of anguish, the horse, the weeping woman, the screaming head, the fallen soldier, the clenched hand on the sword, is to witness one of the supreme dramas of the injection of feeling into conventional subject matter that the century has to offer. Indeed, the effort was such that it carried him past the end of the picture into a series of weeping women's heads, which show, even more clearly than *Guernica,* how Picasso could saturate a motif with meaning, to the point where it could hold no more truth. This free passage from feeling into meaning was the essence of his genius. Even when he was painting below form, he could always find significance in commonplace sensations, however distorted the actual form: the death in a goat's skull or the spikiness of a sea urchin, the feather softness of a dove, the looming stupid menace of a bull, a toad's lumpish slither.

Picasso was 55 when he finished *Guernica,* and up to his 60th birthday or so he remained an artist worthy of comparison (if painters and writers can be compared) with Shakespeare. There was a similar range of feeling, from bawdry to tragedy, coupled with a rhetorical intensity of metaphor and a great depth of experience. After *Guernica* he could still paint very well: *L'Aubade,* in 1942, with its stark intimations of confinement and oppression, seems to distill the mood of occupied France. Some of his portraits of Dora Maar, Marie-Thérèse's successor as his mistress, are of ravishing and edgy beauty.

Yet the inventions of necessity slowly gave way to the needs of mere performance. Picasso's sculpture retained its intensity almost to the end, but his painting did not, and this became clear after 1950. Without doubt, MOMA's great exhibition ends on a dying fall. The Picassian energy is still there, masquerading as inspiration, but too often it ends as a form of visual conjuring. Was he growing bored with his own virtuosity? Impossible to know. Since anything could be converted into a Picasso, and thence into gold, he suffered the dilemma of Midas twice over. This was the inevitable result of the fame he enjoyed in the last quarter-century of his life, a fame such as no artist in history had known. It could only have been created by the pressures of the 20th century, with its mass magazines, its art market, its mania for promiscuity among famous names combining in the most sustained exercise in mythmaking ever to be visited on a painter. In the end he was trapped by his own reputation, the idol and prisoner of his court of toadies and dealers, fawned on and denied the ordinary resistances against which an artist, to survive at all, must push.

It showed in the work. But do the irresolutions of his old age really matter? Picasso shaped his century when it, and he, was younger, and all its possibilities were open to his ravening eye, in those three decades between 1907 and 1937. He was the most influential artist of his own time; for many lesser figures a catastrophic influence, and for those who could deal with him—from Braque, through Giacometti, to de Kooning and Arshile Gorky—an almost indescribably fruitful one.

Today such a career seems inconceivable. No one even shows signs of assuming the empty mantle. If ever a man created his own historical role and was not the pawn of circumstances, it was that Nietzschean monster from Málaga. ∎

M*A*S*H, You Were a Smash

BY RICHARD CORLISS

[
*As it prepared to sign off after 11 seasons, a critic saluted
TV's M*A*S*H as a show whose rare skill, daring humor
and deep humanity touched a national nerve*
]

February 28, 1983

LETTER SENT FROM THE 4077 Mobile Army
Surgical Hospital based in Ouijongbu, Korea:

Dear Mom,
*Well here I am in Korea. It's a long way from Ottumwa,
Iowa, but then I guess it's a long way from everybody else's home
town of the guys around here too. The only thing we're not far from is the front.
Three miles down the road, the war is going full blast. It's our job to patch up the
wounded and, the way they say it around here is, send them back to get wounded again. Actually, I don't do the patching. I'm kind of like what you might sort
of call the company clerk, which is still a pretty good thing for an 18-year-old
farm boy to be if he's gotta be here. They call me Radar on account of because
I can sometimes figure out what somebody's gonna say before they say it—but
you knew that already. Just about all the guys here are great, my boss Colonel
Blake and the surgeons and even the nurses, they're great guys too. But I miss
you, Mom. Enclosed I've put some of my pay, so you can keep up your electroly-
sis. Love to Uncle Ed and all the animals and especially to you.*

Your son, Walter
P.S. They say this war won't last long, Mom. I sure hope they're right.

Stage 9 of the 20th Century-Fox studios in Los Angeles is dark. The backdrop of khaki-drab Korean hills and everything that might serve as inventory, booty or memento have disappeared. Gone are the tables, tubing, clamps and surgical gowns from O.R.; neither the blandly frazzled Lieut. Colonel Henry Blake (McLean Stevenson) nor the avuncular Colonel Sherman Potter (Harry Morgan) will preside any more over that surgeons' battlefield. In the mess hall, the serving trays and cigarette packs are missing; Corporal Klinger (Jamie Farr), the drag queen of 4077, will never again ask Father Mulcahy (William Christopher) to give absolution to the food. The officers' club has been stripped of its jukebox and banners; only the lingering perfume of Major Margaret ("Hot Lips") Houlihan (Loretta Swit) will drive the ghost of Major Frank Burns (Larry Linville) into rages of ecstasy. And in the most famous barracks since Stalag 17—Hawkeye Pierce's Swamp—the cots, footlockers, stove, framed pictures and even the distillery are gone. The giggles and groans of Trapper John (Wayne Rogers) and B.J. Hunnicut (Mike Farrell) and Charles Emerson Winchester III (David Ogden Stiers) are now distant, poignant echoes.

The wish that Corporal Radar O'Reilly (Gary Burghoff) made has come true. In real time, the Korean conflict was over in three years; in CBS's prime time, it lasted eleven increasingly popular years; in syndicated reruns, it has proved so successful that it could outlast the Hundred Years' War. By next Monday, when its 2½-hour send-off episode is aired, *M*A*S*H* will have earned its stars as one of the funniest, most humane and formally adventurous shows ever to leave its mark on TV.

Some of its achievements can be measured in numbers. Since its debut Sept. 17, 1972, *M*A*S*H* has won 14 Emmys and 99 nominations. Its annual rating has climbed from 46th place to third this year (after *60 Minutes* and *Dallas*). In the same time, the show increased the going rate for a 30-second commercial from $30,000 to about $200,000 for a regular episode and, for the feature-length finale, $450,000, topping the rate of last month's Super Bowl by $50,000, to become the most expensive half-minute in TV history. In syndication, *M*A*S*H's* earnings already exceed $200 million, and keep on growing. There is a price for success, and Fox should be happy to pay it: a reported $5 million or so a year to Alan Alda, who anchored the show as Captain Hawkeye Pierce and wrote and directed many of the most memorable episodes in a series whose writing was often of the highest, hippest quality.

No work of popular art can tap the money machine so deftly without touching a national pulse or nerve. *M*A*S*H,* a Viet Nam parable that hit the airwaves three months before the Christmas bombing of Hanoi, surely did so. Like the surgeons whose no-sweat heroism it celebrated, the series began by operating on the wounded American body politic with skill and daring good humor. For half an hour each week, hawk and dove could sit together in front of the TV set and agree: war is an existential hell to which some pretty fine people had been unfairly assigned; now they were doing their best to do good and get out. As the Viet Nam War staggered to a close and *M*A*S*H* generated the momentum any TV series needs to sustain its quality after the first few seasons, the show revealed itself as a gritty romance about the finest American instincts. Here were gruff pragmatism, technical ingenuity, grace under pressure, the saving perspective of wit. The men and women of 4077 MASH could be seen as us at our worst hour, finding the best part of ourselves.

M*A*S*H was about doctors in Korea, and it drew from real life and death as faithfully as many documentaries. Larry Gelbart and Gene Reynolds, who developed the show for TV, talked with dozens of surgeons and nurses who had served in Korea; they even visited a Korean MASH base for more memories. Later, Burt Metcalfe, who took over as producer after Gelbart and Reynolds left, continued the tradition. "We've spoken to almost every doctor who was in Korea," Metcalfe claims. "At least 60% of the plots dealing with medical or military incidents were taken from real life." Says Reynolds: "These guys gave us details we never would have thought of. They kept us honest." Gelbart recalls one doctor's remark: "He said, 'In the winter it is so cold in the O.R. that when the surgeon cuts into a patient, steam rises from the body, and the surgeon will warm his hands over the open wound.' In the last show I wrote and directed, 'The Interview,' I had Father Mulcahy use those exact words when he was asked if the war had changed him."

Dear Dad,

A year in Korea and no end in sight. Last week we suffered a visitation by some brigadier general who tried to boost morale by telling us that we are bringing democracy to this green and peasant land. That was the most ridiculous thing I ever heard. I felt like telling His Belligerence that what this country needs is a good five-cent czar. My tentmate, Major Frank Burns, is even more amusing, if you get your laughs from psychotic paranoia complicated by a spine-wide streak of yellow. He thinks we're here to save Korea from the Koreans, and that when the war is over Seoul will be colonized by the Fort Wayne Kiwanis Club. I couldn't help breaking into a chorus of the Ethel Merman song: "There's no vinism like chauvinism like no vinism I know."

I guess Frank is just the carrier. The disease, the bubonic plague, is knowing that our O.R. is just a three-day pass that wounded kids are given before being shipped back to the front. We knit and purl and offer kind words and jokes so bad even Milton Berle wouldn't steal them. For me, joking is therapeutic. It's the only way I have of opening my mouth without screaming.

Here I am babbling, Dad, and I know you brook no babble. But what can you expect of a barefoot surgeon from Crabapple Cove, Me.? I can't wait to come home, hug you and then log six or seven months' sleep.

Love, Hawkeye

Before it became a television series, *M*A*S*H* had been a mildly successful novel (1968) by Richard Hooker and a surprise hit movie (1970) directed by Robert Altman and written by Ring Lardner Jr. Most of the TV show's major characters were sketched in by the movie, but the tone was '50s frat house, and the emphasis was on the safety-valve sexual high jinks that the heroes perpetrated on some of their uptight colleagues. These droll humiliations would have been too raunchy for TV and too alienating for audiences in search of a weekly identification figure. Enter Alan Alda, who was starring in films and TV movies without having hit it big and who was now ready for the right series. "In talking with Larry Gelbart and Gene Reynolds," Alda recalls, "I wanted to be sure that we weren't making an *Abbott & Costello Go to Korea,* using the war just as a straight line for the jokes. The war had to be a springboard for our best efforts, exploring the horror, not ignoring it." Everyone agreed that this would be, in Reynolds' words, "a different Hawkeye, more sensitive, compassionate and serious than in the film but, through Alan's lovely comic touch, an engaging man withal."

He proved to be something more than that. Like the hero of Fenimore Cooper's *Leatherstocking Tales,* this Hawkeye is an exemplar of the American democrat, the self-reliant nobleman of nature who trail-blazes into a wilderness of the spirit and emerges stronger and wiser. Alda's modern pathfinder is also very much a man of the mid–20th century: liberally educated and not reluctant to parade it, perversely triumphant in a milieu he blithely declares himself unfit to inhabit, japing and shambling after women, with a quip and an invisible cigar, like a Wasp Groucho. In later episodes,

Hawkeye occasionally looked as if he were campaigning for canonization. But he could still bend, and come near breaking, whether in realizing he had a serious drinking problem or in surrendering to the inexplicable but powerful erotic appeal of his longtime nemesis, Hot Lips Houlihan.

Every sitcom must have its bad guys, even as every war finds its black-market profiteers, body-count fanatics and suspicious spooks. *M*A*S*H* had its fair and flaky share, led by Frank Burns, the camp martinet. As Linville notes, Burns had "a mind that's obviously stripped its gears, and yet here he is standing over other human beings with a knife in his hand." At first, locked in a dead-end affair with Frank, Hot Lips was simply a stock shrew, an excellent nurse but a failure as a woman. She was also attracted despite herself to the antic Hawkeye and Trapper John, and Swit and the writers saw possibilities in that. "First she became unhappy with Frank," Swit recalls. "She realized there had to be something more in life for her. Then she started to talk about how lonely her position of authority made her feel. She was married and divorced, and she softened and hardened and grew from that experience. In the episode 'Comrades in Arms,' where she and Hawkeye are stranded and make love, both characters changed: they could never be true archrivals again."

In a superior TV comedy series, familiarity breeds regeneration. The actors become wedded to their characters and, like fond spouses, exchange idiosyncrasies. The writers learn more about the actors and incorporate the nuances into the story lines. *M*A*S*H* had another advantage, although at the time it must have seemed a daunting challenge. Four of the first season's eight regular cast members eventually left the show, and with each replacement the circle of community became tighter. In his rubber-limbed way, Stevenson's Colonel Blake had been as much a MASH misfit as Frank Burns: a suburban doctor reluctant to command, with a fisherman's wily patience and a heart of puppy chow. When Stevenson departed after the third season (his character was reported killed in an airplane crash in the Sea of Japan), Harry Morgan as Colonel Sherman Potter took over. A cavalryman in the first World War who turned medic and was Regular Army to his jodhpurs, Potter became the stern but sentimental father figure every MASHman needed 7,000 miles from home. Similarly, B.J. Hunnicut was an idealistic Marin County version of Trapper John, and Winchester, however smug he might appear to be about his old-money Bostonian lineage, was a Persian pussycat compared with Frank Burns. Each of these characters and actors fed the *M*A*S*H* organism without disrupting it. Each helped keep the show alive and healthy without breaking the circle.

In the post-op of reruns, the members of the 4077 will continue indefinitely to act bonkers, save lives and refresh viewers' spirits. Radar will lose and find his Teddy bear and, maybe, lose his virginity. Klinger will show up in that cunning little chiffon number he bought in Seoul. Frank will fritter and whine and cluck like a chicken. B.J. will keep trying to prove he is *not* the most decent soul south of the 38th parallel. Winchester will open another picnic basket from Mater and savor caviar on a tongue depressor. Father Mulcahy will smile and sigh. Trapper will somehow keep his balance on that second-banana peel. Hot Lips will practice her yoga and do her nails. Henry will accidentally impale himself on a hypodermic needle. Hawkeye will wonder at the insanity of it all, and wonder too whether he is part of the problem or the solution. And Sherman Potter, who has seen it all before in other wars, will grimace like the Sphinx and let the vinegar flow all the way home.

Dear Mildred,

I'm sure you've heard, my dear. The war is over. Horse hockey-pucks! it took longer than I'd've thought. I sometimes wonder whether we're getting better at this sort of thing. The men of the 4077 would surely say we ought to get worse and then give it up. One of them called me—sit down and listen to this—"a tough, bandy-legged little mustang." Donkey doughnuts! That Winchester can get under my old hide. I guess all of them have, and I guess they'll stay there. When I came to this MASH *they looked like a strange new breed of soldier.*

Of course, they're really civilian doctors, and damn good ones too. I'm gonna miss them. Hey, Mother, what say we bring the whole lot of them over to the home for one last schnapps? It'd sure beat watching that thing you've been spending all your time with—what's it, television?

Love forever, Sherman ■

—REPORTED BY DENISE WORRELL/LOS ANGELES

Mainstreaming Allen Ginsberg

BY R.Z. SHEPPARD

[*In a type of critical piece characteristic of* TIME, *the writer assessed a new work, evoked a personality and distilled a career, all within a notably brief compass*]

February 4, 1985

"THE FIRST THING IS to straighten your spine," says Allen Ginsberg, as he starts his *tai chi chuan,* the Chinese exercises he recommends for healthful testicles and liver. With arms extended and hands as graceful as cobra heads, he begins the ritual steps, fluidly shifting his weight from one slippered foot to the other. The martial exercise is based on a subtle principle. "The aggressor is off balance," Ginsberg explains. "The person who is nonaggressive is in balance."

This is a fetching idea and one that applies to America's most public poet. Approaching his autumnal years, the man once feared as a weevil in the nation's moral fiber is in a disarming state of equilibrium. Cultural norms have adjusted in Ginsberg's favor since 1956, when he disturbed the peace with *Howl.* It was a poetic tantrum thrown at the Eisenhower years, at an academic system that rejected his rude unconventionality, at an encompassing conspiracy he imagined had driven his mother and his soul mates crazy. "Moloch! Moloch!" he cried. "Robot apartments! invisible suburbs! skeleton treasuries! blind capitals! demonic industries! spectral nations! invincible madhouses!"

The bearded rebel from Paterson, N.J., also flaunted the subjects of drug

357

use and homosexuality with an explicitness that would have unnerved Walt Whitman, the American bard whose confessional style Ginsberg's most resembles. Yet today, millions of housewives casually tune in to hopheads and gays on *The Phil Donahue Show,* and Allen Ginsberg is a member of the National Institute of Arts and Letters. He is a recipient of fellowships, grants and a National Book Award. He recently returned from a month-long tour of China as guest of the Chinese Writers Association. Once he might have declared the experience groovy. Now he calmly brings the news: "In private the people I spoke with have clear, Mozartian minds. In public they are silent."

Sartorially, Ginsberg meets his fellow citizens halfway: sports jackets, slacks, shirts and ties bought secondhand at the Salvation Army. His $260-a-month apartment in Manhattan's run-down East Village is furnished in Early Struggling Artist: an assortment of old tables and chairs, aging appliances and, for some reason having to do with a previous renovation, a kitchen sink in the living room. The walk-up tenement has no working front bell. To enter, a visitor must call up from the sidewalk and wait for the poet to throw down a key rolled up in a sock.

This charming rite may soon end. Real estate speculators have bought the building, says Ginsberg, and are trying to evict its occupants. The neighborhood, a center for low-income artists, is undergoing gentrification. So, perhaps, is Ginsberg. His earlier works were printed by small presses, notably City Lights Books, Lawrence Ferlinghetti's Beat Generation landmark in San Francisco. Now, for the first time, Ginsberg has an agent and a six-book contract with a major New York publisher.

The initial and most important volume went on sale last month. *Collected Poems 1947-1980* is arranged chronologically, covering the author's days as a Columbia College student, a West Coast beatnik, sexual experimenter, war protester, world traveler and Buddhist. Ginsberg's style harks back to the tradition of popular speech, jazz rhythms and strong imagery. The energy never flags, but the quality is wildly uneven. There are love poems that read like high parodies of rest-room scrawl. *Howl,* once effective as counterculture manifesto, is now an unconvincing historical oddity: "I saw the best minds of my generation destroyed by madness." But *Kaddish,* about Ginsberg's insane mother, who died in 1956, is a masterpiece of candor and emotional persuasion: "The Charity of her hands stinking with Manhattan, madness, desire to please me, cold undercooked fish—pale red near the bones. Her smells—and oft naked in the room, so that I stare ahead, or turn a book ignoring her."

Collected Poems is only the first step in drawing Ginsberg to mainstream publishing and ratifying his presence between hard covers. His $160,000 contract with Harper calls for five more volumes: journals, future poetry, essays and interviews, and letters. There is also a biography of him in the works and a documentary funded by the National Endowment for the Arts. Ginsberg's own visual contributions are 30 years' worth of snapshots of his literary friends. A selection, including the faces of William Burroughs, Jack Kerouac, Gregory Corso and Peter Orlovsky, was recently on display in a Manhattan gallery.

The surviving "hideous human angels," as Ginsberg calls them, keep in touch. Orlovsky, a former lover and longtime companion, lives across the hall. The Ginsberg apartment is a popular rest stop for old companions passing through New York: "I like to keep the place clean, and it's hard, because I'm not here for months at a time," he says, explaining a sign on his bedroom door that asks guests to remove their shoes. Since 1974 much of his time has been spent at the Naropa Institute in Boulder, Colo., a college for Buddhist studies where he teaches poetry and perfects his meditation techniques. He maintains his bank account by giving lectures and readings.

At 58, Ginsberg is confronting one of life's simple truths: one cannot step into the same cash flow twice. His annual income rarely exceeds $40,000, yet for years he has contributed funds to help impoverished friends and artists. "I have some power and money," he says, "but I don't know if I can keep it up much longer. I'm getting too old to run around. I need somewhere I can die in peace." His choice would be a large loft where he could have a Buddhist shrine room and space to organize the books, papers and projects that relentlessly pile up around him. Columbia University receives 20 boxes a year for its Ginsberg archives.

It requires vision and careful work to make a life, let alone leave a literary legacy. This follower in Whitman's footsteps has shown that he is capable of both. One can see it in his eyes: one wide and innocent, gazing at eternity; the other narrowed and scrutinizing, looking for his market share. ∎

A Great Balancing Act

BY STEFAN KANFER

[*After this ingenious review appeared, Theodor Geisel (a.k.a. Dr. Seuss) sent the writer a drawing in which the Cat in the Hat extolled him as "my favorite poet"*]

April 9, 1990

Oh, The Places You'll Go!
by Dr. Seuss; Random House; $12.95

The poetics are tight,
and the drawings are loose
in the forty-three books
that are signed Dr. Seuss.

In the days of the past
he would merrily tell
of the Grinch who took joy
in purloining noel.

Of the Cat in the Hat
and recalcitrant Sam,
who refused any meal
made of Green Eggs and Ham.

And of Horton and Sneetch
and of Yertle and Who
and of Thidwick the Moose
and If I Ran the Zoo.

Every Seusspenseful tale,
every verse that he did,
seemed to land on the bed
or the lap of a kid.

But the doctor of late
has achieved his results
by prescribing for those
who are labeled adults.

In The Lorax *he chose*
as his overall theme
the consumption that eats
at the forest and stream.

And the big Butter Battle
Book *spoke with a roar*
of the lunatic fringes
who trigger a war.

And You're Only Old Once!
pulled the ultimate hat trick:
making readers think twice
about things geriatric.

But the latest of Seuss
fits in no category.
Oh, the Places You'll Go!
is an all-ages story

Of the creature who wins
after being a victim
when it learns how to live
by observing this dictum:

Just "be sure when you step.
Step with care and great tact
and remember that Life's
a Great Balancing Act."

And recalling the thing
left unsaid by the sage:
that surprises may come
on the very last page.

Case in point, Seuss himself,
who is now eighty-six.
Moral: Who says you can't
teach an old Doc new tricks?

■

Hostage of His Own Genius

BY RICHARD SCHICKEL

[*When Marlon Brando died, it became possible to set aside the vagaries and excesses of his later years and refocus on the revolutionary brilliance of his acting and the powerful way he spoke for a generation*]

July 12, 2004

"THERE'S NO ROOM FOR genius in the theater," Laurence Olivier once remarked. "It's too much trouble." He was right. For all the Sturm, Drang and general lunacy that so often attend the production of a play or film, the aim is to mobilize genial craft and polished technique to make something that's easy for producers to budget and schedule, something that clutches the audience's heart but does not send it spiraling into cardiac arrest.

For an important time in his life—and ours—Marlon Brando was touched by genius, by which we mean that he did things in his art that were unprecedented, unduplicable and, finally, inexplicable. And sure enough, for a much longer time, he was "too much trouble" for everyone to bear— including, possibly, himself. The road from self-realization to self-parody is always shorter than we realize.

But let's not talk about that—not yet. Let's think instead about brutal Stanley Kowalski in *A Streetcar Named Desire,* about yearning Terry Malloy in *On the Waterfront,* about the rough voice and silky menace of *The Godfather* and the noble and ignoble ruin of Brando's Paul in *Last Tango in Paris.* Then let's think about how in a minor but still palpable way our lives—especially our imaginative lives—would have been diminished if Brando had not been there to play them. Sometimes in those movies, and in others too, he gave us moments of heartbreaking behavioral reality in which he broke through whatever fictional frame surrounded him and gave us not just the truth of his character but also the truth about ourselves.

One example out of dozens will have to suffice. *Waterfront's* Terry is shyly courting Eva Marie Saint's convent girl. She drops her glove. He picks it up and casually, talking about other things, tries to wriggle his fingers into it. What else of hers might he similarly, clumsily like to invade and possess? And how, we wonder, have we similarly, unconsciously betrayed our truest intentions while pretending that we were just kidding around?

Elia Kazan, who brought Brando to fame in the Broadway production of *Streetcar* (1947) and directed him in *Waterfront*, never took credit for that or any of the other moments Brando achieved for him. "The thing he wanted from me," Kazan later said, "was to get the machine going. And once that machine was going, he didn't need a hell of a lot more." It was, of course, quite a complicated mechanism. Kazan spoke of the contrast, in Brando's work, between "a soft, yearning girlish side to him and a dissatisfaction that is violent and can be dangerous," and observed that it was true of the man himself. "He never knew where the hell he was going to sleep. You didn't know who he was running away from or who he was angry with. You never knew."

No wonder the devotees of Method acting so eagerly claimed him. They believed he was pulling all that conflict out of himself, out of his troubled and rebellious past (cruel and drunken father, wistful and drunken mother) and using it—just as their great guru, Lee Strasberg, preached. In the first years of his fame, that was O.K. with Brando. It saved him a lot of tedious explanations. And it was more than O.K. with the crowd at the Actors Studio, which he briefly joined. It was the headquarters of Stanislavskian acting in America, inheritor of the Group Theater tradition (where in the 1930s Strasberg first came to controversial prominence). They had long needed a star to lead their revolution—against the well-spoken, emotionally disconnected acting style that had long prevailed on stage and film, indeed against the whole slick, corrupt Broadway-Hollywood way of doing show business.

Brando was their stud, possibly the most gorgeous (and authentically sexy) male the movies had ever seen. But he was in his nature ill suited to superstardom. Maybe he didn't want to be anyone's figurehead. He said, truly, that he had an attention span of about seven minutes. Besides, he didn't like delving too deeply into himself. He called that activity "pearl diving," and it upset and scared him. "Actors have to observe," he once said, "and I enjoy that part of it. They have to know how much spit you have in your mouth and where the weight of your elbows is. I could sit all day in the Optimo Cigar Store on Broadway [which he often did] and just watch the people go by."

His first acting teacher, Stella Adler, who also wasn't much for "affective memory" (Strasberg's fancy phrase for pearl diving), agreed. "He's the most keenly aware, empathetic human alive. He just knows. If you have a scar, physical or mental, he goes right to it. He cannot be cheated or fooled. If you left the room, he could be you." In those days, he truly loved acting and was fully devoted to it. His mother said to Adler, "Thank you. You've saved Marlon. He had no direction. Now he has direction."

But not for long. The movies changed. In the '50s, the screen widened to CinemaScope proportions while the audience shrank more than 50% and a panicky Hollywood pretty much abandoned small, tight character-driven dramas. But Brando didn't change. He remained an adolescent idealist, loving the art that had redeemed his incorrigible flakiness but becoming increasingly lost and miserable in this new context. The daring of this work somehow made people laugh uncomfortably. And Hollywood, which will first indulge those it intends to humble, turned against him, blaming him, sometimes unfairly, for cost overruns and box-office failures. Now self-loathing seeped into his interviews. "I've got no respect for acting," he would say. Or, "Acting is the expression of a neurotic impulse." Or, "You get paid for doing nothing, and it all adds up to nothing."

He threw himself distractingly into the great causes of his time, like civil rights. He chose bad movies in which he was trying to be not a leading man but a character actor, hiding in plain sight under pounds of make-up and talking in weird accents. That led directly to the greatness of *The Godfather*. But it was his one full, belated embrace of the Method that led to *Last Tango*, in which he improvised yards of dialogue, based on his own history, to explain his desperately sad character.

THAT WAS IN 1972. He had 32 more years to live, encased in fat and cynicism, enduring personal tragedies (notably the killing of his daughter's lover by one of his sons), emerging occasionally to grab some bucks for reading a few lines off cue cards. It was sad and to some of us infuriating. For if you were young and impressionable in the '50s, he was forever Our Guy—a man whose inarticulate yearnings, whose needs and rages somehow spoke for a silent generation, privately nursing our grievances at the bourgeois serenity of our elders. We would get mad at his fecklessness, but we never quite lost our faith in him, which was occasionally rewarded by the anarchic craziness of *The Missouri Breaks,* by the dainty befuddlements of another Mafia don in *The Freshman.*

Now that he's gone, that faith abides. No, he never did Hamlet or Lear or Uncle Vanya—those were someone else's dreams, not Brando's. He did, without quite knowing it, something grander than that. He gave generations of actors permission to make metaphors of themselves, letting their public find something of themselves in those private moments that, before Brando, no one dared bring forth. Maybe his greatest legacy is named Sean Penn. Or Johnny Depp. Or some nutsy kid whose name we don't yet know. But maybe not. In the end, most acting careers consist of no more than half a dozen great performances and an equal number of near-misses. Those he gave us. The work will abide—while the often foolish and more often misspent life that these performances mysteriously drew upon will fade away, lost at last in the hum and buzz of our infinitely distractible media age. ■

SIGMUND FREUD, 1920

Frontiers of Science and Medicine

Wizard of Menlo

[W R I T E R   U N K N O W N]

[*At 78, having invented—to name just three—the light bulb, the phonograph and the movie camera, Thomas Edison was honored for transforming human life in his time*]

May 25, 1925

ONE DAY LAST WEEK, a large boulder obstructed traffic on the Lincoln Highway at Menlo Park, between New Brunswick and Metuchen, N. J. The boulder was not directly on the cement, nor did it lean menacingly over it. Motorists could have passed by comfortably, save that before the boulder, ranged in rows upon the highway, were some 600 chairs of the folding variety used for church sociables, political meetings and open-air exercises.

Upon the chairs sat notables, upon a platform more notables. Across the boulder rippled two U. S. flags, behind which, fixed in the stone, a bronze tablet mutely announced: "On this site—1876-1882—Thomas Alva Edison began his work of service for the world. . . . This tablet is placed by the Edison Pioneers . . ."

Near Mr. and Mrs. Edison on the platform was John W. Lieb of the New York Edison Co. He dedicated the tablet and presented it to Governor George S. Silzer of New Jersey as a state monument, the latter accepting after Mrs. Edison had unveiled it. President John G. Hibben of Princeton then perorated, with interruptions by a rumbling freight train and a youthful Edisonian who leapt to the fore to declare he would never go to college.* Samuel Insull terminated the speechmaking.

Mr. Insull, when he came to this country from England in 1881, became the private secretary of Mr. Edison. Today he is a living example of the revolution which Mr. Edison has made possible in modern living—for he is President of the Commonwealth Edison Co., which furnishes all of Chicago's electric light, master of a great group of public utilities in the West—many of them grown up out of Mr. Edison's inventions—President of the Chicago Civic Opera Company and in general a magnate of the Middle West. He, with others—aides and witnesses of wholesale changes wrought by Edison inventions—did honor to the inventor. Through it all a big white head nodded modest appreciation, a pair of bright blue eyes twinkled with pleasure.

To the assemblage, no recital of Inventor Edison's history was needful. Too well known was the story of the Ohio youth inept at books, fond of dabbling with chemicals, both greengrocer and publisher in his teens, boxed on the ears (and deafened for life) by a furious conductor because a stick of phosphorus started a fire in the mail car in which he traveled with his printing office and chemicals (he was selling magazines on trains at the time and had a laboratory in one end of the mail car), and later of the young telegraph operator with the itch for invention.

The accomplishments of his life speak for him:

Improvements for the telegraph and for Dr. Bell's telephone of 1875; the electric pen or telescribe, and the mimeograph; the megaphone; an instantaneous vote-recording machine which Congress rejected because "one of the greatest weapons in the hands of a minority to prevent bad legislation ... is the roll-call"; the microtasimeter, for detecting slight changes of temperature; the world's first "talking-machine"; carbon filaments for incandescent electric light bulbs; the "Edison effect," an electric valve; the motion-picture camera; metal filaments for bulbs; the taximeter; an electric street car and numerous minor contrivances that have brought the number of U. S. patents in his name to over 1,000.

During the War, he enlisted his mechanical ingenuity as Chairman of the Naval Consulting Board; his chemical knowledge by producing, in large quantities, carbolic acid and other substances essential to the drug and dye industries, for which the U. S. had been dependent upon Germany.

From Ohio, where he had been born, the scene of his early life, his first

* *Inventor Edison, no college graduate, frequently deprecates the value of a college education.*

experiments and his days as a telegraph operator, Mr. Edison removed to Newark, N. J., in 1873; then to Menlo Park, later to Orange, N. J., where his home and large factories now are. Outside "the old man's" office, a placard advises visitors that he is so busy that he finds it "impossible to grant any personal interviews." Within, an absorbed, absent-minded, gracious, tireless, cheerful individual carries on his work, with the calm open-mindedness of a scientist, from one day to the next of his 79th year. Well might his motto be the one which is the heritage of the Princes of Wales—*"Ich dien"* (I serve).

With but three of his inventions, "the Wizard of Menlo Park" has modified human life more extensively than any man of his time. Most recent figures, for the U. S. alone :

ELECTRIC LIGHTING

Number of customers	13,400,000
Number of employees	300,000
Incandescent lamps per customer	37.85
Residences wired	10,500,000

PHONOGRAPHS

Number of phonographs manufactured per year	981,635
Number of records	98,104,279
Wage earners in the industry	23,505

CINEMA

Feet of film made per month	65,000,000
Miles of film made per year	(over) 150,000
Cinema houses in the U. S.	*17,836
Proportion of U. S. population estimated as attending cinemas regularly	68.2% ■

* In the world there are approximately 47,000 cinema houses.

Intellectual Provocateur

[W R I T E R   U N K N O W N]

[
*A portrait of one of the pioneering thinkers of the
20th century at the end of his immensely influential and
controversial career—ailing, exiled but still indomitable*
]

June 26, 1939

FOR 50 OF HIS 83 years Sigmund Freud has insisted on talking seriously about subjects that other people did not want to discuss. When he began lecturing on the sexual basis of neuroses, in Vienna in 1896, his worldly colleagues regarded him with the embarrassed annoyance reserved for those who hammer away at something people would rather not talk about, even if talking would teach them something. But for laymen, as Freud's theories spread, he emerged as the greatest killjoy in the history of human thought, transforming man's jokes and gentle pleasures into dreary and mysterious repressions, discovering hatreds at the root of love, malice at the heart of tenderness, incest in filial affections, guilt in generosity and the repressed hatred of one's father as a normal human inheritance.

Last week, from his home in exile in London, this 83-year-old disturber of human complacency calmly turned his attention to another topic generally and understandably avoided. This time he psychoanalyzed anti-Semitism. What, he asked, are the reasons for a phenomenon of such intensity and lasting strength as popular hatred of the Jews? Economic and political reasons Freud leaves to others; in *Moses and Monotheism* he is concerned with hidden motives.

Most of the book is given over to an account of the infancy of the Jewish people—not as it is known historically, but as it emerges in their legends, beliefs and religious customs. Its purpose is not to relate a factually, but a psychologically accurate picture, thereby uncovering, Freud believes, the reasons for popular hatred of the Jews and the reasons for the Jewish attitudes toward the persecutions that have darkened their history.

Only in view of the theory and practice of psychoanalysis is *Moses and Monotheism* intelligible. And the history of psychoanalysis is the history of Sigmund Freud.

When young Dr. Freud, fresh from five years' research on the nervous system, returned to his native Vienna and with high hopes hung out his shingle, the gay city was thronged with neurotics, "who hurried, with their troubles unsolved, from one physician to another." Some were afraid of animals; others constantly washed their hands, stammered, endured blinding headaches, lingering illnesses, or even developed strange paralyses of the arms and legs. All balanced precariously on the slender line between sanity and insanity. That the cause of their maladies was psychological, the 30-year-old psychiatrist was certain. But how these maladies arose, and how they could be cured—that was his great problem.

In his Paris clinic, Hypnotist Jean-Martin Charcot had often commanded drowsy neurotics to shed their symptoms. But only a few obeyed the doctor's powerful will and woke up cured. Yet hypnotism was the only scientific light which could prick the deep caverns of the unconscious mind, and even if it brought no lasting cures, young Dr. Freud could not very well do without it.

His first great step toward the development of psychoanalysis came one day when his old friend, Dr. Josef Breuer, a brilliant, popular family doctor, told him the remarkable story of "Anna O."

Anna O. was an intelligent girl of 21, who, while nursing her father during a fatal illness, suddenly developed paralysis of her right arm and both legs. To Dr. Breuer's amazement, when he asked her questions under hypnosis, she explained to him the origin of her symptoms, one by one. While nursing her father, she had suppressed a swarm of impulses as frivolous, selfish or immoral. And each suppressed desire had somehow turned into a physical symptom.

One evening, for instance, as Anna was sitting by her father's bed, she heard dance music floating over from the house next door. She longed to join the party, but sternly repressed the wish. Afterward, whenever she heard the strong rhythm of dance music, she began to cough, almost as though she were beating time. Most astounding part of the case, said Dr. Breuer, was this: as soon as Anna understood the origin and nature of her symptoms, they disappeared.

Greatly excited, Freud joined Breuer, tried the new method of conversing with hypnotized neurotics. Their aim: to "purge" constipated minds of unhealthy, repressed ideas.

Long after Breuer, discouraged by criticism, had left the partnership, Freud continued his attempts to find a more efficient method of mining buried thoughts. One day an alert patient, when asked if he could remember his recent experiences under hypnosis, repeated everything that had been said to him, everything that he himself had said.

This was a crucial discovery. Freud finally abandoned hypnosis, merely invited his patients to lie on a couch in his shaded office and talk of whatever entered their minds. This "free association," Freud soon discovered, was not free at all. For his patients, at first reluctantly mumbling trivialities, gradually wandered back into the past, on to forgotten paths, stumbling painfully over hidden, moss-covered memories, dabbling in streams of old affection. Through sharp observation and almost poetic analysis, Freud was able to interpret the mass of material his patients dredged up, and explain the origin of their symptoms.

Why his patients were "suggestible," why they accepted his explanations, overcame their resistance, strove to know themselves and conquer their symptoms, was at that time a problem to Freud. One day, during her treatment, a woman patient suddenly threw her arms around his neck.

"The unexpected entrance of a servant relieved us from a painful discussion," wrote Freud. "I was modest enough not to attribute the event to my irresistible personal attraction." This emotional "transference," which appeared as passionate, sensual love or fierce hatred, arose in every analysis, accounted for the powerful influence of an analyst over his patients. "[It is] the best instrument of the analytic treatment," Freud wrote, "... and it is resolved by convincing the patient that he is re-experiencing emotional relations which had their origin [in early childhood]." Thus Freud gained, in his patients' minds, the authority of a dearly loved (or violently hated) father or mother.

After examining a large group of neurotics, Freud was surprised to discover that they all had one thing in common: a frustrated sex life. "The neuroses," he declared, "[are] without exception disturbances of the sexual function."

But it was not the unhappy marriages or love affairs of adult life that were mainly responsible for neuroses. For the same experiences that normal persons took in their stride were sufficient to bowl neurotics over. The foundations of neuroses, Freud discovered, were laid in the sex experiences of early childhood. Upon this astonishing fact, which Freud painstakingly confirmed in hundreds of cases, he built his famous theories of the *libido* (Latin for lust) and the Oedipus complex.

Most powerful force which drives human beings, said Freud, is a primeval sex instinct, the libido. During childhood the libido is bound up with such experiences as eating, excreting and thumbsucking. In later years the libido may be transferred to another person (marriage), may remain grounded in childish sex play (perversion), or may overflow as artistic, literary, or musical creation (sublimation). In fact, said Freud, greatest source of creative work is the sex instinct.

Driven by libido, all children fall in love with their mothers, hate and fear their fathers as rivals. Sometimes they may love their fathers too (ambivalence), but the fundamental hostility remains throughout childhood. (Later on girls often fall in love with their fathers.) This Oedipus complex* sets the pattern for a child's response to other persons throughout the rest of his life. Normal persons outgrow the Oedipus situation by the time they reach maturity. But weaker characters cannot tear themselves away from their parents, hence, "fall into neuroses."

There is no escaping the Oedipus complex, said Freud, for it is our heritage from primitive ancestors, who killed their fathers in fits of jealous rage. "We are all omnibuses in which our ancestors ride, and every now and then one of them sticks his head out and embarrasses us," perceptively observed Oliver Wendell Holmes in his pre-Freudian novel *The Guardian Angel* (1867).

In light-hearted pre-War Vienna, which boasted of its sexual freedom, Freud was jeered at and shunned. Prudish physicians complained that he made too much of sex, that he destroyed beautiful illusions (such as the innocence of childhood), that he invaded his patients' privacy.

After the War, when Victorian taboos were thrown aside, and cries of sex freedom rang in every parlor, Freud's doctrines were eagerly gobbled up. Such words as "repression" and "mother fixation" became a part of the common language. Many people still mistakenly think that Freudianism

---

After the old Greek myth of Oedipus, son of the King of Thebes, who killed his father, married his mother.

is a doctrine of licence. On the contrary, Freud believes that self-discipline is essential for civilized living, that there is a middle road between unhealthy repression, which bursts forth as neuroses, and free abandonment to sexual pleasures.

BECAUSE THEY DO NOT believe in the primacy of the Oedipus complex, a small group of analysts have seceded from the Freudian union. Some of them do not agree that men are bound by primeval, rigid instincts. Others hold that society inflicts more wounds upon personality than the sex instinct. For these rebels, orthodox Freudians, whose feelings run high, have nothing but contempt.

Most famed among the secessionists are Carl Jung of Zürich, who has "retreated from psychoanalysis" into semi-religious therapy, and Alfred Adler, who died in Aberdeen two years ago. Adler held that man's mainspring is not sexual desire but a desire for superiority. Physical infirmity or family bullying produces an "inferiority complex." This complex, in turn, forces "overcompensation," or a transformation of weakness into strength. Because Demosthenes stuttered and Beethoven was deaf, said Adler, they developed inferiority complexes. Demosthenes compensated in magnificent oratory, Beethoven in magnificent music.

When the Nazis took Vienna last year they seized Freud's property, money and psychoanalytical publishing house. Although tortured by advanced cancer of the jaw, Freud at first refused to leave his home. In vain did his nephew, Manhattan Publicist Edward Bernays, plead with him to spend his last days in the U. S. He surrendered only when London's famed Dr. Ernest Jones flew to Vienna with a cargo of shrewd arguments.

Early last June Freud went to England "for peace." In a comfortable London house near Regent's Park, filled with his Greek and Egyptian treasures, Freud answers letters, continues his writing, even treats a few old patients. Every Sunday evening he settles down in the parlor, coddles his five young grandchildren, enjoys a lively card game called tarot with his sons. Always at his call is his nine-year-old chow dog, Lun. During his 16 years of suffering, throughout his 15 operations, he has never uttered a word of complaint. Patient and resigned, secure in his fame, he spins out his last thoughts, and basks in the sun.

In the shadow of exile *Moses and Monotheism* was written. But no trace of lamentation shows in the tone of the book. We live, says Freud imperturbably, in remarkable times. For a long period it seemed that progress had made an alliance with barbarism, as in Russia, where a great attempt to lift the people to a higher standard of life was coupled with a ruthless suppression of free speech and thought. But in Germany this unnatural marriage has been dissolved, and barbarism proceeds alone.

In reviewing Jewish history, legends and attitudes, Freud very provocatively suggests: Moses, the founder of the Jewish religion, was no Jew, but an Egyptian.

In the reign of Amenhotep IV, monotheism, the worship of one god, flourished briefly, when Amenhotep drove out the multitude of local deities in which Egypt abounded. After Amenhotep's death his religion was soon overthrown and the older worship returned, but here & there disciples kept alive the monotheistic idea. If Moses was an Egyptian, argues Freud, he must have been one of these; in the period of anarchy that followed Amenhotep's death he must have converted the enslaved Jews, leading them out of Egypt, giving them laws, customs, social order.

For the purposes of Freud's argument, the Jews must eventually have killed Moses. But his memory must have persisted, like the image of the father in childhood, as stern, implacable, good.

Hatred of the Jews, says Freud, is fundamentally hatred of monotheistic religion. The Germans, who now excel in the practice of anti-Semitism, were Christianized within historical times, often to the accompaniment of cruel repressions whose traces persist in their unconscious minds; their latent resentment toward Christianity is diverted against the upholders of another monotheistic religion. And meanwhile, the Jews themselves suffer from a guilt-obsession arising from the forgotten murder of Moses—an unconscious obsession from which they would presumably be freed by the admission of their guilt.

Mankind is not, Freud believes, so far removed from either barbarism or animals as it likes to think. But the mood of his last book is calm. If it does not answer all the questions that anti-Semitism raises, it shows that Freud is no more dismayed by this disorder than by the dark neuroses and perversions that he has studied all his life.   ∎

The Dymaxion American

BY DOUGLAS AUCHINCLOSS

[*Best known for his geodesic domes, R. Buckminster Fuller
was a quirky visionary who, as he saw it, was simply
applying the principles of the universe to practical uses*]

January 10, 1964

HE HAS BEEN CALLED "the first poet of technology," "the greatest living genius of industrial-technical realization in building," "an anticipator of the world to come—which is different from being a prophet," "a seminal thinker," and "an inspired child." But all these encomiums are fairly recent. For most of his life, R. Buckminster Fuller was known simply as a crackpot.

He is also something more than the mere sum of his praise and criticism. He is a throwback to the classic American individualist, a mold which produced Thomas Edison and Thoreau—men with the fresh eye that sees and questions everything anew, and the crotchety mind that refuses to believe there is anything that cannot be done. What Fuller sees excites him with the vision of man's potentialities, and he has made it his mission to help man realize them. Says he: "Man knows so much and does so little."

Last week this crackpot stepped off a plane in London, spouting words the minute his feet touched ground, and headed for a dinner in his honor at the Royal Institute of British Architects. On Sunday he went to Bristol for two days of touring and talking. His next stop: Ghana's University of Science and Technology, which has been waiting a year for his arrival this week to conduct a four-week research and development project.

Today Richard Buckminster Fuller, 68, of Carbondale, Ill.—whose college career never got beyond his freshman midyears—is famous for houses that fly and bathrooms without water, for cars and ways of living bearing the mysterious word "Dymaxion," for things called "octet trusses," "synergetics" and "tensegrity." But he is best known of all for his massive mid-century breakthrough known as the "geodesic dome."

In ten years the famed domes of Bucky Fuller have covered more square feet of the earth than any other single kind of shelter. U.S. Marines have lived and worked in them from Antarctica to Okinawa. Beneath them, radar antennas turn tirelessly along the 4,500 miles of the DEW line, which guards the North American continent against surprise attack. For eight years, the U.S. has been using Fuller domes to house its exhibits at global trade fairs. The Russians were so impressed by the 200-ft.-diameter dome at the 1959 U.S. exhibit in Moscow that they bought it. "Mr. J. Buckingham Fuller must come to Russia and teach our engineers," garbled Premier Khrushchev.

They are being made of almost anything and everything—polyester fiber glass, alloy aluminum, weatherproofed cardboard, plastic, bamboo. More than 50 companies have taken out licenses to make them in the U.S. alone. The small domes are light enough to be lifted by helicopter, and they practically build themselves. The day his company began erecting a geodesic auditorium in Hawaii, Henry J. Kaiser hopped a plane from San Francisco to see the work in progress, but it was finished by the time he got there, and seated an audience of 1,832 at a concert that same night.

Structurally unlimited as to size, cheap to make, requiring no obstructing columns for support, the geodesic dome uses less structural material to cover more space than any other building ever devised. The diameter of the one built for the Union Tank Car Co. in Baton Rouge is the length of a football field. Next year the Union of South Africa expects to be using geodesic huts for low-cost housing. And within a decade it is quite possible, if Bucky has his way, that cities will roof their centers over with vast translucent domes, beneath which mass air conditioning and weatherproofing will enable houses and stores to be constructed only for privacy and aesthetic delight.

Such superdomes are in fact already feasible; several New York designers are still smoldering at World's Fair President Robert Moses for vetoing a proposal to cover the 646 acres of the fair with a Fuller dome a mile or so in diameter. "What an opportunity missed!" says Arthur Drexler, director of architecture and design at Manhattan's Museum of Modern Art. "It would have had the same impact on the world of design as the Crystal Palace at London's great exhibition in 1851—probably more so, because the Crystal Palace prefab pieces had classical roots, whereas Bucky's dome is totally new."

Bucky Fuller, as he calls himself and urges everyone else to call him, is a charismatic man who attracted a cultic following even in the days when he seemed to the unclouded eye little more than some kind of a nut. Today, at 68, he is more charismatic than ever and evokes an impressive chorus of enthusiasm from many of those best qualified to judge his work.

Architect Nathaniel Owings of Skidmore, Owings & Merrill pronounces Fuller "the most creative man in our field; he's the only one that's dealing with something that's totally dissimilar to what everybody else is doing. He's tried to find out how nature really works." Architect Minoru Yamasaki calls him "an intense, devoted genius, whose mind, which is better than an IBM machine, has influenced all of us." Italy's famed Architect Gio Ponti feels that Fuller is "not only a romantic pioneer who sees 50 years ahead, but a genius who has already realized his dreams as to what humanity needs and how the world must look in the future."

Fuller unquestionably agrees with them all. He sees himself quite simply as a kind of technological avatar, come for the liberation of mankind. Says he: "In 1927 I made a bargain with myself that I'd discover the principles operative in the universe and turn them over to my fellow men."

That year of 1927 was the low point of his life, the dark night of the soul in which his real work began, when he stood on the shore of Lake Michigan and tried to decide whether or not to kill himself.

He arrived on that shore with the best New England credentials. His great-great-great-great-grandfather came from the Isle of Wight only ten years after the *Mayflower's* famous landing at Plymouth Rock and fathered a male line of descendants of which every one was a clergyman or a lawyer except Bucky's father, who became a merchant importer. But his most illustrious ancestor was a woman, Transcendentalist Margaret Fuller, the literary friend of Emerson and discoverer of Thoreau, whose strong-minded individualism presaged Bucky's own.

The major influence upon him as a child, he feels, were his summers spent at the small island his family owned, eleven miles off the mainland in Maine's Penobscot Bay. Boats were the chief preoccupation on Bear

Island, and here young Bucky reveled in the lore and learning, puttering and fixing and improvising of the nautical world. Winters he went to prep school as a day pupil at Milton Academy in Massachusetts, an oddball, lonely child whose hazel eyes swam grotesquely behind the thick-lensed glasses he wore to correct the extreme farsightedness he was born with.

When he got to Harvard in 1913, Bucky soon realized that things were going to go badly wrong. His best friend at Milton did not room with him. Other Milton classmates explained that they could not afford to associate with him much because he was obviously not going to make a club. When he tried out for football, he broke his knee. So, as he explains it today, "I deliberately set out to get into trouble."

He cut his midyear exams and took off for New York, where he went on a spending spree that included wining and dining Dancer Marilyn Miller and her chorus line, whom he had got to know by standing outside the stage door in Boston with his family's white wolfhound as conversational bait. When considerably more than his year's allowance had gone up in the heady smoke of this lonely freshman debauch, Bucky cabled a rich cousin and was promptly packed off in disgrace to a cotton mill in Quebec. Harvard gave him a second chance, but Bucky was not having any. "Once again I determined to get fired simply by spending more money than I had. I succeeded."

Fuller was married in 1917—he was 22—to dark and beautiful Anne Hewlett, daughter of a prominent New York architect. In World War I, Bucky, despite his bad eyes, enlisted in the Navy as a chief boatswain, showed such promise that he was sent to the Naval Academy and commissioned an ensign. Studying logistics, ballistics, navigation and early naval aviation, he suddenly found himself in a world rapidly moving from "the wire to the wireless, the track to the trackless, the visible to the invisible, where more and more could be done with less and less."

But the troubles piled up. His daughter Alexandra sickened and died when she was four. For the next five years, Fuller worked out of Chicago for a company set up to market a building material invented by his father-in-law. He was a hopelessly poor executive and as much of a fool about money as he had been at Harvard—living wildly beyond his means and rapidly laocoönizing himself in debts and superdebts. He was also hitting the bottle. "The minute I was through work for the day," he has written of that period, "I would go off and drink all night long, and then I'd go to work again. I had enough health, somehow, to carry on."

But eventually Bucky's father-in-law had to sell his stock in the company, and the directors were delighted to tell Bucky that his services would no longer be required. It was a bad time to be fired; his second daughter, Allegra, had just been born. The year was 1927.

Standing by Lake Michigan "on a jump-or-think basis," as he has put it, he decided that he had faith in what he calls, in Fullerese, "the anticipatory intellectual wisdom which we may call God." His next step was to come to the decision that this meant that there was an "*a priori* wisdom" in the fact of his own being. From there, he decided: "You do not have the right to eliminate yourself. You do not belong to you. You belong to the universe. You and all men are here for the sake of other men." He moved with Anne and their infant daughter into a one-room apartment in a Chicago slum, withdrew completely from all friends and acquaintances for more than a year. And he thought.

BUCKY BEGAN BY EXAMINING the nature of the universe, as a manifestation of God himself. He concluded that it was governed by relatively few principles. Its essence was not matter but design. He began to see man himself as "a complex of patterns. Man is not weight. It isn't the vegetables he eats, because he'll eat seven tons of vegetables in his life. It is a pattern integrity that goes on."

Bucky further reflected that with the huge acceleration of technological capability, mankind was on the verge of tremendous achievements that were not even being attempted because men were stuck in traditional molds of thinking. The time for a great leap forward was at hand, a revolution in which the old Newtonian world would be replaced by Einstein's. "Newton said in the first law of motion that a body persists in a state of rest except as it is affected by other bodies. Normal was 'at rest.' Einstein turned it the other way: 186,000 miles a second is normal. We are living in a world where change is normal."

Bucky first turned his new perceptions on the industry he knew best: building. The traditional building methods seemed to him absurd. Traditional buildings depended on compression on their walls to support the roof. But modern technology has developed tensile materials, which are many times stronger in relation to their weight than compression materials. A house designed to use tension as its basic structural principle could be made infinitely lighter, built with fewer materials, and therefore far more cheaply. If mass-produced, such houses could solve the world's shelter problems.

His first plan was pretty far out: apartment houses built of the aircraft industry's lightweight alloys, each floor hung from a huge central mast. A dirigible would carry the whole building to the selected site, then drop a bomb, plant the building's mast into the resulting crater, and buzz off—leaving a ground crew to fill in the hole around the mast with concrete.

Fuller's next "anticipatory" design was more practical. It was for a single-family house that carried Corbusier's "machine-for-living" concept farther than the Continental avant-garde had dared to think it. The rooms were hung from a central mast. This left free the ground, which could be landscaped to taste. The outer wall was of continuous glass, which enclosed both rooms and garden like a conservatory, with air conditioning from the central mast. The house was supposed to be independent of its location, and therefore easily movable if the family decided to change cities; the whole thing could be picked up and replanted anywhere.

To avoid being tied down by sewage pipes, the bathroom was as nearly waterless as a bathroom can be; a ten-minute "bath" was supplied from a quart of water by means of a Fuller invention called a "fog gun," and provision was made for even this water to be re-collected from the air. The toilets emptied into a waterless device which mechanically packaged and stored the wastes for eventual pickup by a processing plant. Mass-produced, the house was planned to sell at about $1,500 on a 1928 level—approximately $4,800 today.

This "4D House," as he called it, was the launching of the new Bucky Fuller. Though it only existed as a scale model (in which he included a tiny nude doll lying on a bed for verisimilitude and headline-catching purposes), and though it called for alloys, plastics, photoelectric cells and the like, which did not then exist, newspapers wrote it up, and the Marshall Field department store contracted for its display. Fuller's 4D (for Fourth Dimension) title for the house seemed drab to the promotion-minded store executives; they assigned a couple of high-powered word-sculptors to work out a new word for it. After two days of hectic brainstorming, the result was "dymaxion"—vaguely compounded of "dynamic," "maximum" and "ion." Marshall Field copyrighted it in Fuller's name, and in the years to come Bucky turned it into what amounted to a personal trademark. Today he explains that it means the "maximum gain of advantage from the minimal energy input."

In 1930 Fuller moved to a $30-a-month flat in Greenwich Village. When he was not lecturing around town on his Dymaxion House, he liked to hang out at a Village joint called Romany Marie's with artists and writers, talking his and their heads off. Remembers Sculptor Isamu Noguchi: "He used to drink like a fish. He had become a God-possessed man, like a Messiah of ideas. He was a prophet of things to come. Bucky didn't take care of himself, but he had amazing strength. He often went without sleep for several days, and he didn't always eat either."

Bucky's major energies in this period were devoted to trying to improve the lot of mankind by improving two of man's proudest creations: the automobile and the bathroom.

The Dymaxion Car was one of the most dramatic leaps forward in automotive design that have ever been made. In a pre-streamlined world, where the old-fashioned buggy's boxy look prevailed, Fuller's car was built like an airplane fuselage. It had front-wheel drive with the engine in the rear. The steering wheel was connected to its single rear wheel, which enabled the car to run in circles around a man within a radius of a few feet or to drive straight into a parking space and swing in with only inches to spare.

With financial backing from friends, Bucky turned out three prototype Dymaxion Cars between 1933 and 1935. An English group sent over a representative to test its performance. But Bucky's hopes of attracting a manufacturer went glimmering when, with the English visitor on board, the car was rammed by another automobile in Chicago and the driver killed. The car that had hit them, which belonged to a city official, was removed from the scene before the reporters arrived, and early newspaper stories carried screaming headlines, such as THREE-WHEELED CAR KILLS DRIVER. So ended the Dymaxion Car.

The Dymaxion Bathroom, developed in the experimental laboratory of the Phelps Dodge Corp., was designed to slash the cost and increase the ease of installing a bathroom by stamping it out like an automobile body. Fuller really loved this contraption. He mounted it on the back of a truck and rode it out to Long Island. Remembers an old friend: "He went tearing around town, he had some child sitting on the john, and he was throwing toilet paper all over the place." All together, about a dozen bathrooms were made and installed, but Phelps Dodge never bore down very hard on getting them into production—perhaps because of nervousness about the plumbers' union.

With the coming of World War II, Bucky Fuller made a major sacrifice. "I drink very well," he explains, "but I found that if I was talking about my inventions and drinking, people just wrote them off as so much nonsense.

The war was something serious, and I wanted to be properly accredited. So I stopped drinking and smoking." He has done neither since. He got a regular job—as chief of the Mechanical Engineering Section at the Board of Economic Warfare, later as special assistant to the deputy director of the Foreign Economic Administration. The war also brought Fuller another change; for the first time since he started his life over again in 1927, he was able to originate something that was not "anticipatory" but actually put to use: adapting mass-produced grain storage silos for military living units. Hundreds of these "Dymaxion Deployment Units" saw service in the Pacific and the Persian Gulf before restrictions tightened on steel and the project ground to a halt.

"Failure-prone" Fuller had another disappointment in store for him; just as a new version of his Dymaxion House seemed about to go into production in a three-way deal between venture capital, big labor and the aircraft industry, the war's end and a changed economic picture killed the project. But then suddenly, it seemed, he produced the jackpot invention: shelter that was transportable, versatile and cheap—the dome.

BUT IT WAS NOT really sudden, nor was it an invention. It was a slow discovery. And it had begun where Bucky Fuller likes to begin: with a probe into the pattern of the universe. To make that probe, Fuller was struggling to develop a new tool—a geometry of energy. In search of such a geometry, Fuller was using spheres as idealized models of energy fields. Crowding the spheres as close together as possible around a central sphere, he found that instead of forming a still bigger sphere, they made a 14-faced polyhedron—six of the facets in the form of squares, and eight as triangles. Fuller called this figure a vector equilibrium because the outward thrust of its radial vectors is balanced by the restraining force of its circumferential vectors.

Combining a number of vector equilibriums creates a complex of alternating squares and triangles. Dividing the squares once again, he found he had a symmetrical, twenty-sided globe-shaped skin which could be constructed out of tetrahedrons—the triangle-sided pyramid shape that provides the greatest strength for the least volume (or weight). In a sphere made of such interlocked tetrahedrons, the weight load applied to any point was transmitted widely throughout the structure, producing a phenomenal strength-to-weight ratio. Bucky produced his dome by cutting a hollow sphere in half.

Unlike classic domes, Fuller's depends on no heavy vaults or flying buttresses to support it. It is self-sufficient as a butterfly's wing, and as strong as an eggshell. Fuller calls it a geodesic dome because the vertexes of the curved squares and tetrahedrons that form its structure mark the arcs of great circles that are known in geometry as "geodesics."

The geodesic dome, then, is really a kind of benchmark of the universe, what 17th century Mystic Jakob Böhme might call "a signature of God." It crops up all over in nature—in viruses, testicles, the cornea of the eye. And for the time being at least, Bucky Fuller has this signature of God sewed up tight in U.S. patent No. 2,682,235, issued in June 1954. It is almost like having a patent on Archimedes' principle.

And it is making Bucky rich. In the last ten years he has grossed about $1,000,000, and his income is continually rising; this year it will be about $200,000. But the only way Easy Street seems to have changed him is to have eliminated the need for the defiant extravagances that used to burden his family and amuse his friends in the days when the only things that crackled in his pocket were overdue bills. Unquestionably, Bucky could have made much more by incorporating himself or going into organized production. But Bucky is not interested. Says he: "Whatever I do, once done, I leave it alone. Society comes along in due course and needs what I have done. By then, I'd better be on to something else. It is absolutely fundamental for me to work and design myself out of business."

In 1959, he accepted a $12,000 appointment as a research professor at Southern Illinois University, at Carbondale. Bucky's duties are vague and undemanding; he sees students only when he feels like it, and he is in residence no more than a couple of months a year in the medium-sized, blue-and-white plywood dome where he and Anne live in Carbondale. It looks like an overgrown pincushion without pins. But Bucky does not mind, and does not see why anyone else should. Bucky is indebted to S.I.U. for providing him with both a home base and a springboard, and Fuller's fame has helped repay the debt. Sixteen years ago, there were only 3,013 students on the Carbondale campus; today there are no fewer than 18,201 students and a faculty of 1,154. And the university has just been awarded a $10 million, three-year space project, which Bucky will head.

Ten months of the year he spends traveling—and talking. Fuller gets $1,000 per lecture these days, but he gives his audiences an exceptional $1,000 worth. Rare is the lecture that does not run four hours, and often he is still going strong after six—his younger listeners entranced and his older ones falling out of their chairs with fatigue.

In these talks, and in long hours with his friends, Bucky spins off a constant stream of ideas. The project nearest and dearest to his heart these days is the worldwide inventory of the globe's resources. Bucky views this as a matter of war or peace. Says a friend: "Bucky sees the population explosion, man's myths and antagonisms as foretelling a possible new deluge. If resources are not utilized according to Fuller principles of 'comprehensive design,' and therefore become scarce, men will begin to club each other to death."

Bucky sees no reason why mankind should not utilize "the three-quarters of the world that is water." He has projected service stations anchored to the sea bottom for submarines to nestle up to. "It is well known that below 40 feet, turbulence is manageable," he says. He proposes that the automobile may be the next fossil. "We will put little jet wings on our backs and fly out the window on high-frequency beams." Divining that the compression and tension factors can be separated in any structure, he has designed a "tensegrity mast" that seems to be held up by nothing at all. But Fuller insists that with this mast combined with his frame of tetrahedron-octahedron combinations which he calls the "octet truss," he could bridge the Grand Canyon itself.

Bucky's peculiar distinction is that, while many of his fellow intellectuals are depressed by the "materialistic" 20th century, he is exhilarated. He is excited by "humanity's epochal graduation from the inert, materialistic 19th century into the dynamic, abstract 20th century." He feels that there is an "important reorientation of mankind, from the role of an inherent failure, as erroneously reasoned by Malthus, and erroneously accepted by the bootstrap-anchored custodians of civilization's processes, to a new role for mankind, that of an inherent success." He is sure the whole world can be fed, housed and happy, if designers can just put to work all the world's skills with Fuller-like efficiency. He is endlessly excited by the massive strides mankind has made in just the last 50 years, of which one of the most dramatic has been the increase in range of the average man's "toing and froing."

Bucky envisions the day when any man anywhere can jet to work halfway round the world and be home for supper. "Today the world is my backyard. 'Where do you live?' and 'What are you?' are progressively less sensible questions. I live on earth at present, and I don't know what I am. I know that I am not a category. I am not a thing—a noun. I seem to be a verb, an evolutionary process—an integral function of the universe." ■

The Ultimate Operation

BY GILBERT CANT

[*This stirring account of the first human heart transplant—*
the Everest of surgery—placed Dr. Christiaan Barnard's
feat in its historical, ethical and moral context]

December 15, 1967

FOR WEEKS, AND MONTHS, and even years, surgical teams at more than 20 medical centers around the world have been standing ready to make the first transplant of a heart from one human being to another. What they have been waiting for is the simultaneous arrival of two patients with compatible blood types—one doomed to die of some disease that has not involved his heart, and a second doomed to die of incurable, irreversible heart disease.

Last week, in two hospitals separated by almost 8,000 miles of Atlantic Ocean, the historic juxtaposition happened and the heart transplants were performed. The physicians who performed them thus reached the surgical equivalent of Mount Everest, followed automatically by the medical equivalent of the problem of how to get down—in other words, how to keep the patient and transplant alive.

In this, the team at Brooklyn's Maimonides Medical Center, headed by Dr. Adrian Kantrowitz, admitted "unequivocal failure." Their patient, a 19-day-old boy, died 6½ hours after he received a new heart. But the team of Dr. Christiaan Neethling Barnard, 44, which acted first at Cape Town, South Africa, had a more enduring success. Their patient, a 55-year-old man, was feeding himself and making small talk a week after his epochal surgery. At this time, as expected, there appeared the first signs of a tendency by his body to reject the transplant, but the doctors were confident that they could control this reaction.

The Cape Town drama began three months ago, when Louis Washkansky, a wholesale grocer, was admitted to suburban Groote Schuur Hospital with progressive heart failure. Because of two heart attacks, one seven years ago and the other two years ago, the burly patient's heart muscle was not getting enough blood through clogged and closed coronary arteries. He also had diabetes, for which he had been getting insulin. His liver was enlarged. Surgeon Barnard's cardiologist colleagues gave "Washy" (as he was known to World War II buddies in North Africa and Italy) only a few months to live. They shortened it to weeks as his body became edematous (swollen with retained water). Washkansky was dying, and knew it.

Denise Ann Darvall, 25, had no thought of death when she set out with her father and mother to visit friends for Saturday-afternoon tea. In Cape Town's Observatory district, Edward Darvall stopped the car. His wife and daughter started across the street to a bakery to buy a cake when both were struck by a speeding car. Mrs. Darvall was killed instantly. Denise was barely alive, but only barely, on arrival at Groote Schuur Hospital. Her head and brain were almost completely destroyed. The emergency room called Dr. Barnard. The doctors agreed: Denise could not survive. Barnard took Darvall aside and explained what he wanted—the gift of a heart, unprecedented in history. Edward Darvall listened numbly as Barnard told him: "We have done our best, and there is nothing more that can be done to help your daughter. There is no hope for her. You can do us and humanity a great favor if you will let us transplant your daughter's heart." Said Darvall: "If there's no hope for her, then try to save this man's life." He signed the consent.

Dr. Barnard had already told Washkansky what he had in mind, adding: "You can have two days to think it over." Washkansky decided in two minutes: "Go ahead." Dr. Barnard now called in his team of 30 men and women, scattered for the summer weekend.

When did Denise Darvall die? Explains Dr. Marius Barnard, 40, younger brother of Christiaan and his right-hand assistant during surgery: "I know in some places they consider the patient dead when the electroencephalogram shows no more brain function. We are on the conservative side, and consider a patient dead when the heart is no longer working, the lungs are no longer working, and there are no longer any complexes on the ECG."

Though Denise Darvall's heart had stopped beating and she was dead, her heart could not be allowed to degenerate. Irreparable cell damage begins at the temperature of a naturally cooling cadaver in 30 minutes. It can be postponed for two to three hours by cooling. The Barnard team took no chances. By this time, Denise's body was in an operating room a few feet from the operating room in which Washkansky lay. A surgeon opened her chest by a midline incision, snipped some ribs and exposed the heart with its attached blood vessels.

Near the arch of the aorta he inserted a plastic catheter tube, which was connected to a heart-lung machine. Another catheter, similarly connected, went into the right auricle. At this point, the whole body was perfused with oxygenated blood. The surgeons then clamped the aorta beyond the catheter and clamped the pulmonary artery and venae cavae, thus isolating the heart from the rest of the body, which thereafter received no circulation. With the heart-lung machine set at a low flow rate, the heart continued to have oxygenated blood pumped through it. And it was cooled to 73° F.

Meanwhile, Pathologist M. C. Botha was working in his laboratory with a sample of Denise's blood. Washkansky's type was A-positive; Denise's was O-negative. She was the ideal "universal donor." There was no time for Dr. Botha to try matching their white blood cells so that the surgeons could estimate how strong a rejection reaction Washkansky's system would mount against the foreign protein of Denise's heart.

Simultaneously, Washkansky was anesthetized, and at 2:15 a.m. Sunday one of the surgeons opened his chest. Assisting Christiaan Barnard, in addition to his brother Marius, were Drs. Rodney Hewitson and Terry O'Donovan. The main blood vessels were clamped in much the same way as Denise's had been, but in this case the heart-lung machine was to serve a directly opposite purpose: to circulate oxygenated blood through all of Washkansky's body except his about-to-be-discarded heart.

Exercising the captain's prerogative, Dr. Christiaan Barnard moved into the first operating room and cut eight blood vessels to free Denise Darvall's heart; then he severed it from its ligament moorings. It was disconnected from the pump, and was carried to Washkansky's room, where it was connected to a small-capacity heart-lung machine. There it lay, chilled and perfused with oxygenated blood, while Surgeon Barnard removed most—but not quite all—of Washkansky's heart. He left in place part of the outer walls of both the auricles, the right carrying the two entrance holes of the venae cavae, the left carrying the four entrance holes of the pulmonary veins. The rest of the heart, flabby and scarred, he set aside.

In painstaking sequence, Dr. Barnard stitched the donor heart in place. First the left auricle, then the right. He joined the stub of Denise's aorta to Washkansky's, her pulmonary artery to his. Finally, the veins. Assistant surgeons removed the catheters from the implant as Barnard worked.

Now, almost four hours after the first incision, history's first transplanted human heart was in place. But it had not been beating since Denise died. Would it work? Barnard stepped back and ordered electrodes placed on each side of the heart and the current (25 watt-seconds) applied. The heart leaped at the shock and began a swift beat. Dr. Barnard's heart leaped too. Through his mask, he exclaimed unprofessionally but pardonably, "Christ, it's going to work!" Work it did.

The heart-lung pump was still running. Now it was reset to warm the blood. After ten minutes it was switched off to see whether the transplanted heart could carry the whole burden of Washkansky's circulation. It was not yet quite ready, and on went the pump again for another five minutes. This time, when it was stopped, the heart did not falter. It could do the work. The surgeons closed Washkansky's chest. The operation, "from skin to skin," had taken 4¾ hours. It was 7 a.m. "I need a cup of tea," said Dr. Barnard.

An hour later, Washkansky regained consciousness and tried to talk. So carefully isolated from possible infection that even his wife Ann was persuaded not to visit him for four days, he showed improvement day by day. After 36 hours he complained of hunger and ate a typical hospital meal, including a soft-boiled egg. As a further guard against infection, the doctors dosed him with antibiotics. His donated heart, healthy and compact, jumped around somewhat uneasily in the cavity left by his own enlarged heart, but this space would soon shrink naturally. The heart gradually slowed its beat to 100 per minute. (Surgeon Barnard's had been a frenetic 140 when he finished the operation.)

Among the several courses open to them to try to blunt the rejection mechanism, Washkansky's doctors chose to use two drugs, azathioprine (Imuran) and cortisone, plus radiation. At first, to avoid moving their patient, they administered gamma rays with an emergency cobalt-60 unit, somewhat resembling a dentist's X-ray machine, rigged up in his room.

After four days, when Washy was waving at photographers and joshing with doctors and nurses, he was considered strong enough to stand a quarter-mile trundle to the regular radiation treatment center. At week's end, when his white-blood-cell count rose, the doctors still had more drugs in reserve to beat back the rejection mechanism, and they stepped up his cobalt-60 treatments. Washkansky's liver shrank to nearer normal size; Denise's heart and his kidneys worked so well together that he lost 20 lbs. of edema fluid.

Edward Darvall had no reason to regret his decision. Not only was Denise's heart working in Washkansky's chest, but her right kidney was transplanted to a Colored* boy, ten-year-old Jonathan Van Wyk, and was functioning normally at week's end. Washkansky was making wisecracks: "I'm a Frankenstein now. I've got somebody else's heart." (And making the common error of confusing the fictional Dr. Frankenstein with the monster he made.) Washkansky was well enough to go through a radio interview with a doctor. He ate well, and said his only complaint was that he was aching from being kept too long lying in bed.

Dr. Barnard was talking of sending Washkansky home in a couple of weeks. In this he could have been overoptimistic. The possibility remained that he might be as cruelly disappointed as Dr. Kantrowitz by the sudden failure of the transplant. At best, there could be endless complications. Yet the mere performance of the operation set a milestone along the endless road of man's struggle against disability.

SURGEONS HAVE DREAMED FOR centuries of making just the sort of replacement of a diseased or injured limb or organ that Dr. Barnard made last week. But when they tried to make their dreams reality, they found themselves encaged by invisible but seemingly invincible forces, mysterious beyond their understanding. Italian surgeons during the Renaissance occasionally succeeded in repairing a sword-slashed nose or ear with flesh from the patient's own arm, but got nowhere with person-to-person grafts. The first widely attempted transplants were blood transfusions, from lamb to man or man to man. Almost all failed—in many cases, fatally—and no one knew why a few succeeded. Skin grafts, often attempted after burns, slough off after a few weeks unless they are taken from another part of the patient's own body. The first consistently successful hu-

* *The South African designation for one of mixed racial origin.*

man homografts (between two individuals of the same species), beginning in 1905, involved the cornea—the transparent, plastic covering of the eyeball which has no blood circulation.

Not until the present century did it become clear that safe blood transfusions depended on matching at least the A, B and O groups of red cells. The Rh factor came still later. In the early 1900s, U.S. Physiologist Charles Claude Guthrie and French Biologist-Surgeon Alexis Carrel appeared for a while to have broken down the barriers against transplants. They devised most of the basic surgical techniques, notably how to stitch slippery little blood vessels together so that the joints would neither leak nor close down with clots. Guthrie grafted a second head onto a dog half a century before the Russians did it in 1959. Carrel kept part of a chicken's heart "alive" in a laboratory flask. But they still could not get organ grafts between two animals to take for any length of time.

The full explanation of one man's rejection of another's flesh had to wait until 1953, when Britain's Sir Peter Brian Medawar revealed details of the immune mechanism involving the white blood cells. These are the body's main line of defense against viruses, which have protein coatings, and against many other germs. They react just as strongly against any "foreign" (meaning another person's) protein. They make antibody to destroy such invaders.

This explained why the first few kidney transplants, begun at Boston's Peter Bent Brigham Hospital in the early 1950s, had failed. It also explained the success of Dr. Joseph E. Murray's first transplant of a kidney between identical twins, done at the Brigham in 1954. Since only one patient in 300 or more has an identical twin available—let alone willing—to donate a kidney, researchers in a dozen branches of medical science have been trying ever since to devise a way of switching off the immune or rejection mechanism long enough to let a transplant "take," then restore it so that the recipient will not be a helpless prey to every passing infection.

Research doctors have had some, but by no means complete, success with X rays, and with two classes of drugs—the anti-cancer chemicals and cortisone-type hormones. They have devised increasingly complex methods of matching white blood cells to reduce antibody formation, and of making anti-lymphocyte serum in horses to reduce the white cells' activity. This partial success has been sufficient to give today's recipient of a kidney transplant (from close kin or even an unrelated cadaver) at least a 65% chance of surviving.

Every normal person has two kidneys, and since he can live on one, that means he has one to spare. The corpses of healthy people killed in accidents provide two. So although the demand still far exceeds the supply, the kidney transplanter's problem is minor compared with that of the surgeon who would transplant a liver. Each man has only one, and cannot live without it. The world's pioneer in transplanting livers, Dr. Thomas Starzl of the University of Colorado, has obtained 15 so far, with encouraging results in four recent operations on little girls. Comparable problems of supply confront the University of Minnesota's Dr. Richard C. Lillehei, who has transplanted the pancreas with duodenum attached, and an almost complete intestinal tract.

For the surgeon who would transplant a heart, the problems are manifold and more difficult, with moral and ethical as well as medical considerations involved. Since ancient times, the heart has been apostrophized as the throne of the soul, the seat of man's noblest qualities and emotions—as it still is in poetry and love songs. But even the Vatican newspaper *L'Osservatore Romano* noted last week that "the heart is a physiological organ and its function is purely mechanical." In fact, the heart is nothing more than a pump. There is no more soul or personality in a heart than in a slice of calf's liver.

But on one score the ancients were right. The heart is essential to life in a more immediate, temporal sense than any other organ, even the brain. The human body can survive for years in a coma, with no conscious brain function—but only for minutes without a beating heart. So the presence of a heartbeat, along with breathing, has long been the basic criterion for distinguishing life from death. It still is, in the vast majority of cases, despite some special situations in which the brain's electrical activity is a more reliable index. (So far, no surgeon has seriously considered transplanting a brain, because, beyond the forbidding technical difficulties, this would be akin to transplanting a person. Similarly, transplantation of entire gonads—ovaries or testicles—might carry with it a change in hereditary material.)

The real moral and ethical difficulty in heart transplants arises from medical uncertainty. Even when the heart has "stopped cold" and there is no more respiration, the condition is often reversible—as is proved countless times every day by first-aid squads and lifeguards as well as doctors. The surgeon wants the donor's heart as fresh as possible, before lack of oxygen causes deterioration or damage—that is, within minutes of death.

This has raised the specter of surgeons' becoming not only corpse snatchers but, even worse, of encouraging people to become corpses. The question remains: Where should the line be drawn between those to be resuscitated and those not to be?

Equally acute is the ethical problem regarding the proposed recipient of the heart. Obviously he is close to death, or such drastic surgery would not be contemplated. Yet his own heart must be cut out, which is tantamount to killing him, while he still retains vitality enough to withstand the most Draconian of operations. If the transplant should fail, he will certainly die. Thus the surgeons will, in effect, have killed him (as they might in any major operation), no matter how lofty their motive in trying to prolong his life and make it more satisfying.

Stanford University's Dr. Norman E. Shumway introduced a refinement of technique in heart transplants used by both Dr. Barnard and Dr. Kantrowitz last week. In animal surgery, it had been customary to remove the entire heart. This meant severing and later rejoining not only the two great arteries, but also two great veins returning spent blood to the heart and four veins returning oxygenated blood from the lungs. By leaving in place parts of the walls of the upper heart chambers (auricles or atria) to which these six veins return, Dr. Shumway eliminated an enormous amount of delicate suturing in sensitive areas, and cut the operating time virtually in half.

Shumway and Lillehei, like many of today's foremost surgeons and professors of surgery, absorbed much of what they know of the technique and exploratory spirit of their calling from the University of Minnesota's great (and lately retired, at 68) Dr. Owen H. Wangensteen. So did Christiaan Barnard, who was at Minnesota in 1953-1955. Barnard, the son of a Dutch Reformed minister, had always wanted to be a doctor. His father, on a cash income of $56 a month, gave three of his four sons a university education.

Wangensteen, noted as a driver of men, did not have to drive Barnard. He remembers that Barnard once operated on 49 dogs unsuccessfully in an attempt to learn about an intestinal abnormality in the newborn. "On the 50th time he succeeded; that was typical of his singleness of purpose," Wangensteen says. Outside the operating room, then as now, Barnard was tense, and paced with restless energy smoking other people's cigarettes. Inside the operating room Barnard kept himself tightly controlled, talked little, learned much. As a resident in surgery, he crowded into three years the work and experience for which most men take four or five, gaining himself Master of Science and Ph.D. degrees in surgery to add to his Cape Town medical degree.

Back home, Dr. Barnard continued transplant research while practicing heart surgery and running a family. (With two children, he was best known in South Africa, until last week, as the father of a champion water skier, Deirdre, 17.) When he read of the dog onto which the Russians had transplanted a second head, he declared, "There's nothing to it." He did two such operations himself, made movies of the dog operations—and took the movies with him as evidence when he went to Moscow to see whether he could learn anything from the Russians. In fact, he has learned more from former colleagues in the U.S. and from keeping up with their research.

Despite the milestone quality of Barnard's accomplishment, his transplant was only the beginning of the road, not the end. There will continue to be, in the foreseeable future, many more potential heart recipients than donors, and the social problems—such as deciding who shall get a transplant—are even more forbiddingly complex than the surgical. The ultimate solution, Houston's Dr. Michael E. DeBakey insists, is a completely artificial heart. He has been working on such devices for years. Walton Lillehei has a valveless, oxygen-powered device now ready for use as an external "heart assist," which he hopes can eventually be modified for implantation to do the work of both heart and lungs. Last year the National Institutes of Health (N.I.H.) dumped much of the $8,700,000 available into research grants for the perfection of "half-hearts"—devices to assist the left ventricle, or take over its work entirely for a time.

Both DeBakey and Kantrowitz have obtained good results with half-hearts in one or two cases. DeBakey's best patient, Mrs. Esperanza del Valle Vásquez, was on heart assist for ten days after the implantation of two artificial valves in her heart. Now she puts in an eight-hour day on her feet, running her Mexico City beauty parlor. On hearing about Washkansky last week, she burbled: "How marvelous! I want to write to this man—I have so much to tell him." But Shumway insists that in 1,500 operations in which he has opened hearts to correct defects, he has seen not one patient who needed a heart-assist device. The N.I.H. project, he believes, is justifiable only as a step toward the complete artificial heart.

Since that achievement is years away, human-heart transplants will be a valuable intermediate stage. More will now be attempted and with far less misgiving. However stormy Louis Washkansky's near-future course might be, and whatever the ultimate fate of the transplant, the worldwide acclaim for Dr. Barnard's daring and his immediate success have initiated changes in both professional and public attitudes. Surgeons who did not want to take the risks attendant upon being first will now attempt transplants. More medically suitable recipients will be willing to accept a transplant with its inevitable hazards. And more people will be willing to sanction the gift of a heart to help an ailing fellow man. ∎

Unraveling the Double Helix and the Secret of Life

BY FREDERIC GOLDEN

[
*The writer encompassed the epochal 1953 discovery
of the structure of DNA, the master molecule of life,
and the trailblazing exploration of heredity,
disease and human nature that followed*
]

April 19, 1971

WILDLY EXCITED, TWO MEN dashed out of a side door of Cambridge University's Cavendish Laboratory, cut across Free School Lane and ducked into the Eagle, a pub where generations of Cambridge scientists have met to gossip about experiments and celebrate triumphs. Over drinks, James D. Watson, then 24, and Francis Crick, 36, talked excitedly, Crick's booming voice damping out conversations among other Eagle patrons. When friends stopped to ask what the commotion was all about, Crick did not mince words. "We," he announced exultantly, "have discovered the secret of life!"

Brave words—and in a sense, incredibly true. On that late winter day in 1953, the two unknown scientists had finally worked out the double-helical shape of deoxyribonucleic acid, or DNA. In DNA's famed spiral-staircase structure are hidden the mysteries of heredity, of growth, of disease and aging—and in higher creatures like man, perhaps intelligence and memory. As the basic ingredient of the genes in the cells of all living organisms, DNA is truly the master molecule of life.

The unraveling of the DNA double helix was one of the great events in science, comparable to the splitting of the atom or the publication of

Darwin's *Origin of Species.* It also marked the maturation of a bold new science: molecular biology. Under this probing discipline, man could at last explore—and understand—living things at their most fundamental level: that of their atoms and molecules. Once molecular biology was sardonically defined as "the practice of biochemistry without a license." Now it has become one of science's most active, exciting and productive arenas, taking the limelight (and some of the best talent) from that longtime favorite, nuclear physics.

Using laboratory skills that were unheard of a generation ago, scientists have isolated, put together and manipulated genes, and have come close to creating life itself. In 1967 Stanford University's Arthur Kornberg synthesized in a test tube a single strand of DNA that was actually able to make a duplicate of itself. Kornberg's "creation" was only a copy of a virus, a coated bit of genetic material that occupies a twilight zone between the living and inanimate. But many scientists have become convinced that they may eventually be able to create functioning, living cells.

Molecular biology, in part, is rooted in the science of genetics. Ever since Cro-Magnon man, parents have probably wondered why their children resemble them. But not until an obscure Austrian monk named Gregor Mendel began planting peas in his monastery's garden in the mid-19th century were the universal laws of heredity worked out. By tallying up the variations in the offspring peas, Mendel determined that traits are passed from generation to generation with mathematical precision in small, separate packets, which subsequently became known as genes (from the Greek word for race).

Mendel's ideas were so unorthodox that they were ignored for 35 years. But by the time the Mendelian concept was rediscovered at the turn of the century, scientists were better prepared for it. They already suspected that genetic information was hidden inside pairs of tiny, threadlike strands in cell nuclei called chromosomes, or colored bodies (for their ability to pick up dyes). During cell division they always split lengthwise, thereby giving each daughter cell a full share of what was presumed to be hereditary material.

A few years later, the suspicions were dramatically confirmed by the pioneering geneticist Thomas Hunt Morgan in Columbia University's famed "Fly Room." Through ingenious crossbreeding experiments with the fruit fly *Drosophila melanogaster,* Morgan and his students were able to map the relative positions of the genes along the insect's four pairs of chromosomes. Still, the genes' physical nature remained as great a mystery as ever. DNA had been discovered in the nuclei of cells by the Swiss biochemist Friedrich Miescher a few years after Mendel did his work on peas. But since the chromosomes in which the DNA was found also contained proteins—the basic building blocks of life—few scientists had any inkling that DNA might be playing an even more central role to life.

By the 1940s, however, the molecular biologists had come on the scene, and they insisted that fundamental life processes could be fully understood only on the molecular level. In their investigations, some used the electron microscope, which revealed details of structure invisible to ordinary optical instruments. Others specialized in X-ray crystallography, a technique for deducing a crystallized molecule's structure by taking X-ray photographs of it from different angles. Physicist Max Delbrück turned to nature for his investigative tools: bacteriophages (literally, "bacteria eaters"), tiny parasitic viruses that invade their host bacteria and rob them of their genetic heritage.

But the honors for making the breakthrough discovery went to a traditional bacteriologist. Taking purified DNA extracted from the chromosomes of dead pneumonia bacteria, Rockefeller Institute's Oswald T. Avery and his associates showed that it could transform other, normally harmless bacteria into virulent ones. The experiment indicated that it was DNA, and not protein, that carried the genetic message. So unexpected was that finding that even Avery was at first unwilling to accept it. Eight years later, Alfred Hershey and his assistant Martha Chase demonstrated that a virus' DNA could, by taking over a bacterium, also nullify the cell's genetic instructions and replace them with its own. Only then was DNA finally accepted as the magic substance of the genes.

Inspired by these experiments, Watson, then a young Ph.D. in biology from Indiana University, decided to take a crack at the complex structure of DNA itself. The same thought struck Crick, a physicist turned biologist who was preparing for his doctorate at Cambridge. Neither man was particularly well equipped to undertake a task so formidable that it had stymied one of the world's most celebrated chemists, Linus Pauling. Watson, for his part, was deficient in chemistry, crystallography and mathematics. Crick, on the other hand, was almost totally ignorant of genetics. But together, in less than two years of work at Cambridge, these two spirited young scientists showed how it is possible to win a Nobel Prize without really trying.

In 1968 Watson himself produced a highly irreverent, gossipy best-seller, *The Double Helix,* which revealed the human story behind the discovery of DNA's structure: the bickering, the academic rivalries, even the deceits that were practiced to win the great prize. Out of Pauling's earlier work, Watson and Crick got the idea that the extremely long and complicated DNA molecule might take the shape of a helix, or spiral. From the X-ray crystallography laboratory at King's College in London, where Biochemist Maurice Wilkins was also investigating the molecule's structure, they quietly obtained unpublished X-ray data on DNA. Relying as much on luck as logic, they constructed Tinkertoy-like molecular models out of wire and other metal parts. To everyone's astonishment, they suddenly produced a DNA model that not only satisfied the crystallographic evidence but also conformed to the chemical rules for fitting its many atoms together.

OUT OF THE ARCHITECTURE of their precisely constructed double helix emerged the secret of DNA's awesome powers. The banisters of the staircase were fashioned of long links of sugars and phosphates; the steps between them were made of pairs of chemicals called bases, weakly joined at the center by hydrogen atoms. Only four different bases were used—adenine (A), thymine (T), cytosine (C) and guanine (G). But their sequence could vary so widely along the length of the staircase that they made up an almost limitless information-storage system, like the memory bank of a computer. In addition, because the bases were chemically complementary—that is, A paired off only with T, and C only with G—one side of the staircase was in effect a genetic mirror image of the other. Watson and Crick quickly recognized from the structure of their model how DNA worked. But their 900-word announcement in *Nature,* the international weekly published in Britain, concluded with one of the more coy statements in scientific literature. "It has not escaped our notice," they said, "that the specific pairing we have postulated immediately suggests a possible copying mechanism for the genetic material."

In a second letter, they described that mechanism: how the DNA molecule unwinds and unzips itself right down the middle during cell division, its base pairs breaking apart at their hydrogen bonds. Then by drawing on the free-floating material surrounding them in the nucleus of the cell, the two separated strands link up with complementary base-and-strand units along their entire length, forming two exact copies of the original double helix. Thus DNA faithfully passes its genetic information on to new cells and to future generations.

Ingenious as the theory was, scientists still demanded proof that the molecule actually replicated itself. That proof was quick to come. By 1956, Arthur Kornberg, then at Washington University in St. Louis, discovered an enzyme, or natural chemical catalyst (which he named "DNA polymerase"), that was apparently critical to some of the activities of the double helix. Once he obtained enough of the enzyme, he placed it in a test-tube brew with a bit of natural DNA, one of whose strands was incomplete, the four bases (A, T, C, G) and a few other off-the-shelf chemicals. True to his expectations—and the Watson-Crick theory—the incomplete segment picked up its complementary nucleotides from the brew to form a complete double helix.

Implicit in the Watson-Crick model were the workings of DNA's other essential function: how it orders the production of proteins. These are also long and twisted helical molecules, but they are the actual building blocks rather than the genetic blueprints for living things. As such, proteins are immensely varied; there are many thousands of different kinds in the human body alone. The distinctive proteins that make up the cells of the eye, for example, differ from those of the kidneys or muscles. Despite their variety, however, all proteins are built from some of only 20 smaller and simpler molecules, called amino acids. How then, scientists asked themselves, did the isolated double helix, locked in the nucleus of the cell, direct the assembly of amino acids into protein in other parts of the cell?

Scientists suspected that DNA had a helper, a single-stranded chemical first cousin called ribonucleic acid (RNA). Most of the cell's RNA is found in ribosomes. These are globular bodies in the material outside the cell's nucleus that seem to be highly active centers of protein synthesis. But if this ribosomal RNA played a role in protein making, how did it obtain and execute the instructions from the master molecule DNA inside the nucleus?

In 1955, after wrestling with the question, Francis Crick postulated (and Harvard Biochemists Paul Zamecnik and Mahlon Hoagland confirmed) a second form of RNA, which was later found to carry specific amino acids floating in the cytoplasm to the ribosomes; this substance became known as transfer RNA. Then in the early 1960s, biologists discovered a third kind of RNA—shortly after its existence had been theorized by Jacques Monod and François Jacob of France's Pasteur Institute. Called messenger RNA, it provided the missing piece in the molecular puzzle. It was formed on an uncoiled strip of DNA in the nucleus, imprinted with the particular "message" encoded in that portion—or gene—

of the staircase, and then sent off with these instructions to the protein-making ribosomes.

Neat as it was, this scheme still left unanswered one more question: How could DNA or RNA choose from among 20 amino acids to produce complex proteins by using an informational system that had only four code letters—the four bases—at its disposal? An answer to this intriguing problem was suggested by Physicist George Gamow, who likened the four bases to the different suits in a deck of playing cards.

If the cards are dealt one at a time, disregarding the order of the cards within the suits, the player encounters only one of four possibilities on each draw (a heart, diamond, spade or club); clearly, if DNA's code worked this way, there would not be enough choices to encode 20 amino acids. If the cards are dealt in pairs, the number of combinations increases to 16 (since each card may combine with its own kind or one of three other suits). But such a two-unit system also would be inadequate. So Gamow reasoned that DNA's four bases had to be taken at least three at a time: this would yield 64 possible combinations (4 x 4 x 4), more than enough to code for the existing amino acids.

In 1961, Crick's team at Cambridge proved Gamow's ingenious "triplet" theory. They demonstrated that RNA formed from only one or two base units could not effect the manufacture of proteins. But when they added a third base unit, protein formation began immediately. It remained, however, for an unknown young biochemist named Marshall Nirenberg, at the National Institutes of Health, to crack the code itself. That same year Nirenberg had succeeded in building up short, synthetic strands of RNA out of only one type of base. Invariably, this artificial RNA induced the manufacture of chains of proteins consisting of only one type of amino acid, phenylalanine. The conclusion was inescapable: in the genetic code, Nirenberg's triplet had to signify phenylalanine.

Using this clue as their Rosetta stone, Nirenberg and other researchers eventually found one or more three-letter code words, or codons, that could call up every single amino acid—plus other words that acted as punctuation, marking the start or completion of a message ordering the production of a protein. Even more remarkable, they learned that the code was universal: the same four letters, taken three at a time to form a single genetic word, code the same amino acids in all living things. Thus by the mid-1960s, scientists finally understood how DNA passes on genetic information with exquisite precision, and the way it orders up the fabrication of new cellular protein.

DNA is as complex as the system it directs. Even after two decades of intensive study only about one-third of the genes have been mapped along the length of DNA in the chromosome of so elementary a creature as the digestive-tract bacterium *Escherichia coli.* The reason: just a teaspoon of *E. coli* DNA has information capacity approximately equal to that of a computer with a storage capacity of about 100 cu. mi.

Man, for his part, is even more generously endowed—with 1,000 times as much DNA as one *E. coli* in each of his reproductive cells. Even so, the cells of such relatively primitive animals as salamanders, lungfish and even certain one-celled algae contain far more DNA than man's. Does this mean that such lowly beasts have a richer genetic capacity than man? The Carnegie Institution's Roy Britten and David Kohne, after much painstaking investigation, may have found the answer to that embarrassing question. A few years ago they discovered that in the DNA of higher organisms many genes seem to be repeated. In calf cells, they calculated, up to 40% of the DNA consists of segments that are repeated as many as 100,000 times apiece. As a result of this work, some scientists are now convinced that in this seeming redundancy of genes, rather than in the total number, lies the secret of the genetic sophistication of higher organisms.

How would such genetic repetition help man? Some theorists suspect that the "spare" DNA plays a regulatory role, perhaps switching other genes on and off at just the right moment during the involved process of protein manufacturing.

Molecular biologists are also probing ever more deeply into the process of cell differentiation. It has long been known that the DNA in every body cell of an individual organism is identical; this DNA contains all the information necessary to construct the whole organism. Why then, in a human being, for example, is a liver cell so different from a hair cell, a heart cell so different from a skin cell? The answer, Jacob and Monod theorized in 1961, is that only a small percentage of the genes in any cell are giving instructions for the operation of that particular cell. The rest are "turned off" by protein repressers, which wrap themselves around long stretches of DNA and prevent them from transferring their coded information to messenger RNA.

A number of such repressers have since been found in bacteria. Scientists have also isolated enzymes that turn the genes back on. These inducers, as they are called, work by unlocking the repressers on the segment of DNA. It is because of the very complexity of these processes that leading molecular biologists like Crick find the questions arising from cell differentiation so fascinating. How in the human embryo, for instance, are certain genes switched on so that by the end of the first week after conception identical cells have begun to grow into cells with differing characteristics?

So far these fundamental questions are largely unanswerable, although some clues have been uncovered. For one thing, it has been learned that the cell membrane itself appears to play a crucial part in switching genes on and off. When a membrane is merely brushed by certain hormones—a large class of molecules that serve as intercellular messengers—the membrane will respond as though jolted by an electric probe. It will instantly send off a signal to the nucleus, triggering RNA production by the genes. That finding could eventually have medical application for diseases—like diabetes—resulting from vital genes that are inexplicably turned off.

Many more puzzles remain unsolved. In spite of such questions and complications, the basic structure of DNA postulated by Crick and Watson 18 years ago has withstood the test of time remarkably well. More important, it has given man a profound new understanding of basic life processes—and the means to control and alter them. ∎

Fear in a Handful of Numbers

BY DENNIS OVERBYE

[*The gravest danger to the life of the planet and the most destructive enemy of the everyday life of man, a noted science writer argued, was the everyday life of man*]

October 9, 1989

EVERYBODY TALKS ABOUT THE weather, goes the saying (often wrongly attributed to Mark Twain), *but nobody does anything about it.* The word from scientists is that whoever said this was wrong. All of us, as we go about the mundane business of existence, are helping change the weather and every other aspect of life on this fair planet: Los Angelenos whipping their sunny basin into a brown blur on the way to work every morning; South Americans burning and cutting their way through the rain forest in search of a better life; a billion Chinese, their smokestacks belching black coal smoke, marching toward the 21st century and a rendezvous with modernization.

On the flanks of Mauna Loa in Hawaii, an instrument that records the concentration of carbon dioxide dumped into the atmosphere as a result of all this activity traces a wobbly rising line that gets steeper and steeper with time. Sometime in the next 50 years, say climatologists, all that carbon dioxide, trapping the sun's heat like a greenhouse, could begin to smother the planet, raising temperatures, turning farmland to desert, swelling oceans anywhere from four feet to 20 feet. Goodbye Venice, goodbye Bangladesh. Goodbye to millions of species of animals, insects and plants that haven't already succumbed to acid rain, ultraviolet radiation leaking through the damaged ozone layer, spreading toxic wastes or bulldozers.

A species that can change its planet's chemistry just by day-to-day coming and going has, I suppose, achieved a kind of coming-of-age. We could celebrate or tremble. What do we do when it is not war that is killing us but progress? When it is not the actions of a deranged dictator threatening the world but the ordinary business of ordinary people? When there are no bombs dropping, nobody screaming, nothing to fear but a line on a graph or a handful of numbers on a computer printout? Dare we change the world on the basis of a wobbly line on a graph? We can change the world, and those numbers, slowly, painfully—we can ration, recycle, carpool, tax and use the World Bank to bend underdeveloped nations to our will. But the problem is neither the world nor those numbers. The problem is ourselves.

In our relations with nature, we've been playing a deadly game of cowboys and Indians. We all started as Indians. Many primitive cultures—and the indigenous peoples still clinging today to their pockets of underdevelopment—regarded the earth and all its creatures as alive. Nature was a whistling wind tunnel of spirits. With the rise of a scientific, clockwork cosmos and of missionary Christianity, with its message of man's dominion and relentless animus against paganism, nature was metaphorically transformed. It became dead meat.

The West was won, Los Angeles and the 20th century were built, by the cowboy mind. To the cowboy, nature was a vast wilderness waiting to be tamed. The land was a stage, a backdrop against which he could pursue his individual destiny. The story of the world was the story of a man, usually a white man, and its features took their meaning from their relationship to him. A mountain was a place to test one's manhood; an Asian jungle with its rich life and cultures was merely a setting for an ideological battle. The natives are there to be "liberated." By these standards even Communists are cowboys.

The cowboys won—everywhere nature is being tamed—but victory over nature is a kind of suicide. The rules change when there is only one political party allowed in a country or there is only one company selling oil or shoes. So too when a species becomes numerous and powerful enough to gain the illusion of mastery. What we have now is a sort of biological equivalent to a black hole, wherein a star becomes so massive and dense that it bends space and time totally around itself and then pays the ultimate price of domination by disappearing.

Modern science, a cowboy achievement, paradoxically favors the Indian view of life. Nature is alive. The barest Antarctic rock is crawling with microbes. Viruses float on the dust. Bacteria help digest our food for us. According to modern evolutionary biology, our very cells are cities of formerly independent organisms. On the molecular level, the distinction between self and nonself disappears in a blur of semipermeable membranes. Nature goes on within and without us. It wafts through us like a breeze through a screened porch. On the biological level, the world is a seamless continuum of energy and information passing back and forth, a vast complicated network of exchange. Speech, food, posture, infection, respiration, scent are but a few pathways of communication. Most of those circuits are still a mystery, a labyrinth we have barely begun to acknowledge or explore.

The great anthropologist and philosopher Gregory Bateson pointed out 20 years ago that this myriad of feedback circuits resemble the mathematical models of a thinking being developed for the new science of artificial intelligence. A forest or a coral reef or a whole planet, then, with its checks and balances and feedback loops and delicate adjustments always striving for light and equilibrium, is like *a mind.* In this way of thinking, pollution is literal insanity (Bateson was also a psychologist). To dump toxic waste in a swamp, say, is like trying to repress a bad thought or like hitting your wife every night and assuming that because she doesn't fight back, you can abuse her with impunity—30 years later she sets your bed on fire.

Some of these circuits are long and slow, so that consequences may take years or generations to manifest themselves. That helps sustain the cowboy myth that nature is a neutral, unchanging backdrop. Moreover, evolution seems to have wired our brains to respond to rapid changes, the snap of a twig or a movement in the alley, and to ignore slow ones. When these consequences do start to show up, we don't notice them. Anyone who has ever been amazed by an old photograph of himself or herself can attest to the merciful ignorance of slow change, that is, aging—*Where did those clothes and that strange haircut come from? Was I really that skinny?*

We weren't born with the ability to taste carbon dioxide or see the ozone layer, but science and technology have evolved to fill the gap to help us measure what we cannot feel or taste or see. We have old numbers with which, like old photographs, we can gauge the ravages of time and our own folly. In that sense, the "technological fix" that is often wishfully fantasized—cold fusion, anyone?—has already appeared. The genius of technology has already saved us, as surely as the Ghost of Christmas Future saved Scrooge by rattling the miser's tight soul until it cracked. A satellite photograph is technology, and so are the differential equations spinning inside a Cray supercomputer. There is technology in the wobbly rising trace on a piece of graph paper. There is technology in a handful of numbers.

The trick is to become more like Indians without losing the best parts of cowboy culture—rationalism and the spirit of inquiry. We need more science now, not less. How can we stretch our nerves around those numbers and make them as real and as ominous as our cholesterol readings? Repeat them each night on the evening news? We need feedback, as if we were the audience in a giant public radio fund-raising drive hitting the phones and making pledges. Like expert pilots navigating through a foggy night, we need the faith to fly the planet collectively by our instruments and not by the seat of our pants. In the West we need the faith and courage to admit the bitter truth, that our prosperity is based as much on cheap energy as on free markets. A long-postponed part of the payment for that energy and prosperity is coming due if we want to have any hope of dissuading the Chinese and the rest of the Third World from emulating us and swaddling the planet with fumes and wastes.

What if the spirit doesn't hit? We can't afford to wait if we want to survive. While we are waiting for this sea change of attitude, we could pretend—a notion that sounds more whimsical than it is. Scientists have found that certain actions have a feedback effect on the actor. Smilers actually feel happier; debaters become enamored of their own arguments; a good salesman sells himself first. You become what you pretend to be. We can pretend to be unselfish and connected to the earth. We can pretend that 30-ft.-long, black-tinted-glass, air-conditioned limos are unfashionable because we know that real men don't need air conditioning. We can pretend that we believe it is wrong to loot the earth for the benefit of a single generation of a single species. We can pretend to care about our children's world.

The air has been poisoned before, 3 billion years ago, when the blue-green algae began manufacturing oxygen. That was the first ecological crisis. Life survived then. Life will not vanish now, but this may be the last chance for humans to go along gracefully. ∎

Life in Overdrive

BY CLAUDIA WALLIS

[*A new awareness of attention deficit hyperactivity disorder brought relief to many kids and adults but also turned a harsh light on fast-paced, high-stress modern society*]

July 18, 1994

DUSTY NASH, AN ANGELIC-LOOKING blond child of seven, awoke at 5 one recent morning in his Chicago home and proceeded to throw a fit. He wailed. He kicked. Every muscle in his 50-lb. body flew in furious motion. Finally, after about 30 minutes, Dusty pulled himself together sufficiently to head downstairs for breakfast. While his mother bustled about the kitchen, the hyperkinetic child pulled a box of Kix cereal from the cupboard and sat on a chair.

But sitting still was not in the cards this morning. After grabbing some cereal with his hands, he began kicking the box, scattering little round corn puffs across the room. Next he turned his attention to the TV set, or rather, the table supporting it. The table was covered with a checkerboard Con-Tact paper, and Dusty began peeling it off. Then he became intrigued with the spilled cereal and started stomping it to bits. At this point his mother interceded. In a firm but calm voice she told her son to get the stand-up dust pan and broom and clean up the mess. Dusty got out the dust pan but forgot the rest of the order. Within seconds he was dismantling the plastic dust pan, piece by piece. His next project: grabbing three rolls of toilet paper from the bathroom and unraveling them around the house.

It was only 7:30, and his mother Kyle Nash, who teaches a medical-school course on death and dying, was already feeling half dead from exhaustion. Dusty was to see his doctors that day at 4, and they had asked her not to give the boy the drug he usually takes to control his hyperactivity and attention problems, a condition known as attention deficit hyperactivity disorder (ADHD). It was going to be a very long day without help from Ritalin.

Karenne Bloomgarden remembers such days all too well. The peppy, 43-year-old entrepreneur and gym teacher was a disaster as a child growing up in New Jersey. "I did very poorly in school," she recalls. Her teachers and parents were constantly on her case for rowdy behavior. "They just felt I was being bad—too loud, too physical, too everything." A rebellious tomboy with few friends, she saw a psychologist at age 10, "but nobody came up with a diagnosis." As a teenager she began prescribing her own medication: marijuana, Valium and, later, cocaine.

The athletic Bloomgarden managed to get into college, but she admits that she cheated her way to a diploma. "I would study and study, and I wouldn't remember a thing. I really felt it was my fault." After graduating, she did fine in physically active jobs but was flustered with administrative work. Then, four years ago, a doctor put a label on her troubles: ADHD. "It's been such a weight off my shoulders," says Bloomgarden, who takes both the stimulant Ritalin and the antidepressant Zoloft to improve her concentration. "I had 38 years of thinking I was a bad person. Now I'm rewriting the tapes of who I thought I was to who I really am."

Fifteen years ago, no one had ever heard of attention deficit hyperactivity disorder. Today it is the most common behavioral disorder in American children, the subject of thousands of studies and symposiums and no small degree of controversy. Experts on ADHD say it afflicts as many as 3½ million American youngsters, or up to 5% of those under 18. It is two to three times as likely to be diagnosed in boys as in girls. The disorder has replaced what used to be popularly called "hyperactivity," and it includes a broader collection of symptoms. ADHD has three main hallmarks: extreme distractibility, an almost reckless impulsiveness and, in some but not all cases, a knee-jiggling, toe-tapping hyperactivity that makes sitting still all but impossible. (Without hyperactivity, the disorder is called attention deficit disorder, or ADD.)

For children with ADHD, a ticking clock or sounds and sights caught through a window can drown out a teacher's voice, although an intriguing project can absorb them for hours. Such children act before thinking; they blurt out answers in class. They enrage peers with an inability to wait their turn or play by the rules. These are the kids no one wants at a birthday party.

Ten years ago, doctors believed that the symptoms of ADHD faded with maturity. Now it is one of the fastest-growing diagnostic categories for adults. One-third to two-thirds of ADHD kids continue to have symptoms as adults, says psychiatrist Paul Wender, director of the adult ADHD clinic at the University of Utah School of Medicine. Many adults respond to the diagnosis with relief—a sense that "at last my problem has a name and it's not my fault." As more people are diagnosed, the use of Ritalin (or its generic equivalent, methylphenidate), the drug of choice for ADHD, has surged: prescriptions are up more than 390% in just four years.

As the numbers have grown, ADHD awareness has become an industry, a passion, an almost messianic movement. An advocacy and support group called CHADD (Children and Adults with Attention Deficit Disorders) has exploded from its founding in 1987 to 28,000 members in 48 states. Information bulletin boards and support groups for adults have sprung up on CompuServe, Prodigy and America Online. Numerous popular books have been published on the subject. There are summer camps designed to help ADHD kids, videos and children's books with titles like *Jumpin' Johnny Get Back to Work!* and, of course, therapists, tutors and workshops offering their services to the increasingly self-aware ADHD community.

It is a community that views itself with some pride. Popular books and lectures about ADHD often point out positive aspects of the condition. Adults see themselves as creative; their impulsiveness can be viewed as spontaneity; hyperactivity gives them enormous energy and drive; even their distractibility has the virtue of making them alert to changes in the environment. "Kids with ADHD are wild, funny, effervescent. They have a love of life. The rest of us sometimes envy them," says psychologist Russell Barkley of the University of Massachusetts Medical Center. "ADHD adults," he notes, "can be incredibly successful. Sometimes being impulsive means being decisive." Many ADHD adults gravitate into creative fields or work that provides an outlet for emotions.

However creative they may be, people with ADHD don't function particularly well in standard schools and typical office jobs. Increasingly, parents and lobby groups are demanding that accommodations be made. About half the kids diagnosed with ADHD receive help from special-education teachers in their schools, in some cases because they also have other learning disabilities. Where schools have failed to provide services, parents have sometimes sued. Another accommodation requested with increasing frequency: permission to take college-entrance exams without a time limit. Part of what motivates parents to fight for special services is frightening research showing that without proper care, kids with ADHD have an extremely high risk not only of failing at school but also of becoming drug abusers, alcoholics and lawbreakers.

Adults with ADHD are beginning to seek special treatment. Under the 1990 Americans with Disabilities Act, they can insist upon help in the workplace. Usually the interventions are quite modest: an office door or white-noise machine to reduce distractions, or longer deadlines on assignments. Another legal trend that concerns even ADHD advocates: the disorder is being raised as a defense in criminal cases. Psychologist Barkley says he knows of 55 such instances in the U.S., all in the past 10 years.

Some who treat ADHD are worried that the disorder is being embraced with too much gusto. "A lot of people are jumping on the bandwagon," complains psychologist Mark Stein, director of a special ADHD clinic at the University of Chicago. "Parents are putting pressure on health professionals to make the diagnosis." The allure of ADHD is that it is "a label of forgiveness," says Robert Reid, an assistant professor in the department of special education at the University of Nebraska in Lincoln. "The kid's problems are not his parents' fault, not the teacher's fault, not the kid's fault. It's better to say this kid has ADHD than to say this kid drives everybody up the wall." For adults, the diagnosis may provide an excuse for personal or professional failures, observes Richard Bromfield, a psychologist at Harvard Medical School. "Some people like to say, 'The biological devil made me do it.' "

THE MEDICAL RECORD ON ADHD is said to have begun in 1902, when British pediatrician George Still published an account of 20 children in his practice who were "passionate," defiant, spiteful and lacking "inhibitory volition." Still made the then radical suggestion that bad parenting was not to blame; instead he suspected a subtle brain injury. This theory gained greater credence in the years following the 1917-18 epidemic of viral encephalitis, when doctors observed that the infection left some children with impaired attention, memory and control over their impulses. In the 1940s and '50s, the same constellation of symptoms was called minimal brain damage and, later, minimal brain dysfunction. In 1937 a Rhode Island pediatrician reported that giving stimulants called amphetamines to children with these symptoms had the unexpected effect of calming them down. By the mid-1970s, Ritalin had become the most prescribed drug for what was eventually termed, in 1987, attention deficit hyperactivity disorder.

Nobody fully understands how Ritalin and other stimulants work, nor do doctors have a very precise picture of the physiology of ADHD. Researchers generally suspect a defect in the frontal lobes of the brain, which regulate behavior. This region is rich in the neurotransmitters dopamine and norepinephrine, which are influenced by drugs like Ritalin. But the lack of a more specific explanation has led some psychologists to question whether ADHD is truly a disorder at all or merely a set of characteristics that tend to cluster together. Just because something responds to a drug doesn't mean it is a sickness.

ADHD researchers counter the skeptics by pointing to a growing body of biological clues. For instance, several studies have found that people with ADHD have decreased blood flow and lower levels of electrical activity in the frontal lobes than normal adults and children. In 1990 Dr. Alan Zametkin at the National Institute of Mental Health found that in PET scans, adults with ADD showed slightly lower rates of metabolism in areas of the brain's cortex known to be involved in the control of attention, impulses and motor activity. Zametkin's study was hailed as the long-awaited proof of the biological basis of ADD, though Zametkin himself is quite cautious: "I'm absolutely convinced that this disorder has a biological basis, but just what it is we cannot yet say."

What researchers do say with great certainty is that the condition is inherited. External factors such as birth injuries and maternal alcohol or tobacco consumption may play a role in less than 10% of cases. Suspicions that a diet high in sugar might cause hyperactivity have been discounted. But the influence of genes is unmistakable. Barkley estimates that 40% of ADHD kids have a parent who has the trait and 35% have a sibling with the problem; if the sibling is an identical twin, the chances rise to between 80% and 92%.

In the absence of any biological test, diagnosing ADHD is a rather inexact proposition. In most cases, it is a teacher who initiates the process by informing parents that their child is daydreaming in class, failing to complete assignments or driving everyone crazy with thoughtless behavior. "The problem is that the parent then goes to the family doctor, who writes a prescription for Ritalin and doesn't stop to think of the other possibilities," says child psychiatrist Larry Silver of Georgetown University Medical Center. To make a careful diagnosis, Silver argues, one must eliminate other explanations for the symptoms.

The most common cause, he points out, is anxiety. A child who is worried about a problem at home or some other matter "can look hyperactive and distractible." Depression can also cause ADHD-like behavior. "A third cause is another form of neurological dysfunction, like a learning disorder," says Silver. "The child starts doodling because he didn't understand the teacher's instructions." All this is made more complicated by the fact that some kids—and adults—with ADHD also suffer from depression and other problems. To distinguish these symptoms from ADHD, doctors usually rely on interviews with parents and teachers, behavior-ratings scales and psychological tests, which can cost from $500 to $3,000, depending on the thoroughness of the testing. Insurance coverage is spotty.

For kids who are hyperactive, the pattern is unmistakable, says Dr. Bruce Roseman, a pediatric neurologist with several offices in the New York City area, who has ADHD himself. "You say to the mother, 'What kind of personality did the child have as a baby? Was he active, alert? Was he colicky?' She'll say, 'He wouldn't stop—waaah, waaah, waaah!' You ask, 'When did he start to walk?' One mother said to me, 'Walk? My son didn't walk. He got his pilot's license at one year of age. His feet haven't touched the ground since.' You ask, 'Mrs. Smith, how about the terrible twos?' She'll start to cry, 'You mean the terrible twos, threes, fours, the awful fives, the horrendous sixes, the God-awful eights, the divorced nines, the I-want-to-die tens!'"

Most experts say ADHD is a lifelong condition but by late adolescence many people can compensate for their impulsiveness and disorganization. They may channel hyperactivity into sports. In other cases, the symptoms still wreak havoc, says UCLA psychiatrist Walid Shekim. "Patients cannot settle on a career. They cannot keep a job. They procrastinate a lot. They are the kind of people who would tell their boss to take this job and shove it before they've found another job."

Doctors diagnose adults with methods similar to those used with children. Patients are sometimes asked to dig up old report cards for clues to their childhood behavior—an essential indicator. Many adults seek help only after one of their children is diagnosed. Such was the case with Chuck

Pearson of Birmingham, Michigan, who was diagnosed three years ago, at 54. Pearson had struggled for decades in what might be the worst possible career for someone with ADD: accounting. In the first 12 years of his marriage, he was fired from 15 jobs. "I was frightened," says Zoe, his wife of 35 years. "We had two small children, a mortgage. Bill collectors were calling perpetually. We almost lost the house." Chuck admits he had trouble focusing on details, completing tasks and judging how long an assignment would take. He was so distracted behind the wheel that he lost his license for a year after getting 14 traffic tickets. Unwittingly, Pearson began medicating himself: "In my mid-30s, I would drink 30 to 40 cups of coffee a day. The caffeine helped." After he was diagnosed, the Pearsons founded the Adult Attention Deficit Foundation, a clearinghouse for information about ADD; he hopes to spare others some of his own regret: "I had a deep and abiding sadness over the life I could have given my family if I had been treated effectively."

While Chuck Pearson's problems were extreme, many if not all adults have trouble at times sticking with boring tasks, setting priorities and keeping their minds on what they are doing. The furious pace of society, the strain on families, the lack of community support can make anyone feel beset by ADD. "I personally think we are living in a society that is so out of control that we say, 'Give me a stimulant so I can cope,'" says Charlotte Tomaino, a clinical neuropsychologist in White Plains, New York. As word of ADHD spreads, swarms of adults are seeking the diagnosis as an explanation for their troubles. "So many really have symptoms that began in adulthood and reflected depression or other problems," says psychiatrist Silver. In their best-selling new book, *Driven to Distraction*, Edward Hallowell and John Ratey suggest that American life is "ADD-ogenic": "American society tends to create ADD-like symptoms in us all. The fast pace. The sound bite. The quick cuts. The TV remote-control clicker. It is important to keep this in mind, or you may start thinking that everybody you know has ADD."

And that is the conundrum. How do you draw the line between a spontaneous, high-energy person who is feeling overwhelmed by the details of life and someone afflicted with a neurological disorder? Where is the boundary between personality and pathology? Even an expert in the field like the University of Chicago's Mark Stein admits, "We need to find more precise ways of diagnosing it than just saying you have these symptoms." Barkley also concedes the vagueness. The traits that constitute ADHD "are personality characteristics," he agrees. But it becomes pathology, he says, when the traits are so extreme that they interfere with people's lives.

There is no question that ADHD can disrupt lives. Kids with the disorder frequently have few friends. Their parents may be ostracized by neighbors and relatives, who blame them for failing to control the child. School can be a shattering experience for such kids. Frequently reprimanded and tuned out, they lose any sense of self-worth and fall ever further behind in their work.

But the psychological injuries are often greater. By ages five to seven, says Barkley, half to two-thirds are hostile and defiant. By ages 10 to 12, they run the risk of developing what psychologists call "conduct disorder"— lying, stealing, running away from home and ultimately getting into trouble with the law. As adults, says Barkley, 25% to 30% will experience substance-abuse problems, mostly with depressants like marijuana and alcohol. One study of hyperactive boys found that 40% had been arrested at least once by age 18—and these were kids who had been treated with stimulant medication; among those who had been treated with the drug plus other measures, the rate was 20%—still very high.

It is an article of faith among ADHD researchers that the right interventions can prevent such dreadful outcomes. Yet, despite decades of research, no one is certain exactly what the optimal intervention should be. The best-known therapy for ADHD remains stimulant drugs. Doctors can be tempted to throw a little Ritalin at any problem. Swanson has heard of some classrooms where 20% to 30% of the boys are on Ritalin. "That's just ridiculous!" he says.

A rough consensus has emerged among ADHD specialists that whether or not drugs are used, it is best to teach kids—often through behavior modification—how to gain more control over their impulses and restless energy. Also recommended is training in the fine art of being organized: establishing a predictable schedule of activities, learning to use a date book, assigning a location for possessions at school and at home. This takes considerable effort on the part of teachers and parents as well as the kids themselves. Praise, most agree, is vitally important.

Enterprising parents have struggled to find their own answers to attention deficit. Bonnie and Neil Fell of Skokie, Illinois, have three sons, all of whom have been diagnosed with ADD. They have "required more structure and consistency than other kids," says Bonnie. "We had to break down activities into clear time slots." To help their sons, who take Ritalin, the

Fells have employed tutors, psychotherapists and a speech and language specialist. None of this comes cheap: they estimate their current annual ADD-related expenses at $15,000. "Our goal is to get them through school with their self-esteem intact," says Bonnie.

Adults can also train themselves to compensate for ADHD. Therapists working with them typically emphasize organizational skills, time management, stress reduction and ways to monitor their own distractibility and stay focused.

Whether ADHD is a brain disorder or simply a personality type, the degree to which it is a handicap depends not only on the severity of the traits but also on one's environment. The right school, job or home situation can make all the difference. The lessons of ADHD are truisms. All kids do not learn in the same way. Nor are all adults suitable for the same line of work.

Unfortunately, American society seems to have evolved into a one-size-fits-all system. Schools can resemble factories: put the kids on the assembly line, plug in the right components and send 'em out the door. Everyone is supposed to go to college; there is virtually no other route to success. In other times and in other places, there have been alternatives: apprenticeships, settling a new land, starting a business out of the garage, going to sea. In a conformist society, it becomes necessary to medicate some people to make them fit in.

This is not to deny that some people genuinely need Ritalin, just as others need tranquilizers or insulin. But surely an epidemic of attention deficit disorder is a warning to us all. Children need individual supervision. Many of them need more structure than the average helter-skelter household provides. They need a more consistent approach to discipline and schools that tailor teaching to their individual learning styles. Adults too could use a society that's more flexible in its expectations, more accommodating to differences. Most of all, we all need to slow down. And pay attention. ■

—WITH REPORTING BY HANNAH BLOCH/NEW YORK, WENDY COLE/
CHICAGO AND JAMES WILLWERTH/IRVINE

Cosmic Close-Ups

BY MICHAEL D. LEMONICK

[*Images from the Hubble Space Telescope enormously advanced scientific knowledge of—and heightened our eternal awe and wonder at—the vast, mysterious universe*]

November 20, 1995

THEY LOOK REMARKABLY LIKE great towering thunderheads, billowing high into the evening sky as they catch the last rays of the setting sun. They are so sharp, so startlingly three dimensional, that the mind wants to domesticate them, to bring them down to earth, to imagine them rising on the horizon or just beyond the wings of an airliner. These are no ordinary clouds, however. They stand not 30,000 ft. but almost 6 trillion miles high. They are illuminated not with ordinary earthly light but with searing ultraviolet radiation spewing from nuclear fires at the center of a handful of newly formed stars. And they're 7,000 light-years from Earth—more than 400 million times as far away as the sun.

This cosmic vista, seen in a photo released by NASA two weeks ago, is the latest in a series of stunning images captured from the ends of the universe by the Hubble Space Telescope. Once written off as a near total loss because of an inaccurately ground mirror, the Hubble has in the past two years redeemed itself spectacularly. It has offered close-up pictures of distant galaxies that are 10 times as sharp as those produced by earthbound telescopes—pictures that are not just scientifically significant but breathtakingly beautiful as well. In fact, the orbiting observatory has extended our view of the cosmos more dramatically than any single instrument since Galileo first pointed his crude, low-power telescope at the heavens.

The momentous sights revealed by the Hubble can stir anybody's imagination. These are rare glimpses of the outer boundaries of physical reality, and of the fiery cataclysms in which nature perpetually regenerates itself. Even astronomers have trouble keeping their professional cool when pictures like the new one—showing a section of the Eagle Nebula, a knot of interstellar gas and dust in the constellation Serpens—come beaming in from space. "When I saw it, I was just blown away," says NASA's Ed Weiler, the Hubble's chief scientist. The image has such visual impact, in fact, that some researchers tend to overlook its scientific importance.

That importance is immense, however. Some of the smallest features visible in the photo—delicate, stalklike projections reaching out from the clouds—are actually infant star systems the size of our solar system, just now emerging from the gas and dust that shrouded their birth. The ability to see them in such unprecedented detail has told astronomers an enormous amount about how stars are born and why some are circled by planets and others are not. "People had come up with plausible theories about star birth," says Arizona State University astronomer Jeff Hester, leader of the team that took the picture. "Then we got this image—totally out of left field, totally unexpected. And suddenly you could see clearly what's actually happening."

If anyone still harbored lingering doubts about the Hubble's power to do groundbreaking science, the new photograph should put those doubts to rest. Without the Hubble this discovery would not have been possible—and neither would a score of others spanning virtually every branch of astronomy. The telescope has already thrown Big Bang theorists a curve by suggesting that some stars in the universe are older than the universe itself. At the core of one galaxy it has found a black hole as massive as 3 billion suns. It has made scientists front-row spectators at the collision of comet Shoemaker-Levy 9 and the planet Jupiter. And it has begun to unravel the riddle of the brilliant beacons of cosmic light known as quasars. Go to any astronomy conference these days, and you'll find half the scientific papers are based on space-telescope observations. "The Hubble," declares University of Arizona astronomer Rodger Thompson, "is fundamentally altering our view of the universe."

The Hubble still has at least a decade of useful life, and astronomers are convinced that before it's mothballed the telescope will answer many of the most profound mysteries of the cosmos: How big and how old is the universe? What is it made of? How did the galaxies come to exist? Do other Earth-like planets orbit other sunlike stars? "We made Congress a lot of bold promises about how much we'd learn from the Hubble," says John Bahcall, an astrophysicist at the Institute for Advanced Study in Princeton, New Jersey, and an early champion of the idea of a space telescope. "I'm quite relieved to be able to say we were right."

A little more than five years ago, Bahcall was singing a much more melancholy tune. In May 1990, shortly after the Hubble went into orbit, engineers and scientists realized that something was horribly wrong. The telescope simply wouldn't focus properly—the result, it turned out, of a light-gathering mirror that had been ground with exquisite precision, but in the wrong shape. After a lengthy investigation, the disaster was laid to a simple, dumb mistake: a technician had assembled a device that guided the mirror-grinding process with one bolt put on backward. The hobbled Hubble could still do some important science, but much of its research program appeared headed out the window. "I'd been working on this for almost two decades," says Bahcall. "I was devastated."

Others had even more at stake. Bahcall's friend and colleague Lyman Spitzer, an astrophysicist at nearby Princeton University, first began thinking about space telescopes nearly half a century ago. In 1945, just after World War II, a friend approached the young Spitzer asking for help. The Air Force had commissioned a study to look into how Earth-orbiting satellites—still a purely theoretical concept at that point—might be scientifically useful. Would Spitzer be interested in giving an astronomer's perspective? He instantly saw the potential of turning the satellites' gaze away from Earth toward deep space. "I wrote an appendix to the report," he recalls. It was titled "Astronomical Advantages of an Extra-Terrestrial Observatory."

There were, as he reported, two chief advantages. First, the earth's atmosphere is virtually opaque to much of the infrared and ultraviolet radiation that is an important part of the energy output of stars and gas clouds; a telescope orbiting above the atmosphere would be able to see the cosmos in all its colors—not just the ones visible to the human eye. Second, and more important, the atmosphere is like a thick blanket of gas, constantly swirling and churning. That's what makes the stars twinkle. But it also drives astronomers to distraction by blurring the images in their telescopes. A telescope soaring above this roiling sea of air could take crystal-clear pictures and, presumably, lift the veil on some of the universe's deepest secrets.

"I certainly convinced myself that a space telescope would be an important research tool," says Spitzer, still active in astrophysics at 82, "though I don't recall that the report had much impact at the time." All that changed when the Soviets launched Sputnik in 1957; suddenly just about anything involving space took on urgency. Spitzer eventually got a small telescope into orbit in 1972. But by then he and his young colleague Bahcall were thinking about the more ambitious project described in Spitzer's original paper: a much larger space telescope that would—in theory at least—be able see clearly into the outer reaches of the cosmos.

NASA was interested, but Congress was not. "They rejected the first request for funding to study the idea back in 1974," Spitzer recalls. "So astronomers mounted a letter-writing campaign, and John and I testified, and the funding was finally approved." NASA got the official go-ahead in 1977. In 1983 the telescope was formally named after the astronomer Edwin Hubble, who discovered the expanding universe back in the 1920s.

FROM THE START, THE space telescope was designed to be launched from the cargo hold of NASA's new space shuttles—a decision that proved a mixed blessing. The first shuttle had not been launched yet, and as the cost of the shuttle program climbed, so did the cost of launching the Hubble. The telescope's dependence on the shuttle also meant that if launches got backed up, the Hubble likewise got delayed. That was already happening before the *Challenger* disaster; when the *Challenger* went down with its seven-person crew in January 1986, the Hubble launch was pushed back even further.

There were scientific drawbacks to using the shuttle as well. Shuttles carry payloads only a few hundred miles above the earth's surface. At that altitude, the glaringly bright home planet fills nearly half the sky. Any decision about the Hubble's targets had to take Earth's always changing position into account, a scheduling nightmare. And since the Hubble took only 90 minutes to orbit the earth, the telescope could focus on a single object for a few minutes at most before Earth obscured it.

But as a shuttle-launched satellite, the railroad-car-size Hubble had some important advantages. It was designed to be serviced in orbit; the plan was to have shuttle astronauts visit the telescope every few years to replace the original cameras, electronics and other equipment with new, better-performing instruments.

As NASA learned in 1990 with the discovery of the flawed mirror, easy access to the Hubble's innards was crucial. Even so, installation of a complex array of corrective mirrors—essentially fitting the Hubble with a set of eyeglasses—was a high-cost ($700 million), high-risk venture, and some astronomers were dubious. "They considered the whole thing to be rather a Rube Goldberg creation," says Spitzer. On top of that, the list of tasks assigned to the astronauts who flew the repair mission—not just installing the new optics, but replacing an outdated camera, two wobbly solar-energy panels and three faulty gyroscopes, among other balky components—seemed too long. "I don't think anyone except the astronauts themselves thought they could complete the mission," says Bahcall.

But complete it they did, in a series of televised space walks that riveted the nation's attention in December 1993. Floating on the verge of a black void, the crew of the shuttle *Endeavour* checked off one item after another on their impossible list until, in what Bahcall calls a display of "superhuman intelligence and ability," they were done. NASA's badly battered reputation was on the line, but within days the report came in: the images were excellent. "It was hard to believe," Bahcall remembers. "Each instrument worked exactly as it was designed."

Almost immediately thereafter, the dramatic scientific results started rolling in. Among the most significant:

• By measuring with unprecedented precision the distance to the distant galaxy M100 (56 million light-years), a team of researchers led by Wendy Freedman of the Carnegie Observatories in Pasadena, California, provided the most accurate yardstick ever for gauging the expansion rate, and thus the age, of the universe. Their illogical preliminary answer: the cosmos is between 8 billion and 12 billion years old—or about 2 billion years younger than the oldest known stars. While Freedman and others refine their measurements, cosmologists are scrambling to patch up their theories. To save the idea of the Big Bang, the postulated explosive event that created the universe, they are even talking of reviving the idea of the cosmological constant—a sort of universal antigravity force that Einstein proposed and then discarded as inelegant.

• The growing consensus that gigantic black holes lurk at the core of many galaxies—including our own—was confirmed by Holland Ford, now at Johns Hopkins, and his collaborators, who used the Hubble to spot a superheated disk of gas spinning at a dizzying 1.2 million m.p.h. at the very heart of the galaxy M87, 50 million light-years from Earth. The only reasonable explanation: the gas is funneling, like water down a drain, into the gravitational pit of a black hole as massive as 2 million suns.

• Bahcall has used the telescope to take pictures of quasars, starlike objects so bright they can be seen halfway across the universe. Most theorists think quasars are intimately related to giant black holes like the one Ford found; presumably their intense light comes from gas compressed with such force that it explodes in bright bursts of energy. That implies that every quasar should have a galaxy around it, but in several cases Bahcall found no clear evidence of one. "This," he said when he announced his observations, "is a giant leap backward in our understanding of quasars."

• Hubble gave planetary astronomers an unprecedented once-in-a-lifetime view of the mountain-size fragments of comet Shoemaker-Levy 9 smashing one after another into Jupiter. While other telescopes picked up the flashes of light generated by the multimegaton impacts, only the space telescope could see details of the scars they left behind. By carefully observing the dark smudges that the fragments stamped into Jupiter's cloudtops, scientists have begun to understand how the giant planet's stormy atmosphere works.

• More than a score of astronomers working in several teams have taken the sharpest pictures ever of some of the most distant known galaxies—some as much as 10 billion light-years away—and shaken up the conventional wisdom on galactic evolution. Many theorists believed that spiral galaxies—delicate, pinwheel-shape collections of stars like the Milky Way—were the first to evolve in the universe. Occasionally they'd crash into each other, and the resulting amorphous blob would turn into an elliptical galaxy, the second major class of star system. But what the Hubble showed was that there have been elliptical galaxies almost from the beginning, and that the earliest spirals were gnarled and distorted—not spiral at all. "The day that result came out," says Thompson, "one of my colleagues had to quickly rewrite a lecture he was giving later that afternoon."

Indeed, before the Hubble is finished, all sorts of lectures, textbooks and astronomical theories will have to be rewritten. As Robert Williams, director of the Space Telescope Science Institute, in Baltimore, Maryland, points out: "There's long been a belief that whenever you have a tenfold advance in telescope resolving power, you're going to have unexpected discoveries. The Hubble has confirmed it." Right now, in fact, the telescope is taking pictures of a very distant part of the universe that will probe deeper into the cosmos than anyone ever has. Williams expects to release the images sometime this winter—and promises that they will be worth waiting for.

Also worth waiting for are the improvements that will make the telescope many times more powerful than it is today. Shuttle missions are scheduled to dock at the telescope in 1997, 1999 and 2002, each time upgrading the Hubble's cameras and other instruments. "We're going to be replacing the original 1970s and 1980s technology with 1990s instruments," says Weiler. "It'll essentially be a new telescope." Hubble's official working lifetime ends in 2005, when its guaranteed funding runs out. At that point NASA, the astronomers who use the Hubble, and Congress will have to decide whether to keep refurbishing the aging observatory. It may be that in the next generation of ground-based telescopes, new computerized methods of correcting for atmospheric blur will finally make obsolete the notion of putting a telescope in space to take sharp pictures.

But by then the Hubble will have justified its reputation, and its $5 billion-to-$6 billion overall cost, many times over. "That's about the price of a new aircraft carrier," Weiler points out. Spread out over 25 years, he estimates, it comes to about 2¢ a week for every man, woman and child in the U.S. Says Bahcall: "We can take pride in an achievement that no other nation could even consider. It's like our pyramids—but a whole lot more important." And, to our eyes, even more beautiful.   ■

Virologist: Jonas Salk

BY WILFRID SHEED

[
*The author, a novelist and essayist as well as a childhood
victim of polio, sorted out the rivalries and acrimonies
that lay behind the conquest of that dread disease*
]

March 29, 1999

HOW MANY CASES MAKE an epidemic? Survivors of the great polio plagues of the 1940s and '50s will never believe that in the U.S. the average toll in those years was "only" 1 victim out of every 5,000 people. Was that really all it took to scare the nation out of its wits, sending families scurrying in all directions—to the mountains, to the desert, to Europe— in vain hope of sanctuary?

Perhaps polio's other name, infantile paralysis, had something to do with it. Images of babies in wheelchairs and tots on crutches tend to skew one's perception. And just in case anyone wasn't scared enough, the National Foundation for Infantile Paralysis hammered the nightmare home with photos that seemed to show up everywhere of sad-looking children in leg braces. "Please give to the March of Dimes." Oh yes, indeed, five times at the same movie—or so it sometimes felt.

It was inevitable that whoever was first to allay such fears would become a national hero. "The Man Who Saved the Children" should be good for a statue in every town in the world. And since the odds of a microbiologist's becoming even a little bit famous are a lot worse than 5,000 to 1, it was perhaps inevitable that this hero's achievements would immediately be disputed. In a scientific field so heavily manned, findings routinely criss-cross and even minor discoveries can leave a trail of claims and counter-claims, not to mention envy and acrimony, that are truly incurable.

Thus a monument to the conquest of polio faithful to the facts would consist of not one man in a white lab coat but two of them glaring at each other. Both Drs. Jonas Salk and Albert Sabin could and did make convincing cases for themselves and pretty good ones against each other too. But since the public usually prefers one hero to two, and since Salk did get there first, he got the monument.

Between occasional shouts of "Eureka!" even the heroes of science tend to have quiet careers. But Salk's career stands out in at least two respects: the sheer speed with which he outraced all the other tortoises in the field and the honors he did *not* receive for doing so. How could the Man Who Saved the Children be denied a Nobel Prize? Or summarily be turned down for membership in the National Academy of Sciences? What was it about Salk that so annoyed his fellow scientists?

That he was fast, there was no doubt. And hungry too. After taking brilliant advantage of the amazing public education available to New Yorkers in the first half of this century, this son of Orthodox Polish-Jewish immigrants whizzed through his medical training to fetch up at the University of Michigan an enviable fellowship to study virology under the distinguished Dr. Thomas Francis—who, incidentally, would remain in Salk's corner for life, politics or no politics.

Salk's major patron at Michigan, however, proved to be no one man but the whole U.S. Army, which needed a flu vaccine at once to help win World War II and was happy to complete Salk's education in speed under pressure. After that, it was a snap for him to set up his own peacetime lab at the University of Pittsburgh and equip it to the gills for the Great Crusade—the one that every immunologist in the world then had his eye on—against the Great White Whale itself, poliomyelitis.

Fortunately, Salk had somehow found time to do basic research on the virus and write a few theoretical papers, and it was these that caught the eye of Basil O'Connor, the zealous head of the Infantile Paralysis Foundation, who decided to play a hunch and shove some dimes in Salk's direction with instructions to get going.

With that, the seeds of resentment, deep and abiding, were sown. By then, dozens of worthy researchers had been toiling far longer than Salk in the fields of polio and would have given their microscopes for such funding and freedom. Who was this hired gun who appeared from nowhere with a bankroll the size of a special prosecutor's, plus free use of all the backbreaking work that had gone before?

In fact, the key piece of research, available to all, was completed a few years earlier by the one undisputed hero of this story, Harvard's John Enders. It was his team that figured out how to grow polio in test tubes—suddenly giving vaccine hunters everywhere enough virus to work with.

Now the goal was truly in sight, and who got there first was largely a matter of speed—Salk's forte—and luck. "Salk was strictly a kitchen chemist," Sabin used to gripe. "He never had an original idea in his life." But imaginative people perennially underrate efficient ones, and at the time, the kitchen chemist—who prepared his vaccine by marinating the virus in formalin—was just what the doctor ordered.

Salk and Sabin came from the two competing schools of vaccine research. Sabin, like Louis Pasteur, believed the way to produce immunity was to create a mild infection with a "live" but crippled virus, and he concocted his competing vaccine accordingly. Salk, from his flu-fighting days, knew the immune system could be triggered without infection, using deactivated, or "killed," viruses. And, as it turned out, his quick-and-dirty killed viruses were better suited to a crash program than Sabin's carefully attenuated live ones. By 1954, Salk and Francis were ready to launch the largest medical experiment yet carried out in the U.S., vaccinating more than 1 million kids ages six to nine, some with the vaccine, some with a placebo. The children weren't told which they were getting.

The vaccine worked. But the world of science has a protocol for releasing such findings: first publish them in a medical journal, and then spread the credit as widely as possible. Salk took part in a press conference and went on radio but gave credit to nobody, including himself—of course, he was going to get the credit anyway. And that was the mistake that would haunt him.

Radio was right; vanity was wrong. This was not some breakthrough in carbuncle research but hot news that couldn't wait one more minute. Within the brotherhood of researchers, however, Salk had sinned unforgivably by not saluting either Enders or, more seriously, his colleagues at the Pittsburgh lab. Everything he did after that was taken as showboating—when he opened the Salk Institute, a superlab in La Jolla, Calif., for the world's scientists to retreat to and bask in, and even when not long before his death in 1995, he started a search for an AIDS vaccine, to a flourish of trumpets and welcome new funding.

Just as some politicians are at their best when running for office, so Salk came into his own as a spokesman for vaccination. Although it is generally accepted in the field that the real man on the monument should be Enders (who in 1954 shared the only Nobel Prize given for polio research), it seems unlikely that either he or the pugnacious Sabin would have performed half so patiently as Salk the ceremonial chores expected of monuments or would have sat so politely through so many interviews and spread the gospel of disease prevention quite so far and wide and indefatigably.

And one last thing. Like the millions of American veterans who have never ceased thanking Harry Truman for dropping the Bomb and ending World War II, the folks who got their polio shot between the first Salk vaccine and the Sabin model have never had any quarrel with Salk's high place in history. (The two vaccines are now given in alternating booster shots.) There are times when even genius has to give way to the old Yankee virtues of know-how and can-do. And if in this instance these happened to be embodied in the son of a couple of Polish-Jewish immigrants . . . well, a lot of that kind of thing happens in America.   ■

Yes, It Really *Is* Brain Surgery

BY MICHAEL KINSLEY

[A TIME *political columnist suffering from Parkinson's disease was disarmingly frank about his condition while disproving the notion that major surgery is no joke*]

July 24, 2006

LIKE NASA BEFORE THE first moon landing, I have been soliciting advice about what to say when I wake up from brain surgery. That's right, brain surgery—it's a real conversation stopper, isn't it? There aren't many things you can say these days that retain their shock value, but that is one of them. "So, Mike—got any summer plans?" "Why, yes, next Tuesday I'm having brain surgery. How about you?" In the age of angioplasty and Lipitor, even the heart has lost much of its metaphorical power, at least in the medical context. People are willing to accept it as a collection of muscles and blood vessels rather than—or at least in addition to—the seat of various emotions. But the brain remains the seat of the self itself in physical reality as well as in metaphor. And the brain as metaphor looms so large that there isn't much room left for the simultaneous physical reality that the brain is material, performs mechanical functions, can break down and sometimes can be repaired.

So brain surgery remains shocking and mystical. People don't expect to run into someone who's having brain surgery next week squeezing the melons at Whole Foods. (Unless, of course, he's squeezing them and shrieking, "Why don't you answer? Hello? Hello?") Self-indulgently, I've been dropping the conversational bomb of brain surgery more often than absolutely necessary just to enjoy the reaction. And why not? I deserve that treat. After all, I'm going to be having brain surgery.

Brain surgery is a license for self-indulgence. Cancel that dentist's appointment; you've suffered enough. (Though technically, before you go under, you haven't actually suffered at all.) Take out the trash? "C'mon, honey, I've got BRAIN SURGERY next week." Writers devote a lot of creative energy to dreaming up reasons not to write. One of the all-time best came recently from Washington *Post* columnist Anne Applebaum, who told her readers that she was going to stop writing the column for a while because her husband had become Defense Minister of Poland, and she was moving to Warsaw. Sure, Anne, and I'm taking the summer off because I'm having brain surgery. In Cleveland.

But it's true. The operation is called deep-brain stimulation (DBS). They stick a couple of wires into your head, run them around your ears and into batteries that are implanted in your chest. Then current from the batteries zaps some bad signals in your brain so that good signals can be heard by the rest of your body. When it works, as it generally does, it greatly reduces the symptoms of Parkinson's disease. I wrote in TIME $4\frac{1}{2}$ years ago about having PD and adopting a strategy of denial: pretending to myself and others that I didn't have it. By now my symptoms are past the point where dishonesty and self-deception are a useful approach. But maybe this operation will get me back there.

As I write, surgery is a few days off. But you can assume, if you are reading this, that it went well. And thank you for your concern. Now, where was I? Oh, yes, brain surgery. Thinking I would give self-deception one more shot, I tried to convince myself that DBS isn't really brain surgery. They don't crack open your skull; they just drill a couple of small holes to put the wires through. Tiny holes. Itsy-bitsy holes. Teensy-weensy little holes. The propaganda they give you when you sign up for the operation describes the holes as "dime-sized." That took me aback. The dime, there's no denying, is a seriously undersized coin. But frankly, I wasn't thinking coins at all. I was thinking grains of sand. A dime is huge! The hospital printout of all the things you can't do afterward describes it as "major brain surgery." Is there minor brain surgery?

To an American middle-class professional of the 21st century, what is scariest about brain surgery isn't the ever present risk of disaster or even the chance of unexpected side effects. It's the danger that people will look at you differently. We are all brain snobs, and we are all—those of us over 20 or so—losing brain cells. But if you're walking around with wires in your head and batteries flanking your chest, every senior moment when you can't remember the term for, you know, when they drill holes in your skull—right, brain surgery—is . . . is . . . is . . . well, it's going to seem significant to others and to you.

That's why my first words coming out of surgery are so important. They have got to tell the world—and convince myself—that I am all there. Of course, there are the obvious jokes about brain surgery ("Well, it wasn't exactly rocket science") and about those wires in my head ("Can you hear me now?"). There is Dada ("I am the Defense Minister of Poland. Who the hell are you?"). And slapstick ("I feel as if I've lost 10 pounds . . . uh oh"). I'm still working on it.

Editor's note: Kinsley's surgery took place on July 12 and went fine. His first words were, "Well, of course, when you cut taxes, government revenues go up. Why couldn't I see that before?" ∎

AMERICANS LOVE THEIR CARS! ACTRESS JINX FALKENBURG, 1942, BY PETER STACKPOLE

The Great Trial

[W R I T E R   U N K N O W N]

[*The Tennessee prosecution of John Scopes for teaching evolution in school was less a legal than a social and religious watershed—and something of a circus too*]

July 20, 1925

IN THE FASTNESSES OF Tennessee, the quiet of dawn is split asunder by wailing screams from a steam siren. It is the Dayton sawmill, waking up villagers and farmers for miles around. From 5 until 6:30 the blasts continue. The hamlet and the fantastic cross between a circus and a holy war that is in progress there come slowly to life.

Along the main street of the village, where everyone in town sees everyone else within five minutes, peddlers, hucksters, hot-sausage men (they call their wares "hot monkeys" now), pamphleteers, itinerant evangelists, prepare themselves and their goods for another day's trafficking.

The holder of the barbecue concession on the court-house lawn builds up his fire and heaves half an ox on the coals. The field secretary of an anti-Evolution society picks his teeth and adds a note or two of his stock harangue, delivered thrice daily: "Shall we be taxed to damn our children?" An evangelist-bookseller looks proudly up at his billboards: HELL AND THE HIGH SCHOOLS, GOD OR GORILLA, BRYAN'S BOOKS FOR SALE HERE.

A preacher from Georgia in a bungalow on wheels drowsily draws on his outlandish costume—alpaca coat, shabby policeman's trousers and an opera hat—and hopes that the new day may bring him an audience for his weird sermon proving that Negroes are not human beings. The barker for a tent show called *The She-Devil* clears his throat.

In a forest clearing outside the town, exhausted Holy Rollers snore under the shrubbery after a night's orgy of insane gesticulation and acrobatics incited by a mouthing, syncopating professional ecstatic. Sid Strunk, the village policeman, ruminates over his breakfast coffee that it is a good thing they have brought reserves from Chattanooga.

About 8 o'clock, dusty wagons, gigs, buggies and small automobiles come jogging in along the country roads. In them are gaunt farmers, their wives in gingham and children in overalls, who crowd toward the court house to get seats for the day's proceedings in the trial of Teacher John Thomas Scopes, alleged violator of the state's anti-evolution law, bewildered instrument of Science and Faith which have accidentally chosen Dayton as their battleground and in whose wake has come the usual campfollowing of freaks, fakes, mountebanks and parasites of publicity.

Smirking, gabbling, cynical minions of the press throng with the farmers—and that is all of the crowd. For all the publicity she has stirred up, or rather because of it, Dayton has not attracted the visitors she expected—eminent scientists, statesmen, politicians, financiers, society figures.

Events. Two days before the trial, Lawyer William Jennings Bryan, chief of the prosecution, lumbered off a train from Florida. The populace, Bryan's to a moron, yowled a welcome. Going to the house he had rented, Bryan took off his coat, wandered the streets in his shirt sleeves, a panoramic smile of blessing upon his perspiring countenance, an impressive pith helmet covering the bald, pink dome of his head.

He wandered to Robinson's drug store for a strawberry sundae. There sat freckle-faced young Teacher Scopes, in his blue shirt and hand-painted bow tie, grinning with bashful curiosity at passers-by and listening to his proud father, Thomas Scopes of Paducah, Ky., exclaim: "John was always an extraordinary boy." Father Scopes was proceeding to uncomplimentary remarks about Lawyer Bryan when the son interrupted:

"Mr. Bryan, meet my father."

The two shook hands; Bryan consumed his sundae and departed, exuding benevolence.

Lawyer Bryan addressed the Dayton Progressive Club at dinner, shrewdly comparing Dayton to Nazareth and Bethlehem, calling the trial a "duel to death," exhorting men to campaign with him to "put the Bible into the U. S. Constitution."

Slouching Lawyer Clarence Darrow, defense counsel, arrived. Finding shy young Scopes in the crowd, asked Darrow: "Is Bryan here? Is he all right? It would be very painful to me to hear that he had fallen a victim to synthetic sin."

The Courtroom. Fumbling his soiled lavender galluses, slowly masticating a quid of tobacco, Darrow squinted across at Lawyer Bryan, rather voluptuous in a black mohair suit, surrounded by assistant counsel.

By the judge's bench, a cotton-topped, curly-headed boy of four played about, waiting to draw the names of venire-men for the jury from a box, a duty assigned to a young child by state law. The Judge himself, John T. Raulston of Winchester, Tenn., after opening the court and calling a special sitting of the grand jury to reindict Scopes so that there might be no mistake, sat back in his chair chewing gum, waving to friends among the spectators, occasionally calling for order when growls of prejudice greeted the cross-questioning of the venire-men.

A jury was sworn—ten farmers, a shipping clerk and a farmer-teacher, none of whom had ever read a book on Evolution or admitted a prejudice for or against it; all of whom, with the exception of one illiterate, had read the Bible.

Trial. Lawyer Bryan, palm leaf fan in hand, collarless, led the prosecution forces into Court shortly before 9 o'clock. A few of the more courageous clung to their coats, but the heat soon overcame their vanity, with the exception of foppish, double-breasted-coated Dudley Field Malone.

A long fight then began concerning the differences between the caption of the act under which Scopes was indicted and the act itself. Attorney General Tom Stewart led off for the State. He claimed that the Constitution in no way discriminated against religious beliefs. Lawyer Clarence Darrow dominated the proceedings and aggravated in doing so a small rent in his left shirt sleeve into a gigantic tear.

Lawyer Darrow then began his long argument for the defense, basing it on the diversion of the caption of the act from the act itself and on the ambiguity of the indictment. "I am going to argue it [the case] as if it was serious. . . . The Book of Genesis, written when everybody thought the world was flat . . . religious ignorance and bigotry as any that justified the Spanish Inquisition or the hanging of witches in New England. . . . The State of Tennessee has no more right to teach the Bible as the Divine Book than it has the Koran, the Book of Mormon, the Book of Confucius, the Buddha or the Essays of Emerson. . . . Who is the Chief Mogul that can tell us what the Bible means ? . . . Nothing was ever heard of all that [Christian divisions] until the Fundamentalists got into Tennessee. . . . Here is one thing I cannot account for, that is the hatred and the venom and feeling of people with very strong religious convictions. . . . Joshua made the sun stand still. The Fundamentalists will make the ages roll back. . . . This is as brazen and bold an attempt to destroy liberty as was ever seen in the Middle Ages. . . ."

The trial was continued. ■

Midway Man

[WRITER UNKNOWN]

[*Though often criticized as brusque and arrogant,
Robert M. Hutchins was sympathetically profiled here
as a precocious university president and one of the
most radical reformers in American education*]

June 24, 1935

IN CHICAGO THE YEAR'S best-publicized academic
Red scare, having run up against a combination of scorn and
spunk named Robert Maynard Hutchins, ignominiously collapsed. When Drugman Charles R. Walgreen withdrew his
niece from University of Chicago, clamoring that the campus
was rampant with Communism, President Hutchins angrily
refused to dignify his vaporings with a public investigation. Only 75 of the
University's 7,500 full-time students belonged to its two pinko student organizations.* But Drugman Walgreen got his hearing anyway, before the
Illinois Senate and in the Press.

Last week the Senate Committee, after four weeks of chasing marsh
lights, disgustedly called off its investigation for good. President Hutchins,
who had sat through its hearings in blank boredom, calmly went off about
his business. Next week the University will present a series of public lectures by Soviet Ambassador Alexander Troyanovsky and two of his countrymen on "The Soviet Union and World-Problems."

A lucid, original mind, engaging presence and quiet, incisive delivery

---

* *Both were suspended last fortnight for violating the University's rule against off-campus demonstrations.*

make Bob Hutchins one of the ablest and most popular public speakers in the land. In University of Chicago's majestic cathedral-chapel last week he summed up for all liberal educators their case against the patrioteers. His rangy, athletic figure draped in silken gown and the purple hood of a Doctor of Laws, he leaned out from the pulpit to declare:

". . . Almost everybody now is afraid. This is reflected in the hysteria of certain organs of opinion, which insist on free speech for themselves, though nobody has thought of taking it away from them, and at the same time demand that it be denied everybody else. It is reflected in the return of Billingsgate to politics. It is reflected in the general resistance to all uncomfortable truths. It is reflected in the decay of the national reason. Almost the last question you can ask about any proposal nowadays is whether it is wise, just, or reasonable. The question is how much pressure is there behind it or how strong are the vested interests against it.

"Current fears are reflected too in the present attacks on higher education. From one point of view these attacks are justified. From the point of view of those who believe that Heaven is one big country club, universities are dangerous things. If what you want is a dead level of mediocrity, if what you would like is a nation of identical twins, without initiative, intelligence or ideas, you should fear the universities. From this standpoint universities are subversive. They try to make their students think. . . ."

When President Hutchins was done his audience, the first one to behave so in the memory of any chapel-goer, beat their palms.

More than the touch of grey in his close-cropped dark hair, this commencement speech revealed the maturity which is overtaking the golden boy of U. S. Education. Six years ago the nation gasped at the bright promise implied in his prodigious chronology—War-decorated by Italy at 19, Secretary of Yale at 24, Yale Law School lecturer at 26, full professor and dean at 29, President of University of Chicago at 30. To a large section of the U. S. public he is still a brilliant boy theorist, miraculously allowed to tinker a university to his mind's content. But Robert Maynard Hutchins, once the youngest and handsomest big-university president in the land, is now only the handsomest. After six years of guiding a great university through Depression he stands not on his promise but on his performance.

John D. Rockefeller and a prodigious predecessor from Yale gave Bob Hutchins the kind of university he has to run. One "delicious May morning" in 1889 the nation's No. 1 industrialist, trim, erect and in his prime at

49* was pacing up & down before his Manhattan home with the Secretary of the American Baptist Education Society. Suddenly, a few steps from Fifth Avenue, Mr. Rockefeller stopped, faced the Baptist secretary, announced his decision. He would give $600,000 toward founding a Baptist college in Chicago, provided other acceptable donors would give $400,000. When this proposal was announced to a convention of the Education Society in Boston, delegates spontaneously burst out in "Praise God from whom all blessings flow." Mr. Rockefeller concurred in this judgment when he paid his first visit to the Chicago campus seven years later. Said he: "The good Lord gave me the money, and how could I withhold it from Chicago? . . . It is the best investment I ever made in my life."

Before he was through Mr. Rockefeller had increased this best investment to $35,000,000, and his various foundations have since given almost as much again. He thought he was establishing a small Baptist College in the Midwest. It was William Rainey Harper, college student at 10 and Yale Ph. D. at 19, who rid him of that idea. Chosen to bring the embryo institution to birth, fertile, vigorous, 35-year-old First President Harper set his heart on building a great university, scoured the world for its first requisite— great scholars. Before he died of cancer in 1906 he had set the liberal, experimental, scholarly course from which University of Chicago has never departed. Prodigious Yaleman Hutchins now heads the fourth richest (endowment: $59,475,148), sixth largest (enrollment: 13,000) university in the land, with 85 fine buildings, mostly Gothic, strung three-quarters of a mile along South Chicago's spacious Midway Plaisance. Indisputable intellectual leader of the Midwest, it has housed such world-famed scholars as Physicists Albert A. Michelson and Robert A. Millikan, Biologists Jacques Loeb and Frank Rattray Lillie, Philosopher John Dewey, Historian-Ambassador William E. Dodd, Astronomer Edwin Brant Frost, Medical Researchers Alexis Carrel, Frank Billings, Howard Taylor Ricketts.

In the current *Atlantic Monthly,* President Edwin R. Embree of the Rosenwald Fund ranked U. S. universities on the basis of the American Council of Education's investigation of their scholarly eminence in each of 35 academic departments. He found University of Chicago second only to Harvard, its senior by 254 years.

President Hutchins bided only a year before he turned University of

* Beginning his annual summer shuttle from Ormond Beach, Fla. to Lakewood, N. J. last week, Mr. Rockefeller failed for the first time to speak or wave to station bystanders as attendants helped him up a specially-built platform to his private car. His 96th birthday falls on July 8.

Chicago upside down with his New Plan. At one stroke he wiped out the whole conventional university structure and paraphernalia: colleges, graduate schools, credits, course examinations, compulsory class attendance, arbitrary residence requirements. His new structure comprised a College and four Upper Divisions: Biological Sciences, Physical Sciences, Social Sciences, Humanities. A student was to lay a broad cultural foundation in the College, stop there with a certificate if he wished, or proceed to one of the Divisions for advanced work funneling up without interruption through A. B. and A. M. to Ph. D. General examinations would test not his ability to parrot back a set of facts dealt out by one professor, but his thoughtful grasp of a whole field of knowledge. Freed from oldtime academic harness, he could gallop or amble through his course as fast or slowly as he wished.

THERE ARE NO TANGIBLE tests of success for such a scheme as the New Plan, and it is still quite new. But in the enthusiastic judgment of president, faculty and students, the Plan works. University attendance has increased since it started. More important, student calibre has kept step. Dullards are afraid of it. The high-school average of last year's Freshman class was an astounding 90. Applicants write in from all corners of the land, half of them saying they want to enter University of Chicago solely because of the New Plan. Given a chance to proceed under their own steam, students have found that learning is exciting. They pile into extra lecture sessions just for the fun of it, or take examinations without any previous classwork whatsoever and generally pass with higher marks than those of classmembers.

The New Plan has proved itself an administrative blessing. Instead of a regiment of department heads, President Hutchins has only a handful of "vice presidents"—Deans of divisions and professional schools—to deal with on matters of finance and appointments. Individual budgets have dropped from 72 to twelve. Some 400 over-specialized or overlapping courses have been eliminated. To this economy of organization, plus the able assistance of sturdy, white-haired Vice President Frederic Campbell ("Fritz") Woodward, President Hutchins credits his success in bringing the University through Depression relatively unscathed. As income from real estate, mortgages and Standard Oil stock plummeted, he has had to dip heavily into a $1,000,000 reserve fund. But no professors have been discharged, no salaries cut except those of the medical faculty (now mostly restored) and of administrators, including the president.

Aboard a Manhattan-bound express train a fellow passenger once cheerfully asked Chicago's president: "Where are you going?"

"Where," replied Bob Hutchins, "is the train going?"

Chicagoans on & off the campus agree on two facts about President Hutchins: 1) he is exceedingly smart and able; 2) he is entirely too flip and smart-alecky. Friends excuse his brusque manner, his acid impatience with fatuity, on grounds of shyness. But when the Hutchins manner first made itself apparent on the Midway, that explanation did not salve the feelings of oldtime facultymen, already angry at having a youth brought in over their heads. Businessmen in the Loop were equally galled by his domineering ways when he served on Chicago's Unemployment Relief Commission. His popularity reached a nadir in 1931 when he caused the chairman and two members of his philosophy department to quit their jobs in high dudgeon.

Since then Chicago has become better acquainted with Bob Hutchins and his popularity, especially in the past year, has soared. Most facultymen who still dislike him fall into three classifications: 1) mossbacks; 2) peanuts; 3) strangers. Young fellow members of the faculty's X Club (wives have an X's Club) have found him a companion of first-rate wit and charm. Students lucky enough to get into his erudite course on "Classics of the Western World," which he teaches by dialog with smart young Philosophy Professor Mortimer Adler, think it the high spot of their campus lives.

His father is president of Kentucky's Berea College and his younger brother vice president of Yale-in-China, but Bob Hutchins might never have turned to Education if it had not been for beauteous Maude McVeigh. He was 22, penniless and wanted to be a lawyer, but a prep-school teaching job looked like the only way he could earn enough to support a wife. Like nearly all university presidents' wives, Maude Hutchins has been roundly criticized for snobbishness. Mrs. Hutchins, however, is a New Englander with a mind of her own. Scores of faculty folk have sat at her board but she figured out long ago that if she entertained six faculty folk per night, five nights per week, it would take practically a year to go down the list. Hence she and her husband live quietly with their 9-year-old daughter Mary Frances ("Franja") and their Great Dane "Hamlet" on the second floor of the big, yellow-brick President's House overlooking the Midway, entertain intimates there. Instead of an automobile their garage houses a studio where Mrs. Hutchins ably sculpts and draws.

No man could rise so high as President Hutchins has in half his life without causing the world to wonder what the second half may hold for him. Just now not even his intimates can get Bob Hutchins to say any more than that he is vastly interested in Education. Having launched a program which should eventually transform U. S. Education, he is brimful of ideas for extending and improving it. But, though he thinks with vigorous independence about educational problems, he is not primarily a theorist. The New Plan, as he has often pointed out, is the work of many minds. His genius lies in possessing the courage and vision to effect new plans, the ability to administer them to success. ■

The Last Traffic Jam

BY PAUL O'NEIL

[*On the flimsiest of journalistic pretexts, the writer spun a charming fantasia on America's intense—and fundamentally deluded?—love affair with the automobile*]

December 15, 1947

IN HIS LONG AND losing war with machines, modern man has devoted almost as much energy to damning new-fangled contraptions as he has to inventing them. He has cursed the power loom, the steam locomotive, the Welsbach mantle, the airplane and the electric shaver with a vehemence calculated to deliver whole generations of mankind to the greasiest fry cooks of nether Hell. But in half a century of blissful self-delusion he has failed to perceive that the family automobile is the most monstrous engine of all.

The average U.S. citizen completely ignores the regularity with which the automobile kills him, maims him, embroils him with the law and provides mobile shelter for rakes intent on seducing his daughters. He takes it into his garage as fondly as an Arab leading a prize mare into his tent. He woos it with Simoniz, Prestone, Ethyl and rich lubricants—and goes broke trading it in on something flashier an hour after he has made the last payment on the old one.

To a great mass of Americans, the automobile not only represents the keystone of happiness and the hallmark of success but is the only un-shifting goal in a baffling world. Millions who live unscarred through the jalopy or adolescent stage of life toil for decades to progress from Ford to Pontiac, from Pontiac to Buick, and cannot die happy unless guaranteed delivery to the grave in a Packard or Cadillac hearse.

By last week, this peculiar state of mind had not only sucked thousands of American oil wells dry, stripped the rubber groves of Malaya, produced the world's most inhuman industry and its most recalcitrant labor union, but had filled U.S. streets with so many automobiles that it was almost impossible to drive one. In some big cities, vast traffic jams never really got untangled from dawn to midnight; the bray of horns, the stink of exhaust fumes, and the crunch of crumpling metal eddied up from them as insistently as the vaporous roar of Niagara.

Psychiatrists, peering into these lurching, honking, metallic herds, discovered all sorts of aberrations in the clutch-happy humans behind the steering wheels.

Some fell prey to a great, dull hopelessness. In Manhattan's garment district, where it often takes 15 minutes to go a block through trucks, cabs and darting pushcarts, a taxi driver said: "We're beat. We got expressions just like people in Europe. It used to be you could get into a fight, but now even truck drivers take the attitude: 'If you wanna hit me, hit me.' They don't even get out to look at a fender."

But more often, people experienced a wild sense of frustration. Said Dr. J. I. Hilton, a Denver psychiatrist: "The driver behind a traffic crawler gets angry. His reason departs. He wants to ram through, to pass, to punish the object of his anger." Did the doctor feel the same way? "And how," he said, and shuddered. "I dream of wide highways and no automobiles—no automobiles at all."

But though postwar motorists were gradually becoming horn-blowing neurotics with tendencies toward drinking, cat-kicking and wife-beating, there were few who did not believe that the traffic evil would soon be corrected. This enormous delusion has been a part of U.S. folklore since the day of the linen duster, driving goggles and the high tonneau.

Congress and state legislatures had appropriated millions to build super highways on which speeders could kill themselves at higher speeds. The traffic light, the yellow line, the parking lot, the parking meter, the underground garage, the one-way street, the motorcycle cop and the traffic ticket had all blossomed amid the monoxide fumes—and traffic had gone right on getting thicker and noisier year by year.

Unabashed, last week men were still dreaming up panaceas. Only occasionally did they have a wild and honest ring, as when William J. Gottlieb, president of the Automobile Club of New York, jokingly suggested closing down all bridges and tunnels leading to Manhattan and declaring a state of siege. For the most part, man still pinned his hopes on the traffic tag and public works. New York's Police Commissioner Arthur Wallander thought things could be improved if taxicabs were shortened.

Man steadfastly refused to see that nothing could solve the traffic evil but the fast-multiplying automobile itself. The problem would end for good on the day of the last traffic jam—at that shrieking moment when every highway, street, road and lane in the nation was so clogged with cars that none could ever move again. Only then would man be free of the monster. But would he accept his freedom? It seemed doubtful. It would be too easy to lay boards across the tops of a billion sedans and start all over again with jet propulsion, foam rubber wheels and special lighters for the motorist's neon-trimmed opium pipe. ∎

Two Billion Clicks

BY ALEXANDER ELIOT

[*The writer took account of photography as a hobby, even a passion, and a very big business. But he went further, suggesting it was also a national folk art*]

November 2, 1953

THE GREAT SPHINX LAY in fleeting twilight. In the background loomed the Pyramid of Cheops, majestic monument to human striving for eternity. Over the entire scene hovered the breath of the silent desert, the hush of ages. Then a voice spoke.

"For God's sakes, Betsy, stop wiggling," said the voice. "Hold on a minute while I take another light reading . . . Now, smile."

Click.

"Fine. Now just one more, and this time smile as if you mean it."

Before the natural wonders of the world and facing its innumerable small mysteries, before Niagara Falls, Mount Rushmore and the Eiffel Tower, in Siamese temples, French cathedrals and New England general stores, at the bottom of the Grand Canyon and at the top of the Empire State Building, the U.S. amateur photographer pursues his hobby. His camera's combined clicks (he is taking nearly 2 billion pictures this year) would drown the loudest thunder, and the combined light from his flashbulbs (he is using 500 million) would make a major planet pale. The sun to him is chiefly a source of light that often calls for a yellow filter, and the moon merely an object which it is hard to photograph without a tripod;

447

he approaches the highest peaks through a telephoto lens, scans new horizons through his range finder—and if he ever came across the Blue Bird, he would whip out his color chart.

He spent $300 million this year on cameras and gadgets, in order to snap Haitian market women, Manhattan shoeshine boys, Indian fakirs, and (above all) Junior, aged three. Innumerable times he went through the sweet agony of fetching his prints from the corner drugstore or the mailbox,* and if his work did not come out well, he blamed the unknown vandals in the darkroom, the makers of the camera, the film, the subject, and sometimes even himself. He spoiled about 10% of his film, enough to make individual shots of the entire population of the North American continent, and took enough bad pictures to give ulcers to every museum director in the U.S.

Nevertheless, he was practicing an important art, the most typical art of the 20th century, and perhaps the only national folk art yet produced by the U.S.

Oliver Wendell Holmes, in 1859, called the camera "the mirror with a memory." Americans, more than any other people, have become used to seeing the world and themselves in that mirror—staring closely at birth and death, the torment of war and the pleasures of peace, the acts of history and nature, the faces of leaders and of nameless masses. Americans are wrapped in photographs; in newspapers, magazines, movies, billboards, the camera shows them the microbe as big as a face, a face as big as a city block, an entire city as plainly as their own street, their own street as fresh and exciting as a foreign shore. They are caught up (as one photographer put it) in a "fever of reality." Just when and how this fever produces true art has been debated almost since the first daguerreotype appeared more than a century ago.

The difference between *The Last Supper* and the greatest of modern photographs is that Da Vinci's painting is a product of the imagination. The picture came from inside Da Vinci, just as *Hamlet* came from inside Shakespeare. Photographs come from the outside; the camera artist sees something memorable in the world about him, and seizes it from the stream of time into a flat and shadowy sort of permanence. His picture is not so much created as caught. Photography can and often does produce great things without the intercession of genius (many of the finest World

---

* Unless he happened to be one of some 1,000,000 "hypo hounds" who do their own developing.

War II pictures were made without human guidance, by automatically triggered cameras).

Mass production of cameras and film got under way when a Rochester, N.Y. industrialist named George Eastman invented the Kodak. Eastman coined the name to be pronounceable in any language and "snap like a shutter in your face." He also invented the slogan: "You press the button, We do the rest." By 1896, twelve years before Henry Ford started mass-producing autos, Eastman was manufacturing cameras by the thousands, and film by the hundreds of miles. Price of the first Kodak: $25, with a $10 charge for developing and reloading. Twelve years later, Eastman produced a "Brownie" for $1. Photography became a major U.S. fad. "Detective cameras" were disguised as ladies' handbags, muffs, briefcases. President Grover Cleveland delightedly used his Kodak all day long on a fishing trip, was dismayed to learn in the evening that he should have wound the film.

The majority of good professional U.S. photographers work for the printed page. Journalism at its best has found room for both clarity and feeling. It accepts such disparate artists as the lucky amateur who happens to be on the scene of interesting events (*e.g.,* the story in the current LIFE on the student riots at Ames, Iowa was shot almost entirely by amateurs); as well as a professional such as W. Eugene Smith, a chronic agonizer ("I am constantly torn") who traveled 7,500 miles to find the right locale for his *Spanish Village* (1951), shot 500 negatives from which 17 were used.

The printed page is perhaps where photography is truly at home. It seems too restless for museum walls. Says Old Pro Irving Penn: "The photographer belongs to the age of the subway, high-speed cars and tall buildings. His picture is made to be seen amid the haste of contemporary life. Some real folk art appears in journalism or in advertising. A picture that sells a cake of soap can be art too."

By last count, there are 55,000 professional photographers in the U.S., and 35 million amateurs. Of these, about 28 million are "casual," 5,000,000 are "serious" and 2,000,000 are "expert." The casual amateur is the one who takes a picture of his baby from 20 feet away, forgets to wind his film, and cannot tell a thyratron from a réseau.* He is looked down on by experts, but it is he who provides the vast ground swell of enthusiasm for photography, and he has helped pile up the statistics of photography's tremendous growth.

* *Respectively, an electronic tube used in flash equipment, and a color screen used in some printing processes.*

The casual amateur does not worry about producing art, although experts are sure that, scattered in the nation's family albums, there are enough undiscovered masterpieces to fill the National Gallery. The more earnest amateur is organized in a network of 9,000 camera clubs across the U.S. He exhibits his work in museums, at international salons, and, between times, to a captive audience of visiting neighbors. Five major camera magazines with a combined monthly circulation of 806,000 are published for him, as well as 60 camera columns syndicated in hundreds of newspapers. He has made the picture book the hit of the decade in the publishing industry.

How good is the stuff he produces?

One distinguished photographer, Robert Capa, once moodily declared: "Most of the people in this country take pictures, and most of them take better ones than I do." Amateur pictures have made history, *e.g.*, the sinking of the *Vestris* (1928), the explosion of the *Hindenburg* (1937), the Hotel Winecoff fire (1946).

On the other hand, U.S. picture editors complain that amateurs by & large have nothing to say. Many of them seem so exhausted by achieving technical excellence that they have no imagination left to bring to their subjects. Amateurs, like professionals, have their troubles with reality. Part of the difficulty is that they often cannot see reality through all the gadgets which fill their world.

THE SERIOUS U.S. AMATEUR does not yield even to the U.S. driver in his passion for new models and new gimmicks. Foreign cameras with exotic names (Japan's Nikon, Germany's Plaubel Makina and Sweden's Hasselblad) attract him as Jaguars and Lancias attract the motorist ($10 million worth of foreign cameras was imported into the U.S. last year). He is particularly taken with such fairly new products as baby flashbulbs, easily portable strobe lights, and stereoscopic cameras. He pores over catalogues as a gourmet surveys a menu. How can he resist such dishes as the Globetrotter Gadget Bag ("Leather-covered sponge rubber bumper for carrying against body," $42.50); Steineck A-B-C Camera ("Straps to the wrist . . . brilliant finder for sighting at waist level," $150); Flexing Powelites ("Portable Sunshine . . . adjust your lights to any desired position," $10.95-$14.95)?

The camera devotee is apt to lapse into a language all his own. Sample:

Ash-can school (gloomy photography)
baby legs (short-legged tripod)
butterfly (shadow beneath a subject's nose)
darkroom widow (a hypo hound's wife)
Dinky-Inkie (small spotlight)
dynamite (strong developing fluid)
high hat (low camera support for "worm's eye" pictures)
lens louse (he muscles into someone else's picture)
soot & whitewash (a print that has no middle tones)
willy (a soft, fuzzy picture).

And so the amateur strides on, gadget bag bumping against his body, camera on his wrist, portable sunshine at his elbow, the little darkroom widow waiting at home. He lies on his belly in the snow of the Rockies, prowls the Fulton Fish Market at dawn, gets drenched in an inland lake, and hangs from ladders, chasing—with a hunter's relentless zeal—the fleeting moment, to trap it on the silver-coated strip of paper.

Sometimes close to the professional's work, more often miles away from it, he contributes to an art which rivals American painting in quality and interest. Photography does not have (and perhaps cannot have) the quality of slow revelation found in paintings. Its function is quick impact. Yet it sees many things the human eye does not see, in a way the human brain alone cannot retain. It is compiling a vast and brilliant album of the odd, the beautiful and terrible human family. Above all, it is an art form which, for the first time since the art of the Middle Ages, is not reserved to an elite of experts but in which any man with a box camera and an eye for life can shine. ■

Toward a Hidden God

BY JOHN T. ELSON

[
*This story, along with the stark words "Is God Dead?"
on the issue's cover—the first all-type cover in* TIME*'s
history—profoundly stirred readers, who responded with
a then record 3,430 letters to the magazine*
]

April 8, 1966

IS GOD DEAD? It is a question that tantalizes both believers, who perhaps secretly fear that he is, and atheists, who possibly suspect that the answer is no.

Is God dead? The three words represent a summons to reflect on the meaning of existence. No longer is the question the taunting jest of skeptics for whom unbelief is the test of wisdom and for whom Nietzsche is the prophet who gave the right answer a century ago. Even within Christianity, now confidently renewing itself in spirit as well as form, a small band of radical theologians has seriously argued that the churches must accept the fact of God's death, and get along without him. How does the issue differ from the age-old assertion that God does not and never did exist? Nietzsche's thesis was that striving, self-centered man had killed God, and that settled that. The current death-of-God group* believes

---

* *Principally Thomas J. J. Altizer of Emory University, William Hamilton of Colgate Rochester Divinity School, and Paul Van Buren of Temple University. Satirizing the basic premise of their new non-theology, the Methodist student magazine* motive *recently ran an obituary of God in newspaper style: "ATLANTA, Ga., Nov. 9—God, creator of the universe, principal deity of the world's Jews, ultimate reality of Christians, and most eminent of all divinities, died late yesterday during major surgery undertaken to correct a massive diminishing influence. Reaction from the world's great and from the man in the street was uniformly incredulous ... From Independence, Mo., former President Harry S. Truman, who received the news in his Kansas City barbershop, said, 'I'm always sorry to hear somebody is dead. It's a damn shame.'"*

that God is indeed absolutely dead, but proposes to carry on and write a theology without *theos,* without God. Less radical Christian thinkers hold that at the very least God in the image of man, God sitting in heaven, is dead, and—in the central task of religion today—they seek to imagine and define a God who can touch men's emotions and engage men's minds.

If nothing else, the Christian atheists are waking the churches to the brutal reality that the basic premise of faith—the existence of a personal God, who created the world and sustains it with his love—is now subject to profound attack. "What is in question is God himself," warns German Theologian Heinz Zahrnt, "and the churches are fighting a hard defensive battle, fighting for every inch." "The basic theological problem today," says one thinker who has helped define it, Langdon Gilkey of the University of Chicago Divinity School, "is the reality of God."

Some Christians, of course, have long held that Nietzsche was not just a voice crying in the wilderness. Even before Nietzsche, Sören Kierkegaard warned that "the day when Christianity and the world become friends, Christianity is done away with." During World War II, the anti-Nazi Lutheran martyr Dietrich Bonhoeffer wrote prophetically to a friend from his Berlin prison cell: "We are proceeding toward a time of no religion at all."

For many, that time has arrived. Nearly one of every two men on earth lives in thralldom to a brand of totalitarianism that condemns religion as the opiate of the masses—which has stirred some to heroic defense of their faith but has also driven millions from any sense of God's existence. Millions more, in Africa, Asia and South America, seem destined to be born without any expectation of being summoned to the knowledge of the one God.

Princeton Theologian Paul Ramsey observes that "ours is the first attempt in recorded history to build a culture upon the premise that God is dead." In the traditional citadels of Christendom, grey Gothic cathedrals stand empty, mute witnesses to a rejected faith. From the scrofulous hobos of Samuel Beckett to Antonioni's tired-blooded aristocrats, the anti-heroes of modern art endlessly suggest that waiting for God is futile, since life is without meaning.

For some, this thought is a source of existential anguish: the Jew who lost his faith in a providential God at Auschwitz, the Simone de Beauvoir who writes: "It was easier for me to think of a world without a creator than of a creator loaded with all the contradictions of the world." But for others, the God issue—including whether or not he is dead—has been put aside as irrelevant. "Personally, I've never been confronted with the question of God," says one such politely indifferent atheist, Dr. Claude Lévi-Strauss, professor of social anthropology at the Collège de France. "I find it's perfectly possible to spend my life knowing that we will never explain the universe." Jesuit Theologian John Courtney Murray points to another variety of unbelief: the atheism of distraction, people who are just "too damn busy" to worry about God at all.

Yet, along with the new atheism has come a new reformation. The open-window spirit of Pope John XXIII and Vatican II have revitalized the Roman Catholic Church. Less spectacularly but not less decisively, Protestantism has been stirred by a flurry of experimentation in liturgy, church structure, ministry. In this new Christianity, the watchword is witness: Protestant faith now means not intellectual acceptance of an ancient confession, but open commitment—perhaps best symbolized in the U.S. by the civil rights movement—to eradicating the evil and inequality that beset the world.

The institutional strength of the churches is nowhere more apparent than in the U.S., a country where public faith in God seems to be as secure as it was in medieval France. According to a survey by Pollster Lou Harris last year, 97% of the American people say they believe in God. Although clergymen agree that the postwar religious revival is over, a big majority of believers continue to display their faith by joining churches. In 1964, reports the National Council of Churches, denominational allegiance rose about 2%, compared with a population gain of less than 1.5%. More than 120 million Americans now claim a religious affiliation; and a recent Gallup survey indicated that 44% of them report that they attend church services weekly.

Plenty of clergymen, nonetheless, have qualms about the quality and character of contemporary belief. Lutheran Church Historian Martin Marty argues that all too many pews are filled on Sunday with practical atheists—disguised nonbelievers who behave during the rest of the week as if God did not exist. Jesuit Murray qualifies his conviction that the U.S. is basically a God-fearing nation by adding: "The great American proposition is 'religion is good for the kids, though I'm not religious myself.'" Pollster Harris bears him out: of the 97% who said they believed in God, only 27% declared themselves deeply religious.

Christianity and Judaism have always had more than their share of men of little faith or none. "The fool says in his heart, 'there is no God,'" wrote the Psalmist, implying that there were plenty of such fools to be found in ancient Judea. But it is not faintness of spirit that the churches worry about now: it is doubt and bewilderment assailing committed believers.

Particularly among the young, there is an acute feeling that the churches on Sunday are preaching the existence of a God who is nowhere visible in their daily lives. "I love God," cries one anguished teen-ager, "but I hate the church." Theologian Gilkey says that "belief is the area in the modern Protestant church where one finds blankness, silence, people not knowing what to say or merely repeating what their preachers say." Part of the Christian mood today, suggests Christian Atheist William Hamilton, is that faith has become not a possession but a hope.

In search of meaning, some believers have desperately turned to psychiatry, Zen or drugs. Thousands of others have quietly abandoned all but token allegiance to the churches, surrendering themselves to a life of "anonymous Christianity" dedicated to civil rights or the Peace Corps. Speaking for a generation of young Roman Catholics for whom the dogmas of the church have lost much of their power, Philosopher Michael Novak of Stanford writes: "I do not understand God, nor the way in which he works. If, occasionally, I raise my heart in prayer, it is to no God I can see, or hear, or feel. It is to a God in as cold and obscure a polar night as any nonbeliever has known."

Even clergymen seem to be uncertain. "I'm confused as to what God is," says no less a person than Francis B. Sayre, the Episcopal dean of Washington's National Cathedral, "but so is the rest of America." Says Marty's colleague at the Chicago Divinity School, the Rev. Nathan Scott, who is also rector of St. Paul's Episcopal Church in Hyde Park: "I look out at the faces of my people, and I'm not sure what meaning these words, gestures and rituals have for them."

CHRISTIANS ARE SOMETIMES inclined to look back nostalgically at the medieval world as the great age of faith. In his book, *The Death of God,* Gabriel Vahanian of Syracuse University suggests that actually it was the beginning of the divine demise. Christianity, by imposing its faith on the art, politics and even economics of a culture, unconsciously made God part of that culture—and when the world changed, belief in this God was undermined. Now "God has disappeared because of the image of him that the church used for many, many ages," says Dominican Theologian Edward Schillebeeckx.

455

At its worst, the image that the church gave of God was that of a wonder worker who explained the world's mysteries and seemed to have somewhat more interest in punishing men than rewarding them. Life was a vale of tears, said the church; men were urged to shun the pleasure of life if they would serve God, and to avoid any false step or suffer everlasting punishment in hell. It did little to establish the credibility of this "God" that medieval theologians categorized his qualities as confidently as they spelled out different kinds of sin, and that churchmen spoke about him as if they had just finished having lunch with him.

The rebellion against this God of faith is best summed up by the word secularization. In *The Secular City,* Harvey Cox of the Harvard Divinity School defines the term as "the loosing of the world from religious and quasi-religious understandings of itself, the dispelling of all closed world views, the breaking of all supernatural myths and sacred symbols." Slowly but surely, it dawned on men that they did not need God to explain, govern or justify certain areas of life.

The most important agent in the secularizing process was science. The Copernican revolution was a shattering blow to faith in a Bible that assumed the sun went round the earth and could be stopped in its tracks by divine intervention, as Joshua claimed. And while many of the pioneers of modern science—Newton and Descartes, for example—were devout men, they assiduously explained much of nature that previously seemed godly mysteries. Others saw no need for such reverential lip service. When asked by Napoleon why there was no mention of God in his new book about the stars, the French astronomer Laplace coolly answered: "I had no need of the hypothesis." Neither did Charles Darwin, in uncovering the evidence of evolution.

Socialization has immunized man against the wonder and mystery of existence, argues Oxford Theologian Ian Ramsey. "We are now sheltered from all the great crises of life. Birth is a kind of discontinuity between the prenatal and post-natal clinics, while death just takes somebody out of the community, possibly to the tune of prerecorded hymns at the funeral parlor." John Courtney Murray suggests that man has lost touch with the transcendent dimension in the transition from a rural agricultural society to an urbanized, technological world. The effect has been to veil man from what he calls natural symbols—the seasonal pattern of growth—that in the past reminded men of their own finiteness. The question is, says Murray, "whether or not a contemporary industrial civilization can construct symbols that can help us understand God."

What unites the various contemporary approaches to the problem of God is the conviction that the primary question has become not what God is, but how men are justified in using the word. There is no unanimity about how to solve this problem, although theologians seem to have four main options: stop talking about God for a while, stick to what the Bible says, formulate a new image and concept of God using contemporary thought categories, or simply point the way to areas of human experience that indicate the presence of something beyond man in life.

It is not only the Christian Atheists who think it pointless to talk about God. Some contemporary ministers and theologians, who have no doubts that he is alive, suggest that the church should stop using the word for a while, since it is freighted with unfortunate meanings. They take their clue from Bonhoeffer, whose prison-cell attempt to work out a "nonreligious interpretation of Biblical concepts" focused on Jesus as "the man for others." By talking almost exclusively about Christ, the argument goes, the church would be preaching a spiritual hero whom even nonbelievers can admire. Yale's Protestant Chaplain William Sloane Coffin reports that "a girl said to me the other day, 'I don't know whether I'll ever believe in God, but Jesus is my kind of guy.' "

In a sense, no Christian doctrine of God is possible without Jesus, since the suffering redeemer of Calvary is the only certain glimpse of the divine that churches have. But a Christ-centered theology that skirts the question of God raises more questions than it answers. Does it not run the risk of slipping into a variety of ethical humanism? And if Jesus is not clearly related in some way to God, why is he a better focus of faith than Buddha, Socrates or even Albert Camus?

The century's greatest Protestant theologian, Karl Barth of Switzerland, has consistently warned his fellow churchmen that God is a "wholly other" being, whom man can only know by God's self-revelation in the person of Christ, as witnessed by Scripture. Any search for God that starts with human experience, Barth warns, is a vain quest that will discover only an idol, not the true God at all.

The word of God, naked and unadorned, may be fine for the true believer, but some theologians argue that Biblical terminology has ceased to be part of the world's vocabulary, and is in danger of becoming a special jargon as incomprehensible to some as the equations of physicists. To bridge this communications gap, they have tried to reinterpret the concept of God into contemporary philosophical terms. Union Seminary's John Macquarrie, for example, proposes a description of God based on Martin Heidegger's existential philosophy, which is primarily concerned with explaining the nature of "being" as such. To Heidegger, "being" is an incomparable, transcendental mystery, something that confers existence on individual, particular beings. Macquarrie calls Heidegger's mystery "Holy Being," since it represents what Christians have traditionally considered God.

Perhaps the most enthusiastic propagandists for a new image of God are the Tweedledum and Tweedledee of Anglican theology, Bishop Robinson of Woolwich, England, and Bishop James A. Pike of California. Both endorse the late Paul Tillich's concept of God as "the ground of being." Pike, who thinks that the church should have fewer but better dogmas, also suggests that the church should abandon the Trinity, on the ground that it really seems to be preaching three Gods instead of one. Christianity, in his view, should stop attributing specific actions to persons of the Trinity—creation to the Father, redemption to the Son, inspiration to the Holy Spirit—and just say that they were all the work of God.

The contemporary world appears so biased against metaphysics that any attempt to find philosophical equivalents for God may well be doomed to failure. "God," says Jerry Handspicker of the World Council of Churches, "has suffered from too many attempts to define the indefinable." Leaving unanswered the question of what to say God is, some theologians are instead concentrating on an exploration of the ultimate and unconditional in modern life. Their basic point is that while modern men have rejected God as a solution to life, they cannot evade a questioning anxiety about its meaning. The apparent eclipse of God is merely a sign that the world is experiencing what Jesuit Theologian Karl Rahner calls "the anonymous presence" of God, whose word comes to man not on tablets of stone but in the inner murmurings of the heart.

Following Tillich, Langdon Gilkey argues that the area of life dealing with the ultimate and with mystery points the way toward God. "When we ask, 'Why am I?' 'What should I become and be?', 'What is the meaning of my life?'—then we are exploring or encountering that region of experience where language about the ultimate becomes useful and intelligible." To Ian Ramsey of Oxford, this area of ultimate concern offers what he calls "discernment situations"—events that can be the occasion for insight, for awareness of something beyond man. It is during these insight situations, Ramsey says, that the universe "comes alive, declares some transcendence, and to which we respond by ourselves coming alive and finding another dimension."

A discernment situation could be falling in love, suffering cancer, reading a book. But it need not be a private experience. The Rev. Stephen Rose, editor of Chicago's *Renewal* magazine, argues that "whenever the prophetic word breaks in, either as judgment or as premise, that's when the historical God acts." One such situation, he suggests, was the 1965 riots in Watts, a black neighborhood of Los Angeles—an outburst of violence that served to chide men for lack of brotherhood. Harvard's Harvey Cox sees God's hand in history, but in a different way. The one area where empirical man is open to transcendence, he argues, is the future: man can be defined as the creature who hopes, who has taken responsibility for the world. Cox proposes a new theology based on the premise that God is the source and ground of this hope—a God "ahead" of man in history rather than "out there" in space.

For those with a faith that can move mountains, all this tentative groping for God in human experience may seem unnecessary. The man-centered approach to God runs against Barth's warning that a "God" found in human depths may be an imagined idol—or a neurosis that could be dissolved on the psychiatrist's couch. Rudolf Bultmann answers that these human situations of anxiety and discernment represent "transformations of God," and are the only way that secular man is likely to experience any sense of the eternal and unconditional.

This theological approach is not without scriptural roots. A God who writes straight with crooked lines in human history is highly Biblical in outlook. The quest for God in the depths of experience echoes Jesus' words to his Apostles, "The kingdom of God is within you." And the idea of God's anonymous presence suggests Matthew's account of the Last Judgment, when Jesus will separate the nations, telling those on his right: "I was hungry and you gave me food, I was thirsty and you gave me drink." But when? they ask. "And the King will answer them, 'Truly, I say to you, as you did it to one of the least of these my brethren, you did it to me.' "

THE THEOLOGICAL CONVICTION that God is acting anonymously in human history is not likely to turn many atheists toward him. Secular man may be anxious, but he is also convinced that anxiety can be explained away. As always, faith is something of an irrational leap in the dark, a gift of God. And unlike in earlier centuries, there is no way today for churches to threaten or compel men to face that leap; after Dachau's mass sadism and Hiroshima's instant death, there are all too many real possibilities of hell on earth.

The new approaches to the problem of God, then, will have their greatest impact within the church community. They may help shore up the faith of many believers and, possibly, weaken that of others. They may also lead to a more realistic, and somewhat more abstract, conception of God. "God will be seen as the order in which life takes on meaning, as being, as the source of creativity," suggests Langdon Gilkey. "The old-fashioned personal God who merely judges, gives grace and speaks to us in prayer, is, after all, a pretty feeble God." Gilkey does not deny the omnipotence of God, nor undervalue personal language about God as a means of prayer and worship. But he argues that Christianity must go on escaping from its too-strictly anthropomorphic past, and still needs to learn that talk of God is largely symbolic.

The new quest for God, which respects no church boundaries, should also contribute to ecumenism. "These changes make many of the old disputes seem pointless, or at least secondary," says Jesuit Theologian Avery Dulles. The churches, moreover, will also have to accept the empiricism of the modern outlook and become more secular themselves, recognizing that God is not the property of the church, and is acting in history as he wills, in encounters for which man is forever unprepared.

To some, this suggests that the church might well need to take a position of reverent agnosticism regarding some doctrines that it had previously proclaimed with excessive conviction. Many of the theologians attempting to work out a new doctrine of God admit that they are uncertain as to the impact of their ultimate findings on other Christian truths; but they agree that such God-related issues as personal salvation in the afterlife and immortality will need considerable re-study. But Christian history allows the possibility of development in doctrine, and even an admission of ignorance in the face of the divine mystery is part of tradition. St. Thomas Aquinas declared that "we cannot know what God is, but rather what he is not."

Gabriel Vahanian suggests that there may well be no true faith without a measure of doubt, and thus contemporary Christian worry about God could be a necessary and healthy antidote to centuries in which faith was too confident and sure. Perhaps today, the Christian can do no better than echo the prayer of the worried father who pleaded with Christ to heal his spirit-possessed son: "I believe; help my unbelief." ∎

Myth of the Motorcycle Hog

BY ROBERT HUGHES

[
TIME's *erudite art critic revealed another side of his*
personality in this paean to the pleasure and freedom—
and, of course, the thrill—of roaring along on a chopper
]

February 8, 1971

HAS ANY MEANS OF transport ever suffered a worse drubbing than the motorcycle? In the 17 years since Stanley Kramer put Marlon Brando astride a Triumph in *The Wild One,* big bikes and those who ride them have been made into apocalyptic images of aggression and revolt—Greasy Rider on an iron horse with 74-cu.-in. lungs and ape-hanger bars, booming down the freeway to rape John Doe's daughter behind the white clapboard bank: swastikas, burnt rubber, crab lice and filthy denim. It has long been obvious that the bike was heir to the cowboy's horse in movies; but if Trigger had been loaded with the sado-erotic symbolism that now, after dozens of exploitation flicks about Hell's Angels, clings to any Harley chopper, the poor nag could not have moved for groupies. As an object to provoke linked reactions of desire and outrage, the motorcycle has few equals—provided it is big enough.

When *Easy Rider* was released, it looked for a time as though public attitudes might soften. A lot of people were on the side of Captain America and his fringed partner Billy, shotgunned off their glittering, raked choppers on a Southern back road. But for every cinemagoer who vicariously rode with Peter Fonda and Dennis Hopper in that movie, there were probably ten who went with their redneck killers in the pickup truck. The chorus from press and TV remains pretty well unchanged, resembling the bleat of Orwell's sheep in *Animal Farm:* "Four wheels good, two wheels bad!" The image of the biker as delinquent will take a long time to eradicate. "You meet the nicest people on a Honda," proclaims the Japanese firm that has cornered nearly 50% of the bike market in the U.S.; but the general belief is that you still meet the nastiest ones on a chopper.

To the public, the names of the outlaw or semi-outlaw motorcycle clubs is a litany of imps in the pit, from the Animals and Axemen, through the Equalizers and Exterminators, the Marauders and Mongols, the Raiders and Road Vultures, to the Warlocks and Wheels of Soul. The unsavory names with which these gangs have christened themselves are apt to make the public forget that their collective membership is probably no more than 3,000, the merest fraction of the 3,000,000 people who regularly ride bikes in the U.S. In fact, these "outlaws" on the road are infinitely less of a threat than the driver of a station wagon with two martinis under his seat belt.

The myth goes roaring on. Business, though, may kill it, for bikes are big business today. At the end of World War II there were fewer than 200,000 registered motorcycles in the U.S. Today there are nearly 2,500,000, most of them imports from Japan, Germany and Britain. The majority are small, almost civilized creatures, below 500 cc. in engine capacity. But the popularity of the big snorting monsters, which can go from a standstill to 60 m.p.h. in less than six seconds flat and cruise comfortably on freeways at 90 m.p.h., has also ascended. It has its perversities.

To the four-wheeled culture, there is something inexplicable about the very idea of owning such a bike. A big machine is expensive: a new Honda Four costs nearly as much as a Volkswagen; a big Harley, almost $1,000 more. Choppers, the Fabergé Easter eggs of the bike world, are even worse. When all the stripping, chroming, raking, molding, metal flaking and polishing are done, a chopper, righteously gleaming from fishtail exhaust to brakeless front wheel, may have cost its owner $5,000 in materials and labor. Insurance is heavy, since to many companies the fact of owning a bike is prima-facie evidence of irresponsibility. The risk of theft is high, especially in cities, where case-hardened steel chains and medieval-looking padlocks must tether the mount if one so much as stops for a hamburger.

Highway cops dislike bikers and are apt to assume that a Hell's Angel lurks slavering and Benzedrined inside every rider; they take a sour glee in plastering the riders with tickets for the slightest infraction. Worst of all, there are accidents. Big bikes are superb manifestations of engineering skill, but they are utterly vulnerable. There is no body shell, no padding, no safety belt—nothing to cushion the body that wrenched forward over the bars at 50 m.p.h. may be no more than a leaking bag of tissue and bone fragments when the concrete has finished with it. On any long trip, moreover, the biker stands to encounter at least one car-swaddled Milquetoast with blood in his eye whose hope is to run him off the road. Highways are the bullrings of American insecurity and every biker knows it, or ends up in a hospital.

So why ride? There are, of course, impeccable reasons. Bikes are easy to park, they save gas, they pollute the air less than cars. But the impeccable reasons are not always the real ones. Buying a bike, particularly a big motorcycle, is buying an experience that no other form of transport can give: a unique high that like pot has spun its own culture around itself. The name of the game is freedom. A biker, being more mobile, is on a different footing from a driver. The nightmares of traffic afflict him less. Instead of being trapped in a cumbersome padded box, frozen into the glacier of unmoving steel and winking red taillights on the ribboned parking lots that expressways have become, he can slide through the spaces, take off, go . . . And the kick is prodigious.

Instead of insulating its owner like a car, a bike extends him into the environment, all senses alert. Everything that happens on the road and in the air, the inflections of road surface, the shuttle and weave of traffic, the opening and squeezing of space, the cold and heat, the stinks, perfumes, noises and silences—the biker flows into it in a state of heightened consciousness that no driver, with his windows and heater and radio, will ever know. It is this total experience, not the fustian clichés about symbolic penises and deficient father figures that every amateur Freudian trots out when motorcycles are mentioned, that creates bikers. Riding across San Francisco's Golden Gate Bridge on his motorcycle, the biker is sensually receptive every yard of the way: to the bridge drumming under the tires, to the immense Pacific wind, to the cliff of icy blue space below.

"Se tu sarai solo," Leonardo da Vinci remarked five hundred years ago, *"tu sarai tutto tuo"* (If you are alone, you are your own man). Biking, like gliding, is one of the most delightful expressions of this fact. There is nothing secondhand or vicarious about the sense of freedom, which means possessing one's own and unique experiences, that a big bike well ridden confers. Antisocial? Indeed, yes. And being so, a means to sanity. The motorcycle is a charm against the Group Man. ∎

In Pennsylvania:
A Time on the River

BY FRANK TRIPPETT

[*The high school reunion is a rite so familiar as to be a cliché, but the writer turned such an acute yet tender gaze on this one that it yielded a rare truth and poignance*]

July 24, 1978

SOME OF THE GIRLS of the May Court were on board, vestiges of beauty lurking after the erosions of the decades. The boy most likely to succeed was in the crowd, a preacher now. Both of the class's sets of twins were on hand. One of its two black members was present. The other had been glimpsed around town years ago, but where he was now was a mystery here in Kittanning, Pa., a hilly little county seat on the Allegheny River some 45 miles northeast of Pittsburgh, homelike if not home to the members of the Kittanning High School class of 1948.

In all, 119 of the 221 classmates converged on the diesel-powered stern-wheeler *Liberty Belle* for the cruise that was to cap their 30th reunion, a four-hour voyage up the river into the darkness and back, a roast beef dinner and dancing to a three-piece band. It was a starry night of boozy merriment, insistent camaraderie, an interlude of urgent small talk and the irresistible pursuit of ghosts.

There, up from a Washington suburb sporting an ice cream suit fit for Cab Calloway and a wife who made it known she had met Liz Taylor, was the kid who had been the class's best dancer. There, gowned in lavender and telling of an ended marriage while speaking of her new companion as "my fiancé, my roommate, whatever," was the girl who had been head majorette. There, with the conspicuous tan and the bleached hair, baring a leg in a comic chorus-line kick—who could that be?

By now, the 60 or so classmates who had gone to the earlier parties were no longer puzzled. But some 60 more had waited for the climactic boat ride to join in, so the inevitable protests of recognition—"Oh, I remember you!"—still rang out as the passengers mingled among tables and chairs arrayed on the *Liberty Belle's* three decks.

Such cries were first heard five days before, when about 30 gathered in the nearby mountains to drink, sing and roast wienies around a bonfire that set off the most extended reunion ever staged by the class. It was also the most rained-on reunion. Drizzly weather beset the wienie roast and transformed it, and the parties of the next two nights, from al fresco to al canopy (a stately funeral tent was provided by Class Member Jack Kennedy, who had stuck around Kittanning and fulfilled a lifelong dream of becoming an undertaker). There was no sign that the rain damaged the spirits of the celebrators, not even those who had forsaken sunny climes to attend.

In from Fresno, Calif., for his first reunion since graduation, Procter and Gamble Executive Jack Simpson claimed convincingly that he was delighted to be there, jostling hip to hip with dozens of others under a dripping canvas before the bonfire finally got lit. "It's marvelous," said he, and went on to muse on time's familiar way of shrinking one's childhood world: "When I was a kid, that Allegheny Bridge was the Golden Gate. Today I realized I could clear it with a 9-iron."

Old Kittanning (founded 1796) had shrunk not only in mind but in reality, its population down from 7,700 in 1948 to 6,490 today, thanks in part to the migration of people like the class of '48. Fully 100 members wound up living more than 50 miles distant from Kittanning, 56 of those out of state. Other things had gone from town too: Paul's, the soda fountain that had been a favorite hangout; the trains on which some kids had commuted from nearby communities to consolidated Kittanning High School. Still, progress had not made a detour. One brand-new hangout, Winky's, a burger joint of gleaming glass, metal and plastic, had just gone up on a site made available by the demolition of a grand old mansion designed by Stanford White.

The town's civic travails hardly preoccupied these classmates. Indeed, it was rare to hear them allude to even the epochal events—the Korean

War, television, the black revolution, the assassinations, the sexual revolution, the Viet Nam War, inflation, Watergate—that shook and transformed the world into which they graduated in 1948. Mostly, along with beers and highballs and a bit of close-harmony singing, they indulged in chitchat and banter about those things that any sane person of 48 (as they all were, give or take a year) knows to be the important matters of life: marriage, children, divorce, death, friends, health.

It was easy, then, by the clear day of the cruise, for even an outsider who had been hanging around to glimpse some of the private realities that lurked beneath the surface of things. An outsider could learn that there, joyfully swaying to a modish beat on the main deck's dance floor, was a woman whose husband had killed himself not many years ago. And that the bouncy little man assiduously declaring affection for one and all—"I love ya! I love ya!"—had been the shy little-boy-lost-in-the-corner all his high school days. And that the burly farmer looking on would soon marry off his last daughter and would probably never quite cease grieving over the death of his only son, at twelve, in a tractor accident. And that the bleached blonde doing the comic kick was the wittiest girl in the class and had wound up in Florida unmarried and happened to be the twin of that sedate matron who had married a classmate and raised five boys. And that the perky, petite woman with the Myrna Loy face, the one doing the jitterbug, had raised two kids alone on $50 a week and, though cheerfully recalling the name of the man who had sung at her wedding, preferred not to mention the name of the chap she had married and divorced two decades ago.

And there, seemingly all over the place, table-hopping and back-slapping, was the man who had sung at that wedding—Johnny Lindeman, almost bald, clearly the spark of the whole reunion, thoughtful, everybody's friend. Decked out in bright red trousers fit for an interlocutor. Moved back home a few years ago after working as an organizer of high-minded causes down in Washington. Moved back after a divorce that distanced him from his four children. Running the family florist business with a brother now that his father had been immobilized by illness. Looking happy and even jubilant tonight. Good singer, Johnny, best in class. Not a bad actor. Played George Gibbs in the senior production of *Our Town* and still thinks of Grover's Corners when, from soaring Pine Hill across the river, he looks down on the tilted strew of toy buildings that are Kittanning.

The girl who played Emily Webb had married a classmate and settled in town and, though she wanted to come, stayed away from the reunion because she was sorrowing over the recent death of an infant grandchild. Still, it was easy to imagine that the memory of her Emily was hovering about, reminding them all again, as she does in the last act: "It goes so fast. We don't have time to look at one another."

Surely (since what else is a reunion for?) these aging children, most of them, were looking to make up for lost time as their vessel labored up the river into darkness only to come home to Kittanning in darkness still. ■

Football's Supercoach

BY B.J. PHILLIPS

[*This colorful portrait showed why a college coach, if he was as tough, driven and dedicated as "Bear" Bryant, stood as an icon on the American landscape*]

September 29, 1980

HE IS A MAN of dimension, there can be no disputing that, and over the years his friends and foes have praised or damned him in outsize terms. To the rabid, almost reverential followers of his University of Alabama football teams, Paul William ("Bear") Bryant is a nearly mythic figure, a man who embodies the traditional American values: dedication, hard work, honesty and, above all, success. To the frustrated fans of the legions of teams he has defeated, he is a relentlessly slippery recruiter, a ruthless win-at-all-costs tyrant. To some, he is the demigod of the autumn religion, the finest coach of a uniquely American game. To others, he is the proselytizer of a brutal sport, a symbol of a national fixation on violence.

The exaggerations miss the point. For all his drill-field discipline, Bryant is not John Wayne with a whistle, a link to vague frontier tenets presumed lost. The most closely scrutinized coach in America, he could not get away with being a bagman for postadolescent jocks even if he tried. Nor is he a helmet-bashing maniac who views Saturday afternoons in the stadium as the moral equivalent of D-day. He is, at times, treated a bit too royally by those who vest football with more importance than it deserves. But he is also scorned too savagely by those who do not understand that

The Social Fabric

the game has a rightful place in the life of small towns, schools, city back lots, the nation.

Today Bear Bryant unquestionably is the dominant figure in college football, but he began to make his mark in another age—the late 1940s, when Harry Truman was still in the White House. Bryant is that rare man who has changed with his times, the only one of his generation to coach as successfully in an era when football players use hair dryers in the locker room as he did when they wore crew cuts. "Thirty-five years makes a long time," he reflects. "A lot of good, a lot of bad, some things you did that were smart, some things you did that were plain stupid. Thirty-five years makes a lot of changes."

Just one thing has never changed: Bear Bryant has always won football games. In 35 years as a head coach, Bryant has won 298 games, lost 77 and tied 16. Before the 1980 season reaches its midpoint, he will become only the third coach to win 300 games. Late next year he should pass Pop Warner (313) and Amos Alonzo Stagg (314) to become the coach with the most victories in college-football history. His teams have won 23 games in a row, currently the longest winning streak in big-time college football. Bryant has taken teams to bowl games 26 times (a record); last season's Sugar Bowl appearance was the 21st consecutive postseason trip for Alabama's Crimson Tide (also a record). Under his stewardship, the polls gave Alabama the national championship six times. Bryant's teams have won 14 Southeastern Conference titles and a Southwest Conference crown.

Bryant's ability to shape successful teams from the constantly changing lineups has made him a one-man institution of higher learning for football: 42 of his former assistants and players have become head football coaches in the colleges and pros, among them the Houston Oilers' Bum Phillips, L.S.U.'s Paul Dietzel, the Washington Redskins' Jack Pardee, the New York Giants' Ray Perkins and the University of Pittsburgh's Jackie Sherrill. More than 60 former Bryant players have gone on to the pros (including five last year alone), among them former Jets Quarterback Joe Namath, Houston Quarterback Kenny Stabler, former Dallas Linebacker Lee Roy Jordan, New England Patriot Star Offensive Guard John Hannah and current Jets Quarterback Richard Todd.

At 67, Bear Bryant is a massive presence, a powerful man, 6 ft. 3½ in., 205 lbs., with sharp eyes and a sharper wit carefully sheathed by a down-home demeanor. His face is seamed and sunbaked from a lifetime on practice-field towers and stadium sidelines. His voice, a rich Southern drawl, is rarely raised; there is seldom any need.

Alabama's players may not feel close to Bryant ("I don't have time to coach individuals any more. I organize; my assistants coach"), but they are devoted to him. Remarks Defensive End E.J. Junior: "Coach Bryant is a father figure to the team. There's never much rah-rah talk, just plain common sense. In that respect, he's one of the best philosophers of life I've ever met."

The eagerness of impressionable youth? Bryant can dominate grown men the same way. Houston Oilers Coach Phillips recalls staff meetings during his days as one of the Bear's assistants at Texas A & M: "There'd be 16 of us, counting everybody on the staff, and we'd all be talking. When he'd walk in, everyone would just stop right in the middle of a sentence. He'd sit down, take out a pack of cigarettes, beat one on his thumb to pack it down, light it and smoke the whole damn thing without saying a word. He just had that magic about him: if he was going to say anything, you were going to be sure you didn't miss it."

At times, it seems that Bryant can have the same effect on the whole state of Alabama. Bill Baxley, Alabama's former attorney general, calls Bryant "the No. 1 asset of the state." He is certainly treated as though he were: two uniformed state policemen act as bodyguards and chauffeurs on game days. Bryant has achieved a pop-hero status. His face appears on T shirts and bumper stickers, and there are even postcards showing him strolling on water. The inscription: I BELIEVE. Small wonder that former Governor George Wallace says: "He never got into politics. But if he ever did, he could have had anything he wanted in this state."

Bryant's long career began in Moro Bottom, Ark. His father was a hardscrabble farmer struggling to eke out a living in the Depression South. When the elder Bryant was disabled by high blood pressure, his wife Ida kept the family going by selling vegetables from a horse-drawn wagon. Young Paul perched beside her and felt the sting of disparagement from the "city kids" of nearby Fordyce (pop. 3,206). He first won social acceptance as a fiercely combative football player for the state-champ Fordyce Redbugs, and football has since made him the guest of Presidents. "I had to try to get good at football," he says, "because I didn't have anything to go back to, anything else to count on."

When he was 17, University of Alabama Assistant Coach Hank Crisp came to call in a Model A Ford. He offered a way out of the fields with a scholarship. Paul, who was already known as Bear because at age twelve he had lost a wrestling match with a carnival bear, left for college in 1931.

At Alabama, Bryant lived above the gymnasium, going out for a date only when, in those days of relaxed rules, the line coach peeled a few dollars off a roll of bills and rewarded his charges, ostensibly for sweeping the basketball court. Bear played end on the best team the college had ever fielded: in 1934 Alabama beat Stanford in the Rose Bowl, 29-13.

In the fall of his senior year, Bryant met Mary Harmon Black, a campus belle and "the prettiest girl I ever saw." They were married, and after graduation Bryant took a job as an assistant coach at Alabama. He stayed for four years, then took an assistant's post at Vanderbilt. It was the first of many moves over the next two decades as he followed the apprentice coach's itinerant trail. "We've moved 27 times in our married life," says Mary Harmon Bryant. "I used to say I'd put off spring cleaning until I heard whether Paul was going to change jobs. It was easier to move than it was to clean."

Bryant was returning from an interview for the job of head coach at the University of Arkansas when he heard the announcement of the attack on Pearl Harbor. He immediately joined the Navy. After a tour in North Africa as a recreation officer, Bryant spent the war coaching football at a North Carolina preflight school. He left the service five days before the start of the 1945 football season and, at the age of 32, reported as head coach at the University of Maryland, a school with dreams of football grandeur. To be certain that he did not get off to a bad start as a head coach, he took along some of his bull-necked Navy veterans. The record of Bryant's debut: six wins, two losses and one tie. He stayed at Maryland just one season, quitting when the college president, Harry C. ("Curly") Byrd, a former Maryland coach himself, reinstated a suspended player over the Bear's objections.

FOR THE NEXT EIGHT years Bryant was head coach at the University of Kentucky. In 1950 the school won its only outright championship of the Southeastern Conference. He was demanding. All-America Quarterback Babe Parilli, who later played with the Boston Patriots, recalls preseason training camps that began at 5:30 a.m. with orange juice and proceeded to head-on tackling drills at 6 a.m. He also remembers Bryant's coming into his hospital room the day after Parilli underwent surgery and throwing a stack of new plays on the bed. The plays were designed to let Parilli stand back in the shotgun offense and throw the ball after getting a long snap from center. "Learn them," the coach told his quarterback.

Says Parilli: "I thought he was crazy. I could barely move. But I studied the plays. We were playing Louisiana State the next week, and on the day of the game, he said, 'Get into that shotgun and start throwing until I tell you to stop.' I did what I was told, and on the first 16 plays we threw 15 times. I never got touched. We won 14 to 0."

In 1954 the restless Bryant shifted to Texas A & M, at College Station. It was there that his reputation as a football tyrant became truly fixed, largely because of the infamous training camp he conducted at nearby Junction during his first year. Bryant left College Station with 96 football players on scholarship; ten days later, only 27 came back from the crossroads. The rest had quit. Under a merciless Texas sun, they had been drilled hour after hour by a coach who seemed mad. Jack Pardee remembers that the temperature was 110° when the workouts began. "It was an effort to survive. Each player could tell his own story, but mine was simply to make it to the next practice."

A quarter-century later, Bryant still wonders about Junction. "I don't know if what I did was good or bad," he says. "I never will know. It was just the only thing I could have done—at that time, knowing what I knew then. I wouldn't do it now because I know more than I knew then, more about resting players, letting them drink water, more about other ways to lead them. They had to put up with my stupidity. I believe if I'd have been one of those players, I'd have quit too."

The 1954 team, weakened by its trial by fire, was Bryant's only loser, 1-9. Two years later, Texas A & M won the Southwest Conference title. Still Bryant drove his players fiercely. John David Crow, a halfback who won the Heisman Trophy in 1957, recalls going into the dressing room after practice, pulling off his sweat-soaked uniform and, too tired to stand, sitting on a chair in the shower. As he relaxed, Bryant called the team back on the field for another practice. Baking in the sun, Crow fainted and was out for three hours. The first sight he saw upon regaining consciousness was Bryant, hovering anxiously over him.

Bryant had other things to learn about big-time football. During his second year at Texas A & M, the school was put on probation for recruiting violations. Bear now acknowledges that the violations occurred, insisting that they were standard at the time: the usual sorry practices of wealthy alumni giving money, cars, jobs. "All the other schools were doing it, so we did it too," he explains. "I was real bitter about it at the time—I cried all the way home from the meeting where they put us on probation—but looking back, it may have been the best thing that ever happened to me. After that, I always lived by the letter of the law, never won a game anything but the honest way."

In 1958 Bryant returned to his alma mater, which had floundered through four dismal seasons. Before the Auburn game that year, he told the Touchdown Club in Birmingham: "Gentlemen, I wouldn't bet anything but Coca-Cola on tomorrow's game. Next year you can bet a fifth of whisky. And the year after that you can mortgage the damn house." Bryant was right. A bettor would have lost a Coke that first year (Auburn won, 14-8), but the mortgages were safe: Alabama took the next four games in the series without allowing a point.

Bryant's early years at Alabama were stormy. This time the charge was that Bryant coached his teams to play too rough. He taught gang tackling; "pursuit" is the euphemism, and mayhem is occasionally the result, when swarms of tacklers bang into the ball carrier. In 1962 the *Saturday Evening Post* printed a story accusing him of teaching "dirty football," and later ran an article claiming that he and Wally Butts, the University of Georgia athletic director, had conspired to fix a game. Bryant sued in both cases and won settlements out of court totaling $300,000.

Bryant has fed his football machine with generation after generation of blue-chip athletes. "You've got to have chickens," says Bryant, "before you can make chicken salad." He now leaves most of the barnstorming to ten assistants, but in his time he was a courtly and soft-spoken charmer who persuaded parents in order to win over their strong and swift sons.* Says Bryant: "Recruiting is the one thing I hate. I won't do it unless my coaches tell me I've just got to. The whole process is kind of undignified for me and the young man." Not necessarily. Says one former recruit: "Just knowing that that man came into my home to talk to my parents made me an idol around high school."

The man who had once driven players to unconsciousness under the Texas sun hired an expert in tropical medicine to teach him about fluid intake, electrolyte balance and heat-humidity ratios. As the scandals recede in memory, his skills as coach have been increasingly appreciated.

As for his big, grizzly, anything-to-win image, that came into question when he suspended Joe Namath, his most famous player, for breaking

---

* Under N.C.A.A. rules, Division 1A (big college) teams may grant a total of 95 football scholarships. No more than 30 scholarships may be given to an incoming freshman class. Each team is limited to ten assistant coaches.

training rules in 1963. Neither man will reveal the details of the infraction, but whatever its cause, the coach benched his star quarterback before the final regular-season game against Miami and extended the banishment to include the Sugar Bowl. "I don't guess anybody would think much of what Joe did nowadays, including myself," Bryant says. "But he was supposed to be a leader, so he had to live by the rules. It was the hardest thing I ever had to do, and it was to the greatest athlete I ever coached."

Bryant has earned the loyalty of young men as varied as the burly veterans on the G.I. Bill, the obedient crew-cut disciples of the Eisenhower era, the rebellious students of the '60s and the cool careerists of the present generation. Says he: "You can't treat them all equal, but you can treat them fairly. That goes not just for how they're different as individuals, but how they're different from other generations. One player you have to shake up and get mad, but you'll break another player if you treat him like that, so you try to gentle him along, encourage him. The '60s were a rebellious period, and you've got to realize that a player is going to feel that too. Even the places you find good ballplayers can change. I used to think I wanted strong old country boys like I used to be. Now I think the best place to find players is around a Y.M.C.A., where they're playing lots of sports, getting smart and quick, not just strong and dumb."

IN FOOTBALL, WHERE THE top coaches freely trade ideas and theories, a genius is a man who taps the common pool of knowledge and then prepares the best for a game. By that definition, Bryant is a genius. Says Paul Dietzel, athletic director at Louisiana State: "One of his favorite expressions is that 'it's the itty-bitty, teeny-tiny things that beat you.' He'll rehearse problems that might arise in a game over and over again."

They tell the story in the S.E.C. that Bryant has a game plan for a hurricane in the first quarter, a flood in the second, a drought in the third and an eagle swooping down to block a field goal in the fourth. Reminded of the tale, Bryant chuckles, but does not deny it. "Well," the voice rumbles, "we do try to be prepared."

Bryant has worn down his critics—or outcoached and outlived them. He now seems somehow above the fray, a man who has left his past behind. And he has mellowed. His practices are no tougher and his teams tackle no more savagely than those of other top football schools, and the day is long past when he would yank a star quarterback out of a hospital bed and send him out to play.

Bryant became and stayed a winner because his players knew he cared deeply about them and their welfare. Bryant's concern goes deep and lasts long after the athletes have graduated. Against the advice of his business advisers, he has co-signed loans for his former team members and quietly helped them in their careers. Says Royal: "The greatest testimony that any coach can have is those guys who have long since been out of the program. You go ask them how they feel about Bryant, and it's great right down the line. Charisma alone doesn't do it. He's gone out of his way to do favors for these guys for them to be as devoted to him as they are."

As part of his motivation program, Bryant has his players write down a set of goals, then tries to see that they accomplish them. No detail is over-looked. Running Back Major Ogilvie remembers the first things Bryant told his group of freshmen: "Be courteous to everyone, write home to your parents, and keep your rooms neat." Says Ogilvie: "He's so involved in your future. He teaches us as people, not as football players. He relates football to life rather than life to football."

What fascinates Bryant about winning football games is not diagram-ming plays or deciding when to kick a field goal or gamble for a first down, but the challenge of melding 95 very young men into a whole, making each man's vision of himself interdependent with those of his teammates. For all its excesses—and football has more than its share of faults—the sport can be, at its best, a social compact of a high order. Creating this bond is what Bear Bryant excels at, and for this he draws on insights and instincts he has developed over 35 years.

The goal is becoming the best at something, even if it is a game. "I'm just a plow-hand from Arkansas," Bryant insists, "but I have learned over the years how to hold a team together. How to lift some men up, how to calm down others, until finally they've got one heartbeat, together, a team."

The key to building that trust between coaches and players, creating loyalties that have reached beyond a game and into the fabric of a region's culture, is a simple matter of taking care not to act like the biggest animal in the forest. "There's just three things I ever say," sums up Bear Bryant, when he is pushed to explain his philosophy of coaching. "If anything goes bad, then I did it. If anything goes semi-good, then we did it. If anything goes real good, then you did it. That's all it takes to get people to win foot-ball games for you. I can do that better than anybody. That—and I do know a little something about winning." ∎

—REPORTED BY PETER AINSLIE/TUSCALOOSA

Deep Blue Funk

BY CHARLES KRAUTHAMMER

[*When a computer defeated the world's best chess player,
more than a game was lost. The writer asked if machines
were finally (gasp!) taking over human thought*]

February 26, 1996

AS WAS TO BE expected, the end of civilization as we know it was announced on the back pages. On Feb. 10, 1996, in Philadelphia, while America was distracted by the rise of Pat Buchanan, the fall of Phil Gramm and other trifles, something large happened. German philosophers call such large events world-historical. This was larger. It was species-defining. The New York *Times* carried it on page A32.

On Feb. 10, Garry Kasparov, the best chess player in the world and quite possibly the best chess player who ever lived, sat down across a chessboard from a machine, an IBM computer called Deep Blue, and lost.

True, it was only one game. What kind of achievement is that? Well—as Henny Youngman used to say when asked, "How's your wife?"—compared to what? Compared to human challengers for the world championship? Just five months ago, the same Kasparov played a championship match against the next best player of the human species. The No. 2 human played Kasparov 18 games, and won one. Deep Blue played Kasparov and won its very first game. And it was no fluke. Over the first four games, the machine played Kasparov dead even—one win, one loss, two draws—before the champ rallied and came away with the final two games.

Kasparov won the match. That was expected. Game 1, however, was not supposed to happen. True, Kasparov had lost to machines in speed games and other lesser tests. And lesser grand masters have lost regulation games to machines. But never before in a real game played under championship conditions had a machine beaten the best living human.

Indeed, Kasparov, who a few weeks ago single-handedly took on the entire national chess team of Brazil, was so confident of winning that he rejected the offer that the $500,000 purse be split 60-40 between winner and loser. Kasparov insisted on winner-take-all. They settled on 80-20. (What, by the way, does Deep Blue do with its 100-grand purse? New chips?)

Asked when he thought a computer would beat the best human, Kasparov had said 2010 or maybe never. A mutual friend tells me Garry would have gladly offered 1-10, perhaps even 1-100 odds on himself. That was all before Game 1. After Game 1, Kasparov was not offering any odds at all. "He was devastated," said his computer coach, Frederick Friedel. "It was a shattering experience. We didn't know what the game meant. There was the theoretical possibility that the computer would be invincible, and that he would lose all six games."

True, we have already created machines that can run faster, lift better, see farther than we can. But cars, cranes and telescopes shame only our limbs and our senses, not our essence. Thinking is our specialty, or so we think. How could a device capable of nothing more than calculation (of the possible moves) and scoring (of the relative strengths of the resulting positions) possibly beat a human with a lifetime of experience, instant pattern recognition, unfathomable intuition and a killer instinct?

How? With sheer brute force: calculation and evaluation at cosmic speeds. At the height of the game, Deep Blue was seeing about 200 million positions every second. You and I can see one; Kasparov, two. Maybe three. But 200 million? It was style vs. power, and power won. It was like watching Muhammad Ali, floating and stinging, try to box a steamroller in a very small ring. The results aren't pretty.

What is Deep Blue's secret? Grand master Yasser Seirawan put it most succinctly: "The machine has no fear." He did not just mean the obvious, that silicon cannot quake. He meant something deeper: because of its fantastic capacity to see all possible combinations some distance into the future, the machine, once it determines that its own position is safe, can take the kind of attacking chances no human would. The omniscient have no fear.

In Game 1, Blue took what grand master Robert Byrne called "crazy chances." On-site expert commentators labeled one move "insane." It wasn't. It was exactly right.

Here's what happened. Late in the game, Blue's king was under savage attack by Kasparov. Any human player under such assault by a world champion would be staring at his own king trying to figure out how to get away. Instead, Blue ignored the threat and quite nonchalantly went hunting for lowly pawns at the other end of the board. In fact, at the point of maximum peril, Blue expended two moves—many have died giving Kasparov even one—to snap one pawn. It was as if, at Gettysburg, General Meade had sent his soldiers out for a bit of apple picking moments before Pickett's charge because he had calculated that they could get back to their positions with a half-second to spare.

In humans, that is called sangfroid. And if you don't have any sang, you can be very froid. But then again if Meade had known absolutely—by calculating the precise trajectories of all the bullets and all the bayonets and all the cannons in Pickett's division—the time of arrival of the enemy, he could indeed, without fear, have ordered his men to pick apples.

Which is exactly what Deep Blue did. It had calculated every possible combination of Kasparov's available moves and determined with absolute certainty that it could return from its pawn-picking expedition and destroy Kasparov exactly one move before Kasparov could destroy it. Which it did.

It takes more than nerves of steel to do that. It takes a silicon brain. No human can achieve absolute certainty because no human can be sure to have seen everything. Deep Blue can.

Now, it cannot see everything forever—just everything within its horizon, which for Deep Blue means everything that can happen within the next 10 or 15 moves or so. The very best human player could still beat it (as Kasparov did subsequently) because he can intuit—God knows how—what the general shape of things will be 20 moves from now.

But it is only a matter of time before, having acquired yet more sheer computing power, Blue will see farther than Garry can feel. And then it's curtains. Then he gets shut out, 6-0. Then we don't even bother to play the brutes again. The world championship will consist of one box playing another. Men stopped foot racing against automobiles long ago.

Blue's omniscience will make it omnipotent. It can play—fight—with the abandon of an immortal. Wilhelm Steinitz, a world chess champion who was even more eccentric than most, once claimed to have played chess with God, given him an extra pawn and won. Fine. But how would he have done against Blue?

Kasparov himself said that with Deep Blue, quantity had become quality. When you can calculate so fast and so far, you rise to another level. At some point that happened in biology. There are neurons firing in lemmings and squid, but put them together in gigantic enough numbers and fantastic enough array, as in humans—and, behold, a thought, popping up like a cartoon bubble from the brain.

We call that consciousness. Deep Blue is not there yet, though one day we will be tempted to ask him. In the meantime he's done alchemy, turning quantity into quality. That in itself is scary.

At least to me. However, my son, age 10, who lives as comfortably with his computer as he does with his dog, was rooting for Deep Blue all along. "What are you worried about, Dad?" he says. "After all, we made the machine, didn't we? So we're just beating ourselves."

The next generation has gone over to Them. No need to wait for the rematch. It's over. ■

—WITH REPORTING BY WILLIAM DOWELL/PHILADELPHIA

Pride of the Pudgy

BY CALVIN TRILLIN

[
*Turning a sow's ear into barbecued ribs, the author
defied the designation of his hometown as an obese city
by praising its far-from-delicate culinary delicacies*
]

March 24, 1997

WHEN THE COALITION FOR Excess Weight Risk Education announced recently that Kansas City, Missouri, my hometown, was the fourth most obese city in the U.S., I received some congratulatory telephone calls that I suspect were not entirely sincere.

"You must be very proud," I was told by an acquaintance I'll call Ariel, who grew up in San Francisco. My father would have described Ariel as weighing "65 lbs. soaking wet—with her galoshes on." In Kansas City she wouldn't be wide enough to be noticed. I am aware that Ariel probably doesn't think that having the fourth-highest percentage of overweight residents (after New Orleans; Norfolk, Virginia; and San Antonio, Texas) is something to boast about. I am aware that she would not understand the pride I heard in the voice of Arthur Bryant, the legendary Kansas City barbecue man, many years ago when he told me his method of preparing French fries: "I get fresh potatoes and I cook them in pure lard. If you want to do a job, you do a job." Still, the best way to deal with people like Ariel is to play along.

I do think Kansas City has failed to take enough pride in being a mecca for American culinary delicacies that do not happen to be delicate. The

480

city council has never even responded to the suggestion I made years ago, for instance, that one of the Missouri River bridges be named in memory of Chicken Betty Lucas, a virtuoso of the cast-iron skillet.

"National recognition is always gratifying," I said to Ariel. "And 'Fourth Fattest' does have a nice ring, whether or not they decide to put it on the city-limits signs. Don't worry: I'm sure San Francisco will do better next year than 26th."

That was a lie. I don't think that at all. San Francisco is always going to finish out of the money. I would agree with the general manager of Gates Bar-B-Q, in my hometown, who was quoted in the Kansas City *Star* as saying that a lot of people on the coast are skinny because they've developed an interest in eating "roots and bark."

Recently, I was in an ice-cream parlor in San Francisco that served the sort of fresh-fruit drinks sometimes called smoothies, and I noticed that the add-ins you could get in your smoothie (most of them for an extra 50¢), were listed as follows: "spirulina, bee pollen, brewer's yeast, calcium, ginseng, lecithin, protein powder mix, vitamins & minerals, and wheat germ." In Kansas City, people would pay a lot more than 50¢ to have any of those things removed from whatever they were eating and replaced with Betty Lucas' chicken batter.

"I suppose you read that item in the Washington *Post* about the study indicating that patriotism varies in direct proportion to fatness," I said to Ariel, although I knew perfectly well that Ariel is too busy weighing out portions of roots and bark on her kitchen scale to read the Washington *Post*.

I told her about the two social scientists in Virginia, Carl Bowman and James Davison Hunter, who asked American men whether they would fight in a war for this country under any circumstances, and found that 4½ times as many fat ones as skinny ones said yes.

"You must be very proud," Ariel said again.

"Yes," I said, "but it also must make you feel good to know that the few people from San Francisco who did fight for their country would look very trim in their uniforms." Two can play at this insincerity game. ∎

Gasgate

BY GARRISON KEILLOR

[*The celebrated chronicler of Lake Wobegon found that
pious moral indignation is a high horse to get down
from, and sometimes somebody knocks you off*]

November 10, 1997

MONDAY AFTERNOON, I DROVE into town for
gas and stopped at the self-service, and the pump wouldn't
work. Gas wouldn't come out. So I drove down the hill to another self-service, and I got about a dollar's worth in when a
heavy-set woman strode up and said, "You just come from
the Stop 'N Shop?" I said I had. "You drove away without paying for your
gas," she said.

She was the manager of the station up the hill, and she had chased me
in her car. She said I owed her $3.79. I told her that was wrong. The pump
at her station didn't work. No gas came through the nozzle. Not a penny's
worth. The pump dial showed all zeros. "Check my gas gauge," I said.
"The needle is way below empty."

"How do I know your gas gauge works?" she said.

"You can watch it work as I fill up with gas," I said.

"I don't have time for that," she said. "I need $3.79 from you, or I'm
going to have to call the cops."

And then I thought of those aging screen stars over the years who've
been arrested for shoplifting, handcuffed, hauled down to headquarters for

boosting a set of barrettes, and I decided I did not want to end my career that way. The presumption of innocence is not strong in this country. And so I paid up—to avoid bringing shame to my family.

What hurt most was the triumphant crime-stopper look on the heavy-set woman's face, her moral hauteur as she jabbed her finger at me and raised her voice so that she could be heard by passersby 50 ft. away. She wasn't just collecting on a debt, she was testifying before a Senate committee. She was Acting. This hurt me. Especially as I remembered having behaved that way myself. And it struck me that Gasgate was my penance for the *Solidarity Forever* affair.

I did a concert in Chicago on Labor Day Sunday and a week before sent the lyrics of *Solidarity Forever* to be printed in the concert program for the audience to sing. The sponsor sent back a message: "Can't sing *Solidarity Forever*—too political." I looked at that message, and I heard the rattle of drums and the skirl of bagpipes. I heard the Authors Guild lining up behind me. PEN. The A.C.L.U.

Being censored is a high privilege for any American writer, and we experience it approximately zero times in our career. Our great bugaboo is not censorship; it's getting remaindered, seeing our brave writing stacked on the bookstore floor, marked down to $1.89—and nobody buying it at that price either. Writers of today know that the nobility bestowed on Henry Miller and D.H. Lawrence will never be ours, that nobody bothers with repression anymore because everyone knows that to crack down on an artist is to promote him. Even Jesse Helms, not the swiftest intellect in the U.S. Senate, knows this, having personally raised Robert Mapplethorpe from obscurity. Performance artists who languished for years, underwhelming tiny audiences for practically no money, have been rescued by a ringing denunciation from the religious right and given a career.

The suppression of *Solidarity Forever* was the closest I had ever come to being censored, and I was not about to pass up my chance. I sat down and fired off an indignant letter about the meaning of Labor Day, faxed it to Chicago and was thinking how to proceed further (WRITER PLANS SING-IN; POLICE CHIEF THREATENS ARRESTS; MAYOR PLEADS FOR CALM), and it was lovely to contemplate. I mentioned the *Solidarity* affair to a woman friend, and she threw her arms around me and told me she admired me. This is not an everyday occurrence in my life.

The very next day the sponsor called up and said, "Fine. We'll print the lyrics if that's what you want," and my balloon went *pfffffffffft*. I did the concert, and the words to *Solidarity Forever* were there in the program, and the audience sang all four verses lustily, including, "They have taken untold millions that they never toiled to earn./ But without our brain and muscle, not a single wheel can turn./ We can break their haughty power, gain our freedom, when we learn/ That the union makes us strong."

That was that. I came home, and the next day I glanced at the fax I had sent to the sponsor. The tone of self-righteousness was a little mortifying. More than a little. When you write a sanctimonious letter, it is hard to keep it under control; there is a tendency to rise to indecent heights of piety. You don't simply argue the facts at hand, you rise in defense of godliness and decency and the First Amendment and oppressed peoples everywhere. Then, six weeks later, a heavy-set woman jabs her finger at you and accuses you of having filched $3.79 worth of gas and says it in a shrill voice so that a woman filling up her van at a nearby gas pump hears it and looks your way and thinks, "That poor man. I hope he gets some counseling before it's too late." ∎

The Viagra Craze

BY BRUCE HANDY

[*The "potency pill" opened a new chapter in human sexuality, curing genuine disorders and enhancing many relationships, but raised the question of how much of our intimate lives we want quantified and chemically manipulated*]

May 4, 1998

BESIDES ITS PHONY NAME, funny shape and unappetizing color, what's not to like about Viagra, the new pill that conquers impotence? Could there be a product more tailored to the easy-solution-loving, sexually insecure American psyche than this one? The drug, manufactured by Pfizer, went on sale three weeks ago, finally giving talk-show hosts something other than Bill Clinton and Pamela Lee to crack smarmy jokes about.

Spurred, perhaps, by just that sort of publicity, would-be patients have been besieging urologists' offices and sex clinics—men both genuinely dysfunctional and merely dissatisfied, skulking around in hopes of achieving "better" erections through chemistry. Already, a kind of Viagra connoisseurship is beginning to take hold. "The hundreds are absolutely incredible," says a very satisfied user, referring to the drug's 100-mg maximum-strength dosage, "and the effect lasts through the following morning." What else can one say but *Vrooom!* Cheap gas, strong economy, erection pills—what a country! What a time to be alive!

"We've always been waiting for the magic bullet," says Dr. Fernando Borges of the Florida Impotency Center in St. Petersburg, where he has been working with sexually dysfunctional patients for 21 years. "This," he says, "is pretty close to the magic bullet." The very day Viagra became available, Dr. John Stripling, an Atlanta urologist, churned out 300 prescriptions with the help of a rubber stamp he had had the foresight to purchase. At the Urology Health Center in New Port Richey, Fla., which participated in the drug's clinical trials, the waiting time to see a doctor for a Viagra consultation is a month. Not that this has stopped motivated patients. "We've been inundated with emergencies," says Dr. Ramon Perez. "Pain in the kidney. Blood in the urine. But when they get in here, they just want to ask us about Viagra. It's amazing. These people have been impotent for three years, and they cannot wait another few days."

"It's the fastest takeoff of a new drug that I've ever seen, and I've been in this business for 27 years," says Michael Podgurski, director of pharmacy at the 4,000-outlet Rite Aid drugstore chain. After a brief lag, the drug is now being prescribed at the rate of at least 10,000 scripts a day, outpacing such famous quick starters as the antidepressant Prozac (which went on to become one of the biggest-selling drugs in America) and the baldness remedy Rogaine (which has been something of a disappointment after its initial blaze of popularity).

The run on Viagra has been abetted by the likes of David Michael Thomas, a Milwaukee, Wis., osteopath who advertises his services on the Web at *www.penispill.com* and who allegedly prescribed Viagra to some 700 patients after cursory $50 telephone examinations. At a license-suspension hearing in front of Wisconsin regulatory officials last week, Thomas agreed to stop the practice. (Normally a diagnosis of impotence involves a rigorous physical exam, blood tests and an extensive sexual history.) Other entrepreneurs have been offering prescriptions directly over the Internet.

Even supporters of the pill worry about hyped expectations. "People always want a quick fix," complains Dr. Domeena Renshaw, a psychiatrist who directs the Loyola Sex Therapy Clinic outside Chicago. "They think Viagra is magic, just like they thought the G spot worked like a garage-door opener." In the wake of fen/phen and Redux, the diet-drug treatments that were pulled from the market last year after it was learned that they could damage heart valves, caution would be advisable with Viagra. But so far the side effects seem comparatively slight and manageable: chiefly headache, flushed skin, upset stomach and curious vision distortions involving the color blue. Pfizer, leaving nothing to chance, has even requested and received the Vatican's unofficial blessing for Viagra. All in all, a happy ending for American men, their partners and especially Pfizer stockholders, who have seen the value of their shares jump nearly 60% this year alone.

Yet there's something unnerving about Viagra too, not so much on the face of it (the drug's merits appear to be manifold; doctors think it might even improve the sexual response of postmenopausal women) but in the broader philosophical implications. Is sexuality, like the state of happiness or male-pattern baldness, just one more hitherto mysterious and profound area of human-beingness that can be pharmaceutically manipulated, like any other fathomable construct of enzymes and receptors? Another looming question: Since Viagra is taken—at prices ranging from $8 to $12 a pop—not on a day-in, day-out basis but only when one actually wants to have sex, will HMOS and other insurers soon be telling us how much sex is reimbursable? Sufficient? Normal? Necessary?

And what about the impact on the freighted social interactions we euphemistically refer to as dating? "I bet that within a year, you'll see women's-magazine articles saying, 'How to Tell If It's You or Viagra,' " says James R. Petersen, who has written the *Playboy* Advisor column for the past 22 years. He adds, "I think Viagra is going to be as monumental as the birth-control pill." No less an authority than Bob Guccione, publisher of *Penthouse* magazine, believes the drug will "free the American male libido" from the emasculating doings of feminists. And not only that. According to Guccione, "the ability to have sex by older men will make them healthier and live longer. It will fool the biological clock when men are still active in the later years. It is a very significant effect of the drug that many haven't contemplated." There isn't any actual scientific evidence to back up Guccione's claims, but he does do a nice job of illuminating two important subtexts of Viagra's appeal: the chimeras of undiminishable power and perpetual youth.

Of course, the overt appeal is pretty compelling too.

In the past decade there have been great advances in the treatment of impotence, which is now seen by most therapists, in most cases, as a physiological rather than a psychological problem, rejecting the medical establishment's long-held view. The word impotence itself, like "frigidity" for women, is considered suspect in many circles; the more politically correct—or at least clinical—term is erectile dysfunction, or ED, as it is commonly abbreviated. Inspired by a 1992 National Institutes of Health Conference and landmark 1994 study on the problem, the diagnosis has been defined more broadly, from the rather strict criterion of inability to get an erection, period, to the somewhat more elastic and subjective criterion of inability to get an erection adequate for "satisfactory sexual performance." This has led to a tripling of the number of men estimated to be impotent in this country—some 30 million according to the NIH, half of whom are thought to be under the age of 65. ED is associated with age; it affects about 1 in 20 men ages 40 and up, 1 in 4 over 65.

From a drug manufacturer's point of view, this burgeoning of the potential market has coincided quite nicely with the development of pharmaceutical treatments. (At least two more impotence pills are in the pipeline from different companies.) Before Viagra, the most promising therapies involved putting gel suppositories in the urethra and injecting drugs directly into the base of the penis. The downside is not hard to grasp. "You can imagine the look most patients gave when I told them they would have to stick a small needle into the most sensitive portion of their body," says University of Chicago urologist Dr. Gregory Bales. The good news is that the erections resulting from such injections can last an hour or more, even after orgasm, though depending on one's taste and circumstances, this too could be a downside. Other treatments, which involve vacuum pumps, penile implants and penis rings, are no less awkward or, to get to the heart of the matter, no more conducive to the spontaneous, unselfconscious, beautiful sex that Calvin Klein ads imply is our daily right.

THE PROMISE OF VIAGRA is its discretion and ease of use. Doctors recommend taking the pill an hour before sex, which might lead to some wastage among overly optimistic users but shouldn't otherwise interfere too greatly with the normal course of coital events. An even greater advantage, or at least a more naturalistic one: unlike the injectable drugs, which when efficacious produce an erection regardless of context (famously proved by Dr. Giles Brindley, a leading British impotence researcher, who once demonstrated a successful experimental treatment by dropping his trousers in front of hundreds of astonished colleagues at a conference), Viagra merely paves the way for the *possibility* of arousal. Erections must still be achieved the old-fashioned way, whether through desire, attraction, physical stimulation, the guilty thrill of an illicit affair, page 27 of *The Godfather* or what have you.

Loyola psychiatrist Renshaw offers the instructive example of a couple who came to see her the day after the man had taken Viagra for the first time: "They went to bed to wait for something to happen and fell asleep while they were waiting. They forgot to have foreplay. They expected an instant erection." The next night, after Renshaw gently reminded them about the importance of stimulation, they had intercourse for the first time in three years.

During the drug's clinical trials, which as a rule tend to have rosier outcomes than real life, Pfizer reported a 60%-to-80% success rate, depending on the dosage (compared with a 24% success rate for placebos). The anecdotal evidence is even more compelling, if one can put up with a certain amount of crowing. Earl Macklin, a 59-year-old security guard in Chicago, has suffered from impotence on and off for 10 years as a result of diabetes. The first two times he tried Viagra, it produced minimal results; the third time he was able to have intercourse with his girlfriend for the first time in their four-month relationship.

Tom Cannata, a 43-year-old accountant from Springfield, Mass., has been taking Viagra for the past three years as a trial subject. He was suffering from partial impotence brought on, he believes, by years of bicycle riding (an activity, it should be noted, that is not universally held to be a cause of impotence). Cannata was able to achieve erections but felt that they "should have been stronger and much longer-lasting." Viagra worked for him the first time and has worked ever since. "Not only is the frequency of our sex greater," he says, "but for me it is much more intense than it was without the medication. The quality is so much better. Much firmer, stronger erections. And the orgasm is much more explosive." So pleased has Cannata been with the results that he was inspired, he says, to go out and buy a sports car not long after beginning the drug—indicating, perhaps, a soon-to-boom, Viagra-inspired market for souped-up cars, Aramis, over-size stereo equipment and other accoutrements of the virile life-style.

Many doctors insist that more isn't necessarily more with Viagra. Known to chemists by the less evocative name of sildenafil (the word Viagra, redolent of both "vigor" and "Niagara," had been kicking around Pfizer for years, a brand name in search of a product), the drug began life as a heart medication designed to treat angina by increasing blood flow to the heart. Sildenafil, it turned out, wasn't so good at opening coronary arteries, but happy test subjects did notice increased blood flow to their penises, a side effect brought to Pfizer's attention when the test subjects were reluctant to return their leftover pills. The medication works by suppressing the effect of the naturally occurring enzyme phosphodiesterase type 5 (PDE5), which causes an erection to subside after orgasm by breaking down the body chemical known as cyclic GMP. It is cyclic GMP that initiates the muscular and vascular changes that lead to an erection in the first place. While PDE5 is always present in the penis, cyclic GMP is produced only during arousal. The catch in impotent men is that they may not produce enough cyclic GMP to temporarily "win out" over the PDE5. Thus the efficacy of Viagra: by strong-arming PDE5, it allows a little bit of one's cyclic GMP to go a long way.

One more nugget of possibly boring but crucial biochemistry: the erectile tissue in the penis has a finite number of receptors for cyclic GMP. This means that a normally functioning man with adequate levels of the chemical shouldn't get any more bang for his buck by gobbling Viagra; the variations anyone feels in his or her sexual response are due to factors outside the drug's purview. At the same time, Pfizer hasn't done any testing of the drug on nonimpotent men to prove the point, but it's hard to imagine that biochemical nitpicking is going to stop people from experimenting. Certainly it will be hard for wet blankets and smarty-pants to compete with the siren calls coming out of sex clinics around the country from men "feeling 18 again."

"If you can have an erection naturally, you probably won't need Viagra," says Thomas Burnakis, pharmacy clinical coordinator at Baptist Medical Center in Jacksonville, Fla. "It's not going to make your erection harder or last longer. But I can guarantee you that if you walk in and say, 'Doc, I'm having trouble keeping my flag up,' most physicians are not going to insist on testing. What's to keep you from using it? Absolutely nothing. And just as with fen/phen, while a lot of doctors said they would not give that drug, a lot of clinics were prescribing it. It's going to be a moneymaking procedure. They'll give a cursory exam, charge you for that and write the prescription"—a prediction that has already been borne out on the Internet. According to Pfizer, there's no evidence that overeager users could develop a physical addiction to Viagra. But as for a psychological addiction, that is uncharted territory.

It is because of the potential for abuse and, more to the point, the traditionally seedy associations that cling to impotence remedies (witness the ads in the back of low-rent men's magazines for spurious Spanish fly, hard-on creams and the like) that drug companies have only recently turned their attention to sexual dysfunction. This would account for the tone adopted by Pfizer chairman and CEO William Steere even as he figuratively licks his chops over the potential market in "aging baby boomers." He is careful to point out that "quality-of-life drugs are gene-based just like those for serious medical conditions. In areas like impotence, aging skin, baldness and obesity, the science is just as profound as if you were working in cancer, asthma or anti-infectives." In other words, Viagra is sober stuff and not at all akin to Sy Sperling's Hair Club for Men.

Along related lines, a brochure for Pfizer employees points out that while "jokes and puns are often used in conversation about sexual health topics . . . you can redirect humorous remarks to more appropriate discussion by not joining in the humor and pointing out the seriousness of the subject matter, reminding the people with whom you speak that ED is a significant medical condition that affects the lives of millions of men and their partners." This is true, of course. It also speaks to the tricky questions of taste and exploitation that Pfizer will have to navigate in marketing the drug. So far, without an official launch or virtually any promotion, Viagra is doing fine. But why hold back? Advertisements will begin appearing in medical journals in about six weeks, followed by consumer ads this summer. A company spokesman says they will be "tasteful and emotional, emphasizing [impotence] as a couple's condition." One can imagine.

At any rate, it's an emphasis that should remind us that human sexuality is far too rich and complex for the entire subject to be balanced on the delicate fulcrum of an erection. As with the debate in psychiatry between traditional talk therapists and their more pharmacologically minded colleagues, controversy over Viagra and its cousins may well provoke a rift among sex researchers. Raymond Rosen, a professor of psychiatry at the Robert Wood Johnson Medical School in Piscataway, N.J., makes the obvious but necessary point that Viagra will not be the final word on sexual dysfunction or dissatisfaction: "There's a danger that we could lose sight of the fact that a lot of sexual problems relate to poor relationships or poor self-esteem or anxiety, depression or other factors." Or as Petersen, the *Playboy* adviser, puts it, "You can take an angry couple and give them Viagra, and then you have an angry couple with an erection." Oddly, that's reassuring. ∎

—REPORTED BY EDWARD BARNES AND
LAWRENCE MONDI/NEW YORK, WENDY COLE/CHICAGO,
GREG FULTON/ATLANTA AND ARNOLD MANN/WASHINGTON

Left and Gone Away

BY   PAUL   GRAY

[*A wistful salute to the effortless style and reticent dignity of baseball legend Joe DiMaggio, whose death renewed old feelings of admiration, affection and awe*]

March 22, 1999

HE WAS IDOLIZED BY millions who never saw him hit or catch a baseball. During the 13 seasons Joe DiMaggio played center field for the New York Yankees, baseball was still the national pastime, but one that a majority of fans followed from afar. The 16 major league teams were clustered in only 10 cities, with St. Louis as the westernmost outpost. In that pre-television era, sports heroes were made out of words, those spoken over the radio during play-by-play broadcasts and those printed in newspapers the next morning. No wonder legends arose. Most people experienced baseball by reading adventure stories in the daily press or by listening, the way the ancient Greeks did, to the voices of the bards.

Baseball's mythmaking machinery went into overdrive when it encountered DiMaggio. Sportswriters for New York City's nearly a dozen daily papers fell in love with the shy 21-year-old who came up with the Yankees from spring training in 1936. Babe Ruth wasn't around anymore to provide reliably flashy copy, and without him the team lacked charisma. This handsome new kid, the son of a Sicilian immigrant fisherman, looked promising. His awkwardness and reticence with reporters might be portrayed as enigmatic, as might his absolutely deadpan demeanor on the field. And advance word from DiMaggio's minor league exploits with the San Francisco Seals was that he could, in baseball parlance, "do it all": hit, hit for power, run, field and throw.

Whatever pressure the rookie felt from all these ravenous expectations never showed on the diamond. He not only did it all, he did it with a stylishness that awed sportswriters and spectators alike. DiMaggio was the leading American League vote getter for the 1936 All-Star game. That same summer he appeared on the cover of this magazine. His Yankees cruised to the AL pennant, the team's first since 1932, and beat the rival New York Giants in the World Series. (During DiMaggio's 13 years as the Yankees' star player, the team appeared in 10 Series and won nine.)

His successful rookie season confirmed and enhanced the DiMaggio mystique. The next year, a radio broadcaster called him "the Yankee Clipper," a tribute to the way he sailed so majestically while pursuing fly balls across the green expanses of center field. His batting skill won him the sobriquet "Joltin' Joe." Meanwhile, the young man from Fisherman's Wharf was acquiring a Manhattan polish. He took up tailored suits and the high life at Toots Shor's nightclub, where the habitués treated him like a god who had inexplicably deigned to join their mortal company. He dated beautiful women, including actress Dorothy Arnold, whom he later married and with whom he had a son, Joe Jr.

The defining event of DiMaggio's career occurred in 1941, when he got at least one base hit in 56 consecutive games—a feat of consistency no other player has come close to matching. Evolutionary biologist (and sports buff) Stephen Jay Gould once wrote that "DiMaggio's streak is the most extraordinary thing that ever happened in American sports."

DiMaggio retired at the end of the 1951 season, after having been hobbled for several years by painful bone spurs in his right heel. (A few sportswriters did not blush at comparing him to Achilles.) Those who never saw him play and who consult the common statistical benchmarks may wonder at DiMaggio's renown. His lifetime batting average (.325) was good, but not so high as those of his rough contemporaries Stan Musial (.331) and Ted Williams (.344). DiMaggio's career home runs (361) also trailed Musial's (475) and Williams' (521). But Joltin' Joe drove in more runs per game than either man and had far fewer strikeouts than any comparable slugger.

Once out of baseball, DiMaggio did the only thing that would attract more attention than his 1941 streak. Long divorced from his first wife, he courted and in 1954 married Marilyn Monroe. This union was passionate but star-crossed. Freed at last from the demands and expectations created by his on-field heroics, he craved privacy and a quiet life; she attracted, wherever she went, a maelstrom of publicity. He believed in punctuality; she was always late. He expected an Old World housewife; she was a New World sex goddess. He wanted her to abandon the movies and settle with him in San Francisco; she was reveling in a fame that outstripped even her teenage fantasies.

Gay Talese was one of the few journalists to gain a measure of DiMaggio's trust in later years, and an article in his 1970 collection *Fame and Obscurity* called "The Silent Season of a Hero" recounts a telling vignette from the nine-month Monroe-DiMaggio marriage. During their delayed honeymoon in Japan, she was asked by a U.S. Army general to visit the troops in Korea. When she got back, she said, "It was so wonderful, Joe. You never heard such cheering." He replied, "Yes I have."

Being the man who had won and lost Marilyn Monroe added a new dimension to the DiMaggio legend. So did his quiet grief after her death in 1962, when he arranged her funeral—barring the Hollywood types whom he felt had betrayed her—and ordered fresh flowers placed weekly on her grave. The great poker-faced star had a heart after all, and the world could see that it had been broken.

He spent his 48 years after baseball essentially being Joe DiMaggio. The less he said about himself during his dignified public appearances, the more others talked about him. Ernest Hemingway put him into *The Old Man and the Sea* ("I would like to take the great DiMaggio fishing," the old man said. "They say his father was a fisherman."). Paul Simon's song *Mrs. Robinson,* written for the movie *The Graduate* (1967), asked, "Where have you gone, Joe DiMaggio? A nation turns its lonely eyes to you," evoking a '60s sense of vanished heroes.

Now that he has really gone—a longtime three-pack-a-day smoker dead last week of lung cancer at age 84—those of us old enough to remember him in uniform and full glory feel especially bereft. I not only saw the Yankee Clipper play in person; I got his autograph twice. The first time was in the spring of 1951, when I was an 11-year-old fan hanging around with my schoolmates outside the entrance to the Del Prado hotel on Chicago's South Side, where visiting AL teams stayed when they played the White Sox. The Yankees were in town, and I was waiting for my hero Joe DiMaggio. At last he emerged to get on the team bus for a night game at Comiskey. He told all of us to line up, and he signed our books.

Several months later, the Yankees were back at the Del Prado, and so were my buddies and I. When DiMaggio came out, I noticed that none of my friends approached him. Maybe it was because they already had his autograph or because he was injured and hadn't been playing much. But I thought it was wrong for DiMaggio to board the bus unpestered by any worshipers, so I turned over a page in my autograph book—to make sure he wouldn't see that I already had him—and asked him to sign it. He did and got on the bus and took what I realized was his regular seat next to the front window on the right side. I looked up at him. He looked down and noticed me and waved. I waved back then, and I do so now for all of us who admired his graceful career and life. ∎

WINSTON CHURCHILL, 1951, BY ALFRED EISENSTAEDT

Persons
Of the Year

Man of the Year: Franklin D. Roosevelt

BY MANFRED GOTTFRIED

[
*Having launched his New Deal in the teeth of the
Depression, President Franklin D. Roosevelt was the
obvious choice, one already ratified by the American public*
]

January 7, 1935

IN CHAPTER 1934 OF the great visitors book which men call History many a potent human being scrawled his name the twelvemonth past. But no man, however long his arm, could write his name so big as the name written by the longer arm of mankind. Neither micrometer nor yardstick was necessary to determine that the name of Franklin Delano Roosevelt was written bigger, blacker, bolder than all the rest.

While other men in other lands were making 1934 history, the voters of the U. S. took pencil & paper on Nov. 6 and wrote their own ticket for Man of the Year. It was not a new ticket because they had picked Franklin Roosevelt as their Man of 1932 by electing him to the Presidency, but it was a different one. Two years ago a hundred million people looked to this cheerful, charming gentleman to do something in the greatest industrial crisis on record. This year they used their ballots again, not as a desperate hope but as a grateful reward for services rendered. President Roosevelt might not have done all the things he promised to do and all the things he did do might not be for the country's good in the long run— but what he did do seemed so much better than the deeds of any other single citizen in the land that only the narrowest partisan could cavil at his popular selection as The Man of 1934.

In last November's election there was but one national issue—the New Deal. The voters' verdict was not a mere stamp of approval. It was a paean of acclamation. With unqualified popular enthusiasm, New Dealers were swept head over heels into office. For the first time since the Civil War a President in office had his mandate from the people not only renewed but enormously enlarged in an off-year election. The landslide of 1932 was almost submerged and forgotten in the landslide of 1934. What made the name of Franklin Roosevelt so big, so black, so bold, was the fact that the wealthiest single nation of the modern world had committed itself as never before to one man in a do-or-die attempt to pull itself out of a deep, dark economic hole.

In the eyes of oldtime politicians Franklin Roosevelt has bewitched the U. S. people with his smile, the toss of his head, the hearty frankness of his manner. These personal attributes apparently counted for more with the average citizen than did the concrete record of the President's achievements during 1934. By last week that record was still an unfinished story, with the outcome of many of his executive undertakings still dangling between success and failure. He had kept busy; he had put on a good show; he had exuded cheer and optimism; but he had decisively won few major battles in the past twelve months.

Finance. Into the lap of the U. S. the Man of the Year dumped a budget calling for a two-year expenditure of nearly $17,000,000,000, a two-year deficit of $9,000,000,000. By the end of the year the Public Debt had been increased from $23,800,000,000 to $28,300,000,000. And the Treasury actually found it easier to float new loans than it had a year earlier. But after making emergency expenditures of $4,500,000,000 the pump of industrial recovery was not yet primed and the prospect of a balanced budget was still very remote.

Money. The Man of the Year lopped 41¢ off the gold value of the dollar, called in all gold, nationalized all silver bullion in the U. S. and set the Treasury to buying 1,300,000,000 oz. of silver. But little if any general price-rise followed, and the President admitted to newshawks that his gold policy was a disappointment.

Farmers. With the help of the Agricultural Adjustment Administration, farm prices were boosted back 45% of the way from their Depression bottom to 1929 highs. Farm income was upped to $6,000,000,000, a round billion above 1933, exclusive of $500,000,000 paid by AAA for restricting production. But the biggest scarcity factor in boosting farm prices was the Drought, an act of God.

Employment. The Man of the Year spent $1,400,000,000 to relieve the unemployed, not counting $814,000,000 for the Civil Works Administration*—his first work relief project, wound up because it was too expensive. But the American Federation of Labor last week reported that the unemployed for December totaled 11,459,000 which was 400,000 more than a year earlier.

Labor. The Man of the Year scrapped one Labor Board and founded another to enforce industrial-labor peace through collective bargaining. He labored diligently to prevent automobile, steel and cotton textile strikes, to settle bloody labor altercations in San Francisco, Minneapolis, Toledo. But strikes cost the lost of 20,888,000 man-days of work in the first nine months of 1934 compared to 9,456,000 man-days loss in the same period of 1933.

International. Too busy at home to give much attention to foreign policy the Man of the Year nonetheless concluded a new treaty with Cuba which wiped out the Platt Amendment, put U. S. relations with that country on a new basis, improved relations with all Latin-America. From Congress he got power to make reciprocal tariff agreements to promote foreign trade. But up to last week only one such agreement (with Cuba) had been signed. In November U. S. exports were worth $195,000,000 (devalued dollars), up $11,000,000 from a year earlier, although, calculated in old gold dollars, U. S. foreign trade was at ebb, touching its Depression low in July.

Industry. The Man of the Year launched a 1934 drive in behalf of half-dead heavy industry by setting up the National Housing Administration which by year-end had induced householders to spend $100,000,000 on home renovation. But the Federal Reserve's latest index of industrial production stood at 74%, almost the exact level of a year earlier, while the National Recovery Administration broke like a wave on the beach; its price-fixing efforts abandoned; its collective bargaining feature challenged in the courts; its funeral oration read by Alfred P. Sloan of General Motors: "Today the magic possibilities of industrial regimentation and the so-called planned economy no longer cast the spell of yesterday—that spell is broken. That is the most important thing. . . . It is real progress."

Travels & Talks. The Man of the Year went yachting off Florida; attended the Harvard-Yale crew races at New London; cruised for a month aboard

---

* For the four and one-half months that CWA was in operation. Part of it was spent in the closing weeks of 1933.

the *U. S. S. Houston* from Annapolis to Puerto Rico and the Virgin Islands, through the Panama Canal to Hawaii and back to Portland, Ore.; traveled across the continent with the cheers of multitudes in his ears and the news of drought-slaking rains in his wake; relaxed as the country squire at Hyde Park; toured the Tennessee Valley; sunned himself in the pool at Warm Springs. And during 1934, he spoke 23 times over the radio, more than any previous President in any previous year. But in the same time his wife managed to make five more broadcasts than her husband.

Such were Franklin Roosevelt's most notable doings and concerns of 1934. They brought him in touch with as many kinds of men as there are in the old jingle:

Richman Vincent Astor provided the yacht which carried the Man of the Year to sea, fishing for bonefish and barracuda off the Bahama Keys while Congress was overriding his veto of veterans' pension increases.

Poorman Fred C. Perkins, maker of automobile batteries in a factory shed at York, Pa. was fined $1,500 because he could not afford to pay 40¢ an hour wages commanded by the New Deal's NRA.

Beggarman Elmer Thomas, putting aside his Senatorial cutaway for tattered overalls, asked again & again for alms, in the form of a few billions of greenbacks.

Thief John Dillinger, on whose grave near Indianapolis last week appeared a spray of greens inscribed "Merry Christmas, Old Pal," was the No. 1 catch of a New Deal's crime drive which in one year landed every major public enemy save one in jail or grave, solved seven out of eleven kidnappings, convicted three kidnappers.

But these persons and these events, of themselves, could not nominate a Man of the Year. One prime statistic takes rank above those listed. On Nov. 6, 17,300,000 Democratic votes were cast against 13,370,000 Republican votes. That result, reckoned by the standards of off-year elections and the huge Democratic majority returned in Congress, was every inch a landslide. The disparity between cause and effect represents Roosevelt Magic, the craftsmanship of a man who is master of the art of politics.

The persuasive quality of his smile is not reducible to Magic, but the persuasive quality of his words is well exemplified in his speeches. When he spoke last spring at Gettysburg he struck his keynote of popularity: "We are all brothers now in a new understanding." He struck it in a sterner mood when reproving the old order at Green Bay: "My friends, the people of the United States will not restore that ancient order!" He struck it sentimentally in his radio speech last September: "My friends, I still believe in ideals." He struck it in Tupelo where he defended his power program: "This is not regimentation—it is community rugged individualism." And with more inspiration at Harrodsburg: "We pioneers of 1934. . . . We, too, are hewing out a commonwealth."

Thus to mankind who always love a doer of great deeds, Franklin Roosevelt showed himself in the figure of a Hercules striving to perform immense but modern labors, of a hero who in the U. S. tradition does all his labors on a neighborly basis. He himself expressed as nearly as it is likely to be expressed, the result of this attitude, the reason for the vote of Nov. 6 when he declared:

"The people of this nation understand what we are trying to do. . . ." ∎

Man of the Year: Adolf Hitler

[W R I T E R   U N K N O W N]

[*Adolf Hitler was the first figure picked by* TIME *for his evil impact on world events. The choice was tragically apt, for the Führer would soon ignite World War II*]

January 2, 1939

GREATEST SINGLE NEWS EVENT of 1938 took place on September 29, when four statesmen met at the *Führerhaus,* in Munich, to redraw the map of Europe. The three visiting statesmen at that historic conference were Prime Minister Neville Chamberlain of Great Britain, Premier Edouard Daladier of France, and Dictator Benito Mussolini of Italy. But by all odds the dominating figure at Munich was the German host, Adolf Hitler.

Führer of the German people, Commander-in-Chief of the German Army, Navy & Air Force, Chancellor of the Third Reich, Herr Hitler reaped on that day at Munich the harvest of an audacious, defiant, ruthless foreign policy he had pursued for five and a half years. He had torn the Treaty of Versailles to shreds. He had rearmed Germany to the teeth—or as close to the teeth as he was able. He had stolen Austria before the eyes of a horrified and apparently impotent world.

All these events were shocking to nations which had defeated Germany on the battlefield only 20 years before, but nothing so terrified the world as the ruthless, methodical, Nazi-directed events which during late summer and early autumn threatened a world war over Czechoslovakia. When without loss of blood he reduced Czechoslovakia to a German puppet state, forced a drastic revision of Europe's defensive alliances, and won a free hand for himself in Eastern Europe by getting a "hands-off" promise from powerful Britain (and later France), Adolf Hitler without doubt became 1938's Man of the Year.

Most other world figures of 1938 faded in importance as the year drew to a close. Prime Minister Chamberlain's "peace with honor" seemed more than ever to have achieved neither. An increasing number of Britons ridiculed his appease-the-dictators policy, believed that nothing save abject surrender could satisfy the dictators' ambitions.

The figure of Adolf Hitler strode over a cringing Europe with all the swagger of a conqueror. Not the mere fact that the Führer brought 10,500,000 more people (7,000,000 Austrians, 3,500,000 Sudetens) under his absolute rule made him the Man of 1938. Japan during the same time added tens of millions of Chinese to her empire. More significant was the fact Hitler became in 1938 the greatest threatening force that the democratic, freedom-loving world faces today.

The Fascintern, with Hitler in the driver's seat, with Mussolini, Franco and the Japanese military cabal riding behind, emerged in 1938 as an international, revolutionary movement. Rant as he might against the machinations of international Communism and international Jewry, or rave as he would that he was just a Pan-German trying to get all the Germans back in one nation, Führer Hitler had himself become the world's No. 1 International Revolutionist—so much so that if the oft-predicted struggle between Fascism and Communism now takes place it will be only because two revolutionist dictators, Hitler and Stalin, are too big to let each other live in the same world.

A generation ago western civilization had apparently outgrown the major evils of barbarism except for war between nations. The Russian Communist Revolution promoted the evil of class war. Hitler topped it by another, race war. Fascism and Communism both resurrected religious war. These multiple forms of barbarism gave shape in 1938 to an issue over which men may again, perhaps soon, shed blood: the issue of civilized liberty *v.* barbaric authoritarianism.

The man most responsible for this world tragedy is a moody, brooding, unprepossessing, 49-year-old Austrian-born ascetic with a Charlie Chaplin mustache. The son of an Austrian petty customs official, Adolf Hitler was raised as a spoiled child by a doting mother. Consistently failing to pass even the most elementary studies, he grew up a half-educated young man, untrained for any trade or profession, seemingly doomed to failure. Brilliant, charming, cosmopolitan Vienna he learned to loathe for what he called its Semitism; more to his liking was homogeneous Munich, his real home after 1912. To this man of no trade and few interests the Great War was a welcome event which gave him some purpose in life. Corporal Hitler took part in 48 engagements, won the German Iron Cross (first class), was wounded once and gassed once, was in a hospital when the Armistice of November 11, 1918 was declared.

His political career began in 1919 when he became Member No. 7 of the midget German Labor Party. Discovering his powers of oratory, Hitler soon became the party's leader, changed its name to the National Socialist German Labor Party, wrote its anti-Semitic, anti-democratic, authoritarian program. The party's first mass meeting took place in Munich in February 1920. The famed Munich Beer Hall *Putsch* of 1923 provided the party with dead martyrs, landed Herr Hitler in jail. His incarceration at Landsberg Fortress gave him time to write the first volume of *Mein Kampf,* now a "must" on every German bookshelf.*

Outlawed in many German districts, the National Socialist Party nevertheless climbed steadily in membership. Time-honored Tammany Hall methods of handing out many small favors were combined with rowdy terrorism and lurid, patriotic propaganda. The picture of a mystic, abstemious, charismatic Führer was assiduously cultivated.

The situation which gave rise to this demagogic, ignorant, desperate movement was inherent in the German Republic's birth and in the craving of large sections of the politically immature German people for strong, masterful leadership. Democracy in Germany was conceived in the womb of military defeat. It was the Republic which put its signature (unwillingly) to the humiliating Versailles Treaty, a brand of shame which it never lived down in German minds.

That the German people love uniforms, parades, military formations, and submit easily to authority is no secret. Führer Hitler's own hero is Frederick the Great. That admiration stems undoubtedly from Frederick's military prowess and autocratic rule rather than from Frederick's love of French culture and his hatred of Prussian boorishness. But unlike the pol-

---

* *Deputy Führer Rudolf Hess helped write it. Imprisonment also gave Hitler time to perfect his tactics. Even before that time he got from his Communist opponents the idea of gangsterlike party storm troopers; after this the principle of the small cell groups of devoted party workers.*

ished Frederick, Führer Hitler, whose reading has always been very limited, invites few great minds to visit him, nor would Führer Hitler agree with Frederick's contention that he was "tired of ruling over slaves."*

In bad straits even in fair weather, the German Republic collapsed under the weight of the 1929–34 depression in which German unemployment soared to 7,000,000 above a nationwide wind drift of bankruptcies and failures. Called to power as Chancellor of the Third Reich on January 30, 1933 by aged, senile President Paul von Hindenburg, Chancellor Hitler began to turn the Reich inside out. Unemployment was solved by: 1) a far-reaching program of public works; 2) an intense rearmament program, including a huge standing army; 3) enforced labor in the service of the State (the German Labor Corps); 4) putting political enemies and Jewish, Communist and Socialist jobholders in concentration camps.

What Adolf Hitler & Co. did to Germany in less than six years was applauded wildly and ecstatically by most Germans. He lifted the nation from post-War defeatism. Under the swastika Germany was unified. His was no ordinary dictatorship, but rather one of great energy and magnificent planning. The "socialist" part of National Socialism might be scoffed at by hard-&-fast Marxists, but the Nazi movement nevertheless had a mass basis. The 1,500 miles of magnificent highways built, schemes for cheap cars and simple workers' benefits, grandiose plans for rebuilding German cities made Germans burst with pride. Germans might eat many substitute foods or wear ersatz clothes but they did eat.

What Adolf Hitler & Co. did to the German people in that time left civilized men and women aghast. Civil rights and liberties have disappeared. Opposition to the Nazi regime has become tantamount to suicide or worse. Free speech and free assembly are anachronisms. The reputations of the once-vaunted German centres of learning have vanished. Education has been reduced to a National Socialist catechism.

Germany's 700,000 Jews have been tortured physically, robbed of homes and properties, denied a chance to earn a living, chased off the streets. Now they are being held for "ransom," a gangster trick through the ages. But not only Jews have suffered. Out of Germany has come a steady, ever-swelling stream of refugees, Jews and Gentiles, liberals and conservatives, Catholics as well as Protestants, who could stand Naziism no longer. TIME's cover, showing Organist Adolf Hitler playing his hymn of hate

---

* *Bismarck, the Iron Chancellor, also complained of the submissiveness of German character.*

in a desecrated cathedral while victims dangle on a St. Catherine's wheel and the Nazi hierarchy looks on, was drawn by Baron Rudolph Charles von Ripper, a Catholic who found Germany intolerable.

Meanwhile, Germany has become a nation of uniforms, goose-stepping to Hitler's tune, where boys of ten are taught to throw hand grenades, where women are regarded as breeding machines. Most cruel joke of all, however, has been played by Hitler & Co. on those German capitalists and small businessmen who once backed National Socialism as a means of saving Germany's bourgeois economic structure from radicalism. The Nazi credo that the individual belongs to the state also applies to business. Some businesses have been confiscated outright, on others what amounts to a capital tax has been levied. Profits have been strictly controlled. Some idea of the increasing Governmental control and interference in business could be deduced from the fact that 80% of all building and 50% of all industrial orders in Germany originated last year with the Government. Hard-pressed for food-stuffs as well as funds, the Nazi regime has taken over large estates and in many instances collectivized agriculture, a procedure fundamentally similar to Russian Communism.

As 1938 drew to a close many were the signs that the Nazi economy of exchange control, barter trade, lowered standard of living, "self-sufficiency," was cracking. Nor were signs lacking that many Germans disliked the cruelties of their Government, but were afraid to protest them. Having a hard time to provide enough bread to go round, Führer Hitler was being driven to give the German people another diverting circus. The Nazi-controlled press, jumping the rope at the count of Propaganda Minister Paul Joseph Goebbels, shrieked insults at real and imagined enemies. And the pace of the German dictatorship quickened as more & more guns rolled from factories and little more butter was produced.

In five years under the Man of 1938, regimented Germany had made itself one of the great military powers of the world today. Despite a shortage of trained officers and a lack of materials, the Germany Army has become a formidable machine which could probably be beaten only by a combination of opposing armies.

Meanwhile an estimated 1,133 streets and squares, notably Rathaus Platz in Vienna, acquired the name of Adolf Hitler. He delivered 96 public speeches, attended eleven opera performances (way below par), sold 900,000 new copies of *Mein Kampf* in Germany besides selling it widely in Italy and Insurgent Spain. His only loss was in eyesight: he had to begin wearing spectacles for work. Last week Herr Hitler entertained at a Christmas party 7,000 workmen now building Berlin's new mammoth Chancellery, told them: "The next decade will show those countries with their patent democracy where true culture is to be found."

But other nations have emphatically joined the armaments race and among military men the poser is: "Will Hitler fight when it becomes definitely certain that he is losing that race?" The dynamics of dictatorship are such that few who have studied Fascism and its leaders can envision sexless, restless, instinctive Adolf Hitler rounding out a mellow middle age in his mountain chalet at Berchtesgaden while a satisfied German people drink beer and sing folk songs. There is no guarantee that the have-not nations will go to sleep when they have taken what they now want from the haves. To those who watched the closing events of the year it seemed more than probable that the Man of 1938 may make 1939 a year to be remembered. ∎

Through War & Peace

BY MAX WAYS

[
*Over five tumultuous decades, Winston Churchill's
eloquence and abilities were never in doubt, especially
by him. For his long record of bold leadership,
TIME chose him as its Man of the Half-Century*
]

January 2, 1950

STARTING WITH SUPERB CONFIDENCE, the 20th Century plunged vigorously forward from ambush to ambush. Other ages may have suffered greater agonies; none suffered greater surprises. Much that seemed for the best turned out for the worst. Germany's progress led to Sarajevo and later to Buchenwald. Japan's progress became Pearl Harbor. The overthrow of the Czar became Communist dictatorship. The greatest triumphs of capitalism fell prey to socialism and bureaucracy. Science led to Hiroshima.

Shock after shock threw civilization into confusion. As the 20th Century plunged on, long-familiar bearings were lost in the mists of change. Some of the age's great leaders called for more & more speed ahead; some tried to reverse the course. Winston Churchill had a different function: his chief contribution was to warn of rocks ahead, and to lead the rescue parties. He was not the man who designed the ship; what he did was to launch the lifeboats. That a free world survived in 1950, with a hope of more progress and less calamity, was due in large measure to his exertions.

Churchill first came to public attention as the victim of an ambush and he never forgot the lesson. As a correspondent with British forces in the Boer War, he accepted an invitation to join a rash reconnaissance by armored railway train into enemy territory. The Boers waylaid the train. Churchill managed to get some wounded men to safety and started back alone toward his besieged comrades. A mounted Boer (Louis Botha, who later became Prime Minister of the Union of South Africa, and Churchill's good friend) rode up, aiming a rifle. Churchill remembers that what went through his mind then was a magnanimous statement of Napoleon: "When one is alone and unarmed, a surrender may be pardoned."

Whether or not his sense of history was already that active, Churchill did surrender. But his life was to be full of pleasant as well as unpleasant surprises. Within five weeks he made a hair-raising escape from the Boer prison at Pretoria, walked unnoticed through the crowded town, hid all day in a copse tenanted by a large vulture, stumbled upon the only English settlement in 20 miles, and was smuggled under a carload of wool to safety in Portuguese territory. All Britain acclaimed Churchill as a national hero.

Late in 1900, the hero was elected a Tory member of the House of Commons. There, three weeks after Victoria's death had opened the new era, he rose, inwardly quaking and outwardly calm, to make his first speech. His subject: the Boer War. He favored reinforcement of the army in South Africa, but his main point was to urge civil rather than military government of conquered areas. He wanted "to make it easy and honorable for the Boers to surrender, and painful and perilous for them to continue in the field."

These Churchillian themes would recur in succeeding decades: no appeasement of the armed enemy; no revenge on the beaten enemy; no military encroachments on civilian responsibility; look ahead to what you want and remember that every action has consequences which affect the goal. In short, Churchill at 26 was already a serious politician.

In Britain, the Liberal Party was the first channel of those who sought State help against the rigors of capitalism. Sidney and Beatrice Webb and their Fabians went further than the Liberals: they worked for gradual change toward the socialist state. (The grade turned out to be steeper than they thought.)

Churchill, as president of the Board of Trade (1908-10)* and Home

---

* In 1908 Churchill married Clementine Hozier "and," he reported, "lived happily ever afterwards." Mrs. Webb noted that Churchill's bride had no fortune, "which is to Winston's credit." Mrs. Webb had inherited money and, like other similarly fortunate 20th Century characters (including Franklin Roosevelt), she had a deep-seated prejudice against the accumulation of money by any other means.

Secretary (1910-11), was in the front ranks of the early Liberal drive for social security. He fought for old-age pensions and a job-finding service for the unemployed. But even in those Liberal salad days there were limits beyond which Churchill would not go. Offered the Local Government Board (now part of the Health Ministry), he recoiled: "I decline to be shut up in a soup kitchen with Mrs. Sidney Webb!"

In 1911 Churchill was appointed First Lord of the Admiralty. He plunged wholeheartedly into the navy's fathomless sea of details, visited every major naval installation in the British Isles and the Mediterranean. "I could put my hand on anything that was wanted," he recalls. He knew how to put the technicalities into memorable metaphors. In a 1914 debate on naval estimates, he told the House of Commons: "If you want a true picture in your mind of a battle between great modern ironclad ships, you must not think of it as if it were two men in armor striking at each other with heavy swords. It is more like a battle between two eggshells striking at each other with hammers."

Churchill gives this picture of the summer of 1914: "The world on the verge of its catastrophe was very brilliant. Nations and Empires crowned with princes and potentates rose majestically on every side, lapped in the accumulated treasures of the long peace. All were fitted and fastened—it seemed securely—into an immense cantilever. The two mighty European systems faced each other glittering and clanking in their panoply, but with a tranquil gaze ... But there was a strange temper in the air ... Almost one might think the world wished to suffer ..."

The world did not wish nor foresee the suffering of 1914-18. Blindly, the peoples acquiesced in World War I. The generals of 1914 knew as little as the peoples about what lay ahead. Trenches were dug from Switzerland to the sea, and a four-year siege of war which neither side sought or foresaw developed. Early in the war, Churchill suggested "interposing a thin plate of steel" to protect troops from machine-gun fire. He ordered experimental tanks in 1915. The paternity of the tank is disputed; Churchill is at least its uncle.

His other major effort to end the Western Front deadlock was the Dardanelles campaign, later known by a tragic name—Gallipoli. He wanted to force the Dardanelles, knock Turkey out of the war, tip the Balkan states to the side of the Allies and open a supply line through the Black Sea to exhausted Russia. Gallipoli was bungled by lack of coordination between the services and a piecemeal, too-little, too-late scale of attack.

Churchill got the blame. He was fired from the Admiralty in May 1915 and six months later was dropped from the cabinet. For the next six months he saw trench warfare at firsthand as a lieutenant colonel in France. After Lloyd George became Prime Minister, he called Churchill back to head the Munitions Ministry in 1917.

After the war, the shame of the dole, the misery of the depressed areas, settled, like coal dust, on the power and glory and glitter of the British Empire. Churchill, who had defected to the Liberals in 1904, went back to the Tory Party in 1925. From 1924 to 1929 he served as Chancellor of the Exchequer. To this post he brought his amazing administrative ability and his infirm grasp of the decimal system ("those damn little dots"). He put Britain back on the gold standard (1925) and helped break the General Strike of 1926. It was not one of his better decades; in 1922 he was even beaten for Parliament by a Mr. Scrimgeour, a Prohibitionist and Christian Socialist who had unsuccessfully contested the seat at Dundee against Churchill in five elections since 1908.

FROM 1930 TO 1950, Churchill was four men, working in close partnership.

The personal Churchill was happy, reveling in the good things of life, both the simple and the complex. He laid bricks and built dams at his country home, enjoyed the best food and sampled, thoroughly, the best brandy. From painting, for years his main hobby, he derived "a tremendous new pleasure." Only Winston Churchill could have said: "Painting a picture is like fighting a battle . . . It is the same kind of problem as unfolding a long, sustained, interlocked argument." Churchill's happiness is an important element in his political leadership. The forces of dictatorship are pessimistic and sullen. Churchill loves freedom partly because he has got so much fun out of it. As Lord Birkenhead once said: "Mr. Churchill is easily satisfied with the best."

Churchill the journalist maintained a fairly high average of quality, and his quantitative achievement was prodigious. During the '30s, which friendly biographers have called his "wasted years," he averaged a million words (equivalent to ten novel-length books) a year.

Churchill the historian in the '20s wrote *The World Crisis,* professionally regarded as the best account of World War I. His *Marlborough* is not just a tribute to a famous ancestor. It abounds with new glimpses of an age with many lessons for the 20th Century.

Churchill the politician has the other three, especially the historian, working for him. He is not obsessed with the past, but with the application of the past to the present and future. The business of a serious politician is to foretell; he uses history as an instrument of prophecy.

Churchill spotted Hitler early as the main enemy of Britain and of civilization. He also foresaw that the crucial point of danger would be met when Germany's air power overhauled Britain's. In & out of the House of Commons Churchill began to hammer this home. Out of sheer apathy, the Tories ignored him. The Laborites, out of a deeply ingrained pacifism, did the same. Both parties pursued disarmament in the teeth of Hitler's rising might. In 1932, Churchill said: "Do not [believe] that all Germany is asking for is equal status . . . All these bands of sturdy Teutonic youths . . . are not looking for status. They are looking for weapons."

When Chamberlain came home from Munich with "Peace for our time," Churchill called it by its right name: "A total and unmitigated defeat."* Churchill's warnings had two effects of transcendent importance: 1) they speeded up expansion of the R.A.F. to the point that saved Britain, 2) they left Churchill with a clear record, giving the free world a man to trust, after so many other leaders stood disgraced by unpreparedness and appeasement.

The disasters of early 1940 had finished Chamberlain. Calling in Churchill and Lord Halifax, he told them that a coalition government had to be formed. Labor Party leaders would not serve under other Conservatives tainted with appeasement; the new Prime Minister had to be either Churchill or Halifax. For once, the voluble Churchill was silent. For a long minute he stared fixedly into space until Halifax modestly declined the task. Churchill, at 65, had attained the supreme responsibility at a moment of supreme crisis. He thought that was just as it should be: "As I went to bed at about 3 a.m. I was conscious of a profound sense of relief . . . Impatient for the morning, I slept soundly and had no need for cheering dreams. Facts are better than dreams."

What Churchill said and did thereafter is still famous and fresh in the world's memory. Some of the passages of his wartime speeches are as ready to the tongue of 1950 as anything in Shakespeare, and the deeds to which he was a party are still better known.

---

* *An interlude in Churchill's Cassandra years was his defense of King Edward VIII in the 1936 abdication crisis over Wallis Simpson. When the abdication was decided upon Churchill walked weeping from Buckingham Palace. He wrote Edward's speech: "At long last . . ."*

From his study of Marlborough's times (in which some British leaders dealt secretly with the enemy, France, and thereby consolidated Britain's reputation as "perfidious Albion"), Churchill brought a deep sense of the moral and political necessity of good faith between wartime allies. Although he was never misled about Communism's character or ultimate aims, he dealt loyally with his ally, Stalin. Through the darkest months, working more & more closely with Roosevelt, Churchill hoped for and expected that an even greater ally, the U.S., would come in. After the Japanese attack on Pearl Harbor in 1941, it did. In the succeeding four years it mobilized 14,000,000 men, built 4,900 merchant ships, sent 76,000 planes overseas with 2,000,000 tons of bombs. Soon Japan's sun—and Hitler's—began to set.

In July 1945, after Hitler's defeat, Britain held its first general election in ten years. Churchill has described the surprising result: "I acquired [in 1940] the chief power in the State, which ... I wielded in ever-growing measure for five years and three months of world war, at the end of which time, all our enemies having surrendered unconditionally, or being about to do so, I was immediately dismissed by the British electorate from all further conduct of their affairs." Britain at that point preferred Clement Attlee (Churchill called him: "That sheep in sheep's clothing") and his Socialists, who continued the grim, grey wartime regime of "fair shares for all"—and not much for anybody.

Attlee presided resolutely over the partial dissolution of the Empire on which Churchill cast a Cassandra eye: "It is with deep grief that I watch the clattering down of the British Empire, with all its glories and all the services it has rendered to mankind." It was too late for such regrets. Asians were determined to break the imperialist tether even at the risk of chaos and subsequent Communist control. The Communist menace hung over all the East, the gravest long-range threat to the world's peace.

In March 1946 Churchill performed one of his greatest services for Western civilization in a speech at Fulton, Mo. He flourished his membership card in the union of practicing prophets: "Last time I saw it all coming and cried aloud to my own fellow countrymen and to the world, but no one paid any attention." He said: "There is nothing [the Russians] admire so much as strength, and there is nothing for which they have less respect than for weakness, especially military weakness ... If the Western democracies stand together in strict adherence to the principles of the United Nations Charter, their influence for furthering those principles will be immense, and no one is likely to molest them. If, however, they become divided or falter in their duty and if these all-important years are allowed to slip away—then indeed catastrophe may overwhelm us all."

The Fulton speech defined the main issue hanging over the world as the half-century closed. Out of Fulton came the Marshall Plan, Western Union, the military aid program, the decline of the Communist threat to Western Europe, and the spirit of defiance that inspired the great airlift to Berlin in the teeth of the Russian blockade.

Harry Truman had been with Churchill at Fulton. He agreed with what Churchill said—but Harry Truman did not make the speech. He was another kind of politician, unsurpassed at guessing what the people wanted—as he was to prove in a memorable surprise on Nov. 2, 1948. Truman's kind of leadership might not be able to mobilize the free world against ambushes ahead. Now that the center of power had shifted to Washington, a Churchill was needed there. But no Churchill was visible on the U.S. horizon. In 1941 he had warned: "Nothing is more dangerous in wartime than to live in the temperamental atmosphere of a Gallup poll, always feeling one's pulse and taking one's temperature. I see [it said that] leaders should keep their ears to the ground. All I can say is that the British nation will find it very hard to look up to leaders who are detected in that somewhat ungainly posture." Leadership in the cold war called for more than Harry Truman's exquisitely sensitive, ground-gripping ear.

As the half-century ended, Churchill was getting ready for his 13th British general election. He would fight it—as he had fought all his other great battles—on the issue of freedom. Churchill likes freedom. He has been with freedom on some of its darkest and brightest days. ∎

Never Again
Where He Was

BY JESSE BIRNBAUM

[*Equal rights for blacks became more than an issue; it was a cause, a movement, and* TIME *singled out Martin Luther King Jr. for bravely leading and symbolizing it*]

January 3, 1964

THE JETLINER LEFT ATLANTA and raced through the night toward Los Angeles. From his window seat, the black man gazed down at the shadowed outlines of the Appalachians, then leaned back against a white pillow. In the dimmed cabin light, his dark, impassive face seemed enlivened only by his big, shiny, compelling eyes. Suddenly, the plane shuddered in a pocket of severe turbulence. The Rev. Martin Luther King Jr. turned a wisp of a smile to his companion and said: "I guess that's Birmingham down below."

It was, and the reminder of Vulcan's city set King to talking quietly of the events of 1963. "In 1963," he said, "there arose a great Negro disappointment and disillusionment and discontent. It was the year of Birmingham, when the civil rights issue was impressed on the nation in a way that nothing else before had been able to do. It was the most decisive year in the Negro's fight for equality. Never before had there been such a coalition of conscience on this issue."

In 1963, the centennial of the Emancipation Proclamation, that coalition of conscience ineradicably changed the course of U.S. life. Nineteen million Negro citizens forced the nation to take stock of itself—in the

Congress as in the corporation, in factory and field and pulpit and playground, in kitchen and classroom. The U.S. Negro, shedding the thousand fears that have encumbered his generations, made 1963 the year of his outcry for equality, of massive demonstrations, of sit-ins and speeches and street fighting, of soul searching in the suburbs and psalm singing in the jail cells.

And there was Birmingham with its bombs and snarling dogs; its shots in the night and death in the streets and in the churches; its lashing fire hoses that washed human beings along slippery avenues without washing away their dignity; its men and women pinned to the ground by officers of the law.

All this was the Negro revolution. Birmingham was its main battleground, and Martin Luther King Jr., the leader of the Negroes in Birmingham, became to millions, black and white, in South and North, the symbol of that revolution—and the Man of the Year.

King is in many ways the unlikely leader of an unlikely organization—the Southern Christian Leadership Conference, a loose alliance of 100 or so church-oriented groups. King has neither the quiet brilliance nor the sharp administrative capabilities of the N.A.A.C.P.'s Roy Wilkins. He has none of the sophistication of the National Urban League's Whitney Young Jr., lacks Young's experience in dealing with high echelons of the U.S. business community. He has neither the inventiveness of CORE's James Farmer nor the raw militancy of SNICK's John Lewis nor the bristling wit of Author James Baldwin. He did not make his mark in the entertainment field, where talented Negroes have long been prominent, or in the sciences and professions where Negroes have, almost unnoticed, been coming into their own. He earns no more money than some plumbers ($10,000 a year), and possesses little in the way of material things.

He presents an unimposing figure: he is 5 ft. 7 in., weighs a heavy-chested 173 lbs., dresses with funereal conservatism (five of six suits are black, as are most of his neckties). He has very little sense of humor. He never heard of Y. A. Tittle or George Shearing, but he can discourse by the hour about Thoreau, Hegel, Kant and Gandhi.

King preaches endlessly about nonviolence, but his protest movements often lead to violence. He himself has been stabbed in the chest, and physically attacked three more times; his home has been bombed three times, and he has been pitched into jail 14 times. His mail brings him a daily dosage of opinion in which he is by turn vilified and glorified. One letter says:

"This isn't a threat but a promise—your head will be blown off as sure as Christ made green apples." But another ecstatically calls him a "Moses, sent to lead his people to the Promised Land of first-class citizenship."

Some cynics call King "De Lawd." He does have an upper-air way about him, and, for a man who has earned fame with speeches, his metaphors can be downright embarrassing. For Negroes, he says, "the word 'wait' has been a tranquilizing Thalidomide," giving "birth to an ill-formed infant of frustration." Yet when he mounts the platform or pulpit, the actual words seem unimportant. And King, by some quality of that limpid voice or by some secret of cadence, exercises control as can few others over his audiences, black or white. He has proved this ability on countless occasions, ranging from the Negroes' huge summer March on Washington to a little meeting one recent Friday night in Gadsden, Ala. There, the exchange went like this:

King: I hear they are beating you!

Response: Yes, yes.

King: I hear they are cursing you!

Response: Yes, yes.

King: I hear they are going into your homes and doing nasty things and beating you!

Response: Yes, yes.

King: Some of you have knives, and I ask you to put them up. Some of you may have arms, and I ask you to put them up. Get the weapon of nonviolence, the breastplate of righteousness, the armor of truth, and just keep marching.

Few can explain the extraordinary King mystique. Yet he has an indescribable capacity for empathy that is the touchstone of leadership. By deed and by preachment, he has stirred in his people a Christian forbearance that nourishes hope and smothers injustice. Says Atlanta's Negro Minister Ralph D. Abernathy, whom King calls "my dearest friend and cellmate": "The people make Dr. King great. He articulates the longings, the hopes, the aspirations of his people in a most earnest and profound manner. He is a humble man, down to earth, honest. He has proved his commitment to Judaeo-Christian ideals. He seeks to save the nation and its soul, not just the Negro."

Whatever his greatness, it was thrust upon him. He was born on Jan. 15 nearly 35 years ago, at a time when the myth of the subhuman Negro flourished, and when as cultivated an observer as H. L. Mencken could write that "the educated Negro of today is a failure, not because he meets insuperable difficulties in life, but because he is a Negro. His brain is not fitted for the higher forms of mental effort; his ideals, no matter how laboriously he is trained and sheltered, remain those of a clown."

Mencken had never met the King family of Atlanta. King's maternal grandfather, the Rev. A. D. Williams, was one of Georgia's first N.A.A.C.P. leaders, helped organize a boycott against an Atlanta newspaper that had disparaged Negro voters. His preacher father was in the forefront of civil rights battles aimed at securing equal salaries for Negro teachers and the abolition of Jim Crow elevators in the Atlanta courthouse.

As a boy, Martin Luther King Jr. suffered those cumulative experiences in discrimination that demoralize and outrage human dignity. He still recalls the curtains that were used on the dining cars of trains to separate white from black. "I was very young when I had my first experience in sitting behind the curtain," he says. "I felt just as if a curtain had come down across my whole life. The insult of it I will never forget."

Raised in the warmth of a tightly knit family, King developed from his earliest years a raw-nerved sensitivity that bordered on self-destruction. Twice, before he was 13, he tried to commit suicide. Once his brother, "A. D.," accidentally knocked his grandmother unconscious when he slid down a banister. Martin thought she was dead, and in despair ran to a second-floor window and jumped out—only to land unhurt. He did the same thing, with the same result, on the day his grandmother died.

A bright student, he skipped through high school and at 15 entered Atlanta's Negro Morehouse College. His father wanted him to study for the ministry. King himself thought he wanted medicine or the law. "I had doubts that religion was intellectually respectable. I revolted against the emotionalism of Negro religion, the shouting and the stamping. I didn't understand it and it embarrassed me." At Morehouse, King searched for "some intellectual basis for a social philosophy." He read and reread Thoreau's essay, *Civil Disobedience,* concluded that the ministry was the only framework in which he could properly position his growing ideas on social protest.

At Crozer Theological Seminary in Chester, Pa., King built the underpinnings of his philosophy. Hegel and Kant impressed him, but a lecture on Gandhi transported him, sent him foraging insatiably into Gandhi's books. "From my background," he says, "I gained my regulating Christian ideals. From Gandhi I learned my operational technique."

The first big test of King's philosophy—or of his operating technique—came in 1955, after he had married a talented young soprano named Coretta Scott and accepted the pastorate of the Dexter Avenue Baptist Church in Montgomery, Ala.

On Dec. 1 of that year, a seamstress named Rosa Parks boarded a Montgomery bus and took a seat. As the bus continued along its route, picking up more passengers, the Negroes aboard rose on the driver's orders to give their seats to white people. When the driver told Mrs. Parks to get up, she refused. "I don't really know why I wouldn't move," she said later. "There was no plot or plan at all. I was just tired from shopping. My feet hurt." She was arrested and fined $10.

For some reason, that small incident triggered the frustrations of Montgomery's Negroes, who for years had bent subserviently beneath the prejudices of the white community. Within hours, the Negroes were embarked upon a bus boycott that was more than 99% effective, almost ruined Montgomery's bus line. The boycott committee soon became the Montgomery Improvement Association, with Martin Luther King Jr. as president. His leadership was more inspirational than administrative; he is, as an observer says, "more at home with a conception than he is with the details of its application." King's home was bombed, and when his enraged people seemed ready to take to the streets in a riot of protest, he controlled them with his calm preaching of nonviolence. King became world-famous, and in less than a year the Supreme Court upheld an earlier order forbidding Jim Crow seating in Alabama buses.*

In December 1961, King joined a mass protest demonstration in Albany, Ga., was arrested, and dramatically declared that he would stay in jail until Albany consented to desegregate its public facilities. But just two days after his arrest, King came out on bail. The Albany movement collapsed, and King was bitterly criticized for helping to kill it. But King learned a lesson in Albany. "We attacked the political power structure instead of the economic power structure," he says. "You don't win against a political power structure where you don't have the votes. But you can win against an economic power structure when you have the economic power to make the difference between a merchant's profit and loss."

It was while he was in his post-Albany eclipse that King began planning for his most massive assault on the barricades of segregation. The tar-

* The desegregation order still holds, but older Montgomery Negroes have since reverted to a somewhat loose pattern of segregated seating. Rarely, for example, will a white rider and a Negro sit beside each other.

get: Birmingham, citadel of blind, die-hard segregation. King's lieutenant, Wyatt Tee Walker, has explained the theory that governs King's planning: "We've got to have a crisis to bargain with. To take a moderate approach, hoping to get white help, doesn't work. They nail you to the cross, and it saps the enthusiasm of the followers. You've got to have a crisis."

The Negroes made their crisis, but it was no spur-of-the-moment matter. King himself went to Birmingham to conduct workshops in nonviolent techniques. He recruited 200 people who were willing to go to jail for the cause, carefully planned his strategy in ten meetings with local Negro leaders. Then, declaring that Birmingham is the "most thoroughly segregated big city in the U.S.," he announced early in 1963 that he would lead demonstrations there until "Pharaoh lets God's people go."

Awaiting King in Birmingham was Public Safety Commissioner Theophilus Eugene ("Bull") Connor, a man who was to become a symbol of police brutality yet who, in fact, merely reflected the seething hatreds in a city where acts of violence were as common as chitlins and ham hocks. Bull Connor sent his spies into the Negro community to seek information. Fearing that their phones were tapped, King and his friends worked up a code. He became "J.F.K.," Ralph Abernathy "Dean Rusk," Birmingham Preacher Fred Shuttlesworth "Bull," and Negro Businessman John Drew "Pope John." Demonstrators were called "baptismal candidates," and the whole operation was labeled "Project C"—for "Confrontation."

THE PROTEST BEGAN. Day after day, Negro men, women and children in their Sunday best paraded cheerfully downtown to be hauled off to jail for demonstrating. The sight and sound of so many people filling his jail so triumphantly made Bull Connor nearly apoplectic. He arrested them at lunch counters and in the streets, wherever they gathered. Still they came, rank on rank. At length, on Tuesday, May 7, 2,500 Negroes poured out of church, surged through the police lines and swarmed downtown. Connor furiously ordered the fire hoses turned on. Armed with clubs, cops beat their way into the crowds. An armored car menacingly bulldozed the milling throngs. Fire hoses swept them down the streets. In all, the Birmingham demonstrations resulted in the jailing of more than 3,300 Negroes, including King himself.

The Negroes had created their crisis—and Connor had made it a success. Because of Connor, the riots seared the front pages of the world press, outraged millions of people. Everywhere, King's presence, in the pulpit or at rallies, was demanded. But while he preached nonviolence, violence spread. "Freedom Walker" William Moore was shot and killed in Alabama. Mississippi's N.A.A.C.P. Leader Medgar Evers was assassinated outside his home. There was violence in Jackson, Miss., in Cambridge, Md., in Danville, Va. In Birmingham, later in the year, a church bombing killed four Negro Sunday-school children, while two other youngsters were shot and killed the same day.

Those events awakened long-slumbering Negro resentments, from which a fresh Negro urgency drew strength. For the first time, a unanimity of purpose slammed into the Negro consciousness with the force of a fire hose. Class lines began to shatter. Middle-class Negroes, who were aspiring for acceptance by the white community, suddenly found a point of identity with Negroes at the bottom of the economic heap. Many wealthy Negroes, once reluctant to join the fight, pitched in.

Now sit-in campaigns and demonstrations erupted like machine-gun fire in every major city in the North, as well as in hundreds of new places in the South. Negroes demanded better job opportunities, an end to the *de facto* school segregation that ghetto life had forced upon them.

Many whites also began to participate, particularly the white clergy, which cast off its lethargy as ministers, priests and rabbis tucked the Scriptures under their arms and marched to jails with Negroes whom they had never seen before. The Rev. Dr. Eugene Carson Blake, executive head of the United Presbyterian Church in the U.S.A., declared: "Some time or other, we are all going to have to stand and be on the receiving end of a fire hose." Blake thereupon joined two dozen other clergymen in a protest march—and was arrested.

In the months following Birmingham, Negroes paraded, demonstrated, sat in, stormed and fought through civil rights sorties in 800 cities and towns in the land. The revolt's basic and startling new assumption—that the black man can read and understand the Constitution, and can demand his equal rights without fear—was not lost on Washington. President Kennedy, who had been in no great hurry to produce a civil rights bill, now moved swiftly. The Justice Department drew up a tight and tough bill, aimed particularly at voting rights, employment, and the end of segregation in public facilities.

To cap the summer's great storm of protest, the Negro leaders sponsored the now famous March on Washington. It was a remarkable spectacle, one of disorganized order, with a stateliness that no amount of planning could have produced. Some 200,000 strong, whites and blacks of all ages walked from the Washington Monument to the Lincoln Memorial. There, the Negro leaders spoke—Wilkins, A. Philip Randolph, Young and SNICK's Lewis.

But it was King who most dramatically articulated the Negro's grievances, and it was he whom those present, as well as millions who watched on television, would remember longest. "When we let freedom ring," he cried, "when we let it ring from every village and every hamlet, from every state and every city, we will be able to speed up that day when all of God's children, black men and white men, Jews and Gentiles, Protestants and Catholics, will be able to join hands and sing, in the words of the old Negro spiritual,

> *"Free at last,*
> *Free at last.*
> *Thank God Almighty,*
> *We are free at last."*

The march made irreversible all that had gone before in the year of the Negro revolution. In that year, the Negroes made more gains than they had achieved in any year since the end of the Civil War. A speed-up in school integration in the South brought to 1,141 the number of desegregated school districts. In the North, city after city re-examined *de facto* school segregation and set up plans to redress the balance. In 300 cities in the South, public facilities—from swimming pools to restaurants—were integrated, and in scores of cities across the nation, leaders established biracial committees as a start toward resolving local inequities.

Still, for every tortuous inch gained, there are miles of progress left to be covered. There remain 1,888 Southern school districts where segregation is the rule—and scores of other districts where desegregation sits uneasily in token form. Though Montgomery buses are technically integrated, the city's other public facilities still are not. Team sports are still carefully segregated in a large number of Southern institutions; the NBC television network recently canceled coverage of the annual Blue-Gray football game because Negroes are not eligible to participate. Only 22 states have enforceable fair-employment laws on the books. And not counting Mississippi, where there is a total absence of integrated public facilities, those in other Southern states are so spotty and inconsistent (a downtown lunch counter, yes; the city swimming pool, no) that it is hard for a Negro nowadays to know where he may go and where he may not.

One natural consequence of the Negro's militant position: a backlash reaction, derived from the notion that "the Negro is pushing too far, too fast," and that he is also threatening the unskilled white man's job security. James P. Mitchell, Eisenhower's onetime Labor Secretary, now San Francisco's human-relations coordinator and a friend of the Negro, feels that "militancy could quite easily antagonize important people who are now prepared or preparing to do something. What Negroes have to remember is something they tend to forget: that they are a minority, and that they can only achieve what they want with the support of the majority."

What the Negroes expect, and what they are getting to a degree that would have been astonishing at the start of 1963, is a change of attitude. "A lot of people," says Chicago's Negro Baptist Minister Arthur Brazier, "are re-examining their motives. Even if this means that a lot of hidden prejudices have been uncovered in Northerners, good will be gained from the fact that Americans have been forced to act on days other than Brotherhood Days and Weeks."

Often the changes in attitudes are tiny in scope but broad in meaning. No longer do the starters at Miami's municipal golf courses ask a trio of white men if they will accept a Negro fourth; they merely assign the Negro, and the foursome heads onto the course. A New York adoption agency is asking white families to take Negro children. Louise Morgan, a former Chicago advertising executive, says: "I had conned myself into thinking I was a liberal. The rude awakening occurred less than a year ago, when a Negro writer and his family sought an apartment in my building and were turned down. I had met him. He was bright and a gentleman. Yet I didn't lift a finger to help him. That's all changed now."

In addition to marching in demonstrations, clergymen are welcoming Negroes to their all-white congregations in many places, and are mounting mail campaigns to Congress in support of the civil rights bill. Several Roman Catholic archdioceses now require a specific number of sermons on race relations. The National Council of Churches has budgeted $300,000 to support civil rights activities.

The most striking aspect of the revolt, however, is the change in Negroes themselves. The Invisible Man has now become plainly visible—in bars, restaurants, boards of education, city commissions, civic committees, theaters and mixed social activities, as well as in jobs. Says Mississippi's N.A.A.C.P. President Aaron Henry: "There has been a re-evaluation of our slave philosophy that permitted us to be satisfied with the leftovers at the back door rather than demand a full serving at the family dinner table." With this has come a new pride in race. Explains Dr. John R. Larkins, a Negro consultant in North Carolina's Department of Public Welfare: "Negroes have a feeling of self-respect that I've never seen in all my life. They are more sophisticated now. They have begun to think, to form positive opinions of themselves. There's none of that defeatism. The American Negro has a different image of himself." Moreover, says U.C.L.A.'s Negro Psychiatrist J. Alfred Cannon, "We've got to look within ourselves for some of the answers. We must be able to identify with ourselves as Negroes. Most Negro crimes of violence are directed against other Negroes; it's a way of expressing the Negro's self-hatred. Nonviolent demonstrations are a healthy way of channeling these feelings. But they won't be effective unless the Negro accepts his own identity."

Where most Negroes once deliberately ignored their African beginnings and looked down on the blacks of that continent, many now identify strongly with Africa—though not to the point where they would repudiate their American loyalties– and take pride in the emergence of the new nations there. Some Negro women are affecting African-style hairdos; Negroes are decorating their homes with paintings and sculpture that reflect interest in African culture. There has been a decline in sales of "whitening" creams, hair straighteners and pomades, which for years found a big market among Negroes obsessed with ridding themselves of their racial identity.

King's preparations for 1964 are well under way. "More and more," he says, "I have come to feel that our next attack will have to be more than just getting a lunch counter integrated or a department store to take down discriminatory signs. I feel we will have to assault the whole system of segregation in a community."

King's most intensive efforts will be centered on Alabama and Mississippi, "because there the problem is greatest. The Negro suffers more and more. How to deliver an all-out attack? This is what we have to think about. I'm thinking now in terms of thousands and thousands of people. They would have to be students, mainly because, for financial reasons, working adults find it difficult to remain in jail." King's mission is to turn the potential for violence into successful, direct, nonviolent action, and he works at the job 20 hours a day. He has moved back with his wife and four children to Atlanta, where he shares the pulpit of the Ebenezer Baptist Church with his father. His house, near the church, is an old, two-story, four-bedroom place. Paintings with African themes and a photograph of Gandhi hang on the walls. There is a threadbare scatter rug in the living room, two chairs protected with plastic, and a couch in need of a new slip cover. One of the keys is missing on the old grand piano. King likes to play the piano, although, as his wife says, "he starts off the *Moonlight Sonata* as if you're really going to hear something, but he fades out."

King rises at 6:30 a.m. and goes to his study for 45 minutes of reading. Then he has fruit juice and coffee for breakfast, and at 9 o'clock drives to his office in one of his two cars (a 1960 Ford and a 1963 Rambler). There he goes to work in a 16-ft.-square room filled with perhaps 200 volumes on Negro and religious subjects; he checks his mail (about 70 letters a day), writes his speeches and sermons, confers with aides and, by telephone, with civil rights leaders around the country. He usually eats his lunch at his desk, then continues working, often until 2 or 3 o'clock the next morning.

More and more, King spends his time in airplanes, journeying to the far corners of the U.S. to speak and preach to huge audiences. He traveled about 275,000 miles in 1963 and made more than 350 speeches. Wherever he goes, the threat of death hovers in the form of crackpots. "I just don't worry about things like this," he says. "If I did, I just couldn't get anything done. One time I did have a gun in Montgomery. I don't know why I got it in the first place. I sat down with Coretta one night and we talked about it. I pointed out that as a leader of a nonviolent movement, I had no right to have a gun, so I got rid of it. The quality, not the longevity, of one's life is what is important. If you are cut down in a movement that is designed to save the soul of a nation, then no other death could be more redemptive."

It is with this inner strength, tenaciously rooted in Christian concepts, that King has made himself the unchallenged voice of the Negro people—and the disquieting conscience of the whites. That voice in turn has infused the Negroes themselves with the fiber that gives their revolution its true stature. In Los Angeles recently, King finished a talk by saying: "I say good night to you by quoting the words of an old Negro slave preacher, who said, 'We ain't what we ought to be and we ain't what we want to be and we ain't what we're going to be. But thank God, we ain't what we was.' "

After 1963, with the help of Martin Luther King Jr., the Negro will never again be where or what he was. ■

Driving Toward a New World Order

BY MARSHALL LOEB

[
With Saudi Arabia's King Faisal at their head, the
OPEC *nations wielded the weapon of oil as never before,*
bringing about a historic global shift of power
]

January 6, 1975

IN EVERY CAR AND tractor, in every tank and plane—oil. Behind almost every lighted glass tower, giant industrial plant or little workshop, computer and moon rocket and television signal—oil. Behind fertilizers, drugs, chemicals, synthetic textiles and thousands of other products—the same substance that until recently was taken for granted as a seemingly inexhaustible and obedient treasure. Few noted the considerable historic irony that the world's most advanced civilizations depended for this treasure on countries generally considered weak, compliant and disunited. Now all that has changed, and the result has been a major economic and political dislocation throughout the world.

The change became dramatically apparent in 1974, a pivotal year that saw the decline of old powers, old alliances, old philosophies—and the rise of new ones. The West's belief in the inevitability of human progress and material growth was badly shaken as inflation spread oppressively across the world, several industrial societies tumbled into recession, and famine plagued a score of nations. There was a marked erosion in the wealth, might and cohesiveness of North America, Europe and Japan. In the developing world, 40 or more countries with few natural resources fell increas-

527

ingly into destitution and dependency. Meanwhile, a handful of resource-rich nations gravely compounded the problems and challenged the vital interests of the rest of the world by skillfully wielding a most potent weapon: the power of oil.

United in history's most efficient cartel, these nations exploited modern civilization's dependence on oil. Their power came from the uniqueness of oil, an exhaustible and not quickly replaceable resource that has long been shamefully wasted by much of the world. Because oil is not usually found where it is most consumed, and demand for it is so great, it is the most widely traded commodity in world commerce as well as a highly volatile element in world politics.

Again and again, the cartel formed by the Organization of Petroleum Exporting Countries raised the price of oil until it reached unprecedented and numbing heights. The producing nations' "take" from a barrel of oil, less than $1 at the start of the decade, was lifted from $1.99 before the Arab-Israeli war 15 months ago to $3.44 at the end of 1973 to more than $10 at the end of 1974. The result is the greatest and swiftest transfer of wealth in all history: the 13 OPEC countries earned $112 billion from the rest of the world last year. Because they could not begin to spend it all, they ran up a payments surplus of $60 billion. This sudden shift of money shook the whole fragile structure of the international financial system, severely weakened the already troubled economies of the oil-importing nations and gave great new political strength to the exporters.

The beneficiaries of this transfer were a disparate group of oil-possessing Africans, Asians, Latin Americans and, most favored of all, Arabs, who provided two-thirds of the petroleum exports and have more than three-fifths of the proven petroleum reserves in the non-Communist world. One bleak, sparsely populated country is by far the world's greatest seller and reservoir of oil, and one dour, ascetic and shrewd man is its undisputed ruler. He was a principal factor in raising oil prices, and now holds more power than any other leader to lower them or raise them anew. He is completing arrangements to nationalize the vast U.S.-owned oil properties within his country, bringing an end to an era in which the international oil companies dominated the Persian Gulf and helped to transform its face and fortune. Both in his own right and as a symbol of the other newly powerful potentates of oil, Saudi Arabia's King Faisal is the Man of the Year.

Last year Faisal's Saudi Arabia earned $28.9 billion by selling nearly one-fifth of all the oil consumed by non-Communist countries. The King channeled part of these funds into a massive development program that aims at building factories, refineries, harbors, hospitals and schools for his 5.7 million people. Faisal also spent about $2 billion on modern weapons for his small but growing armed forces. He granted a large part of the $2.35 billion that the Arab oil producers pledged at Rabat to the "confrontation states" in the battle against Israel; last year he was the primary outside bankroller of the Egyptians, Syrians, Jordanians and the Palestine Liberation Organization. He also made $1.2 billion in multilateral loans and grants and pledged to give some $200 million to poor countries outside the Arab world. But all the King's spending and all the King's plans could not come close to using up Saudi Arabia's wealth. The new financial giant of the world, Saudi Arabia in 1974 stood to accumulate a surplus of about $23 billion—a potentially unsettling force in global finance.

Moreover, Saudi Arabia's new wealth is simply the most spectacular symbol of the rising fortunes of the OPEC nations. With their surplus of some $60 billion last year, they took in $164 million more each day and $6.8 million more each hour than, by best estimates, they can currently spend. At that rate of accumulation, the *Economist* of London calculates, OPEC could buy out all companies on the world's major stock exchanges in 15.6 years (at present quotations), all companies on the New York Stock Exchange in 9.2 years, all central banks' gold (at $170 an ounce) in 3.2 years, all U.S. direct investments abroad in 1.8 years, all companies quoted on stock exchanges in Britain, France and West Germany in 1.7 years, all IBM stock in 143 days, all Exxon stock in 79 days, the Rockefeller family's wealth in six days and 14% of Germany's Daimler-Benz in two days (which in fact Kuwait did in November—though for that little country, the purchase represented all of 15 days of oil earnings).

King Faisal is not merely the richest of the OPEC leaders. He is also a spiritual leader of the world's 600 million Moslems because his kingdom encompasses Islam's two holiest cities, Mecca and Medina. The King, who is 68, wants to pray within his lifetime in the third most holy city, in Jerusalem at the Dome of the Rock,* and to walk there without setting foot on Israeli-held territory. Unless and until he gets his wish, peace is unlikely to have much future in the Middle East. Faisal hates Zionism with a cold passion and often argues, despite the Soviet Union's pro-Arab, anti-Israel

---

* From which, according to Moslem legend, the prophet Mohammed ascended into heaven astride his favorite white steed, Buraq.

policies, that Zionists and Communists are allied to control the world.

In 1974 Faisal used his political authority to aid Secretary of State Henry Kissinger in moving toward an interim agreement in the Middle East. He helped persuade the Syrians, for example, to agree to the disengagement pact with the Israelis on the Golan Heights. Acknowledging Faisal's role, Kissinger told TIME Correspondent Strobe Talbott: "The King is a sort of moral conscience for many Arab leaders. By having great religious stature, he can act as a kind of pure representative of Arab nationalism." And, Kissinger adds, "Faisal has been able to maneuver Saudi Arabia from being a conservative state into a political bellwether."

One of the causes of the West's woes is that for too long it underestimated the will and power of Faisal and other rulers of oil-producing nations to act together. The cries for higher prices had been rising for 15 years, first from the Venezuelans and Iranians, then from the radical Arab leaders of Libya, Algeria and Iraq. Faisal, a conservative and a longtime friend of the U.S., at first resisted—and then changed his mind because of U.S. political and military support of Israel.

For many frustrating months in 1973, the King, and his spokesmen, warned the U.S. that unless it forced Israel to withdraw from occupied Arab territories and settle the Palestinians' grievances, he would slow down oil production. The State Department thought that the threat was hollow; President Nixon warned on television that the Arabs risked losing their oil markets if they tried to act too tough.

The Arab-Israeli war of October 1973 moved the Arabs to impose a reduction in oil output—and do much more. Within ten days after the Egyptians and Syrians had attacked Israeli-occupied territory, the Arabs and Iranians in OPEC*—long derided in the West for their disunity—coalesced and raised prices from $1.99 to $3.44 per bbl. A few days after that, King Faisal led an even stronger move. Angered by the U.S. military resupplying of Israel, the Saudis and the other Arabs embargoed all oil shipments to the U.S. and started cutting production. Very quickly their output dropped 28%. When the West made no response, OPEC realized its own strength and kept right on raising prices through 1974.

This huge success gave new pride and political power to all the Arabs

---

* The members of OPEC, in order of last year's earnings are: Saudi Arabia, Iran, Venezuela, Nigeria, Libya, Kuwait, Iraq, United Arab Emirates, Algeria, Indonesia, Qatar, Ecuador and Gabon, which is an associate member. The United Arab Emirates is a federation of Abu Dhabi, Dubai, Sharjah, Ajman, Umm al Quwain, Ras al Khaimah and Fujairah.

and brought King Faisal widespread respect in the Arab world, many of whose leaders had earlier scorned him as an unregenerate conservative. Suddenly the Arabs found themselves avidly courted by people who for long had condescended to them. The hotels of Riyadh, Dubai and Baghdad overflowed with Western businessmen hawking Idaho potatoes, cement plants, color television systems and gas-fired steel mills. The Middle East also became a magnet for Western bankers, each with his own creative plan for dispensing the Arabs' cash. Elite American universities, from Stanford to Chicago to Columbia, searched for Arab professors and added courses in Arabic history, culture, language, religion. Western governments vied with the Soviets over which side could sell the Arabs more—and more destructive—fighter jets, tanks and missiles.

SO MUCH FOREIGN MONEY washed into Arab oil-producing countries that ordinary statistics no longer made sense. Estimated gross national product per capita ran to $13,000 in Kuwait, $14,000 in Qatar and more than $23,000 in Abu Dhabi. But those figures did not reflect living standards because the quick cash has not had time to filter down to the people. Bureaucracies strained to figure out ways to spend at home. Kuwait expanded one of the world's most all-encompassing welfare states. To hold down food prices, most of the big oil producers subsidized imports of staples. Office buildings, low-rent apartments and supermarkets rose almost everywhere. Some planners worried about keeping a work ethic going. Said a Saudi government minister: "We will have to be very careful not to spoil our citizens. Our people will have to deserve what they earn. We will furnish them with basic requirements, but nobody should live on charity."

The Europeans and the Japanese, umbilically dependent on the Middle East for respectively 70% and 80% of their oil, not only pressed their most modern technology on the Arab states but also granted them strong diplomatic support. Some European political leaders called for a new Euro–Middle East alliance, perhaps to replace the Atlantic Alliance. The French, responding to what they call the "New Reality" of oil-based Arab power, were especially obsequious in their attentions. The Dutch, long outspoken defenders of Israel, fell silent in fear of Arab wrath.

Indeed, the Arabs' ultimate weapon, oil, did much to change the entire balance of their conflict with Israel. Within the United Nations, a bloc of Arab, African, Latin American and Communist countries banded into a new majority, pushing through resolutions that isolated Israel and antagonized the U.S. Only the Dominican Republic and Bolivia voted with the U.S. and Israel when the General Assembly, by a margin of 105 to 4, invited the P.L.O.—with its long record of terrorism—to join in the debate over the Palestine issue. The U.N. welcomed P.L.O. Leader Yasser Arafat as a conquering hero and gave his organization permanent observer status.

Several other countries rose on petropower. Oil made Nigeria not only black Africa's wealthiest nation ($9.2 billion in earnings) but unquestionably its strongest political force. Indonesia, though still abysmally poor, is showing the first glimmerings of its potential as Southeast Asia's economic leader, thanks to oil exports. Oil-endowed Venezuela at midyear trebled its national budget, to almost $10 billion, to take account of rising revenues. The Venezuelans are expanding their state-owned steel industry in the Orinoco backlands, paying to educate thousands of future leaders at U.S. universities and gaining great influence among Central American republics by promising them loans. Says Venezuela's President Carlos Andrés Pérez: "This is our opportunity to create a new international economic order."

A new order is the ultimate goal of the petrocrats. Their aim is to lead many of the Third World nations in an economic revolution that is already bringing a radical redistribution of the world's wealth and political power. The transfer of riches to the oil producers has helped slow or stop the rise of living standards in many other countries—a development that has potentially grave social consequences. The steep economic growth that the industrial nations have enjoyed since World War II tended to soften social and economic inequalities because even the poor and deprived made visible progress year by year and could discern a brighter future. Now, if there is slow growth or no growth, demands for social justice will be more urgent—and harder to fulfill. Democratic governments will have to find ways to redistribute the existing wealth, or else face dissension and perhaps chaos.

The sudden, sharp rise in oil prices inflamed all sorts of problems, increasing government controls, intensifying nationalism and calling into question the future of free economies. People were gripped with the fear that events had overtaken their ability—or their government's ability—to cope. Otherwise sober men spoke of extreme solutions: repudiation of international debts, massive currency devaluations, the suspension of parliamentary government, even military intervention in the producing countries.

It was possible to blame too much of this malaise on oil. Many countries have long suffered from high inflation because they were living beyond their means for years. Particularly in the West's mass-consumer societies, the poor wanted to live like the middle class, and the middle class wanted to live like the rich. Demands piled up—for more goods, fatter wages, higher social welfare—and prices soared. Still, by best estimates, the rise in energy prices caused one-quarter to one-third of the world's inflation last year. As the price of oil increased, it kicked up the prices of countless oil-based products, including fertilizers, petrochemicals and synthetic textiles. To battle inflation, all Western nations clamped on restrictive budget and credit policies, causing their economies to slow down simultaneously for the first time since the 1930s.

The danger of a global recession grew because, as people spent more for oil, they had less money left over to spend on other things. The overall decline in demand reduced production and jobs. Because non-OPEC nations had to pay out so much for foreign oil, they moderated their buying of other imports; that slowed the growth of world trade, which has been a major source of international cooperation since World War II. The U.S.'s relations with its allies also came under strain, and the West seemed without will or unity. For most of the year, Western European nations and Japan refused to follow the U.S.'s call for a united front against the oil producers, essentially because European leaders considered the consumers' bargaining power too feeble.

The U.S. was a major oil exporter through the late 1950s, but then its own demands raced so far ahead of production that it now has to import more than one-third of its supply. The nation's bill for foreign oil pyramided from $3.9 billion in 1972* to $24 billion last year. The $20 billion jump meant that Americans either had to increase their foreign debts greatly or produce and export $20 billion more in goods and services—food, steel, planes, machinery, technology—to pay for oil imports. Unless the oil price comes down or the country sharply reduces its oil imports or substantially increases production, the U.S. will have to spend that extra $20 billion or more every year. This will drain off more of the nation's resources and build up trade debts that future generations will have to pay. In 1974 the rippling effects of rising oil prices contributed three or four percentage points to the U.S. inflation rate of 12%. The oil rise, which Yale Economist Richard Cooper called "King Faisal's tax," reduced Americans' purchasing

* For comparison, 1972 is used because it was the last "normal" year before the embargo and the biggest increases.

power and consumption of goods as much as a 10% increase in personal income taxes would have done.

For Europeans, life became a little darker, slower, chillier. Heating-oil prices went up 60% to 100%, and thermostats were turned down. In the midst of a French conservation drive in October, President Valéry Giscard d'Estaing found his Elysée Palace dining room so cold that he lunched with Premier Jacques Chirac in the library by a crackling fire. Throughout Western Europe, energy costs were a cause of the slump in sales of autos, houses and electrical appliances. Layoffs spread in those and other industries. Unemployment hit a postwar high in France. In Germany, foreign workers were being paid bonuses to quit and go back home to Spain, Turkey and Yugoslavia.

The poorest countries of Africa, Asia and Latin America were the worst hurt victims of the oil squeeze. Indeed, the developing countries' extra costs for oil last year totaled $10 billion, wiping out most of their foreign aid income of $11.4 billion from the industrialized world. In black Africa, only Nigeria has any big known reserves of oil, and Gabon, the Congo Republic and Angola possess some oil. For the other black African countries, the petrobill came to $1.3 billion last year. Development plans were stymied because so much money was drained off for oil. Drought-induced hunger became worse, in part because those countries could no longer afford as much gasoline to run their tractors, or fertilizers to nourish their fields. Inflation raced at rates averaging 45%.

The poorest countries—those with scant resources to finance their needed imports—descended into a new category, now known as the Fourth World. The old Third World became a more exclusive, OPEC-led grouping, limited to those nations that are exploiting their rich mineral or agricultural resources.

In sum, the world has entered an era in which natural resources will count for much more than before, conservation will gain a premium over consumption, and more attention will be paid to exploiting resources than curbing pollution. All this will bring many changes in lifestyles: slower gains in real purchasing power, stricter controls on energy use, smaller cars. It remains to be seen to what extent the changes will be accepted by such disparate forces as labor unions, auto manufacturers, and consumer and environmental groups.

With passion, the oil producers defend their price increases on the ground that it is high time that the producers of raw materials get a fair shake from the richer industrial nations. For too long, the terms of trade were stacked against the materials producers. While they were forced to pay ever inflating prices for their machines, medicines, food and other goods bought from the West, the developed countries not only imported oil at low, stable prices but also built industrial and consumer booms on it. Now the oil producers must build their own industries, both to get a more equitable share of the world's income and to insure themselves against the day when their petroleum resources run out. Furthermore, by keeping prices high, the producers argue they are really doing the rest of the world a favor by forcing both energy conservation and the search for alternative resources.

IN ALL THIS, THE role of the oil companies is growing weaker. The companies not only discovered and developed the oil but also put up billions of dollars to build rigs, pipelines, refineries and harbors. They have done so for more than 40 years, since long before the Saudis had much interest in oil, let alone the means to exploit it. The first prospectors—from Standard Oil of California—went to Saudi Arabia in 1933 and brought in the first well in 1938. They and later prospectors had a rugged frontier existence, living in tents and huts, relying on an 11,000-mile-long logistics line from the U.S., and coping with desert sand, burning heat and loneliness. In the late 1930s and early 1940s, they were joined by Exxon, Texaco and Mobil to form the Arabian American Oil Co. Oil prices were relatively low—$1.40 to $2 and the governments' take ranged from 20¢ to less than $1 a bbl.—because Middle East production costs were modest, oil was in surplus in the world, and the producers' governments were weak and disunited. Company earnings were huge. When supplies tightened and producers began to get together in the late 1960s, the governments' split of production profits rose from 50-50 to 67-33. Even before the price rises since 1973, Middle East governments profited nicely from oil; Saudi Arabia's take from 1965 to 1972 totaled $10 billion.

The companies, in fact, were among the biggest losers of 1974. The four U.S. partners in Aramco had to agree late in the year to sell their remaining 40% ownership to Faisal's government. It will pay the partners $2 billion for almost all their facilities, a price that the Saudis can meet with less than one month's oil earnings. The Saudi takeover will move Kuwait, Qatar, Oman and the United Arab Emirates to nationalize the last of the Western oil operations in those areas, probably this year. The companies will become mere agents, selling technical and marketing services to the governments for a fee.

If Faisal and his allies hold prices up, the rest of the world could encounter such compounded problems that 1974 would be remembered as an easy year. With oil at $10 a bbl., OPEC would charge the world another $600 billion in the next five years. To pay the bill, the 137 nations outside the cartel would have to deliver one-quarter of their total exports to OPEC's elite 13 countries. It would be impossible for the oil importers to transfer so much of their production—or for OPEC nations to absorb it all. The most frightening figure for the future is that OPEC nations stand to accumulate payments surpluses of $250 billion to $325 billion by 1980, and the rest of the world would run up exactly that much of a deficit.* For the countries that have them, surpluses create huge purchasing—and political—power. Conversely, deficits usually lead to recessions, devaluations and decline.

Naturally, the Saudis are piling up the biggest surpluses. At present prices and production levels, they will collect a staggering $150 billion over the next five years. But they will be unable to buy or build fast enough to use up even one-third of their oil money on domestic development. By 1980, they stand to have well over $100 billion in surplus—to lend, give away or invest in foreign countries.

In the chancelleries and countinghouses, everybody is seeking ways for the OPEC countries to lend their surpluses back to the oil importers in a massive "recycling." A hypothetical example of recycling: Italy pays several billions of dollars to Aramco, the marketing agent, for Saudi Arabian oil; Aramco then pays this money to Saudi Arabia, which in turn deposits it in Western banks; the banks then lend it back to the government of Italy. Trouble is, the petrodollar deposits are short-term (the oil countries want the power to pull their money out at a moment's notice), while most loans, to be useful to a government or business, must be for the longer term—anywhere from one to ten years. A further difficulty is that many of the big borrowers are chancy credit risks. More and more bankers fear that their institutions will go under if the OPEC depositors withdraw their money or the borrowers default on their loans.

One long-lasting problem is that recycling is really a euphemism for indebtedness, and interest payments must find their way back to the oil

* By contrast, West Germany now has the world's highest accumulated surplus, $36 billion. It will be surpassed this year by Saudi Arabia. The highest surplus ever accumulated by the U.S. was $26 billion in 1949; the total for the U.S. now is $16 billion.

countries. In the 1980s some OPEC members may be earning as much from interest on their loans and bank deposits as from oil. This added wealth would give them more flexibility to reduce oil production if they want to conserve their liquid gold or to punish importers by reductions for political reasons. Meanwhile, to pay the interest, the borrowers may have to print more and more money, fueling inflation.

Thus, even with the best of recycling, the importing nations will be vulnerable. Says Walter Levy, the world's leading oil consultant: "The world economy cannot survive in a healthy or remotely healthy condition if cartel pricing and actual or threatened supply restraints of oil continue."

The Western nations will have no real bargaining strength until they show that they are taking strong measures to conserve. By significantly reducing demand, the big buyers of oil might force OPEC into production cuts that some cartel members may eventually find intolerable. Cutbacks would be particularly rough for Iran and Iraq, both of which plan substantial production increases in the next few years to finance their grand development programs. Rather than reduce output, other populous countries with ambitious development schemes—Nigeria, Venezuela, Indonesia—might be tempted to buck the cartel by selling below the fixed price.

OPEC, however, has not been at all damaged by a world oil surplus of one to two million bbl. a day, which has shown up because high prices reduced consumption last year. In the non-Communist world, consumption fell from 48 million bbl. a day in 1973 to 46.5 million bbl. last year; in the U.S., it declined from 17 million bbl. to 16.2 million bbl. Partly in response, OPEC is now producing at 20% below capacity with no visible problems. Again, it is Saudi Arabia that holds the key. The country has accumulated so much money that it could stop production for two or three years and still have more than enough cash to import food, provide free medical care and education, finance new industry and subsidize other Arab nations. But unless and until the industrial nations get together, much of the non-Communist world could not long function without Saudi Arabia's 8.5 million bbl. per day.

Even so, the consumers must conserve to show OPEC that they are serious and to hold down their payments to the cartel. Kissinger has urged that they hold their oil imports essentially flat over the next decade. Certainly the U.S. can and must lead the way by making the severest cuts because it wastes so much energy. A nation that has one-twentieth of the world's population should not expect to go on burning one-third of the world's oil.

Through taxes and other mandatory measures, the U.S. could switch from profligacy to a new conservation ethic. The remedies are well known. Much energy could be saved by increasing federal taxes on gasoline, clamping a steeply graduated tax on heavy, thirsty cars, pumping many more millions into mass transit, and granting tax credits for purchases of building insulation. In addition, the U.S. could and should expand its domestic supplies of energy by increasing the capacity of the Alaska pipeline, opening the Navy's petroleum reserves in California and Alaska, encouraging offshore drilling, liberalizing controls on the strip-mining of coal (but adding guarantees that the lands would be reclaimed) and allowing natural gas prices to double or more.

Beyond conserving energy and recycling OPEC's money, the oil importers have no feasible weapons against the cartel. Military intervention could be extremely risky. There is always the danger that the Soviets would step in on the side of the Arabs—or extract a high political price from the West for staying out. Pipelines might be vulnerable to sabotage, though captured oilfields could be fairly easily protected. In any event, U.S. authorities condemn the wave of fantasizing about oil wars as "highly irresponsible." Military intervention, says a Washington policymaker, would be considered "only as absolutely a last resort to prevent the collapse of the industrialized world and not just to get the oil price down."

A settlement with Israel would not itself lead to a price reduction. The non-Arab nations—Iran, Venezuela, Nigeria, Indonesia—though not part of the conflict, still want to maintain or increase prices. Yet marked progress toward peace on terms acceptable to the Arabs is absolutely essential before prices can soften; the Arabs will insist on that. There is virtual consensus among Western policymakers that Israel must give up almost all of its 1967 conquests and accept a homeland for the Palestinians. Otherwise, wars are likely to continue, and Israel cannot win the last round against 120 million Arabs enriched and armed by oil money.

A most positive step would be for oil producers and consumers to seek common and reciprocal interests going far beyond energy. The producers should be given greater responsibilities and more high offices in international councils. For example, they should get far more than the 5% of the voting strength that they now have in the World Bank and the International Monetary Fund. This would give them a larger voice in setting international monetary policies, which they deserve, and would also oblige them to put up quite a bit more than the 5% that they now give to underwrite those groups. The producers have been increasing their foreign aid fairly rapidly, but they probably should give much more in grants, low-interest loans and concessionary prices to the neediest countries. Last year OPEC members made aid commitments totaling $9.6 billion and actually disbursed $2.6 billion in gifts, concessionary loans and other aid—roughly half of it to Egypt, Syria and Jordan.

Whatever devices are created to put OPEC capital to work in the rest of the world, the Western countries should help the oil producers build up their own agriculture and industries. Faisal notes, for example, that his rich country badly needs industrialization. To help prepare the producers for the day, however distant, when their oil runs out, the West should also join them in developing alternative forms of energy and should send technology and experts to OPEC countries. Fast development is inevitable in the oil countries, and it will help work off their surpluses by spurring their imports. For their part, OPEC members may lend or invest some of the huge sums of capital that oil importers will need to develop energy supplies from the atom, from shale and sands and, probably many years from now, from the sun and wind.

In the difficult decade ahead, the best hope is that all sides will realize that they are really interdependent—for resources, technologies, goods, capital, ideas. The old world of Western dominance is dead, but if the oil powers try to dominate the new world of interdependencies, the result will be bankruptcies and deflation in the West, and even worse poverty and hunger in the have-not developing countries.

The oil producers, who talk a great deal about past exploitation and their future aspirations, might consider the implications for themselves of the havoc that their monopoly pricing is causing the rest of humankind. The oil consumers, who are the victims of that upheaval, would do well to ponder with more sympathy the OPEC countries' deeply felt desire for a larger share of the world's wealth. In this great global clash of interests, it is time for both sides to soften their anger and seek new ways to get along with each other. If sanity is to prevail, the guiding policy must be not confrontation but cooperation and conservation. ∎

The Computer Moves In

BY OTTO FRIEDRICH

[*On rare occasions* TIME's *annual choice was not a person but a thing—here, the machine that was revolutionizing the way people worked, played, learned and lived*]

January 3, 1983

WILL SOMEONE PLEASE TELL ME, the bright red advertisement asks in mock irritation, WHAT A PERSONAL COMPUTER CAN DO? The ad provides not merely an answer, but 100 of them. A personal computer, it says, can send letters at the speed of light, diagnose a sick poodle, custom-tailor an insurance program in minutes, test recipes for beer. Testimonials abound. Michael Lamb of Tucson figured out how a personal computer could monitor anesthesia during surgery; the rock group Earth, Wind and Fire uses one to explode smoke bombs onstage during concerts; the Rev. Ron Jaenisch of Sunnyvale, Calif., programmed his machine so it can recite an entire wedding ceremony.

In the cavernous Las Vegas Convention Center a month ago, more than 1,000 computer companies large and small were showing off their wares, their floppy discs and disc drives, joy sticks and modems, to a mob of some 50,000 buyers, middlemen and assorted technology buffs. Look! Here is Hewlett-Packard's HP9000, on which you can sketch a new airplane, say, and immediately see the results in 3-D through holograph imaging; here is how the Votan can answer and act on a telephone call in the middle of the night from a salesman on the other side of the country; here is the

Olivetti M20 that entertains bystanders by drawing garishly colored pictures of Marilyn Monroe; here is a program designed by The Alien Group that enables an Atari computer to say aloud anything typed on its keyboard in any language. It also sings, in a buzzing humanoid voice, *Amazing Grace* and *When I'm 64* or anything else that anyone wants to teach it.

As both the Apple Computer advertisement and the Las Vegas circus indicate, the enduring American love affairs with the automobile and the television set are now being transformed into a giddy passion for the personal computer. This passion is partly fad, partly a sense of how life could be made better, partly a gigantic sales campaign. Above all, it is the end result of a technological revolution that has been in the making for four decades and is now, quite literally, hitting home.

Americans are receptive to the revolution and optimistic about its impact. A new poll* for TIME by Yankelovich, Skelly and White indicates that nearly 80% of Americans expect that in the fairly near future, home computers will be as commonplace as television sets or dishwashers. Although they see dangers of unemployment and dehumanization, solid majorities feel that the computer revolution will ultimately raise production and therefore living standards (67%), and that it will improve the quality of their children's education (68%).

The sales figures are awesome and will become more so. In 1980 some two dozen firms sold 724,000 personal computers for $1.8 billion. The following year 20 more companies joined the stampede, including giant IBM, and sales doubled to 1.4 million units at just under $3 billion. When the final figures are in for 1982, according to Dataquest, a California research firm, more than 100 companies will probably have sold 2.8 million units for $4.9 billion.

To be sure, the big, complex, costly "mainframe" computer has been playing an increasingly important role in practically everyone's life for the past quarter-century. It predicts the weather, processes checks, scrutinizes tax returns, guides intercontinental missiles and performs innumerable other operations for governments and corporations. The computer has made possible the exploration of space. It has changed the way wars are fought. Despite its size, however, the mainframe does its work all but invisibly, behind the closed doors of a special, climate-controlled room.

Now, thanks to the transistor and the silicon chip, the computer has

---

* *The telephone survey of 1,019 registered voters was conducted on Dec. 8 and 9. The margin of sampling error is plus or minus 3%.*

been reduced so dramatically in both bulk and price that it is accessible to millions. In 1982 a cascade of computers beeped and blipped their way into the American office, the American school, the American home. The "information revolution" that futurists have long predicted has arrived, bringing with it the promise of dramatic changes in the way people live and work, perhaps even in the way they think. America will never be the same.

In a larger perspective, the entire world will never be the same. The industrialized nations of the West are already scrambling to computerize (1982 sales: 435,000 in Japan, 392,000 in Western Europe). The effect of the machines on the Third World is more uncertain. Some experts argue that computers will, if anything, widen the gap between haves and have-nots. But the prophets of high technology believe the computer is so cheap and so powerful that it could enable underdeveloped nations to bypass the whole industrial revolution. While robot factories could fill the need for manufactured goods, the microprocessor would create myriad new industries, and an international computer network could bring important agricultural and medical information to even the most remote villages. "What networks of railroads, highways and canals were in another age, networks of telecommunications, information and computerization... are today," says Austrian Chancellor Bruno Kreisky. Says French Editor Jean-Jacques Servan-Schreiber, who believes that the computer's teaching capability can conquer the Third World's illiteracy and even its tradition of high birth rates: "It is the source of new life that has been delivered to us."

There are some occasions when the most significant force in a year's news is not a single individual but a process, and a widespread recognition by a whole society that this process is changing the course of all other processes. That is why, after weighing the ebb and flow of events around the world, TIME has decided that 1982 is the year of the computer. It would have been possible to single out as Man of the Year one of the engineers or entrepreneurs who masterminded this technological revolution, but no one person has clearly dominated those turbulent events. More important, such a selection would obscure the main point. TIME's Man of the Year for 1982, the greatest influence for good or evil, is not a man at all. It is a machine: the computer.

It is easy enough to look at the world around us and conclude that the computer has not changed things all that drastically. But one can conclude from similar observations that the earth is flat, and that the sun circles it every 24 hours. Although everything seems much the same from one day to the next, changes under the surface of life's routines are actually occurring at almost unimaginable speed. Just 100 years ago, parts of New York City were lighted for the first time by a strange new force called electricity; just 100 years ago, the German Engineer Gottlieb Daimler began building a gasoline-fueled internal combustion engine (three more years passed before he fitted it to a bicycle). So it is with the computer.

THE FIRST FULLY ELECTRONIC digital computer built in the U.S. dates back only to the end of World War II. Created at the University of Pennsylvania, ENIAC weighed 30 tons and contained 18,000 vacuum tubes, which failed at an average of one every seven minutes. The arrival of the transistor and the miniaturized circuit in the 1950s made it possible to reduce a room-size computer to a silicon chip the size of a pea. And prices kept dropping. In contrast to the $487,000 paid for ENIAC, a top IBM personal computer today costs about $4,000, and some discounters offer a basic Timex-Sinclair 1000 for $77.95. One computer expert illustrates the trend by estimating that if the automobile business had developed like the computer business, a Rolls-Royce would now cost $2.75 and run 3 million miles on a gallon of gas.

Looking ahead, the computer industry sees pure gold. There are 83 million U.S. homes with TV sets, 54 million white-collar workers, 26 million professionals, 4 million small businesses. Computer salesmen are hungrily eyeing every one of them. Estimates for the number of personal computers in use by the end of the century run as high as 80 million. Then there are all the auxiliary industries: desks to hold computers, luggage to carry them, cleansers to polish them. "The surface is barely scratched," says Ulric Weil, an analyst for Morgan Stanley.

Beyond the computer hardware lies the virtually limitless market for software, all those prerecorded programs that tell the willing but mindless computer what to do. These discs and cassettes range from John Wiley & Sons' investment analysis program for $59.95 (some run as high as $5,000) to Control Data's PLATO programs that teach Spanish or physics ($45 for the first lesson, $35 for succeeding ones) to a profusion of space wars, treasure hunts and other electronic games.

This most visible aspect of the computer revolution, the video game, is its least significant. But even if the buzz and clang of the arcades is largely a teen-age fad, doomed to go the way of Rubik's Cube and the Hula Hoop, it is nonetheless a remarkable phenomenon. About 20 corporations are selling some 250 different game cassettes for roughly $2 billion this year. According to some estimates, more than half of all the personal computers bought for home use are devoted mainly to games.

Computer enthusiasts argue that these games have educational value, by teaching logic, or vocabulary, or something. Some are even used for medical therapy. Probably the most important effect of these games, however, is that they have brought a form of the computer into millions of homes and convinced millions of people that it is both pleasant and easy to operate, what computer buffs call "user friendly." Games, says Philip D. Estridge, head of IBM's personal computer operations, "aid in the discovery process."

Apart from games, the two things that the computer does best have wide implications but are quite basic. One is simply computation, manipulating thousands of numbers per second. The other is the ability to store, sort through and rapidly retrieve immense amounts of information. More than half of all employed Americans now earn their living not by producing things but as "knowledge workers," exchanging various kinds of information, and the personal computer stands ready to change how all of them do their jobs.

• Frank Herringer, a group vice president of Transamerica Corp., installed an Apple in his suburban home in Lafayette, Calif., and spent a weekend analyzing various proposals for Transamerica's $300 million takeover of the New York insurance brokerage firm of Fred S. James Co. Inc. "It allowed me to get a good feel for the critical numbers," says Herringer. "I could work through alternative options, and there were no leaks."

• Terry Howard, 44, used to have a long commute to his job at a San Francisco stock brokerage, where all his work involved computer data and telephoning. With a personal computer, he set up his own firm at home in San Rafael. Instead of rising at 6 a.m. to drive to the city, he runs five miles before settling down to work. Says he: "It didn't make sense to spend two hours of every day burning up gas, when my customers on the telephone don't care whether I'm sitting at home or in a high rise in San Francisco."

• John Watkins, safety director at Harriet & Henderson Yarns, in Henderson, N.C., is one of 20 key employees whom the company helped to buy home computers and paid to get trained this year. Watkins is trying to design a program that will record and analyze all mill accidents: who was injured, how, when, why. Says he: "I keep track of all the cases that are referred to a doctor, but for every doctor case, there are 25 times as many first-aid cases that should be recorded." Meantime, he has designed a math program for his son Brent and is shopping for a word-processing program to help his wife Mary Edith write her master's thesis in psychology. Says he: "I don't know what it can't do. It's like asking yourself, 'What's the most exciting thing you've ever done?' Well, I don't know because I haven't done it yet."

Aaron Brown, a former defensive end for the Kansas City Chiefs and now an office-furniture salesman in Minneapolis, was converted to the computer by his son Sean, 15, who was converted at a summer course in computer math. "I thought of computers very much as toys," says Brown, "but Sean started telling me, 'You could use a computer in your work.' I said, 'Yeah, yeah, yeah.' " Three years ago, the family took a vote on whether to go to California for a vacation or to buy an Apple. The Apple won, 3 to 1, and to prove its value, Sean wrote his father a program that computes gross profits and commissions on any sale.

Brown started with "simple things," like filing the names and telephone numbers of potential customers. "Say I was going to a particular area of the city," Brown says. "I would ask the computer to pull up the accounts in a certain zip-code area, or if I wanted all the customers who were interested in whole office systems, I could pull that up too." The payoff: since he started using the computer, he has doubled his annual sales to more than $1 million.

Reatha Brown has been lobbying for a new carpet, but she is becoming resigned to the prospect that the family will acquire a new hard-disc drive instead. "The video-cassette recorder," she sighs, pointing across the room, "that was my other carpet." Replies her husband, setting forth an argument that is likely to be replayed in millions of households in the years just ahead: "We make money with the computer, but all we can do with a new carpet is walk on it. Somebody once said there were five reasons to spend money: on necessities, on investments, on self-improvement, on memories and to impress your friends. The carpet falls in that last category, but the computer falls in all five."

By itself, the personal computer is a machine with formidable capabilities for tabulating, modeling or recording. Those capabilities can be multiplied almost indefinitely by plugging it into a network of other computers. This is generally done by attaching a desktop model to a telephone line (two-way cables and earth satellites are coming increasingly into use). One can then dial an electronic data base, which not only provides all manner of information but also collects and transmits messages: electronic mail.

Just as the term personal computer can apply to both a home machine and an office machine (and indeed blurs the distinction between the two places), many of the first enthusiastic users of these devices have been people who do much of their work at home: doctors, lawyers, small businessmen, writers, engineers. Such people also have special needs for the networks of specialized data.

The personal computer and its networks are even changing that oldest of all home businesses, the family farm. Though only about 3% of commercial farmers and ranchers now have computers, that number is expected to rise to nearly 20% within the next five years. One who has grasped the true faith is Bob Johnson, who helps run his family's 2,800-acre pig farm near De Kalb, Ill. Outside, the winter's first snowflakes have dusted the low-slung roofs of the six red-and-white barns and the brown fields specked with corn stubble. Inside the two-room office building, Johnson slips a disc into his computer and types "D" (for dial) and a telephone number. He is immediately connected to the Illinois farm bureau's newly computerized AgriVisor service. It not only gives him weather conditions to the west and the latest hog prices on the Chicago commodities exchange, but also offers advice. Should farmers continue to postpone the sale of their newly harvested corn? "Remember," the computer counsels, "that holding on for a dime or a nickel may not be worth the long-term wait."

Johnson's computer now knows the yields on 35 test plots of corn, the breeding records of his 300 sows, how much feed his hogs have eaten (2,787,260 lbs.) and at what cost ($166,047.73). "This way, you can charge your hogs the cost of the feed when you sell them and figure out if you're making any money," says Johnson. "We never had this kind of information before. It would have taken too long to calculate. But we knew we needed it."

Just as the computer is changing the way work is done in home offices, so it is revolutionizing the office. Routine tasks like managing payrolls and checking inventories have long since been turned over to computers, but now the typewriter is giving way to the word processor, and every office thus becomes part of a network. This change has barely begun; about 10% of the typewriters in the 500 largest industrial corporations have so far been replaced. But the economic imperatives are inescapable. All told, office professionals could save about 15% of their time if they used the technology now available, says a study by Booz, Allen & Hamilton, and that technology is constantly improving. In one survey of corporations, 55% said they were planning to acquire the latest equipment. This technology involves not just word processors but computerized electronic message systems that could eventually make paper obsolete, and wall-size, two-way TV teleconference screens that will obviate traveling to meetings.

The standard home computer can seem menacing when it appears in an office. Secretaries are often suspicious of new equipment, particularly if it appears to threaten their jobs, and so are executives. Some senior officials resist using a keyboard on the ground that such work is demeaning. Two executives in a large firm reportedly refuse to read any computer print-out until their secretaries have retyped it into the form of a standard memo. "The biggest problem in introducing computers into an office is management itself," says Ted Stout of National Systems Inc., an office design firm in Atlanta. "They don't understand it, and they are scared to death of it."

But there is an opposite fear that drives anxious executives toward the machines: the worry that younger and more sophisticated rivals will push ahead of them. "All you have to do," says Alexander Horniman, an industrial psychologist at the University of Virginia's Darden School of Business, "is walk down the hall and see people using the computer and imagine they have access to all sorts of information you don't." Argues Harold Todd, executive vice president at First Atlanta Bank: "Managers who do not have the ability to use a terminal within three to five years may become organizationally dysfunctional." That is to say, useless.

If more and more offices do most of their work on computers, and if a personal computer can be put in a living room, why should anyone have to go to work in an office at all? The question can bring a stab of hope to anybody who spends hours every day on the San Diego Freeway or the Long Island Rail Road. Nor is "telecommuting" as unrealistic as it sounds. In his 1980 book, *The Third Wave*, futurist Alvin Toffler portrays a 21st century world in which the computer revolution has canceled out many of the fundamental changes wrought by the Industrial Revolution: the centralization and standardization of work in the factory, the office, the assembly line. These changes may seem eternal, but they are less than two centuries old. Instead, Toffler imagines a revived version of pre-industrial life in what he has named "the electronic cottage," a utopian abode where all members of the family work, learn and enjoy their leisure around the electronic hearth, the computer.

Continental Illinois Bank and Trust Co. of Chicago has experimented with such electronic cottages by providing half a dozen workers with word processors so they could stay at home. Control Data tried a similar experiment and ran into a problem: some of its 50 "alternate site workers" felt isolated, deprived of their social life around the water cooler. The company decided to ask them to the office for lunch and meetings every week. "People are like ants, they're communal creatures," says Dean Scheff, chairman and founder of CPT Corp., a word-processing firm near Minneapolis. "They need to interact to get the creative juices flowing. Very few of us are hermits."

TIME's Yankelovich poll underlines the point. Some 73% of the respondents believed that the computer revolution would enable more people to work at home. But only 31% said they would prefer to do so themselves. Most work no longer involves a hayfield, a coal mine or a sweatshop, but a field for social intercourse. This is not just a matter of trading gossip in the corridors; work itself, particularly in the information industries, requires the stimulation of personal contact in the exchange of ideas: sometimes organized conferences, sometimes simply what is called "the schmooze factor." Says Sociologist Robert Schrank: "The workplace performs the function of community."

PROPHETS OF THE ELECTRONIC cottage predict that it will once again enable people to find community where they once did: in their communities. Continental Illinois Bank, for one, has opened a suburban "satellite work station" that gets employees out of the house but not all the way downtown. Ford, Atlantic Richfield and Merrill Lynch have found that teleconferencing can reach far more people for far less money than traditional sales conferences.

To the nation's 10 million physically handicapped, telecommuting encourages new hopes of earning a livelihood. A Chicago-area organization called Lift has taught computer programming to 50 people with such devastating afflictions as polio, cerebral palsy and spinal damage. Lift President Charles Schmidt cites a 46-year-old man paralyzed by polio: "He never held a job in his life until he entered our program three years ago, and now he's a programmer for Walgreens."

In the home, computer enthusiasts delight in imagining machines performing the domestic chores. A little of that fantasy is already reality. New York City Real Estate Executive David Rose, for example, uses his Apple in business deals, to catalogue his 4,000 books and to write fund-raising letters to his Yale classmates. But he also uses it to wake him in the morning with soft music, turn on the TV, adjust the lights and make the coffee.

In medicine, the computer, which started by keeping records and sending bills, now suggests diagnoses. CADUCEUS knows some 4,000 symptoms of more than 500 diseases; MYCIN specializes in infectious diseases; PUFF measures lung functions. All can be plugged into a master network called SUMEX-AIM, with headquarters at Stanford in the West and Rutgers in the East. This may all sound like another step toward the disappearance of the friendly neighborhood G.P., but while it is possible that a family doctor would recognize 4,000 different symptoms, CADUCEUS is more likely to see patterns in what patients report and can then suggest a diagnosis. The process may sound dehumanized, but in one hospital where the computer specializes in peptic ulcers, a survey of patients showed that they found the machine "more friendly, polite, relaxing and comprehensible" than the average physician.

The microcomputer is achieving dramatic effects on the ailing human body. These devices control the pacemakers implanted in victims of heart disease; they pump carefully measured quantities of insulin into the bodies of diabetics; they test blood samples for hundreds of different allergies; they translate sounds into vibrations that the deaf can "hear"; they stimulate deadened muscles with electric impulses that may eventually enable the paralyzed to walk. In all the technologists' images of the future, however, there are elements of exaggeration and wishful thinking. Though the speed of change is extraordinary, so is the vastness of the landscape to be changed.

Certainly the personal computer is not without its flaws. As most new buyers soon learn, it is not that easy for a novice to use, particularly when the manuals contain instructions like this specimen from Apple: "This character prevents script from terminating the currently forming output line when it encounters the script command in the input stream." Another problem is that most personal computers end up costing considerably more than the ads imply. The $100 model does not really do very much, and the $1,000 version usually requires additional payments for the disc drive or the printer or the modem.

It is becoming increasingly evident that a fool assigned to work with a computer can conceal his own foolishness in the guise of high-tech authority. Lives there a single citizen who has not been commanded by a misguided computer to pay an income tax installment or department store bill that he has already paid?

What is true for fools is no less true for criminals, who are now able to commit electronic larceny from the comfort of their living rooms. The probable champion is Stanley Mark Rifkin, a computer analyst in Los Angeles, who tricked the machines at the Security Pacific National Bank into giving him $10 million. While free on bail for that in 1979 (he was eventually sentenced to eight years), he was arrested for trying to steal $50 million from Union Bank (the charges were eventually dropped). According to Donn Parker, a specialist in computer abuse at SRI International (formerly the Stanford Research Institute), "Nobody seems to know exactly what computer crime is, how much of it there is, and whether it is increasing or decreasing. We do know that computers are changing the nature of business crime significantly."

Even if all the technical and intellectual problems can be solved, there are major social problems inherent in the computer revolution. The most obvious is unemployment, since the basic purpose of commercial computerization is to get more work done by fewer people. One British study predicts that "automation-induced unemployment" in Western Europe could reach 16% in the next decade, but most analyses are more optimistic. The general rule seems to be that new technology eventually creates as many jobs as it destroys, and often more. "People who put in computers usually increase their staffs as well," says CPT's Scheff. "Of course," he adds, "one industry may kill another industry. That's tough on some people."

Such social problems are not the fault of the computer, of course, but a consequence of the way the American society might use the computer. "Even in the days of the big mainframe computers, they were a machine for the few," says Katharine Davis Fishman, author of *The Computer Establishment.* "It was a tool to help the rich get richer. It still is to a large extent. One of the great values of the personal computer is that smaller concerns, smaller organizations can now have some of the advantages of the bigger organizations."

How society uses its computers depends greatly on what kind of computers are made and sold, and that depends, in turn, on an industry in a state of chaotic growth. Innovators are pushing off in different directions. Hewlett-Packard is experimenting with machines that respond to vocal commands; Osborne is leading a rush toward portable computers, ideally no larger than a book. And for every innovator, there are at least five imitators selling copies.

Whatever its variations, there is an inevitability about the computerization of America. Commercial efficiency requires it, Big Government requires it, modern life requires it, and so it is coming to pass. But the essential element in this sense of inevitability is the way in which the young take to computers: not as just another obligation imposed by adult society but as a game, a pleasure, a tool, a system that fits naturally into their lives. Unlike anyone over 40, these children have grown up with TV screens; the computer is a screen that responds to them, hooked to a machine that can be programmed to respond the way they want it to. That is power.

Many Americans concerned about the erosion of the schools put faith in the computer as a possible savior of their children's education, at school and at home. The Yankelovich poll showed that 57% thought personal computers would enable children to read and to do arithmetic better. Claims William Ridley, Control Data's vice president for education strategy: "If you want to improve youngsters one grade level in reading, our PLATO program with teacher supervision can do it up to four times faster and for 40% less expense than teachers alone."

No less important than this kind of drill is the use of computers to teach children about computers. They like to learn programming, and they are good at it, often better than their teachers, even in the early grades. They treat it as play, a secret skill, unknown among many of their parents. They delight in cracking corporate security and filching financial secrets, inventing new games and playing them on military networks, inserting obscene jokes into other people's programs. In soberer versions that sort of skill will become a necessity in thousands of jobs opening up in the future.

This transformation of the young raises a fundamental and sometimes menacing question: Will the computer change the very nature of human thought? And if so, for better or worse? There has been much time wasted on the debate over whether computers can be made to think, as HAL seemed to be doing in *2001,* when it murdered the astronauts who might challenge its command of the spaceflight. That answer is simple: computers do not think, but they do simulate many of the processes of the human brain: remembering, comparing, analyzing. And as people rely on the computer to do things that they used to do inside their heads, what happens to their heads?

Will the computer's ability to do routine work mean that human thinking will shift to a higher level? Will IQs rise? Will there be more intellectuals? The computer may make a lot of learning as unnecessary as memorizing the multiplication tables. But if a dictionary stored in the computer's memory can easily correct any spelling mistakes, what is the point of learning to spell? And if the mind is freed from intellectual routine, will it race off in pursuit of important ideas or lazily spend its time on more video games?

Charles P. Lecht, president of the New York consulting firm Lecht Scientific, argues that "what the lever was to the body, the computer system is to the mind." Says he: "Computers help teach kids to think. Beyond that, they motivate people to think. There is a great difference between intelligence and manipulative capacity. Computers help us to realize that difference."

For all such prophecies, M.I.T. Computer Professor Joseph Weizenbaum has answers ranging from disapproval to scorn. He has insisted that "giving children computers to play with . . . cannot touch . . . any real problem," and he has described the new computer generation as "bright young men of disheveled appearance [playing out] megalomaniacal fantasies of omnipotence."

Weizenbaum's basic objection to the computer enthusiasts is that they have no sense of limits. Says he: "The assertion that all human knowledge is encodable in streams of zeros and ones—philosophically, that's very hard to swallow. In effect, the whole world is made to seem computable. This generates a kind of tunnel vision, where the only problems that seem legitimate are problems that can be put on a computer. There is a whole world of real problems, of human problems, which is essentially ignored."

So the revolution has begun, and as usually happens with revolutions, nobody can agree on where it is going or how it will end. Nils Nilsson, director of the Artificial Intelligence Center at SRI International, believes the personal computer, like television, can "greatly increase the forces of both good and evil." Marvin Minsky, another of M.I.T.'s computer experts, believes the key significance of the personal computer is not the establishment of an intellectual ruling class, as some fear, but rather a kind of democratization of the new technology. Says he: "The desktop revolution has brought the tools that only professionals have had into the hands of the public. God knows what will happen now."

Perhaps the revolution will fulfill itself only when people no longer see anything unusual in the brave New World, when they see their computer not as a fearsome challenger to their intelligence but as a useful linkup of some everyday gadgets: the calculator, the TV and the typewriter. Or as Osborne's Adam Osborne puts it: "The future lies in designing and selling computers that people don't realize are computers at all." ∎

—REPORTED BY MICHAEL MORITZ/SAN FRANCISCO, J. MADELEINE NASH/
CHICAGO AND PETER STOLER/NEW YORK

A Brief History of Relativity

BY STEPHEN HAWKING

[
*To explain the ideas of Albert Einstein that transformed
our sense of the universe and made him the choice as
Man of the Century, TIME tapped a popular writer who
was himself a distinguished theoretical physicist*
]

December 31, 1999

TOWARD THE END OF the 19th century scientists believed they were close to a complete description of the universe. They imagined that space was filled everywhere by a continuous medium called the ether. Light rays and radio signals were waves in this ether just as sound is pressure waves in air. All that was needed to complete the theory was careful measurements of the elastic properties of the ether; once they had those nailed down, everything else would fall into place.

Soon, however, discrepancies with the idea of an all-pervading ether began to appear. You would expect light to travel at a fixed speed through the ether. So if you were traveling in the same direction as the light, you would expect that its speed would appear to be lower, and if you were traveling in the opposite direction to the light, that its speed would appear to be higher. Yet a series of experiments failed to find any evidence for differences in speed due to motion through the ether.

The most careful and accurate of these experiments was carried out by Albert Michelson and Edward Morley at the Case Institute in Cleveland, Ohio, in 1887. They compared the speed of light in two beams at right angles to each other. As the earth rotates on its axis and orbits the sun, they reasoned, it will move through the ether, and the speed of light in these two beams should diverge. But Michelson and Morley found no daily or yearly differences between the two beams of light. It was as if light always traveled at the same speed relative to you, no matter how you were moving.

The Irish physicist George FitzGerald and the Dutch physicist Hendrik Lorentz were the first to suggest that bodies moving through the ether would contract and that clocks would slow. This shrinking and slowing would be such that everyone would measure the same speed for light no matter how they were moving with respect to the ether, which FitzGerald and Lorentz regarded as a real substance.

But it was a young clerk named Albert Einstein, working in the Swiss Patent Office in Bern, who cut through the ether and solved the speed-of-light problem once and for all. In June 1905 he wrote one of three papers that would establish him as one of the world's leading scientists—and in the process start two conceptual revolutions that changed our understanding of time, space and reality.

In that 1905 paper, Einstein pointed out that because you could not detect whether or not you were moving through the ether, the whole notion of an ether was redundant. Instead, Einstein started from the postulate that the laws of science should appear the same to all freely moving observers. In particular, observers should all measure the same speed for light, no matter how they were moving.

This required abandoning the idea that there is a universal quantity called time that all clocks measure. Instead, everyone would have his own personal time. The clocks of two people would agree if they were at rest with respect to each other but not if they were moving. This has been confirmed by a number of experiments, including one in which an extremely accurate timepiece was flown around the world and then compared with one that had stayed in place. If you wanted to live longer, you could keep flying to the east so the speed of the plane added to the earth's rotation. However, the tiny fraction of a second you gained would be more than offset by eating airline meals.

Einstein's postulate that the laws of nature should appear the same to all freely moving observers was the foundation of the theory of relativity, so called because it implies that only relative motion is important. Its beauty and simplicity were convincing to many scientists and philosophers. But there remained a lot of opposition. Einstein had overthrown two of the Absolutes (with a capital A) of 19th century science: Absolute

Rest as represented by the ether, and Absolute or Universal Time that all clocks would measure. Did this imply, people asked, that there were no absolute moral standards, that everything was relative?

This unease continued through the 1920s and '30s. When Einstein was awarded the Nobel Prize in 1921, the citation was for important—but by Einstein's standards comparatively minor—work also carried out in 1905. There was no mention of relativity, which was considered too controversial. I still get two or three letters a week telling me Einstein was wrong. Nevertheless, the theory of relativity is now completely accepted by the scientific community, and its predictions have been verified in countless applications.

A very important consequence of relativity is the relation between mass and energy. Einstein's postulate that the speed of light should appear the same to everyone implied that nothing could be moving faster than light. What happens is that as energy is used to accelerate a particle or a spaceship, the object's mass increases, making it harder to accelerate any more. To accelerate the particle to the speed of light is impossible because it would take an infinite amount of energy. The equivalence of mass and energy is summed up in Einstein's famous equation $E=mc^2$, probably the only physics equation to have recognition on the street.

Among the consequences of this law is that if the nucleus of a uranium atom fissions (splits) into two nuclei with slightly less total mass, a tremendous amount of energy is released. In 1939, with World War II looming, a group of scientists who realized the implications of this persuaded Einstein to overcome his pacifist scruples and write a letter to President Roosevelt urging the U.S. to start a program of nuclear research. This led to the Manhattan Project and the atom bomb that exploded over Hiroshima in 1945. Some people blame the atom bomb on Einstein because he discovered the relation between mass and energy. But that's like blaming Newton for the gravity that causes airplanes to crash. Einstein took no part in the Manhattan Project and was horrified by the explosion.

Although the theory of relativity fit well with the laws that govern electricity and magnetism, it wasn't compatible with Newton's law of gravity. This law said that if you changed the distribution of matter in one region of space, the change in the gravitational field would be felt instantaneously everywhere else in the universe. Not only would this mean you could send signals faster than light (something that was forbidden by relativity), but it also required the Absolute or Universal Time that relativity had abolished in favor of personal or relativistic time.

Einstein was aware of this difficulty in 1907, while he was still at the patent office in Bern, but didn't begin to think seriously about the problem until he was at the German University in Prague in 1911. He realized that there is a close relationship between acceleration and a gravitational field. Someone in a closed box cannot tell whether he is sitting at rest in the earth's gravitational field or being accelerated by a rocket in free space. (This being before the age of *Star Trek,* Einstein thought of people in elevators rather than spaceships. But you cannot accelerate or fall freely very far in an elevator before disaster strikes.)

If the earth were flat, one could equally well say that the apple fell on Newton's head because of gravity or that Newton's head hit the apple because he and the surface of the earth were accelerating upward. This equivalence between acceleration and gravity didn't seem to work for a round earth, however; people on the other side of the world would have to be accelerating in the opposite direction but staying at a constant distance from us.

On his return to Zurich in 1912 Einstein had a brainstorm. He realized that the equivalence of gravity and acceleration could work if there was some give-and-take in the geometry of reality. What if space-time—an entity Einstein invented to incorporate the three familiar dimensions of space with a fourth dimension, time—was curved, and not flat, as had been assumed? His idea was that mass and energy would warp space-time in some manner yet to be determined. Objects like apples or planets would try to move in straight lines through space-time, but their paths would appear to be bent by a gravitational field because space-time is curved.

With the help of his friend Marcel Grossmann, Einstein studied the theory of curved spaces and surfaces that had been developed by Bernhard Riemann as a piece of abstract mathematics, without any thought that it would be relevant to the real world. In 1913, Einstein and Grossmann wrote a paper in which they put forward the idea that what we think of as gravitational forces are just an expression of the fact that space-time is curved. However, because of a mistake by Einstein (who was quite human and fallible), they weren't able to find the equations that related the curvature of space-time to the mass and energy in it.

Einstein continued to work on the problem in Berlin, undisturbed by domestic matters and largely unaffected by the war, until he finally found the right equations, in November 1915. Einstein had discussed his ideas with the mathematician David Hilbert during a visit to the University of Göttingen in the summer of 1915, and Hilbert independently found the same equations a few days before Einstein. Nevertheless, as Hilbert admitted, the credit for the new theory belonged to Einstein. It was his idea to relate gravity to the warping of space-time. It is a tribute to the civilized state of Germany in this period that such scientific discussions and exchanges could go on undisturbed even in wartime. What a contrast to 20 years later!

The new theory of curved space-time was called general relativity to distinguish it from the original theory without gravity, which was now known as special relativity. It was confirmed in spectacular fashion in 1919, when a British expedition to West Africa observed a slight shift in the position of stars near the sun during an eclipse. Their light, as Einstein had predicted, was bent as it passed the sun. Here was direct evidence that space and time are warped, the greatest change in our perception of the arena in which we live since Euclid wrote his *Elements* about 300 B.C.

EINSTEIN'S GENERAL THEORY OF relativity transformed space and time from a passive background in which events take place to active participants in the dynamics of the cosmos. This led to a great problem that is still at the forefront of physics at the end of the 20th century. The universe is full of matter, and matter warps space-time so that bodies fall together. Einstein found that his equations didn't have a solution that described a universe that was unchanging in time. Rather than give up a static and everlasting universe, which he and most other people believed in at that time, he fudged the equations by adding a term called the cosmological constant, which warped space-time the other way so that bodies move apart. The repulsive effect of the cosmological constant would balance the attractive effect of matter and allow for a universe that lasts for all time.

This turned out to be one of the great missed opportunities of theoretical physics. If Einstein had stuck with his original equations, he could have predicted that the universe must be either expanding or contracting. As it was, the possibility of a time-dependent universe wasn't taken seriously until observations were made in the 1920s with the 100-in. telescope on Mount Wilson. These revealed that the farther other galaxies are from us, the faster they are moving away. In other words, the universe is expanding and the distance between any two galaxies is steadily increasing with time. Einstein later called the cosmological constant the greatest mistake of his life.

General relativity completely changed the discussion of the origin and fate of the universe. A static universe could have existed forever or could have been created in its present form at some time in the past. On the other hand, if galaxies are moving apart today, they must have been closer together in the past. About 15 billion years ago, they would all have been on top of one another and their density would have been infinite. According to the general theory, this Big Bang was the beginning of the universe and of time itself. So maybe Einstein deserves to be the person of a longer period than just the past 100 years.

General relativity also predicts that time comes to a stop inside black holes, regions of space-time that are so warped that light cannot escape them. But both the beginning and the end of time are places where the equations of general relativity fall apart. Thus the theory cannot predict what should emerge from the Big Bang. Some see this as an indication of God's freedom to start the universe off any way God wanted. Others (myself included) feel that the beginning of the universe should be governed by the same laws that hold at all other times. We have made some progress toward this goal, but we don't yet have a complete understanding of the origin of the universe.

The reason general relativity broke down at the Big Bang was that it was not compatible with quantum theory, the other great conceptual revolution of the early 20th century. The first step toward quantum theory came in 1900, when Max Planck, working in Berlin, discovered that the radiation from a body that was glowing red hot could be explained if light came only in packets of a certain size, called quanta. It was as if radiation were packaged like sugar; you cannot buy an arbitrary amount of loose sugar in a supermarket but can only buy it in 1-lb. bags. In one of his groundbreaking papers written in 1905, when he was still at the patent office, Einstein showed that Planck's quantum hypothesis could explain what is called the photoelectric effect, the way certain metals give off electrons when light falls on them. This is the basis of modern light detectors and television cameras, and it was for this work that Einstein was awarded the 1921 Nobel Prize in Physics.

Einstein continued to work on the quantum idea into the 1920s but was deeply disturbed by the work of Werner Heisenberg in Copenhagen, Paul Dirac in Cambridge and Erwin Schrödinger in Zurich, who developed a new picture of reality called quantum mechanics. No longer did tiny particles have a definite position and speed. On the contrary, the more accurately you determined the particle's position, the less accurately you could determine its speed, and vice versa.

Einstein was horrified by this random, unpredictable element in the basic laws and never fully accepted quantum mechanics. His feelings were expressed in his famous God-does-not-play-dice dictum. Most other scientists, however, accepted the validity of the new quantum laws because they showed excellent agreement with observations and because they seemed to explain a whole range of previously unaccounted-for phenomena. They are the basis of modern developments in chemistry, molecular biology and electronics and the foundation of the technology that has transformed the world in the past half-century.

When the Nazis came to power in Germany in 1933, Einstein left the country and renounced his German citizenship. He spent the last 22 years of his life at the Institute for Advanced Study in Princeton, N.J. The Nazis launched a campaign against "Jewish science" and the many German scientists who were Jews (their exodus is part of the reason Germany was not able to build an atom bomb). Einstein and relativity were principal targets for this campaign. When told of the publication of the book *One Hundred Authors Against Einstein,* he replied, Why 100? If I were wrong, one would have been enough.

After World War II, he urged the Allies to set up a world government to control the atom bomb. He was offered the presidency of the new state of Israel in 1952 but turned it down. "Politics is for the moment," he once wrote, "while . . . an equation is for eternity." The equations of general relativity are his best epitaph and memorial. They should last as long as the universe. ∎

A Note on the Type

THE TEXT TYPE FOR this book is called Kingfisher™, designed by the British type designer Jeremy Tankard. It is an elegant, readable typeface designed to facilitate legibility in text-heavy books. Tankard, 39, tells why he was motivated to create a new typeface when thousands already exist. From his website, *www.typography.net:*

> A few years ago I went to buy a novel. Choosing the right book became a torturous exercise. While attracted to various titles by their covers, time and again I was put off by the interior design of the books. Text suffered from being crammed on the page; inking was often inconsistent, resulting in gray pages; the type size was invariably too small and, more often than not, set in one of only a few seemingly standard typefaces.
>
> So I didn't buy a novel. Instead I asked myself, "Why aren't more new text types used today?" Surely there are enough of them around.
>
> I asked the freelance book typographer Dale Tomlinson why the quality of so much book setting should still be so poor. He explained that many of the "classic" book faces had suffered through digital interpretation and that, often, new types were simply not formal enough for continuous text reading.
>
> All this prompted me to look more closely at the design requirements of a typeface that would be able to address these concerns. The result is Kingfisher™.